The Guide to
IT Service
Management
Volume I

The Guide to IT Service Management
Volume I

edited by Jan van Bon

 Addison-Wesley

An imprint of **Pearson Education**

London ■ Boston ■ Indianapolis ■ New York ■ Mexico City ■ Toronto ■ Sydney ■ Tokyo ■ Singapore ■ Hong Kong ■ Cape Town ■ New Delhi ■ Madrid ■ Paris ■ Amsterdam ■ Munich ■ Milan ■ Stockholm

PEARSON EDUCATION LIMITED

Head Office
Edinburgh Gate
Harlow CM20 2JE
Tel: +44 (0)1279 623623
Fax: +44 (0)1279 431059

London Office:
128 Long Acre, London WC2E 9AN
Tel: +44 (0)20 7447 2000
Fax: +44 (0)20 7447 2170
Website:www.it-minds.com

First published in Great Britain in 2002

© Pearson Education Limited 2002

The right of Jan van Bon to be identified as author of this work has been asserted by him in accordance with the Copyright, Designs and Patents Act 1988.

ISBN 0 201 73792 2

British Library Cataloguing in Publication Data
A CIP catalogue record for this book can be obtained from the British Library

Library of Congress Cataloguing in Publication Data
Applied for

All rights reserved; no part of this publication may be reproduced, stored in a retrieval system, or transmitted in any form or by any means, electronic, mechanical, photocopying, recording, or otherwise without either the prior written permission of the Publishers or a licence permitting restricted copying in the United Kingdom issued by the Copyright Licensing Agency Ltd, 90 Tottenham Court Road, London W1P 0LP. This book may not be lent, resold, hired out or otherwise disposed of by way of trade in any form of binding or cover other than that in which it is published, without the prior consent of the Publishers.

Many of the designations used by manufacturers and sellers to distinguish their products are claimed as trademarks. Pearson Education Limited has made every attempt to supply trademark information about manufacturers and their products mentioned in this book.

10 9 8 7 6 5 4 3 2 1

Designed by Sue Lamble
Typeset by Pantek Arts Ltd, Maidstone, Kent.
Printed and bound in Great Britain by Biddles Ltd of Guildford and King's Lynn.

Jan van Bon, chief editor of the Guide, can be contacted at jvbon@wxs.nl

The Publishers' policy is to use paper manufactured from sustainable forests.

Contents

Acknowledgements — x
Introduction to IT Service Management and the Guide — xii

part 1

Models for managing information systems — 1

1. ASL, second-generation application management — 7
   Remko van der Pols and Machteld Meijer-Veldman

2. BDM®: IT-enabled business development and management methodolgy — 24
   Djoen Tan and Aad Uijttenbroek

3. BiOOlogic™ — 34
   Johann Schreurs and DirkJan van der Hoven

4. CobiT® — 51
   A.C.P. van Nijnatten, A.M. Dohmen and P.N.A. Broshuis

5. A model for functional management — 70
   Frank van Outvorst

6. The HP IT Service Management Reference Model — 81
   Jeff Drake

7. IPW™ and IPW Stadia Model™ — 97
   Hans van Herwaarden and Frank Grift

8. Integrated Service management (ISM)® — 116
   H. van den Elskamp, W.J.J. Kuiper, H. Wanders, J. van Bon and W. Hoving

9. ITIL: best practice in IT Service Management — 131
   Lex Hendriks and Martin Carr

10. Information Technology Process Model — 151
    Paul Hertroys and Bart van Rooijen

11. A 'Managerial Step-by-Step Plan' — 158
    Maarten Looijen and Wouter de Jong

12. Managing the delivery of business information — 165
    Leo Ruijs and Albert Schotanus

13 MIP: managing the information provision — 178
Dirk Jan van der Hoven, Guido Hegger and Jan van Bon

14 Microsoft Operations Framework (MOF) — 190
Dave Pultorak

15 The SIMA: a practical approach to information technology management — 204
Louis van Hemmen, Michiel Borgers and Rick Klompé

Review of part 1 — 216

part 2

Sourcing and procurement — 227

16 Methodological ERP acquisitions: the SHERPA experience — 231
Joan A. Pastor, Xavier Franch and Francesc Sistach

17 Relationship management: delivering on the promise of outsourcing — 247
John Buscher

18 Chinese walls in IT outsourcing — 263
Roger Leenders, Johan Duim, Albert van Houwelingen, Mario Paalvast and Gregg Shaffer

19 Best practice in acquisition and procurement management: the Information Services Procurement Library — 277
John Dekker and Lex Hendriks

Review of part 2 — 297

part 3

Metrics — 299

20 Enforcing performance guarantees based on performance service levels — 302
André Scholz and Klaus Turowski

21 GQM applied in IT Service Management — 312
Wouter de Jong

22 Service level measurement: checkpoint 2000 — 324
Mike Tsykin

23 How to improve the quality of your support centre by certification — 335
Eppo Luppes, Bill Sheehan and Jackie Kuflik

24 A standard for IT Service Management — 344
Jenny Dugmore

Review of part 3 — 358

Contents

part 4

Maturity 363

25 The future of the IT organization 366
Guus Delen, Mark Griep, Daam Grund and John Roelofs

26 Professionalization of ICT-management organizations:
a roadmap for ICT managers 383
Gertrud Blauwhof, Christine Praasterink, Frank van Outvorst,
Leen van Stappen, Marco Postma, Ger Manders and Wim van Haaren

27 Improvement of the test process using TPI® 408
T. Koomen and M. Pol

28 Securing information now or never 420
Anton Griffoen and Jaap van der Wel

29 Quality of software development 431
Paul Hendriks

Review of part 4 442

part 5

Processes 447

30 Service Level Management 450
Rocky Kostick, Justin Williams and Matt Arnold

31 An integrated environment for managing software maintenance projects 460
Francisco Ruiz, Mario Piattini and Macario Polo

32 Kwintes project: results of a multidisciplinary research project in the
field of IT Service Management 478
L.J. Ruijs

33 Integrated life-cycle management 489
Wim van den Boomgaard and Ton Pijpers

34 Hunting the mammoth 507
Jan F. Bouman and Michel van Dijk

Review of part 5 519

part 6

Organizational aspects 521

35 Embedding and managing IT processes in an organization 525
Richard van Bavel and Jeroen Bronkhorst

36 Patching the blind spot in implementation of IT process models 542
Peter A.J. Bootsma and Jan van Bon

37 Competence management 558
Renée Kamphuis

38 Knowledge management and the IT Service Management organization — 567
A.P. Kuiper, P.M. Los and J. Sietsma

39 Organizational improvement and culture ... growth deserves space! — 583
Jolanda Meijers and Hans van Herwaarden

Review of part 6 — 593

part 7

Practical guidance — 599

40 The process approach: managing chaos? — 604
Frank van Elsdingen and Bram de Landtsheer

41 IT Service Management: the IT management ERP solution — 617
Michael D. Loo

42 End-to-end Service Level Management — 627
J. den Boer, P.R. Leeuwenburg, J.J. Vilé and A.C. Otterman

43 IT Service Management: a pragmatic direction — 642
John Gilbey

44 Beauty is in the eye of the beholder — 651
Barry J.M.A. Meesters and Jan F. Bouman

45 Service Level Management — 667
Peter Sullivan

46 The management of IT service expectations — 678
Rhion Jones and Mike Fox

47 Is there life after ITIL? — 687
Lisette Favier

48 Russian roulette — 698
Dick Costeris

Review of part 7 — 713

part 8

E-management — 719

49 Service Management and the Internet: managing e-services — 721
Jeroen Wiebolt and Ingewang Wong

50 Management of a website: what's new? — 731
C.D. Deurloo, R.J.C. Donatz, R. van der Pols and F.J. Snels

Contents

51 Vision in the BLUR of eManagement — 742
Michiel Borgers and Paul van der Spek

Review of part 8 — 753

part 9

Tools and instruments — 755

52 Enterprise Management Software implementation — 757
Niranjan Prasad, Sankaran Velunathan and Shyam Sundar V

53 A business-focused Service Level Management Framework — 778
Paul Maestranzi, Ron Aay and Richard Seery

Review of part 9 — 799

part 10

Compendium for IT Service Management — 801

54 IT management glossary — 802

Acknowledgements

Many experts from the field of IT Service Management have assisted in putting together this first edition of *The Guide to IT Service Management Volume I*. Without these authors, who have done a lot of work to formulate their knowledge and insights and put them down on paper, a book like this would not be possible. I owe these authors my gratitude. The names of the authors are mentioned in their respective contributions, but you can be assured that many more were involved in the writing and evaluating of the final texts.

The authors of the chapters in this Guide are not the only ones who have put effort into this book. Many others wrote proposals that didn't make it. Only part of those proposed chapters were rejected for reasons of quality or because they fell outside the scope of the book we wanted to make. The other major reason for rejection was the limitation on size. We think that the Guide has the right number of contributions for a first edition. Depending on the way the Guide is received, we will determine the structure of the next edition. For that reason all readers are invited to give their feedback to the editor in chief, preferably by e-mail: jvbon@wxs.nl. We hope that many of the authors whose articles were not selected for this edition will be willing to try again for the next edition. To make a well-balanced Guide it is necessary to have a great number of proposals. Those proposals reflect the highlights of the global interest in this field and make it possible to choose the best-fitting contributions for the final book.

Another group of people who played a major role in composing this Guide was the Advisory Board. To build a true world-class Guide we needed a selection mechanism for the proposals that reflected a global perspective on the subject of IT Service Management. Therefore we set up an international Advisory Board, consisting of a great number of specialists from all over the world. The members of this Advisory Board have been reading all proposed contributions, which were made completely anonymous. All these proposals were carefully evaluated. From the comparison of these evaluations, which reflected the views of a very diverse group, the final selection of papers was made. I thank the members of this Advisory Board especially for their sophisticated and unbiased evaluations, in alphabetical order:

CCTA/OCG, Best Practice Division: John Groom
Compaq Computer Corporation, Operations Management Services: Sjaak van den Broek
Ernst & Young, Information Technology Infrastructure: Theo Schrammeijer
EXIN, Examination Institute for Information Science: Lex Hendriks

Acknowledgements

GartnerGroup, Research Advisory Service: Colleen Young
Hewlett-Packard: Chris Harris
IBM, Global Services EMEA: Juan Antonio Zufiria
ITSMF-Americas: Ken Hamilton
ITSMF-Australia: Bob Philipson
ITSMF-Belgium: Stef Knaepkens
ITSMF-International: Jos Brusse
ITSMF-South Africa: David Cannon
ITSMF-Switzerland/Austria/Germany: Walter Vogt
ITSMF-The Netherlands: Foppe Vogd
ITSMF-United Kingdom: Aidan Lawes
META Group, Services Management Strategies: Stratos Sarissamlis
University of Technology Delft, Information Strategy and Management of Information Systems: Maarten Looijen

Creating a Guide like the one you have before you now takes quite an effort, which one shouldn't take on alone. I couldn't have done this without the help of my two colleagues Wil Haasdijk and Rolf Akker, who were a great help in managing and editing the content of the Guide. I owe them my respect.

Finally I want to thank Ivo van Haren, professional publisher and personal friend, who stimulated me to develop this Guide. Ivo finds a real challenge in the distribution of knowledge in the discipline of IT Service Management. He has made a difference by helping me to overcome a lot of hurdles that an editor encounters on the road to publishing a complex book.

Jan van Bon,
Chief editor,
May 2002

Introduction to IT Service Management and the Guide

The importance of IT Service Management is becoming widely recognized. Whereas in the 1960s and 1970s interest was still focused mainly on the improvement of hardware, and whereas the development of software was the major concern until well into the 1980s, the 1990s was the decade that saw the rise of service management.

For decades, Service Management had been seen as an extension of development, more of a necessary evil than a valuable element in automation. But recent years have been characterized by a turnaround in this view, supported not least by Gartner Group publications, which show that around 70–80 percent of the life-cycle costs of an information system are incurred in the exploitation phase.

This shows that the exploitation area is a rewarding area of activity when it comes to cost control. This is further supported by the discovery that developers spend around 60 per cent of their time on maintenance. In addition, it is evident that there is a strong growth in the awareness that many primary business processes can no longer function without the contributions made by information systems; in many industries, IT is already one of the primary business processes. Think, for instance, of telecommunications, banking, insurance and other data-intensive industries. The developments in e-commerce also show that IT has become a crucial factor for operational management. And on closer inspection it will be found that the main day-to-day activities of a very large number of IT staff seem to consist of management activities. Therefore the business needs to get control of information technology and the services based on it.

All in all, there is a flood of signals showing that the organization of IT Service Management is a field to which very careful attention should be paid. And this is in a world that is characterized by an avalanche of technological developments and increasing demands on the time-to-market, flexibility and performance of information systems.

Motivation for the Guide

The motivation for compiling *The Guide to IT Service Management* came up some years ago, when the editor became aware that a clear synchronization in the development of concepts on the theme of IT Service Management was taking place in part of Europe. However, there was still no question of worldwide synchronization. Quite the contrary: further investigation showed that different approaches to implementing care for the quality of information provision were to be found in different parts of the world.

On the basis of discussions with the IT Service Management Forum (ITSMF), the first steps towards this Guide were taken in 1998. The publication of this Guide is intended to make information on the various approaches to IT Service Management more generally available and to provide a platform on which concepts can develop. The very latest developments in the subject can be followed continuously in editions to be brought out annually. In addition, discussion of the developments identified and the various approaches to them will be encouraged in international discussion forums on the Internet (http://itsmportal.net). This combination of initiatives can make a contribution to the desired global synchronization of concepts in the field of IT Service Management.

Scope of the Guide

The subject of this Guide is IT Service Management. But what is IT Service Management? There are many definitions, of which I prefer the following: 'IT Service Management is a set of processes that cooperate to ensure the quality of live IT services, according to the levels of service agreed with the customer.' It is superposed on management domains such as systems management, network management, systems development and on many process domains such as change management, asset management and problem management.

This new specialist area is gradually becoming fully mature. This can be seen, for instance, from the fact that different theoretical frameworks with substantial content are coming into existence alongside each other. Theory formation is always a sign of the growth of a specialist area. We also see this in the discipline of IT Service Management. In the relatively short history of the field of IT Service Management, one approach has managed to become established as the *de facto* standard in several countries: ITIL, the IT Infrastructure Library. The market in a rapidly increasing number of countries is focused on the application of this approach at present. But there are also various other methodological approaches, which you will find listed in this book. Many of the approaches have a strong relationship to the best practices defined in ITIL and continue to embroider on that theme. Each of the approaches has its own advantage in different situations.

Standardization and certification

As is usual in the development of a 'new' discipline, regulations and standardization are following some distance behind practice. Therefore there is still hardly any regulation on the part of government and the standardization organizations in this case. The concept of a 'standard' does not go much further than a *de facto* standard such as ITIL.

The only formal regulation which can be applied is effectively the antiquated ISO range. Although not specifically designed for the management area, many regulations apply to a wide quality area, and so also to IT Service Management. But certification initiatives relating to management organizations are beginning to appear here and there. In addition, a number of initiatives for individual-oriented certification are to be found in the Service Management field. These are the first signs that standardization is arising. It is still too early to say what form of certification will lead to standardization in the longer term. Certification indicates a stable situation:

- **Individual-oriented**: the job must be generally recognized and acknowledged. The professional group must be homogenous and measurable.
- **Organization-oriented**: there must be a stable picture of what the organization is, its goals, performance pattern etc.

There is no point in certification if a stable situation of this kind has not been achieved. After all, in that case the value of the certificate will not be recognized; it is not founded on the recognition of a goal to be pursued. It is quite evident that the desired stability is not yet within the reach of the field of IT Service Management. Metrics (Part 3 of this book) deals in more detail with recent developments.

Missing dictionary

While the subject is flourishing, there are also some teething troubles for this relatively young discipline. One of these is the lack of a settled, stable, terminology framework. There are synchronized definitions across the world for many technical terms, but when two IT specialists speak about issues such as 'management', 'problem', 'application' or 'infrastructure', just to take some obvious terms, there is immediately an enormous risk that they each have a different semantic framework and have different meanings in mind, with all the negative consequences this involves. This has resulted in the development of a standard terminological framework in the Netherlands, one of the first countries to fully adopt ITIL and IT Service Management practices since the early 1990s. The definitions and the framework are part of this Guide, and they will help you to get acquainted with new terminology.

Industry formation

The fact that the field of IT Service Management is experiencing strong growth is also evident from the development taking place in dedicated industry organizations in this area. The explosive growth of an organization such as the IT Service Management Forum is typical. Specialized organizations such as the Help Desk Institute (HDI), Help Desk 2000, ISACA and the International Information Systems Security Certification Consortium (IISSCC) are also showing a growth which is providing a higher profile for sections of the specialist area. Just recently an initiative of market leaders and infrastructure organizations in the IT services branch has led to installing a new IT Service Fund. The Fund, managed by leading authorities in the IT services industry, will stimulate and finance initiatives that will benefit the IT services market and emphasize its innovative nature.

Organization of the Guide

This Guide is an international publication in the field of IT Service Management, after the example of the Dutch *IT Beheer Jaarboek*, the IT Service Management Yearbook. This Yearbook has been published annually since 1997 and is a highly appreciated source of state-of-the-art insights, methods, glossaries, cases etc. in the field of IT Service Management. This *Guide to IT Service Management* will also be published regularly. The book is a compilation of chapters contributed by researchers and practitioners addressing issues, trends, and challenges facing the management of IT services.

The Guide was created by distributing a worldwide call for chapters on a large scale. From the proposals which were submitted for the Guide, a series of 53 were selected in an intensive selection process. Selection was carried out according to strict standards;

there was an international editorial board consisting of specialists from various organizations: ITSMF representatives, global research and consultancy organizations, global providers, examination institutes, quality organizations and universities. The participating organizations were OGC (formerly CCTA, UK), Delft University of Technology (NL), Compaq, IBM, HP, Ernst & Young, Meta Group, Gartner Group, EXIN (NL) and representatives from ITSMF Chapters in the United Kingdom, the Netherlands, the United States, Switzerland, Germany, Austria, South Africa, Australia, Belgium and the umbrella organization ITSMF International. This board received a large number of totally anonymous proposals for contributions to the Guide. On the basis of its commentaries on the subject content, a selection was made and the authors then further developed their contributions. This method has ensured that the texts you now have in front of you are the most interesting ones we gathered worldwide. The fact that a strikingly large proportion of the authors are from Dutch organizations not only shows the importance attached to the field in that country, but also illustrates the stage of development it has progressed to in the Netherlands. It is also noticeable that two or more contributions have been included by some organizations from various countries (HP, KPN, Origin, PinkRoccade, Quint Wellington Redwood, The Art of Service). The anonymous treatment of the proposals means that this reflects these organizations' concentration on the theme of IT Service Management.

Publications in the Netherlands

In the Netherlands, the fast-growing demand for information sources about this subject has led to the development of the Annual Yearbook and various other books, two dedicated magazines (*IT Beheer Magazine* and *IT Service Magazine*), a series of pocket guides (*ICT Management Pocket Guides*) and the development of a website dedicated to the subject of IT Service Management (http://nl.itsmportal.net). After a cautious start in 1997, the later editions of the Yearbook captured tremendous attention. Over a short period of time, the book has been acknowledged as the standard work on IT Service Management in the Netherlands. The main reason for this success is believed to be the simple and thorough entry level this book is offering to newcomers as well as to experienced service management specialists regarding the question 'What is IT Service Management all about?'. The book does not contain in-depth studies of specific processes in the same way that ITIL does, but instead offers an overview of the model-wise approach one could use in implementing a service management strategy. It also presents an annual hot-list of items which have drawn serious attention.

The main part of the Dutch Yearbook discusses approaches for IT Service Management (next to ITIL), as well as other methods that build upon ITIL, and it describes the main benefits in a wider context.

Furthermore, the book contains a compendium: a glossary of IT Service Management terminology. This glossary was based upon: a thorough survey of several hundred companies in the Netherlands; ITIL documentation; and several existing glossaries derived from international sources. A Compendium Committee is reviewing the glossary on an annual basis.

This historical sketch emphasizes the great attention IT Service Management has been receiving in the Netherlands. Although it is hard to find an explanation, the subject is very much more alive in the Netherlands than in most other countries. Therefore, you will find a relatively high proportion of Dutch sources among the contributions in this Guide. This emphasizes – taking into consideration the broadly international face of the editorial board that was used to select the anonymous proposals for this Guide – the ideas developed in the productive Dutch Service Management climate.

Structure of the Guide

The Guide begins in **part 1** with a survey of methodological approaches to designing IT Service Management. In the frameworks presented, considerable use is made of in-house vocabulary. For example, the terms 'IT' and 'ICT' are used as synonyms, depending on the preference of the various authors. There is a range of different emphases in the frameworks, and in some cases the framework has more the character of a vision while in others it is a fully fledged method. The frameworks will be of varying use in different circumstances, depending on the reader's local situation.

The Parts following this are subdivided by theme. An important trend is dealt with in **part 2**; because of the increasing complexity and the high demands placed on service provision, more and more companies are faced with the question of whether to do it themselves or outsource it.

Part 3 contains contributions dealing with the real need for quantification. It is necessary for us to learn to deal with measurable variables (metrics) so that we can render the service provision quantifiable and be able to direct the required improvement in its quality.

Part 4 goes into the issue of quality improvement in IT service organizations. A stepwise improvement approach often leads to what has been recognized as the 'maturity' of the organization.

In **part 5** you will find an elaboration of some of the most important single processes in IT Service Management.

Part 6 deals with an aspect of IT Service Management which is attracting increasing interest. The less hard aspects of the field are increasingly coming to be recognized as important variables within a service provision company. Whereas other industries have already been working with this awareness for many years, the IT service industry still has a lot to learn in this area. And this is particularly difficult for an industry which is characterized by people who have come into the field because of a mainly technological interest.

Part 7 provides a number of practical illustrations and aids for the application of various frameworks. These contributions bridge the gap between theory and practice. They will provide you with valuable ideas on how other organizations have solved their service management problems, emphasizing the aspect of organizing people.

Part 8 deals with the latest development in e-business: what are the effects of e-business developments on the solutions we found in the 'traditional' IT world?

In **part 9**, we present some structures for the matter of tooling, found to be so very important in many organizations.

We finish the Guide with the Compendium for IT Service Management, **part 10**. The Compendium defines hundreds of terms used throughout this Guide. The

Compendium doesn't have an official status but reflects most of the terms used in an integrated and consistent way. It covers various IT service management domains and is compatible with ITIL and the Delft school.

Target audience and ambition

The intention in preparing this Guide is to make a contribution to the development of concepts in the field of IT Service Management. By exchanging experiences and insights on these subjects, IT specialists in all parts of the world can find out about the relevant developments which are taking place in the field. The inclusion of a wide, representative range of concepts from different parts of the world enables readers to follow up those matters which are in line with the approaches appropriate for their cultures. It is hoped that by including these carefully selected contributions in a single book, there will be a kind of 'mutual infection' which will stimulate and synchronize developments in the field. This book contains instructive elements for everyone involved in the organization and delivery of IT services, and so its target audience includes the majority of people working in IT. Because of the growing awareness that the function of IT is solely to support the primary business processes, it can be expected that the frameworks provided for that purpose in this Guide will make a useful contribution to the development of state-of-the-art IT service providers.

part 1

Models for managing information systems

Introduction to the theme

The importance of IT Service Management is increasingly recognized and acknowledged. This is evident, for example, from the number of periodicals, publications and events in this area. That is a logical consequence of the amount of money being spent on IT Service Management; the costs of management and maintenance are a multiple of the development and implementation cost. As an extension of this development, many suppliers and large user organizations have developed methods to give shape to IT Service Management. Further analysis of these methods shows that there is a great deal of overlap, but also many differences: management processes are named and sequenced in a particular way, the IT Infrastructure Library (ITIL) and the Capability Maturity Model are followed to a greater or lesser extent, and the objects to be managed are arranged in different ways.

Readers will find the concepts presented more or less immediately accessible depending on their local situation. But the wide variation in what is included makes it very improbable that among all the frameworks presented not one way of thinking will be found which is in line with the reader's view or can be used by the reader as a guideline for future growth. The fifteen (!) frameworks which are documented in this part for that purpose have been included in alphabetical order.

Focus on process and customer

All the frameworks provided for designing IT Service Management adopt a process-oriented approach. Function-oriented and organization-oriented approaches have quite definitely had their day. The focus is on the customer, and there is the general belief that to pursue that principle efficiently a process-oriented approach has to be adopted. In many cases the ITIL specifications, which describe a series of fundamental best practices in the IT Service Management field, are further embroidered. At the same time, it can be concluded that a great deal more is needed in addition to ITIL to arrive at a reasonable management model. It is recommended that a coherent process model in which the various processes are positioned with respect to each other should be developed. This is recognized even within the ITIL world, as is demonstrated by the adoption of PD 0005, the Code of Practice for IT Service Management, which is closely based on ITIL, by the British Standards Institute.

Survey

By comparison with ITIL, some of the frameworks presented have a different subdivision of the activities into processes: IBM's Information Technology Process Model (ITPM) distinguishes explicitly between the strategic, tactical and operational levels and speaks of process groups such as customer relations maintenance, realize solutions, deliver solutions and deliver operational services; the Integrated Service Management model (ISM) and IPW emphatically name a production process; BiOOlogic distinguishes several pragmatic 'pipelines' from ITIL processes; Microsoft's Operations Framework (MOF) and ISM apply a different definition of problem management. However, most of the methods presented are based closely on the best practice definitions which are documented in ITIL.

And whatever grouping of activities is adopted, the activities are managed in accordance with a process order in all the modern frameworks. This shows the importance of a customer-oriented approach in IT service provision; focusing on the service process suggests that the customer will be served as efficiently and effectively as possible. It would be very strange if this approach did not include one framework in which you can find valuable points of reference for your own problem areas, whether these are 'sealing the gap', flattening the 'drama triangle' or one of the other current problems. The various contributions are introduced briefly below.

Content

This part contains 16 chapters, describing various frameworks for IT service management. The frameworks differ in scope, detail, etc., but all are relevant for the understanding of management issues in IT service management. One contribution is an analysis of one of the frameworks presented (i.e. ITIL) and appears right after the presentation of ITIL. Thus:

ASL, second-generation application management
Remko van der Pols and Machteld Meijer-Veldman

BDM®: IT-enabled business development and management methodology
Djoen Tan and Aad Uijttenbroek

BiOOlogic™
Johann Schreurs and DirkJan van der Hoven

CobiT®
A.C.P. van Nijnatten, A.M. Dohmen and P.N.A. Broshuis

A model for functional management
Frank van Outvorst

Part 1: Models for managing information systems

The HP IT Service Management Reference Model
Jeff Drake

IPW™ and IPW Stadia Model™
Hans van Herwaarden and Frank Grift

Integrated Service Management (ISM)®
H. van den Elskamp, W.J.J. Kuiper, H. Wanders, J. van Bon and W. Hoving

ITIL: best practice in IT Service Management
Lex Hendriks and Martin Carr

Information Technology Process Model
Paul Hertroys and Bart van Rooijen

A 'Managerial Step-by-Step Plan'
Maarten Looijen and Wouter de Jong

Managing the delivery of business information
Leo Ruijs and Albert Schotanus

MIP: managing the information provision
Dirk Jan van der Hoven, Guido Hegger and Jan van Bon

Microsoft Operations Framework (MOF)
Dave Pultorak

The SIMA: a practical approach to information technology management
Louis van Hemmen, Michiel Borgers and Rick Klompé

Review of part 1

Reading instructions

The frameworks are presented in alphabetical order. They are not independent: several frameworks are 'extensions' to either ITIL or the Delft school method. It might be worthwhile to start with these two ('ITIL and IT Service Management' and 'A Managerial Step-by-Step Plan'), and then read one or more of the other frameworks.

Introduction to the chapters

ASL, the Application Services Library, makes use of the experience with R2C (Redirection, Control and Continuity), a management method developed by PinkRoccade for the direction and management of operational processes. You will find PinkRoccade's vision of management and innovation in this model. Even though the methodology has been developed by a very large IT service provider, it is equally applicable to a smaller organization. The methodology concentrates on the organization and on the design of the service (level) management process. The service team plays a key role in the model. R2C is based substantially on the ITIL definitions, and it includes a maturity levelling analysis which can be used to introduce the method step by step.

BDM: IT-enabled business development and management methodology, is a framework that provides a number of standard IT business processes which may be used in the design of organizations. It is aimed at creating supportive IT organizations that focus on the core business processes. The framework has a very broad scope and is formulated in a generic, academic style, making it especially suitable as a visonary starting point in the (re)design of IT organizations.

BiOOlogic offers a very different and innovative management framework for developing, establishing and organizing IT organizations in line with management and customer organizations. BiOOlogic combines object-oriented modelling techniques with e.g. CMM/SPICE, ITIL and UML. ITIL processes are interpreted in smaller, more manageable flows, and in this way BiOOlogic provides a very pragmatic interpretation of a design method for IT service providers.

CoBiT (Control objectives for information and related technology) has been developed as a generically applicable and widely accepted standard of best practices for auditing IT management. CoBiT was developed by the Information Security Audit & Control Association (ISACA), an international organization of IT management specialists (including IT auditors). PricewaterhouseCoopers uses CoBiT frequently and described the framework, focusing on business processes (and the information required for this). CoBiT is based in part on the ITIL definitions.

Implementation of ASL (see above) brings application management to a higher, more professional level. With an ICT services provider that operates more professionally, the shortcomings of functional management in the customer organization become more manifest. This leads to a demand for a structural approach to the functional management processes. To meet this demand, PinkRoccade Atribit developed **a model for functional (application) management**.

Hewlett-Packard's vision is described and explained in the **HP IT Service Management Reference Model**. The IT Service Management processes are illustrated using the model, while the organizational aspects and the management tools to be used are addressed in the model. A step-by-step plan to achieve Service Management forms part of the model. The IT Service Management Reference Model incorporates many ITIL best practices.

The **IPW** model was developed as the first ITIL-based process model for IT Service Management. It originated from the implementation of a process- oriented approach in the national Dutch telecommunications IT department in 1992. It then evolved into a more complete model, covering tactical and strategic processes. This was achieved by using it in various companies and later on in the consultancy practice of Quint Wellington Redwood. The model has been extended with a CMM-like staged maturity approach, the **IPW Stadia Model**, which can help in improving the way service management processes are executed.

In 1992, the national Dutch telecommunications company developed the first successful application of ITIL in the Netherlands. In an increasingly complex environment, its present liberated IT company is acting more and more often as a system integrator. A reference model known as **Integrated Service Management (ISM)** is used in this approach. ISM records how a supplier can offer a number of sub-services to a customer as a single integrated service, taking account of all the insights which are at a premium in modern IT Service Management.

In the late 1980s, the British government's Central Computer and Telecommunications Agency (CCTA, now OGC) started developing the **IT Infrastructure Library (ITIL)**. ITIL was the term used to designate the OGC's manuals. ITIL contains descriptions of a collection of best practices for the management of information systems infrastructure. The chapter on ITIL demonstrates that ITIL also refers to the approach, philosophy and objective behind the ITIL books. The IT Infrastructure Library can be seen as the 'works' of many other frameworks. At present, ITIL's ideas are being disseminated rapidly right across the world, and ITIL interest groups are being set up in many countries. (There is further discussion, in chapter 47, part 7, by Lisette Favier, of how ITIL has developed in recent years.)

The **IT Process Model (ITPM)** is the model-based approach which is applied globally by IBM. Characteristic features of ITPM are the difference in approach from ITIL and also the associated difference in choice of words. For instance, because of its international character it refers consistently to 'IT management' rather than to 'IT Service Management'. The model is characterized by a different subdivision of activities into processes; it has its roots in the Information Systems Management Architecture (ISMA) which IBM published in 1979. In itself, the IT Process Model is not an applicable model but, rather, a framework within which an applicable model can be developed. ITPM and ITIL complement each other well. ITPM is a reference model for controlling IT, indicating the relationships and information flows between the processes. ITIL is a description of best practices, which shows how these processes can be implemented.

The **Managerial Step-by-Step Plan (MSP)** presents a step-by-step plan by which the management of information systems can be designed, in line with the way in which the management of information systems is presented at the Delft University of Technology by Professor M. Looijen. The attitude towards IT Service Management as taught at the Delft University of Technology shows a connection with the principles of service management. To this end, the Triple Model is placed in the perspective of service provision to the customer. ITIL has also been given its place in this approach.

Cap Gemini Ernst & Young collects all its methods and standards in the areas of management, system development and strategy in the quality system Perform, including the standard for **managing the delivery of business information**. When concluding service level agreements, Cap Gemini Ernst & Young applies a special method, developed jointly with the Universities of Technology of Delft and Eindhoven and the Vrije Universiteit Amsterdam. The further development of the model takes account of best practices as these are documented in ITIL.

The **management of information provision (MIP)** states how the information requirement of the business processes can be translated into IT provision. The service concept is central to this view of internal information provision. In this model, the basic processes in information provision are grouped logically into organizational processes, information management processes and the processes relating to the delivery of information services. In this simple model, you will find points of reference for most of the other models and processes which are elaborated in the Guide. The model provides a starting point for discussions on the many other process models which are useful in organizing the management of information technology.

Microsoft recently came up with its vision of IT Service Management, in **MOF: the Microsoft Operations Framework**. Given its presence as a world leader in software products, it is important to take notice of this vision, in which Microsoft openly declares how important it thinks IT Service Management is. MOF is composed of three core models – Process, Team and Risk – that incorporate the principles and practices that business people and IT practitioners need in order to manage IT service delivery and infrastructure effectively on the Microsoft platform. MOF '… provides comprehensive technical guidance for achieving mission-critical production system reliability, availability, supportability, and manageability on Microsoft's products and technologies'. This chapter describes MOF, and shows its relationship to ITIL.

The **Standard Integrated Management Approach (SIMA)** is used by InterProm as its own approach to the design of management and security for open, multi-vendor IT infrastructures. The SIMA was developed to support the design of IT Service Management at all phases of the reorganization process. The approach combines practical experience with existing and internally developed methods, techniques and standards, not only in the sphere of IT Service Management but also on the organizational and business administration levels. This chapter gives an illustration of the approach to change which can be adopted when designing IT Service Management. SIMA includes a focus on processes, in which various interpretations, including ITIL, can be adopted.

ASL, second-generation application management

Remko van der Pols and **Machteld E.E. Meijer-Veldman**
PinkRoccade, The Netherlands

Summary

During the past few years much has been published about, and practical experience gained with, a process-wise set-up of application management organizations. This experience and a theoretical study of several other models led to a new framework called ASL, the Application Services Library, which consists of a framework and a library of best practices in the field of application management. In the framework, attention is not only paid to operational and tactical processes, but to strategic considerations as well. In this chapter the new framework is introduced and the relationship with, for instance, a framework for functional management is described.

1.1 Introduction

Most businesses are now to some extent critically dependent on their application systems to support their business processes and provide pertinent management information in order to facilitate executive decisions. Organizations make significant investments in application systems. Formerly the emphasis of management attention was on the initial *development*. During the past six years or so application management, the continued maintenance of the applications, has gained more attention. Indeed software maintenance is the most important contributory factor to system life-cycle costs. Maintenance and support of an application can amount to between 50% and 67% of the overall life-cycle costs. Continual maintenance and evolution of existing applications is a wise investment and is necessary to ensure that existing systems continue to meet the needs of the business and function dependably. For many years, maintenance was perceived as a problem area; however, competent management can now ensure that the maintenance and evolutive processes are efficient, effective and provide value for money. Furthermore, awareness has grown that innovation of applications and innovation of application management organizations will be the key to the success of information-intensive organizations.

The growing attention to application management has resulted in various publications and the development of a number of models for application management. Lessons learned from a number of implementations of the R2C process model (Meijer, 2000), the study of other application management models (Hinley, 2000) and the consequences of the present developments led to a new framework and a library of best practices, the Application Services Library (ASL). Some lessons learned are outlined, the new model is introduced and the relationship with other models (such as the model for functional management) is described.

1.2 Analysis of R2C and other models

The ASL model is based on five years' experience with R2C on the one hand and on a theoretical study of other models for application management on the other.

TABLE 1.1
The ASL model

Term	Description
Application management	The contracted responsibility for the management and execution of all activities related to the maintenance and evolution of existing applications, within well-defined service levels
Enhancement	The result of a request for change in functional or non-functional requirements that were not specified originally for the existing application system
Maintenance	The coordinated activities that enable an existing system to be sustained, operated and used, according to agreed rules and procedures
Operation	The technical operating of an application in, for instance, a computer centre during the use of the system
Renovation	Considerable changes made to an existing application in order to extend its life cycle

Experience with R2C

Performance

The maintenance and enhancement processes perform well on the operational and tactical levels. They give good support in implementing an application management organization (Figure 1.1).

Distinction between maintenance and enhancement

Making a concrete distinction between continuous maintenance processes and enhancement/renovation (the left-hand and the right-hand cluster respectively on the operational level) has been an important eye-opener and has made it possible to optimize organizations. The maintenance activities, the continuous activities that are aimed at an optimal and faultless use of the application, usually do not comprise the biggest part of the application management activities. In many organizations they get little attention. However, they are of vital importance for user satisfaction. By distinguishing them from the project-wise enhancement activities, they get the attention they deserve.

Coordinating management of maintenance and enhancement

The coordinating character of the management processes, the integral steering on maintenance and enhancement, has been proven to be of major importance. When changes

FIGURE 1.1

R2C model

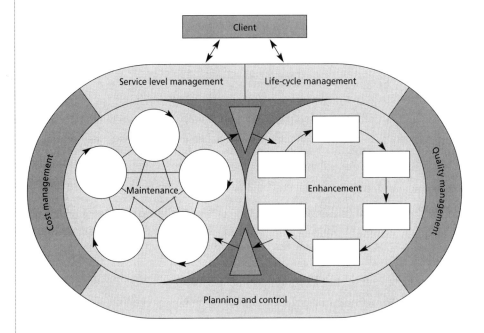

had to be made to applications, the everyday maintenance activities got too little attention. The ability to maintain and run the enhanced application got too little attention as well. There was not enough emphasis on the fact that applications are made to be used. This led to (new versions of) applications that were 'thrown across a wall', with the accompanying frustration for technical management.

The service team principle

A business manager is responsible for business, an ICT manager for ICT service. Both business and ICT service are isolated concepts, with a lack of consciously shared values. Therein lies a significant cause of coordination problems. The solution speaks for itself. By determining the importance of an application in consultation, it is made clear to both parties what has to be done by the application manager and what returns can be expected by the application owner. One way of reducing coordination problems between functional management, application management and technical management is to organize mutual responsibility more clearly. This is achieved by making one body responsible for the overall information provision per client. This body, the service team, bears responsibility for steering the entire life cycle of information provision. The team thus builds a bridge between the client organization and the automation specialists. An unequivocal platform is created for the client.

The service team functions initially as a partner of the client organization. The primary contact point for the service team is the functional management. The service team is responsible for the overall quality (both technical and functional) of the information provision to a client, defines the desired service and supervises it. The service team coordinates mutual agreements, checks whether they are complied with and reports on this to the client organization. This is how the team manages the overall information provision: development, innovation, usage and operation. As a result the business manager can concentrate on his or her primary business.

Service level agreements

A professional client–supplier relationship requires that business managers can steer their ICT service providers, especially regarding output. Services and products are then laid down in a service level agreement (SLA).

An SLA defines the obligations and responsibilities of both the supplier and the purchaser of the services. The starting point is that the current and future needs of the client are met as well as possible at a realistic price. An SLA contains guarantees regarding the service, but also sets criteria against which the quality of the service can be measured. The service team sets the criteria in consultation with the business manager. This is done as much as possible in units that the business manager (and the end user) can recognize and steer. Service levels for maintenance and enhancement, for instance, contain requirements regarding the availability of applications, the accessibility of the service desk, the response times for certain functions and the speed at which incidents are resolved. ICT services are thus made clear, measurable, verifiable and steerable by a service level agreement. Agreements are also laid down concerning the way in which the client organization and the ICT service provider work together. These more operational agreements and procedures structure the collaboration and determine the quality of the service to an important extent. The agreements relate to various areas, such as the submission and settlement of change proposals and/or incidents and the checking and acceptance of products. Reports and evaluations enhance the ability to steer processes.

A glimpse of the future

Anticipating developments in good time ensures the continuity of the support and precludes the need for divestment. The Life Cycle Management process was defined to support this vision. The past few years have proven that applications live far longer than expected during their development. Issues like Y2K and the euro clearly show this. Replacement of existing applications by newly built substitutes requires years. During their life cycle, applications define the possibilities of the business process. The need to have a long-term view during enhancement has only increased. An annual renewal plan is drawn up on this basis. This serves to provide a continuous, systematically managed renewal of the entire ICT infrastructure. The quality and continuity of the information provision are thus guaranteed.

Weaknesses

Although Life Cycle Management was described a couple of years ago, in practice it has mainly been used on a tactical level. The concept was regarded as valuable, however.

Up to now, the renewal of a company's own ICT organization did not get much attention in application management. Improvement of services took place within a defined scope. But the scope itself was hardly ever renovated. Clients considered service delivery to be rigid, and service levels seemed to be used as an argument to prove that the wishes of a client could not be met. Usually, there is little attention to cooperation, outsourcing and commercial considerations.

This leads to an organization that acts professionally, and rigidly. This was also experienced during implementations of R2C. The organizations act more professionally but have difficulties with structural change. The motivation for the new framework is: not only do things well, but keep on doing the good things.

Other models

David Hinley (2000) has made a study of other models for application management and their strengths and weaknesses. The models examined are:

- Software Maintenance Management (SWM) (Hinley and Bennett, Centre for Software Maintenance, 1992);
- The Capability Maturity Model (CMM) applied to maintenance (SEI-Carnegie Mellon);
- Maintenance Assistant Capability for Software (MACS), Esprit II Project (No. 2570);
- European Platform for Software Maintenance (EPSOM), Eureka Software Factory;
- Reverse Engineering into CASE Technology (RECAST), OGC and CSM and LBMS Ltd;
- Software Life-cycle Support (ITIL Publication);
- Application Management Environments and Support (AMES), Esprit: Intecs Sistemi SpA, Matra Marconi Space, Valation Teknillinen Tutkimuskeskus (VTT), and the CSM;
- Foster's 7-model (British Telecom);
- R2C (PinkRoccade);

and some less well-known models such as Boehm etc.

The conclusion was that application management still gets relatively little attention in the scientific world. It confirmed that all models have more or less the same weaknesses and strengths.

The study pointed out that models concerning the maintenance and enhancement of applications have seen an evolution. At first, the models were especially concerned with application development; subsequently they were concerned with technical (infrastructure) management and mainly derived from ITIL.

Furthermore, it became clear that it will be essential to bring future frameworks and methodologies into the public domain. New developments like chain automation, outsourcing, ERP and ASP make an open application management infrastructure more important.

In the study the following challenges for future models have been defined:

- Evolution of the applications portfolio is facilitated when the applications managers have visibility of the business; this can best be achieved through mutual trust and cooperation, and hence a new framework must support the development of a mature relationship between the client and the service provider in terms of a strong partnership.
- In establishing such partnerships, applications managers need to transcend standard IS service management metrics and track performance and client satisfaction in such a way that there is visibility and accountability in the management of software assets.
- The framework library has demonstrated that there are a number of de facto standards, e.g. ITIL for Service Management, SEI-CMM for software process

assessment etc. Application management can benefit from a more holistic approach which not only considers the process, people and technology but also orthogonal views of strategic, tactical and operational issues.

- The model should be sufficiently flexible to be used in all application management scenarios, and to deal with the diverse and complex problems in providing an application service.
- The proposed framework must provide a traceable pathway in which changes to individual applications and the evolution of the application portfolio may be managed successfully.
- For many organizations, ICT is not considered a core skill or competency, although it may in fact be critically dependent upon IS for a number of its business processes. This presents one of a number of opportunities for ICT service organizations to meet the changes in their client's organizational structure, by recognizing the potential demands placed upon them not only to maintain the applications systems which are critical to the client's business, but to work more closely in partnership with the client's organization to provide a higher level of quality service in relation to applications support, evolutionary change and redevelopment.
- To 'win' business in the application services market, it is necessary to have a clear and consistent strategy which minimizes both customer and supplier risk. An application management strategy is required which can be presented to the client and which demonstrates that the applications which are critical to the business are being managed like any other business asset.
- The framework needs to be sufficiently robust to deal with legacy applications in all environments in terms of renewal, replacement and retirement. Previous attempts have either focused on particular software environments or have been hindered by the lack of tool support.
- The application management framework must clearly focus on the provision of an application service as a value-added activity. Service provider and customer risks need to be recognized and are effectively managed through timely assessment and mitigation. The reliance and cooperation necessary between the various roles should be made explicit, in order that the relationships between the various disciplines and application management can be defined.

The experiences with older frameworks and the challenges outlined above led to the framework that is described in the next sections.

1.3 The new framework

Basic principles

Some of the basic elements for the new framework are a number of strengths of the R2C model:

- service team;
- controllable service by means of service level agreements and insight into costs;

- a forward-looking vision of applications by evolutionary changes;
- integral management of maintenance and enhancement/renovation.

For wide use, the framework had to meet some conditions:

- the presence of a number of best practices;
- independence of suppliers by means of bringing the framework into the public domain;
- a vast knowledge network and knowledge organization in which experiences in the field of application management can be easily shared.

This chapter does not pay attention to the latter aspects. However, they have been filled in in practice.

The framework

The framework for application management is derived from the principles and ideas presented earlier. The purpose of the management framework is to be able to describe application management in depth as well as in breadth, so that readers can appreciate the activity domains and the aspects which are of interest to them or require management attention. It may also be used to facilitate awareness and understanding. The framework supports three perspectives (levels of management): strategic, tactical and technical (or operational). A second criterion for the several clusters in the framework implies the distinction of whether a process is supporting a service function or an application function (Table 1.2).

TABLE 1.2 Service vs. application view

	Service view	Application view
Goal	Provide optimal services to users	Provide optimal applications
Focus	User organization	Business process of user organization
Most important knowledge	Knowledge of the users and their organization	Knowledge of the market and the process of the user organization
Important terms	Service, up time, ……	Market terms such as assurance product, invoice etc.
Renewal	Which developments are seen in the client's organization; which technology; which future services	The direction in which the client's market is moving; the implications for the client's business process and the supporting applications

Application management is defined as: the contracted responsibility for the management and execution of all activities related to the maintenance and evolution of existing applications, within well-defined service levels. In other words: the management of the maintenance, enhancement and renovation of applications in a business-economically sound manner. The key principle here is to support the business processes using information systems for the life cycle of the business processes.

Two essential viewpoints can be distinguished here:

1. The first is the perspective of '*supporting the business processes using information systems*'. This means keeping the applications up and running and making sure that they support an organization's day-to-day activities. In practical terms, this involves providing a continuous service by making firm agreements about the service level and restoring the agreed service level as soon as possible if deviations are established; creating a high level of accessibility for questions and remarks by clients about the service; and preventing disruptions and facilitating new services by responding as an ICT service provider in good time. The focus is therefore on service, the service that is supplied and that (together with infrastructure management) facilitates the use of applications. In cost terms this generally amounts to 10–20% of the overall costs of application management.

2. The second viewpoint is '*the life cycle of the business processes*'. Organizations evolve; environments and markets change. To continue functioning optimally, the supporting information systems have to grow with the organization. This involves enhancing the applications to the current and future technical and functional requirements. The application-related processes generally account for the majority of the costs of application management.

We can distinguish operational, tactical and strategic processes in these two areas. This results in the ASL framework depicted in Figure 1.2. The ovals and the rectangle in the middle each represent a cluster of processes. Three levels are distinguished: operational, tactical and strategic.

FIGURE 1.2

ASL framework

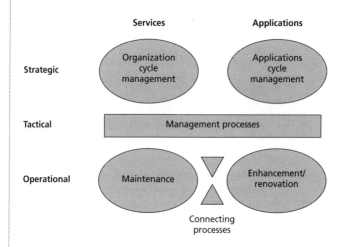

The **operational level** recognizes two clusters of processes:

1. **'maintenance' of applications**: processes that ensure the optimum availability of the applications currently being used to support the business process with a minimum of resources and disruption in the operation;

2 *'enhancement/renovation'* of applications: processes that adapt applications to new wishes and requirements in response to changes to the organization and its environment. The necessary adjustments are made to the software, the data model and the documentation.

The steering **tactical level** comprises the overall management processes. These processes provide for the collective steering of the operational processes for 'services' on the one hand and 'applications' on the other. Both the strategic and the operational levels supply the management processes. The future and day-to-day reality are thus secured in these processes.

The directive **strategic level** also distinguishes two clusters of processes, based on subdivision into the 'service angle' and the 'application angle'. In these days of making services and service providers more flexible, the service provider of today (for both operational services and systems enhancement) is not necessarily the service provider for ever. There are countless reasons why these tasks could also be performed by another service provider. Competition between service providers regarding the services being supplied is increasing. Separating the two angles makes it possible to make an individual choice for each area.

The clusters of processes at strategic level are:

- **Organization Cycle Management (OCM)**: processes that are aimed at developing a future vision of the ICT service organization and translating that vision into a policy for its renewal;
- **Applications Cycle Management (ACM)**: processes that serve to shape a long-term strategy for the various applications that fit within the entirety of an organization's information provision in relation to the organization's long-term policy.

1.4 More detailed description of the framework

This section discusses the processes per cluster.

Maintenance processes at operational level

At the operational level, the following areas of attention can be identified for managing information systems:

- the **identification and maintenance** of various objects (e.g. application, interface between two applications, component, database, etc.) of service;
- the **availability** and the **quality** of these objects;
- the deployment of the right **capacities** and **assets**, the right resources and the right quantities that are required for the service;
- the **questions**, *wishes and defects* concerning the objects or the agreed service.

These areas of attention can be traced back to the definitions of the maintenance processes:

- **Incident management** is the process that provides for the settlement of incidents or service calls. In this context, a service call is a question, a wish, a disruption, etc., concerning the existing application(s). Incident management provides a service desk process, for example. The service desk provides contact with the functional managers and/or end users. The service desk also provides users with information about the implications of (changes in) the ICT service. In the incident management process the service calls are taken and registered, and actions are set in motion to deal with them. The result is also monitored. Making structural analyses of the registered service calls provides insight into the desired improvement activities.
- **Configuration management** covers the processes concerned with the registration, storing and maintenance of information about (versions of) configuration components that are being used, such as software and documentation.
- **Availability management** concerns the processes that provide, monitor and guarantee the availability of services and ICT components.
- **Capacity management** provides for the optimum deployment of resources, i.e. right time, right place, right quantity and at a realistic price.
- **Continuity management** relates to the range of measures needed to guarantee the continuity of the service, e.g. in the event of a calamity, for which fallback facilities and backups have to be arranged, or prevention of fraud.

Enhancement/renovation processes at operational level

The enhancement and/or renovation of ICT objects such as software, documentation and design take place in a project-based manner within the framework of a renewal scenario. In general terms, the following activities are carried out (Figure 1.3):

FIGURE 1.3

The operational processes

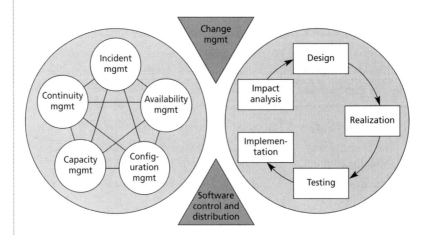

- ***impact analysis***: the activities for conditioning and charting the implications of a change proposal;
- ***design***: further information analysis and design;
- ***realization***: the realization and/or assembly of the changed objects;
- ***testing***: the testing of the changed objects with the following end result: completed products for acceptance, acceptance tests and discharge from the client;
- ***implementation***: the introduction of the changed objects focusing on conversion, training, instruction and migration, followed by discharge from the client.

Before the actual realization is started, much attention is paid to project definition and initiation: setting down the project, process and product requirements, schedule, budget and project organization.

Connecting processes between 'maintenance' and 'enhancement/renovation'

The following processes are distinguished at operational level as connections between the maintenance cycle on the one hand and the enhancement/renovation cycle on the other:

- **Change management** relates to the process that determines which requests for change are introduced in a 'release'. In consultation with the client, and validated by impact analysis, this process results in an agreement on the alterations that will be made, on the scheduling, costs and completion dates. In actual fact, change management forms the incoming channel to enhancement and renovation.
- **Software control and distribution** covers the processes involved with the control and distribution of software objects and additional objects (such as documentation) during development and testing and during the transfer to operation. Control means: a safe working method that must limit the risks of unauthorized use, unauthorized change or deletion. This process can be described as the outgoing channel: adapted ICT components are transferred to operation and use.

The management processes at tactical level

The management processes at tactical level comprise the following areas of attention:

- ***time***: delivery time, required capacity and effort;
- ***money***: finances involved in the entirety of the service provision;
- the ***quality*** of the services provided and the monitoring method;
- ***agreements*** with clients and suppliers.

The results from the other process clusters provide input to the management processes. Integral planning and management are thus made possible, both for releases of the applications and for services. The situation that this creates also secures the strategy on the shop floor and translates the experiences from maintenance and enhancement back to higher levels. These processes have a monitoring and foreseeing angle. Identifying possible risks and taking appropriate measures (parts of risk management) form an integral part of the management processes.

The four areas of attention mentioned are reflected in the defined management processes (Figure 1.4):

- *Planning and control*: the management of time and capacity relating to all activities that are involved in maintenance, enhancement and renovation of applications. The simultaneous steering of the project-based renewal activities and the continuous maintenance activities – often performed by the same department and people – is one of the major challenges of application management.
- *Cost management*: the processes concerned with the managing and charging of ICT costs. Cost management yields business-economic data so that an optimum balance can be found between price and quality. Good cost control, and possibly returns control, from an integral angle, highlight the financial implications of the various choices. The best choice is made in consultation with the client(s).
- *Quality management*: concerned with the quality of the application management processes, the products, the service and the organization. Testing the products, actively monitoring the application management processes and experiences of maintenance and renovation provide insight into the bottlenecks and, accordingly, into the structural improvement options. The organization-wide standards, new requirements and future developments also form input to this process. The quality of the resources deployed (including auxiliary equipment and personnel) also come under quality management.
- *Service level management*: comprises the activities that specify in more detail the desired services and lay down and monitor the desired service level. The purpose of service level management is therefore to make the service level transparent, and to control and account for it.

FIGURE 1.4
The tactical processes

Planning and control	Cost management	Quality management	Service level management

Applications Cycle Management (ACM) processes at strategic level

In the present hectic time in the market and in organizations, it is hard to gain a clear understanding of the desired ICT support in the long term (10 years). Therefore, there is little sense in designing a complete blueprint for the ICT structure. The emphasis should be on a stepwise growth path from the existing situation to a new situation, which will probably be changed after a couple of years in its turn. The scope of the ACM processes that are defined in ASL is the next 3–5 years. They can lead to improvement activities in a comparable or even longer term.

ACM concentrates on the future of information provision, on the life cycle of the objects in information provision. This takes place at two levels: at the level of 'the application' and at the level of 'the complete application portfolio' that supports a business process. ACM calls for trend watching in the areas of technology, the business processes within the client organization and the environment of the client organization – in other words, the entire process chain.

The ACM processes are (Figure 1.5):

- ***ICT portfolio management*** charts the significance and the performance of the various existing applications for the organization, translates the company policy into the various objects and sets out a strategy for the future of the objects in the ICT portfolio. In many client organizations this process forms part of information management or information planning.

- ***Life-cycle management*** matches the existing options of, and the future requirements for, one or more applications that support a business process. A strategy is then drawn up to meet the future requirements. This process is deeper, more substantive and – in comparison with the previous process – more sharply focused on the specific business process.

- ***ICT developments strategy*** examines which ICT developments could be of interest to the client organization and its information provision. Application development technology, but also new infrastructures such as networking and audio/visual, could create possibilities that have an impact on the applications.

- ***Customer environment strategy*** provides an image of process chain developments and the resulting requirements and opportunities for the applications and information provision of the client organization. Organizations function as a link in a chain of organizations. This creates a strong mutual connection between the applications. The possibilities of the organization's own information provision determine the place and position of the organization in these chain processes.

- ***Customer organization strategy*** charts the developments within the client organization as well as the obstacles, the impact on the applications and the ways of responding to them.

FIGURE 1.5
Strategic processes within Applications Cycle Management

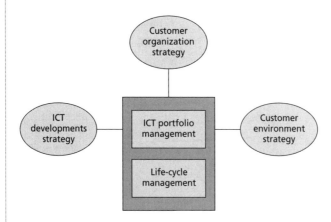

Organization Cycle Management (OCM) processes at strategic level

These processes concern the life cycle of the services provided by the internal and external ICT service provider(s) and adjustment of how the ICT service is organized.

The relationship between the ICT service providers and the client organization is not a constant factor: consider outsourcing, privatization and application service provision (ASP). These developments have a significant impact on the client organization, but also of course on the way in which the ICT service is organized. In this cluster the strategy is defined:

- Which services does the ICT service provider wish to provide in the future?
- What does the ICT service provider have to do to continue to guarantee the desired service level in the long term?
- What does the ICT service provider have to do to operate successfully in the market (how to keep it or replace it)?

The following processes are distinguished here (Figure 1.6):

- **Account definition** determines the image, strategy, and organizational form for the realization of the approach to the desired markets.
- **Market definition** determines the market segments to which the services will be provided in the future on the basis of an analysis of the market, supply chain and client developments.
- **Service delivery definition** charts the service that the market wants and that the ICT service provider can supply using relevant skills, and translates it into policy and strategy.
- **Skills definition** determines skills, knowledge and expertise called for by the future service of the organization.
- **Technology definition** determines the (development) tools, technology and methods that the organization wants to use to realize the future service.

FIGURE 1.6

Strategic processes within Organization Cycle Management

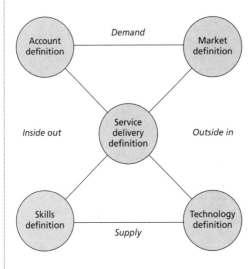

It all relates to demand, supply and delivery. Figure 1.6's top is occupied with demand from the market and the clients, and the bottom indicates which technologies and services are feasible and could be delivered. The delivery is the final result, in which the service profile that will be desired in due course is defined on the basis of demand, supply and resources present.

1.5 Relationships with models for technical and functional management

The distinction that was made between the service provider and the renovator of an application can be made as well in other forms of management, namely technical management and functional management. Processes such as incident management, continuity management etc. can also be recognized in functional management (Deurloo, 1998, 2000; Van Outvorst, 2000). The content of these processes differs of course; the goals are comparable, however.

Other processes can be identified that depend strongly on the type of management. Functional management concerns, among other things, the business processes. In functional management, knowledge of the business process and the user organization is most important, since functional management translates the developments therein to requirements and wishes for information provision and applications.

The relationship between the various models can be outlined easily (see Figure 1.7).

FIGURE 1.7

Relations between models on the operational level

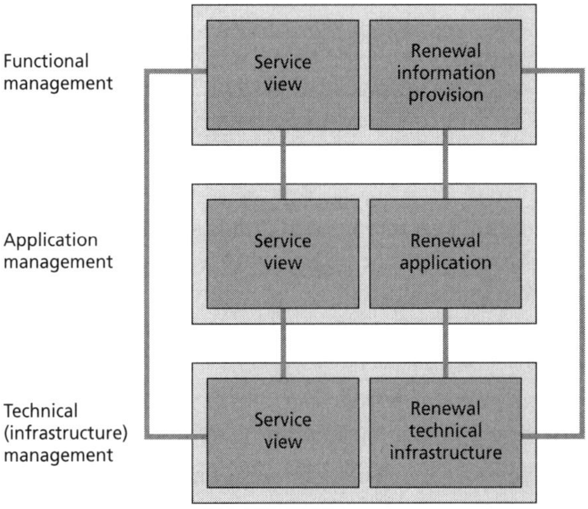

Cooperation between the continuous operational processes of functional management and application management is intensive. The same goes for cooperation with technical (infrastructure) management. For instance, the help desk within functional management has a firm relation with the help desks within application and technical management. The same goes for processes like availability management.

In office automation a strong link between functional management and technical management can be recognized, and the processes concerned with enhancement and renovation also have a strong mutual relation.

These relations are also present on the tactical and strategic levels. The link between the process cluster Applications Cycle Management in application management and a similar process cluster concerning the future of the information provision in functional management is very strong, as is the cooperation in Service Level Management. This is depicted in Figure 1.8 in which the upper layer depicts a perspective view on application management, the lower layer on functional management. The stronger links are symbolically represented by the bold lines.

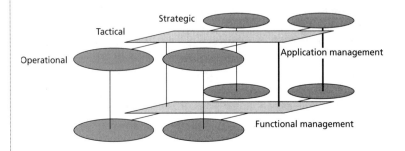

FIGURE 1.8
Relations between functional management and application management

A relation to the ITIL processes for technical infrastructure management can be easily defined, since the (mainly operational) processes in ASL that are recognized in ITIL as well are based on these ITIL processes.

A detailed description of the differences between ITIL and ASL has been given.

1.6 Conclusions

The application management framework highlights a number of requirements in order to provide a professional applications service. It also provides three perspectives which are aimed broadly at strategic, tactical and technical management.

To summarize the ASL framework, it is proposed that to provide a high-quality professional applications service it is necessary to:

- manage applications in portfolio terms, i.e. recognize that applications are a business asset that can justify financial support in order to sustain their value;
- identify and assess the risks of maintenance and ensure that customer benefits are realized;
- have a valid maintenance strategy for the maintenance and renewal of legacy systems, with the purpose of extending the useful life of existing applications, in a cost-effective and timely manner;
- ensure that IT infrastructure management requirements are incorporated during the design and development stages of applications and that maintainability and other quality attributes are considered throughout the application's life.

The ASL framework has also addressed challenges for application management, such as:

- the development of mature relationships between client and service provider;
- visibility of and accountability for the management of software assets;
- closing the gap between development, enhancement and operation of applications;
- meeting business needs through the timely recognition of potential demands to be placed on applications in support of business processes by means of the defined strategic processes.

These processes will become more and more important in a period in which e-commerce, outsourcing, ERP, middleware and many other products come to market. The framework offers much support in implementing an application management organization. It can be used very well in connection with models for technical management (ITIL) and functional management.

The framework overcomes some of the limitations recognized in former models such as R2C, including: scalability, the lack of strategic direction and visibility of business plans, and benefits realization. The first reactions to the framework are very positive. In cooperation with several organizations the framework is being developed in more detail and founded on best practices.

Literature

Deurloo, Kees, Van Outvorst, Frank and Van der Pols, Remko (2002) 'Een niew functioneel beheermodel', *IT Beheer Jaarboek 2002*, ten Hagen & Stam, Den Haag.

Deurloo, C. D, Meijer-Veldman, M.E.E. and van der Pols, R. (1998), 'Model voor Functioneel Beheer', *IT Beheer Jaarboek 1998*, ten Hagen & Stam, Den Haag (in Dutch).

Hinley, David S. (2000) *Barracuda Content Design, a methodology for the provision of Application Services* (Chapter 6 with Remko van der Pols and Machteld Meijer), PinkRoccade.

Looijen, Maarten (1999) *Information Systems – Management, Control and Maintenance*, ISBN 90 267 2846 8, Kluwer, Deventer.

Meijer, Machteld, van Outvorst Frank, Hoogland, Dolf and Fris, Barbara (2000) 'Application Services with R2C', *World Class IT Service Management Guide 2000*, p. 133, ten Hagen & Stam, Den Haag.

van Outvorst, Frank *et al.* 'A model for functional management', chapter 5 of this Guide.

Pastors, Marco, Knetsch, Jack *et al.* (eds) (2001) *Application Services Library, Introduction Best Practices and Framework for Application Management*, ISBN 90-806050-2-6, PinkRoccade, Voorburg.

van der Pols, Remko (2001) *ASL: een framework voor applicatiebeheer*, ten Hagen & Stam, Den Haag.

Thiadens, Theo (1999) *Beheer van ICT-voorzieningen*, Academic Services (in Dutch).

2 BDM®: IT-enabled business development and management methodology

A new approach to managing modern (network) organizations in a dynamic environment

Djoen Tan Tansconsult
Aad Uijttenbroek Lansa Publishing

Summary

Rapid changes in the marketplace and the progress of the development of information technology (IT) require companies to exhibit ever greater flexibility and alertness. Because almost everything depends on everything else, it becomes increasingly difficult for senior management to acquire a complete picture of the situation and to make the right decisions. This is even more difficult because of the use of various methodologies for the management, development, maintenance and use of the different types of resources, such as people, machines, money and information. BDM offers a consistent overall approach to managing complex (network) organizations in a dynamic environment.

2.1 Towards a new economy

The transfer of labour-intensive activities to low-income countries is causing a continuing shift in industrial countries from labour-intensive companies to knowledge-intensive companies whose products have an added value based on know-how and creativity. The industrial economy, based on raw materials and physical labour, is becoming an information economy, based on knowledge and communication. The characteristics of the information economy are:

- accelerated technological developments;
- enhanced information and knowledge intensity of activities;
- reduced time-to-market and life cycle of products and services;
- increased possibilities to split the value chain of an organization into smaller pieces;
- globalization of the marketplace;
- mass customization;
- fading boundaries between branches of industry.

The acceleration of technological developments is caused by spiralling IT supply and demand, stimulated by the ever-improving cost–performance ratio of the main hardware components. Continuing rapid progress enables the enhancement of the information and knowledge intensity of activities and a continued reduction in time-to-market and the life cycle of products and services. Businesses seize these opportunities to distinguish themselves from their competitors. The compression of space and time, caused by growing worldwide communications and stimulated by e-business (Shim *et al.*, 2000), gives rise to a globalization of the marketplace and an intensification of global competition. Global companies are emerging which develop their products and services in countries where the appropriate know-how is available, buy materials and components where these are cheapest and produce in countries with the lowest costs for labour and distribution. The geographic devolution of business activities results in network organizations or boundaryless organizations (Ashkenas *et al.*, 1995; Markus *et al.*, 2000) with relatively independent units having strategic alliances with suppliers and customers. In this way these companies are large enough to be able to make the required investments and small enough to respond to local markets. IT also enables mass customization. With mass customization, producers aim to manufacture their product not only as cheaply as possible but also with enough variety, so that almost everybody can get the exact product they need. The innovation of products and services, made possible by IT, erases the boundaries between branches of industry. A slew of competitors can suddenly emerge from the most unexpected corners at unforeseen moments.

To survive in the information economy, companies need to apply IT pro-actively instead of reactively. This means that the existing organizational characteristics, such as business strategy, organization structure and business processes, are not taken as given facts but are changed so as to profit fully from the possibilities of IT (Tan, 1996). This can be business process redesign or even business scope redefinition or business redesign (Venkatraman, 1994).

2.2 The necessity of a new methodology

The rapid developments described above, together with many mutually dependent factors, make it difficult for managers to obtain a complete overview and make the right decisions. Furthermore, resource managers, such as controllers, human resource managers and information systems (IS) managers, use different methods. In the new economy, (senior) managers therefore need a new methodology that meets the following demands:

- must be aimed directly at achieving the business goals;
- must be based on the business processes;
- must assume a (rapid) continuous change in the organization;
- must be suitable for all types of resources;
- must be applicable in all types of organizations (from traditional hierarchical organizations to modern network organizations);
- must be able to incorporate current methods and techniques.

BDM meets these requirements. BDM is based on the IIM Information Infrastructure Management methodology originally developed by the authors for IS management (Uijttenbroek, Tan and De Jong, 2000).

2.3 The BDM frame of reference

According to the BDM frame of reference, activities are carried out in organizations to achieve organizational goals. Activities consist of actions and the various types of resources or components needed to perform these actions. Related actions can be clustered into business processes and organizational units.

BDM identifies the following six types of infrastructure consisting of components and their relationships (see Figure 2.1):

1. the *human infrastructure*: individuals, groups/teams, groups of groups and communities;
2. the (knowledge and) *information infrastructure*: knowledge and information systems, knowledge bases and databases, computers and communication networks;
3. the *financial infrastructure*: accounts, sets of accounts, cost centres and budgets;
4. the *legal infrastructure*: corporate bodies, agreements, contracts, laws, regulations, rules, etc;
5. the *production means infrastructure*: primary production means, such as machines, equipment, plants and means of transport;
6. the *support infrastructure*: secondary production means, such as buildings, energy and water supplies, and so on.

With the exception of the legal and financial infrastructures, the infrastructures generally consist of concrete (visible) components as opposed to activities and processes. Unambiguity is improved by considering the infrastructures together with the business processes. Persons or machines cannot overlap each other physically, for instance.

The transition towards an information economy causes the human and information infrastructures to become more and more important; the core competencies of an enterprise are often based to a large extent on these infrastructures. These infrastructures are also more difficult to imitate by competitors than the other infrastructures.

FIGURE 2.1
Organizational units, processes and infrastructures

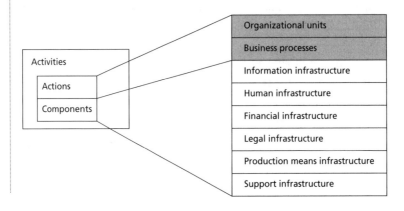

FIGURE 2.2

BDM management model

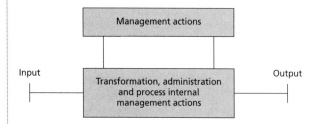

The BDM frame of reference also recognizes a simple two-layered management model, shown in Figure 2.2. The two layers consist of (strategic) management actions and operational transformation actions (to transform inputs into outputs), combined with operational management and administrative support to assess performance or quality. Each process always contains a certain amount of internal management (internal process management). There should always be a balance between internal process management and external process management, depending on the situation.

2.4 The BDM process diagram

As mentioned before, related actions can be combined into business processes. BDM has defined 20 generic processes for the management, development, maintenance and production/operation/use of organizational units, processes and infrastructure components (see Figure 2.3). The BDM processes are generic because they can be applied to all kinds of organizations and to all kinds of resources (infrastructures). The development of the BDM process structure is aimed at achieving maximum coherence between the distinct BDM process activities and minimal interdependence between the processes.

FIGURE 2.3

BDM process diagram

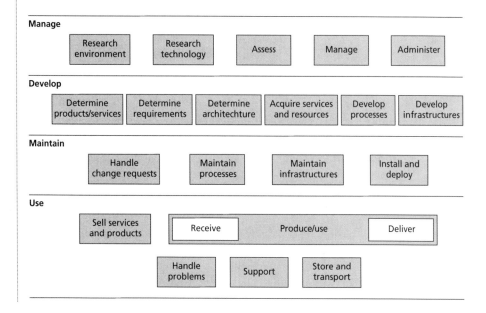

The 20 generic processes can be arranged into four main processes or levels:

1. **Manage**: research environment, research technology, assess, manage, administer.
2. **Develop**: determine products/services, determine requirements, determine architecture, acquire services and resources, develop organizational units and processes, develop infrastructures.
3. **Maintain**: handle change requests, maintain organizational units and processes, maintain infrastructures, install and deploy.
4. **Operate/use**: sell products and services, produce/operate/use, handle problems, support use, store and transport.

The BDM processes can be applied to the manufacturing of any product (buildings, cars, food, energy, IT products, etc.) or the delivery of any service (financial, government, health, legal, engineering, real estate, media, communication and IT services).

With the 'administer' process an organization configuration database (OCDB) can be realized that presents an overview of the performance or quality of processes and resources for strategic and operational decisions (Prahalad and Krishnan, 1999). A software tool will be available in the near future. This tool will make it possible to build and operate process networks and will assist management in automatically keeping information about process and resource performance. The basis for maintaining information will be the OCDB mentioned above.

The BDM processes are continuous processes aimed at continuous performance improvement. In other words, the model offers a 'continuous improvement mechanism' in which the performance or quality of the processes and infrastructure components in a changing environment is central. Because the model can be applied to all of the six infrastructures, the management, development, maintenance and operation/use of all types of resources are brought together in one integral approach.

2.5 Service management and product management

Figure 2.4 shows the BDM management model as a model in which services and products are acquired and delivered. Strategic management takes care of adaptation of the organization to changing circumstances. Operational management controls the transformation of inputs into outputs. The idea is that an organization (or organizational unit) supplies services (s) and/or products (p) to another organization (or organizational unit) and that management controls quality. One can distinguish two types of management:

1. **service management**, which makes sure that a service (provided by a number of processes) complies with an agreed Service Capability Level Agreement;
2. **product management**, which makes sure that a product (a collection of components) complies with an agreed Product Capability Level Agreement.

The abbreviations II, HI, FI, LI, PI and SI refer respectively to information infrastructure, human infrastructure, financial infrastructure, legal infrastructure, production means infrastructure and support infrastructure. In this view the infrastructures also deliver services and products to the actions needed to transform inputs from suppliers to outputs for clients.

FIGURE 2.4

Management model in which services and products are acquired and delivered

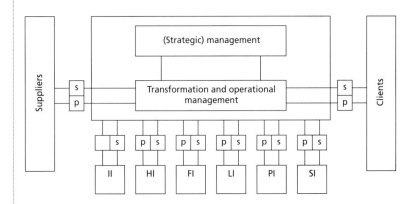

2.6 Assessing and improving the quality of services and products

To assess the quality or 'capability' of services (processes) and products (components), use is made of existing international ISO standards. To assess processes, BDM uses the ISO15504 (SPICE) capability assessment approach; for products, use is made of an approach based on ISO9126 (Uijttenbroek *et al.*, 1998). Although ISO15504 has been developed for capability assessment of IT processes, the standard is also applicable to the assessment of all kinds of processes. Processes can have processes or products as result or output. A product can be used as a resource in another process or can be a component to be used to make a complete product to be sold to clients.

The quality of a process is determined by a level from 0 to 5. To determine the level, a number of attributes must be scored. These are shown in Table 2.1. Each attribute is scored on a four-point scale: Not Achieved, Partially Achieved, Largely Achieved and Fully Achieved (the NPLF score). Every next level must have L or F scores from previous attributes. A process is, for instance, at level 3 when the first five attributes have L or F scores.

TABLE 2.1

Process capability levels according to ISO 15504 (SPICE)

Capability or quality levels	Process attributes	Score
Level 0: Incomplete process	No attributes	
Level 1: Performed process	Process performance	L or F
Level 2: Managed process	Performance management Work product management	L or F L or F
Level 3: Established process	Process definition Process resources	L or F L or F
Level 4: Predictable process	Process measurement Process control	L or F L or F
Level 5: Optimizing process	Process change Continuous improvement	L or F L or F

To determine scores, one can make use of an adapted version of the balanced scorecard approach (Kaplan and Norton, 1996). For each attribute, a scorecard is determined consisting of the following elements, for instance:

1. Process Performance Scorecard: The degree to which inputs and outputs of the process have been consistently and clearly described.
2. Performance Management Scorecard: The degree to which the user of the result of the process is satisfied with it and receives it in a timely fashion.
3. Work Product Management Scorecard: The degree to which planning of activities is available and approved; the degree to which all steps, delivery times and resources to be used have been administered; the degree to which internal and external process management has been described.
4. Process Definition Scorecard: The degree to which the process has been described according to an organizational standard, is being kept up to date and all concerned are being informed.
5. Process Resources Scorecard: The degree to which human and other resources needed for the process have been described and actually used.
6. Process Measurement Scorecard: The degree to which performance metrics have been determined and periodic assessments take place on the basis of these metrics. The degree to which human and other resources are being assessed.
7. Process Control Scorecard: The degree to which periodic assessments and analysis of performance are used to determine actions to improve process performance, risk analysis takes place and improvements are evaluated.
8. Process Change Scorecard: The degree to which changes in organizational objectives, performance and resources in use are being identified and result in proposed process changes.
9. Continuous Improvement Scorecard: The degree to which implementation of changes is being managed and controlled.

Each element of an attribute is scored, which leads to a total score for each attribute. N and P scores result in proposed actions to improve the scores to L or F. Depending on the situation, more detailed scores can be developed and more elements can be scored.

A product or product component is the result of a process and is used as input in a following process. Products are also resources in carrying out process steps. IT products and resources can be assessed in a similar fashion on the basis of ISO 9126 (see Table 2.2). The ISO 9126 standard defines product quality as scores to a collection of attributes. An attribute can be detailed as a number of levels of sub-attributes. For instance, usability can be detailed in terms of clarity, understandability, user friendliness and attractiveness of the product for the user. Each attribute should be scored according to an appropriate scheme. The ISO 9126 attributes can be grouped in a capability-level approach as used in ISO 15504, to give a capability level to products.

TABLE 2.2 Product quality levels on the basis of ISO 9126

Capability or quality levels	Product attributes	Score
Level 0: Incomplete product	No attributes	
Level 1: Performed product	Functionality	L or F
Level 2: Applicable product	Usability	L or F
Level 3: Established product	Reliability	L or F
Level 4: Predictable product	Efficiency	L or F
Level 5: Optimized product	Portability Maintainability	L or F L or F

2.7 BDM and ITIL

The ITIL (IT Infrastructure Library) methodology is currently popular in larger organizations in the UK and the Netherlands. ITIL is primarily focused on the maintenance and operations of the IT infrastructure. To compare the BDM processes with the ITIL processes, one should limit the BDM processes to the IT infrastructure. In Table 2.3 the most important ITIL processes from the Service Delivery Set and the Service Support Set are related to the BDM processes applied to the maintenance and operation/use of the IT infrastructure.

TABLE 2.3 Relationship between ITIL and BDM processes

ITIL processes	BDM processes
Service delivery set	
Service level management	Manage, determine requirements, handle change requests, assess
Capacity management	Determine requirements, determine architecture, develop infrastructure, handle change requests, install and deploy, operate/use
Contingency planning	Determine requirements, develop infrastructure, operate/use, support use
Availability management	Determine requirements, develop infrastructure, assess, operate/use, support use
Cost management	Administer, determine requirements, determine architecture
Service support set	
Configuration management	Administer, handle change requests, install and deploy, support use
Help desk	Administer, handle change requests, assess, operate/use, handle problems, support use
Problem management	Develop infrastructure, assess, maintain infrastructure, operate/use, handle problems, support use
Change management	Handle change requests, maintain infrastructure, install and deploy, operate/use, support use
Software control and distribution	Administer, assess, maintain infrastructure, install and deploy, operate/use

Table 2.3 shows that a number of BDM processes are not available in the ITIL approach. These are: research environment, research technology, determine products and services, acquire services and resources, develop processes, maintain processes, sell products and services, and store and transport. This is because ITIL is limited to the maintenance and use of the IT infrastructure. BDM has a much greater scope than ITIL and offers a consistent overall approach, in which ITIL publications have a place as elaborations of (parts of) BDM processes.

2.8 BDM use

A few examples of BDM applications are as follows:

- BDM has been used to improve customer relations processes, using the 'research environment', 'determine products/services', 'sell products/services', 'product development' and 'support' processes. This has resulted in an intranet (to become an internet) application intended to bring customers together with the organization, in a community, in order to share new customer product requirements with product development.

- In another case BDM, or rather its predecessor IIM, has been used to set up service level agreements for IT hardware installation and maintenance, using the processes 'maintain infrastructure', 'manage processes/infrastructure', 'handle problems', 'support' and 'install and deploy' processes.

- BDM has been used to set up configuration management for IT requirements, processes and infrastructure architectures, using the processes 'determine requirements', 'determine architecture', 'manage' and 'administer'.

- In user environments, BDM is being used to develop a process-based, componentized enterprise resource planning (ERP) application.

2.9 Conclusions

BDM aims to provide a number of standard business processes which may be used in the design of organizations, large and small, traditional and advanced. It often serves as a checklist to make sure important aspects of organizational practice are not forgotten. BDM also provides a consistent approach to the management of business processes and all types of resources, in particular with respect to planning, administration and management. BDM-type management assumes the use of performance/quality assessment and improvement, and it is very much based on well-designed and proven approaches and international ISO standards. Service level management and product capability management are natural concepts. BDM is a tool to build process-based organizations. Processes may extend beyond the borders of the organization without loss of control of actions and resources.

BDM is aimed at achieving business goals through improved processes and improved management of processes; processes are the most basic ingredient of the approach. Rapid organizational change is easier to achieve using BDM, because of the architectural approach, meaning that processes, process steps and resources are meticulously administered as components in an organization configuration database. This allows for better maintenance of organizational know-how. The components may be used to build different types of organizations, from the traditionally hierarchical to the completely networked. The approach is open to other methods and techniques. BDM is used by senior managers and consultants.

Literature

Ashkenas, R., Jick, T, Kerr, S. and Ulrich, D. (1995) *The boundaryless organization*, Josseyn-Bass, San Fransisco.

Kaplan, R.S. and Norton, D.P. (1996) *The Balanced Scorecard: translating strategy into action*, Harvard Business School Press, Boston.

Markus, M.L., Manville, B. and Agres, C.E. (2000) 'What makes virtual organizations work', *Sloan Management Review*, Fall.

Pralahad, C.K. and Krishnan, M.S. (1999) 'The new meaning of quality in the Information Age', *Harvard Business Review*, June.

Shim, S., Pedayala, V. Sundaraman, M. and Gao, J. (2000) 'Business-to-business e-commerce frameworks', *Computer*, October.

Tan, D.S. (1996) *IIM: From information systems management to information infrastructure management*, Lansa Publishing, Leiderdorp, The Netherlands (ISBN 90-5590-029-X).

Uijttenbroek, A.A., Tan, D.S. *et al.* (1998) *Assessment and Improvement of Modern Information Services*, Lansa Publishing, Leiderdorp, The Netherlands (ISBN 90-5590-037-0).

Uijttenbroek, A.A., Tan, D.S. and De Jong, W. (2000) *IIM: Information Infrastructure Management*, Lansa Publishing, Leiderdorp, The Netherlands (ISBN 90-5590-045-1).

Venkatraman, N. (1994) 'IT-enabled business transformation: from automation to business scope redefinition', *Sloan Management Review*, Winter.

3 BiOOlogic™

Business-aligned integrated management of IT organizations and supporting tools through natural object-oriented logic

Johann Schreurs ICT division of Treasury Department,
DirkJan van der Hoven HIT, The Netherlands

Summary

In order to survive in the global market today, businesses need to be capable of adapting their corporate strategies rapidly to changing market requirements. Their success depends on their capability to put strategy into operation. Strategies have to be realized in the business by both culture and structure. BiOOlogic is an architectural style to guide the translation of strategy into structure. This structure gives views and specifications by which the strategy can be put into operation.

3.1 Introduction

Information and communication technology (ICT) has become a critical enabler to realize business strategies. IT Service Management covers a wide range of management aspects to structure and align ICT with the business. The ITIL best practices for processes to service and operate ICT for the business are well known. But ITIL does not address all required management aspects. Quality to the business customers can only be realized by analysing and designing processes in conjunction with the organization, personnel competencies, products and services.

IT Service Management applies to many different kinds of organizations with different strategies, from traditional IT departments of large organizations to internet service providers. The authors selected a business case from their own experience to explain in a practical way how theory can be put to work. The business case is the step-by-step translation of strategy into structure for the ICT division of a government organization. The case applies to large businesses as well.

3.2 BiOOlogic modelling

Modelling for products like cars, buildings and information systems is quite common. Great products don't just happen; they're designed to be that way. According to the authors, analysis and design are even more important for complex systems such as organizations. Analysis determines 70% of the end result.

The foundation of BiOOlogic is object-oriented business engineering (OOBE). The Unified Process (UP) is used to organize analysis-and-design activities. The Unified Modelling Language (UML) is used for modelling. Besides process and language it's advisable to use tools, especially tools that support entire teams. Various tools are available on the market to support this process and language. Using OOBE, BiOOlogic has put ITIL and other best practices, models and methods into new perspectives or views, which make their usage more practical as well as better applied in specific situations.

BiOOlogic modelling is based on analysing organizations through different views on proper levels of abstraction. The key views presented here are:

- *process view*: design of business processes by standardization of process flows and process roles;
- *product view*: structure of ICT products such as hardware and software in relation to their added value ('functionality') for customers;
- *organization view*: organizational structure with positioning of personnel functions/human resources, their knowledge and skills.

These views deliver two products: management views (virtual organizations) and models to organize the ICT organization.

Management views

Management views put the reader in the pilot's seat. Each view provides an insight into the various aspects of the virtual organization. These aspects are logical abstracts of real-world concepts. The views are a method for ICT management, consultants, architects, analysts and designers to focus on the different aspects of the organization. Ideas and solutions can be discussed, tested and decided upon based on these views. The virtual organizations can be formed in advance of the physical formation of the real-world organization and remain as a tool for evaluation and adjustment after physical formation. They form a knowledge base for strategic, tactical and operational management of the organization.

Organization models

These views are also instruments to make the transformation from the virtual to the physical organization and to the reality to be achieved. Together, these views form the model for both the business and ICT organization.

Application

BiOOlogic can be applied to both the design and redesign of ICT organizations, from strategy to production and operation of information systems. The scope can be varied from the whole organization to its individual parts. Furthermore, it can be used to develop the supporting information systems, whether the ICT organization is to be changed or not. BiOOlogic can also be used for non-ICT organizations such as the supported business organization.

3.3 The case

The case applies to a government organization with roughly 30,000 users and an ICT division with 3000 ICT personnel. Users and front-office ICT personnel are geographically spread over dozens of locations in the Netherlands. ICT management and back-office ICT personnel work in a central location. Various platforms (mainframe and mid-range enterprise-servers and local servers), connected through LAN and WAN, support in-house-developed legacy and client–server business applications as well as packaged software. The authors cooperated in various projects to provide the ICT division with supporting tools. The whole of the content (presented here), work processes, management style and teamwork by which these projects are realized is known as the 'Deventer Model'.

3.4 Roadmap

The business and ICT organizations are designed from their respective strategies, as specified by objectives and preconditions. For redesign, the present organizations are modelled as well. The model is produced not just by the act of charting everything, but by analysing and modelling the essential topics, as addressed and prioritized by the objectives set. This model enables all parties involved to discuss the present situation and evaluate it against the objectives. In the case of redesign, the path of successive planning levels for the change management of the organization(s) can be drawn from the model(s) of the present to the future organization(s).

This case provides a step-by-step roadmap on how to structure and organize ICT organizations that produce and service ICT products, with consideration for the development, service and system management of ICT products. The roadmap is as follows:

1. Analysis of business requirements
2. Answer strategic challenges
3. Define overall structure for strategic answers (Quality Management)
4. Identify type(s) of organization(s)
5. Design process structure
6. Design product structure
7. Design organizational structure
8. Design the real organization
9. Culture

Figure 3.1 puts all steps in the perspective of the three management cycles of organization, quality and department management. Organization management adapts customer requirements to the strategy of the ICT division. That strategy is put into operation in the departments through structure and culture. The cultural line, though, is the most important, for it determines about 70% of the final result! Forget about structure when the right culture is not adopted. For cultural changes, BiOOlogic includes intervention strategies based on social-psychological concepts. These are not listed here, because the scope of this chapter is structure.

FIGURE 3.1

Case roadmap

3.5 Step 1: Analyse business requirements

Design of the business and the ICT organization starts with envisioning the objectives and preconditions of the supported business organization. The purpose of the ICT organization is to facilitate the business organization. The ICT objectives and preconditions are derived from the business objectives and preconditions in order to design the ICT organization.

The ICT division in this case provides two groups of services to the business: business cases and use cases. The ICT products provide use cases to the customer, such as *collect data*, *print report* and *signal exception* to support the execution of business processes. Before we get there, the ICT division has to produce these ICT products. For that, the ICT division provides business cases such as *develop business application*. The difference is that a use case is delivered by a product and a business case is delivered by people in the organization. Business cases hook up own-business processes with business processes of other organizations. An objective of the business cases to produce ICT products might be to reduce the time-to-market to produce ICT products.

After the ICT products have been produced, they have to be put into and kept in operation. For that, the ICT division provides a second group of business cases such as *supply ICT product*, *restore ICT product* and *support usage of ICT product*. These business cases are commonly addressed by the concept of *IT Service Management*. This is the main area where ITIL is applied. Objectives of the business cases to operate and service ICT products are:

- Reduce response time of service desk to register and plan handling of service calls.
- Reduce time-to-market in the supply (procurement, assembly, logistics and installation) of ICT products.
- Reduce number of incidents.
- Reduce restore-times.
- Increase online opening hours.

To follow up on these customer requirements, more internal ICT objectives can be set, such as:

- planning capacity and availability of products through the whole infrastructure, on the basis of service levels required by the customers;

- being able to calculate and offer TCO quotations on all relevant parts of the infrastructure and the provision of services to the customers;
- immediate knowledge of what the negative impact, caused by a product error, would be on the service to the customers;
- knowing in advance what possible negative impact a change can have and what fallback scenarios are to be in place, before a change is executed.

3.6 Step 2: Answer strategic challenges

The challenges to enable the ICT division to meet the objectives listed above are customer-focus, effectivity, efficiency, low cost, and control. The strategic answers to these challenges are *integrated approach*, *reduction of complexity*, *organizational flexibility*, *social-technical choices* and *advanced technology*.

An *integrated approach* can be achieved vertically by connecting strategy with organizational characteristics and horizontally by integrated analysis of all business processes in relation to the realized services on the external interfaces of the ICT division.

Complexity can be reduced by using transparent structures and different views to focus on specific subjects. In BiOOlogic, different views are used to simplify the structuring of end products, business and supporting processes, production and control means, and organizational elements.

Fewer management levels enable a quick response in reaction to external changes, less functionalization by, for example, integration instead of separation of support personnel into line departments, and a small-scale approach to large or complex projects, thus making the ICT division more *flexible*.

The ICT division needs motivated employees to achieve success in customer relations, access to information, etc. Required *social-technical choices* are clarity on responsibilities in conjunction with the required authorizations, career planning and development based on competence-management of skills and knowledge and a facilitating management style.

The ICT division should not fall behind in the use of *advanced technology* in comparison with its potential competitors. The ICT division is a business by itself and is even more dependent on advanced technology than non-ICT businesses.

3.7 Step 3: Define overall structure for strategic answers (QM)

The answers from step 1 can be associated with different aspects of management. These aspects can be placed into one context with the BiOOlogic ICT aspect management model™ shown in Figure 3.2.

The ICT organization provides the customer with two kinds of services: use cases and business cases. The main goal of course is to provide use cases from ICT products. Products depend on quality management (QM).

Customer requests to get ICT products are handled through business cases. Business cases are realized by the execution of business processes within the ICT organization. Quality management has to ensure proper realization of the business cases. Aspects to be handled by QM are processes, human resources and organization, and specifications for supporting tools (information systems).

FIGURE 3.2

BiOOlogic ICT aspect management model™

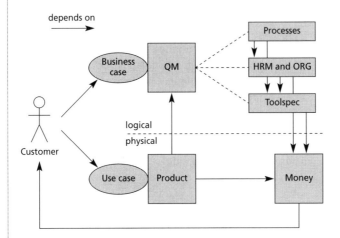

The realization of business cases through the ICT division is structured by processes. The performance of processes depends on the (human) resources in the organization. The structuring of processes, (human) resources and organization is the responsibility of ICT management. Both processes and human resources depend on supporting tools. Information management takes the structure of processess and organization into analysis to specify the required supporting tools.

In the design of ICT information systems, a distinction is made between service management and system management tooling. Service management tools support the provision of services and realizing processes. System management tools support the operation of ICT products and can automate processes. ICT products are constructed, installed and put at the customers' disposal according to the tool specification.

Human resources, tool specifications (development and implementation activities) and products cost money. The ICT division depends on its customer(s) to cover this. The ICT division in our case used to get direct coverage of costs through a budget system. Over recent years this has been changing towards pricing, where the customer pays for realized business cases and use cases. The difference between cost and pricing is profit for the ICT division. BiOOlogic uses its concept of service-based costing, called BiOOlogic-SBC™, to calculate the cost of business and use cases to help pricing. By taking the business objects that realize the services as the focal point, it's much easier to relate the costs of resources to services.

This in contrast to activity-based costing, which takes the activities as its focal point, which leads to far more complex calculations.

3.8 Step 4: Identify type(s) of organization(s)

The next step is to design the structure for the different aspects of quality management. The ICT division in our case is responsible for producing, operating and servicing ICT products. Logically, there are two organizations with their own structure: one to produce and integrate ICT products and one to operate produced and installed ICT products. By the operation of ICT products, the ICT organization processes and produces data and provides other use cases for the customer. Roughly, the two organizations are the 'production of ICT products' and the 'production of data'. This can be compared to a company that produces washing machines in a plant and then operates the produced machines in a chain of launderettes (Figure 3.3).

This metaphor is of course hypothetical when we look at the real world of washing clothes. In the ICT business, though, there are many ICT organizations that work just like that. Therefore this metaphor makes it clear that organizations in the ICT market can be far more complex than organizations in other lines of business.

The first step to reduce this complexity is to divide the ICT division into a product organization (production, sales and service of ICT products) and a service organization (production, sales and service of data by operating the ICT products). Both organizations have to organize their primary and supporting activities, as shown by the two Porter value chains in Figure 3.3, where we focus on the 'O' that stands for 'operation' and the 'S' that stands for 'service'. The operation of the product organization is organized through development, integration and packaging processes. The operation of the service organization is concerned with the delivery of end services, for example data processing.

FIGURE 3.3

Two organizations in one

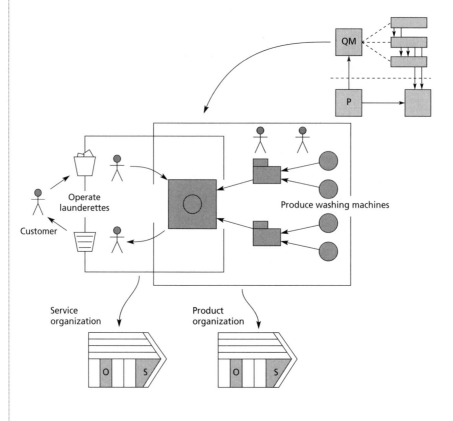

3.9 Step 5: Design process structure

The most popular standards, such as ITIL, focus on the processes to be performed by the ICT organization. When the focus is limited to looking at only the processes and the organization, applying ITIL can lead to major problems when:

- process roles are appointed directly to organizational functions (process and organization are flattened);
- formalized ITIL processes are confused with the processes that already exist in an organization.

As a result of this, many ICT organizations are organized around processes, with departments such as 'change management' or 'problem management' and functions such as 'change manager' and 'problem manager'. Having departments and functions such as these tends to cause people in these organizations to fight for the ITIL processes for which they feel responsible, instead of focusing on delivering services.

There is a lot of literature naming processes that are responsible for services and related concepts such as 'incidents' and 'problems'. In fact, it is the resources, especially human resources, and not processes that are to be held responsible. The point is that processes are nothing more than activity flows, which are nothing more than 'air' and therefore cannot be held responsible. 'Change manager' and 'problem manager' should be seen as process roles and not as personnel functions.

The second imperfection is that ITIL processes are positioned as the real processes that flow through organizations. Inputs and outputs to customers and suppliers are drawn based on the ITIL processes, resulting in spaghetti-like flow patterns that are complex and confusing. The reason is that traditional process-modelling puts the focal point on the flow of activities.

A much better way is to use ITIL processes as formalized flows of activity. The required competencies to perform these activities should be formalized in process roles. In doing so, ITIL processes form a means for quality management of the processes that really flow through the organization.

In BiOOlogic, ITIL processes are assembled into standardized templates for process flow and process roles. Other activities that are not covered by ITIL, such as inbound and outbound logistics, can be assembled like this as well. BiOOlogic makes a distinction between *business* and *standardized processes*.

A *business process* should be seen as the flow of activities that are really being performed by the resources of the organization. In the real world, processes are the successive operations that resources perform in a collaboration to realize a business case (or use case). Therefore BiOOlogic puts the focal point on the collaborating resources to model business processes. From the UML scenario and collaboration, diagrams are used that express the cooperation of business objects, like resources, to realize business cases. In the BiOOlogic business-process view, the successive operations are extracted in a round-trip sequence that starts and ends at the communication with the customer of the business case. In this view the activities are grouped by the business objects that perform these activities. To keep the focus on the business cases, it's a good idea to name business processes likewise. Business cases are often called service calls.

Standardized processes consist of reusable patterns of activities and the skills required to take responsibility for these activities. The required skills are defined in process roles. These patterns are reused in the design of business processes. The relations between business and standardized processes form a means for quality management.

Figure 3.4 shows an example of a business process in relation to applied standardized processes. This simplified example shows the business process to supply a new ICT product to a customer:

1. The customer calls the front office with a service request to supply a terminal. To begin with, the service support desk conducts help-desk activities such as registering and classifying the call as a request for change (RFC) and identifying the end product (terminal) to be supplied. A check is also performed to see whether the customer is authorized for this service (SLM: service level management). If the customer is authorized, the customer receives a promise such as: 'Your terminal will be up and running in 5 working days,' or whatever service level has been planned and agreed on this.

2. Next, the possible impact of performing the change is analysed, based on which rollback scenarios can be set ready (change management). A check is made whether a terminal (CI) is already available and, if so, installed (configuration management). If not, the stock is checked; and if nothing is in stock, a product is ordered, received and distributed (inbound and outbound logistics).

3. After installation of the CI, the change is administered (change management) and the operation of the terminal is checked (help desk). The terminal is delivered to the customer and after acceptance of this delivery by the customer the call 'supply new terminal' is closed.

The most important business processes realize business cases for the customers. Some business cases to produce, operate and service ICT products are shown in Table 3.1.

Further, the ICT organization performs business processes to handle calls from external suppliers, such as technology pushes, orders and deliveries. Within the ICT organization there can also be internal triggers to start business processes, with process concepts such as *changes* to replace sold ICT products and *problems* to analyse and solve faults.

FIGURE 3.4
Business process view

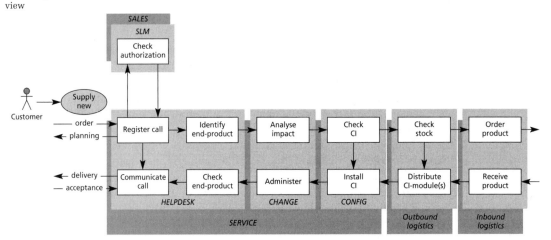

TABLE 3.1

Business cases of ICT division

Organization	Business case
Product organization	Plan and agree development of ICT products [1] Develop ICT products, such as business applications and workplaces (Internally) restore and support faults in ICT products (resolve problems).
Service organization	Plan and agree implementation and following operation of ICT products [1] Supply (sell) ICT products (new, update and delete) Maintain ICT products (keep them going, keep available). Produce ICT products (perform tasks the users can't do themselves). Restore and support ICT products (resolve incidents and help usage of ICT products)

3.10 Step 6: Design product structure

BiOOlogic makes a distinction between products and the added value that products provide. The added value is modelled as the provision role a product plays to other products and the (functional) use case to the customers.

A PC, for example, is a product described according to its manufacturer, model and type. The provision role of that product depends on its deployment, for example the role of workplace, workgroup server, gateway or firewall.

From the *system management* point of view, the physical environment is of interest. For example, to what patch port is it connected and what patch cables are used? Relationships such as these are important to manage and operate the physical products, the ICT resources. This can be compared to human resource management, which is focused on human resources.

Most important for IT Service Management, though, are logical dependencies. The solution for the internal ICT objectives from step 1 is a clear view of the dependencies between ICT products. The essence of this is to show what product depends on which other product. It is the dependencies that have to be managed. The customer depends on the business applications and the services that are provided on those applications. In order to achieve that, the ICT organization has to ensure that all products on which these business applications rely are managed well. The ICT organization has to link up the dependencies by organizing internal ICT provision with internal services.

For example, business application BA1 exists for a client and a server-application that depend on generic application SAP for HR data, on client (PC), DBMS and enterprise server (mainframe, Unix, etc.). SAP depends on client, DBMS and enterprise server. DBMS depends on enterprise server. Client depends on local server (for example, Novell). Client, local server and enterprise server all depend on local area network (LAN). LAN depends on wide area network (WAN). This example is illustrated in Figure 3.5.

First, it is necessary to reduce the complexity in the forest of ICT products. The objective of clustering is to reduce complexity in the mass of ICT products, in order to provide an overview for management and communication. This can be done by clustering ICT products with many internal and minimal external dependencies. Here you can make good use of object-oriented techniques. The criteria for clustering are derived from basic system theories:

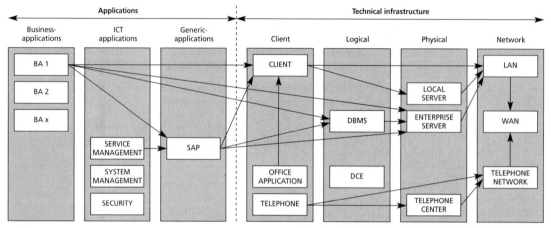

FIGURE 3.5

BiOOlogic product view (simplified example)

- **Focus on customer markets** The main clustering criterion is the market of the customer's business. In our case, this is taxation and the collection of taxes, on which the business applications are clustered in the above example. Differentiate between products that are used in direct contact with the customer/user and products that are employed transparently to the customer, for instance between a client and a server product.
- **Product properties** Differentiate on product properties such as hardware and software. Cluster products which can replace one another in time. For example, Novell and NT, Oracle and Sybase, mid-range and mainframe, etc.
- **Knowledge** Cluster products that require specialist personnel knowledge and skills required to develop and operate these products. For example, DBA knowledge and skills in the management of Oracle and Sybase.
- **Specific use** Differentiate between fixed, mobile and distributed products.

In BiOOlogic, the following clusters are used, in the order of dependencies:

- **application services:** business applications and tools for the ICT organization itself;
- **client services:** workplaces (workstations, telephony and basic office applications);
- **logical services:** database management systems (Oracle, Sybase, DB2), DCE, middleware, internet, intranet, etc;
- **physical services:** enterprise and local servers (server hardware and operating systems);
- **network services:** network connections (network hardware, network operating systems and protocols).

Clustering helps to reduce complexity; however, different ways of clustering can be used. Dependencies are not changed by the way that ICT products are clustered. Smart clustering, though, reduces the web of dependency arrows, thus helping to make it easier to view and manage dependencies. Aspects other than dependencies could be viewed as well. In essence, 'dependency' is just one role that any resource can play. Other roles can be based on, for example, environmental issues. Many virtual organizations can be drawn from reality, depending on what aspect is focused upon.

3.11 Step 7: Design organizational structure

Node organization structure for the back office

To produce washing machines or, in our case, ICT products, the organization needs a variety of specific knowledge on the various components of applications and technical infrastructure (TIS). However, different skills are required for analysis, design and construction; the key competence to address here is knowledge of the products (Figure 3.6).

The production of ICT products requires high levels of knowledge and horizontal coordination of activities. Knowledge is decisive for the required structure. The best organizational structure for that is the node organization, where knowledge is clustered in nodes that interact on the dependencies between the products they produce. This is a typical back-office organization that can be accommodated in one central location.

The nodes of the product organization can be structured in the same clusters as in step 6. The result is a one-on-one mapping of organization and product infrastructure. Advantages are:

FIGURE 3.6

The node organization

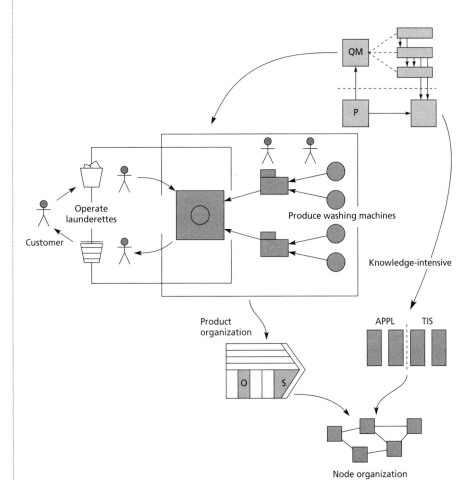

- Clarity concerning what node of the product organization is responsible for what part of the infrastructure and, from that, what the internal customer/supplier relations are.
- That makes it easier to address the right unit for the right job in the execution of processes to deliver services to the customer.
- By grouping human resources with knowledge on the clustered ICT products, the sharing and management of that knowledge becomes more efficient. By grouping, for example, DB2, Sybase and Oracle specialists into one node, all these specialists can more easily gain knowledge to manage all the products.

The dependencies between the clusters identify the internal service-relations, on which the thus organized nodes have to agree in order to provide service to the customer at the front door.

Clone organization structure for the front office

For the delivery of service to the customers, it is mainly skills that are required and not knowledge. Like the launderettes, the service organization has to be accommodated near to the customers and other partners. 'Near' means optimal from a geographic or logistic point of view. Because the customers are located in different offices in the country, the service organization also should be dispersed. As with the launderettes, one successful concept is cloned throughout the country. The service organization is shaped by the clone organization (Figure 3.7).

FIGURE 3.7

The clone organization

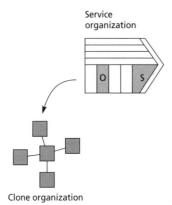

Group the logical structure of the organization

Now the two types of organization can be combined into one logical structure (Figure 3.8). Sales and service for both organizations are placed on the interface with the customer in the front office. Operation activities of the product organization to produce ICT products are organized by nodes in one central back office (BO). Operation activities of the service organization to operate the ICT products, in order to process and produce data, are allocated to the operations organization (OPER).

FIGURE 3.8

The logical organization

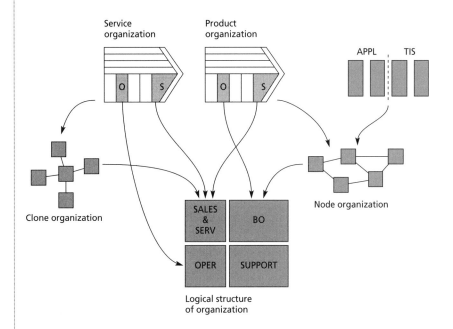

In the organization view, topics such as boundaries and interfaces of the organizational structure are addressed. Basic system theories apply here as well, but to organizational systems.

In relation to organizational systems and units, personnel functions are put in place. In this view, the emphasis is on what basic competencies, knowledge and skills are required for different functions; for example, the difference between the functions that have direct contact with customers and those that only have to communicate internally.

The basic organizational structure from BiOOlogic for ICT-organizations consists of four organizational units (Figure 3.9):

- front office (FO): intake of service request (human-to-human interaction);
- operations (OPER): delivery of ICT provision (product-to-human interaction);
- back office (BO): control of ICT provision and support of front office and production;
- support (SUP): functions that are not specific to ICT, such as logistics and warehousing.

The front office forms the interface with the supported organizations. The service broker or account manager agrees and plans the required services. The service broker is responsible for integrated planning of production, implementation, operation and service of ICT products. In order to do this, the service broker makes internal agreements with FO, OPER, BO and SUP.

This addresses the biggest problem of ICT management today. Development projects are usually made responsible for the development and implementation of information systems. Although the customer will require operation and service of the developed information systems, the management of service and operations is not always involved to agree and plan service levels on this before implementation.

FIGURE 3.9

BiOOlogic organization view

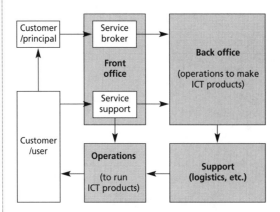

ICT organizations should offer so-called 'TCO' quotations based on the net total costs through the whole life cycle of an information system. The operational phase of information systems costs 70–80% of the total costs for maintenance, depreciation/replacement and service personnel. This should be taken into consideration when deciding on the development of information systems. ICT management needs to have a budget and the resources for that in place when implementing information systems.

Service Support takes in the service requests from the customer. Depending on the type of call, these calls are handled by themselves or by Operations. Service Support and Operations form the 'shop' of the ICT organization. Internally, these external services are supported by internal back-office services.

The back office has to provide an unskilled front office with standardized service solutions. These are standard RFCs, standard incident solutions and standard operation orders, which the front office can apply to received service calls without interference or further support from the back office.

In case there are no standard solutions available to satisfy the customer on agreed service levels, Service Support calls upon the back office to deliver the service. After that, the back office can build a new standard solution for the next identical service request.

Skilled front offices perform these back-office tasks for ICT products that they have knowledge and skills for, although the building of standard solutions should, preferably, be left to the back office.

Standardized solutions also form the basis for the automation of delivery of these services. For ICT organizations, the supporting services such as logistics include software and hardware distribution. Software control by a definitive software library (DSL) can be considered as a software warehouse. Owing to its sensitive nature, software control and distribution would usually be located in the back office of the physical organization.

More organizational functions can be added to this view, like the process owner, staff and organization. Management can be specialized into separate functions as well. A process owner is the person responsible for organizing the execution of processes in the organization. In the organization view, a function for this can be positioned as the central process control between FO, OPER, BO and SUP.

3.12 Step 8: Design the real organization

From the above logical structure it's an easy step to localize organizational units (Figure 3.10) in order to design the organization as most people know it.

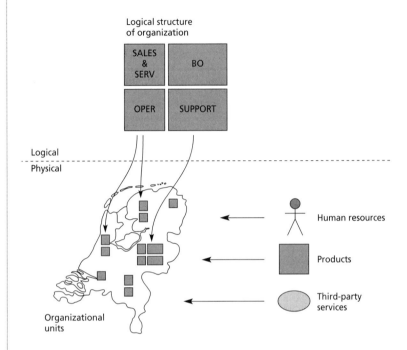

FIGURE 3.10
The physical organization

The back office and the main parts of support (logistics of software, procurement) are accommodated in a central location. The front office and operations are cloned to the central and decentralized locations. The logistics of hardware is not specific to ICT and can therefore be outsourced.

3.13 Conclusion

In ICT management the importance lies in responsibility and authorization. In reality it is the organizational resources that are responsible for providing services and, because of this, are authorized regarding other resources and services from others. Processes are the activities that these resources execute to establish the services they are responsible for.

The key problem in today's application of standards such as ITIL is that the focus is placed solely on processes. This focus should be balanced with a focus on services to deliver to the supported business and the resources which are responsible for providing these services.

More information, such as the literature consulted for this chapter, can be found on the BiOOlogic website www.bioologic.com.

Note

1 Planning and agreement of development, implementation and subsequent operation should be combined to plan and agree the total service of use cases and business cases over the full life cycle of the ICT product.

4 COBIT®

A.C.P. van Nijnatten CISA,
P.N.A. Broshuis, PricewaterhouseCoopers Global Risk Management Solutions

Summary

In the global information society, effective management of information and related technology (IT) is critical to the success and survival of an organization.

CoBiT (Control objectives for information and related technology) is designed to be the breakthrough IT-governance tool that helps in understanding and managing the risks and benefits associated with information and related IT. It has become a generic and widely accepted standard. CoBiT has been developed by the Information Security Audit & Control Association (ISACA), an international organization of IT governance and controls.

In this chapter, the CoBiT framework is presented as well as the services that PricewaterhouseCoopers developed around this framework to provide the IT manager with the means to take operational control over the IT issues at hand.

4.1 The world of IT

Nowadays, IT is a point on the agenda of many management meetings. There are two major reasons for this. Firstly, during recent decades, IT usage grew dramatically as a result of the introduction of ERP (enterprize resource planning), data warehousing, EDI, the internet and e-business solutions (Figure 4.1). Secondly, the goal of IT investments has shifted from the automation of basic back-office processes towards using IT throughout the business to gain competitive advantage. The business world is facing an ever growing dependency on IT and, as a result of these developments, responsibility for IT has moved into the business domain.

As IT appears on the agenda, interest in IT management models grows rapidly. Many organizations realize that to be successful and to survive means that they have to understand and manage the risks of implementing new IT solutions and of maintaining the current portfolio. One framework that can support management in addressing these risks is CoBiT.

Within enterprise governance, IT governance is becoming more and more prominent. CoBiT defines IT governance as a structure of relationships and processes to direct and control the enterprise in order to achieve the enterprise's goals by adding value while balancing risk versus return over IT and its processes. IT governance is integral to the success of enterprise governance by assuring efficient and effective measurable improvements in related enterprise processes.

FIGURE 4.1

The world of IT

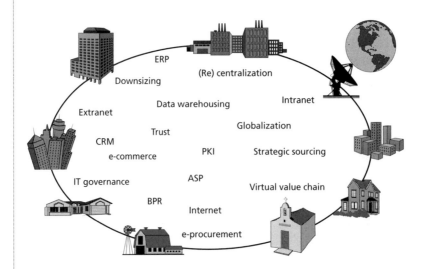

IT governance provides the structure that links IT processes, IT resources and information to enterprise strategies and objectives. It integrates and institutionalizes good practices of planning and organizing, acquiring and implementing, delivering and supporting, and monitoring IT performance to ensure that an enterprise's information and related technology support its business objectives. IT governance thus enables the enterprise to take full advantage of its information, thereby maximizing benefits, capitalizing on opportunities and gaining competitive advantage.

4.2 The COBIT framework

Some history: the ISACA project

In 1996, the Information Security Audit & Control Association (ISACA) started a project to develop the COBIT framework for IT governance and control.

COBIT was originally based on ISACA's control objectives, and it has been enhanced with existing and emerging international technical, professional, regulatory and industry-specific standards. The resulting control objectives have been developed for application to organization-wide information systems. The term 'generally applicable and accepted' is explicitly used in the same sense as Generally Accepted Accounting Principles (GAAP).

COBIT is relatively small in size and attempts to be both pragmatic and responsive to business needs while being independent of the technical IT platforms adopted in an organization.

While not excluding any other accepted standard in the information systems control field that may have come to light during the research, sources identified are:

- ***technical standards*** from ISO, EDIFACT, etc;
- ***codes of conduct*** issued by the Council of Europe, OECD, ISACA, etc;
- ***qualification criteria*** for IT systems and processes: ITSEC, TCSEC, ISO 9000, SPICE, TickIT, Common Criteria, etc;

- ***professional standards*** for internal control and auditing: COSO, IFAC, AICPA, CICA, ISACA, IIA, PCIE, GAO, etc;
- ***industry practices and requirements*** from industry forums (ESF, I4) and government-sponsored platforms (IBAG, NIST, DTI), etc; and
- ***emerging industry specific requirements*** from banking, electronic commerce and IT manufacturing.

In July 2000, the third edition of CoBiT was released, which is currently the most recent edition. The third edition was developed by ISACA in close collaboration with Gartner Group Research and the GRMS practice of PricewaterhouseCoopers. Nowadays, the CoBiT family of products consists of several booklets; see Figure 4.2.

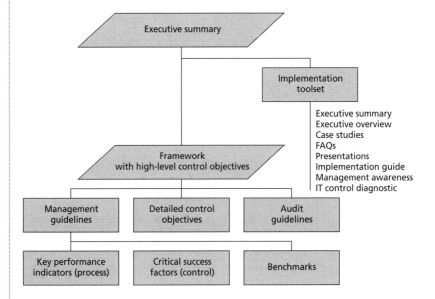

FIGURE 4.2

COBIT product family

The third edition marks the entry of a new primary publisher for CoBiT: the IT Governance Institute, which was formed in 1998 by the Information System Audit and Control Association (ISACA) and its related Foundation in order to advance the understanding and adoption of IT governance principles. Therefore, the third edition is deemed an open standard and can be downloaded from the IT Governance Institute's website (www.ITgovernance.org), except for the Audit Guidelines which can only be downloaded by ISACA members.

The CoBiT principle

Business orientation is CoBiT's main theme. CoBiT is designed to be employed not only by auditors but also, and more importantly, as comprehensive guidance for management and business process owners. Increasingly, business practice involves the full empowerment of business process owners so they have total responsibility for all aspects of the business process. In particular, this includes providing adequate controls.

COBIT defines 'control' as the policies, procedures, practices and organizational structures designed to provide reasonable assurance that business objectives will be achieved and that undesired events will be prevented or detected and corrected. This definition is adapted from the COSO Report.[1]

The underpinning concept of the COBIT framework is that control in IT is approached by looking at information that is needed to support the business objectives or requirements, and by looking at information as being the result of the combined application of IT-related resources that need to be managed by IT processes. This concept is depicted in Figure 4.3.

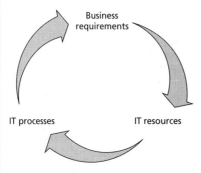

FIGURE 4.3
The underpinning concept of the COBIT framework

Business requirements for information

To achieve business objectives, information needs to conform to certain criteria, which COBIT refers to as business requirements for information. COBIT defines seven distinct yet certainly overlapping categories (Table 4.1).

TABLE 4.1
COBIT categories

Effectivity	Deals with information being relevant and pertinent to the business process as well as being delivered in a timely, correct, consistent and usable manner.
Efficiency	Concerns the provision of information through the optimal use of resources.
Confidentiality	Concerns the protection of sensitive information from unauthorized disclosure.
Integrity	Relates to the accuracy and completeness of information as well as to its validity in accordance with business values and expectations.
Availability	Relates to information being available when required by the business processes now and in the future. It also concerns the safeguarding of necessary resources and associated capabilities.
Compliance	Deals with complying with laws, regulations and contractual arrangements to which the business is subject.
Reliability of information	Relates to the provision of appropriate information for management to operate the entity and for management to exercise its financial anD compliance reporting responsibilities.

For the fiduciary requirements, CobiT did not attempt to reinvent the wheel – COSO's definitions for effectiveness and efficiency of operations, reliability of information and compliance with laws and regulations were used. However, reliability of information was expanded to include all information – not just financial information.

CobiT identified confidentiality, integrity and availability as the key elements for security, since they are used worldwide to describe IT security requirements.

Quality of information is captured to a large extent by the integrity criterion. The usability aspect of quality is covered by the effectiveness criterion, while cost is considered to be covered by efficiency.

IT resources

The IT resources identified in CobiT, whose combined application results in information, can be explained and defined as set out in Table 4.2.

TABLE 4.2 IT resources in CobiT

Data	Objects in their widest sense (i.e., external and internal), structured and non-structured, graphics, sound, etc.
Application systems	Understood to be the sum of manual and programmed procedures.
Technology	Hardware, operating systems, database management systems, networking, multimedia, etc.
Facilities	All the resources to house and support information systems.
People	Staff skills, awareness and productivity to plan, organize, acquire, deliver, support and monitor information systems and services, etc.

IT processes

CobiT contains 34 IT processes, required to manage the IT resources which are needed to produce information. Each IT process is defined in a high-level control objective, which is a statement of the desired result or purpose to be achieved by implementing control procedures in a particular IT activity. This definition of control objective has been adapted from the so-called SAC report.[2]

For each of the 34 IT processes, there are from 3 to 30 detailed control objectives, 318 in total. Appendix I to this chapter includes a description of the high-level control objective and detailed control objectives as listed in CobiT for change management.

The IT processes are classified into four logical domains in order to use wording that management would use in day-to-day activities – not auditor jargon. These domains are:

- planning and organization;
- acquisition and implementation;
- delivery and support;
- monitoring.

In the following paragraphs each domain and the processes it includes are presented.

Planning and organization

Both strategy and policies are made to realize the company goals using automated data processing. The strategy is transformed into an IT policy covering various areas (see Table 4.3). An important part of the policy is the organization, information and technology architecture.

TABLE 4.3 IT policy areas

1	Define a strategic plan
2	Define an information architecture
3	Define a technology policy
4	Define the IT organization
5	Manage investments
6	Communicate goals policy and strategy
7	Human resources management
8	Guarantee compliance to external demands
9	Risk management
10	Project management
11	Quality management

Acquisition and implementation

To realize the strategy, the IT infrastructure needs to be identified, developed, built and integrally implemented. Managing changes to information systems and the IT infrastructure is a very important process in this domain (Table 4.4).

TABLE 4.4 Areas of change

1	Identify IT solutions
2	Acquire information systems
3	Acquire an IT infrastructure
4	Develop and maintain procedures
5	Approve IT solutions
6	Change management

Delivery and support

The delivery and support of the IT services and the IT infrastructure is covered in this domain. The different processes (Table 4.5) handle determination and maintenance of service levels and ensure price performance and availability. The agreed service levels apply to all the processes.

TABLE 4.5
IT services

1	Service level management
2	Manage supplier relations
3	Performance and capacity management
4	Guarantee continuity
5	Guarantee security of information
6	Identify, assign and manage costs
7	Training and education of users
8	Assist, advise and consult users
9	Configuration management
10	Manage problems and incidents
11	Manage data
12	Manage facilities
13	Manage operations

This is the domain that has most in common with ITIL. In addition to the service management processes, the actual processing of data and facilities management are positioned in this domain.

Monitoring

Monitoring the process is a continuous process to gain management control. It is one of four processes in this domain (Table 4.6). The other processes are externally oriented and concern an independent audit of the IT organization.

TABLE 4.6
Monitoring processes

1	Monitor the processes
2	Assess adequacy of internal control
3	Obtain independent assurance
4	Provide for independent audit

The CobiT summary table

It is clear that not all control measures will satisfy the different business requirements to the same degree. Similarly, not all control measures will necessarily impact the different IT resources to the same degree. Therefore, the CobiT summary table indicates the applicability of the IT resources that are specifically managed by the process under consideration. This classification is based on a rigorous process of input from researchers, experts and reviewers.

For the relation between IT processes and business requirements, the following levels of degree are used:

- **primary** is the degree to which the defined control objective directly impacts the information criterion concerned.
- **secondary** is the degree to which the defined control objective satisfies only to a lesser extent or indirectly the information criterion concerned.
- **blank** could be applicable; however, requirements are more appropriately satisfied by another criterion in this process and/or by another process.

The COBIT summary table, which reflects these relationships, is included as Appendix II to this chapter.

The COBIT cube

In order to provide the information that the organization needs to achieve its objectives, IT governance must be exercised by the organization to ensure that IT resources are managed by a set of naturally grouped IT processes. The COBIT framework is designed to support this. It can be approached from three vantage points: information criteria, IT resources and IT processes. These three vantage points are depicted in the COBIT cube (Figure 4.4).

FIGURE 4.4

The COBIT Cube

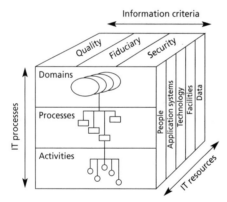

New in COBIT third edition: the management guidelines

A basic need for every organization is to understand the status of its own IT systems and to decide what security and control they should provide. However, to obtain an objective view of an organization's own level is not easy. What should be measured and how? In addition to the need for measuring where an organization is, there is the importance of continuous improvement in the areas of IT security and control. Deciding on the right level is equally difficult. Senior managers in corporate and public organizations are frequently asked to consider a business case for expenditure to improve the control and security of the information infrastructure. While few would argue that this is not a good thing, all must occasionally ask themselves: *'How far should we go, and is the cost justified by the benefit?'*

Management is continuously searching for condensed and up-to-date information in order to make difficult decisions on risk and control, fast and successfully. Some traditional questions and management information tool-kits used to find the response are set out in Table 4.7.

TABLE 4.7 Management questions

Management's questions	Toolkit
How do I 'keep the ship on course'?	Dashboards
How do I achieve results that are satisfactory for the largest possible segment of our stakeholders?	Scorecards
How do I adapt the organization, in a timely manner, to trends and developments in its environment?	Benchmarking

However, dashboards need indicators, scorecards need measures and benchmarking needs a scale for comparison. The response is provided by the CoBiT management guidelines, which are generic and action-oriented for the purpose of addressing the following types of management concerns:

- **Performance measurement** – What are the indicators of good performance?
- **IT control profiling** – What's important? What are the critical success factors for control?
- **Awareness** – What are the risks of not achieving our objectives?
- **Benchmarking** – What do others do? How do we measure and compare?

An answer to these requirements to determine and monitor the appropriate IT security and control level is the definition of specific:

- **benchmarking** of IT control practices (expressed as maturity models);
- **critical success factors**, which define the most important issues or actions for management to achieve control over and within its IT processes;
- **key goal indicators**, which tell management – after the fact – whether an IT process has achieved its business requirements, usually expressed in terms of:
  - availability of information needed to support the business needs
  - absence of integrity and confidentiality risks
  - cost-efficiency of processes and operations
  - confirmation of reliability, effectiveness and compliance;
- **key performance indicators**, which are measures of how well the IT process is performing.

Maturity model

In order to determine the level of security and control to be provided, managers asks themselves questions such as:

'What internationally recognized standards exist, and how are we placed in relation to them?'

'What are other people doing, and how are we placed in relation to them?'

'What is regarded as industry best practice, and how are we placed with regard to that best practice?'

'Based upon these external comparisons, can we be said to be taking "reasonable" precautions to safeguard our information assets?'

To supply meaningful answers to questions like these, CobiT has been provided with a maturity model. For each of the 34 IT processes, there is an incremental measurement scale (see Table 4.8).

TABLE 4.8

CobiT generic maturity model

Generic maturity model	
0	**Non-existent**. Complete lack of any recognizable processes. The organization has not even recognized that there is an issue to be addressed.
1	**Initial**. There is evidence that the organization has recognized that the issues exist and need to be addressed. There are, however, no standardized processes but instead there are ad hoc approaches that tend to be applied on an individual or case-by-case basis. The overall approach to management is disorganized.
2	**Repeatable**. Processes have developed to the stage where similar procedures are followed by different people undertaking the same task. There is no formal training or communication of standard procedures and responsibility is left to the individual. There is a high degree of reliance on the knowledge of individuals and therefore errors are likely.
3	**Defined**. Procedures have been standardized and documented, and communicated through training. It is, however, left to the individual to follow these processes, and it is unlikely that deviations will be detected. The procedures themselves are not sophisticated but are the formalization of existing practices.
4	**Managed**. It is possible to monitor and measure compliance with procedures and to take action where processes appear not to be working effectively. Processes are under constant improvement and provide good practice. Automation and tools are used in a limited or fragmented way.
5	**Optimized**. Processes have been refined to a level of best practice, based on the results of continuous improvement and maturity modelling with other organizations. IT is used in an integrated way to automate the workflow, providing tools to improve quality and effectiveness, making the enterprise quick to adapt.

Using the maturity model, management can map:

- the current status of the organization – where the organization is today;
- the current status of (best-in-class in) the industry – the comparison;
- the current status of international standard guidelines – additional comparison;
- the organization's strategy for improvement – where the organization wants to be.

This process is summarized in Figure 4.5.

Critical success factors

Critical success factors are the most important issues or actions for management to achieve control over and within its IT processes. CobiT provides management with

FIGURE 4.5

Benchmarking

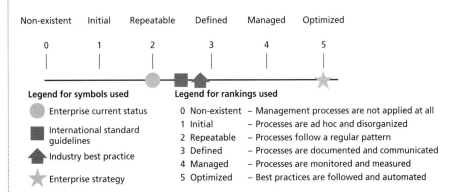

predefined critical success factors for each of the 34 IT processes. The critical success factors defined for change management are:

- Change policies are clear and known and they are rigorously and systematically implemented.
- Change management is strongly integrated with release management and is an integral part of configuration management.
- There is a rapid and efficient planning, approval and initiation process covering identification, categorization, impact assessment and prioritization of changes.
- Automated process tools are available to support workflow definition, pro-forma workplans, approval templates, testing, configuration and distribution.
- Expedient and comprehensive acceptance test procedures are applied prior to making the change.
- A system for tracking and following individual changes, as well as change process parameters, is in place.
- A formal process for hand-over from development to operations is defined.
- Changes take the impact on capacity and performance requirements into account.
- Complete and up-to-date application and configuration documentation is available.
- A process is in place to manage coordination between changes, recognizing interdependencies.
- An independent process for verification of the success or failure of change is implemented.
- There is segregation of duties between development and production.

Key goal indicators and key performance indicators

A key goal indicator is a measure of 'what' has to be accomplished. Therefore, it needs to be defined as a target to achieve.

Key performance indicators are measures that tell management 'how well' an IT process is achieving its business requirements by monitoring the performance of the enablers of that particular IT process.

In a balanced business scorecard, key goal indicators will be set at overall business level and IT will be an enabler, whose performance will be measured by key performance indicators, as depicted in Figure 4.6.

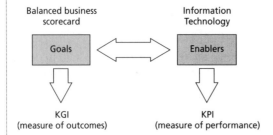

FIGURE 4.6

Balanced business scorecard

Since IT is one of the major enablers for any business, it will have its own scorecard and therefore its own key goal indicators and key performance indicators. The performance measures of the enablers become the goal for IT, which in turn will have a number of enablers. These could be the COBIT domains. Here again, the measures can be cascaded, the performance measure of the domain becoming a goal for the process. This principle is shown in Figure 4.7.

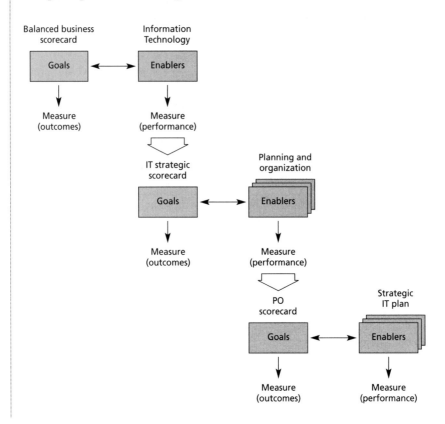

FIGURE 4.7

Cascaded balanced scorecards

But how are the business and IT goals and measures linked? The COBIT framework expresses the objectives for IT in terms of the information criteria that the business needs in order to achieve the business objectives. The goal for IT can then be expressed as delivering the information that the business needs in line with the business requirements (Table 4.9). After the business has defined its requirements, the COBIT summary table can be used to identify the IT processes having primary or secondary importance.

TABLE 4.9 COBIT summary table

Key goal indicators	Key performance indicators
● Reduced number of errors introduced into systems due to changes	● Number of different versions installed at the same time
● Reduced number of disruptions (loss of availability) caused by poorly managed change	● Number of software release and distribution methods per platform
● Reduced impact of disruptions caused by change	● Number of deviations from the standard configuration
● Reduced level of resources and time required as a ratio to number of changes	● Number of emergency fixes for which the normal change-management process was not applied retroactively
● Number of emergency fixes	● Time lag between the availability of the fix and its implementation
	● Ratio of accepted to refused change-implementation requests

4.3 Implementing control over IT using Tr-ICS

It is said that COBIT is a competitor in the market of IT service management models. We feel that COBIT provides more than ITIL, ISO900X, COSO or ITSEC. It incorporates the principles of all these models and methods. After determining which IT processes are relevant for your organization, it is recommended that the models and methods that COBIT incorporates are used. Very often COBIT is too generic to make the control objectives operational. Standards such as the following can be used in translating the control objectives to concrete measures:

● CMM, SDM for development;
● ITIL for IT Service Management;
● ISO for general quality management;
● ITSEC and BS7799 for logical and physical security of data and systems.

In general, however, COBIT is too generic as a framework and reference guide to be applied as such. Hence, its IT processes and control framework have to be tailored into a model for a given (IT) organization. Therefore, PricewaterhouseCoopers has developed a control assessment and modelling tool called Tr-ICS (Technology related – In Control Services). Tr-ICS supports IT organizations to reach an optimum in providing added value to the business by identifying the appropriate IT processes and level of controls required to meet the business requirements.

To implement control over IT using COBIT, it is essential that management is actively involved and there is a clear vision, strategy, policy and set of guidelines, paying attention to:

- the risks involved by using IT;
- the implementation of control measures to limit the defined risks.

It is not only the responsibility of the IT organization to implement control. Nowadays we see the embodiment of IT deep within the business processes. A business manager must understand the contribution of IT to his or her processes to manage related risks properly and to ensure the information received meets the business requirements.

The Tr-ICS method is broadly defined. It can be used in almost all kinds of organization using a variety of technology and information systems. Tr-ICS is divided into four modules. Depending on the situation that the IT organization is in, all or just a subset of the modules can be employed. An overview is provided in Figure 4.8, and each module is described a little further in turn hereafter.

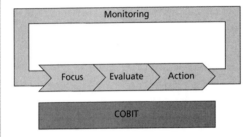

FIGURE 4.8
Overview of Tr-ICS

Focus

This module identifies the business drivers for IT and assesses the level of business risks involved with the deployment of information technology for each of the seven business requirements by:

1. asking business management to determine the impact on the business if the business requirements for information are not met;
2. asking IT management to perform a high-level assessment of the likelihood that business requirements for information are not met.

The combination of the business requirement and the extent that the organization is risk-averse results in a materiality factor for each business requirement. The seven materiality factors, one for each business requirement, are needed during the evaluation phase.

Furthermore, the focus phase provides an opportunity to scope the review in terms of which of the 34 IT processes will be taken into account during the review.

Evaluate

The most important part of the evaluation phase is an assessment of the level of control for each IT process selected during the focus phase. Depending on the situation, this can consist of a self-evaluation based on the maturity levels as defined in CobiT, or an independent IT audit can be performed.

In order to define actions and agree on priorities during the next phase, the evaluation phase concludes with a gap analysis. For each IT process, it is determined to what extent the level of control meets the business requirements. This is done by matching the current level of control for the IT process with the materiality of each business requirement for information, using the CobiT summary table in which the importance of well-controlled IT processes for meeting the business requirements has been specified. Tr-ICS uses several gradations to specify the gap between the current and preferred level of control, ranging from exposure, concern, housekeeping, okay, to concern+.

For example, an exposure would be the following situation: an organization assigned high materiality to availability of information, meaning that the impact on the business would be high if information is not available, which was not considered impossible. According to the CobiT summary table, the change management process has primary importance for the availability of information. However, the controls assessment learned that change management is operating at level 1 of the maturity model.

Concern+, in contrast, refers to the situation where an IT process is over-controlled. For example, when efficiency and reliability are not that important for the organization, and the IT process of identifying and attributing costs is operating at level 4 of the maturity model, the organization could ask itself whether that is necessary or whether resources could better be spent otherwise.

The evaluation leads to the identification of areas where risk is not been adequately addressed, given the relative importance of business requirements. It could also result in the identification of IT processes which are over-controlled.

Action

The action phase starts with defining the action plan to address control deficiencies identified during the previous phase. Two very important activities in this phase are creating awareness and defining a suitable control model. The analysis, as mentioned during the evaluation phase, plays an important role.

The control model itself can be based on the 34 IT processes and related control objectives as defined in CobiT, supplemented with other frameworks and standards but also with specific needs and input that the organization already has.

The most important activity within this phase, however, is implementing the actions defined.

Monitoring

Since both business and IT are continuously changing, the 'fit' of the control model needs to be re-evaluated on a continuous basis. This is the only way to ensure that business requirements will be met not only now but also tomorrow and the day after.

Final remarks

With the introduction of COBIT, a new framework is available claiming a special position between other service management and IT auditing frameworks and standards. COBIT combines the views of business and IT management, as well as IT auditors. COBIT has proven to be successful in bridging the gap between IT management and IT auditors. Firstly, it is a very extensive repository for IT auditors, ensuring their effectiveness to the business. Secondly, the framework focuses on the business instead of IT in such a way that business management understands its responsibility for IT governance and control, creating a breeding ground for recommendations made by the IT auditor. Last but not least, the COBIT framework is aligned with other popular models such as ITIL for IT service management, CMM for software development and ITSEC for security. This enables management to use COBIT in order to assess the effectiveness of improvement programmes using these kinds of frameworks and standards.

Appendix I

Control objectives for change management
High-level control objective

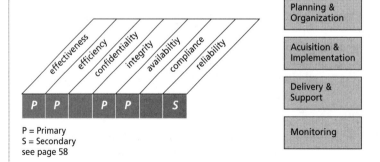

P = Primary
S = Secondary
see page 58

Control over the IT process of
managing changes

that satisfies the business requirement
to minimize the likelihood of disruption, unauthorized alterations and errors

is enabled by
a management system which provides for the analysis, implementation and follow-up of all changes requested and made to the existing IT infrastructure

and takes into consideration

- identification of changes
- categorization, prioritization and emergency procedures
- impact assessment
- change authorization
- release management
- software distribution
- use of automated tools
- configuration management
- business process redesign

Detailed control objectives

AI 6.1. Change Request Initiation and Control	IT management should ensure that all requests for changes, system maintenance and supplier maintenance are standardized and are subject to formal change-management procedures. Changes should be categorized and prioritized and specific procedures should be in place to handle urgent matters. Change requesters should be kept informed about the status of their request.
AI 6.2. Impact Assessment	A procedure should be in place to ensure that all requests for change are assessed in a structured way for all possible impacts on the operational system and its functionality.
AI 6.3. Control of Changes	IT management should ensure that change management and software control and distribution are properly integrated with a comprehensive configuration management system. The system used to monitor changes to application systems should be automated to support the recording and tracking of changes made to large, complex information systems.
AI 6.4. Emergency Changes	IT management should establish parameters defining emergency changes and procedures to control these changes when they circumvent the normal process of technical, operational and management assessment prior to implementation. The emergency changes should be recorded and authorized by IT management prior to implementation.
AI 6.5. Documentation and Procedures	The change process should ensure that whenever system changes are implemented, the associated documentation and procedures are updated accordingly.
AI 6.6. Authorized Maintenance	IT management should ensure that maintenance personnel have specific assignments and that their work is properly monitored. In addition, their system access rights should be controlled to avoid risks of unauthorized access to automated systems.
AI 6.7. Software Release Policy	IT management should ensure that the release of software is governed by formal procedures ensuring sign-off, packaging, regression testing, hand-over, etc.
AI 6.8. Distribution of Software	Specific internal control measures should be established to ensure distribution of the correct software element to the right place, with integrity, and in a timely manner with adequate audit trails.

CobiT summary table

Appendix II

Information criteria: effectiveness, efficiency, confidentiality, integrity, availability, compliance, reliability

Domain		Process	effectiveness	efficiency	confidentiality	integrity	availability	compliance	reliability
Planning & Organization	PO1	Define a strategic IT plan	P	S					
	PO2	Define the information architecture	P	S	S	S			
	PO3	Determine the technological direction	P	S					
	PO4	Define the IT organization and relationships	P	S					
	PO5	Manage the IT investment	P	P					S
	PO6	Communicate management aims and direction	P					S	
	PO7	Manage human resources	P	P					
	PO8	Ensure compliance with external requirements	P					P	S
	PO9	Assess risks	S	S	P	P	P	S	S
	PO10	Manage projects	P	P					
	PO11	Manage quality	P	P		P		S	
Acquisition & Implementation	AI1	Identify solutions	P	S					
	AI2	Acquire and maintain application software	P	P		S		S	S
	AI3	Acquire and maintain technology architecture	P	P		S			
	AI4	Develop and maintain IT procedures	P	P		S		S	S
	AI5	Install and accredit systems	P			S	S		
	AI6	Manage changes	P	P		P	P		S
Delivery & Support	DS1	Define service levels	P	P	S	S	S	S	S
	DS2	Manage third-party services	P	P	S	S	S	S	S
	DS3	Manage performance and capacity	P	P			S		
	DS4	Ensure continuous service	P	S			P		
	DS5	Ensure systems security			P	P	S	S	S
	DS6	Identify and attribute costs		P					P
	DS7	Educate and train users	P	S					
	DS8	Assist and advise IT customers	P						
	DS9	Manage the configuration	P				S		S
	DS10	Manage problems and incidents	P	P			S		
	DS11	Manage data				P			P
	DS12	Manage facilities					P	P	
	DS13	Manage operations	P	P			S	S	
Monitoring	M1	Monitor the processes	P	S	S	S	S	S	S
	M2	Assess internal control adequacy	P	P	S	S	S	S	S
	M3	Obtain independent assurance	P	P	S	S	S	S	S
	M4	Provide for independent audit	P	P	S	S	S	S	S

Notes

1 *Internal Control-Integrated Framework*, Committee of Sponsoring Organizations of the Treadway Commission, 1992.
2 *Systems Auditability and Control Report*, The Institute of Internal Auditors Research Foundation, 1991 and 1994.

5 A model for functional management

Frank van Outvorst PinkRoccade Atribit

Summary

On the basis of ITIL and many years of experience with software development and maintenance, PinkRoccade Atribit developed a model for application management, called Application Services Library (ASL). ASL (described in Chapter 1) is a further development of an earlier model for application management, R2C.

Implementation of ASL or R2C brings application management to a higher, more professional level. With an ICT services provider that operates more professionally, the shortcomings of functional management within the customer organization become more apparent. This leads to a demand for a structural approach to functional management processes. To meet this demand, we developed a model for functional management. This chapter, based on Deurloo et al. (1998), elaborates on this model for functional management.

5.1 Introduction

In practice, both ITIL and ASL (or R2C) lack sufficient guidelines and content in the field of functional management. What was needed was a framework for functional management. This framework should take into consideration the growing importance of ICT and proper ICT management for effective and efficient information provision within the customer organization.

It is evident that such a framework for functional management must match with the frameworks for infrastructure management and application management (respectively ITIL and ASL/R2C).

The framework for functional management is expected to result in:

- performance indicators;
- improved output of functional management;
- transparency for end users and management;
- better understanding of the value of functional management for business processes;
- improved performance of application and infrastructure management;
- improved support of the business processes and therefore improved business results and user satisfaction.

5.2 Background

In his book *Information Systems – Management, Control and Maintenance*, Looijen (1998) introduced a threefold model for information systems management (Figure 5.1). In the model, Looijen distinguishes three different areas in information systems management:

1. infrastructure management;
2. application management;
3. functional management.

Infrastructure management is responsible for the management and execution of the technical implementation of an information system. This implementation consists of hardware, executable software and operational databases.

FIGURE 5.1 Threefold model for information systems management (simplified illustration)

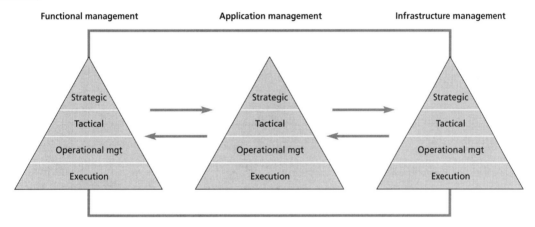

Infrastructure management can be divided into

- operational control;
- technical support and services;
- maintenance of the technical infrastructure.

A widely-used common model for technical infrastructure management is ITIL. It is evident that any framework for either application management or functional management should connect properly with ITIL.

Application management is responsible for maintaining the application software and databases. It has the contracted responsibility for the management and execution of all activities relating to the maintenance and evolution of existing applications, within well-defined service levels (see Chapter 1).

Based on an earlier model, namely R2C, ASL was developed as an important step towards a model for application management that can be used widely. The model for functional management as described in this chapter fits well on both R2C and ASL.

Functional management acts on behalf of the business organization and is responsible for providing sufficient ICT support in an intermediate role between the business and the ICT services provider.

In our daily practice we find Looijen's threefold model quite useful (van Outvorst *et al.*, 2000). It gives good directions to organizations on how to design their information systems management. It emphasizes the three areas that should be covered and the fact that they are strongly related.

5.3 Relations of functional management

We have already stated that functional management has an intermediate role between the ICT services provider on the one hand and the user and the business organization on the other. The ICT services provider is responsible for infrastructure management and application management and acts by order of functional management. Functional management represents the customer of the ICT services provided.

In accordance with R2C/ASL, the service team is the single point of entry to the ICT services provider. The counterpart of the service team is functional management, which acts as the single point of contact on ICT topics for management, users and other parties in or around the business organization. For the service team, functional management is their only entry point to the business organization. On behalf of the business organization, functional management formulates the requirements that have to be met by the ICT services provider (Figure 5.2).

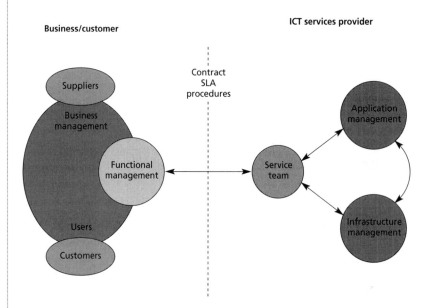

FIGURE 5.2
Functional management and its relations

Business processes and the user organization are the primary concerns of functional management. In particular:

- Functional management regards information systems (the total set of hardware and software) as a normal but essential part of the business processes. Therefore the way systems fit onto the business processes, their effectiveness and efficiency, and their cohesion with the organization policies are monitored by functional management.

- The most important expertise for functional management is knowledge of the business and the working methods of the users. Communication takes place in terms that are totally related to the business processes, such as invoice, order, delivery, bill of materials, decree, etc.
- Another very important area of expertise for functional management is knowledge of information technology. Functional management must be able to assess the possibilities that arise from technological developments. Also, the solutions suggested and applied by the ICT services provider must be reviewed and discussed by functional management.
- Besides users and management, functional management will have working relationships with other internal and external parties. This is needed because usually an information system and its supported process are part of a large chain of processes. Such a chain can stretch outside the boundaries of one organization.
- Functional management reports to business management concerning operation, fit and investments in the field of information systems.

5.4 Information systems as important means of production

An important aspect of our framework for functional management is our premise that ICT is considered as a regular means of production. As with other means of production (labour, machinery, etc.), the current status and performance of information systems must be taken into consideration in making plans for the future. We find this to be a relatively new point of view. It involves a continuous and two-way evaluation and adaptation of information systems to the business organization and vice versa. This must take place based on the current situation of both the information system and the organization, which is projected into the expected future.

The premise mentioned above is an essential part of our framework for functional management. Functional management plays an important role in this process, which we call life-cycle management (Figure 5.3).

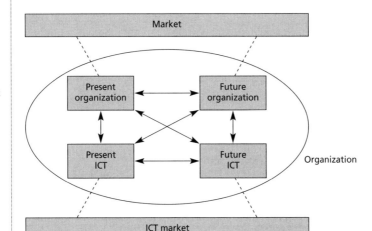

FIGURE 5.3
Strategic assessment of information systems and organization: life-cycle management

5.5 Model for functional management

Functional management administers the information systems and their fit to the business processes on behalf of the user organization. Three key areas are recognized within functional management (Figure 5.4):

1. user support (left circle);
2. managing system enhancements (right circle);
3. control (outer layer).

Each of these three is described further below. It should be noted that control is an essential area that is performed on behalf of the (business) management.

FIGURE 5.4
Model for functional management

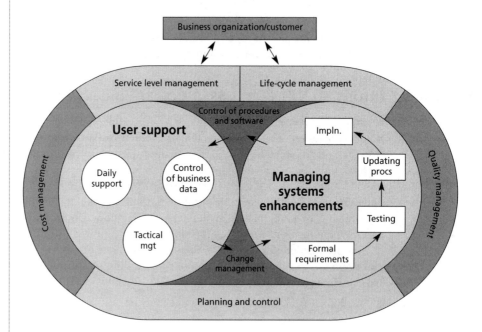

User support

The goal of user support is to keep the information system up and running. As well as daily support, this means several tactical management processes as well.

Daily support

Daily support comprises all activities necessary for undisturbed use of, and processing by, the information system.
Sub-processes of daily support comprise:

1. *Call management*: the help-desk process where users are directly supported in their use of the information systems. Call management consists of activities such as registration of incidents/complaints, resolving complaints, handling one-off requests

(e.g. ad hoc information retrieval or incidental processing jobs), instructing the service team in case of extra production, disruptions or recoveries, answering questions about use of the information system, etc.

2. *User communications*: providing training, publishing newsletters or announcements, organizing and presiding over user groups, etc.

Tactical management

Tactical management focuses on the operations of the information systems over a longer term. Tactical management processes have their counterparts in application management (ASL) and infrastructure management (ITIL). However, within functional management the emphasis is on the needs of the business organization. Functional management controls these needs from a business point of view. The needs may affect the availability and usability of the information systems and the IT services provided by internal and external providers, the resource capacities that are needed and disaster recovery.

Tactical management is concerned with the management of:

1. **availability**: taking care of current and future availability of the information systems for the users. This involves authorization control as well.
2. **capacities**: making an inventory of the capacities needed in business terms and securing and monitoring optimum deployment of ICT resources.
3. **problems**: analysing the different incidents and finding solutions to prevent the incidents from occurring again in the future.
4. **disasters**: taking care to be prepared for disasters such as a total breakdown of all information systems. This requires the development and updating of measures aimed at recovery of the information systems. The business needs and cycles must be taken into consideration, so that a proper focus for recovery is possible.

Functional management must express itself in business terms, for example:

- availability of system functions that are familiar to the users, e.g. order input, invoices, payments, forecast calculation, etc;
- sizing, e.g. number of clients in the database, number of transactions, length of time required to print invoices, etc;
- business cycles such as payment period, invoice period, annual reporting period, etc.

Control of business data

Control of business data is concerned with management of:

1. **data definitions**: producing and monitoring organization-wide data definitions for the objects in the object model as part of the information architecture; this is the role of the database administrator;
2. **content management**: managing all kinds of values in system tables, parameter settings, etc. that are used by the information system.

Managing system enhancements

Organizations and their information must evolve as the organizational environment changes. This means that information systems must evolve as well, which requires management of the evolving functionalities. This is the purpose of managing system enhancements, which has similarities with projects for developing new information systems and consists of several stages.

Formulating requirements

The results of formulating requirements form the basis on which application management or infrastructure management can go to work. The subprocesses are:

1. determination of the information needs of the business organization and its end users;
2. outlining the (changed) functionalities that the information system will have to perform, including determination of (changed) system functions needed as well as determination of the (changed) object model needed;
3. stating requirements for the (changed) system in terms of availability, dependability, capacity, robustness, performance, cost, flexibility, portability, maintainability, security, etc;
4. managing interfaces with other information systems and/or other organizations.

Testing

Testing has a number of sub-processes:

1. testing the functional specifications drawn up by application management on the basis of the requirements formulated at an earlier stage;
2. preparation and execution or coordination of acceptance testing, performance testing, user testing, etc;
3. reporting problems that came up during testing, and prioritizing the problem-solving activities;
4. final and formal acceptance of the information system.

Updating procedures

Updating procedures is concerned with updating (the documentation of) procedures, working methods, user manuals and so on.

Implementing

Implementing the information system consists of the following:

1. putting the information system into operation within the user organization;
2. coordination of conversion activities if necessary;
3. instruction and training in the operations using the information system;
4. setting up facilities and organization (ordering of furniture and other materials, implementation of new working methods).

Control

Control is a management role that is performed by functional management on behalf of business management. It focuses both on functional management itself and the total information provision within the organization, and it consists of several processes.

Life-cycle management

Life-cycle management aims at a perfect match between the information systems and the business organization and processes. One of the elements of life-cycle management is a periodic assessment of the information system. In such an assessment the technical, functional and exploitation quality of the system are analysed. Also, the fit of the system onto the policies and the expected future of the organization is examined, together with new opportunities offered by ICT developments. This assessment is necessary to create a realistic scenario for the future of the information system.

Planning and control

Planning and control is an important control process. Life-cycle management and planning and control have most links with business planning for the business organization and information planning. Planning and control is concerned with all processes regarding planning and monitoring of the activities that are related to functional management and ICT services provision (Figure 5.5).

FIGURE 5.5

Planning and control

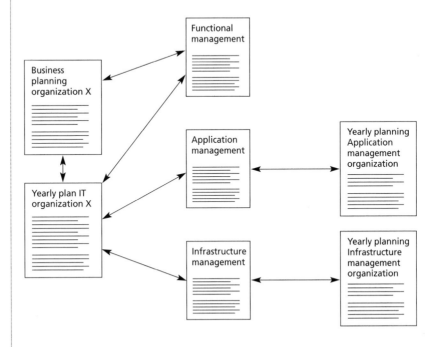

Cost management
Performing cost calculations, planning financial budgets and monitoring actual costs are part of cost management, which also comprises allocation of ICT costs to the final customer (business organization) and sending formal invoices for the use of certain applications.

Quality management
Quality management is the development, deployment and monitoring of a quality system together with a quality plan regarding the entire information provision. Topics addressed are the quality of the processes of information systems management, the quality of their outputs, user satisfaction and employee contentment.

Service level management
Service level agreements are a well-known instrument in information systems management. Service level management, as part of functional management, acts as the counterpart of the ICT services provider on behalf of the business organization.

Connecting processes
Similar to the models for application and infrastructure management, the model for functional management distinguishes connecting processes. These processes interface between the user support processes, which are concerned with providing a stable, unchanging information system, and the processes related to managing the systems enhancements.

Two main connecting processes can be distinguished, as set out next.

Control of procedures and software
This process has a similar role to software distribution and control in application or infrastructure management, but its focus is different. This process consists of the following:

1. control and distribution of documentation of procedures, working methods and manuals for the use of the information system;
2. issuing instructions to the ICT service team that result in actual technical operations of the information system;
3. coordination of software distribution and data conversion.

Change management
In the change management process, functional management is the intermediary between the ICT services provider and the user organization. In change management within functional management, the following processes can be distinguished:

1. Formulating change requests. Change requests may emerge as a result of the user support process or of organizational changes. Organizational changes may be caused by changed regulations, changes in the market, new technologies, etc.

2. Evaluation, approval and prioritizing of changes suggested by application management. On this point, there are strong relations with impact analysis and release planning.
3. Monitoring of progress in the realization of changes by application management and infrastructure management.

5.6 Functional management process scan

On the basis of the model for functional management, a functional management process scan has been developed. This scan provides insights into the presence and quality of functional management processes as well as problems that occur in this context.

This scan shows the maturity of the processes of functional management. Six maturity levels can be distinguished:

1. *absence*: the process is fully absent and not recognized in the organization;
2. *initiation*: the process is highly dependent on personal initiatives; there is no organization-wide commitment to the process;
3. *awareness*: the process is perceived but not yet clearly defined;
4. *control*: the process is defined and controlled;
5. *integration*: metrics are used and processes facilitate one another;
6. *optimization*: continuous controlled improvement.

Figure 5.6 gives an example of how the maturity levels for (groups of) functional management processes can be reported. Very large differences between the different sections of the 'rose' shape give an indication of possible problems.

The findings of the scan (perception of the processes, quality of the processes and problems) are very useful in further professionalizing functional management.

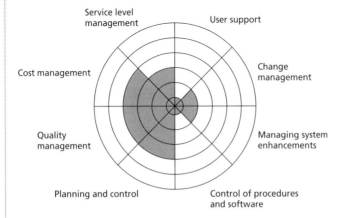

FIGURE 5.6
Maturity levels for functional management

5.7 Finally

More professional application and infrastructure management lead to the need for more professional functional management. To support this development, the model for functional management is very useful. It gives guidelines on how to fulfil the role of functional management. The strong points of the model are the explicit attention to user support and managing system enhancements. User support is a continuous, indefinite, ongoing process, whereas managing system enhancements is a definite, one-off project. The model clearly points out that both areas are important and should be managed integrally by a central control layer.

Furthermore, the model has proven a good basis for a process scan. With the use of this scan, the shortcomings of functional management can be clearly identified. The scan is very useful for planning improvements in functional management.

The model for functional management is stable, though subject to continuous evaluation and improvement. Currently we are working on improvements to the model. We expect to present the improved model in the near future.

Improvements focus on the role of strategic information processes in the organization and their relation to the model. The improved model should pay explicit attention to areas such as information management and information policy.

Literature

Deurloo, C.D., Meijer-Veldman, M.E.E. and van der Pols, R. (1998) 'Model voor Functioneel Beheer', in *IT Beheer Jaarboek 1998*, Den Haag: Ten Hagen Stam (in Dutch).

Looijen, Maarten (1998) *Information Systems – Management, Control and Maintenance*, ISBN 90 267 2846 8, Deventer: Kluwer.

Meijer, M., van Outvorst, F. Hoogland, D. and Fris, B. (2000) 'Application services with R2C', in *World Class IT Service Management Guide 2000*, The Hague: Ten Hagen Stam.

Van Outvorst, F. Van der Zee, P. and Deurloo, C. (2000) 'De praktijk van functioneel beheer – het model voor functioneel beheer in de praktijk', in *IT Beheer Jaarboek 2001*, Den Haag: Ten Hagen Stam (in Dutch).

6 The HP IT Service Management Reference Model

Jeff Drake Hewlett-Packard Consulting, USA

Summary

This chapter describes the HP IT Service Management Reference Model. This model is a significant tool proven to be useful in presenting and describing the many IT management processes, inter-process relationships, and business linkages IT needs to put in place for the successful development, deployment and support of services in the e-world (Figure 6.1).

FIGURE 6.1
Process + people + technology

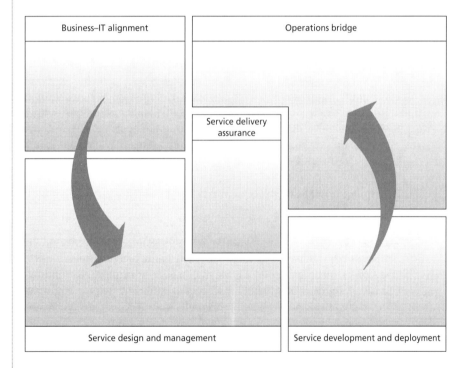

As we take our first few steps into the new millennium, corporate IT organizations are once again being forced to deal with another challenge: 'e-everything' – brought about by the emergence of new technology, the pervasiveness of the Internet, and an ever-increasing competitive marketplace. E-commerce,[1] e-business[2] and e-services[3] are already making fundamental changes to the way businesses are created and operated and to how we live and work. Figure 6.2 shows the relationship between these three terms. Buying a home or car, shopping for books or groceries, managing your personal

FIGURE 6.2

The relationship between e-commerce, e-business and e-services

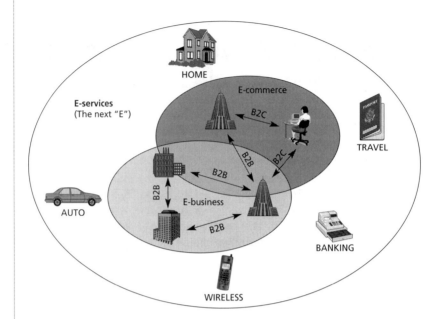

finances and trading stock, planning a trip or mapping your family genealogy are activities that are done significantly differently today compared with just two years ago. Companies like eBay, Amazon.com, AutoMall.com, Charles Schwab and Yahoo represent just a few success stories of the companies that have been in the forefront of the e-services revolution.

6.1 Supporting e-services through IT Service Management (ITSM) e-services

IT Service Management (ITSM) is an approach that combines proven methods such as process management and known industry best practices together with forward-thinking concepts such as running IT 'as a business' (as opposed to running IT 'within' a business). Adopting ITSM enables IT organizations to deliver quality services that satisfy customer business needs, are process-driven, meet cost targets, and achieve performance targets specified within service level agreements (SLAs). It is an approach that is vital to all IT organizations, big or small, that are currently supporting, or planning to support, an e-business venture. Imagine that a major business unit has just informed IT management that they want to quickly provide retail shopping to customers directly – via the Internet. Those of us who might use such a method to purchase products, the end-customers, will see only one service – call it 'online shopping'. But hidden from our view, behind the firewall and inside the company, many different IT services have to be delivered to support this new e-business venture and make it successful. For example:

● **Datacentre services**
   – Hardware procurement
   – Software licence management

- Performance and capacity planning
- Database administration and computer operations
- Etc.

Security services
- Virus protection
- Data security
- Security audits
- Etc.

Desktop services
- Workstation installation and setup
- Etc.

Network services
- Internet/intranet access
- Remote access
- Network management
- Site connectivity
- Etc.

However, this is just the tip of the iceberg! These crucial, supporting IT services cannot be delivered consistently, let alone guaranteed, without the aforementioned well-defined, measurable IT processes, integrated technologies, clearly defined roles and trained staff. And if the quality of these fundamental IT services cannot be guaranteed, then neither can the end-customer's online shopping service! There is an undeniable dependency of the quality and performance of the 'one' on the quality and performance of the 'many'. Offering the public a usable online shopping service requires an incredibly stable IT environment if you want to keep customers from beating down your door with complaints, or worse – taking their business elsewhere. And in the world of e-business, your competition is only one mouse-click away. This means that underlying IT services, just like the e-services they support, have to be carefully planned, deployed, and maintained. Changes to the production IT environment must be carefully monitored and controlled, service-related assets must be tracked, incidents handled quickly, service level commitments must be met, potential service outages addressed before they happen, computer operations must continue uninterrupted, etc.

The bottom line is that if IT doesn't have its own service 'act' together, delivering successful e-services to customers just isn't going to happen.

Herein lies a dangerous trap. For with the entire industry in an uproar as everyone started marching to the e-services drumbeat, it was soon seen (before the e-bubble burst) to be easier than ever for corporations to forget their basic support requirements (e.g. stabilizing their infrastructure, implementing process management, etc.) in all the excitement around developing an e-business – at a time when those basic support requirements are more important then ever before. IT organizations need to be vigilant and continue asking themselves: 'What do we need to have in place in order to support our business objectives?' Answering this question serves to re-emphasize the continuing importance of some of the major challenges facing IT organizations today, as IT strives to identify:

- what IT processes are required to deliver quality IT services;
- what inter-process relationships and business linkages are required to deliver quality IT services;
- what appropriate technologies are available that are process-enabling and provide tight process integration;
- what IT organizational structure will allow the efficient delivery of customer services.

But answering questions as to 'what' IT needs begs other questions regarding 'how' and 'where'. For example:

- knowing how to design and implement IT processes that enable quality IT service delivery and support to customers;
- knowing how to implement process-enabling technologies quickly and cost-effectively;
- knowing how to identify which IT functions to insource and which (if any) to consider for selective outsourcing;
- knowing where to start.

Knowing 'when' you should start planning for IT Service Management is perhaps the easiest question to answer – you should have started yesterday!

6.2 The need for a model

Given these difficult questions that IT organizations are trying to answer, chief executives and the IT managers who report to them have all been in need of a clear picture that depicts the IT processes required to deliver quality IT services in support of their emerging e-services. Without a clear picture, IT organizations will continue to struggle as they try to determine:

- the current state of IT with regard to process (the 'as is');
- the desired future state of IT (the 'to be');
- the gaps between the current and future states of IT;
- the steps needed to bridge those gaps.

Therefore, the need for a concise picture – one that reflects an enterprise service management capability – is very real for most IT organizations and critical to their success.

6.3 The HP IT Service Management Reference Model

In 2000, Hewlett-Packard (HP) developed such a picture and called it the IT Service Management Reference Model. HP, in its work with IT organizations around the world, was acutely aware of the difficulty in identifying:

- the needed IT processes;
- service management organizational requirements;
- process-enabling technologies;

problems associated with communicating critical needs and possible solutions across the enterprise.

To this end, HP focused considerable time and energy to assist customers in this effort by assembling a team of IT Service Management experts, whose goal was to develop a model that could be used as an enterprise reference for corporate IT organizations. This model, which functions as a high-level fully-integrated IT process relationship map, has proved to be invaluable to companies around the world as they seek an understanding of both their problems and their possible solutions. Additionally, this reference model is extremely useful in initiating a meaningful dialogue between all parties interested in IT process requirements and solutions by providing a coherent representation of IT processes and a common language. The HP IT Service Management (ITSM) Reference Model incorporates many of the IT Infrastructure Library (ITIL) best practices. ITIL was originally developed by the government of the United Kingdom in an effort to better manage service delivery to its IT customers. Consisting of a series of published books, ITIL has been adopted and implemented throughout Europe and is in the midst of a migration to the Americas. The ITSM Reference Model development team took the ITIL practices that could be applied to the enterprise and built them into the model, while adding the experience of HP consultants around the world, gained through their own efforts at developing and implementing service management solutions, both within HP and for HP customers. The result is a model that combines the best that ITIL has to offer with the best that industry experience has to offer. The team also designed the model to reflect the need to run IT 'as a business' rather than merely running IT 'within a business'. Therefore, the ITSM Reference Model has several processes not found in ITIL. However, many ITIL terms and definitions are used throughout the model, while others have been modified to reflect HP experience and perspective. This was a conscious effort to enable better organizational communication by adopting a common glossary of terms, definitions, and concepts that are already in use globally. Note that the HP ITSM Reference Model can be applied to any IT enterprise, regardless of size or distribution, whether you are supporting an e-business or not. Although its focus is on distributed environments, the model is still valid for traditional data centres because it addresses the non-integration issues that are prevalent in existing mainframe-centric process models. Hewlett-Packard is also using this model internally, as a vehicle for interdivisional communication and both product and service development.

As a high-level IT process relationship map that depicts a common service life cycle, the model can be used to do the following:

- **Define and assess the current IT environment**. Utilizing the model, IT staff can quickly identify the processes currently in place and begin an immediate discussion regarding their status, value, and relationships with other key IT processes.
- **Identify process 'gaps' and the desired future state of the IT organization**. The model is a quick reference tool that demonstrates the desired future end-point to be achieved by IT, and provides a framework for planning the accomplishments needed to get there.

- **Prioritize work efforts**. Although the model represents the processes that IT must have in place to deliver quality services, in reality every corporation differs in its immediate needs. IT organizations must therefore consider a variety of process implementation priorities for their specific situations. The ITSM Reference Model expedites this effort due to its emphasis on inter-process relationships and linkages, thereby helping IT staff judge the impact and value of one implementation approach versus another.

- **Identify critical process linkages**. Recognizing required process linkages further assists process design and implementation efforts by serving as a guide to understanding which processes need to be linked and what types of information need to be shared.

- **Begin organizational realignment discussions**. While the model is in fact a process map and not an organizational model, it can still be used quite effectively to discuss and plan for organizational change within IT. Given the service life-cycle orientation of the model, it can be a useful starting point and reference for restructuring IT along both process and service lines.

- **Identify areas to apply process-enabling technologies**. Drilling down into the model and analysing process hand-offs and integration points provides IT with an ability to target potential areas to which time-saving process-enabling technologies can be applied.

- **Identify insourcing and outsourcing opportunities**. Utilizing the model to better grasp critical IT process interrelationships can help IT staff decide which services make business sense to insource, and which should be considered opportunities for selective outsourcing. Additionally, such knowledge can provide IT with an understanding of how their insourced IT processes must interface to those that are outsourced to another service provider.

The HP IT Service Management Reference Model can really provide immediate value and be used in many different ways. The model continues to evolve based on real-world experience, and to reflect industry direction. Recently, given the e-services revolution the industry is currently experiencing, Hewlett-Packard updated the ITSM Reference Model to reflect the enhanced perception of, and need for, Security Management.

6.4 Model content

Five process groups

Over the years, there have been many different lists and descriptions of IT processes and just as many different opinions about their importance. Given the goal of IT Service Management to provide quality services to customers, the processes in the ITSM Reference Model have been organized into five process groups, each focused on a different key aspect of the service life cycle (see Figure 6.3). These groups are discussed briefly below and a description of all the processes they contain follows.

FIGURE 6.3

The ITSM Reference Model process groups

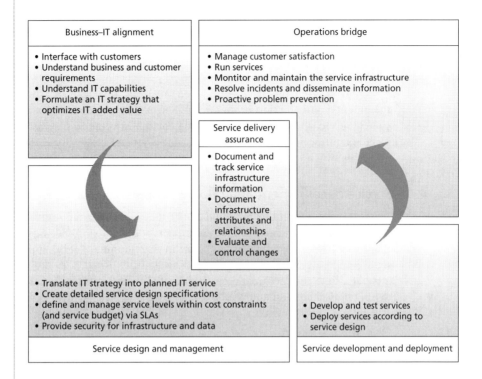

Service delivery assurance

This process group occupies the centre of the ITSM Reference Model for several reasons, and the illusion that the other four process groups appear to revolve around this central 'hub' is intentional (refer to the arrows in Figure 6.3). Firstly, the processes in this group are what provide the necessary stability to the IT environment required by all of the other processes in the model. Without the processes in Service Delivery Assurance, none of the other IT processes in the model will ever operate efficiently. How can they, when 'fire fighting' will be the primary activity occupying everyone's time? And this is exactly the result you get when these processes are missing. Secondly, the Service Delivery Assurance processes reach out and 'touch' every other process in the model at some point in time, and usually more than once. For these reasons, it makes sense to place this very important process group in the centre of the model.

Business–IT alignment

The processes contained in this group are focused on running IT 'as a business'. The activities performed by these processes determine service market potential; seek and achieve a common understanding between IT and its customers regarding business needs and IT capabilities; and, in the end, formulate an IT strategy that will optimize IT added value. These processes are therefore quite strategic in nature.

Service design and management

The processes in this group enable IT to translate the IT strategy (i.e. the 'vision' developed as a result of Business–IT Alignment process performance) into planned services (i.e. 'reality') via detailed design specifications. Activities involving the definition of service levels; the creation, negotiation, and signing of service level agreements; and infrastructure and data security, are also performed. Service availability, service capacity, and IT service costing information are all incorporated into service contracts via the interaction of the processes within this group with other processes in the model.

Service development and deployment

The processes within this group enable IT to update existing services and develop new services and their related infrastructure components (e.g. procedures, tools, hardware staging, software installation, application development, training plans, etc.). Once a service and its components have been successfully tested, they are then deployed and integrated into the production environment to experience another battery of tests prior to final project sign-off and production release.

Operations bridge

Similar to the nautical concept of a 'bridge' on a ship, the processes in this group work together to provide the required command, control, and support of the IT environment. These processes also manage customer satisfaction. Focused on service delivery, they enable the ongoing running, monitoring, and maintenance of the IT enterprise environment.

6.5 The HP ITSM Reference Model Processes[4]

Figure 6.4 shows the processes contained within the ITSM Reference Model. Experience dictates that the life cycle of a service is much more dynamic and complex than can be described by any two-dimensional picture; that is, the processes being executed at different points during this life cycle may be iterative in nature, involve numerous interactions with other IT processes, require various feedback loops to ensure quality, etc. Even recognizing this, from the time a service is no more than a gleam in a customer's eye to the point at which the service is being delivered, the structure of the ITSM Reference Model can still provide high-level guidance on the general flow of activities performed during the service life cycle. The following brief descriptions of each of the processes within the model will describe the general workflow of the model.

Business–IT alignment

Business assessment
The Business Assessment process assesses the market for IT services, and based on business need defines the business requirements that will drive IT's contribution to

FIGURE 6.4

The Reference Model processes

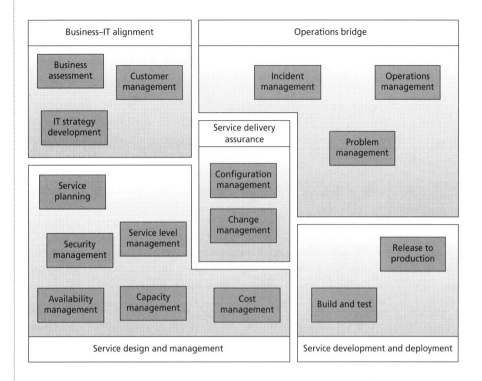

the corporate value chain. The activities performed by this process are very important when attempting to run IT 'as a business' rather than merely 'within a business'. Periodic business planning sessions and/or changes within the industry can trigger this process to execute, often exposing opportunities for new service developments or improvements. This process requires a sound understanding of service markets and interaction with a number of other IT processes, including Customer Management and IT Strategy Development.

Customer management

The Customer Management process enables IT to function as a business partner with its customers. Performing this process allows IT to anticipate new customer requirements, communicate service value to the customer, measure customer satisfaction, and engage in joint problem-solving efforts. The Business Assessment process, when doing competitive and market analyses, can utilize much of the customer information gained as a result of this process, while the findings of both the Business Assessment and Customer Management processes provide much of the substance that fuels the IT Strategy Development process.

IT strategy development

This process enables IT to derive and establish the overall value proposition for the IT services organization by consolidating the market segment value statements discovered by the Business Assessment process. It aligns customer business planning with

IT business planning, helps IT to articulate a broad plan for achieving its goals and objectives, and enables IT to act decisively. Utilizing much of the information developed by the Business Assessment and Customer Management processes, this process translates customer business requirements into a coherent IT strategy. This strategy should include a well-defined IT architecture and relevant organizational models. IT Strategy Development, Business Assessment and Customer Management (i.e. the Business–IT Alignment processes) will all be required to interact in order to derive a sound IT strategy. Together, these processes will output the business cases and requirements that will be consumed as inputs by the Service Planning process.

Service design and management

Service planning

Using the results of the Business–IT Alignment processes, the Service Planning process can define, track, and control services that can be leveraged across multiple customers (i.e. standard services) and include them in a service portfolio. If needed, standard services can then be modified (i.e. custom services) to fit the needs of different business units or sets of customers. This process enhances IT added value by ensuring that the services planned by IT match customer business requirements and IT delivery capabilities. This process develops detailed service specifications that are then used by all of the other processes in Service Design and Management as they contribute to the overall service life cycle.

Service level management

The Service Level Management process enables IT to define, negotiate, monitor, report, and control customer-specific service levels within predefined standard service parameters. Of special significance is the interaction between Service Planning and Service Level Management. With a detailed service specification at its disposal, the Service Level Management process can hammer out measurable service-level objectives with potential customers and allow IT management to eventually sign and commit to meaningful service level agreements (SLAs). As might be imagined, both Service Planning and Service Level Management are dependent on the results of, and interactions with, other related IT processes (see below) in order to execute successfully.

Security management

The Security Management process enables IT to define, track and control the security of corporate information and services. This process accounts for the implementation, control and maintenance of the total security infrastructure. All services (current, newly developed and planned) must adhere to strict corporate standards pertaining to information security. In this day and age of e-commerce, data security is of the greatest importance.

Availability management

The Availability Management process allows IT to define, track and control service availability to its customers and manage supplier contributions to overall service availability. It should be noted that considerations like system availability and network availability are vital 'components' enabling service availability. Service plans (i.e. specifications) generated by Service Planning are reviewed and analysed as a result of the Availability Management process and modified if needed to reflect service availability requirements. Service level agreements (SLAs) must contain a negotiated understanding of predicted service usage, how the service will be delivered in the event of a disaster (e.g. off-site computing, emergency response, etc.), what types of service contingencies IT has prepared for (e.g. on-site inventory of spare parts, etc.). The Availability Management process will deliver this important information to the Service Level Management process for SLA development.

Capacity management

This process enables IT to define, track and control service capacities to ensure service workloads are ready to meet the demands of customers at agreed-upon performance levels. It should be noted that considerations like system capacity and network capacity are vital 'components' enabling overall service capacity. Service capacity information is also critical to successful new services and service level agreements; therefore this process interacts with Service Planning and Service Level Management in a similar way to Availability Management.

Cost management

The Cost Management process enables IT to define IT cost and charging allocation structures that support service budgets and ensure cost recovery. This process includes tracking and controlling actual costs by service and by customer. It also includes charging customers for service delivery. It will be important for each IT process to track the costs accrued and pass this information to Cost Management. In turn, Cost Management will be required to interact with the Business–IT Alignment processes for budgeting purposes, and with Service Planning and Service Level Management for service pricing estimates.

Service development and deployment

Build and test

This process allows IT to develop and validate a functional version of a component, service function, or end-to-end service and documents instructions for replication and implementation of a production copy as needed. When a service specification has been completed, the Build and Test process will be needed to acquire the necessary components, build components (in some cases) and/or service functions (like a backup capability, web functionality, etc.), or even complete end-to-end service solutions (like SAP Financials, etc.). Once assembled, the component, function, or end-to-end service will need to be thoroughly tested. This process interacts extensively with the Change Management, Configuration Management and Release to Production processes, among others. (Note that an important part of this process is testing for adherence to security policies and guidelines.)

Release to production

Performing the Release to Production process enables IT to create one or more production copies of a new or updated component, service function, or end-to-end service for a specific customer, based on a detailed production plan referred to here as a 'master blueprint'. Required components are procured and the production copy is staged, implemented in the production environment, tested, and activated for customer use (this means it is ready for billing). The Release to Production process interacts with the Build and Test, Change Management and Configuration Management processes, as well as other processes in the model.

Operations bridge

Operations management

More a collection of many various tasks and procedures than a single process, together they enable IT to manage and perform the normal, day-to-day processing activities required for IT service delivery in accordance with agreed-upon service levels. Essentially they allow IT to 'operate' the production environment required to deliver services. This process is closely tied to Incident Management (includes the Helpdesk) and Problem Management processes, and valuable information is shared between them. There is also a close connection between this process and the Change and Configuration Management processes as well.

Incident management

Purely *reactive* in nature, this process, often simply called Help Desk or Service Desk, is focused on quickly restoring service availability by handling incidents occurring in the infrastructure or reported by customers and seeks to minimize service disruptions. This process manages the day-to-day support interface between customers and service providers, and as such it is critical to successfully managing customer satisfaction. Call management and efficient first-, second- and third-level support are encompassed in this process. Again, Change and Configuration Management interact heavily with this process.

Problem management

Purely *proactive* in nature, this process is focused on reducing the number of incidents occurring in the production environment by addressing the root causes of failures (based on closed incidents). It also includes ongoing trend analysis and known error control, concerned with ensuring that long-term solutions addressing root causes are implemented. This process is closely tied to Incident Management, as it operates in part on the closed incidents generated by the help desk, as well as informing other processes about potential problems with the infrastructure.

Service delivery assurance

Change management

This IT process logs all significant changes to the enterprise environment, coordinates change-related work orders, prioritizes change requests, authorizes production changes, schedules resources, and assesses the risk and impact of all changes to the IT environment. Given the scope of this process, it is easy to see why it interacts with every other process in the ITSM Reference Model. As processes are performed they will inevitably create some kind of change in the IT environment. Change Management is the one process that regulates these changes, controls them and records them, thereby dramatically reducing infrastructure instability.

Configuration management

This IT process centrally registers and controls information about the infrastructure, such as configuration item (CI) attributes (e.g. identifying system and network hardware, production software, people (staff), documentation, etc.), CI status (e.g. in stock, in repair, in production, etc.), and their relationships (e.g. this user has PC 'A' on her desk, printers 'B,' C', and 'D' available for use, is covered by 'Online Shopping SLA 10.1', etc.).[5] Note that upon first glance it is easy to mistake this process for standard asset management. This is wrong. The Configuration Management process is distinct from corporate asset management in that it is focused entirely on the IT infrastructure and allows interrogation of infrastructure data based on relationships. Any other IT process that will be affecting the infrastructure will be interacting with this process.

6.6 So where do you start?

Hewlett-Packard's experience of sharing this model with clients has repeatedly confirmed its validity, and following initial presentations of the model one of the most common questions is: 'Where do we start?' Herein lies one of the most powerful aspects of the ITSM Reference Model, for the model has neither a beginning nor an end. In other words, you can start using the model from any point, but most IT organizations typically choose to start where their company is hurting the most. Following are three common real-world scenarios that illustrate this point and the flexibility of the model.

Scenario 1: My help desk is broken!

One of the most significant areas of 'pain' for businesses involves the help desk that is not working properly, the symptoms of which can manifest themselves in several different ways: complaints that the help desk is unresponsive, end users experiencing the same problems over and over, a growing list of unresolved issues, etc. The cause of these problems is often the fact that the Incident and Problem Management processes either do not exist (i.e. no metrics in place, non-existent procedures, continual reinvention of solutions, etc.) or are poorly understood and considered to be the same, when in fact Incident Management should be reactive while Problem Management should be uniquely proactive. The Reference Model separates these processes distinctly. Few things will throw a help desk into chaos faster than assigning help desk staff the responsibility for both resolving reported incidents (a reactive effort applied to incoming calls) and doing in-depth root-cause analysis (a proactive effort applied to the results of exhaustive trend analyses and/or incident correlation on closed incidents). Experience demonstrates that whenever help desk personnel are expected to do both reactive and proactive tasks, the reactive tasks almost always take precedence (i.e. the 'squeaky wheel gets the grease'). With staff focused on reactively putting out 'fires', there is little time left to proactively do trend analysis or search the database of closed incidents for pointers to potential future incidents and root causes. The Reference Model notes and describes the differences between the Incident Management and Problem Management processes, and these differences are further detailed in the ITSM process and design guides (based on the ITSM Reference Model) used by Hewlett-Packard Consulting.

Scenario 2: My customers are asking us to write SLAs!

With businesses being pressured to become more customer-oriented (a factor required for long-term success), many IT organizations are being asked to provide performance and quality guarantees for the services being delivered (i.e. defined service levels). However, many IT organizations are quick to realize that they are unprepared and/or unable to make serious commitments regarding service quality without significant work. Why? If asked to define the relationship between IT and the business, most IT organizations would describe it as 'technology provider', rather than 'service provider'. Unfortunately, this internally focused thinking will not support the requirements of the business in the new e-world. Businesses want choices in the services they purchase and are willing to pay for packaged services they can understand. But making this happen requires something of a paradigm shift for IT, as even attempting to create a list of existing IT services in business language is a non-trivial undertaking (especially the first time IT is forced to do so). Add to this the facts (discussed earlier) regarding the necessary robust infrastructure, tools, etc. that are required to deliver quality services, and it becomes obvious why IT managers can't make serious commitments to their customers about service. Yet, still they are on the hook, so to speak, to write service level agreements (SLAs) and make guarantees. This is a difficult situation to say the least. The Reference Model helps IT organizations understand what is required to be both customer and service-oriented. It describes the relationships between Service Level Management (the process which results in signed SLAs) and other IT processes in the model, identifies the necessary business and process linkages, and provides a totally integrated view of overall service quality. Again, this process, like all of the other processes in the Reference Model, is further detailed in process design guides used by Hewlett-Packard Consulting.

Scenario 3: We need better control of our production environment!

If asked whether they have a Change Management process or not, most IT managers would state with certainty that they do have such a process. Yet, experience shows that it usually does not take any time at all to find numerous examples in these same companies of recent situations where serious production problems have occurred due to either unscheduled changes or poorly planned changes. What is usually meant by the statement 'We have a Change Management process' is that at some point in time (perhaps distant) a team was formed to think about change management; they may have even developed real process-flow diagrams, written procedures, etc. In most cases it does NOT mean nor guarantee that staff are actually following the process today, or that the process has been continually improved to match business requirements. In other words – sure, they have a Change Management process (on paper somewhere), but in reality the process is broken. And let's face it; having a broken Change Management process can have the same effect on the business as having no Change Management process at all. Sometimes problems with Change Management are discovered when analysing other processes, like Incident Management. It is not uncommon to find out that when the help desk is 'on fire' because it can't handle the call load, one of the primary reasons is that the Change Management process is either non-existent or seriously broken. High percentages of reported incidents can sometimes be tracked to just a few unscheduled changes or situations where a change was not executed properly. Without a solid Change Management process, the IT environment cannot be stabilized, and IT will not be able to make any serious commitments to customers regarding service levels. Unlike Change Management, most IT managers realize quickly that they are not currently using a Configuration Management process. But once the concept of Configuration Management is explained (see Service Delivery Assurance above), they also realize that such a process would benefit their organizations greatly. Providing the Change Manager with the ability to easily determine the relationships between configuration items (CIs) that are facing a significant change, thus greatly aiding risk and impact analysis; providing the help desk with the ability to quickly associate callers with the IT with assets they are using (e.g. PCs, applications, service level agreements, etc.); providing IT the capability to immediately assess the current state of IT assets (i.e. in stock, in repair, in production, on order, etc.) – these are all benefits to be gleaned from implementing a Configuration Management process. The Reference Model is a valuable tool that can be used when making a case to focus IT on Change and Configuration Management, as these two processes occupy the centre of the model due to their importance. The Reference Model process relationship maps can be easily used to further explain the necessary information exchanges and integrations that must occur between these two processes and every other process in the model.

6.7 The bottom line

Which IT process you decide to implement or improve first is going to differ from company to company, and to some degree is less important than the decision you need to make to really do something to get your IT organization ready to support the 21st-century e-business initiatives your company will be pursuing. The HP ITSM Reference Model is a tool that can be used throughout the entire life cycle of service development, enabling your business to have the capability to deliver the quality services required to beat the competition in the new e-world.

Acknowledgements

The development of the Hewlett-Packard IT Service Management Reference Model was an aggressive team effort, involving many people from different HP entities and countries during the project, too many to mention each and every one here. Yet, certain contributors provided such value that they must be mentioned by name. It is with great pride that I call them my peers. Special thanks to: Yvonne Bentley and Dorene Matney. Additional key contributors were: Bert Van Barneveld, Paul Ham, Colin Henderson, Peter Kane, Joe Kouba, Karen Klukiewicz, Paul Miller, Jens Ritter, Jeff Swann, Mark Taguma, Ron Tarver, Georg Bock, Tjerk Feenstra, Karl Tomlinson, Steve Lochner, Monica Hasegawa, Steve Helper, Christian de Ryss, Larry Hicks, Masashi Fujita, Gavin Runnalls, Arjan Middendorp, Onno Van Kooten and Erik Laboulbenne. I am also especially grateful for the assistance given to me by Brad Wasson, Tjerk Feenstra, Paul Miller and Hans Linschooten in the development of this chapter.

Notes

1. 'E-commerce' is a term that refers to the buying and selling of goods and services over the Internet – both business-to-business (B2B) and business-to-consumer (B2C) transactions.
2. E-business ('electronic business', derived from such terms as 'e-mail' and 'e-commerce') embraces e-commerce, but also includes Internet-based communications and Web-enabled business processes.
3. An e-service is a service or resource available on the Internet that conducts a transaction, completes a task, or solves a problem – and can be used by people, businesses and 'things' (such as our cars, our homes, manufacturing lines, anything with a microchip in it). E-services are easily understood from the end-customer viewpoint, i.e. buying a car online, trading stock online, arranging a trip online, etc. But e-services can also refer to IT resources offered via the Net, such as storage, MIPS on demand, enterprise applications, etc. Note that e-commerce and e-business were essential foundations required before e-services could be used successfully.
4. Note that Hewlett-Packard Consulting has developed detailed progress-design guides for each of the processes in the model.
5. Configuration data are typically stored in a Configuration Management database (CMDB).

7 IPW™ and the IPW Stadia Model™ (IPWSM)

Hans van Herwaarden and **Frank Grift MBA**
Quint Wellington Redwood, the Netherlands

Summary

IPW is a method for the implementation of a process-oriented workflow in an ICT organization, which is used by an increasing number of companies. Traditionally, the focus of IPW was on the management processes (operational and tactical), but over the past few years the scope of IPW has been broadened to include the strategic and development processes as well. For the practical elaboration of the processes, so-called best practices are used. The implementation model uses the best practices of models such as ITIL, CMM^{SM} and/or SPICE in addition to the best practices collected by Quint. Using the so-called 'maturity levels' defined in CMM and SPICE, a phased approach can be used in the development domain. Up until now, this was not the case for the management domain (operational, tactical and strategic), as ITIL had always assumed an all-or-nothing situation (compliant or not). In this contribution the IPW Stadia Model is described, which, based on IPW and analogous to the philosophies of CMM and SPICE, defines a number of stages for the execution of management processes as well as for management organizations.

7.1 A brief review of IPW

The IPW model is a process model for an ICT organization, which connects the ITIL processes: Help Desk, Configuration Management, Change Management, Problem Management, Software Control and Distribution (service support set) and Capacity Management, Cost Management, Availability Management, Contingency Planning, Service Level Management (service delivery set). The purpose of the model is to gain insight into the relationships between the ITIL processes and to provide a framework for an ICT organization. Without such a model it is often very difficult to start an ITIL improvement process. ICT management must deal with questions such as: Where do we start? To what extent are these processes demanding to each other? Which processes are critical? That is why many of our clients use the IPW model as a reference model for communication within the ICT organization as well as to their customers. For example, the IPW model appears in publications, posters and memos etc. Therefore, everybody is acquainted with the IPW model and many discussions about the introduction of ITIL processes will be related to this model. The IPW model is not a theoretical model; it originates from practice. On the one hand, it is based on the known ITIL classification of IT Management and on the other hand based on the 'best practices' in many organizations. Implementation of Process-oriented Workflow (IPW) is seen as a de facto standard for the implementation of ITIL processes in an ICT organization. In 1997, the Gartner Group characterized the IPW model as a highly usable model to set up an ICT organization and therefore a worthwhile investment. This has led to a strong and rapid increase in the international awareness of IPW, which has caused a number of large multinationals to apply the model worldwide. Over the past few years, the model has proved to be extremely successful in transforming both large and small ICT organizations from product, functionally and technologically oriented organizations to customer, process and service-oriented organizations. Also, when (parts of) the IT services are outsourced, IPW has proved to be of great practical use to both the outsourcing organization and the outsourcing partner. These organizations achieve clearly defined services, division of processes over several organizations, and entry into agreements on matters such as communication, the execution of processes, or reporting. Furthermore, the use of IPW has had an important synergetic effect on the certification of ICT organizations (ISO 9000) and the introduction of other quality systems (NKM, EFQM).

7.2 The evolution of IPW

A decade of experience has been gained with IPW and the model has been adjusted, extended, adapted and refined many times by Quint Wellington Redwood. Quint Wellington Redwood and KPN Telecom developed the basic version (Figure 7.1) of IPW in 1992. This model consists only of incident, problem and change management concentrated around the production process. Configuration management was placed within this model as a support function.

The purpose of this version was to show the most important relationships between the processes mentioned. During the development of this model, choices of the level of modelling were made. On a certain level of abstraction, only the main streams of information between and within the processes are shown. This is done for two reasons. On the one hand, to retain the overview, because a full, complex process model is very difficult to use as a communication method within an ICT organization. On the other hand, the IPW model was designed to recognize the ITIL

FIGURE 7.1

IPW in 1992

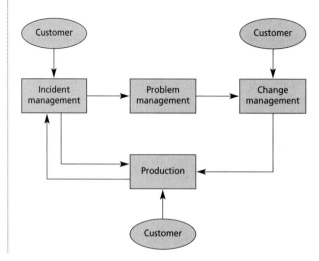

7 ■ IPW™ and the IPW Stadia Model™ (IPWSM)

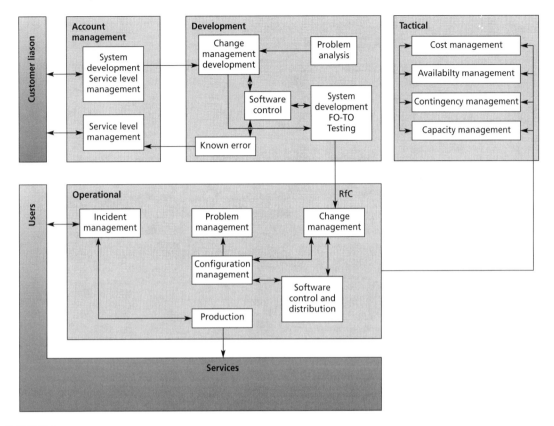

FIGURE 7.2

IPW in 1994

processes easily. By the adoption of ITIL as a de facto standard, a conscious choice was made for an IPW model with a recognizable process from the ITIL books. This particular criterion of development has modified the success of the IPW model in relation to other models. If users do not see the relationship between IPW and ITIL easily, a new barrier is created, which conflicts with the most important aim of the IPW model: to create an overview of ITIL processes. In 1993, the need to expand IPW with the service delivery processes arose. The reason was that users wanted IPW as a reference model for the entire ICT organization, maintaining the identification with the ITIL books. However, the precise boundaries and relationships between the service delivery processes are less clear than with the service support processes. When the ITIL books about the service delivery processes are read, it is clear that the consistency that characterized the service support process (from incident to problem, to known error to request for change) is largely missing in the service delivery books. Since almost no implementation went further than the service support processes, the second version of the IPW model presented the service delivery processes as one block of processes. Figure 7.2 shows the IPW model in 1994.

In 1997, the strategic processes of an ICT organization were also assigned to the IPW model. In this model the Service Delivery processes were also shown

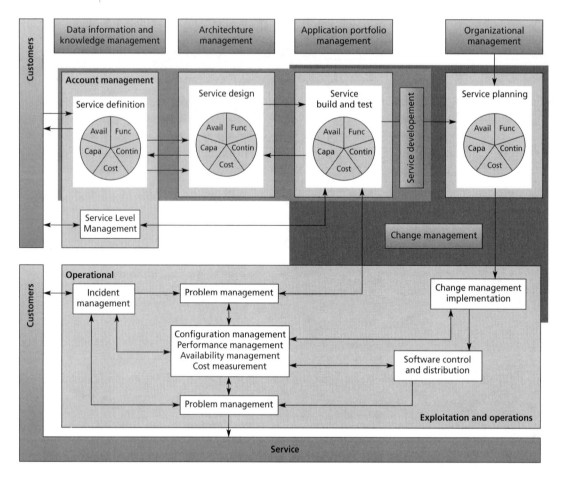

FIGURE 7.3

IPW in 1997

in one block, but were placed in the Service Planning, Development and Account Management processes. In this version it was assumed that the Delivery processes were passed through Service Planning as well as Development. A further specification of the Service Delivery processes was left undone. Figure 7.3 shows the IPW model in 1997. In October 1998, the booklet 'The ABC to IPW' was published, which describes the IPW model on two levels: (1) the highest level of abstraction; (2) the elaboration of every process in a separate process model. This booklet also provided a description of the further specification of the Service Delivery processes. The latest version, developed in 1999, is shown in Figure 7.4. Supplier Management and Security Management processes were integrated into the model, following the latest developments within the ITIL Library and the publication of the Information Systems Procurement Library (ISPL).

7.3 Organizational improvement

It appears that during the implementation and evaluation of a large number of projects for the transformation of an ICT organization, a number of issues always surface. For instance, the cultural aspects, the human resource aspects and the issues regarding the technology to be used are elements that play a part in each transformation. These aspects and their interrelationship must be given due attention when an organization improvement project is conducted. Management of Organizational Change (MOC) forms the thread of all phases. The Analyse Unfreeze–Reconfigure–Refreeze (AURRA) phasing forms an extremely practical framework for planning and implementing organizational changes. Conscious use of this AURRA phasing (Figure 7.5) has already prevented many organizations from planning courses, new procedures or changes in the hierarchy and implementing them inappropriately. In the Analyse phase the current situation in which the organization finds itself is assessed. This phase is essential for identifying improvement priorities, obtaining a baseline, and for planning and obtaining the necessary pre-conditions for an improvement project.

FIGURE 7.4
IPW in 1999

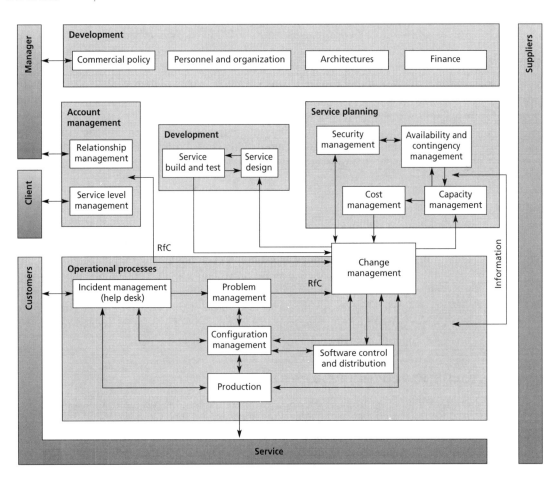

FIGURE 7.5

The AURRA organization improvement cycle

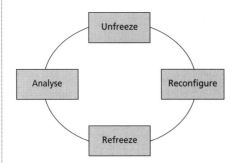

The Unfreeze phase is important for obtaining general support in the organization for the necessary changes. As many people as possible should gain an understanding of the necessity of the changes, after which the desired situation can be sketched. During the Reconfigure phase, changes in the organisation, systems, working methods and procedures can be implemented. In the Refreeze phase measures are taken to prevent the organization from reverting to the old working methods and thereby losing the improvements already established. Once this cycle has been completed, it starts again – the Refreeze phase is simply followed by another Analysis phase. The cycle is repeated, on the one hand to measure the improvement, and on the other hand to prepare the next improvement. Using this cycle to improve organizations prevents the introduction of new procedures or working methods that soon become 'shelfware' and consequently lead to no improvement. Experience shows that quick wins are indeed often possible but that, for a lasting result, the typical time span of an integral change project is 1 to 3 years, depending on the size of the organization and the complexity of the environment. This contribution will focus entirely on the processes of such an improvement project.

7.4 Phasing

The question of which processes should be improved first presents itself with each transformation. This question cannot be answered at a generic level for all organizations. After all, each organization is different, each has its own unique problems, and each operates in a specific environment. So when setting up an improvement project, these elements have to be taken into account. This requires an organization-specific insight, which is obtained in the 'Analyse' phase of the AURRA frame. This ensures that the priorities for the organization's improvement are tuned accordingly to the successful operation of the ICT organization in question.

7.5 Generic dependencies

Without detracting from anything mentioned above, at the same time a more generic statement can be made about the logical order of the IPW processes on the basis of the relationships and the dependencies (input/output) in the model. For instance, the problem management process is largely dependent on the incident information supplied by the incident management process (input) in order to be able to identify the underlying causes. Also, the problem management process is dependent on the place of delivery for RFCs (output) to be facilitated by the change management process. Therefore, the workflow defined in the model already indicates some logical order for the improvement of the processes (Figure 7.6).

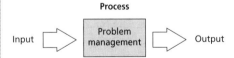

FIGURE 7.6
Process dependencies

7.6 Generic process characteristics

A logical improvement order can also often be found in the IPW processes themselves (in each separate box). In practice it appeared that, for an improvement project to run optimally, the process should be assigned a number of generic process characteristics, which are then worked out using the best practices for the process. Owing to the assigning of generic process characteristics, the execution of the process reaches an increasing level of quality. This is sometimes also called a 'higher' development stage. The generic process characteristics apply to all IPW processes. An example of a generic process characteristic is the performance of the primary process activities. For the incident management process these primary process activities are the best practices in the field of taking in, registering, routing, solving, and completing incidents. For the incident management process, the generic process characteristic use of standards translates into the use of reaction and solution times for incidents. By adding this angle to IPW, the process improvement phases are worked out based on the arrangement of the generic characteristics of each process according to a logical improvement sequence. Table 7.1 on page 107 shows a full enumeration of the generic process characteristics. By defining combinations and/or selections of processes with associated levels, a number of development stages can be identified for an ICT organization as a whole. The definition of stages per process and for an organization as a whole, based on IPW, forms the core of the IPW Stadia Model. The resulting generic phasing of process improvement projects is partly inspired by the ideas behind CMM and SPICE. CMM and SPICE are specifically tuned to software development and distinguish a number of maturity levels (stages) for the execution of processes. As the development processes of IPW are already worked out using models such as CMM and SPICE, these can be automatically used. However, the management processes in IPW did not yet have such an arrangement. Drawing on experience with the improvement of management processes, the IPWSM provides for this. In order to be able to show the relationship between IPWSM and CMM and SPICE, the essence of both concepts is described in a broad outline.

7.7 CMM

The Capability Maturity Model^{SM}, developed and maintained by the Software Engineering Institute (SEI), which is part of Carnegie Mellon University in Pittsburgh, provides five maturity levels for software development. The first version of the model became available in 1991. In 1993 version 1.1 was introduced, and the final draft for version 2.0 has been available since 1997. CMM distinguishes the following levels: initial, repeatable, defined, managed, and optimizing. Each level of maturity is associated with a number of so-called key process areas, which are worked out using common features that in their turn are worked out using key practices. The CMM thus enables the software development organization to consciously select a certain target level of maturity, and then to work towards that level. CMM has a strongly prescriptive character, and an official assessment (which is centrally registered worldwide) will result in 'fully satisfied' only at a certain level when all necessary elements of that level have been completely worked out. Whether this is indeed the case is assessed under the direction of certified lead assessors, who have been specially trained for this purpose by the SEI. The elements associated with a certain level are explicit and specifically defined. In the USA, organizations such as the Ministry of Defense and Boeing require that software suppliers have reached at least the CMM 3 level, or can show that they will reach this level within an acceptable period of time. Many software development organizations have, therefore, started software process improvement (SPI) projects to reach a higher CMM level. Also, the number of professional software development organizations in Europe that do so is on the increase, not least because these projects (like improvement projects in the management domain) yield enormous savings and boost overall effectiveness. Since the introduction of version 1.1 of CMM, a number of derivatives have become available, including the Personal Software Process^{SM} (PSP), which unlike the more organization-oriented CMM is specifically tuned to the improvement of the maturity level of individual software developers.

7.8 SPICE

Software Process Improvement and Capability dEtermination is a reference process model for software development developed by order of the International Standards Organization (ISO). The SEI was one of the organizations to assist in its development, which was initiated in 1992. SPICE is partly based on CMM, but it is less specific in determining the elements that must be worked out for an organization to reach a certain maturity level. The first official release of SPICE is now available (ISO 15504). If we compare this version with the CMM on the basis of the information now available, then we see that SPICE distinguishes five process categories, which can be divided into a total of 35 processes, which in their turn are worked out using some 200 base practices in total. Thus far, there is not much difference from CMM, apart from the fact that the scope of SPICE is wider than that of CMM and that some aspects have been elaborated upon in more detail. The process categories have a so-called thematic arrangement (customer/supplier, engineering, project, organization, and support). Six maturity levels are distinguished (not performed, informal, planned and tracked, well defined, quantitatively controlled, and continuously improving). An important difference with CMM is that these levels are applied by process and not to organizations as a whole. The six levels are worked out with a total of 11 so-called common features and 26 generic practices. The model, therefore, offers a much more generic way of reaching a certain maturity level (stage) that links up well with the generic process characteristics that form the basis of the IPW Stadia Model.

7.9 IPWSM

The IPW Stadia Model is a model that divides the IPW management processes, which form a superset of the processes from the ITIL library, into five process categories and that defines a number of process activities and best practices for all of these processes. Most of the best practices are taken from the ITIL library. Other best practices have been added for fields not provided for by ITIL. So far nothing is new, as this was also the case in the IPW model. Apart from the fact that it mainly concerns management processes and not development processes, the arrangement is comparable with the arrangements used in CMM and SPICE. However, the IPWSM adds the maturity level component, which is again comparable with that of CMM and SPICE. In the IPWSM, six process stages are distinguished. These stages are: 'not performed', 'not identified', 'monitored', 'controlled', 'proactive', and 'improving' (Figure 7.7). The stages are worked out using the generic process characteristics already mentioned, which indicate the maturity level reached by the IPW process.

FIGURE 7.7
The IPWSM process stages

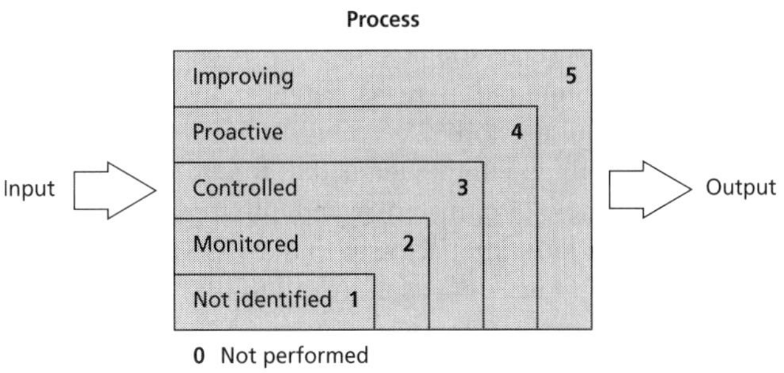

- **Stage 0: Not performed.** In this stage, a process is not carried out at all, not even in an informal or implicit manner.

- **Stage 1: Not identified.** In this stage, the primary process activities are (partially) carried out, but it is not recognized in any way. People are not aware that the process is being conducted. The performance of the process takes place on an ad hoc basis and has an implicit and informal character. The process is not described and there is no process registration.

- **Stage 2: Monitored.** In this stage, the process is not only carried out but also recognized as such. Furthermore, the course of the process is measured. Although the process can in no way be controlled and therefore no corrective action can be taken, the course of the process is recorded. The process is partially described but not yet standardized. In most cases the course of the process is monitored. The course of the process is also recorded. It is important that all actors are aware of and committed to the performance of the process. No roles have yet been defined for all process actors. No objectives have been set for the process and therefore there are no process standards either. The process is not geared to other processes. In a crisis situation there is still a realistic risk of the process being bypassed.

- **Stage 3: Controlled.** In this stage, the process is under control. This means that, in addition to the performance of the process (which is now standardized), registration and reporting, there is also control of the process. Corrective action is taken during the course of the process and the performance of the process is planned. Resources (people, means and technology) become available. All necessary process actors have been given explicit roles. However, there still is an internal and retrospective approach. There are objectives and therefore standards for the process, but these have been established internally and they are not tuned to the external environment. Nevertheless, the process is geared to other related processes. In this stage, the process is also always applied in crisis situations.

- **Stage 4: Proactive.** In this stage, the process is tuned to the external (customer) environment, which means that certain external objectives have been set for the process. There is an outside-in approach. During the process, surprise effects are reduced and the planning develops a more prospective character. The organization of the processes is reactive as well as proactive so that, whenever possible, action is taken before something goes wrong.

- **Stage 5: Improving.** In this stage, the course of the process is continuously adjusted based on planning, implementation, measurements, evaluation, audits and reviews. This process improvement capability is embedded in the process itself. There is a so-called 'double-loop learning', which means that the process not only corrects itself but also adapts itself to new circumstances (adaptive process). Table 7.1 indicates the generic process characteristics that are associated with each stage. In IPWSM these generic process characteristics have been linked to IPW best practices by process.

Table 7.1 has been translated this way into a complete set of tables for the IPW processes (one for each process). The stages or maturity levels are directly linked with the (perceived) added value of the process for the customer (customer value), and they are worked out using the generic process characteristics. To indicate the added value, a Levitt-based model is used. This model describes the added value of products, but is just as much applicable to services. In this model the following layers are distinguished: generic, extended, exceeding, and excelling (Figure 7.8). As processes reach a higher IPWSM stage, more layers of the service are filled in and the added value of the process for the customer increases. Compared with CMM and SPICE, the process maturity approach of the IPWSM is more similar to the SPICE approach than to the CMM approach, as CMM is more oriented towards the organization as a whole. However, the organization-wide CMM approach can be found in the IPWSM model, although the arrangement is focused more on management organizations. On the basis of a selection of processes and a maturity level associated with each process, five maturity levels have been defined for an ICT management organization as a whole. These stages, in which an

TABLE 7.1

Process stages, generic process characteristics, customer value and capability

Process stage	Generic process characteristics	Customer value	Capability
0. Not performed	• N/A	• No value	• N/A
1. Not identified	• Ad hoc performance of (parts of) primary process activities	• No or little perceived value	• Depending on chance, informal agreements and 'heroes'
2. Monitored	• (Management) awareness and commitment • Performance of primary process activities • Measurement and analysis of the process • Process reporting	• Generic value	• To measure is to know • Relevant activities take place primarily as part of the process and are, therefore, perceived • Reporting forms the basis for thoughts about improvements
3. Controlled	• Defined standard course of the process • Process roles have been allocated • Training of process actors • Resources available (people, means, tools) • Planning of the process • Process control • Action if taken to correct the course of the process when (internal) standards are exceeded • (Periodic) process audits	• Extended value	• The (standard) course of the process can be controlled, and can, therefore, be corrected in case the standards are exceeded • The necessary capacity, in terms of people and means, is available and can be planned
4. Proactive	• The process is tuned to the external environment • Action is taken to correct the course of the process even before (external) standards are exceeded • Course of the process initiates communication with (customer) environment • (Periodic) process reviews	• Exceeding value	• The performance level required by the customer is perceived and is consciously and predictably aimed at • SLAs can be entered into that can also be fulfilled
5. Improving	• Corrective measures for the organization of the process, embedded in the process itself (adaptive process) • Continual audits and reviews • Continual increase in effectiveness and efficiently	• Excelling value	• The service level required by the client can be exceeded

organization can find itself, are: 'initial', 'operational monitoring', 'operational control', 'service control', and 'service improving' (Figure 7.9). The arrangement can be used together with, or in addition to, the process maturity levels mentioned earlier.

FIGURE 7.8

Levitt layered customer value

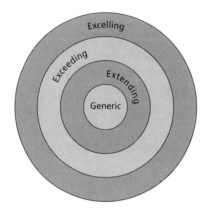

FIGURE 7.9

IPWSM organizational stages

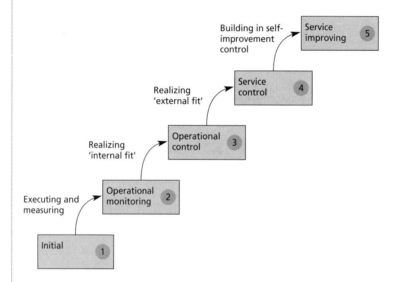

Stage 1: Initial

This stage is the 'safety net' of the model. Each organization immediately qualifies for this quality level. Characteristics of an organization on this level are non-performance of agreements and a type of control that is very much department-oriented. The organization displays compartmentalization, it is a functional 'stovepiped' organization, work is carried out very reactively, little or nothing has been documented, and the organization is blind to the environment in which it operates. Solving problems (which are often passed on), the provision of a service or the supply of a product is reserved to a limited number of 'heroes', who do everything in their power to keep it this way. There is no process registration or reporting and activities are not planned. So people hardly know what they are doing. Work is mainly reactive and production with a possible alternative is considered to be the only process. Most processes have the level of 'not performed' in these organizations. The key production process is carried out and large-scale 'fire fighting' (incident management) takes place. Although these processes are performed, people are not aware of them. This is also true for the processes of change management and software control and distribution. They are categorized as being on the 'not identified' level. To the extent that any arrangements have been made, in crisis situations people immediately revert to the behaviour described. An ICT organization in this stage often has no idea of its situation and is, therefore, ironically enough, generally quite satisfied with it. The organization in question often finds it very difficult to commence improvement activities. To get the organization to do so often requires external intervention (merger, outsourcing, reorganization, downsizing, etc.). The motto of this stage is: 'The butterfly leads a happy life, because it is unaware that it only lives for one day.'

Stage 2: Operational monitoring

In this stage, the organization is in much better shape than in stage 1, although the perception of it may be different. The most important difference is that a number of processes that should be carried out by every ICT organization are indeed conducted. These processes are not yet present to their full extent, but (as the name of this stage implies) they have been worked out on the monitored level. This means that the basic course of the process is present and that, in any case, data are collected about the activities carried out so that reporting can take place. Also, a number of the tactical processes can already be performed, although they are often still in the not-identified stage. The organization is not yet able also to control its processes. There are no standards yet for the course of the process and therefore no corrective actions are taken. The most important value of reaching this stage is that data becomes available about the activities that are being carried out, so that, in the next stage, plans can be made on the basis of the data. Furthermore, the different processes distinguished are not yet geared to one another. The ICT organization that has reached this stage becomes aware of what is actually going on, without it being able to do something about it right away. Although organizations are often given a rude shock from this stage, the feeling they tend to be left with after the shock is that it is still good to know what is happening. The motto of this stage is: 'It's better to know what's happening than to wonder why it happened.'

Stage 3: Operational control

In this stage, there is a so-called 'internal fit'. Most of the processes are planned and controlled on the basis of objectives and standards. Corrective action can be taken during the course of the process, although internal, self-chosen standards may still be used for this. The key operational processes and the primary process have reached the controlled stage, while a number of the tactical processes have reached the monitored stage. The ICT organization has its operational processes under control (hence the name of this stage), although this control exists in an isolated, closed environment. Nevertheless, it is quite an achievement to have reached this stage. In the following stage, the robustness of the process arrangement and the control can be tested against, and geared to, the external (customer) environment. An ICT organization that has reached this level will, in all probability, celebrate – and rightly so, as now finally both the management and the employees are beginning to have a 'hands-on' feeling. The mottoes of this stage are: 'The horizon is the limit' and 'We have saddled the horse and we know how to ride IT.'

Stage 4: Service control

In this stage, there is a so-called 'external fit' in addition to the 'internal fit'. This means that the organization has geared its internal control to the external (customer) environment in which it operates. The standards applied to the processes have been set by the customers. The customers also have an influence on the service provided. The focus of an organization in this stage is, therefore, shifted from controlling the operation (organization, processes, technology) to controlling the service (tuning it according to the customers). The planning has a proactive and forward-looking character and the processes themselves trigger the intended customer orientation by always operating from this point of view. Many operational processes have already reached the proactive stage, while an important part of the tactical processes is in the controlled stage. Also, a number of the strategic processes have come into the picture by now, of which the majority are in the controlled stage. An organization that has reached this stage can be proud – with good reason, as it is probably setting the standard in the market now. The mottoes of this stage are: 'The sky is the limit' and 'World-class service is the standard.'

Stage 5: Service improving

An organization that has reached this stage adds to all quality characteristics reached in the previous stages, the capability to continuously adapt the course of the process itself to the internal and external environment. The operational, tactical and strategic processes have all reached the proactive or improving level. No organization improvement project is required any more, because the individual processes themselves have reached a level at which they continually improve themselves. The mottoes of this stage are: 'The universe is the limit' and 'Galaxy-class service is the standard.'

7.10 Best of both worlds

When the CMM and SPICE concepts were applied to the IPW management processes, a 'best of both worlds' approach was used, where the process-oriented approach (SPICE) forms the basis, and the organization-oriented approach (CMM) has added value if the situation of the relevant ICT organization gives cause for it. The first approach makes it possible to shape process improvement in the management domain with maximum flexibility, taking into account the specific context. The latter approach allows the ICT organization, as a whole, to be certified at a certain level. For instance, this latter possibility may be interesting when the ICT organization also wants to offer its services to third parties (outsourcing organizations). Table 7.2 shows a survey of the different organizational stages and the associated process levels, based on an extended version of IPW.

7 ■ IPW™ and the IPW Stadia Model™ (IPWSM)

TABLE 7.2 Organizational stages and process stages, for extended version of IPW

IPW processes		IPWSM organisation maturity levels				
Process group	Process	Initial	Operational monitoring	Operational control	Service control	Service improving
Operations	Production	Not identified	Monitored	Controlled	Proactive	Improving
Service support	Incident management	Not identified	Monitored	Controlled	Proactive	Improving
	Problem management	Not performed	Not performed	Monitored	Controlled	Proactive/ improving
	Change management	Not identified	Monitored	Controlled	Proactive	Improving
	Software control and distribution	Not identified	Not identified	Controlled	Proactive	Improving
	Configuration management	Not performed	Not performed	Monitored	Controlled	Proactive/ improving
Service Delivery	Service level management	Not performed	Not performed	Monitored	Controlled	Proactive/ improving
	Capacity management	Not identified	Not identified	Monitored	Controlled	Proactive/ improving
	Availability management	Not performed	Not performed	Monitored	Controlled	Proactive/ improving
	Cost management	Not performed	Not performed	Monitored	Controlled	Proactive/ improving
	Contingency planning	Not performed/ not identified	Monitored	Controlled	Proactive	Improving
Strategic planning	Commercial policy	Not performed	Not performed	Monitored	Controlled	Proactive/ improving
	Personnel & organization	Not performed	Not performed	Monitored	Controlled	Proactive/ improving
	Architectures	Not performed	Not performed	Monitored	Controlled	Proactive/ improving
	Finance	Not performed	Not performed	Monitored	Controlled	Proactive/ Improving
Service development	Depending on situation. Worked out using CMM of SPICE and a custom arrangement					

7.11 Skipping stages

When defining improvement projects, there may be the tendency to skip a level when improving processes. There is no point in doing so, however, as in each stage the processes are assigned generic process characteristics that build on the level reached in the previous stage. Nevertheless, it is possible to work out some of the aspects of a subsequent stage while not all criteria of the current stage have yet been satisfied. Also, when choosing target levels for each process, the organization stages do not have to be the only aspects to be considered. After all, these are generic, while a specific ICT organization may have different priorities due to its own unique problems or special circumstances. In this way, the process stages can be used to define 'custom' organization stages. In doing so, the external reference to the IPWSM organization stages is indeed lost, but this reference is certainly not relevant for all organizations.

7.12 Additional value of IPWSM

IPWSM should not be seen as a replacement of the IPW model, but merely as an addition to it. Using the maturity levels (stages) for each process, the seemingly unmanageable 1-to-3 year project required to achieve an integral and lasting result can be made more manageable. The IPWSM model also allows the definition of a target level of maturity for each separate process of a transition project. It also allows any interim results to be made explicit as different sets of processes together with the maturity levels defined for them, while previously processes as a whole were often chosen for this purpose. In addition, the definition of the generic process characteristics stores a treasury of knowledge about the logical order to follow in order to reach a higher process level. This means that the generic process characteristics, as well as the list of ITIL/IPW activities and best practices, also offer a valuable reference for drawing up plans for improvement projects. This knowledge was, of course, already an implicit part of the baggage of the organization improvers involved, but in this way the relevant experience is also made explicit. The IPWSM can also be an excellent tool for assessing the capability of providers of IT services, such as outsourcing companies. This is because an IPWSM assessment may predict which service level they are able to provide. This is relevant for both the outsourcing organization and the outsourcing partner.

Table 7.3 shows, once again, how the development of the processes leads to higher organization stages. Just to be perfectly clear, we state again that the IPW Stadia Model does not dictate a specific order of processes. The priorities still depend on the logical order and the interrelationship of the processes in IPW, as well as the specific circumstances of the target organization. These priorities can be established on the basis of the analysis phase. Once these priorities have been established, however, a logical development path is still sketched by the different maturity levels and the associated generic process characteristics. In line with practical experience, this makes it possible to start with more processes while still keeping the project manageable and well defined in terms of time. Figure 7.10 is a graphical representation of the relationship between IPW

TABLE 7.3
Development of process stages in relation to the development of the organization

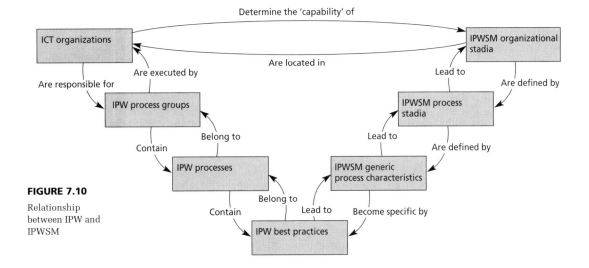

FIGURE 7.10

Relationship between IPW and IPWSM

and IPWSM. For the analysis phase, a powerful assessment method is available (QuintQuest), which can be used to evaluate the process stages and, therefore, the organization stage. The assessment can be visualized in a so-called stages profile, which can be considered as a snapshot of the situation at a certain point in time.

7.13 Product portfolio and future

The product portfolio of IPW and IPWSM includes the process model, the process groups, the processes, the best practices, the division into stages of maturity on process and organizational level, the cross-reference to CMM, and the associated assessment method (QuintQuest). Courses in process improvement using IPWSM and the cross-reference to SPICE are available now. For ICT organizations, IPWSM is partly publicly available. The other part is available if an organization improvement project is commenced under the supervision or direction of Quint Wellington Redwood organization improvers. The future may also see the development of courses in the use of the complete product portfolio, intended for assessors and organization improvers. A certification programme will then be essential. In that way, the entire IPW Stadia Model, including assessment method and best practices library, could be licensed to ICT organizations. Automated support for organisation improvement on the basis of IPWSM is one of the options being studied. Spin-off products such as a personal management process – following PSP – may also be possible. Depending on the success of IPWSM and the enthusiasm of the market, these possibilities will be given the appropriate follow-up.

7.14 Conclusions

IPWSM is an extremely powerful tool for structuring and shaping improvement projects in ICT organizations in a non-authoritative manner. To this end, the model distinguishes a number of stages of maturity, both at process level and at organizational level. Following an assessment to evaluate the organization and/or the processes it performs, an improvement plan is drawn up, taking into account the specific circumstances unique to the organization. After realization of the improvement plan (or in between), the situation can once again be tested against the model by carrying out a repeat assessment. Naturally, the success of an ICT organization depends on a multitude of factors. For instance, the ability to attract and keep competent professionals, the technology used, and the knowledge of the market for which the organization has been established are all just as important as the maturity stage of the execution of the processes. Yet in practice it turns out that once organizations have come to know the flywheel effect of process improvement, these organizations are able to accomplish a dramatic improvement in performance and success. 'Fix the process, not the problem!' is what Sirkin and Stalk already said in 1990. In 1998, this appears to be more applicable than ever. The power of the IPW Stadia Model is mainly based on the fact that it is not a theoretical frame but a model that originated from actual practice and the experience of leading organization improvers. In addition, it is consistent with the ideas prevailing in the world of process improvement in the development domain and with the ideas regarding quality management in general. The all-important thing, however, is that it really works!

Although the basic version of the model was already defined in 1995, it was only published for the first time in 1998. In the intervening time, behind the scenes of many key ICT organization improvement projects, it has been continuously tested on consistency and applicability and adapted to the latest developments. The current product portfolio offers interesting possibilities for extension or the development of spin-off products. The model has proven to be as successful as IPW itself. If you would like to know more about IPW, IPWSM, SPI, PSP CMM, or SPICE, please contact Quint Wellington Redwood organizational improvement (Internet: **www.quintgroup.com**, e-mail: **hans.van.herwaarden@quint.nl**).

Acknowledgement

The authors of this article are Hans van Herwaarden MIM MMC RI and engineer Frank Grift MBA of Quint Wellington Redwood. Frank is one of the founders of Quint, and was highly involved in developing and evolving the range of IPW models. He also wrote the booklet 'ABC to IPW'. Hans is the mastermind behind the IPW Stadia Model, a model that enables a structured and staged approach using the model to improve the performance of ICT organizations. This chapter is a combination of two articles on these topics, the articles having been published in the Dutch IT-Yearbooks of 1998 and 1999.

Literature

Grift, F.U. and de Vreeze, M. (1998). *The ABC of IPW*, The Hague: Ten Hagen & Stam Uitgevers.

'Fix the process, not the problem', *Harvard Business Review*, July/August 1990.

Hendriks, P.R.H. 'Kwaliteitszorg van software-ontwikkeling' in *IT Beheer Jaarboek*, (1998).

Magee, F. (1997) 'Quint Wellington Redwood's IPW: Processes for IT', Gartner Group Research note, pp 220–194, April.

SPICE, consolidated product, part 1: concepts and introductory guide version 1.0, 1997.

Watts S. (1990). *Managing the Software Process*, Humphrey, Addison-Wesley SEI (1997).

deWit, Theo. (1997) *The Capability Maturity Model: guidelines for improving the software process*, SEI. SPICE baseline practices guide, Version 1.0, September 1994.

deWit, Theo. (1997) 'IPW Invoering van een procesgerichte werkwijze', *IT Beheer Jaarboek 1997*, Ten Hagen & Stam.

Integrated Service Management (ISM)®

H. van den Elskamp, W.J.J Kuiper and **H. Wanders**
KPN Datacenter

J. van Bon and **W. Hoving**
Bureau Hoving & Van Bon, the Netherlands

Summary

In 1992, KPN (Royal PTT Telecom) developed the IPW model to achieve one of the Netherlands' first successful ITIL implementations. In an increasingly complex environment, the current KPN Datacenter aims to contract the highest service level, the so-called Full Service Management (often by means of a gradual growth), thereby acting as a systems integrator. To realize the required service a reference model, known as Integrated Service Management (ISM), was developed. This model embodies the way in which several sub-services can be offered to a client as a single integrated service, and it includes all of the premium insights of modern IT service management. The model incorporates all that has been learned during the past six years of experience with process-based service management. In developing the model, KPN used a highly structured approach. By establishing a number of building blocks (paradigms), the final model is gradually revealed. Since the model is limited to the theoretical fundamentals, it offers a set of tools instead of a definitive solution to a specific situation.

8.1 Introduction

KPN Telecom has successfully applied the IPW model since 1992. In doing so, IPW has contributed greatly to the improvement of KPN Datacenter's IT service. During this period, it became apparent that an increasing number of questions required different answers. Some of the questions came out of the experience with IPW, which led to the development of new insights. Other questions were the result of new possibilities arising from improved technology. Further technological developments, changing requirements and the demands of customers, in particular, led to more questions. In order to provide an adequate answer to these questions, a project was started within KPN Datacenter, applying the existing knowledge and experience to the development of a new model. This model was to include all activities from product development through to delivery. The development of the model took place in close collaboration with Bureau Hoving & Van Bon. This article discusses the nature of the identified bottlenecks, the approach towards the establishment of the description of the model, the paradigms and their value to the end model, and the end model itself.

8.2 Bottlenecks

The bottlenecks discussed are partly based on experiences during the ten years in which IPW has been applied and are partly those that are most likely to manifest themselves at the moment the service is to be professionalized further. These bottlenecks also come to light, maybe more clearly then ever, when implementing new services based on technological innovations such as client/server and Web applications that require platform-transcending IT management. The bottlenecks mentioned have their origin partly in the fact that the described process model was not applied consistently and partly in the fact that certain aspects of the process model are difficult to apply. Even more important, however, is the progressive insight that is the result of ten years' experience with a process-based working method. This insight leads to demands that are difficult to establish within the classic process model. Furthermore, there have been two relevant external developments. Firstly, the number of buyers requiring a higher level of service is growing. The role of IT support within their company objectives is so crucial that they require a guaranteed service. The second external development is the availability of ever-improving service management tools, making models applicable that were formerly only theoretical. The value of IPW is not questioned by the above. This classic process model has been successfully applied to many services. However, the fact that an increasing number of buyers are demanding a higher standard of service and the fact that the Datacenter wants to offer a higher quality of service result in the following inventory of bottlenecks.

Bottleneck 1: Difficult integration of services

End-to-end IT service to the customer is the result of a large number of integrated sub-services. Examples of this are sub-services keeping the central system operational, or the network or the workstation. Sub-services may also include hardware and software maintenance. Other applications interactively communicating by means of interfaces and adding new functionality are other types of sub-services. These sub-services are provided by various internal or external organizations. System management is often provided internally and the same applies to LAN and workstation management. WAN management and especially hardware maintenance are often brought in from outside. Maintenance of custom applications is generally provided by the developer, either from within or from outside the organization. The quality of the end product, the service that is provided to the customer, depends on the quality of these various sub-services. To be able to provide service to the standard required by the customer, the 'purchasing' of all sub-services needs to be attuned to the requirements of the end product and monitored throughout the life cycle of the service. Offering an integrated service requires a large degree of fine-tuning between the suppliers involved. *To ensure that the end product is excellent, exceptional effort must be applied to the integration of sub-services.*

Bottleneck 2: Quality improvement collapses under operational pressure

ITIL designates a number of quality improvement processes of which Problem Management is one of the most important. Within ITIL, the objective of the Problem

Management process is twofold: (1) to reduce the impact of incidents – an operational task; (2) to find out the cause of incidents to prevent (re)occurrence – a task aimed at structural quality improvement. As both objectives fall under one process description (even under IPW) and also under one process control, the objective of quality improvement is pushed into the background under the pressure of operational activities. The current disruption of the service quickly gains a higher priority than investigation for the sake of quality improvement. However, solving incidents without structurally improving quality is like mopping the floor while the sink is still flooding over. *The absence of a structure in which a proactive, quality-improving objective has a chance of success means that permanent quality improvement has been neglected.*

Bottleneck 3: The difficult relationship between service agreement and delivery

With the implementation of a process-based approach, it was hoped that contracts (SLAs) would primarily include a service description, coupled with a number of parameters concerning availability, response time, set-up times etc. However, in practice, the service provider often finds it easier to simply charge a couple of easily allocated costs, either with or without commercial surcharge. The customer, on the other hand, still appears to be looking for the safety of a recognizable costing structure based on matters such as hardware (type of computer, number of megabytes, network capacity), software and hours of support, instead of recognizable performance units in terms of operational processes. The resulting bottleneck is that both parties still come to an agreement but that this agreement does not describe the actual needs of the customer, namely the required IT service and the associated support. The supplier, on the other hand, is left with the problem that he or she might deliver what was contractually agreed upon, but that the customer is still not satisfied. The cause of this problem is twofold. The customer is not IT-conscious enough to properly evaluate a service and therefore tries to find safety in the description of the resources to be deployed (hardware, software and staffware). Not only does the supplier find it difficult to determine the cost of the service, but even more to steer the organization towards service parameters. *The absence of SLAs with clear, controllable and measurable service parameters serves to worsen the classic discontent of IT buyers.*

Bottleneck 4: Limited additional value of configuration management

Often, an ITIL 'implementation' will start at an early stage, setting up and fleshing out a configuration management database. According to the developers, this CMDB should serve many purposes, such as configuration management, asset management, resource management, cost management, etc. and should support practically all processes. This creates a database full of detailed information that contains many interrelationships. Maintaining such a database is often very time-consuming, making it almost impossible to verify data. The problem is aggravated further by the fact that those who are responsible for the detailed maintenance of changes, i.e. system managers, operators and/or change support staff, do not see the full benefit of their efforts in their daily work. Proper maintenance of a CMDB, therefore, requires a great deal of discipline and effort. The returns are further diminished as, in the case of many of the larger actions, the CMDB often does not contain the information required, making further stock-taking necessary. *The CMDB offers limited support for activities, while its maintenance requires a disproportionately large amount of effort.*

Bottleneck 5: Questionable added value of process

Process descriptions establish the sequence of activities. Often, this is not the shortest route from A to B. A number of activities described in the processes, such as checks, authorizations and registrations, form part of the process itself, to ensure quality, and are not aimed at the establishing of the main objective of the process. Certain other activities are necessary for facilitating other processes. The importance and the execution of these processes are not always obvious to the persons who actually do the work. This problem occurs especially if the objective of the process, the description and the total picture of the full model, are not clear enough. *The absence of clarity regarding the position of activities within the process and the absence of the understanding of the importance of those activities within the framework of the total service cause lack of motivation.*

Bottleneck 6: Slowing-down effect of over-documentation

Descriptions of processes, procedures and work instructions are not generally fun to read, especially for those who are required to execute them. The same goes for descriptions of processes within process models. Descriptions often tend to list all of the variants and exceptions occurring within a process in one go, often giving a detailed exchange of information. If the processes, procedures and working instructions are also recorded in a single, all-encompassing document, this results in a document that is very inacces-sible, both in use and maintenance. Many people, especially beginners, are overwhelmed by the number of rules and regulations that seem to push the actual work into the background. *Brief, simple and clear descriptions of the working method, and summaries of the main points, are usually absent.*

Bottleneck 7: Process and procedures only cover part of the activities

The original IPW description focuses on a number of operationally positioned processes. The strategic and tactical processes are acknowledged but have not been designed with the operational processes in mind. This causes a breakdown in communication at the borderlines of the processes, leading to errors and delays. This gap is also the cause of the lack of grip on, and understanding of management in relation to, the operational activities. *The lack of coherence between operational processes on the one hand, and tactical and strategic processes on the other, causes too large a gap within the organization.*

Bottleneck 8: Customization is difficult

It is the aim of every manager to improve continuously. Until recently, an availability of 99% was a veritable achievement. Due to continuous improvements to the quality of hardware and software, and certainly also in the standard of managers, the realization of better performance by components of the technological infrastructure is proving more and more achievable. The infrastructure, on the other hand, is becoming increasingly complex and service levels are becoming more specialized. Performance is crucial to some applications, whereas to other applications it is data integrity and recovery up to the last second, or simply availability. For some services, the standard level of the service is too high for the nature of the business it supports. For example, not all disks need to be doubled up, the failure of one of the ten workstations may not need to be resolved within 8 hours, or the loss of one day of production may be less costly than the costs of prevention. If the service level is properly attuned to the business, it suffices to deliver simply what is requested. The same applies here: `You can have too much of a good thing!' *Unlimited service leads to unnecessarily high costs, possibly endangering the competitive position.*

Bottleneck 9: Projects/taskforces/escalations

The complexity and dynamics of ICT management require proper fine-tuning of all those involved. A good process model and clearly worked out procedures, work instructions and good supporting tools are suitable aids. Owing to time pressure or size, the performance of certain actions is sometimes kept outside the process control. These activities are then organized in the form of task forces, projects or escalations. Placing activities in these organizational forms is often a good and necessary means to ensure a practical implementation. These activities are placed outside the process because the way in which the regular process is described and executed does not instil sufficient trust concerning the establishing of the desired objective. However, the necessary registrations are often not performed, resulting in incorrect or incomplete data for future processes. The result is twofold. Firstly, the risk of disruption to the progression of the project, as well as to the quality assurance of the future production, increases due to the fact that the facilitating processes are not properly activated. The second risk is that the project's or the task force's claim to resources makes those essential resources unavailable to other IT services. This bottleneck arises especially if the project or task force is automatically given a priority that is higher than that of the execution of the process. *Under pressure, the agreed working method is (too) often deviated from, causing the activation of two conflicting control mechanisms and causing damage to the quality of service.*

Bottleneck 10: Steering towards processes

Maintaining process-based working methods requires just as much innovation as their initial implementation. Process-based working methods also require process-based management. The way in which objectives are introduced into the organization is still predominantly from the top down. Organizations arranging their operational activities through processes fail to utilize the full added value. The choice for process-based working methods should be followed by the choice for process-based control and also process-based rewards. *Control and award systems 'from the top down' have the effect of placing the interest of the department before the process-based establish- ment of the service.*

8.3 Approach

In developing the model, a highly structured approach was used. The model is approached step by step by establishing a number of building blocks (paradigms). Since the model is limited to the theoretical fundamentals, it offers a set of tools instead of a definitive solution for a specific situation. The use of the model easily facilitates the creation of a varying number of organizational elaborations. The development of the model is based on a number of limiting conditions constituting the minimum requirements for the model. The model must: be acceptable and simple; be recognizable and practicable; be maintainable; be process-based, service-oriented and customer-oriented; be traceable and reproducible; describe variants according to their nature, not per case; and make a clear contribution to controlling the increasing complexity of the IT service. The ISM model was deliberately limited to those processes directly leading to the provision of a service. As a result of this, a number of organizational, financial and facilitary processes, essential to the company, have not been included in the model. The model was deliberately not developed in detail. By describing the main processes and putting them foremost, a well-organized, clear and well-implemented model has been created. *A model that works is better than 'the right model'.*

An organization can be viewed in many ways and dimensions. Each dimension in itself provides information important to the layout of the organization. The description of the main service dimensions provides the paradigms forming the building blocks of the ISM model. Each paradigm describes a dimension of the IT service management or part of the service. The paradigms employed are individually recognizable and have as such been adopted and accepted within the IT management field. To be able to use the various paradigms for the development of one integrated model, each paradigm should be described in view of this purpose; in this case, the creation, provision and continuation of an integrated IT service. This results in a consistent elaboration, complementary to an organization that strives for the same goals.

The delivery paradigm

Elaboration of the delivery paradigm

The client is supplied with a service. This service is continuous in nature, consisting of the provision of an information system and its support (Figure 8.1). A good service necessitates an effective and coherent management of the interaction between customer and supplier.

FIGURE 8.1

The delivery paradigm

The impact of the delivery paradigm on the ISM model

The ISM processes have been selected in such a way that there is a continuous relationship to the delivery of the information system and its interactions. Each interaction with the customer is directly linked with a specific process within the supplier domain.

The infrastructure paradigm

Elaboration of the infrastructure paradigm

ISM focuses on the delivery and maintenance of an integrated service. The infrastructure paradigm delivers an image of the infrastructure used for this purpose: what it comprises and which part of the infrastructure is important to the implementation and control of the service, always related to the level of the IT service. According to the delivery paradigm, a service consists of an information system with the associated interaction support.

According to the infrastructure paradigm, each information system can be split into a large number of components, as shown in the information system tree (Figure 8.2). This information system tree shows the components constituting an information system. An information system consists of an infrastructure of 'human resources' and an infrastructure of information technology (IT). Other dimensions such as procedures and documentation are always applicable to this and other components of the information system tree. The information technology is again made up of the technical infrastructure, the application infrastructure and the technical facilities infrastructure.

FIGURE 8.2

The information system tree

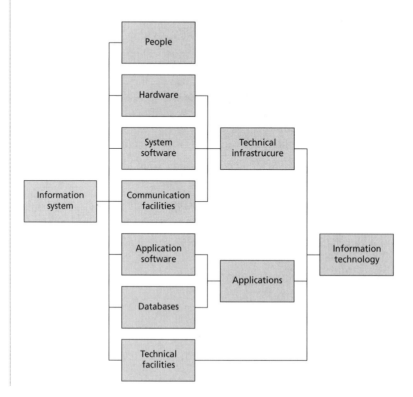

The technical infrastructure consists of hardware, System software and communication facilities. Depending on the architecture, the application infrastructure may consist of application software and databases. Technical facilities include buildings, computer floors and energy facilities.

The impact of the infrastructure paradigm on the ISM model

The scope of the ISM model covers the information system and thereby all its components. This means that, for all processes, one or more components of the infrastructures constitute an object that the process is working on. So the 'incident recovery' process processes all incidents, regardless of the component or domain of the information system infrastructure to which they are applicable. Therefore, no distinction is made between the equipment-related incidents and the application software-related incidents.

The same applies to the change process. By nature, the infrastructure paradigm provides important guidelines for the service-oriented populating of the CMDB. By showing the information system per service, a meaningful specification of the various necessary resources is created. This is important for both the preparation of a new service and for its continuous delivery.

The organization paradigm

Elaboration of the organization paradigm

The organization paradigm starts with the view that each organization can be seen as a system of cooperating infrastructures (Figure 8.3):

- people – who;
- processes – what;
- products – how and with what.

The impact of the organization paradigm on the ISM model

Of course, the design of an ISM model focuses on a process-based approach. It is first determined which processes need to be executed within an organization. Next, the optimum combination of people and products infrastructure is determined. Environmental factors (culture, financial position, etc.) play an important role in the latter. ISM always discriminates between these information system, people, hardware, system software, communication facilities, application software, databases, technical infrastructure applications, information technology, and technical facilities infrastruc-

FIGURE 8.3

The organization paradigm

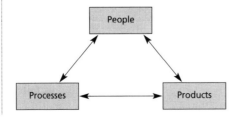

tures. A process model is defined which consciously excludes all influences of the people, the organization infrastructure. As an implementation is greatly determined by the environmental factors and by subjective issues such as the preference of the current manager or by culture, this document remains limited to the indication of several implementation variants. Requirements concerning the products infrastructure to be employed may also be derived from the process infrastructure. The nature and character of the products depend on many environmental factors and are, therefore, not developed further.

The control paradigm

Elaboration of the control paradigm

Within each organization, a number of control levels can be distinguished. The control paradigm assumes that three control levels can be distinguished within each organization (Figure 8.4):

- **the strategic level**, which mainly determines the long-term information policy and provides a global vision and direction for the organization;
- **the tactical level**, which translates the vision and policy, as defined at the strategic level, into a medium-term specification of the infrastructure facilities;
- **the operational level**, which transforms the infrastructure specifications into the information systems being used.

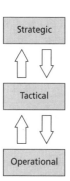

FIGURE 8.4
The control paradigm

The impact of the control paradigm on the ISM model

On the one hand, applying the control paradigm leads to the typification of the recognized processes according to one of three levels, as indicated. The ISM processes are always chosen in such a way that they will fit univocally into one control level. For example, the Problem Management process is characterized as a tactical process: it determines which improvements must be made to the infrastructure to facilitate the required service quality, or in the case of internal improvements, to efficiency. This process, therefore, does not include operational activities regarding the infrastructure. This is contrary to the relevant ITIL definition. In ISM, the reactive activities contributed by ITIL for the Problem Management process always fall under the Incident Handling process, regardless of the incidents in question.

The integration paradigm

Elaboration of the integration paradigm

The integration paradigm ensures the delivery of the service, as seen from the point of view of the supplier. The customer is not concerned with this division of the components and it is, therefore, hidden: the customer only 'sees' the 'total supplier'. The supplier is responsible for managing the interface(s) with the sub-supplier(s). The supplier hereby assumes the role of system integrator for the sub-suppliers of components constituting the integrated service (Figure 8.5). The domain of the supplier can consist of one or more sub-domains. The integrated service to be delivered is then divided into components of the various sub-suppliers.

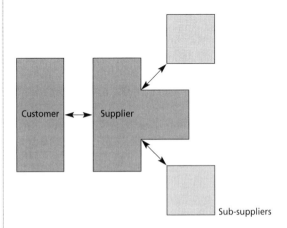

FIGURE 8.5
The integration paradigm

The impact of the integration paradigm on the ISM model

Each sub-domain that is to be put into practice can be specified and split off as an independent domain. The requirements for the total service are translated into requirements applicable to the delivery of the sub-services from the split domain. The ISM model has the customer specify requirements for the total service in terms of behaviour, functionality and support. The requirements derived from these characteristics are translated into the sub-domain by the service integrator, without further requirements regarding the internal working method of the sub-supplier. Therefore, a sub-domain can be seen as a 'black box'. Communications between customer, supplier and sub-supplier are kept uniform, however, to facilitate the composite structure. It therefore concerns agreements on the level of process interfaces and inter-process communication. The generic model

8.4 The generic model

The considerations and paradigms presented above lead to *the generic model* for Integrated Service Management® (Figure 8.6). For the IT service supplier to be able to deliver a composite service, it is essential to take the role of integrator if the service is to be split into components. The integrator manages the interfaces with the

FIGURE 8.6

The generic model

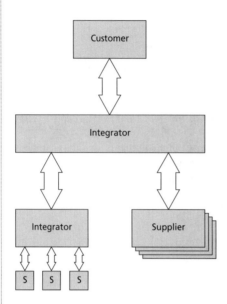

component suppliers. This model does not necessitate agreements among the sub-suppliers themselves, as this is the responsibility of the integrator. For complex services, the model may be 'repeated', the sub-supplier taking the role of integrator for the components under his or her responsibility.

Customer–supplier relations

If we combine the control paradigm and the delivery paradigm, we arrive at the conclusion that the customer–supplier relationships take place on three control levels as well. Each level knows its own specific customer–supplier interactions. The interactions on each of these levels are characterized by two-way traffic and can be described as follows (Figure 8.7).

FIGURE 8.7

Combination of delivery paradigm and control paradigm

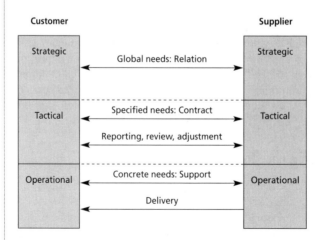

Strategic

The customer sets up an information plan to facilitate the information of the customer domain. Based on this information plan, the supplier provides information about the (im)possibilities, the standards and the requirements used in the service policy. This is an iterative process, its objective being the fine-tuning of the information plan and the delivery options. Here, the object of attention is the *relationship* between customer and supplier.

Tactical

The customer sets up the specifications of the information system, be it new or to be amended, and also sets up the requirements linked with the delivery. The supplier quotes for the service, either new or to be amended, and/or maintenance takes place within the terms and conditions of existing SLAs (adjusting specifications, reporting). Here, the object of attention is always the *specification* of the information system and its support.

Operational

The customer uses the integrated service delivered by the supplier. The user generates complaints (incident reports), questions (information) and (standard) orders. The actions of the supplier consist of solving complaints, providing information and the results of orders. Here, the object of attention is always the assured *delivery* of the information system.

Processes within the model

After the paradigms have been established, the following step may be taken. This step consists of the specification of the interactions and the definition of the associated processes that are operative within the ISM model (Figure 8.8). On a *strategic level*, the information plans of the customers, market research and innovation lead to service requirements (in the form of service plans and standards). On a *tactical level*, the infrastructure requirements and delivery are formulated from this, together with the

FIGURE 8.8

Elaboration of the most impotant interactions between customer and supplier

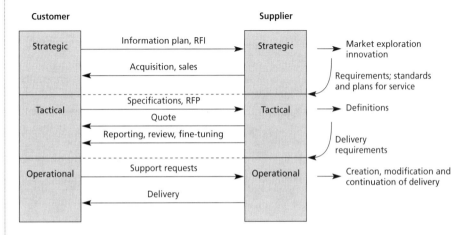

specifications of the customer. Adjustments are constantly made based on customer requirements and/or internal efficiency considerations. On an *operational level*, the delivery is created, modified and, of course, continued.

8.5 The Integrated Service Management Process model

The previous section established the paradigms, creating a generic model for the delivery of an integrated service. At this stage, the processes occurring on a strategic, tactical and operational level need to be completed. The model shows three levels as well (Figure 8.9).

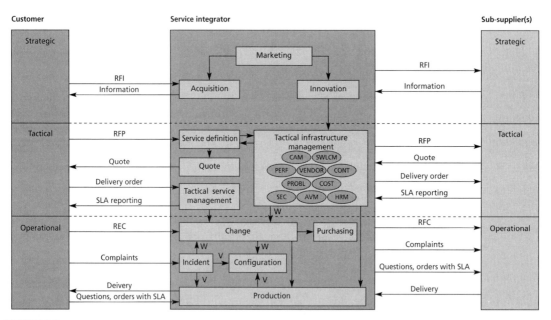

FIGURE 8.9

The Integrated Service Management model. Arrows represent triggers for the next process.

Strategic processes

The strategic level includes the Marketing, Innovation and Acquisition processes, Marketing being in the sense of researching the market, not only to sell the services to be delivered, but also to explore the market for developments, especially those that are relevant for further improvement of management tools for the services to be delivered. This specifically controls the Innovation process, as this may see the creation of measures that will improve the efficiency of IT management. From the Acquisition process, the strategic contacts with the customer are maintained. Based on a Request For Information (RFI), the iterative interaction with the customer finally determines the shape and form of the service to be delivered, the information the customer needs and how it is to be achieved. As soon as the customer decides that the supplier might be able to meet the information needs, a Request For Proposal (RFP) is drawn up.

Tactical processes

On a tactical level, this RFP provides the input for the Service Definition process. This process needs to see the specified information requirements translated into infrastructure terms used to deliver the service. The specification of this infrastructure is based on the information system tree. After consultation with sub-suppliers, a quote will be issued, stating the specifications and costs of the service to be delivered. Again, an iterative interaction concerning these costs and specifications will take place between the customer and the supplier. This may finally lead to a delivery order: the input for the Tactical Service Management process (group). This delivery order is in the form of an agreement (contract) stating the terms and conditions and the specifications of the service to be delivered, i.e. the service level agreement (SLA). The Tactical Service Management process is aimed at the achievement and continuation of the requested service. It might also lead to organizational adjustments, e.g. setting up a 7×24-hour support. The tactical level also sees processes concerning the care of the infrastructure. The model has 10 processes included within the Tactical Infrastructure Management (TIM) process group. TIM is the total of all processes ensuring that the layout of the infrastructure remains such that the integrated service is delivered in conformity with the agreements. The following processes are distinguished within TIM:

- Availability Management
- Capacity Management
- Contingency Management
- Cost Management
- Vendor Management
- Performance Management
- Security Management
- Problem Management
- Life Cycle Management
- Human Resource Management.

Operational processes

The *operational* level sees the delivery of the service in conformity with the specifications as agreed with the customer. Of course, no information system is perfect and the ISM model also has the necessary processes in place to deal with disruptions and adjustments in a correct and adequate manner. To enable proper implementation of the ISM model, it is essential that each user has a clear picture of the definition of *managed infrastructure*. This requires agreements being made within the whole of the organization, to prevent confusion. The fact is that the ISM model only concerns this managed infrastructure.

The model can further distinguish between changes to copies and types. Objects for which the type (a characteristic feature of the object) changes are processed using the change process. Changes relating to (identical) copies are not processed using the

Change process, but are processed in the Production process and registered in the CMDB. The Production process executes all operational activities related to the service to be delivered. These activities can be triggered from the Incident and Change processes and lead to adjustments to the daily planning in the Production process.

The customer domain will also produce questions and small orders, however, directly interfering with the Production process. Examples of small orders include a one-time production of a database query and the addition of a user profile to an authorization database. One final trigger (series) for the Production process originates from the TIM processes (e.g. problem solving and innovation projects).

Process integration between domains

Interactions with sub-suppliers of the integrated service are controlled from the processes described in the ISM model. The model does not dictate any requirements to the working process or method within the sub-domains, apart from the fact that each of the identified ISM processes requires uniform input by sub-suppliers. This way, the interaction can be specified clearly and the agreements can be guaranteed by means of a quality system.

ITIL: best practice in IT Service Management

Lex Hendriks and **Martin Carr**
EXIN, the Netherlands and OGC, the United Kingdom

Summary

ITIL, the IT Infrastructure Library, has become the de facto international standard for IT Service Management. Its focus on the quality of service and best practice has made the ITIL framework the most popular common language for planning and managing processes, roles and activities in IT Service Management. The public availability of the OGC/CCTA books, the international support by a user platform (the itSMF) and an internationally recognized qualification structure with training and examination, ITIL, attracted consultants, tool developers and practitioners from all over the world.

The success of ITIL stimulated the development of IT Service Management as an important management field within the ICT industry. In fact, many models and approaches in IT Service Management have been developed as extensions on ITIL, combining best practice found in the ITIL books with the experience and knowledge of consultants and academics.

9.1 IT Service Management

IT Service Management can be described as the art of managing the entire ICT sector of an organization, its infrastructure and its activities, as a coherent set of interrelated processes aimed at providing business-justified services to the organization.

In the past, many IT organisations were internally focused and concentrated on technical issues. These days, businesses expect high service quality coupled with the ability to change requirements rapidly and effectively. This means that, for IT organizations to live up to these expectations, they need to concentrate on service quality and a more customer-oriented approach. Financial issues are now high on the agenda and IT organizations need to develop a more businesslike attitude to provision of service.

One way of presenting an overview of the subject of IT Service Management is depicted in Figure 9.1. This diagram is reproduced from *A Code of Practice for IT Service Management (PD0005)*,[1] published by the British Standards Institute. It shows the main areas in IT Service Management. It is a pictorial description of some simple but important principles of Service Management:

- Service Management is about services based on automation that have to be designed and managed.
- Services need agreements between customers and suppliers.
- Services need to be released.
- Resolution is needed in case of any interruption of the service.

FIGURE 9.1
Service Management according to PD0005

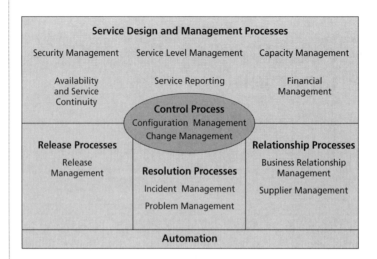

9.2 Benefits and problems

Having recognized that IT organizations are in the business of service provision, they must now adopt a whole new way of thinking and embrace the same business concepts used by all service providers. There is a lot of catching up to do.

But before entering the subject in some more detail, let us consider what are the benefits for an organization of having a clearer definition of its Service Management function and adopting a more structural approach. Some of the benefits are:

- a more conscious alignment of IT services with the actual business needs of the organization;
- improved quality of service – more reliable business support;
- reduced costs in managing and delivering IT services;
- IT service continuity procedures more focused, coupled with more confidence in the ability to follow them when required;
- clearer view of current IT capability;
- better information on current services (and possibly on where changes would bring most benefits);
- greater flexibility for the business through improved understanding of IT support;
- better motivated staff with improved job satisfaction through better understanding of capability and better management of expectations;
- enhanced customer satisfaction as Service Management staff know and deliver what is expected of them;
- increased flexibility and adaptability within IT service provision;
- system-led benefits, e.g. improvements in security, accuracy, speed and availability, as required for the required level of service;
- improved cycle time for changes and greater success rate.

9 ITIL: best practice in IT Service Management

The importance and level of these will vary between organizations. An issue comes in defining these benefits for any organization in a way that will be measurable later on. Following ITIL guidance can help to quantify some of these benefits.
Successful Service Management should:

- provide a good understanding of the customer's requirements, concerns and business activities and deliver business-led, rather than technology-driven, services;
- improve customer satisfaction;
- improve value for money, resource utilization and service quality;
- deliver an infrastructure for the controlled operation of ongoing services by formalized and disciplined processes;
- equip staff with goals and an understanding of the customer's needs.

If there were only benefits, IT Service Management would be a simple common-sense activity, with no need for any framework or guidance whatsoever. However, in practice, organizations encounter problems with service management processes, for example:

- excessively bureaucratic processes, with a high percentage of the total support headcount dedicated to Service Management;
- inconsistent staff performance for the same process (often accompanied by noticeable lack of commitment to the process from the responsible staff);
- lack of understanding on what each process should deliver;
- no real benefits, service cost reductions, or quality improvements arising from the implementation of Service Management processes;
- unrealistic expectations, e.g. service targets rarely hit;
- wasted effort or, worse, confused and poorly serviced customers because of no or poor change management;
- no visible improvement.

Avoiding these problems, or overcoming them when they occur, is part of the rationale of the ITIL framework.

9.3 ITIL

Originally developed in the late 1980s and now undergoing a refresh and consolidation, ITIL documents industry best-practice guidance. It has proved its value from the very beginning. Initially, CCTA (the UK Government's Central Computer and Telecommunications Agency) collected information on how various organizations addressed Service Management, analysed this and filtered those issues that would prove useful within the UK public sector. As this guidance was found to be more widely applicable, very soon markets for consultancy, training, formal qualifications and tools were created by the international service industry.

The concept of managing services for the improvement of business functions is not new; it predates the Infrastructure Library. The idea to bring all of the Service Management best practice together under one roof, however, was both radical *and* new.

Being a framework, ITIL describes the contours of organizing Service Management. It shows the goals, general activities, inputs and outputs of the various processes, which can be incorporated within IT organizations. However, ITIL is not a methodology – it does not cast in stone every action you should do on a day-to-day basis because that is something that will differ from organization to organization. Instead, it focuses on best practice that can be utilized in different ways according to need. ITIL provides a proven method for planning common processes, roles and activities with appropriate reference to each other and shows how the communication lines should exist between them.

ITIL focuses on providing high-quality services with a particular focus on business relationships and meeting business needs. This means that the IT organization must provide whatever is agreed with customers, which implies a strong relationship between the IT organization and their customers and partners.

Tactical processes are centred on the relationships between the IT organization and its customers, setting up agreements on service delivery and monitoring these, while on the operational level the service support processes are about delivering the services according to these agreements. On both levels you will find a strong relationship with quality systems such as ISO 9000 and a total quality framework such as the Malcolm Baldridge Award or the European Framework for Quality Management (EFQM). ITIL supports these quality systems by providing defined processes and best practice for the management of IT services, enabling a fast track towards ISO certification.

ITIL is relevant to anyone involved in the delivery or support of services. It is applicable to anyone involved in the management or day-to-day practice of Service Management, in-house or outsourced, as well as anyone defining new processes or refining existing processes. Business managers will find ITIL helpful in understanding and establishing best-practice IT services and support, whether provided internally or through a contracted external service provider. Managers from supplier organizations will also find it relevant when setting up agreements for the delivery and support of services.

9.4 ITIL update

ITIL originally consisted of ten core guides covering the two main areas of Service Support and Service Delivery, supported by over 30 complementary guides covering a range of issues from cabling to business continuity management.

The first series of the Infrastructure Library amalgamated Service Management from an IT standpoint but could have done more to capture the interest of the business. The business perspective series was published to bridge the gap between business and management and, although a success, the series was published at a time when the original IT Infrastructure Library guidance was perceived as being outdated in some respects.

Recently, the core guides of ITIL have been revised, updated, restructured and published in both paper and electronic form, to make it simpler to access the information needed to manage services. The core guides have now been merged to create two books, covering the areas of Service Support and Service Delivery, in order to eliminate duplication and enhance navigation. The new ITIL books concentrate on processes rather than roles ('management' rather than 'manager'). The message from this is that ITIL is applicable not just to the larger IT organizations, but also to the smaller IT organizations where staff undertake many different roles. Indeed, one of the newer aspects of these books is that care has been taken to indicate which roles can be undertaken by the same person and which should be kept separate.

To complement these first two new books, additional material is being written, some new and some formed by bringing together material from some of the existing ITIL complementary books. To ease the navigation through ITIL for such a broad audience, the diagram in Figure 9.2 has been developed, to show the five principal elements covered in the restructured library. Each of these elements will have interfaces and overlaps with each of the other four. The elements are:

- the business perspective;
- managing applications;
- delivery of IT services;
- support of IT services;
- managing the infrastructure.

FIGURE 9.2

Jigsaw diagram

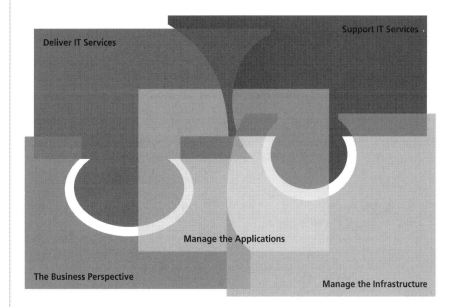

The major elements of the ITIL books can be likened to overlapping jigsaw puzzle pieces (or perhaps better as tectonic plates), some of which have a precise fit, and some of which overlap or do not fit together accurately. The movement of one piece may affect one or more of its neighbouring pieces. At the highest level, there are no strict demarcation lines. Indeed, if we consider further the analogy of tectonic plates, sliding over and under one another, joining and separating, then the Earthly problem of points of instability or friction caused by the imprecise nature of the pieces has an IT Infrastructure Library equivalent. It is precisely where process domains overlap or where demarcation lines cannot be clearly drawn that many management problems arise. We cannot stop all the problems from occurring (just as we cannot stop earthquakes resulting from the movement of tectonic plates) but we can provide advice about how to prepare for and deal with them.

The business perspective book will cover a range of issues concerned with understanding and improving IT service provision, as an integral part of an overall business requirement for high-quality IS management. These issues include:

- customer liaison;
- managing facilities management;
- managing supplier relationships;
- third party and single source management;
- understanding and improving IT service management;
- surviving IT infrastructure transitions.

The ICT infrastructure management book includes:

- network service management;
- operations management;
- management of local processors;
- computer installation and acceptance;
- systems management (covered here for the first time).

The book on applications management will embrace the software development life cycle, expanding the issues touched upon in software life cycle, support and testing of IT services. Applications Management will expand on the issues of business change, with emphasis on clear requirement definition and implementation of the solution to meet business needs.

9.5 Service delivery

As previously mentioned, the ITIL books on Service Support and Service Delivery cover the core of the ITIL framework on IT Service Management.

The Service Delivery book looks at what service the business requires of the provider in order to provide adequate support to the business users. To provide the necessary support, the book covers the following topics:

- capacity management;
- financial management for IT services;
- availability management;
- service level management;
- IT service continuity management.

These topics had been covered in the previous delivery set. However, the topic of contingency planning is now addressed more closely and related to the subject of business continuity management, reflecting the shift from an IT view on continuity to a business view on the continuity of IT services, while the subject of cost management is covered under the broader topic of financial management for IT services in order to consider the wider, related, costs of running an IT service.

To avoid confusion regarding roles and terminology, the terms 'customer' and 'user' are used throughout the new books to differentiate between those people (generally senior managers) who commission, pay for and own the IT Services (the customers) and those people who use the services on a day-to-day basis (the users). The semantics are less important than the reason for differentiation.

The primary point of contact for customers is the service level manager, or the business relationship manager, while the primary point of contact for users is the service desk. A poorly functioning Incident Management process will affect the user population immediately. A service that is poor value for money will have a greater impact on the customer.

The days when staff in IT organizations regarded their 'customers' as a *necessary evil* or just *difficult colleagues* have (hopefully) passed. There is a growing awareness that, in order to succeed as an IT facility, the IT organization has to stay close to its customers, understand and predict their requirements, and satisfy them. IT organizations are now raising the priority of customer satisfaction from being merely 'nice to have' to 'essential'.

The provision of quality IT services with high levels of availability and performance can be achieved with the correct hardware, software and underlying support disciplines. This level of service may satisfy, but may not delight, the customer! Extra effort is needed for the customer to enjoy the experience and want to come back for more. The way in which the service is delivered is dependent on the people delivering the service. Customer and user delight will only be achieved if the people involved are responsive to their customers' and users' needs, are attentive, reliable and courteous, delivering the service in the way they themselves would like to receive it.

The processes in Service Delivery are all involved in the overall process of planning the delivery of IT services in agreement with the needs of the business (Figure 9.3).

Service Level Management

The goal of Service Level Management is to maintain and improve IT service quality through a constant cycle of agreeing, monitoring, reporting and reviewing IT service achievements. The Service Level Management (SLM) process is responsible for ensuring that service level agreements (SLAs) and any underpinning operational level agreements (OLAs) or contracts are met, and for ensuring that any adverse impact on service quality is kept to a minimum (Figure 9.4). The process involves assessing the impact of changes upon service quality and SLAs, both when changes are proposed and after they have been implemented. Some of the most important targets set in the SLAs will relate to service availability and thus require incident resolution within agreed periods.

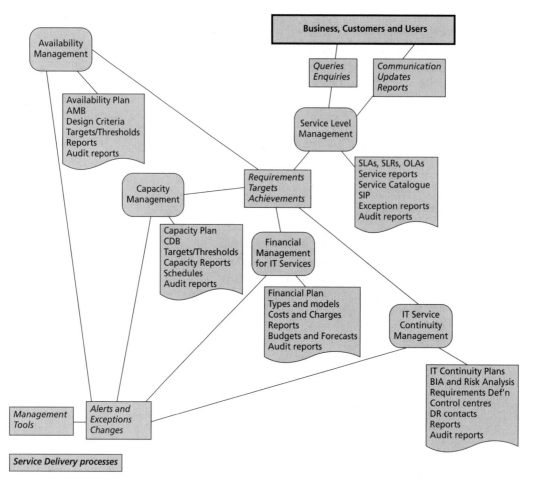

FIGURE 9.3
Overview of the Delivery processes

SLM is the hinge for Service Support and Service Delivery. It cannot function in isolation as it relies on the existence and effective and efficient working of other processes. An SLA without underpinning support processes is useless, as there is no basis for agreeing its content.

Financial Management for IT services

The process of Financial Management aims at providing cost-effective stewardship of IT assets and resources used in providing IT services. Financial Management is responsible for accounting for the costs (costing) and return on IT service investments (IT portfolio management), and for any aspects of recovering costs from the customers (charging). It requires good interfaces with Capacity Management, Configuration Management (asset data) and Service Level Management to identify the true costs of service. Financial Management is likely to work closely with Business Relationship Management and the IT organization during the negotiations of the IT organization's budgets and individual customer's IT spend.

FIGURE 9.4

The Service Level Management process

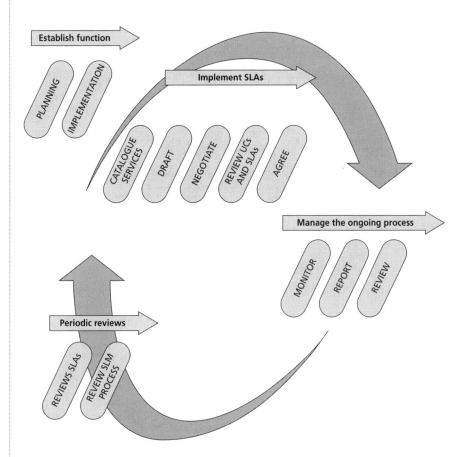

Capacity Management

The goal of the process of Capacity Management is to ensure that capacity and performance aspects of the business requirements are providing timely and cost-effective manner (Figure 9.5). It is directly related to the business requirements and is not simply about the performance of the system's components, individually or collectively. Capacity Management is involved in incident resolution and problem identification for those difficulties relating to capacity issues.

Capacity Management activities raise Requests for Change (RFCs) to ensure that appropriate capacity is available. These RFCs are subject to the Change Management process, and implementation may affect several CIs, including hardware, software and documentation, requiring effective Release Management.

Capacity Management should be involved in evaluating all changes, to establish the effect on capacity and performance. This should occur both when changes are proposed and after they are implemented. Capacity Management should pay particular attention to the cumulative effect of changes over a period of time. The negligible effect of single changes can often combine to cause degraded response times, file storage problems, and excess demand for processing capacity.

FIGURE 9.5

The Capacity Management process

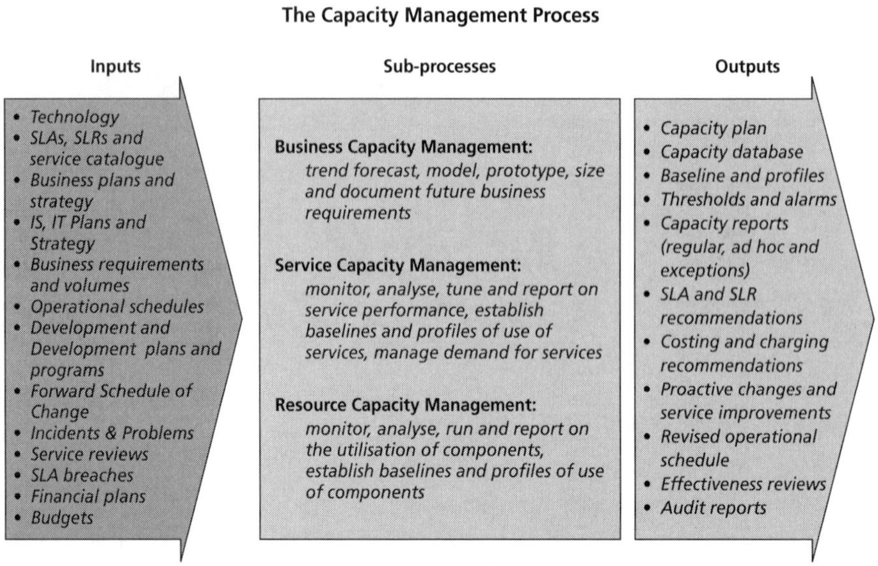

The Capacity Management Process

Inputs
- Technology
- SLAs, SLRs and service catalogue
- Business plans and strategy
- IS, IT Plans and Strategy
- Business requirements and volumes
- Operational schedules
- Development and Development plans and programs
- Forward Schedule of Change
- Incidents & Problems
- Service reviews
- SLA breaches
- Financial plans
- Budgets

Sub-processes

Business Capacity Management:
trend forecast, model, prototype, size and document future business requirements

Service Capacity Management:
monitor, analyse, tune and report on service performance, establish baselines and profiles of use of services, manage demand for services

Resource Capacity Management:
monitor, analyse, run and report on the utilisation of components, establish baselines and profiles of use of components

Outputs
- Capacity plan
- Capacity database
- Baseline and profiles
- Thresholds and alarms
- Capacity reports (regular, ad hoc and exceptions)
- SLA and SLR recommendations
- Costing and charging recommendations
- Proactive changes and service improvements
- Revised operational schedule
- Effectiveness reviews
- Audit reports

IT Service Continuity Management

IT Service Continuity Management will ensure that the required IT technical and service facilities can be recovered within the timescales required by Business Continuity Management. It is concerned with managing an organization's ability to continue to provide a predetermined and agreed level of IT services to support the minimum business requirements following an interruption to the business. Effective IT service continuity requires a balance of risk reduction measures such as resilient systems and recovery options, including backup facilities. Configuration management data is required to facilitate this prevention and planning. Infrastructure and business changes need to be assessed for their potential impact on the continuity plans, and the IT and business plans should be subject to Change Management procedures. The Service Desk has an important role to play if business continuity is invoked.

Availability Management

Availability Management will optimize the capability of the IT infrastructure and supporting organization to deliver a cost-effective and sustained level of availability to satisfy business objectives. Availability Management is concerned with the design, implementation, measurement and management of IT services to ensure the stated business requirements for availability are consistently met. Availability Management requires an understanding of the reasons why IT service failures occur and the time taken to resume service. Incident Management and Problem Management provide a key input to ensure the appropriate corrective actions are being progressed.

Availability targets specified in SLAs are monitored and reported on as part of the Availability Management process. Additionally, Availability Management supports the Service Level Management process in providing measurements and reporting to support service reviews.

9.6 Service Support

The Service Support book is concerned with ensuring that the customers and users have access to the appropriate services to support the business functions. Issues discussed in this book are:

- Service Desk
- Incident Management
- Problem Management
- Configuration Management
- Change Management
- Release Management.

The list of issues above, compared with the previous Service Support Set in ITIL, reflects some interesting developments in IT Service Management best practice that have taken place over the past few years.

The distinction between an incident (an event that prevents using the service properly) and a problem (a possible error in the infrastructure that could be the cause of one or more incidents) is sometimes considered one of the hallmarks of ITIL terminology. It often causes some confusion, certainly in organizations that have just started working with the ITIL framework, but it has an important benefit: separating quick service restoration from getting at the source of the trouble and fixing it.

It has become best practice in many organizations to group the activities related to resolving incidents and problems in processes of their own. In the original Service Support Set, one part of Incident Management was treated as a task of the Help Desk and another as a sub-process of Problem Management. The recent update brought ITIL again in line with best practice and defined the Service Desk as a function in the organization, bringing together activities from several IT Service Management processes that have to do with the day-to-day contacts with the users of the IT services. This also reflected a development in many organizations where the IT Help Desk was transformed into a broader IT Service Desk.

Release Management now not only captures the activities from Software Control and Distribution but those related to releasing all kinds of items and 'packages' of software and hardware in support of the IT services.

The overall goal of the processes in Service Support is to ensure that the IT services are provided in agreement with the business needs and especially to provide procedures for controlled changes in the IT infrastructure and resolution of incidents and problems (Figure 9.6).

Service Desk

The Service Desk is an important function for the different Service Management processes. It is a single point of contact between service providers and users, on a day-to-day basis. It is also a focal point for reporting incidents and making service requests. As such, the Service Desk has an obligation to keep users informed of service events, actions and opportunities that are likely to impact their ability to pursue their day-to-

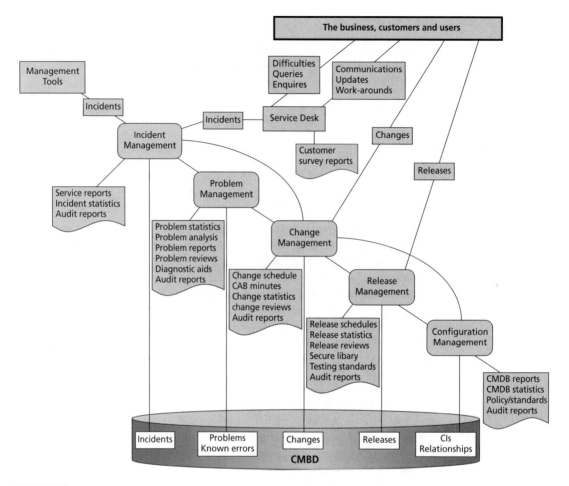

FIGURE 9.6
Overview of the Support processes

day activities. For example, the Service Desk might act as the focal point for change requests from users, issuing change schedules on behalf of Change Management, and keeping users informed of progress on changes. Change Management should therefore ensure that the Service Desk is kept constantly aware of change activities.

The Service Desk is in the direct firing line of any impact on the SLAs and as such needs rapid information flows.

The Service Desk may be given delegation to implement changes to circumvent incidents within its sphere of authority. The scope of such changes should be predefined and the Change Management function should be informed about all such changes. Prior approval of Change Management is essential before changes of specification of any CI are implemented.

Incident Management

The primary goal of the Incident Management process is to restore normal service operation as quickly as possible and minimize the adverse impact on business opera-

FIGURE 9.7

The process of incident investigation

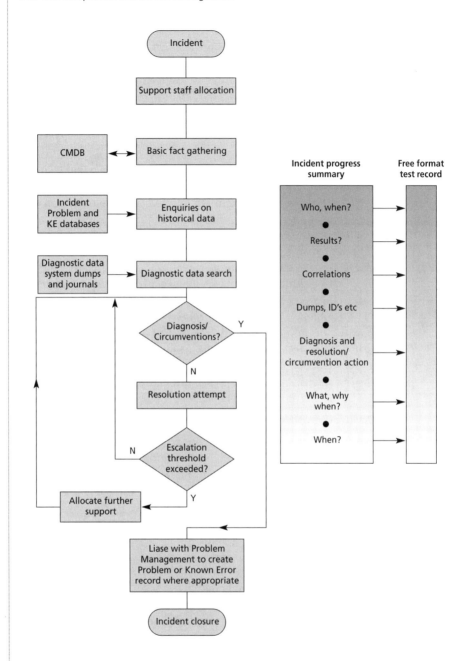

tions, thus ensuring that the best possible levels of service quality and availability are maintained (Figure 9.7). 'Normal service operation' is defined here as service operation within service level agreement limits.

There should be a close interface between the Incident Management process and the Problem Management and Change Management processes as well as the function of the Service Desk. If not properly controlled, changes may introduce new incidents. A way of tracking back is required. It is therefore recommended that the incident records should be held on the same CMDB as the problem, known error and change records, or at least linked without the need for rekeying, to improve the interfaces and ease interrogation and reporting.

Incident priorities and escalation procedures need to be agreed as part of the Service Level Management process and documented in the SLAs.

Problem Management

The goal of Problem Management is to minimize the adverse impact of incidents and problems on the business that are caused by errors within the IT infrastructure, and to prevent recurrence of incidents related to these errors. In order to achieve this goal, Problem Management seeks to get to the root cause of incidents and then initiate actions to improve or correct the situation. The Problem Management process has both reactive and proactive aspects. The reactive aspect is concerned with solving problems in response to one or more incidents. Proactive problem management is concerned with identifying and solving problems and known errors before incidents occur in the first place.

The Problem Management process requires the accurate and comprehensive recording of incidents in order to identify effectively and efficiently the cause of the incidents and trends. Problem Management also needs to liaise closely with the Availability Management process to identify these trends and instigate remedial action.

Configuration Management

Businesses require quality IT services provided economically. To be efficient and effective, all organizations need to control their IT infrastructure and services. Configuration Management provides a logical model of the infrastructure or a service by identifying, controlling, maintaining and verifying the versions of configuration items (CIs) in existence.

Configuration Management is an integral part of all other Service Management processes. With current, accurate and comprehensive information about all components of the infrastructure, the management of change, in particular, is more effective and efficient. Change Management can be integrated with Configuration Management. As a *minimum*, it is recommended that the logging and implementation of changes be done under the control of a comprehensive Configuration Management system and that the impact assessment of changes is also done with the aid of the Configuration Management system. All change requests should therefore be entered in the Configuration Management Database (CMDB) and the records updated as the change request progresses through to implementation.

The Configuration Management system identifies relationships between an item that is to be changed and any other components of the infrastructure, thus allowing the owners of these components to be involved in the impact assessment process. Whenever a change is made to the infrastructure and/or services, associated Configuration Management records should be updated in the CMDB. Where possible, this is best accomplished by use of integrated tools that update records automatically as changes are made.

The CMDB should be made available to the entire Service Support group so that incidents and problems can be resolved more easily by understanding the possible cause of the failing component. The CMDB should also be used to link the incident and problem records to other appropriate records such as the failing configuration item and the user. Release Management will be difficult and error-prone without the integration of the Configuration Management process.

Change Management

The goal of the Change Management process is to ensure that standardized methods and procedures are used for efficient, prompt and authorized handling of all changes in the IT infrastructure. Change Management aims at minimizing the impact of change-related incidents upon service quality, and consequently to improve the day-to-day operations of the organization.

To make an appropriate response to a change request entails a considered approach to assessment of risk and business continuity, change impact, resource requirements and change approval. This considered approach is essential to maintain a proper balance between the need for change and the impact of the change.

The Change Management process depends on the accuracy of the configuration data to ensure the full impact of making changes is known. There is therefore a very close relationship between Configuration Management, Release Management and Change Management (Figure 9.8).

Details of the change process are documented in SLAs to ensure that users know the procedure for requesting changes and the projected target times for, and impact of, the implementation of changes.

Details of changes need to be made known to the Service Desk. Even with comprehensive testing, there is an increased likelihood of difficulties occurring following change implementation, either because the change is not working as required or expected, or because of queries on the change in functionality.

The Change Advisory Board (CAB) is a group of people who can give expert advice to a Change Management team on the implementation of changes. This board is likely to be made up of representatives from all areas within IT and representatives from business units.

Release Management

Many service providers and suppliers may be involved in the release of hardware and software in a distributed environment. Good resource planning and management are essential to package and distribute a release successfully to the customer. Release Management takes a holistic view of a change to an IT service and should ensure that all aspects of a release, both technical and non-technical, are considered together.

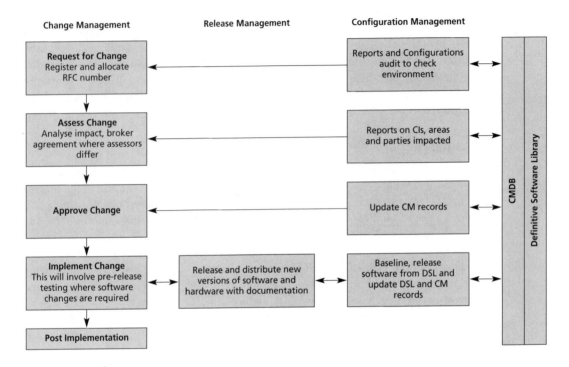

FIGURE 9.8

The relationship between Configuration, Change and Release Management

Changes may often result in the need for new hardware, new versions of software, and/or new documentation, created in-house or bought in, to be controlled and distributed, as part of a new 'packaged release'. The procedures for achieving secure, managed rollout should be closely integrated with those for Change Management and Configuration Management. Release procedures may also be an integral part of Incident Management and Problem Management, as well as being closely linked to the CMDB in order to maintain up-to-date records.

9.7 A process-led approach

To clarify how the guidance in ITIL yields a comprehensive framework for continuous improvement of IT services, many process models have been developed. The CCTA/OGC produced a set of process models to describe the make-up of ITIL and many organizations felt a need to enhance these to make them fit to their needs.

The main benefit of such a process-led approach is its focus on roles and activities grouped in a comprehensive way to facilitate communication, co-operation, management and control. In periods of radical changes in the organizational structure, process models proved to be a sound basis of keeping track of the necessary relationships between the activities in IT Service Management.

Although process models now form the cornerstones in the ITIL framework, it should be stressed that there is no one-and-only model available fit for all purposes, all organizations and all circumstances.

The process elements for management of services can be defined precisely. However, in practice, when analysing the processes in more detail, elements overlap. This situation illustrates the need for both consistency across the guidance, and advice on how to deal with management problems that may arise. The cause of these management problems may be the result of boundaries drawn that perhaps have more to do with the span of control than with logical grouping of related processes.

Fundamental to the process-led approach in IT Service Management is the need for continuous improvement of the ICT services provided. The process improvement model in Figure 9.9 illustrates how business objectives are translated in an improvement plan, using an analysis of the current state of affairs. To make such an improvement continuous, it is crucial that there is a loop back to the original question, 'Where do we want to be?', which is only possible if some metrics are available on the results of the improvement plan.

FIGURE 9.9
Process improvement model

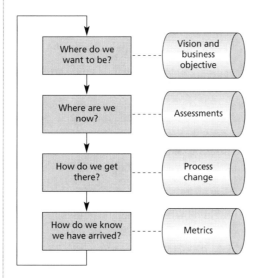

In short, if you can draw up a process model of best practice (or any practice in fact that is more effective than your current way of doing things), you can compare that model with a description of your current practice and use it to define improvements. If you do this in the light of your business direction or critical success factors, you can define measures of how you can demonstrate improvements and achievements that are truly useful.

Much of the essentials of the ITIL framework can be understood from this process improvement model. For example, improvement of the processes of IT Service Management in general is needed for improvement of the ICT services. ITIL provides guidance on improving these processes, based on best practice in the IT industry.

9.8 Planning and implementation

More and more organizations are recognizing the importance of Service Management to their business. However, it is common for working practices to be based on historical or political considerations rather than the current needs of the business or best practice. It is therefore essential, before implementing any or all of the components of Service Management, to gain management commitment, to understand the working culture of the organization, and to assess any existing processes and to compare these to the needs of the business and to best practice.

To analyse the needs of the organization and implement the desired solution is not a trivial task. Implementation is likely to be incremental and will certainly involve changes in culture as well as changes in processes, and perhaps changes in organization structure. To undertake these changes requires a programme and/or project approach.

One of the benefits of adopting a programme and/or project approach is that you can undertake the necessary investigations, identify what, why, where, when and how changes will need to be made, and how much they will cost. In a programme and/or project approach, you will also have designated decision points where you can opt to continue with the programme or project, change direction, or stop.

OGC's Managing Successful Programmes (MSP) and PRINCE2 (PRojects IN Controlled Environments), both widely adopted internationally, provide integrated and structured approaches to managing those change activities.

The change programme or project needs to consider your current position, where you would like to be, and plot the path between these states. For each option identified, you can begin to articulate:

- the business benefits;
- the risks, obstacles and potential problems;
- the costs of the move plus longer-term running costs;
- the costs of continuing with the current structure.

You can then begin to see how the business needs can be supported and see the associated costs. The benefits can then be balanced against costs and risks. Undertaking the investigative work could be considered to be one project that can then be followed by a series of implementation projects.

Some advice before you start: the ITIL is not a magic wand. Do not expect miracles to happen when you implement the process framework. In the past, many organizations have tried to use process implementations as the basis for company reorganizations, or to assist with company mergers. Too many disparate goals for the project will lead to failure and disappointment. The targets and objectives associated with a Service Management project must relate to the delivery of quality IT services aligned to business need.

A 'health check' based on ITIL's best practice for the processes can be used as an objective way of assessing the capability, maturity and effectiveness of Service Management processes in an organization. This assessment should aim to identify those aspects that are functioning well, thus determining which best practices are in current use and should be retained, and also to pinpoint gaps, problem areas and constraints. Using the outputs from a health check, you will be better equipped to define your implementation or improvement priorities.

Non-IT-specific issues which can influence your performance in delivering services, such as people management and resource management, can be assessed by using (self) assessment methods provided by Total Quality Management methods. Be aware that in many cases it is these factors which have the major effect upon the actual performance from the Service Management processes.

9.9 The ITIL infrastructure

ITIL now stands for much more than merely a library of useful books. The framework of best practice in IT Service Management has to be disseminated and organizations starting to work with it need support, consultancy, training and tools. Since the mid-1990s the term ITIL has stood not just for the framework but also for the approach and philosophy shared by its practitioners.

A range of organizations cooperate internationally to support ITIL as a de facto international standard in IT Service Management. The diagram in Figure 9.10 illustrates which parties are involved in the dissemination and development of ITIL. Apart from the OGC, these range from commercial companies providing training, consultancy and tools to the international user forum itSMF, a platform for exchange of best practices in IT Service Management, and examination bodies such as EXIN and ISEB.

FIGURE 9.10

The ITIL infrastructure

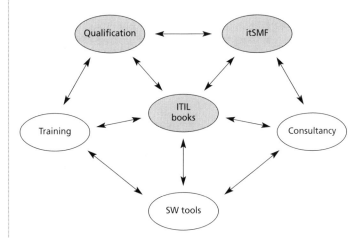

The Dutch IT examination institute EXIN and ISEB, the examination body of the British Computer Society, have developed a global ITIL-based qualification structure for IT Service Management which has three levels of proficiency: Foundation, Practitioner and Manager. Exams for the certificates of this qualification scheme have been held in over 30 countries. By the end of 2000, over 30,000 people held a qualification in IT service management worldwide, and many more have received training.

The examination bodies, OGC and itSMF, cooperate in managing the qualification scheme with a shared responsibility in keeping it up to date and relevant for organizations involved in IT service management. As with the ITIL guides, the specification of the qualification scheme – its requirements and certification processes – is publicly available.

The above ITIL infrastructure not only contributed to the success of ITIL all over the world and made the ITIL framework the de facto international standard in IT Service Management, but it also assures feedback on the guidance in the library from a best practice point of view. The update of ITIL that recently took place is part of this feedback for continuous improvement. In using the framework, practitioners in all kind of organizations (small, large, commercial, public, and with centralized or distributed systems) have both proved its value and extended it for their particular needs.

Some extensions of ITIL became methods or frameworks of their own in IT Service Management. There obviously is a need for these and one may also recognise the wisdom of their guidance, especially if such guidance is adequate for specific groups of organizations. The guidance in ITIL, although open to improvement based on the experience of practitioners, is meant to be applicable generically. It is unique in offering a core for IT Service Management based on the best practice in a worldwide infrastructure of practitioners.

Note

1 PD0005 is based on ITIL and provides a management introduction to IT Service Management. It is the basis for the British Standard *BS15000:2000 Specification for IT Service Management*.

10 Information Technology Process Model

Paul Hertroys and **Bart van Rooijen**
IBM Global Services

10.1 What is ITPM, and what can it do for you?

The IT Process Model is a reference model for controlling information technology within an organization (Figure 10.1). The model was developed when studies of various IT environments showed that many processes featured a recurrent common denominator (Figure 10.2). The model can act as a starting point for understanding the current processes, and, where necessary, form a basis for the design and restructuring of these processes. In addition, it can pinpoint the processes required to set up a new management system.

FIGURE 10.1
The IT Process Model

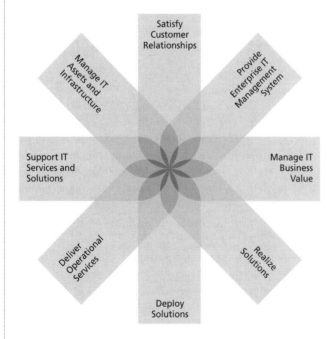

FIGURE 10.2

Survey into the contribution of IT to company management with ITMP

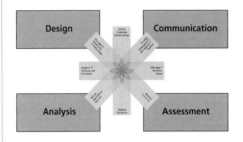

The IT Process Model is also suitable for use as an assessment system, both for determining the current strengths and weaknesses of the IT organization and for selecting the processes that, once restructured, will yield the best performance. For example, a European bank has used the model to determine its priorities for improving management-support processes in a number of business units. Many Dutch companies have used the IT Process Model in combination with ITIL to structure their IT management.

The IT Process Model can be used for the analysis of job performance and information flows. The IT Process Model played a major role in a recent multi-client survey by IBM Global Services into the way IT contributes to company management.

10.2 ITPM in practice

The IT Process Model is not an implementation model, so it doesn't say how things should be done. The IT Process Model shows what should be happening, i.e. the processes shown form a starting point for designing the processes and procedures of the IT organization itself. The model does not constitute a set of instructions to be blindly followed: although the processes are being presented in a certain order, the model remains flexible and easy to adapt. Depending on the existing situation and conditions, the model described can be used to bring about concrete improvements. This makes the model eminently suitable in combination with a best-practice model such as ITIL.

Even though the order in which the actions take place is not fixed, the relationships between the processes form a fixed factor. For each process, the IT Process Model shows the activities and information flows between the processes and activities. In this way, the processes form a framework into which the best practices, i.e. the way the processes should work, may be implemented. In this respect, the processes of the IT Process Model lend themselves well for inclusion in a quality framework of choice, e.g. ISO9000 or EFQM (Figure 10.3).

IBM Global Services has developed a number of tools and techniques for applying the IT Process Model in the analysis of IT organizations: workshops and maturity matrices, providing insight into the way the current IT processes work within the organization, statistical tools to identify problem areas and priorities, and user surveys that link up with the processes in the model. In addition, the IT Process Model can be used as a basis for designing the management framework for Systems Management Framework Design, a method for designing an entire management framework, complete with tooling, roles and responsibilities, and procedures.

FIGURE 10.3
ITPM and the relationships with other frameworks

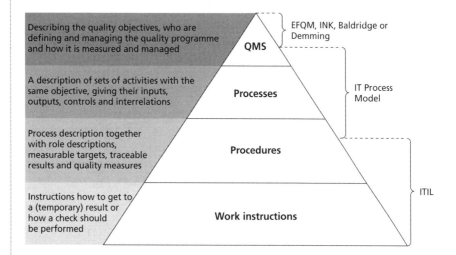

10.3 ITPM and ITIL

In the Netherlands, the Information Technology Infrastructure Library (ITIL) has become the industry standard for setting up IT management. What is the relationship between ITPM and ITIL?

ITPM and ITIL complement each other well. ITPM is a reference model for controlling IT, indicating the relationships and information flows between the processes. ITIL is a description of best practices, showing how these processes can be implemented.

ITPM is aimed at designing, monitoring, and controlling processes within the current environment, at strategic planning for the future environment and relationships between the processes, whereas ITIL focuses on filling in certain primary areas in order to maintain the current environment as effectively as possible. An example of this relationship is shown in Figure 10.4, illustrating the relationship between the sub-processes within the 'Provide IT Operational Support to Customers' process and the ITIL Help Desk module.

10.4 ITPM and SMFD

While ITPM provides a model for analysing and designing processes for an IT organization, the actual design process itself will also have to be structured. For this purpose, IBM has developed Systems Management Framework Design (SMFD). Using this method, the management activities required for various IT elements and their implementation can be determined. The process is based on a company-wide and overall overview of the IT services. Since SMFD can be used with a number of different process models, the analysis and the general design obtained with ITPM can serve as the perfect basis for a design created with the aid of SMFD. Figure 10.5 shows the five stages comprising the SMFD process. For detailed information on the model, in-depth documentation is available.

FIGURE 10.4

Relationships between an ITPM process and an ITIL process

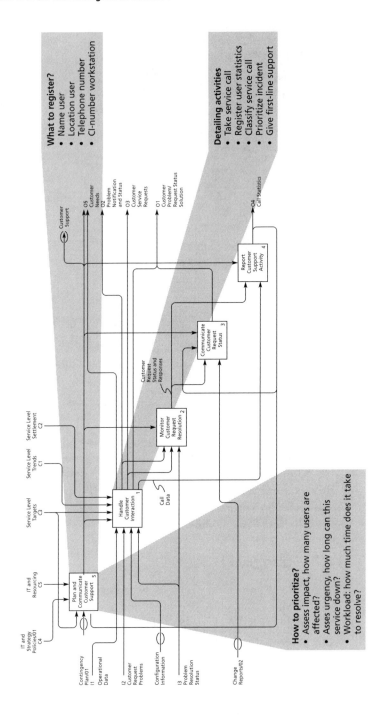

FIGURE 10.5

The five stages of the SMFD process

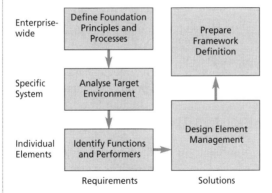

10.5 Implementing processes

All presented models have in common that they cover the wide range of the IT services domains. From a pragmatic point of view, these models will assist in the what's and how's but still contain abstract views of reality.

IBM's Intellectual Capital Management System shows numerous examples where these models were applied to specific customer requirements and where the models assisted in achieving significant improvements on customers' issues.

Most of the cases, however, show specific customer situations where issues were experienced or at least suspected. Very few examples were found where these models could be applied for initial start-up of IT organizations.[1]

Issue- or solution-based consultancy practices will encounter difficulties during their engagements when no clear agreement can be reached concerning where to start and from which angle issues will be engaged. Where ITPM advertises to start at a solid understanding and appreciation of the customers' wants and needs and of the services they value enabling to define a portfolio of IT services that will address these needs, ITIL will recommend starting with Configuration Management, once the bottom-up approach is elected.

FIGURE 10.6

Interaction between Service Demand and Service Supply in Service Entry Points

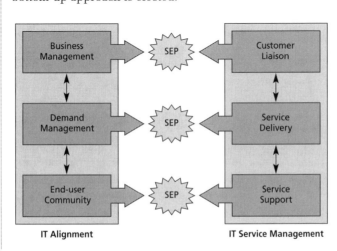

Meanwhile, many lessons learned from process implementations are available. These bring us to the conclusion that the best starting points are the Service Entry Points (SEPs) within the area of IT services supply and demand. Supply and demand are interacting in these SEPs on operational, tactical and strategic levels. Figure 10.6 shows the SEPs for operational, tactical and strategic levels of supply and demand.

All interactors are represented by their points of contact (PoC). On an operational level, the end-user community triggers the Incident Management process for Service Support, while on a tactical level Demand Management triggers the Service Level Management process in Service Delivery.

For the bottom-up approach, the Incident Management and Service Level Management processes are the ones to start with. An additional benefit in this implementation strategy is the involvement of the counterpart PoCs. Project and implementation ambitions can more easily be communicated to those who will benefit. Within the business environment the allocated PoCs can actively be involved in process design and implementation of IT Service Management.

10.6 Measurement of process effectiveness

'If you can't measure it, you can't manage it' can be regarded as a statement that will attract much sympathy. Whereas in process design it is relatively easy to determine input and output for the processes, it becomes more complex when performance indicators[2] for these processes need to be determined. We have seen evidence of cases where, for each IT Service Management process, 5 to 10 performance indicators were designed. This adds up to a grand total of almost 100 indicators for 10 processes (both operational and tactical).

Doubts arise at to whether such a size can be managed effectively, not to mention whether a management system is available that controls this number of indicators.

Nevertheless, IT Service organizations develop the need to have measures implemented that drive their performance. There is a significant similarity with the Balanced Scorecard (Kaplan, Norton, 1996).[3] From a business point of view, the four angles for business performance are not disputed, and the same can be argued for IT Service organizations. The four angles – the Financial, Customer, Internal and Innovation and Learning perspectives – are equally suitable for the provision of IT Services.

If there is a positive answer to the question 'Why does business need a Balanced Scorecard?', probably the same positive answer can be found for the question: 'Why do IT organizations need an IT scorecard?'

An organization's measurement system strongly affects the behaviour of people both inside and outside the organization. The same logic can be applied to the behaviour of IT Service Management and the people contributing to it. If the objective is to improve the effectiveness of processes, achievement of this objective will involve changing people's behaviour and in particular the behaviour of those who actively deploy activities that are an integral part of that process.

It is on this subject that business management consultants and IT Management consultants should work together to align a Business Scorecard and an IT Scorecard. Figure 10.7 shows the relationship between them.

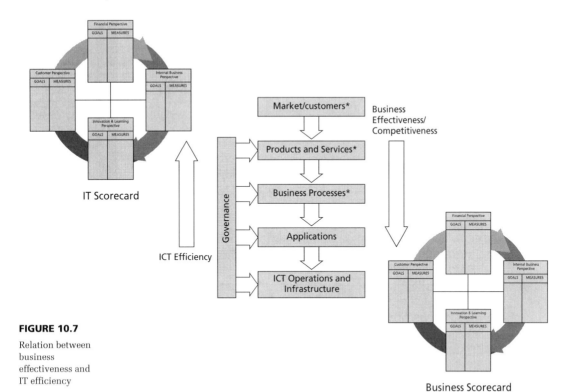

FIGURE 10.7

Relation between business effectiveness and IT efficiency

Business management should be responsible for the business requirement definition for IT and should advise the chief executive on IT strategy, mission and architecture, IT and business strategy alignment, and pricing policies and methodologies. When this can be accomplished, the designing, building and implementing of IT Service Management processes, using ITIL and ITPM, will have a good chance of delivering as required.

In fact, it will answer the question of what ITIL and ITPM can do for you.

Notes

1 The exception to this rule is the initial start-ups of e-business.
2 Also referred to as Key Performance Indicators, e.g. KPIs.
3 Kaplan, R.S. and Norton, D.P. (1996) *The Balanced Scorecard: translating strategy into action*, Harvard Business School Press, Boston.

11
A 'Managerial Step-by-Step Plan'

Maarten Looijen and **Wouter de Jong**
Delft University of Technology

11.1 Introduction

At Delft University of Technology in the Netherlands, the subject of 'Information Systems Management, Control and Maintenance' belongs to the curriculum of Technical Informatics. The whole subject is covered by a translation of the book *Beheer van Informatiesystemen*, first published in 1995. In a short time it became quite popular in the Netherlands and by 1999 the fourth edition had been published. Each edition is a revision of the preceding one because new developments in information and communication technology and in management, control and maintenance of that technology are continually taking place.

In the course of more than 10 years, the management aspects of information systems in business and industry became more and more important, and as a result the education and research in this field developed at the same rate. The issues include technical, organizational and economical subjects. They cover a number of models to support practical situations. These models together with techniques have been brought together in a logical sense by a number of steps to realize and to assess the management, control and maintenance of information systems. All these steps are represented by a 'Managerial Step-by-Step Plan'.

11.2 The MSP

The 'Managerial Step-by-Step Plan', or MSP, provides a number of steps by means of which, in a systematic way, the organization of the management, control and maintenance (MCM) of information systems can be realized. Furthermore, these steps express the relationships existing between the various subjects.

MSP assumes that the building blocks for the realization of MCM can be identified and therefore it will be possible to arrive at a finished product. Moreover, MSP aims at critically analysing the existing MCM situations. On the basis of the results obtained, it will then be possible to decide whether an adaptation of MCM or parts of it is necessary. This means that MSP aims at the realization of a totally new MCM organization as well as at a possible adjustment of existing MCM organizations and everything involved. Each step includes a description of the activities to be done. The approach is based on the book *Information Systems Management, Control and Maintenance* by M. Looijen, published in the Netherlands (see literature).

Step 1: the object of MCM

Describe the object to be managed, controlled and maintained, namely one or more information systems and the business processes connected with these. The object is expressed in hardware, software, data sets, procedures and the people using it. All characteristics of the object should be described. Moreover, it is important to know in what way the object presents itself physically; often this is, for instance, distribution, diversity and quantity. Also, the technical facilities for electricity, cooling and the like have to be known. As to the business processes, of which the information systems are derivatives, type and size have to be mapped.

Step 2: the user organization

Describe the demands on hardware, software, data sets, procedures and the relevant data processing procedures being made in relation to practical applications. The technical facilities should also be involved here. The preconditions concerning the financial, material and human resources that are needed have to be known; these are related to the demands formulated in this step.

The situational factors (or contingency factors) are also important in this step. They describe the company to which the object of MCM belongs. Characteristics of the company, such as nature, size, location and age, are used. Together with the requirements and the preconditions, they form the starting points for the following step, which anticipates the details of these more fully.

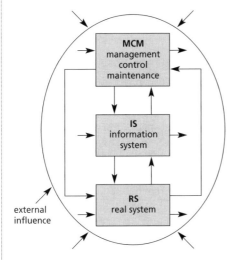

FIGURE 11.1

The MCM paradigm

Step 3: the MCM tasks

Select the task fields by means of which the demands made by the user organization in step 2 can be met. A task field is a coherent cluster of tasks. The prevailing preconditions as well as the situational factors of the company have to be taken into account. This may imply that the entire task field does not need to be selected, just one or more MCM tasks belonging to the task field in question. When selecting, the relationship between task fields has to be identified as soon as it appears that an independent task field cannot meet a certain demand. For, in practice, there is a great coherence between task fields. The relationship between user organizations, the object of MCM and MCM itself is depicted by the so-called MCM paradigm (see Figure 11.1).

The life cycle of the object of MCM is illustrated by the Extended State Model, which includes all relevant states of any information system (see Figure 11.2). Each state has relationships with one or more task fields. The meaning of the states is:

IPP: information policy and planning
D: development
A/I: acceptance and implementation
U: utilization
E: exploitation
M: maintenance.

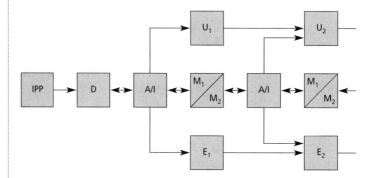

FIGURE 11.2
The Extended State Model

Step 4: the MCM processes

Translate the task fields of step 3 into MCM processes. This implies that the task fields must be described in more detail so these can coherently be presented as processes. ITIL, i.e. the IT Infrastructure Library, can be used here. The library includes nine sets, each of which focuses on a number of MCM processes. In practice, almost always only two of the nine ITIL sets are used. These are the Service Support set (Configuration Management, Problem Management, Change Management, Help Desk, and Software Control & Distribution) and the Service Delivery set (Service Level Management, Capacity Management, Contingency Planning, Availability Management and Cost Management for IT services).

Step 5: the generic process approach

All processes of step 4 are worked out in the so-called Basic Process Model, which is a generic process approach. This consists in its most elementary form of a transformation. It is preceded by input, which is transformed into output. Both input and output are filtered. The input that passes the filter is buffered for transformation, analogously to queuing. The input that does not pass the filter goes elsewhere (another transformation).

After filtering, feedback to the input filter may be generated that is again considered for transformation. If there is no feedback, buffering takes place and the process is then brought to an end or continued elsewhere (see Figure 11.3). Proceeding from the generic process approach, each MCM process will be realized. On the basis of this,

11 ■ A 'Managerial Step-by-Step Plan'

FIGURE 11.3
The generic process model

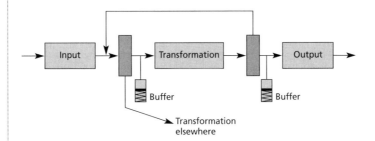

each MCM process can be worked out unambiguously. Relationships between the processes are established wherever necessary. These relationships need not be the same for each management situation. However, for a number of processes this is the case, because certain processes are clearly interrelated – for instance, Problem Management and Change Management.

Step 6: the three forms of MCM

Describe the three MCM forms Functional Management, Application Management and Technical Management on the basis of the task fields selected in step 3. Distinguish the three levels, i.e. the strategic level, the tactical level and the operational level. The approach is two-dimensional or three-dimensional, depending on the number of occurrences of each management form (Figure 11.4), the Triple Model of MCM. The approach is rather theoretical by nature and is used as a basis for a more practical extension. We extend the model by relating this step to steps 3 and 4, and by using the Extended Triple Model of MCM (see Figure 11.5). This model derives from the Triple Model of MCM all relevant MCM tasks needed to form the MCM processes. The acronyms refer to so-called task areas: clusters of task fields.

Step 7: the organization of MCM

Realize the organic MCM units which are responsible for Functional Management, Application Management and Technical Management. This may have as a result that the three MCM forms distinguished in step 6 occur more than once. Take into consideration the problems involved in centralization, decentralization and outsourcing of MCM. The result is an overall picture of how MCM is distributed over organic MCM units.

Step 8: the integration model

Relate the result of step 5, namely the MCM processes, to the organization of MCM. As a result, the MCM processes are embedded in the organic MCM units of step 7.

FIGURE 11.4
The Triple Model of MCM

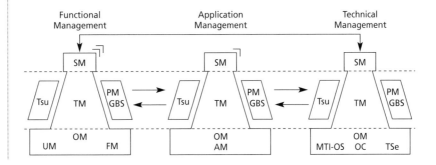

FIGURE 11.5

The Extended Triple Model of MCM

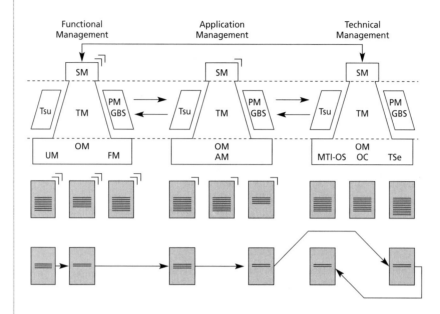

This expresses the responsibilities of the MCM units and the MCM tasks in the MCM processes to be performed – see example in Figure 11.6. This example illustrates the performing of a request for change in relation to the three forms of MCM.

Step 9: functions and employees

Establish the functions to be performed, and also the required knowledge, understanding and skills that are needed to carry out the MCM tasks within the MCM processes. Assign the functions to the employees who will be responsible for the performance of the MCM tasks. The ultimate result is an MCM organization that may be considered capable of interpreting MCM as expressed in the preceding steps. This is an organization where MCM is attuned to the requirements and preconditions made in relation to the user organization, and where the identified situational factors are taken into account. At the same time the MCM organization has to be considered capable of contributing to the realization of organizational objectives, as information systems increasingly form an integral part of the business processes. In order to improve the above and to carry it out professionally, one needs to complete the following step.

Step 10: service management

Draw up the service level agreements between utilization and MCM of information systems on the basis of the requirements and preconditions formulated in step 2. Equip the MCM organization with methods and techniques so that it can verify whether the services agreed upon are delivered and, if necessary, can adjust the services. Wherever possible, MCM has to be proactive. This implies observation and analysis of trends in the progress of the quality level of the services. Along with quality and control, economic and legal aspects play a part as a service level agreement is a contract representing rights and duties for users and management. Furthermore, measuring and comparing of services play an important part.

FIGURE 11.6

The Integration Model

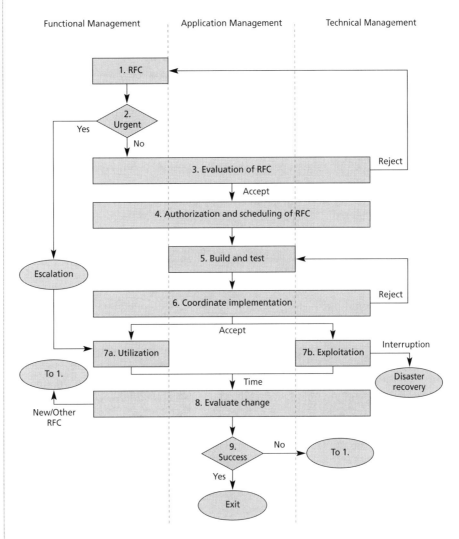

Step 11: assessment and simulation

Evaluate regularly how well the MCM functions and take into account changes within the user organization and external changes. It must be understood that MCM is managing, controlling and maintaining information systems in accordance with requirements and preconditions agreed upon in relation to practical applications and to the characteristics of the information system components; it also contributes to the realization of business objectives. An important aid here is the application of MCM simulation. With the help of this the management can, in its totality, be investigated at animation level. At Delft University of Technology, simulation of MCM is an ongoing project. It includes a dynamic presentation and game of MCM processes such as Help Desk and Problem Management, Performance Management and Operations, Network Management and Availability Management (see Figure 11.7). One of the main objectives is to show real MCM situations in contrast to reports explaining complicated situations. Another objective is offering an instrument to manage and to influence the performance of MCM processes.

FIGURE 11.7

Simulation of MCM processes

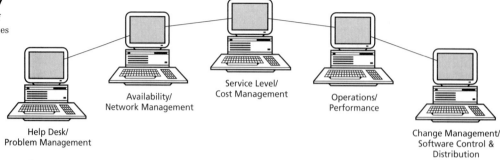

All 11 steps are depicted in Figure 11.8.

FIGURE 11.8

The Managerial Step-byStep Plan (MSP)

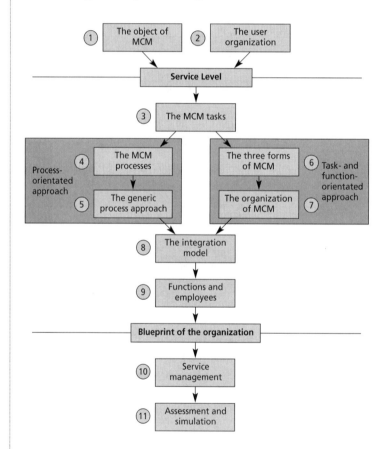

Literature

Looijen, M., (1998) *Information Systems – Management, Control and Maintenance*, ISBN 90-267-2846-8, Kluwer Bedrijfsinformatie, the Netherlands.

12 Managing the delivery of business information

Leo Ruijs and **Albert Schotanus**
Cap Gemini Ernst & Young (CGEY), the Netherlands

Summary

IT Service Management is seen by Cap Gemini Ernst & Young (CGEY) as a continuing activity growing both in importance and in complexity. In this chapter we specify how to control this increasing complexity. The suggested methodology is developed in cooperation with the Delft University of Technology, the Eindhoven University of Technology and the Vrije Universiteit Amsterdam and is based on CGEY's quality system PERFORM.

12.1 Introduction

An optimum organization of the primary business processes is a precondition for a successful organization. Often the manner in which these business processes are supported by the information technology is a crucial factor. After all, the world around us is continually changing and that has consequences for the business processes. Owing to the effect of market movements, improvements in efficiency and quality, and the necessary cost reductions, these business processes must regularly be modified. The degree to which the supporting information technology (IT) – flexibly and without adversely affecting the continuity of the processes – can be used to support the required changes often determines the success of such changes. However, changes in the primary process are often delayed if the IT organization is not able to deal adequately with these changes. In addition, changes within IT itself can also play a role. By using new development techniques, companies are better able to shorten the development time for new functionalities. Statements such as 'nine months become nine weeks become nine days' are seen much more often in the professional magazines. This makes it increasingly difficult for competitors to differentiate amongst themselves on the basis of functionality. Companies have to differentiate themselves on the basis of quality – on the basis of the organization that provides the service and at the same time guarantees the quality of that service. A second important aspect is the increasing complexity which is becoming possible as a result of the new methods. 'Dumb' terminals have been replaced by local networks with intelligent workstations and servers. Furthermore, the computing centre of the past now consists of several linked (internal and external) computing centres, which together with the servers form either an inter-regional or worldwide network, often using the Internet. As a result, multiple systems and companies are involved in the delivery of business information. For every company, it is therefore essential that in addition to the organization of the overall company operations, the necessary attention is also paid to the operational management of the information delivery processes.

12.2 The vision

We do not talk about 'administering' but of 'managing the delivery of business information' and of 'IT Service Management', indicating the proactive role covering the complete subject. We approach the delivery of business information from the perspective of the overall operations of the company. From this perspective, the delivery of business information should, in a businesslike manner, provide support for the primary business processes. In our vision of the management of the delivery of business information, the reference point is providing and receiving services. The manner in which these services are built up and delivered is, in short, what IT service management is all about. Managing the delivery of business information is the overall framework within which the implementation of service management is carried out. To an increasing degree, organizational structures are linked to a specific situation and are also continually subject to change in order to adapt to the environment of the organization. However, regardless of the manner in which they are organized, companies continue to implement the same types of processes. That is why we have chosen a process-centred approach, which, in so far as is possible, makes management of the delivery of business information independent of the type of organization. Fundamental to this vision is the so-called Lemniscate model for IT Service Management.

Lemniscate model

The following three concepts are central to the Lemniscate model for IT Service Management (Figure 12.1):

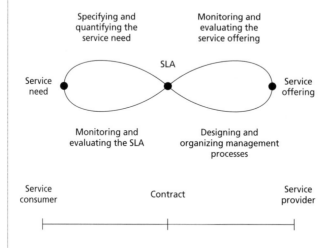

FIGURE 12.1

The Lemniscate model

- the IT service needs of the customer;
- the services provided by the IT service provider;
- the agreements with regard to the services desired and the services to be provided.

In the Lemniscate model, IT Service Management contains a left loop, Service Level Management (SLM), and a right loop, Service Process Management (SPM). Within SLM, the IT organization negotiates with its customers with regard to the services to be delivered and the conditions under which these are to be delivered (specifying and quantifying). The agreements that result from these negotiations are set down in a service level agreement (SLA). Then the IT organization organizes the delivery of services such that these agreements can be complied with (designing/organizing management processes). Within the framework of SPM, measurements and evaluations are then conducted to determine whether the agreements are actually being carried out. If it is necessary to adjust the process, then the implementation processes are organized differently (monitoring/evaluating management processes). Another possibility is that the agreements are modified (monitoring/implementing SLAs). In short: IT Service Management consists of methods for dealing with and translating the IT needs of a customer into an SLA and then embedding the SLA in the IT service organization. The former takes place in a process between customer and service provider, the latter within the management organization itself. The approach involves continuous management and improvement and thus becomes a tool for quality assurance.

12.3 The approach

Based on the Lemniscate model, the approach we use consists of four phases:

- Phase 1: Specifying and quantifying SLAs;
- Phase 2: Designing and organizing management processes;
- Phase 3: Monitoring and evaluating management processes;
- Phase 4: Monitoring and evaluating the SLAs.

Phase 1: Formulating workable SLAs for service provider and customer (according to the SLA specification method)

In actual practice, formulating SLAs turns out to be a difficult process. In addition, the SLAs formulated are often quite different – for example, regarding the area covered, the degree of detail, and the quantification and evaluation options. Often it is not exactly clear which services are to be provided, the conditions are complex and dynamic, and there is no unequivocal list of terminology or framework of concepts to be applied. In many cases there is no structured approach for recognition of services and specification of SLAs. The result is often confusion, misunderstandings and a limited role for SLAs as the basis for organizing and evaluating management processes. In the Lemniscate model, the service level agreement has a central role within IT Service Management. The SLA links the specification of the customer's needs to the IT services delivered by the service provider.

The desired level of service

An effective SLA assumes that the customer has a good picture of their specific company situation and the IT services that they need. First we must map out their organization and their business processes and determine the IT services they presently receive and what they actually need. Then the customer will have to make clear what they require of the IT services and which service level they need. In order to determine the desired service level of the IT services, we distinguish several steps (Figure 12.2).

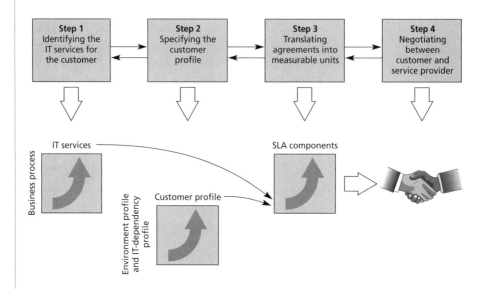

FIGURE 12.2

Four steps to specify an SLA

Step 1: Identifying the IT services for the customer

First we must determine which IT services the customer needs. We consider a service to be a tool to help the customer carry out his or her work, such as 'the ability to create invoices'. The service must be clearly defined for both the customer and the service provider. In this respect, the service provider must take into account what they can and cannot or do not wish to provide in the way of services. The customer should know exactly what he or she really needs and what added value that will offer him or her. For each service, it is possible to formulate specifications that have to be met. For example, for the 'option of creating invoices', one of the specifications is that the invoices must be ready each day by a certain time, so that they can be delivered in a timely fashion. The specifications, or requirements, with which IT services have to comply can be classified in a number of fixed 'SLA components': Availability, Integrity, Exclusiveness, Calamities, Performance, Training, User Support and Change Management. The formulation of these specifications depends, among other things, on the type of business that needs the IT service. So the next step in the SLA specification method is aimed at determining the 'customer profile'.

Step 2: Specifying the customer profile

In the method we derive the specifications for the IT service to be provided from the characteristics and the IT dependence of the customer. The characteristics that have to be taken into account include the size of the organization, the dynamics of the company's operational management, the type of business process (for example, primary or supporting) and the type of user group (experience, training, number etc). The degree of IT dependence is the extent to which an organization can continue to operate in case the IT infrastructure should happen to be disrupted. Each characteristic can influence the agreements that are made within an SLA. For example, a dynamic company management demands flexibility and adaptability from the IT service provider. A large company will more often need IT services in the area of security. An innovative company with sophisticated and rapidly changing IT applications will require intensive and specialist help-desk support. Within the customer profile, two factors will receive specific attention:

- *Formulating the 'environment profile'.* In order to characterize an organization, we analyse the users and the user group as well as the business processes and environment.
- *Determining IT dependence.* Some organizations can better maintain the continuity of their operations than others if IT services and/or IT infrastructure are disrupted. As an example, we can express the IT dependence as the (physical) danger that disruption would cause for people, as economic damage or as the degree to which confidential information would be leaked.

Step 3: Translating agreements into measurable units

To determine the management profile we combine the 'environment profile' with the 'IT dependence profile'. Using four standard environment profiles (as in Mintzberg (1992): Simple structure, Machine bureaucracy, Professional organization and Innovative organization), four IT dependency profiles (completely dependent, dependent, less dependent and completely independent) and a distinction between very confidential and not so confidential, we can theoretically arrive at a total of 32 standard management profiles or types. In practice, however, different variants and subvariants also occur. We can link the management types to relevant SLA components (Availability, Integrity, Exclusiveness, Calamities, Performance, Training, User Support, Change Management). They are, just like the environment types and the dependence types, meant to support and structure the process of specifying the services needed. For each business process that is supported by an IT service, the components are listed for which agreements have to be made. These agreements are strengthened by determining the so-called 'service attributes'. These attributes, which are developed through experience in the real world, are displayed in 'service catalogues'. A catalogue provides both the customer and the service provider with something to go by when negotiating prices and service levels or performance characteristics of the IT services to be provided.

Step 4: Negotiating between customer and service provider

The last step in the SLA specification method is the negotiations between customer and supplier. In this step, we must determine whether the service provider can actually meet the requirements of the customer. The supplier must also consider whether he or she wants to comply with the customer's request. This will depend to a large extent on the supplier's ability to structure the organization and processes in such a way as to be able to comply with the agreements made.

Phase 2: The design and organization of the management processes

The point of departure for the organization of the management processes and activities is the mutual agreements made by customer and supplier regarding the service to be provided. In phase 1, Service Level Management translates the requirements and specifications into norms, which have to be established in phase 2 by Service Process Management. The model 'managing the delivery of business information' provides a tool for the design and organization of management processes. The party responsible for the management organization will use this as a point of departure for giving form to his or her organizational structure. The manner in which this takes place depends very much on the specific situation: no two service providers are identical and every service provider is continually subject to change in order to adapt to the environment of the organization. This means that there are no ready-made solutions for translating the model into an organogram.

Model 'managing the delivery of business information'

The management of the delivery of business information is used as an overall framework for the implementation of service management (Figure 12.3). Within this framework we make distinctions in two directions. First, we distinguish on the basis of the environment in which the activities take place: Usage, Development/maintenance, and Exploitation. This makes it possible to define responsibilities and powers, which results in businesslike agreements. It becomes easier to control the flow of information and, as a result, also its effectiveness and efficiency. Quality assurance is an important motive in this regard. Secondly, we make distinctions based on the nature of the processes: Operational, Supporting, and Management-level processes.

Operational level
In the approach taken, all operational activities are placed at the level of implementation. This can vary from, for example, defining functional specifications for applications, which support a business process, to the development of both applications and infrastructure or daily operational maintenance of applications and systems. To fill in this level we utilize a combination of assignment fields from Looijen and the functions of the NGI (Dutch Society of Information Management). We supplement these with several activities that are the result of new technologies, such as the developments surrounding internets, intranets and extranets, which have been introduced as the result of new activities such as Content Management.

Supporting level
The management processes are found at the supporting level. These processes form the link between activities, which take place in the various functional columns and stand on their own but have a relationship to each other. An example is the request by a user to implement a change, the establishment of this change by a programmer and the implementation of the change by a production employee. The coordination of these various activities is carried out via the Change Management process. For the description of the processes that are found at this level, our point of departure is the internationally accepted IT Infrastructure Library (ITIL):

FIGURE 12.3

The framework

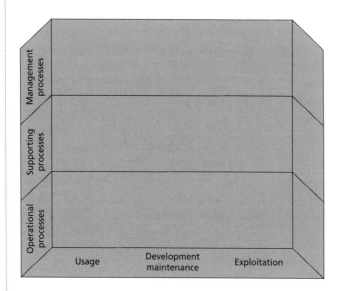

- Service Support Incident Management, Problem Management, Change Management, Configuration Management, Software Control and Distribution
- Service Delivery Availability Management, Capacity Management, Cost Management, Contingency Planning.

At this level, we also find the business-support processes and general resource management.

Management level
The point of departure for the organization of management processes and activities is the mutual agreements between customer and supplier regarding the services provided. The process of Service Level Management is seen as a management-layer process. In support of the Service Level Management process, as described in phase 1, we use the 'SLA Specification Method'. This method starts by determining, on the basis of the customer business process, the desired IT services. Requirements can be specified for each service. The requirements specified for services can be classified in a number of fixed 'SLA components'. For example, these can concern availability, performance or support. Within Service Level Management, requirements and specifications are translated into norms, which are applied to the supporting processes and operational activities. For example, a requirement regarding availability of a service such as e-mail will be translated into availability norms for workstation, servers and networks. By making use of a matrix, which lays out the relationship between the SLA components on the one hand and the supporting and operational activities on the other, it is possible to derive the management functions that have to be organized. This is the responsibility of the general company management function, which can also be found at this level (Figure 12.4).

FIGURE 12.4

The model 'Managing the delivery of business information'

This figure is the developed framework of Figure 12.3 but has been rotated for readability.

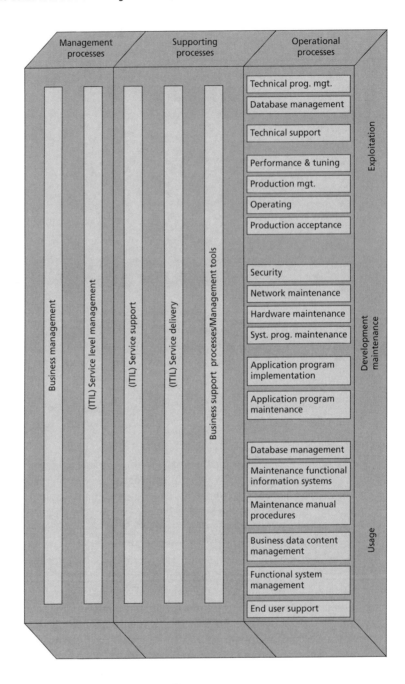

The organization

Regardless of the organizational structure, the form chosen for the management-level processes and the supporting processes is vital. This is often implemented as follows: the customer is assigned a contact person (customer liaison) within the IT organization for making service agreements (e.g. a Service or Contract Manager). Within the IT organization the Service Manager ensures that the agreements made are embedded in the organization and carried out. The Service Manager does this by making it clear, to all parties concerned, what is expected of them and monitoring the process (Figure 12.5).

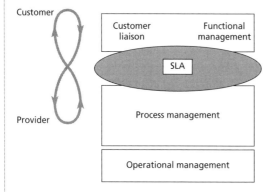

FIGURE 12.5 The liaison between the IT department and its customer

In addition, within the IT organization process, managers are responsible for the organization of the supporting processes. They ensure that the agreements made are translated into norms that are applied to the process in question. They report to the Service Manager responsible who, in turn, informs the customer. In large organizations these activities are found in a Service Management department. In smaller organizations these process managers will devote part of their time to this assignment. This can work very well, provided that the persons involved distinguish between the various responsibilities and tasks they have to carry out and act accordingly (Figure 12.6).

FIGURE 12.6 The liaison in detail

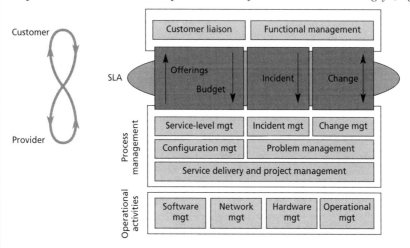

More recently, it is becoming increasingly common to see some of the Information Technology tasks being contracted out. The activities that are primarily involved in such cases are the operational activities at the lowest level in the model representing 'managing the delivery of business information'. Examples of these are application development activities and management activities with regard to technical infrastructure. Of course, this has consequences for the internal IT department: staff who previously carried out these activities become 'superfluous' or are transferred, 'together with their work', to the IT service provider. On the other hand, this also leads to new positions. The activities that have been contracted out must be guided and monitored, especially if they involve a situation in which several suppliers each provide a part of the total service package supplied by the IT department to its customers (Figure 12.7). In such a case, we see that the role of the management- and supporting-layer processes becomes increasingly evident. Depending on the frequency with which such activities occur, it can even develop into a kind of 'service brokerage'. On the one hand, agreements will be made with customers regarding the IT support to be provided and, on the other, providers will be sought who can play a role in providing the services.

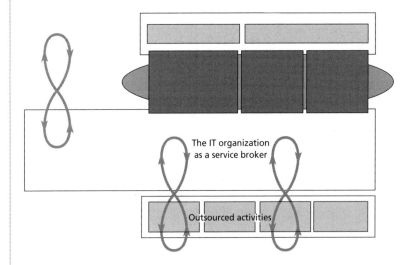

FIGURE 12.7

The IT organization and its suppliers: outsourcing

Phase 3: Monitoring and evaluating the management processes

Phase 3 includes activities such as Measurement/registration, Reporting, and Judging/evaluating. Together with phase 2, phase 3 activities such as Deciding, Modifying/Changing, and Determination of requirements/norms form the quality control cycle of Service Process Management. The emphasis in phase 3 is on measuring. In this section, we describe a framework for measuring. This framework enables us to introduce the various aspects of measuring, such as attributes, units, type of measurement scale etc. and to relate them to each other. It also enables us to indicate how we can use measuring systems to describe and predict characteristics of products and processes and how we can verify these predictions.

A framework for measuring

The framework for measuring as described here is derived from the 'structural model for measurement' (Figure 12.8; Kitchenham *et al.*, 1995). This framework contains seven components, namely:

- **Entity**: an object in the 'real world' whose characteristics we would like to know or predict.
- **Attribute**: a characteristic or trait of an entity. Different entities can have the same attribute and an entity can have various attributes. The relation involved is thus of the 'n to m' type.
- **Attribute relation**: between different attributes of one or more entities.
- **Value**: that which is 'measured' and recorded of an attribute.
- **Unit**: the measuring unit of the 'value'.

FIGURE 12.8 The structural model for measurement

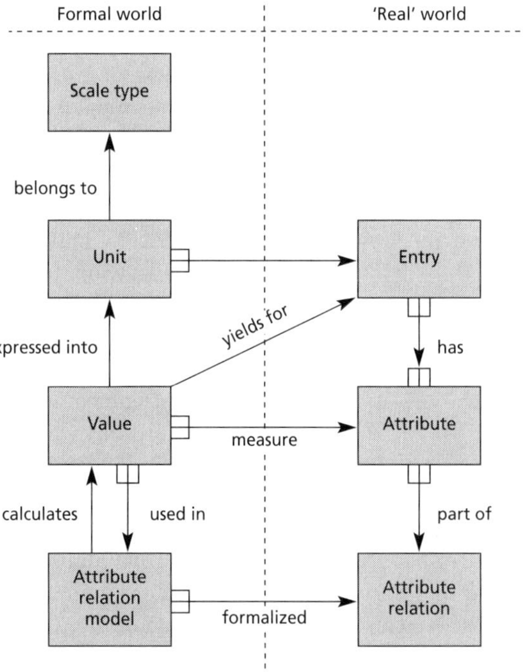

- **Scale type**: the type to which the 'unit' belongs. The following scale types can be distinguished (going from weak to strong):
    - nominal: attributes are only classified;
    - ordinal: a (linear) ranking order is indicated with regard to the possible values of an attribute;
    - interval: as for ordinal, but in addition the 'distance' between two successive values is equal;
    - ratio: as for interval, but in addition the value of 'zero' exists for the attribute;
    - absolute: only the number of times something occurs is counted.

Attribute relation model: a formal model in which the relations are determined that exist in the 'real world' between various attributes of possibly different entities. This model calculates (predicts) the value of an attribute in which we are interested using the values of other attributes in the relational model.

Measuring can be described as the 'assignment' of a number (or symbol) to an entity in an empirical and objective manner in order to characterize a specific attribute. We assign a value to an attribute of an entity. This assigning is called 'measuring'. The value assigned has, of course, a certain unit, and the unit belongs to a particular measurement scale. The term 'measurement system' here is considered to be composed of:

- an attribute of an entity;
- the function which assigns a value to an attribute;
- the unit in which the value is expressed;
- the type of measurement scale.

Measurement systems are divided into direct and indirect systems. In the case of a direct system, the function mentioned above is a measurement. In the case of an indirect system, the function is identical to the relation determined in the attribute relation model and the value is calculated using the values of several other attributes.

Measurable agreements

As an example, we have an SLA that relates to software maintenance and we want to distinguish between the seriousness of errors. We want to make this distinction because errors in one particular category must be solved more quickly than errors in other categories. This means that for every error (entity) we must determine (measure/register) how great the seriousness (attribute) of the matter is. We can agree that the level of seriousness may assume three different values, for example 'not critical', 'critical' and 'very critical'. These values lie on an ordinal scale and the exact description of the labels not critical, critical and very critical functions as the unit for the values measured. The descriptions of these terms must be precise and unequivocal enough so that it is possible to assign each error objectively to one of the three categories. Of course, we also have to define precisely what an error is. Often we will also measure attributes indirectly: to determine the value of an attribute we make use of several other attributes. We can, for example, measure the availability of a help desk by dividing the number of missed calls by the number of calls answered. Of course, we also have to determine how to classify the telephone calls into the two categories of 'missed' and 'answered'. The attribute relation model makes clear how we can calculate the value of an attribute in which we are interested (availability) by using the values of the other attributes (number of missed calls and answered calls). In doing this, we should realize that the measurement systems used should be a correct representation of the actual entities and attributes. If, for example, the help desk can be reached via e-mail as well as by telephone, the above-mentioned measure of availability is of course not complete. This requirement – if the measured availability in month x is less than in month y, then the actual availability in month x must also be less than in month y – is called the representation condition.

Phase 4: Monitoring and evaluating the SLAs

The last phase of the IT Service Management Lemniscate model closes the double cycle of providing services. After agreements have been made, processes set up and implemented, and the agreements made continuously monitored for compliance in the earlier phases, in this last phase the service level provided is judged and evaluated. The basis for this is formed by a report of the service actually provided. This is compared with the agreements made in the SLA. If necessary, this evaluation will be used to fine-tune or modify the agreements. For each service provided, requirements will be specified which can be measured. For example, with respect to the 'ability to create invoices', the requirement applies that the invoices must be ready each day by a specified time so that they can be forwarded in a timely fashion. The requirements specified for IT services can be classified in several fixed SLA components: Availability, Integrity, Exclusiveness, Calamities, Performance, Training, User Support and Change Management. If we assume that the agreements made in the SLA regarding these components are clear and effective, then we can also assume that the report to be made must also deal with these components. The Service Level Report (SLR) will then have a structure that largely corresponds to the SLA components agreed upon from the SLA. The only relevant addition is an extra column containing the measured and/or established value of the SLA component. If all the previous activities have been properly structured, then the evaluation is a simple affair. On the basis of agreements, which can be properly measured, the customer and supplier both know exactly what to expect of each other and misunderstandings can be prevented. If the supplier structures the organization in such a manner that the supplier can comply with the agreements made and regularly monitors and guides this process, then the supplier has the tools in house to deliver on the agreements made. If the supplier is not able to satisfy expectations, the measurements will at any rate provide insight into how this occurred, allowing the supplier to get a handle on the situation and ensure that the agreements will be complied with in the following period.

Literature

Kitchenham, B., Pfleeger, S. L., and Fenton, N., (1995) 'Towards a framework for software measurement validation', in *IEEE Trans. on Software Engineering*, 21(12):929–944, December 1995.

Looijen, M., (1998) *Information Systems – Management, Control and Maintenance*, ISBN 90-267-2846-8, Deventer: Kluwer.

Mintzberg, H., (1992) *Structure in Fives: Designing Effective Organizations*, ISBN 01-385-5479-X, Upper Saddle River: Prentice Hall.

13 MIP: managing the information provision

Dirk Jan van der Hoven HIT B.V.
Guido Hegger KPN
Jan van Bon Inform-IT, the Netherlands

Summary

Here, you will find a process model for management of internal provision of information. This model states how the information needs of organizational processes can be translated into IT facilities which can be used in the organization. In considering internal provision of information, service is of the essence. The model is defined in terms of processes and acts as a stepping stone for discussions concerning many other process models used for fleshing out IT management.

13.1 Introduction

In recent years, the approach to IT management has taken a turn for the better. Until the early 1990s, the focus was on developing applications, and building systems and networks. Models such as ITIL, ISM and IPW helped lay more emphasis on continuous delivery and adjustment of IT facilities for the customer organization. The model for management of internal provision (MIP) of information builds on that thought. The purpose of the model is to:

- create insight into the interrelationships of the processes involved in provision of information, by narrowing down the complexity to a few process groups;
- create an understanding with which to achieve the provision of information.

The model was set up because of the existing need for a model that provides clear insight into the relationship between various organizational processes and their support, by means of simple IT facilities. It can be used for putting the IT organization into practice, determining the players in the 'management' field and in applying various other models for fleshing out IT management. In fact, MIP 'recycles' ITIL for the purpose of functional management (solving functionality incidents, changing functionality, etc.). So where MIP provides added value is in the separation and management of information, copy, type and functionality (specification) – in other words, better modulated configuration management. In doing so, the management/planning and control cycle of: Change (planning + changing) and Rest (exploitation + evaluation) is applied at every level. It is important to pass on and control the necessary changes from the higher levels down to the lower levels, through the configuration abstraction levels, in a structured and controlled manner.

13.2 Overview

The model consists of three main process groups:

- Business Processes;
- Information Management;
- Information Technology Management.

The organization requires information in order to plan and control its services and activities and to apply resources. Deployment of IT facilities (application software, office applications, data storage processing tools, etc.) provides this information. In order to obtain an optimal connection between business processes and various IT facilities, it is necessary for the information needs in an organization to be managed in a structured manner. Therefore, three main groups are created in the management model (Figure 13.1). With regard to the primary processes, the management model remains limited to the indication of connecting levels that are necessary to be able to determine the information needs and to deliver IT facilities in the supporting field. To ensure an optimum link between the IT facility, IT products and services and the business process, insight is required into the principal organization objects, functions and processes group. This insight enables continuous identification, specification, completion and provision of the information needed for the business process. Within the Information Management process, objects and information needed from those objects are maintained in structured information models and specified, where possible, on a component basis to the IT service provider, so that they can be incorporated into the IT facilities portfolio. These main groups can each be further decomposed to Strategic, Tactical and Operational processes.

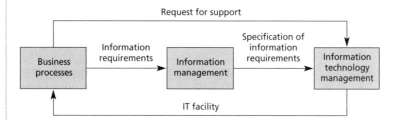

FIGURE 13.1
Main management model groups

This division produces the 3 × 3 matrix for management of the information provision (Figure 13.2). The main task of management of the information provision is to deliver, through IT facilities, the right messages, in the right context, at the right moment, to the right business function in order to support it in the planning and control of its activities and services. All other processes aim to ensure that the implementation runs smoothly. The IT facility is provided by the *IT Facilities Delivery and Maintenance* process group. This process group ensures that the facility is available to the users in accordance with agreements. If the existing facilities are no longer adequate, they will be altered or extended to include new facilities. The purpose of *Functional Support for Use* (or *application*) of the *IT Facilities* process group is to allow users to fully utilize the IT facilities on offer. This process supports colleagues carrying out business processes by helping them with the use of IT facilities and the translation of information requirements into automation terms. The process group *Information Requirements Management* exists on a tactical level. All of the organization's information requirements are managed here. The *Business process management* poses information questions. The *Information Requirements Management* process analyses these questions, compares them to existing information requirements and assigns them a priority (according to information planning guidelines from the Information Policy). Finally, it specifies the information requirements that require fleshing out. The specified information requirements are passed on to the *IT Facilities Management* process. This process explores the ways in which the information requirements can be achieved, the consequences (if any) and the price of meeting those requirements. Furthermore, this process involves the setting-up of agreements concerning the delivery of the IT facilities, in the form of service level agreements (SLAs), and it controls the service with respect to these IT facilities. Standards for this process are set by means of the *Information Technology Policy* process. The strategic framework is determined in the *Information Policy* and *Information Technology Policy* process groups. The input for these processes is the *Business Policy* of the organization, in the form of a business plan for instance. Examples of this framework include prioritization in new facilities development, choices in development methods (e.g. data- or process-oriented) and supplier choices.

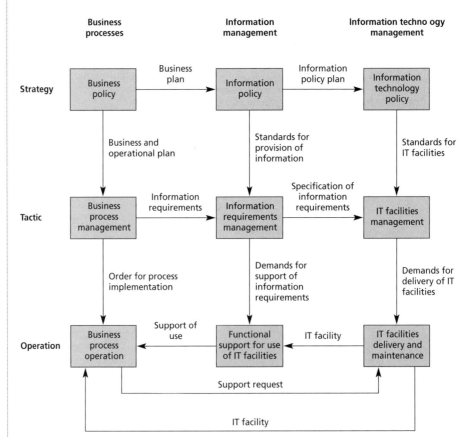

FIGURE 13.2

The 3 × 3 matrix for management of the information provision

13.3 Business processes

In the 'Managing the Information Provision' model, the processes which are relevant to the production of the IT facilities are highlighted in the centre and right-hand columns. All remaining business processes can be found in the left-hand column. Of these remaining business processes, only the interfaces with processes for provision of information are considered:

1. Objectives for the organization are set down on the basis of the Business Policy. These objectives act as input when setting up an Information Policy and Plan. In most cases, the most significant document in this framework will be the business plan.

2. Tactical Management (business process management) indicates the information which is necessary in order to control and implement a business process efficiently.

3. From the Operation (business process operation) arises the request for support of the execution of a business process. One solution to this demand is to provide information by means of an IT facility, but another is to provide some training or alternative solutions. Only the principal inputs and outputs of the described processes are dealt with. In almost all cases, it is a matter of full interaction instead of a one-way flow.

13.4 Information management

The Information Management process group translates the demands brought forward in the business processes into requirements or tasks that can be met with IT facilities. Given the questions of those responsible for a process and given the information plan, the most important step is that of prioritizing the requests for information facilities.

Information policy

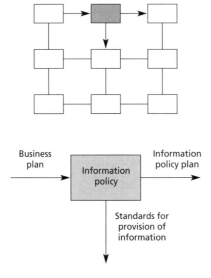

FIGURE 13.3

Information policy

Process outline/activities

This process translates the organization's objectives and strategy into standards and plans for the information infrastructure. It also draws up guidelines that the adjoining processes should comply with.

Output process

- The Information Policy Plan contain a framework which determines whether or not requests for IT facilities should be honoured. This framework can be set up as a blueprint for the information infrastructure. In more dynamic situations, it is more likely that a structure will be set up, which determines the urgency and priority on a case-to-case basis.

- The Information Policy provides guidelines for the way in which information requirements are to be modelled. An important guideline in this framework could be that the needs should suit the corporate data model. The long-term vision and priorities of automation are captured in the Information Plan.

Information requirements management

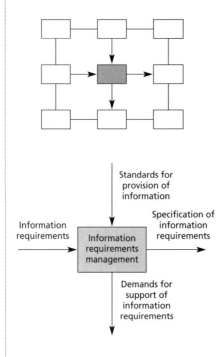

FIGURE 13.4 Information requirements management

13 ■ MIP: managing the information provision

Process outline

This process looks at ways in which the information requirements of the organization processes can be fulfilled. In doing so, the various requirements are interrelated, and which requirements are suitable or unsuitable for automation are determined on the basis of the Information Policy. Requirements which are suitable for automation are then modelled and specified in greater detail.

Activities

This process focuses on carrying out information analysis and analysis of the processes that are necessary in order to collect and record the information. The information analysis not only concentrates on the information required for a specific question, but that information is then also analysed in relation to other (existing) databanks. A corporate information model is of great value to the successful implementation of this process. After it is determined which information is necessary, and which processes can be used to collect and record information, it is possible to determine, on the basis of the Information Policy, whether these requirements are of sufficient priority to be supported by an automated tool. If this is the case, the requirements are then specified in greater detail so as to be translated into an IT facility.

Output process

1 *Information requirements specification*

The functional specification consists of a description of the data (entities, attributes and relationships), the necessary transactions using this data, and the presentation of it. The transactions are specified in functions, control and behaviour in time, process rules and organization. It is possible to limit the specification of the transactions to that of facilities with which the user can define the transaction. The necessary behaviour and support is specified in relation to the transactions and the general IT facilities:

– availability and performance;
– technical support and delivery.

2 *Demands for information requirements support*

The following demands are made for Functional Support for Use of IT Facilities:

– business help desk opening hours and response times;
– handling method and times for user incidents;
– demands for user training;
– handling method and times for amendments;
– the deployment and use of facilities in order to be able to adapt functionality, communication and presentation;
– handling method and times for production orders.

Functional support for use of IT facility

FIGURE 13.5
Information requirements support

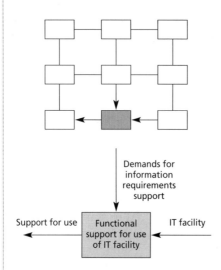

Process outline

This process provides *Business Processes Operation* with direct support in the use of IT facilities. The process in operation poses questions regarding the functionality of the service and simple change requests to *Functional Support for Use of IT Facilities*. Functional questions are answered here. Requests for change (delivery of standard copies, simple queries and the like) are transformed into orders for *IT Facilities Delivery and Maintenance*. Requests for change relating to information are transferred to *Information Requirements Management* and decided upon after consulting with management.

Activities

Incident management
- to accept and register 'functional incidents';
- to diagnose incidents (is the user unsure about how to use the service, or does the service fail to work?);
- to help the user find a solution through giving advice;
- to report an incident in the IT facility to the IT facility's incident management;
- to monitor fault progression.

Problem management
- to classify registered functional incidents and problems;
- to investigate the causes of functional incidents and problems;
- to develop suggestions for removing the causes. For example, these suggestions could be functionality changes, user interface improvements or organizing training.

13 ■ MIP: managing the information provision

● *Change management*
- to deal directly with requests for functionality communication and presentation changes (building queries, modifying screens and fields, etc.);
- to hand out orders for simple changes (quick services);
- to implement new functionality in the user organization (acceptance tests, training, data conversion etc.).

● *Operation*
- training;
- report production;
- to provide and/or deal with processing orders;
- to maintain core data and user settings.

This process is very similar to the *IT facilities Delivery and Maintenance* process (functionality versus technology) and should be completed coherently.

13.5 Information technology management

In the process group *Information Technology Management*, the existing services are kept in existence according to set service levels, developing new services if necessary.

Information technology policy

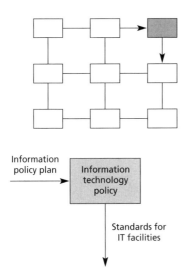

FIGURE 13.6
Information technology policy

Process outline/activities

Based upon the Information Policy, knowledge of information technology, new technological advances and existing IT facilities, this process creates standards and plans for management and development of the IT facilities.

Output process

The standards concern:

- current and desired system architecture;
- current and desired data structure (what data where);
- current and desired infrastructure;
- management methods (e.g. ITIL, IPW, ISM);
- development methods;
- hardware and software to be used;
- generic set-up and quality parameters for service levels;
- guidelines in accordance with the decision of how and when new technology is to be used.

IT facilities management

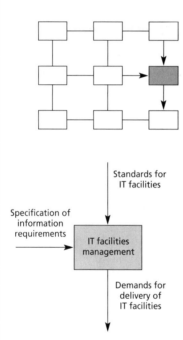

FIGURE 13.7 IT facility management

Process outline

IT Facilities Management meets information requirements with IT facilities, according to the same architecture as was specified for that process. After IT facilities have been defined, this process ensures that the facilities continue to be provided according to the agreed service levels.

Activities

The *IT Facilities Management* and *IT Facilities Delivery and Maintenance* processes contain tactical and operational processes, as documented in the ITIL/IPW/ISM standards. The most significant activity in this process is the integration of several components into a single IT facility which meets the information requirements. The components include technical infrastructure, application software and processes, and services. The various components will often be delivered by various internal and external parties.

Output process

Agreements and reports for the benefit of Information Requirements Management.

The way in which the information requirements are met with IT facilities is specified in a service level agreement by means of *Information Requirements Management*. This agreement specifies:

- functionality (which operations should be executed with what data?);
- behaviour (the where, what and when of data);
- support (batch processing, fault fixing, implementation of changes and the like).

Specifications for the purpose of IT Facilities Delivery and Maintenance
Specifications are given for each individual component belonging to the IT facility, regarding:

- functionality;
- behaviour;
- support.

Naturally, the agreements with the suppliers of various components should provide sufficient guarantees that the agreements concerning the entire IT facility can be met.

IT facilities deliveries and maintenance

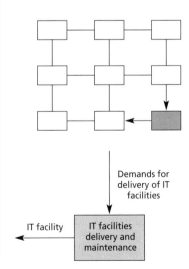

FIGURE 13.8
IT facilities delivery and maintenance

Process outline

This process provides the *Business Process Operation* processes with IT facilities directly and through *Functional Support for Use of IT Facilities*. This is determined via the *IT Facilities Management* process. The process structure can be based on ITIL, IPW and ISM.

Activities

The actual delivery takes place on the basis of the IT facility agreed upon in the *IT Facilities Management* process. Therefore, the primary activity is to maintain the IT facilities as they were initially agreed upon. However, it is possible that the delivery of an IT facility no longer meets the agreed service level. The incident process is then triggered. This process drives the service back to the required level as quickly as agreed. If necessary, the underlying causes of the disruption can then be investigated in the Problem Handling process. Finally, the Change process makes alterations to the IT facilities agreed upon so as to ensure that the IT facility remains in keeping with the organization processes. In this respect, introduction of a new IT facility would be considered as an initial change. Such major changes usually take place in the context of a project; however, naturally, they do remain part of a process. Regarding the Change processes, an important distinction is made regarding the IPW model. Recent versions of the IPW model mention 'development and maintenance (projects)' and 'implementation management'. In the above process model, these processes have been replaced with 'implementation of type changes' and 'implementation of copy changes'. Both processes are applicable to either software changes or hardware changes, or another component of the information system. It is of critical importance that only tried and tested copies are installed in the production environment. If there is a type available that is certified in this manner, it is possible to implement copies of that type directly. If not, a new type or version of an existing type should be developed first.

Output process

- *IT copies*
  - hardware, systems software, network, databases, and application software copies provided by the production environment to users which, individually and/or collectively, deliver the agreed functionality and behaviour.

- *IT support*
  - handling change requests through to delivery of existing or yet to be developed IT copies;
  - execution of operations orders;
  - handling and solving IT incidents.

13.6 Conclusions

The MIP model's 3 × 3 matrix (see Figure 13.2 again) provides a foundation for management issues such as:

- installation and connection of IT management processes and organizations;
- outsourcing;
- suitability and cover of other methods.

The comparison between other process models and MIP provides a context for those models. In this way, the operational ITIL processes from the Service Support set can be found in the *IT Facilities Delivery and Maintenance* unit at the bottom right. The tactical ITIL processes from the Service Delivery set are placed in the process unit at the centre right: *IT facilities management* and the strategic ITIL processes from the Managers set are placed in the process unit at the top right: *Information Technology Policy*. Assigning a destination to elements from the triple maintenance model (Looijen) and process models such as ITPM, IPW and ISM (refer to the relevant contributions elsewhere in this volume) is also fairly straightforward. Note that ITIL's Problem Management is qualified as a tactical process in ISM, and as an operational process in ITIL and IPW. The MIP model does not imply anything about the organization. It does outline the processes (process groups) which require fleshing out. Therefore, entirely in keeping with ISM's organization paradigm, MIP only fleshes out the process infrastructure (see Figure 13.9).

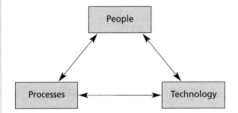

FIGURE 13.9
ISM's organization paradigm

14 Microsoft Operations Framework (MOF)

Dave Pultorak
Pultorak & Associates Ltd, USA

Summary

Any book on world-class IT Service Management today would be incomplete without Microsoft's perspective. Business people and IT practitioners are becoming increasingly reliant on Microsoft's products and technologies as a foundation for mission-critical IT services. Given this, and given Microsoft's market presence and installed base of products and technologies, virtually all business people and IT practitioners need to understand Microsoft's vision for IT Service Management.

Microsoft Operations Framework (MOF) is Microsoft's vision for IT Service Management. MOF is composed of three core models – process, team and risk – that incorporate principles and practices that business people and IT practitioners need in order to manage IT service delivery and infrastructure effectively on the Microsoft platform. MOF '… provides comprehensive technical guidance for achieving mission-critical production system reliability, availability, supportability, and manageability on Microsoft's products and technologies.'[1] This chapter describes MOF.

14.1 Introduction

MOF is Microsoft's articulation of how to effectively operate solutions – developed applications or deployed infrastructure – based on Microsoft products and technologies. Before MOF, Microsoft articulated its operational guidance at the level of the individual product or technology. IT practitioners seeking to organize IT operations effectively around Microsoft products and technologies had to do the work of extracting Microsoft-specific guidance from these materials and mapping that guidance to an overarching framework such as ITIL. Without Microsoft's vision for IT operations, IT service providers who ran their businesses on the Microsoft platform struggled to assess and articulate where they were as organizations, where they wanted to go, and how they planned to get there, in a way that made 'the sky meet the road'.

With the introduction of Microsoft Operations Framework (MOF), all that has changed. Now at last we IT practitioners have Microsoft's strategic vision of how to operate their products and technologies effectively. This chapter introduces that vision: Microsoft Operations Framework.

What MOF is

Microsoft Operations Framework (MOF) is Microsoft's vision for IT Service Management. It is Microsoft's guidance for managing production systems (developed application and deployed infrastructure solutions) within today's complex distributed IT environments.[2] It is important to note that MOF is an extension of, and not a replacement for, the generally accepted industry best practices spelled out in ITIL. Microsoft built MOF on the 'common sense' language and guidance of ITIL, promoting industry alignment. While MOF provides guidance specific to Microsoft products and technologies, it is a model that IT practitioners can use across the entire enterprise, and across the distributed and heterogeneous IT infrastructures and services that are the hallmark of today's IT landscape.

MOF is composed of three core models – process, team and risk – that include the principles and practices that business people and IT practitioners need in order to manage IT operations effectively on the Microsoft platform. MOF '... provides comprehensive technical guidance for achieving mission-critical production system reliability, availability, supportability, and manageability on Microsoft's products and technologies'.[3]

What MOF is not

It is important for IT practitioners to understand not just what MOF is, but what it is not. It is not different from ITIL; rather, it builds on and extends ITIL. It is not just for Microsoft-centric environments, or applicable only to Microsoft products and technologies. While MOF does contain specific guidance for Microsoft products and technologies, IT practitioners can apply MOF across the entire enterprise for managing IT service delivery and infrastructure. Perhaps most importantly for IT practitioners, MOF is not an attempt to create a proprietary IT Service Management framework specific to Microsoft products and technologies. It is instead a bridge between generally accepted standard IT Service Management best practices so well articulated in ITIL, and the everyday realities and specifics of operating an IT platform that includes Microsoft products and technologies.

Why Microsoft created MOF

Microsoft created MOF to address the growing dependence of businesses on mission-critical IT systems, and the increasing use of Microsoft products and technologies for such systems. Studies indicated that the quality of service achieved by customers on the same products and technologies varied as a function of how well those customers organized to operate those products and technologies. To address this need, Microsoft felt it was important to articulate a framework for operations best practices, and subsequently create MOF. They chose to base MOF on ITIL best practices because they felt that ITIL captures the discipline of IT operations well. In addition, they recognized the growing significance of systems that run across organizational boundaries, and the fact that these systems and the organizations that depend on them could benefit from the common organizational architecture that adopting and adapting ITIL provides.[4]

How MOF relates to other Microsoft Enterprise Services frameworks

MOF is one of three Microsoft Enterprise Services frameworks, each of which provides guidance for a distinct part of the IT life cycle as follows:[5]

- Microsoft Readiness Framework (MRF) focuses on preparing individuals and organizations to use Microsoft products and technologies.
- Microsoft Solutions Framework (MSF) focuses on solution development, including both developed applications and deployed infrastructure.
- Microsoft Operations Framework (MOF) focuses on the management of production IT operations, i.e. the effective operation of developed applications and deployed infrastructure.

How MOF relates to ITIL

Microsoft recognizes that the IT Infrastructure Library (ITIL)[6] captures current industry best practices for IT Service Management well.[7] MOF builds on ITIL, and does the work of adapting ITIL with specific guidelines for using Microsoft's products and technologies.[8] MOF also extends the ITIL code of practice to support distributed IT environments and emerging IT solutions such as application hosting, mobile-device computing, and Web-based transaction and e-commerce systems. MOF is intended for business people and IT practitioners who run their businesses on a Microsoft platform, who need to interoperate with other technology platforms, and who depend on systems that run across organizational boundaries. Consequently, it includes specific guidelines for running on the Microsoft platform in a variety of business scenarios.[9]

Like ITIL, IT practitioners from around the world developed MOF. The difference is that in the case of MOF the practitioners were individuals focused largely on operating solutions centred on Microsoft products and technologies, such as practitioners from Microsoft's customers, partners, internal IT groups, and consulting services.

The ITIL philosophy includes the notions that organizations should adopt and adapt ITIL, not just apply it 'off-the-shelf' without customizing it to the organization and its IT infrastructure. Accordingly, Microsoft adopted and adapted ITIL, and the result is MOF.

The sections that follow will illustrate the fact that MOF is essentially an extension of ITIL. If you are familiar with the ITIL Service Delivery and Service Support modules, you will recognize all of these modules as represented in the MOF Process Model (see Figure 14.2). MOF refers to these modules as Service Management Functions (SMFs).

Three core models constitute MOF: The MOF Process Model, mentioned above, and two complementary models, namely, the MOF Team Model and the MOF Risk Model. The section that follows provides an overview of these three core models and how they help IT practitioners achieve operations success in today's complex distributed IT environment.

14.2 The three MOF core models that constitute MOF: tools for achieving operations success in today's complex distributed IT environment

So how does one manage production systems in today's complex distributed IT environment? What is needed is:

1 the right service solutions (developed applications and deployed infrastructure), released and operated using disciplined IT processes,

2 by skilled qualified people who know the processes and their role relative to them,

3 who systematically work to reduce or eliminate risks that would threaten the release and ongoing production operation of service solutions.

These needs map directly to the three core models that constitute MOF, as follows (Diagrams of these models are shown in Figure 14.1):

1	*The right service solutions (developed applications and deployed infrastructure), released and operated using disciplined IT processes*
	The MOF Process Model frames the processes that operations teams perform to manage and maintain IT services
2	*By skilled qualified people who know the processes and their role relative to them*
	The MOF Team Model frames team roles vital to IT operations, including key activities and competencies of those teams, and how to organize those teams effectively, including how to scale the team roles for different sizes and types of organizations
3	*Who systematically work to reduce or eliminate risks that would threaten the release and ongoing production operation of service solutions*
	The MOF Risk Model frames a risk management approach specifically tailored to IT practitioners in organizations that run their businesses on Microsoft products and technologies

Together, the three models provide a strategic framework detailing the processes and organizational roles required to minimize risk and achieve high systems availability, reliability, supportability and manageability in IT operations environments built on Microsoft products and technologies.

The three sections that follow outline the MOF Process Model, Team Model and Risk Model, respectively.

The MOF Process Model

The MOF Process Model (Figure 14.2) frames the processes that operations teams perform to manage and maintain IT services. It provides a simplified, generalized way to think about complex distributed IT environments.[10]

If you are familiar with the ITIL Service Delivery and Service Support modules, you will recognize these ten modules among the MOF Process Model Service Management

FIGURE 14.1

The three core models that constitute MOF: tools for achieving operations success in today's complex distributed IT environment

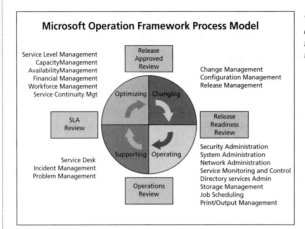

The right service solutions (developed applications and deployed infrastructure), released and operated using disciplined IT processes,

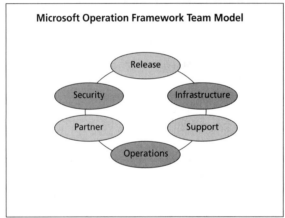

by skilled qualified people who know the processes and their role relative to them,

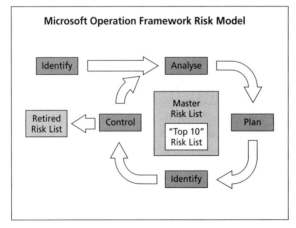

who systematically work to reduce or eliminate risks that would threaten the release and ongoing production operation of service solutions.

FIGURE 14.2

Microsoft Operations Framework Process Model

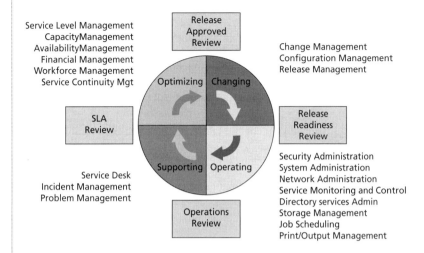

Functions (SMFs) (see Figure 14.5, 'New and deeper SMFs' for additional details). MOF refers to these modules as Service Management Functions (SMFs).

You can think of the MOF process model of an extension and high-order reorganization of the ITIL Service Delivery and Service Support process modules. The section of this chapter entitled 'MOF contributions to IT Service Management' provides an overview of the key features of the MOF process model and how it extends ITIL. For now, please note that:

- The MOF Process Model features 20 SMFs grouped into four quadrants of concurrent operations activity, with each quadrant having a specific mission of service, and an explicit review that evaluates the performance of that quadrant's activities (see Table 14.1 [11]).

- The life cycle of a release of service solution (developed application or deployed infrastructure), including its introduction and ongoing maintenance and operation, is central to the MOF Process Model and symbolized by the arrows on the face of the diagram.

TABLE 14.1 MOF Process Model quadrants

Quadrant	Mission of service	Review
Changing	Introduce new service solutions, technologies, systems, applications, hardware, and processes	Release readiness
Operating	Execute day-to-day tasks effectively and efficiently	Operations
Supporting	Resolve incidents, problems and inquiries quickly	Service level agreement
Optimizing	Drive changes to optimize cost, performance, capacity and availability in the delivery of IT services	Release approved

The MOF Team Model

The MOF Team Model (figure 14.3) frames the team roles associated with operations activity. Microsoft included the Team Model as a tool for ensuring that the people engaged in operational activity are well organized and coordinated.[12]

FIGURE 14.3
Microsoft Operations Framework Team Model

If you are familiar with the Microsoft Solutions Framework, you will recognize that the MOF Team Model is similar to the MSF Team Model. In fact, Microsoft created the MOF team model based in part on lessons learned from MSF.[13] The difference is one of focus – the MSF Team Model focuses on development team roles and goals, whereas the MOF Team Model focuses on operations activity.

The six roles of the MOF Team Model correspond to the key quality goals as shown in Table 14.2.[14]

TABLE 14.2
The six roles of the MOF Team Model

Team role	Quality goal
Release	Effective planning and implementation of releases and changes
Infrastructure	Effective management of physical environments and infrastructure tools
Support	Timely, efficient and accurate customer support
Operations	Predictable, repeatable and automated system management
Security	Protection of corporate assets, controlled authorization and proactive security planning
Partner	Mutually beneficial relationships with service and supply partners

It is important to note that these roles are groups of activities that share a common goal and process ownership, which is not necessarily (or even usually) the same as functional organization. As such, Team Model roles are not intended as functional job descriptions, and the Team Model is not intended as an organizational chart.[15] Actual functional titles and organizational charts will vary widely by organization and team, and a number of people may be involved in performing a role, or one person may perform multiple roles, depending on the scale and requirements of the organization.[16]

The MOF Team Model describes:[17]

- best-practice role clusters to structure operations teams;
- the key activities and competencies of each role cluster;
- how to scale the teams for different sizes and types of organizations;
- which roles can be effectively combined;
- guiding principles that help run and operate distributed computing environments on the Microsoft platform;
- how the MOF team relates to the other Enterprise Services team models.

Communication is at the centre of the MOF Team Model by design, as effective communications is a key component of an effective and efficient IT operations organization.[18]

The MOF Risk Model

The MOF Risk Model (figure 14.4) is a framework for managing risks in an operations environment. Microsoft included the Risk Model in MOF to provide a tool to ensure that:

- proactive risk-management practices are embedded into every IT operations role and process;
- IT operations staff apply proven risk-management techniques to the problems they face every day.[19]

If you are familiar with the Microsoft Solutions Framework, you will recognize that the MOF Risk Model is similar to the MSF Risk Model. In fact, the MOF Risk Model is based on the MSF Risk Model. As with the MOF and MSF Team Models, the difference between the MOF and MSF Risk Models is one of focus. Whereas the MSF Team Model focuses on risks associated with development projects, the MOF Team Model focuses on the risks specific to operations activity.

The five steps in the risk model are as follows:[20]

- **Step 1: identify.** Determine the source of risk, mode of failure, condition, operational consequence, and business consequence.
- **Step 2: analyse.** Determine the risk's probability and impact, and use these to calculate an exposure value to help rank risks against each other.
- **Step 3: plan.** Define mitigations that avoid the risk entirely, transfer it to another party, or reduce the impact or probability or both. Define contingencies to execute if the risk occurs. Define triggers that indicate the risk is about to occur.

FIGURE 14.4 Microsoft Operations Framework Risk Model

- **Step 4: track.** Gather information about how various elements of the risk are changing over time.
- **Step 5: control.** Execute a planned reaction to certain changes. For example, if a trigger value becomes true, execute the contingency plan. If a risk is no longer relevant, retire it. If the impact has changed, restart the cycle at step 2 (analyse) to re-evaluate the impact.

14.3 MOF contributions to IT Service Management

So far, we have discussed the three models that comprise MOF. We saw how the MOF Process Model is an extension of ITIL Service Delivery and Service Support process modules, and how the MOF Team Model and Risk Model complement the MOF Process Model. This discussion was intended as a very high-level introduction to the topic; please be sure to see the documents referenced in the endnotes of this chapter for further details.

Now we turn our attention to the contributions MOF makes to the literature and practice of IT Service Management.

MOF extends ITIL by including a number of innovations intended to help the IT practitioner better organize IT operations, including:

- new and deeper SMFs;
- new organizing concepts for IT operations processes;
- Team and Risk models;
- more prescriptive, relevant, and adaptable guidance.

The section that follows details these innovations.

New and deeper SMFs

New SMFs: workforce management, all operating quadrant SMFs

Figure 14.5 depicts the MOF Process Model with the new SMFs that it adds to the basic set that constitutes the ITIL Service Delivery and Service Support process modules.

MOF draws directly from ITIL for many of the Process Model Service Management Functions (SMFs). This is as it should be; ITIL is generally accepted best practice, meant to serve as a common language for the industry and 'adopted and adapted' as it is in MOF. MOF bases these SMFs on ITIL and extends them to include Microsoft-specific practices and additional industry best practices.[21]

MOF also extends ITIL by adding all the SMFs in the operating quadrant. These SMFs and their goals are as follows:[22]

- **Security administration.** Responsible for maintaining a safe computing environment by developing, implementing and managing security controls.
- **System administration.** Responsible for day-to-day tasks of keeping enterprise systems running, and for assessing the impact of planned releases.
- **Network administration.** Responsible for the design and maintenance of the physical components that make up the organization's network, such as servers, routers, switches and firewalls.

FIGURE 14.5
New and deeper SMFs

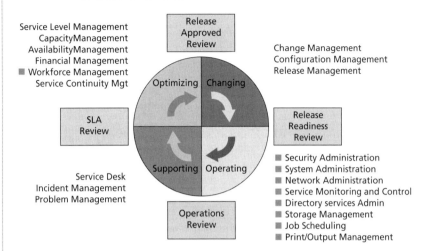

- **Service monitoring and control.** Observes the health of an IT service, and acts when necessary to maintain compliance.
- **Directory services administration.** Responsible for day-to-day operations, maintenance and support of the enterprise directory.
- **Storage management.** Deals with on-site and off-site data storage for the purposes of data restoration and historical archiving, and ensures the physical security of backups and archives.
- **Job scheduling.** Assigns batch processing tasks at different times to maximize the use of system resources while not compromising business and system functions.
- **Print/output management.** Manages the costs and resources associated with business output, and ensures security of sensitive output.

MOF adds one other SMF, namely workforce management, to the Optimizing quadrant, the goal of which is as follows:

- **Workforce management.** Recommends best practices to recruit, retain, maintain, and motivate the IT workforce.

While ITIL emphasizes the need for good workforce management across all operations processes, MOF highlights workforce management by explicitly promoting it to the status of an SMF.

Descriptions of the goals of SMFs that map directly to ITIL Service Delivery and Service Support process modules are omitted here in the interest of brevity. For detailed descriptions of these SMFs, see the MOF Process Model White Paper available at www.microsoft.com/mof.

The operating quadrant SMFs do not appear in ITIL, as ITIL is platform-independent. The operating quadrant is where MOF provides the majority of the operations guidance specific to Microsoft products and technologies.

Deeper SMFs

MOF not only adds SMFs, but adds depth to SMFs, as follows:

- deeper SMFs with guidance specific to Microsoft products and technologies (primarily in the operating quadrant) that automate or improve SMF delivery;
- deeper SMFs based on the experience of Microsoft, its partners and customers;
- deeper SMFs specific to Microsoft products through case studies, examples and toolkits.

New organizing concepts for IT operations processes

The MOF Process Model (Figure 14.6) introduces the following organizing concepts for IT Operations processes.

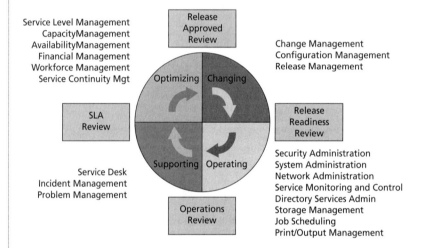

FIGURE 14.6 Microsoft Operations Framework Process Model

The service solution as the central 'unit of work'

MOF focuses on the service solution as the central 'unit of work': MOF organizes around the release and life cycle of a particular service solution, i.e. a particular developed application or deployed infrastructure, where as ITIL focuses at the level of IT operations as a whole. While the primary focus of MOF is on the specific service solution, MOF can also be applied at higher-order structures such as a data centre, an entire operations environment with multiple data centres, outsourced operations and hosted applications.

The fact that MOF focuses on the service solution as the central 'unit of work' is a significant innovation of MOF over ITIL. It allows for tighter integration with solution development frameworks such as MSF, since these frameworks focus on the service solution and its life cycle (in this case, the development, rather than the operational, phase of the service solution's life cycle).

Operations as quadrants of concurrent operational activity with explicit review activities

The MOF Process Model groups related SMFs into quadrants of concurrent operational activity, and orders that activity along a life cycle that links with development frameworks such as Microsoft Solutions Framework (MSF), encouraging 'design for operability'.

The grouping of SMFs into the Changing, Operating, Supporting, and Optimizing quadrants is significant because it recognizes that while operational processes operate concurrently, all service solutions move through operations along a life cycle continuum.

The MOF Process Model associates explicit review activities with each quadrant, including built-in explicit process review points in its process model; while ITIL can be used to assess IT operations, the ten core ITIL Service Support and Service Delivery modules include no such explicit checkpoints. The association of explicit review activities with these quadrants is a key innovation because it builds in specific checkpoints where IT practitioners can evaluate and 'tweak' IT processes.

A final organizing concept that MOF introduces is the placement of all MOF SMFs on a single diagram. As simple as this may seem, the fact that the entire MOF process model is represented on one diagram is important. MOF 'keeps it simple', an acknowledgement that overly complex models are difficult to implement in real-world operations environments.

Operations as ordered activity along a life cycle that links with development, encouraging 'design for operability'

'Design for operability' is an important concept. Too often developers develop solutions without involving operations staff up front, without having in the front of their minds how the solution will be operated once it goes 'live'. As a result, the solution can underperform or be 'high maintenance' once it goes into production. MOF is an important contribution to Microsoft's Enterprise Systems Frameworks because it explicitly articulates 'what's on the other side of the fence' for developers, providing developers with a target for designing their solutions with operations in mind.

Team and Risk Models to complement the Process Model

MOF introduces two additional models to complement the Process Model it has in common with ITIL, namely the Team Model and the Risk Model. If you are familiar with the Microsoft Solutions Framework (MSF), you know that MSF contains team and risk models as well.

Where ITIL identifies roles for process owner for each IT operations process, it does not identify roles commonly associated with clusters of related IT operations activity. This is the contribution of the MOF Team Model – a clearer mapping of roles, not just to processes, but also to common sets of operations activity.

Where ITIL embeds a discussion of handling risks in each IT operations process description, MOF elevates the management of risk to its own process model. This is meant to encourage IT operations managers to consider risk assessment an ongoing process, not a one-time event, and to integrate risk management into the day-to-day work of the IT operations staff.[23]

More prescriptive, relevant, adaptable operations guidance

MOF extends ITIL by providing more prescriptive ('how to') versus descriptive guidance, especially for the Operating quadrant SMFs.

MOF also extends ITIL by providing guidance beyond the traditional IT shop. The landscape for IT service providers, whether in-house or providing service as a business, has radically changed over the past few years. New technologies and new business trends have driven this change, which is grounded in the business use of the Internet, and the ongoing trend of both IT infrastructure and IT organizations increasingly becoming more and more distributed or 'virtual'. In templates, examples and sidebars, MOF provides content that speaks to the specific needs of IT service providers in this new landscape.

Lastly, MOF is available electronically. This makes customization to your particular situation very easy.

14.4 Acknowledgements

Microsoft Process Model for Operations, Microsoft Team Model for Operations, and Microsoft Risk Model for Operations diagrams are © 2001 Microsoft Corporation. All rights reserved.

The author would like to gratefully acknowledge the following individuals for the insight into MOF that they have provided him in preparing this chapter. Please note that any errors of either commission or omission are entirely those of the author.

Neal Fairhead, Product Manager, Microsoft Operations Framework

Bret Clark, Group Program Manager, MOF

Kathryn Rupchock, Lead Program Manager, MOF

Mark Short, Program Manager, Enterprise Services Framework Training

14.5 For more information

For more information on Microsoft's enterprise frameworks and offerings, see:
http://www.microsoft.com/mof
http://www.microsoft.com/msf
http://www.microsoft.com/es
A MOF course is in development. For course availability, see
http://www.microsoft.com/es
For more information on ITIL, see
http://www.itil.co.uk/

Notes

1 *Microsoft Operations Framework White Paper Executive Overview*, Microsoft Corporation, February 2001 version 2.0.
2 Adapted from *Microsoft Operations Framework White Paper Executive Overview*, Microsoft Corporation, February 2001 version 2.0.

3 *Microsoft Operations Framework White Paper Executive Overview*, Microsoft Corporation, February 2001 version 2.0.
4 Adapted from a conversation with the author in January 2001.
5 Adapted from *Microsoft Operations Framework White Paper Executive Overview*, Microsoft Corporation, February 2001 version 2.0.
6 ITIL is an IT service management best-practice framework intended as a tool for IT practitioners to increase business effectiveness and efficiency in the use of IT. ITIL is the international de facto standard framework for IT Service Management. It is a public domain framework developed by IT practitioner drawn from the public and private sectors around the globe under the auspices of the Central Computer and Telecommunications Agency (CCTA). The CCTA (now OGC) is a United Kingdom government executive agency chartered with development of best practice advice and guidance on the use of information technology in service management and operations.
7 *Microsoft Operations Framework White Paper Executive Overview*, Microsoft Corporation, February 2001 version 2.0.
8 Microsoft Operations Framework Datasheet, Microsoft Corporation.
9 Adapted from *Microsoft Operations Framework White Paper Executive Overview*, Microsoft Corporation, February 2001 version 2.0.
10 Adapted from *Microsoft Operations Framework White Paper Process Model for Operations*, Microsoft Corporation, January 2001 version 2.0.
11 *Microsoft Operations Framework White Paper Executive Overview*, Microsoft Corporation, February 2001 version 2.0.
12 Adapted from *Microsoft Operations Framework White Paper Executive Overview*, Microsoft Corporation, February 2001 version 2.0.
13 *Microsoft Operations Framework White Paper Executive Overview*, Microsoft Corporation, February 2001 version 2.0.
14 Adapted from *Microsoft Operations Framework White Paper Team Model for Operations*, Microsoft Corporation, November 2000 version 2.0.
15 Adapted from *Microsoft Operations Framework White Paper Team Model for Operations*, Microsoft Corporation, November 2000 version 2.0.
16 *Microsoft Operations Framework White Paper Executive Overview*, Microsoft Corporation, February 2001 version 2.0.
17 *Microsoft Operations Framework White Paper Team Model for Operations*, Microsoft Corporation, November 2000 version 2.0.
18 Adapted from *Microsoft Operations Framework White Paper Team Model for Operations*, Microsoft Corporation, November 2000 version 2.0.
19 Adapted from *Microsoft Operations Framework White Paper Risk Model for Operations*, Microsoft Corporation, December 2000 version 2.0.
20 *Microsoft Operations Framework White Paper Executive Overview*, Microsoft Corporation, February 2001 version 2.0.
21 Adapted from *Microsoft Operations Framework White Paper Process Model for Operations*, Microsoft Corporation, January 2001 version 2.0.
22 *Microsoft Operations Framework White Paper Executive Overview*, Microsoft Corporation, February 2001 version 2.0.
23 Adapted from *Microsoft Operations Framework White Paper Risk Model for Operations*, Microsoft Corporation, December 2000 version 2.0.

15 The SIMA: a practical approach to information technology management

Louis van Hemmen BitAll b.v.
Michiel Borgers Cap Gemini Ernst & Young
Rick Klompé Inter Acces

Summary

Management of an information and communication technology (IT) infrastructure must be organized efficiently and most of all effectively, in order to support the organization's business processes optimally. The IT department has to focus more on its customers and the services provided to support their business processes, thus enabling customers to gain competitive advantages from IT. Therefore, the IT department should be organized according to its characteristic services, having its own business processes. The complexity of the IT infrastructure must be reduced by breaking it down into pieces according to the types of function that its components perform. This chapter shows a way to do so by using the Standard Integrated Management Approach (SIMA). The SIMA provides a pragmatic approach to organizing the IT management function and effecting the inevitable organizational changes to keep up with changing technologies and customer requirements.

15.1 Introduction

The IT management (ITM) function is responsible for the management of all IT components supporting an organization's business processes. The set of IT components to be managed can be very complex and dynamic. The ITM function has to deal with continuous changes and developments in technology as well as in the organization. Main movements influencing the ITM function as we see them both in literature (Langsford and Moffett, 1993; Sprague and McNurlin, 1993; Tschichholz et al., 1996) and in practice are:

- rapid evolution of technology;
- distribution of processing power;
- diversification of products and suppliers;
- outsourcing of IT tasks;
- integration of IT with business processes;
- increasing maturity of end users;
- increasing costs;
- increasing customer orientation.

IT components are rapidly evolving. Hardware prices are dropping continuously whereas the complexity and influence of IT on the organization's business processes are increasing rapidly. Processing power is distributed from mainframes to networked computers with cooperative processing functions. Systems can stretch over several organizations and components and services can be physically distributed. The size and complexity of these distributed systems introduce problems due to the number of components. Corporations are moving to a combination of centralized and decentralized modes of work both existing simultaneously, as downsizing and in particular client–server techniques do not meet the users' requirements in all situations. Since this movement is like a pendulum continuously swinging between centralization and decentralization, the IT infrastructure will remain dynamic and continuously changing (Sprague and McNurlin, 1993). For both modes, various types of components from various suppliers are used. Organizations are confronted more often with different suppliers specializing in fewer and more specific products or services. Equally, Stajano states that there is a movement away from proprietary systems towards open systems and standards and away from a reliance on single-vendor solutions towards open, multi-vendor, heterogeneous systems (in: Langsford and Moffett, 1993; Hemmen, 1996). Outsourcing of both development and ITM tasks increases and it will become a matter of interest as an increasing number of organization's turn back to their core business. As a result of outsourcing, the number of parties involved in the development and management of the organization's IT infrastructure grows, also influencing relations with external suppliers. Despite growing decentralization and diversification of products and suppliers, organizations want to integrate all IT components into an IT infrastructure, making all available facilities accessible from every point in the organization. Although IT components can differ considerably from one another and may provide very diversed facilities, they all can interact. End users are maturing and becoming more aware of the possibilities of IT, resulting in growing demands for functionality, availability and performance. Owing to a considerable decrease in costs and an increase in performance of hardware and software, the range of application of IT has become far greater in the past few years. This leads to higher user demands, resulting in larger and more complex information systems and in increasing instead of decreasing IT costs. Anticipating these changed demands, the customer and thus the organization's business objectives become central, characterizing the latest innovation wave: reaching the customer. Another characteristic feature of (most) IT infrastructures, apart from their complexity and dynamic nature, is the evolution of systems and working methods over the years. Many networks and systems have been developed in an ad hoc manner and many distributed systems often evolve by implementing existing services on new equipment (Langsford and Moffett, 1993). Despite the fact that information systems are often outdated, they are hard to replace as they perform a critical function in the organization's business processes. Many organizations are confronted with these issues, putting a heavy load on the ITM function. However, most organizations only experience two main consequences, i.e. excessively high IT costs and disappointing contributions of IT to their business processes. This can be explained by the fact that most organizations are managed mainly on input and output, namely financial aspects such as number of staff, budget, turnover and profit, and the range and level of services provided to the customers. IT costs increase disproportionately when compared with, for instance, growth of turnover. As the contribution of IT to business processes is hard to quantify, costs are easily considered to be too high. However, costs can only be cut down safely and effectively when their cause and impact are fully understood. An organization's ITM function has to handle these continuous developments so as to be able to respond to changed user demands. This requires the ITM function to change as well.

15.2 Underlying principles of the SIMA

The major lesson of the 1980s is that technology alone does not yield success and that strategy, people, business operations and technology should be aligned (Sprague and McNurlin, 1993). As 60% of the effectiveness of ITM can be attributed to organizational alignment of people and processes (Gartner Group, 1994), improvements in ITM should start from an organizational point of view. The necessary savings on operating expenses mean that traditional methods no longer work and old rules and assumptions must be challenged (Sprague and McNurlin, 1993). Broadhead (1996) states that one should search for a way for ITM that is linked closely to how the organization and the business are managed. However, in reality we see that most organizations still believe they can organize their ITM function in the old way just by implementing one or more tools for network and systems management. This idea might be reinforced by the absence of practically applicable methods for ITM and the wide variety of tools, e.g. to automate operator tasks or to monitor the performance or capacity of IT components. In spite of a wide range of ITM tools, the maturity of the tools is far from satisfactory, making process and organizational alignment the most critical factors in ITM effectiveness (Gartner Group, 1994). To reorganize the ITM function, according to these basics, into an efficient and effective operating function means accepting diversity and turning it to the users' advantage while presenting an integrated and complete picture to managers. The solution must take into account technology as well as environmental factors, business objectives and the external business environment. It is very important to organize the ITM function around outcomes, not tasks, whereas geographically dispersed resources should be treated as if they were centralized. Therefore, parallel activities should be linked rather than integrated and the areas of decision making and responsibilities should be put where the work is done. The ITM function should be treated as a separate business unit with its own products, services and business processes to provide them. On the other hand, the ITM function must always be aware of the fact that is just a supporting unit being part of a larger organization. The production chain as a whole, not just the interests of the ITM function, should be leading. The confidentiality, integrity and availability of the IT components and the information processed by them, is very important regarding the whole production chain. These three issues are the main scope of security management, which is frequently indicated as a separate ITM function. As the availability and correctness of the IT functionality is a responsibility of the ITM function, security management should be incorporated into the ITM function. Therefore, within the SIMA, security management is integrated into the ITM function and parts of the SIMA have already been applied for security management. This all requires major changes in both the organizational structure of the ITM function, the way of working and thinking of its employees, and the position of the ITM function in the overall IT department. The SIMA has been developed to support organizations (re)designing their ITM function.

15.3 Standard Integrated Management Approach

The Standard Integrated Management Approach (SIMA) was developed to (re)organize the ITM function. The SIMA has been developed from practice in addition to a variety of methods, techniques and standards of ITM. The SIMA consists of two main building blocks, namely the SPOT areas and the ITM Project Approach. Both building blocks contain a number of supporting tools such as the Six-layer Model, a Service Management Framework and an incremental implementation method (3-IMß). The Service Management Framework provides a structured means to (re)design the ITM function.

SPOT

SPOT represents the basis of the SIMA, namely the proposition that (re)organizing the function requires an integrated approach from four perspectives. These four perspectives are Services, Processes, Organization and Tools, which together describe the complete ITM function. Each of these perspectives has to be incorporated into the project activities to establish an adequate ITM.

Services

When designing a customer-oriented ITM function, one has to study the services provided to the end user supporting the customers' business processes. The ITM function must have a clear picture of its customers, the services it delivers to them and how these services are built together with IT components. A number of tools are available to describe the services, such as a layered model and outsourcing principles/agreements.

Layered Model
The most straightforward and also most effective model is the Layered Model, represented in Figure 15.1. This model can be used to determine how the services are built with a variety of IT components. The Layered Model is based on the DUneTManagement Model (Daalen *et al.*, 1995) and the OSI Reference Model (ISO, 1994), and divides the IT infrastructure into six layers. The top of this model represents the Service as delivered to the customer. In a number of cases there will be a one-to-one mapping to an application, as services usually consist of just one application. The Application layer represents the actual application visible to the end user. The Data layer contains both the application databases and the database management system, whereas the System layer represents operating systems to run the application on (e.g. DOS, UNIX or Windows). Communication protocols are positioned in the Network layer and, finally, physical network components (e.g. cables, routers and gateways) are represented in the Cableware layer.

Outsourcing principles/agreements
The Layered Model can also be used to determine which (internal or external) organization unit is responsible for what layers. The layers and their relationships with the other components of the infrastructure have to be described to ensure an end-to-end service to the customer. The definition of the interfaces is very important, when a layer is outsourced to an external organization unit. For internal organization units

FIGURE 15.1

Layered Model

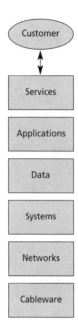

the contents, activities and tasks of the layer itself have to be defined too. For internal organization units it is also important to describe the layer itself. More often, the services delivered to the customer have to be described in contracts. Those contracts between the ITM function and users can be divided into four agreements, each of these agreements having their own scope: Overall or General Agreement, Service Level Agreement, Financial Agreement and Procedure Agreement. Besides the contract(s) with the user organization, the ITM function will also be confronted with Underpinning Contracts and Operational Level Agreements. Underpinning Contracts are agreements between the ITM function and external suppliers, while Operational Level Agreements are agreements between organization units within the ITM function. The link between all these contracts is essential also to ensure an end-to-end service. Within the SIMA standard, templates for all those agreements are made and checklists for outsourcing projects are also described.

Processes

In many branches, production lines are commonly organized around business processes. Although this appeared to be a much more practical approach than a functional or organizational point of view, it took quite some time before IT organizations began describing their activities in business processes. The SPOT area Processes represent the ITM processes that have to be described and implemented for the ITM function. Nowadays, there are several process models that are commonly accepted to describe the ITM function in business processes (Hemmen, 1996). Examples are the OSI Reference Model, the Telecommunications Management Network (TMN, 1992), NMF's business process model (NMF, 1995) and the IT Infrastructure Library (CCTA, 1989). Since ITIL is very popular among a large number of organizations in the

Netherlands, it is frequently used in the SIMA projects. However, as ITIL is just a set of best practices describing each process in view of a specific situation, it has to be customized to the situation concerned. Still, other process models are incorporated in the SIMA as well. Whether an organization is organized around tasks or processes, the activities that it performs have to be described unambiguously. The SIMA has standard (ITIL) process descriptions and standard procedures, which can be easily adjusted to the specific situation of the organization. This saves a lot of time during the process design stage and supports a pragmatic approach for organizational change.

Organization

The SPOT area Organization is underestimated in many models for organizing and improving the ITM function (Hemmen, 1996). The success of the improvements strongly depends on this area, as the adjustments have to be made to the way of working within the ITM function. The Organization area focuses on the organizational settings and the allocation of tasks, responsibilities and authorities. It may have serious consequences, particularly for the final implementation of changes or new activities or processes when not enough attention is given to the organizational setting and an adequate allocation. The implementation method is described later in this chapter. To embed tasks, responsibilities and authorities in the organization, they have to be positioned within the organizational structure describing the distribution of management responsibilities and authorities. Often, changes have to be made to this structure as well. The organizational structure and hierarchical settings are more apparent in contrast with, for example, the culture of an organization. This aspect has to be considered when designing and implementing changes. The design of the new ITM function has to be adapted to the characteristics of the specific organization. In a more bureaucratic organization, for example, there will be many checks and procedures, compared with a very small and young organization that is not used to working with checks and procedures. So the design of the ITM function should, among other things, depend on the organizational culture. Tools, like matrices, checklists and courses, are available for the SPOT area Organization (Figure 15.2). Matrices have been developed to ensure that all necessary tasks, responsibilities and authorities regarding all services or service components have been allocated. The matrices can be applied to both the current and the desired situation, so that the departments involved can be identified easily. These same matrices can be applied to check whether the allocation of tasks and responsibilities is understood by the employees. Furthermore, the SPOT area Organization contains tools to determine the cultural characteristics of the organization as well. Besides the matrices and checklists, many courses have also been developed. These courses ensure that the ITM staff receive an adequate education to perform their tasks. These courses range from those discussing the ITM processes to those that allocate soft skills such as presenting and handling difficult conversations.

Tools

The ITM staff must have all relevant information available to carry out the designed ITM processes and tasks. Nowadays, there are numerous tools to measure, monitor or manage certain aspects of applications and the technical infrastructure. Platforms such

FIGURE 15.2

Two examples of the usage of matrices

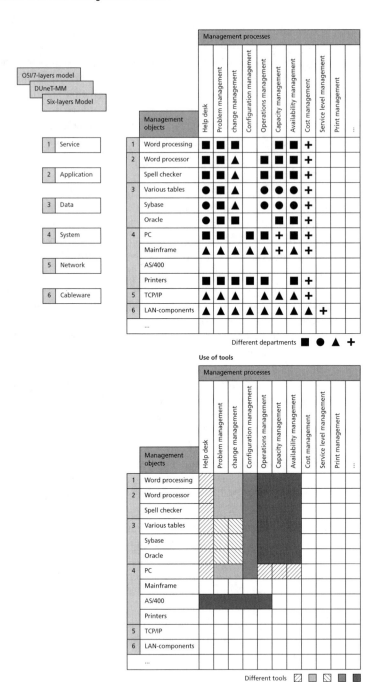

FIGURE 15.3

The Implementation Roadmap

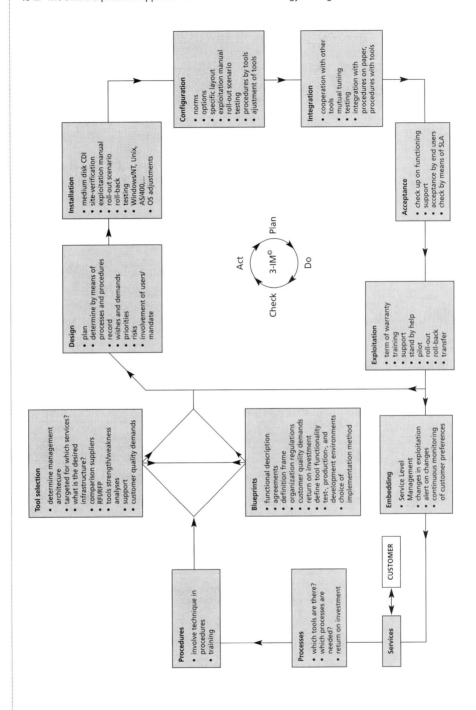

as OpenView, CA Unicentre TNG or Tivoli make it possible to perform the ITM function centrally. In order to use the available tools optimally, the information required should be described in detail and the operator tasks should be analysed to determine which tasks can best be automated. Within each organization or independent business unit, one must strive for an integrated ITM information system with, if necessary, a link to similar systems of suppliers and customers. The main purpose of this integrated system is supporting the ITM function in providing the defined services according to the service levels recorded in the agreements with the customers. This information system must be designed carefully before buying tools. The most important issue in this design process is that one selects tools that fit, not tools that can do most. The Implementation Roadmap, which is part of this area, describes all activities that have to be carried out, from tool selection to an operational tool (Figure 15.3).

ITM Project Approach

The (re)organization of an ITM function requires a structured and thought-out approach. Therefore, the SIMA contains project planning as well. This Project Approach identifies three main stages as being Audit, Design and Implementation. The Project Approach starts with the analysis of the current situation, designs a new ITM function and ends with implementing the design within the ITM function (Figure 15.4).

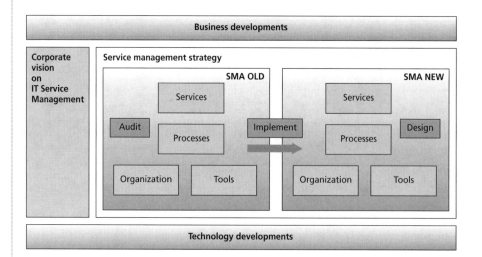

FIGURE 15.4
Mapping the SIMA with the Service Management Framework

Audit

The current situation within the ITM function has to be observed and analysed first. During the Audit stage an inventory of the ITM function is made on all four SPOT areas. The listed situation is compared to an 'ideal' organization of the ITM function to identify problem areas and points for improvement. The 'ideal' organization is then finely tuned using conversations with the customer according to the five CMM levels. The Audit stage can be carried out as a QuickScan as well as a detailed full-sized inventory. For both methods, checklists and questionnaires are available to determine the maturity level of the ITM function on the SPOT areas. Sometimes it is useful to start with a QuickScan for all SPOT areas and perform a full-sized inventory on those areas that need to be improved. As a result, it is possible to focus on the weaker parts of the ITM function without investigating all well-functioning parts. The way of working in an improvement project is determined according to the outcome of the Audit stage. Usually the Audit is the starting point of an improvement project. It will also provide input to the Design stage. The Audit can also be used as a measuring activity that is performed at the beginning and during the project to show the progress of the project.

Design

Starting from the findings from the Audit stage, a design is made for the desired situation that solves a number of the problems identified and marked as important. The desired ITM function is described by means of the Service Management Framework (SMF). The SMF is developed to support (the communication on) the design of an ITM function. However, it can be used likewise to describe and analyse the current situation. The SMF distinguishes four levels of abstraction:

- The *IT Service Management environment* describes the position of the ITM function in relation to its environment and the organisational and technological developments it is faced with.
- The *IT Service Management strategy* defines the ITM function's strategy, being a deduction of the strategy and demands of the overall organization it is part of.
- The *IT Service Management architecture* translates the ITM strategy into an organizational design in terms of the four SPOT areas.
- The *IT Service Management blueprints* provide detailed descriptions of the Service management architecture for each of the SPOT areas.

The purpose of the SMF is to provide a coherent description of the ITM function by providing several perspectives and positioning these perspectives in relation to each other into a complete picture. The SMF aims to provide a means of doing so that is logical, pragmatic, practical and relatively simple to understand, instead of a more theoretical and abstract perspective. The SMF can be compared with the functional design within software development. At the end of the Design stage, a specific SMF is made with the solutions for the identified problems.

Implementation

The Implementation stage represents the actual realization of the improvements. Both Audit and Design may have provided a lot of insight and knowledge, but benefits are only gained when adjustments have been made to the way of working. The blueprints defined in the Design stage have to be put into practice. However, changing an organization can be difficult due to – for example, opposition from within the organization, the long duration of projects or the complexity of translating the blueprints into practical issues. An Integrated Incremental Implementation method (3I-M) has been developed to implement changes in the ITM function (Figure 15.5). This method con-

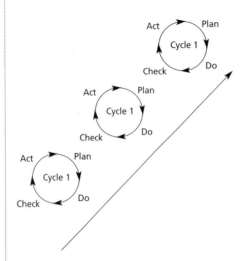

FIGURE 15.5
The 3I-M approach

tains, among others, several practical tools to reduce oppositions. The implementation method 3I-M is based on the principles of Rapid Application Development and Total Quality Management. The main basics of 3I-M are a short, stepwise realization of the changes and frequent interaction with the employees involved. The method consists of a number of cycles according to the principles of Plan–Do–Check–Act. Applying the principles of time-boxing, each cycle has a fixed duration. During the Plan stage of each cycle the changes to be realized during that stage are established. These changes than are designed, checked and implemented. When the time to realize changes exceeds planning, the change is forwarded to the next implementation cycle. The improvements have to be secured within the organization. Documentation and education are essential elements to realize this. Among others, procedures, manuals and service level agreements have to be written. The SIMA contains templates for these documents and the InterpromIS© method can be applied to produce clear and readable documentation. The education programmes contain several courses that can be followed by the employees of the ITM function. The result of the Implementation stage is an improved ITM function on all SPOT areas.

15.4 Concluding remarks

The world of ITM is continuously changing and therefore the ITM function has to improve too. The SIMA is an approach that can be used to (re)organize the ITM function. The two building blocks, the SPOT areas and the ITM Project Approach, make the SIMA unique compared with other approaches and methodologies. The complete ITM function is described by the four SPOT areas, enabling an integrated approach that can be modelled using the Service Management Framework. Besides a descriptive model, the SIMA consists of a project method that supports the implementation of the improvements in the ITM function. Although the SIMA incorporates a large number of pragmatic methods, tools and theories, further research is necessary to improve the approach and to incorporate new developments. Currently, research projects are dealing with the relationships between the SIMA and e.g. Functional Management, CRM, e-commerce and ERP. The SIMA has been improved over more than five years and has proved its success in the improvement of many ITM functions in different organizations.

Literature

Broadhead, S. (1996), 'Het beheer van uw netwerk, virtueel of niet', in Dutch, *LAN Internetworking Magazine*, 8 (3), 28–35.

CCTA (1989) *IT Infrastructure Library*, Central Computer and Telecommunications Agency, United Kingdom.

Daalen, P. van, Koo, N. de, Leeuwen, A. van and Stappershoef, L. (1995) 'Het DUneT Management Model', in Dutch, *Informatie*, *37* (3), 201–8.

Davenport, T.H. (1993) *Process Innovation: Reengineering Work Through Information Technology*, Harvard Business School Press, Boston, USA.

Gartner Group (1994) 'Pragmatic NSM Management', Research Note, K-ORG-097, Sannerud.

Hemmen B. (1996) 'Modelling change management of evolving heterogeneous networks', PhD thesis, Technical University of Delft.

ISO (1994) 'Reference Model of Open Distributed Processing', ITU-T X.900 series recs., ISO/IEC 10476 series.

Klompé, Rick and Pothuizen, Leon (1997) 'The SIMA: a practical approach to information technology management', *Journal of Information Technology*, 12, 121–9.

Langsford, A. and Moffett, J.D. (1993) *Distributed Systems Management*, Addison-Wesley.

NMF (1995) *A Service Management Business Process Model*, Network Management Forum.

Sprague, R.H. and McNurlin, B.C. (1993) *Information Systems Management in Practice*, Prentice Hall International Editions.

Swanson, E.B. and Beath, C.M. (1989) *Maintaining Information Systems in Organizations*, John Wiley & Sons.

TMN (1992) 'Principles for a Telecommunications Management Network', CCITT Recommendation M.3010.

Tschichholz, M., Tschammer, V. and Dittrich, A. (1996) 'Integrated approach to open distributed management', *Computer Communications*, 19(1), 76–87.

For more detailed information on SIMA, please contact Inter Access InterProm: P.O. Box 8003, 3900 CA Veenendaal, The Netherlands (+31)318-541940.

Review of part 1

Meijer and Van der Pols describe the recently developed **ASL framework**. A striking difference between ASL and most of the other frameworks (except for the R2C model, which constitutes the original base for ASL) is the point of view: the IT management world is approached from the perspective of the application manager. That way, the authors choose a position near the functionality of the software, i.e. the application. This fits the demands that seem to be most important in an evolving IT environment: a close association with business processes. On the other hand, it ignores to some extent the role of the rest of the infrastructure. It only incidentally covers the position of the technical infrastructure, while more and more functionality of information systems is today built into commodities, the basic characteristics of the infrastructure.

It is good to see that the authors ackowledge the fact that operational services are provided through the integration of a lot of separated IT domains, thus supporting the views on Integrated Service Management.

The ASL modelling concentrates on the rather traditional environment where the software code is maintained. This explicit separation between technical infrastructure and application infrastructure fits the practice of many traditionally organized IT organizations: separate departments for development/maintenance of software and for exploitation of the information systems. In that exploitation environment, the production versions of the application run in combination with the hardware, system software, networks and facilities. In that same practice we have recognized for several years now what has been called '*the drama triangle*': the troublesome communication between customer, application management and exploitation (Production/Operations). This leads to the 'throwing over the wall' syndrome, responsible for lots of trouble in IT for decades now.

This problem is recognized in ASL. In the underpinning R2C model, years ago, a solution was provided in terms of 'the service team'. In fact this was the first publication we could find that mentioned such an apparent integrating task in the IT service domain. This cohesion was also recognized in other models, especially KPN's Integrated Service Management (ISM), that explicitly emphasized the role of the service integrator. By acknowledging the integration element the ASL framework can now be regarded to be the modelling of a sub-domain in the IT landscape: the domain where the software is maintained. And because a large proportion of the market is still separated according to these rules, the framework will fit practice very well. It is, however, of equal importance to focus on the shortcomings of the model, because it is exactly that organizational barrier that caused so many IT problems for so many years. Especially in 'the new age', speed and flexibility are important issues and any lack of cooperation will frustrate those factors. Advice to anyone applying ASL is therefore:

beware of organizational problems; communication, culture and cooperation will be the decisive factors for the success of IT companies. For the rest, the model can provide you with a detailed management structure, to be used as a reference in the organization of your IT service management.

In **BDM: IT-enabled business development and management methodology**, the authors choose a position close to business interest: they emphasize that IT should be supporting business efficiency ('activities are carried out in organizations to achieve organizational goals'). BDM is based upon the Information Infrastructure Management (IIM) model. IIM was initially designed as a model for managing information systems, with a special focus on resource management and aimed strongly at supporting business processes. IIM differed from most other IT management models in the way that it took more types of resources into consideration than most other models did: human resources, financial resources, legal resources, facilities – they all were covered by the generic approach of IIM. This made IIM the IT management model with the broadest scope for several years.

BDM follows that line: a firm respect for resources, a wide scope, a generic nature, using widely accepted building blocks from other disciplines. BDM doesn't stop at that generic level, however. The framework gets more interesting; at the moment, it specifies the 20 processes that are really important in management, development, maintenance and operations. There, the model chooses its position by stating what is important according to the authors. In these processes and process groups we can recognize several aspects that are covered by other frameworks in this part, but none of them has the wide scope of BDM. For example, BDM uses the stepwise quality-improvement method of capability maturity mechanisms (in this case, SPICE), it uses the customer–provider paradigm (typical for frameworks at the third, service-focused level of those maturity models) and it applies the integration paradigm: there are always suppliers and customers for any organization. Furthermore, the authors made sure that BDM fits quality frameworks such as ISO and best practices such as ITIL.

The level of detail in the documentation around BDM (and IIM, in a series of publications) makes it more of a method than many other frameworks. On the other hand, the model is formulated in a very generic style, making it especially suitable for use as a vision framework: if you follow the checklist nature of BDM in a quality improvement project, you can be sure that many important aspects are covered. That makes it especially useful in combination with more specific models for specific problem areas.

BiOOlogic is a rather unusual framework in the range of models in this chapter. It has an architectural approach that gives it a firm base. By using a language structure (UML) and building blocks that are made very explicit, it provides a highly structured approach to organizing IT organizations. BiOOlogic adapts the process–people–product triad in a flexible way: it can be applied to the whole organization, but also to specific limited domains within an organization.

One of the most attractive aspects of BiOOlogic is that it reduces the complex game of (re)designing IT service organizations to some simple rules, which – if followed adequately – will lead you simply to a result that suits your organization. The step-by-step approach that the authors describe can help in a very practical way.

Schreurs and van der Hoven warn the reader about the pitfalls of ITIL, emphasizing that ITIL is misunderstood and misused by many, in the way that it is used as a prescriptive framework of processes. The process modelling approach used in BiOOlogic is much more coherent since it has a singular architectural base.

There is a danger in BiOOlogic as well: the (still) 'unusual' elements require a strong commitment to this approach, and will cost participants some extra energy to get used to. As is normally the case with new approaches, it requires something of a 'proven application' before it will be adopted by others. In this case, the succesful and long-term application of BiOOlogic in a Dutch government organization may just provide such a 'proof of concept'.

CobiT focuses on the quality of information, as a means of reaching quality IT services, and it makes a case for the supportive nature of IT on behalf of the business processes. The framework is process-oriented, has a broad scope, and can be used especially in auditing. Based upon CobiT analysis results, an organization can assess or be assessed in terms of quality.

CobiT uses four domains for the processes it recognizes in IT organizations, one of them – Delivery and Support – being especially relevant from the Service Management point of view. This domain contains 13 processes, largely compatible with ITIL definitions.

The combination of management goals, information, business processes and resources makes CobiT an adequate set of service management mechanisms. It provides the modelling equipment and is extensively documented. ISACA, the owner of CobiT, makes a lot of those documents freely accessible through Web channels, although some of the more template-like materials are not free. CobiT is attracting attention all over the world, and is well managed in a structure of national chapters of ISACA, the organization for IT auditing professionals.

In **A model for functional management**, Deurloo, Meijer-Veldman and Van der Pols follow the ideas of Professor Maarten Looijen, by dividing IT management into three major domains: technical management, application management and functional management (the 'threefold model'). Functional management is recognized as a specific discipline in other frameworks as well. With their description of functional management, the authors define a responsibility area that is complementary to ITIL (for infrastructure management) and ASL/R2C (for application management). Since ITIL covers only the domain of the service provider, this functional management is not part of ITIL. Nevertheless, it is of the utmost importance to manage this domain very well, since it is of great importance to the quality of the relationship between provider and customer.

The modelling of the functional management domain by the authors differs slightly from that in the generic MIP model (see later in this review). MIP simply divides the functional management domain into a strategic, a tactical and an operational level. The division into *user support*, *system enhancements* and *control* has to some extent the same structure. Nevertheless the Model for Functional Management presented here can be regarded as a thorough description of the middle column in the MIP model.

By supplying a maturity assessment paragraph, the authors support the recognition of the reader of their own relative position in this discipline. You can identify the shortcomings of functional management in your organization, and get an idea of the improvements you should make to get control of the demand for IT services as well.

By focusing on 'the demand side' – the authors make a very valuable contribution to this Guide, one that everyone should have in mind when reading the other frameworks that describe the supplier side of the service game.

The **HP ITSM Reference Model** is figured with motion: Service Design and Management is triggered by Business–IT Alignment, and the Operations Bridge is triggered by Service Development and Deployment. The effect has some analogy with the Microsoft Operations Framework (MOF; see below). Unlike the illustration in MOF, however, the core illustration in the HP ITSM Reference Model is not based on the PDCA cycle of continuous improvement but on a segmentation, a subdivision, of the IT service management processes into coherent process groups. This is quite similar to the approach of the British Standards Institute, when it developed its *PD0005 Code of Practice for IT Service Management* (1998). Nevertheless, HP's model differs enough from PD0005 to show an original face, while both models are compliant with ITIL. At the centre of the modelling we find the usual twins in ITSM model ling: change management and configuration management. Both processes are focused on controlling the IT infrastructure, the way they are defined in ITIL. Another example makes clear that the Reference Model is compliant with ITIL: although problem management is called 'proactive in nature', the process is positioned as an Operations Bridge process (as in IPW), instead of a (tactical) management process (as in ISM).

The model, like most of the models presented here, is typically a reference model – an image to be used in determining specific modelling – and therefore it is available in various levels of detail. The four domains at the periphery are well explained, and have a management perspective: strategy, tactics and operations are used as the determination factors. The last domain, operations, is split between development/deployment and the production environment, as is usual in IT organizations.

The description of the models stops at the level of process grouping, leaving the explicit relations between the individual process to your own imagination. For that purpose, however, you can turn to several other reference models presented in this part.

In 1992 the midrange data centre of Dutch Telecom succesfully implemented a process-oriented workflow, with the support of a consulting agency, Quint Wellington Redwood. After this succesful initiative, many organizations in the Netherlands used the model that was developed here: **IPW, Implementation of a Process-oriented Workflow**. Quint Wellington Redwood developed the model further in its consultancy practice, and regularly published details of the model. Apart from the quality of the model, this open mind regarding publication was probably one of the most important reasons for the model being used in so many companies, and led to the recognition by Gartner (1997, research note P-220-194) as a standard for modelling IT Service Management processes.

From the beginning, IPW was built on ITIL definitions; and although ITIL wasn't followed to the letter in all implementations, it always stayed compatible with ITIL. Thus, it was complementary to the ITIL books and provided practitioners exactly what was missing in ITIL: the process model. In recent years, IPW has been used in other countries as well.

IPW has undergone a serious evolution in the decade that it has existed. The scope of the model has been widened several times, and a supporting mechanism for step-by-step maturity improvement, the IPW Stadia Model, has been added. The latest version covers both the demand and the supply side, and is compatible with a number of other public-domain modelling perspectives such as ASL, CMM and SPICE.

The fact that the model follows ITIL has advantages: it can be applied by organizations adopting ITIL, all over the world. On the other hand, ITIL documentation is not always state of the art, as Favier states. For example, the position of the Problem Management process in the model is designed differently in some other models that do not follow ITIL definitions so strictly, as well as the position of Development. However, simply applying rule one: 'keep an open mind when you're using a reference model', will enable you to build your own model. And that is what makes IPW valuable: it can be used as a reference model by everyone applying ITIL definitions in their organization. And it will do more: it enables you to incorporate several of the other detailed frameworks in this part, helping you to find a broad perspective on the management of information systems.

The same telecom company that was involved in the creation of IPW developed a somewhat different approach a couple of years later: **ISM, Integrated Service Management**. After applying IPW for a number of years, the changing circumstances had led to a situation of specialization: more and more specific sub-tasks in the supply domain were taken care of by specialist organizations, leaving more and more of a service integrator role for the data centre. This situation was modelled in ISM, using all that had been learned by applying ITIL and IPW for a number of years.

ISM was applied in several other companies as well and, like IPW, evolved into a more sophisticated approach. The contribution of Van den Elskamp *et al.* zooms in to the practical bottlenecks that existed when the need for ISM arose. Having previously had experience with the development of such a model, the authors used a highly structured set of building blocks, so-called paradigms, to create ISM. This approach should make it easy to reproduce the same or a different model by applying a particular set of management paradigms.

ISM, like all frameworks in this part, has its own specific value. In this case it is the focus on the service integrator role that makes it a special model, differing from the others. But the model has its own characteristics in other ways as well. For example, it groups a series of ITIL titles as a single tactical process and uses a full proactive definition of problem management, thereby deviating from ITIL definitions more than most of the other models presented here.

At present, **ITIL's** remarkable advance seems unstoppable. This is also evident from the strong growth in demand for ITIL examinations. The international qualification structure for IT Service Management developed by EXIN and ISEB brings a number of elements of ITIL's winning formula to light. One of the most important is surely the fact that ITIL is much more than just a collection of useful books. It is a combined force of books, training, certificates, tools, services etc. That makes it more of a method than any of the other frameworks presented in this part of the book.

There is a lot of confusion about ITIL, stemming from all kinds of misunderstandings over its nature. ITIL is, as the OCG states, a set of best practices. The OCG doesn't claim that ITIL's best practices describe pure processes. The OCG also doesn't claim that ITIL is a framework, designed as one coherent model. That is what most of its users make of it, probably because they have such a great need for such a model. Perhaps one of the most powerful characteristics of ITIL is exactly that fact: it doesn't prescribe a model for your IT service-delivery processes to a high level of detail. In

Review of part 1

ITIL's best practices, a series of relationships between processes are suggested but there remains a significant degree of freedom. There are plenty of models built on the ITIL elements, each giving a somewhat different accent or approach. Therefore ITIL can be used as a set of building blocks in the model you choose or develop.

ITIL is a definite buzzword now. It started out in the late 1980s, and it was adopted fast in the UK and even faster in the Netherlands. There was a lot of experience gained in the 1990s, leading to a firm understanding of the strengths, weaknesses, opportunities and threats applicable to ITIL, as the SWOT analysis has learned. Some of the most important issues from that SWOT analysis are worthwhile mentioning here:

1. Always build your own process model around the ITIL basic definitions. If you can't think of a model yourself, then just copy the most appealing one from the available models, mentioned in e.g. this part.

2. Make clear what parts of ITIL fit your organization and what parts don't. Since your company will probably differ from all others, you can't simply copy any 'best practice'.

3. Add a management perspective on operations management in your modelling, because ITIL doesn't cover that area as a single process.

4. Beware of the so-called ITIL specialist. Keep an open mind and don't believe everything they tell you: the hype will cause a lot of people to think that '*this is it*', meanwhile losing their perspective on reality.

5. If you rely on ITIL for an implementation of your IT management philosophy, always add knowledge from the field of organization management. Most of the organizational changes are led by IT specialists, and they are simply not aces in organization consultancy.

ITIL is a very useful library of best practices for anyone who is willing to keep an open mind. It will probably grow into the most widely used framework for IT management in the next couple of years, worldwide. It is clear, however, that you will need more than ITIL to solve all your IT management problems. On the other hand, many of the broader models are built on ITIL. Used in this way, ITIL can be of great use to this world for many years to come.

ITPM, the IT Process Model, is a recent version of IBM's perspective on IT management. IBM was one of the very first IT organizations ever to use process perspectives in its management methods. The publication of ISMA, the Information Systems Management Architecture, in 1979, was the first publication of a process model in IT management that received any serious attention. In the late 1980s the CCTA, now OCG, used ISMA as a base for the definition of ITIL. From ISMA, IBM developed a new model for IT management, starting in 1994. That project resulted in the IT Process Model: process- and customer- focused, independent of technology using an integrated structured modelling of processes and fit for measurement and control. IBM stated that it was not a model that could be implemented, but more a reference for modelling components that could be used to solve practical management issues.

In this recognition IBM showed more self-knowledge than many other providers of proprietary models. As is the case with most of the models presented here, they are more vision than method, and they merely provide elements that you can use in your own environment. There is no doubt that this is useful, but if you are looking for a true method, then much more is needed.

In the ITPM model we see a grouping of processes that is remarkably different from most of the other frameworks presented in the Guide. It focuses on the most important management issues in IT management. By taking that approach it uses process titles that are different from ITIL. Since the scope of ITPM is broader than that of ITIL, you can give ITIL processes a place within ITPM. In the chapter on ITPM there is another interesting statement: ITPM is concentrated on processes and ITIL is concentrated on the level of procedures and working instructions. And although this opinion will not easily find much support, they are probably right. In the ITIL books we can find descriptions of functions, procedures, tools, etc., while ITPM concentrates on more abstract values in IT management. This leads to a situation in which ITPM and ITIL might just team up very well. If you can locate yourself in the high-level process grouping of the IT Process Model, the model may exactly provide what is says it does: a reference model for controlling information technology within your organization.

A Managerial Step-by-Step Plan is more than a proprietary model for the management of information systems. It is the result of an academic school that started in the late 1980s, at the Department of Information Strategy and Management of Information Systems, Delft University of Technology, in the Netherlands. Professor Maarten Looijen was the initiator of a formalized theory on the management of information systems that was very successful in the Netherlands for a long period, and was exported to several countries in Africa and Asia in the following years. At the centre of the approach of this school was the Threefold Management Model: functional management, application management, technical management. All these management forms concentrate on the object of the information system.

This management method is more of a method than any of the other models presented in this part:

- It has a very clear *view*, placing the object of the information system at the centre of the model.
- It has a highly sophisticated *modelling strategy*, ranging from the Task Reference Model and the Threefold Management Model to the Extended State Model.
- It is accompanied by an *implementation* approach: the Step-by-Step Plan.

Like most of the other frameworks, it lacks a management method for its own use, and it doesn't specify extensive supporting mechanisms (except for the simulation tooling). The framework, however, has proven its usefulness in many cases, and has been the basic training for IT management academics for many years.

The Step-by-Step Plan gives you a quite straightforward approach for the determination and the implementation of IT management structures in your organization, admitting the use of specific process templates and organizational aspects as they are preferred in your organization. This way, it offers a generic approach to the management, control and maintenance (MCM) of information systems.

In **Managing the delivery of business information** we find a model that is highly compatible with the Delft school, as described above. It concentrates on the information system (the object to be managed) and is concerned with the complete domain of information servicing. Core to this model is the Lemniscate: a two-winged process of aligning IT service requirements to IT performance. This way, the formalized relation between customer and provider is central in the view of the Cap Gemini Ernst & Young's (CGEY) model, and hence it is concerned with service level management. The model is based on ITIL and therefore has the abovementioned pros and cons.

The model is also based on the results of a long-term academic study on IT Service Management (Kwintes – see Chapter 32), which has resulted in a strong theoretical base for the model. And because the Kwintes project also had participants from service providers and user organizations it has kept to a pragmatic level. For example, the SLA templates generated from this project belong to the best available in this field. They explicitly cover quality parameters such as Availability, Integrity, Exclusiveness, Calamities, Performance, Training, User Support and Change Management. Another interesting result from this project was the initiative to create an IT Service Capability Maturity Model (ITS CMM). Level 2 of this model was included in the result of Kwintes. The following levels were taken up in the DOCIS project, initiated by the Vrije Universiteit of Amsterdam.

The model is well structured, as could be expected in the case of an academic research result: SLA reports are tightly in line with SLA quality parameters. Comparison with the chapter by Meesters and Bouman in Part 7, and with Rhion Jones' chapter in the same part, reveals that the SLA is focused on the tangible aspects of service quality. Meesters and Bouman, as well as Jones, emphasize the intangible factors that are of the utmost importance in managing customer satisfaction. Quote: 'Therefore an SLA should not only cover the rational specification, but also the emotional aspects should be addressed. A traditional Service Level Agreement covers the tangibles and sometimes some communication, reliability, competence and access aspects (as Meesters and Bouman state). Looking at the total picture, there can still be a lot of reasons for the customer to be unhappy.' In the CGEY model, there are formally no service levels formulated in terms of 'expectations'. However, the model is supposed to support the management of expectations in an implicit way, by facilitating discussion about the requirements: any discrepancies between actual and expected performance will be subject to regular discussion between customer and supplier. Looking at all the other gaps in this customer–supplier minefield (as is illustrated in the GAP model of Parasuraman, Zeithaml and Berry) raises the question of whether they are all covered by this model. The illustrated focus on expectations is definitely a valid one, but it will probably work best when combined with a formal contract that covers the measurable metrics. And that is well covered by the CGEY model.

The **Management of Information Provision (MIP) model** is a very simple model that provides some help in discussions about roles and responsibilities in terms of information management: use, management and provisioning. The model is typically process-based, like most of the other models presented here, and offers a high-level framework, leaving all the organizational aspects out of the picture. In this framework you can easily position the ITIL processes, as well as most of the other models and model components that are discussed in the other chapters (e.g. IPW, ISM, ITPM, HP's ITSM Reference Model, etc.). Dividing the information management playground into three columns (responsibility areas) and three rows (management layers) produces the MIP model, a.k.a. **the 3 × 3 matrix for information management**. Each of the nine resulting cells is defined in terms of input/output in all directions of the surrounding cells, as well as in terms of the activities in the cell.

The value of this model is rather limited, although it provides a fine framework for discussions on domains of responsibilities, e.g. in cases of outsourcing and process modelling. Furthermore, it is in line with the threefold model of the Delft school, clearly showing the domain for Application Management, as it is described in the first model in this Guide.

When Microsoft recently published its vision of IT Service Management in **MOF: Microsoft's Operations Framework**, it attracted a lot of surprise. Until that time, the management aspects of Microsoft's product portfolio had to be covered by other management frameworks, such as ITIL, making Microsoft a typical software house. But, as Mike Pultorak, one of the participants in the development process of MOF, explains, Microsoft realized that its products had to be incorporated into a management vision in order to achieve its goals in terms of IT 'any place, any time, on every device'. This vision had to be realized in the .Net philosophy, which brought development tools and software for servers, clients and services together in one integrated set that had to be available for users in many shapes and at many devices, at extremely high availability rates.

To achieve such a goal, Microsoft had to choose a management framework that would enable this: the perception of its product quality appeared to be highly determined by the maturity of the management environment that used these products. And it did. By combining some of the best management elements available, Microsoft built its own framework, concentrated on the production environment of products. And although it was claimed that MOF was developed as guidance, specific to Microsoft products and technologies, in practice it appears to be a model that can be used for all platforms.

The model was based on ITIL, as so many of the models presented here are, and it adds its own characteristics to it. Again this emphasizes that ITIL is the industry's best practice at the moment, widely accepted throughout the world. On the other hand, by building on ITIL so explicitly, MOF also lays itself open the threat of incorporating some of the flaws of ITIL, which are not yet widely recognized as such (see the remarks on ITIL).

Since MOF is officially aimed only at Microsoft products, it can afford to wander off the traditional People/Process/Products triad and exchange products for the risk factor. The Risk Model is the complement to the Process Model, and the triad is now completed by the Team Model.

The Process Model differs from other models such as the BSI Code of Practice and the HP ITSM Reference Model:

- MOF gives security an operational character; this seems to be a matter of preference, since many other processes could shift to another management layer as well.
- MOF doesn't cover the integration aspects with customers and suppliers in the Process Model; instead, both are covered in a different perspective, namely the Team Model (support and partner).
- MOF mentions the service desk, whereas BSI and ITIL stepped away from the process character of the service desk: it is an organizational team, with tasks in many (operational) processes.
- MOF lacks the strategic management layer, the way the HP model does. That is made explicit by choosing a position near the operations team.

Review of part 1

MOF shows much more detail in the operations sector, with processes such as System Administration, Service Monitoring & Control, Job Scheduling, etc.

MOF creates its own character this way. It is not aiming at management layers, like the HP model does, nor is it a segmentation model like the BSI standard, but it emphasizes the life cycle of continuous improvement in accordance with well-known mechanisms such as Deming's PDCA cycle. By building on the Team Model and the Risk Model, as they were developed in the adjacent model domain (MSF, Microsoft's Solutions Framework), it continues on a road already taken.

MOF claims to be building on ITIL. That obviously is true. It also claims to be extending ITIL. That also is true: it adds a Workforce Management process in the 'optimizing' stage (comparable to ITIL tactical levels). This is recognized in other frameworks as well (e.g. ISM). But MOF especially goes into much more detail in the operations sector. That sector is the one ITIL domain that was never constructed well, and is still not covered in the latest ITIL publications. In fact, it can be called 'the missing ITIL domain'. In several frameworks this domain is positioned as the Operations Process (see e.g. IPW and ISM). In the MOF this domain is analysed in even more detail, making the claim for 'extensions' very clear. Pultorak explains that the reason for this omission is the platform-dependent nature of these processes, but the processes listed in MOF do not seem to be platform bound in any way: Storage Management, Network Management, Security Administration, etc. are very generic activities. In this case, MOF seems to add more to ITIL than it realizes … .

'Design for operability' is recognized as an important aspect. In several other models, e.g. ASL, this is also the case. It is definitely a sign of practical maturity to have such a procedure in place, at least if you want to prevent the traditional 'over the fence' behaviour of development teams, and the accompanying 'ravine' between development and operations teams.

The Risk Model, presented as an extension to ITIL, seems to be largely covered by IT Service Continuity Management, as it is defined in the latest ITIL publications. Indeed, this is an ongoing process, as MOF states.

Altogether, Microsoft's Operations Framework seems to be a very serious attempt to create a management environment for Microsoft products, stimulating better use of the features and the application of these products. The framework Microsoft developed this way is no less than any of the other frameworks presented here. In fact, by choosing such a specific nature, it is refreshing to see the innovative nature of the framework, as compared with many other frameworks that blindly copy some of the more general mistakes in modelling IT service management.

In the view of **SIMA, the Standard Integrated Management Approach**, four areas of interest for IT management are recognized, called the SPOT areas: Services, Processes, Organization and Tools. SPOT adds the Services factor to the classic Process/People/Products triad. In this way SIMA is typically an analytical model that breaks the complex IT management field down to manageable pieces. It recognizes the fact that technology alone doesn't do the trick: you need people and processes to be aligned effectively, in order to reach high-quality services. This view can also be found in several other frameworks in this part of the book.

The layered model that breaks down the service into several components is largely compatible with the infrastructure paradigm of ISM, also used in the Compendium IT Service Management. The model incorporates a series of existing reference models: ITIL, NMF, TMN, etc., but still has its own characteristics: high-level but practical and ITSM-focused.

Strictly speaking, SIMA is independent of ITIL: any model of processes can be chosen. The model incorporates some guidance for its application, in the three-step model: audit/design/implementation.

Concluding remarks

The frameworks presented in this part cannot be seen as methods; therefore we use the title 'frameworks'. In most frameworks the visions – the views – are specified in detail, but most frameworks lack a structure for modelling and application of the framework, and lack information about the management of the framework itself and the way it is supported. In sum, the frameworks are predominantly high-level views of the management of IT (services).

The frameworks have several characteristics in common. The available specifications of the frameworks are limited to rather high-level, abstract descriptions. They all speak of processes, and of objects to be managed, although they differ in the decomposition and in the way the two domains are related. The influence of ITIL and the Delft school is significant: not only in terms of compatibility, but also in the way most frameworks have increasingly adopted one or both in the last three years.

The same applies to CMM: more and more frameworks incorporate certain levels of maturity in the practice of the framework. The CMM model is used to add a stepwise improvement plan to the framework. Most frameworks now have a stepwise plan, a phasing, an implementation strategy, a change management approach or an audit and control cycle.

All frameworks have taken the process focus on board. This fits the evolution of upgrading from the technology-focused data center of the past towards the service-focused organization of this decade.

The differences in terminology conceal the strong similarities of the frameworks. It is not clear what the added value of these proprietary languages is, apart from the obvious desire of the providers to distinguish themselves from others. It also is not clear in what way this leads to a new understanding of IT service management. But maybe this is the practical road towards a common insight into the universal principles of IT Service Management.

One advantage from the wide range of frameworks is clear: wherever you are, whatever your business is, the wide range of frameworks makes it very improbable that you will not be able to find one framework or a combination of frameworks that would help you in choosing your own approach to organizing IT service management.

part 2

Sourcing and procurement

Introduction to the theme

The ICT sourcing issue is still a topical subject. There are different types of sourcing (i.e. insourcing, outsourcing, co-sourcing) of which outsourcing is the most actively used term. ICT outsourcing implies commissioning an external ICT service provider to perform certain ICT activities for an organization, such as information planning, system development, or maintenance and exploitation of information systems (IS).

Pros and contras

The pros of outsourcing have a strong relationship with the motives of an organization to outsource business functions: the pros form the motive. Beulen (1994), in his collaborative work on outsourcing decisions, gives an overview of motives subdivided into traditional and specialistic motives for outsourcing:

- **Traditional motives**
  These motives concern the lack of capacity of the organization to perform an ITSM process itself and the strategic considerations as to whether the organization should perform the ITSM process.
- **Specialist motives**
  These motives are further subdivided into five categories:

  – *Quality motive*
  The higher quality standards demanded by the organization cannot be fulfilled by the IT department, but can be fulfilled by an external ICT service provider.

  – *Costs motive*
  Costs of IT are increasing; an ICT service provider could deliver services at lower costs as a result of economies of scale.

  – *Financial motive*
  An enterprise has limited investment possibilities: investment in ICT means that no investment in other business resources can be made. An ICT service provider could deliver the ICT service without the need for long-term investments.

– Core business motive
Enterprises, having made the strategic decision to 'go back to core business', will outsource their ICT services when this is not their core business.

– Cooperation motive
Joint ventures and mergers can lead to problem situations between the participating parties: outsourcing could be used for rapid integration of the information systems involved.

Next to the positive contributions of outsourcing to the business goals, a number of negative influences can be depicted: the contras or risks of outsourcing.
Klepper and Jones (1998) give a great number of risks. A few examples:

- Outsourcing can involve some loss of control over the timely delivery of services and the quality of the service, both in respect to costs; in the case of outsourcing services, an organization depends on the ICT provider but doesn't have control over the behaviour of the provider.
- Flexibility is reduced. Any change in requirements must be accomplished through, and with the consent of, the ICT provider.
- Cost savings may not be realized: the costs of outsourcing are higher than expected.
- Corporate secrets and confidential information may be accessible to ICT providers.
- The time, effort and labour necessary to manage outsourcing may be larger than anticipated.
- By outsourcing, you are cut off from learning about new developments in technology, and the application of the technology is made harder.

The responses to the risks can be categorized into

- controlling the outsourcing decision;
- choosing the right provider;
- limiting opportunism on the part of the provider; and
- managing the outsourcing relationship.

Content

This part contains four chapters. Two of these relate directly to the subject of outsourcing on two different themes: competences at the client side needed in outsourcing structures, and influences of culture on outsourcing. The other two chapters are focused on procurement, a subject very close to outsourcing. One contribution has a primary focus on the procurement of ERP software, the other on the procurement of IT services. Thus we have:

Methodological ERP acquisition: the SHERPA experience
Joan A. Pastor, Xavier Franch and Francesc Sistach

Relationship management: delivering on the promise of outsourcing
John Buscher

Part 2: Sourcing and procurement

Chinese walls in IT outsourcing
Roger Leenders, Johan Duim, Albert van Houwelingen, Mario Paalvast and Gregg Shaffer

Best practice in acquisition and procurement management: the Information Services Procurement Library
John Dekker and Lex Hendriks

A review of part 2 follows thereafter.

Reading instructions

There is no specific sequence in which the articles should be read owing to the fact that there is no real interdependency between them. However, the contributions on procurement (acquisition) are somehow interconnected. It would therefore be worthwhile first to read the chapter on the more general procurement method descibed in 'Best practice in acquisition and procurement management' to get a notion of procurement, followed by the more specific ERP acquisition method in 'Methodological ERP Acquisition: The SHERPA Experience'.

Introduction to the chapters

The title of the first chapter, **Methodological ERP acquisition: the SHERPA experience**, gives a clear representation of the contents of Pastor, Franch and Sistach's contribution. The main subject in this chapter is SHERPA, a procurement method especially designed for enterprise resource planning (ERP) software. The authors give insight into the SHERPA procurement method by describing in depth its different phases, stages, organization, evaluation criteria, etc., as well as explaining several experiences in its application to real ERP procurement cases.

Many authors of publications on the subject of outsourcing at least agree on one thing: you need certain expertise inside an organization to control the external ICT service provider. In **Relationship management: delivering on the promise of outsourcing**, Buscher explores the different kinds of expertise needed in order to make a success of outsourcing.

In **Chinese walls in IT outsourcing** Leenders *et al.* investigate the problematic IT outsourcing market in Taiwan and give a clear insight into the Taiwanese business culture by trying to explain the stagnating outsourcing business. The basis of their research is formed by a comprehensive research of literature followed by a period of thorough field work.

In **Best practice in acquisition and procurement management**, Dekker and Hendriks give insight in the Information System Procurement Library (ISPL). The ISPL is, like ITIL, a best practices library of books, this time on the subject of procurement of ICT services. ISPL contains a series of books, tools and services to give the client and provider organization the ability to draw up effective ICT contracts.

Literature

Beulen, E. *et al.* (1994) *Outsourcing van IT-dienstverlening: een make or buy beslissing.* Kluwer Bedrijfswetenschappen (in Dutch)

Klepper, R. and Jones, W. O. (1998) *Outsourcing Information Technology, Systems and Services.* Prentice Hall

De Looff, L. A. de (1997) *Information Systems Outsourcing Decision Making: A Managerial Approach.* Idea Group Publishing. Series in Information Technology Management

16 Methodological ERP acquisition: the SHERPA experience

Joan A. Pastor, Xavier Franch and Francesc Sistach
Universitat Politècnica de Catalunya, Barcelona, Spain

Summary

In the area of information systems and software engineering, models, methods and methodologies have focused mainly on systems development, and much less effort has been put into systems acquisition. With regard to this last issue, we can find, on the one hand, simple methods which give generic advice on the acquisition of software, hardware and related services and, on the other, methods of a very complex and demanding nature. To try to fill this gap, we propose SHERPA, a new method for the acquisition of an enterprise resource planning (ERP) solution, which requires a medium-level effort while maintaining a high level of rigour and is specific for ERP. SHERPA stems from industrial experience, and it has been and is being used in various contexts, which is yielding some valuable feedback to the method.

16.1 Enterprise resource planning systems and their acquisition

In recent years, many organizations across most industries have acquired and implemented enterprise resource planning software solutions (ERPs). ERPs are customizable software packages with company-wide comprehensive functionality from which to build highly integrated management information systems (IS) for supporting both vertical functional areas and horizontal business processes across an enterprise. There are many reasons and consequences of the recent but significant trend of implementing ERP-based ISs; among these are:

- Organizations aim at implementing ERPs to enable the overall informational integration of functional areas across their – re-engineered – business processes, replacing most of their proprietary legacy systems, and thus reducing their future needs for in-house bespoke IS development.

- Usually, an ERP-based IS is set to become the back-office transactional foundation upon which to build the remaining decisional and communicational ISs, at both intra- and inter-organizational levels.

- Thus, in order to reach most or all of the organization's functional units and business processes, the implementation and maintenance of an ERP-based IS usually becomes a risk- and change-intensive project requiring significant economic, temporal and labour investments.

The important implications of an ERP solution for any organization make its acquisition a critical process, given that it can reach most or all departments and functions, and that it usually requires a significant economic and temporal investment in terms of implementation and maintenance. However, to the best of our knowledge, only very recently have some public acquisition methods specifically tailored for ERP software solutions appeared.

For the purposes of this chapter, we define *ERP acquisition* (also known as *ERP software procurement* or *selection*) as the following decision process: to clearly define the need that could be fulfilled with the help of an ERP product and/or related service; to find suitable products and services in the market that may help in the fulfilment of such a need; to establish appropriate criteria for the evaluation of ERPs; to evaluate products and services in the light of these criteria; to select the best available product and service, or the best possible combination of products and services; and to negotiate the final contract with the product vendor or service provider.

Once the strategic nature of ERP acquisiton is accepted, we can conclude that any organization pursuing a successful ERP experience should start by following a well-established ERP system procurement process, defined in terms which are as systematic and formal as possible, within the level of resources deemed adequate by the organization. This statement is based on reasons that, although obvious, seem often to be overlooked or only superficially considered:

- A well-established ERP procurement process can be a good starting point and set a good standard for the remaining ERP life-cycle phases within the hosting organization.
- Furthermore, it can help to determine organizational, business and user requirements that will facilitate more mature evaluations of ERP alternatives, as well as clarify how the ERP solution eventually selected fits these requirements.
- An early clear vision of required customizations, bespoke extensions and integration with preserved legacy systems will ease the definition of the scope of the subsequent ERP implementation process and of what the users should expect from the ERP-based IS.
- An early vision of the ERP-based transactional IS will facilitate IS strategic planning with regard to subsequent decisional and communicational, intra- and inter-organizational IS domains, such as so-called 'business intelligence', 'customer relationships management', 'supply chain management' and, more generally, 'electronic business'.
- In other words, a well-established ERP procurement process is a good foundation for successful ERP implementation and usage.

The strategic importance of ERP acquisition, the lack of methods for ERP acquisition and the euphoria around this kind of software solution are the main reasons that motivated us to develop SHERPA (*Systematic Help for an ERP Acquisition*) (Sistach et al., 1999; Sistach and Pastor, 2000). SHERPA is a method for acquiring ERPs that is rigorous and sufficiently complete but not too complex for the task in hand. Its goal is to be useful to managers, or consultants working for them, who want to acquire an ERP solution using a methodological and systematic approach, and who may find other methods too generic, complex or expensive. It is worth mentioning that SHERPA was first derived from a real experience of an ERP acquisition for a midsize company, and that so far it has been used and improved in three more ERP acquisition cases. Furthermore, the four companies which have applied SHERPA in their respective ERP acquisition decisions belong to four different industries.

The rest of this chapter is organized as follows. We first contextualize SHERPA within other related procurement methods. Then we provide an overview of the phased structure used with SHERPA, and comment on project management issues. Next, we give more details of its core evaluation phase, the classified evaluation criteria, and criteria formalization. Finally, we provide some conclusions and describe our most recent experiences with ERP acquisition by combining SHERPA with some modelling tools.

16.2 Related procurement methods

If we analyse previous works on software acquisition, we can distinguish two dimensions for classifying them: generality and level of effort required. That is, we can find methods focused on acquiring any type of IS product or service and methods focused on one specific type; and we can find works that present some ideas and steps to follow (these can hardly be considered methods) and complete and complex methods. Table 16.1 shows some methods that we have studied, classifies them according to these two dimensions and shows the relative position of SHERPA.

TABLE 16.1 Classification of IS procurement methods

	Generic	Specific
Higher effort	Euromethod PORE	Verville and Halingten (2001)
		SHERPA
Lower effort	Conger (1994) Mayrand and Coallier (1996)	Chaffey (1999) Reimann and Waren (1985), Lucks and Gladwell (1992) Hlupic and Mann (1995)

Euromethod (European Software Institute, 1996; Helmerich, 1998) is the best example of a very complete and complex method (its description takes nearly 250 pages) of a generic nature (it covers any kind of IS products and services). It is mainly suitable for public administrations which have to acquire products or services following a process of tendering.

PORE or Procurement Oriented Requirements Engineering Method (Maiden and Ncube, 1998) is devoted to select COTS (commercial on-the-shelf) software. PORE is a quite elaborated and generic iterative method, which provides templates for its five processes and for its documents and guidelines for the project team, and gathers techniques from many other works.

Conger (1994) proposes a generic, semi-structured acquisition method, including some tasks, tables and checklists. Mayrand and Coallier (1996) base their work on the eight phases of the acquisition process proposed by standards ISO/IEC-12207 and ISO/IEC 9126 (ISO/IEC, 1991, 1995), but focusing on large-scale software, risk management and quality assurance.

Regarding more specific methods, Chaffey (1999) offers long checklists devoted to select groupware, workflow and intranet solutions as a part of a book devoted to this kind of collaborative software; Reimann and Waren (1985) propose a method also based on long checklists for acquiring decision support systems; Hlupic and Mann (1995) have developed a tool that assists the user to select simulation software; and Lucks and Gladwell (1992) study the automatic selection of mathematical software.

Besides SHERPA (Sistach *et al.*, 1999; Sistach and Pastor, 2000), and to the best of our knowledge, only very recently (Verville and Halingten, 2001) has there appeared another public acquisition approach specifically tailored to ERP software solutions. In this book, the authors present several justifications and advice on ERP acquisition, as well as general evaluation criteria and reflections on some real ERP acquisition cases in big companies. Readers may build their particular ERP acquisition method from this book. At the other extreme, Stefanou (2000) presents, rather than a detailed method, a brief research framework of the critical issues involved in ERP system adoption and selection processes.

Other work that may be related to ERP acquisition is SA-CMM or Software Acquisition Capability Maturity Model (SEI, 1996), which is the equivalent of CMM applied to software acquisition. This model helps an organization to evaluate its general software-acquisition process, obtaining a maturity level, and to improve it progressively.

16.3 Overview of SHERPA

SHERPA within the general ERP life cycle

SHERPA covers all of the ERP acquisition process, from the search for candidate ERPs to the signing of the contract with the provider of the selected ERP and related services. SHERPA divides this process into five phases. Furthermore, for completeness and for practical considerations, instead of assuming that the decision to acquire an ERP has already been taken, we have decided to include, as an optional phase 0, one devoted to the analysis of the opportunity of acquiring an ERP. In the other end of the acquisition process, SHERPA does not cover the implementation of the selected ERP, nor its usage, maintenance, extension, evolution or retirement. Figure 16.1 shows the role of SHERPA within a general ERP life cycle.

FIGURE 16.1

SHERPA within an ERP life cycle

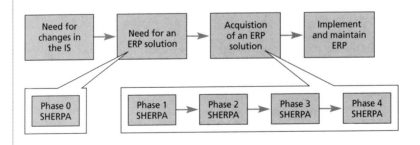

Phases within SHERPA

The five phases of SHERPA are described briefly here. Phase 0 is divided into two sub-phases: one that SHERPA does not cover and another that SHERPA covers in less detail but with the same structure as the other phases. Each of the remaining four phases is divided into stages and begins with an organization stage, followed by some stages specific to the phase and a final review and approval stage. This final stage is devoted to reviewing and gathering all the results of the phase, generating a final document and discussing it with a project committee, which will eventually approve it. Table 16.2 shows briefly the phases and stages of SHERPA.

TABLE 16.2 Phases and stages of SHERPA

Phases	Stages
Phase 0.1: Study the strategy and business processes	Not covered by SHERPA.
Phase 0.2: Decide to acquire an ERP	A) Organization B) Review the organization C) Evaluate the options D) Select an option
Phase 1: Search for candidates and first filter	A) Organization B) Review organization and IS C) Develop minimum requirements D) Study the ERP market E) Market research F) First selection G) Review and approval
Phase 2: Research the candidates and second filter	A) Organization B) Refine evaluation criteria C) Evaluate candidates in detail D) Second selection E) Review and approval
Phase 3: Analysis of and demonstrations by candidates, and visits to the providers	A) Organization B) Review evaluation criteria C) Prepare and attend ERP demos D) Final evaluation of candidates E) Third selection F) Review and approval
Phase 4: Final decision, negotiation and planning	A) Organization B) Negotiate the contract C) Review and approval

Phase 0: Study the strategy and business processes and decide to acquire an ERP

This phase is divided into two very different stages. In the first stage, the project team (whose characteristics are described below) studies the business (mission, strategy, etc.), its departments and business processes. This is something that we consider fundamental if the team is to evaluate how well each ERP adapts to the organization. All this can be achieved by studying internal documents of the company or, if these documents do not exist or are insufficient, by conducting interviews with employees – mainly executives and functional directors. In any case, since there are plenty of methods to achieve this purpose, we will not cover this stage in more detail here.

In the second stage, a committee has to decide whether the company is to acquire an ERP. This decision can be part of an IS plan or an isolated decision. It consists on a deep study of each alternative (internal or external custom development, best of breed, maintaining existing systems, etc), looking for its benefits, disadvantages and costs, in order to adopt one of them (or a combination of them). Since this is something that is addressed in depth by some methods specific to IS strategic planning, we have not developed a complete method ourselves. Instead, we propose a framework which can be embedded in other IS planning methods or used as a guideline if the organization is not following any particular IS planning method.

We propose the following tasks for the ERP adoption decision: describe each of the alternatives based on the specific situation of the organization and its IS; evaluate each alternative with the help of a list of criteria; analyse each alternative with respect to other specific considerations of the organization; and select one alternative.

The list of criteria that we have developed includes three main categories:

- *future criteria*: aligning with the strategy of the organization, usefulness and usability, adaptability to changes, integration capabilities, robustness, out-of-date risk, external dependency and maintenance support by the provider;
- *transition criteria*: type of implementation, implementation support, implementation time, change time, change impact, adaptability of users, business process re-engineering, users' participation, risk of interfaces, investment, ROI and risk of failure;
- *present criteria*: usefulness of existing IS, risk of maintaining existing problems, IS team participation.

For example, and as a first approach, acquiring an ERP could be evaluated as: strong external dependency, strong integration capabilities, big-bang implementation, strong impact on users and business processes, medium risk of failure, low risk of maintaining existing problems, etc.

Phase1: Search for candidates and first filter

Based on the knowledge of the company, obtained in Phase 0, and on some minimum requirements for candidate ERPs (price, platform, etc.), the project team conducts market research looking for ERPs suitable for the organization. This means getting references to ERP providers (professional magazines, software buying guides, trade shows, etc.) – perhaps dozens of them. By contacting the providers (by telephone, e-mail or some other way, but not necessarily an interview), the project team has to obtain enough information on each ERP so that, applying the minimum requirements, the number of candidates can be reduced to a number between 5 and 8 approximately. This reduction is necessary, as in the next phase each ERP will be studied deeply (having many ERP candidates obviously increases the effort required later).

Phase 2: Research the candidates and second filter

Here the project team needs much more information about the ERPs obtained in Phase 1. This information should be obtained from one or more interviews with the providers, getting as many fact sheets, catalogues, articles, etc. as possible. By applying a long list of more detailed selection criteria – which has to be refined and adapted to the organization – the project team should select two or three ERP candidate solutions. Again, here the selection criteria have to be considered as useful guidelines, not as exclusion criteria. If an ERP solution seems adequate but implies important changes in the IT infrastructure or in any other part of the organization, or simply does not comply with some criteria, it should not be eliminated immediately.

Phase 3: Analysis of and demonstrations by candidates, and visits to the providers

At this point the ERP providers have to demonstrate their products to the project team, the company top management, the mid-level management (department managers) and a selected group of future end users. The purpose here is to obtain a much deeper knowledge of each solution, specifically of its functionality and adaptability to the organization. The phase can include generic or customized demos at the provider installations or at the company itself, and can be cyclic, so people attend more focused demos of each ERP. Customized demos take longer to prepare and thus delay the completion of this phase, but they provide a much sounder baseline from which to compare the various ERP products considered. The project team gathers all the opinions, reviews and refines the application of the list of criteria to each candidate ERP and prepares a selection proposal, which has to be approved first by IT management and, finally, by top management.

Phase 4: Final decision, negotiation and planning

The project team negotiates the contract with the selected ERP provider, including the estimation of the cost and the schedule for the implementation, two very important aspects that should be estimated by the ERP provider, and a contingency plan. Finally, IT management and top management give their final approval, and the signing of the contract with the ERP provider may proceed.

Project team

Given that most mid-sized companies have never acquired an ERP solution in the past and on the assumption that they will face the acquisition of an ERP only occasionally (every several years), it would be naive to assume the presence of experts on ERP selection within these companies. Hence, it seems wise to try to include external ERP consultants in the project team. Preferably, these external consultants should be neutral with regard to ERP products and should offer knowledge of, and experience with, structured acquisition methods such as SHERPA.

Also, it is recommended, if not mandatory, to include in the project team some key internal people with knowledge of the organization and its IS. This points, at the least, to the IS/IT manager and to somebody else with a broad vision of the company (general manager, quality manager, controllers, internal auditors, organization manager, etc.).

Thus, we propose a project team of 3–5 people with a broad range of knowledge and experience, including: business strategy and business processes of the company, local ERP market, a systematic method for acquiring ERPs, previous acquisition experiences, and general business and IS knowledge.

In Phase 3, it is necessary to include many managers and users in the selection process, but they are participants and not full project-team members. Also, each of phases 1–4 finishes with a *Review and approval stage*, where a project steering committee must evaluate the work done so far. This committee should include top management and some other managers, and it could be the usual IS/IT committee that many companies have.

Effort estimation and project planning

Regarding effort, measured in total hours devoted to the project, and the planning of these hours in light of the tasks of the overall project, obviously they will depend on each case. The number of people in the project team, the number of managers and users involved in demos, the number and detail of these demos and the number of ERPs selected in each phase are some important factors of the effort equation.

Overall, and only as an indicator of the duration of ERP acquisition projects for mid-sized companies, it seems reasonable to complete the acquisition project in a few months (hardly less than two, three is easily achievable, and less than six). The total effort should be in the region of 'hundreds' of hours, assuming that the project committee, managers and users would contribute about half of them. It must also be noted that good management of the project schedule is a critical factor, as there are a lot of interviews and demos which must be attended by many people. Also, dedication to the project is variable for all the participants in the project.

16.4 Phase 2 in detail

Internal structure

Phase 2 may be considered the most demanding phase and the one where nearly all of the selection criteria are introduced and applied for the first time within the overall ERP acquisition process. For these reasons, we have selected Phase 2 as the one to be explained in more detail, describing each of its five stages.

A) Organization

The project was organized in Phase 1; at this point, it is only necessary to review all the documentation generated in that phase, and to review and detail the planning for Phase 2. The project team meets to start Phase 2.

B) Refine evaluation criteria

Taking into consideration the minimum requirements decided in Phase 1, Tables 16.3–16.7 containing selection criteria must be tuned for the particular company. These tables provide a list of around 30 first-level evaluation criteria, which become many more when refined, and which we have grouped in six categories: strategy, functionality, technical, provider, services and economic. Overall, they cover all the typical aspects that can affect a decision to buy an ERP.

Tables 16.3–16.7 give criteria for all the categories except strategy. Each table lists the criteria plus some explanations on each one. For the strategy criteria, there is no guide, and the project team must elaborate a table from scratch based on the present and future business strategy of the company, as explicitly stated in its mission statement and business plan, or drawn from interviews with top management. As a guideline, this table may include aspects such as: generic competitive strategy, main strategic focus on producing or on selling, break barriers between departments, improve the quality management, change a hierarchical organization into a matrix one, develop business units, support for e-business, advanced supply-chain management, etc.

TABLE 16.3 Functionality criteria

Criterion	Definition
Includes functionality by areas, processes, levels, priorities: • Commercial • Logistics • Manufacturing • Accounting • Finances • Human resources • Quality • Technical (Engineering, R&D) • Top management	Functionality requirements may be described, classified and evaluated along several dimensions: • requirements by functional areas that the ERP has to serve and how it covers each one; • requirements by inter-departmental and inter-organizational business processes; • requirements by organizational levels; • all requirements described, classified and evaluated at a level of detail in accordance with their relative business priorities.
Main target	Functional area/s for which the ERP is specially oriented
Adaptability	Possible level of customization in general and for the company
Openness for: • custom developments • working with other systems	Level of openness to additional bespoke development (internal or external) and to other existing applications (for example, vertical applications), API, etc.
Specific supports	For example: Y2K, euro, ISO9000

The project team must analyse all criteria contained in the tables and produce new tables adapted to the particular application. For the functionality criteria, the project team must analyse the functional needs of the organization and develop a much longer list of specific functions or business processes that the candidate ERP should support – or that would be recommended.

TABLE 16.4

Functionality criteria

Criterion	Definition
Platforms	IT platforms supported
Database management systems	DBMSs used as database for the ERP
Languages and development	Languages and development tools used to customize the ERP
User management levels, roles, authorizations, etc	Management capabilities: users, user groups, access
User documentation ● Printed manual ● Online help ● Tutorials	Type of user documentation for training and helping users to use the ERP.
Technical documentation ● Database schema ● Source code ● Design	Technical documentation on the internal structure of ERP master databases and programs
External connectivity ● Internet/Web ● Remote ● EDI	Types of external connectivity supported

TABLE 16.5

Provider criteria

Criterion	Definition
Provider characteristics: history, staff, clients, income, benefits…	Characteristics of the main provider as a company
Localization	Localization of provider's offices (headquarters, offices, etc.)
Similar implementations	Similar customers that use the ERP
References company, which use the ERP and could be	One or more clients, similar to the customer asked for comments
Experience sector of the company	Experience of the provider in general and in the
Confidence	Confidence of the project team in the provider and its ERP

TABLE 16.6 Services criteria

Criterion	Definition
Implementation method and implementation experience	Existence of an organized, documented and tested implementation method
Implementation services: • Installation, Adaptation, • Training, Support, • Custom development, • Connection to other systems, • Maintenance, • Platform, Others.	Services offered by the provider during and after the implementation and regarding ERP and global IS issues
Type of implementation	Strategy or strategies proposed by the provider for the implementation
Implementation estimated time	Provider estimation to implementation time

TABLE 16.7 Economics criteria

Criterion	Definition
Pricing method	Methods used by the provider to evaluate the price of the ERP and its implementation, maintenance, etc. (by users, modules, platform, …)
Cost	Cost of ERP software, implementation, maintenance, custom development, changes in IT infrastructure, etc.
Contract	Type of contracts offered and/or acceptable

C) Evaluate candidates in detail

Following the work initiated in the market research stage (E) of Phase 1, the project team must get much more information about each of the ERP candidates selected in that phase. This can be achieved through closer direct contacts with the providers, and also by studying all relevant documentation. We strongly recommend visiting the provider's offices and talking with commercial, technical and management staff. As a result, the tables generated in the previous stage should be updated and completed with the information in hand, although some details may be left for the next phase.

D) Second selection

With all the information available so far about candidate ERPs, organized around the above criteria tables, the project team must select two or three candidate ERPs. Metrics for each criteria item and category may be used, as well as relative weights.

E) Review and approval

Finally, the project team gathers all documents generated in the phase and writes a report for the project steering committee, including an approximate plan for the next phase. The project team presents the report and, if it is approved, starts the next phase. Since the next phase will involve the participation of many users, its planning must be discussed in detail at this point. More specifically, the report can include the following chapters: definition and description of evaluation criteria tables, all the tables with the information on each ERP (selected or not), list of selected ERPs, and planning for the next phase.

Desirable formalization of evaluation criteria

Once evaluation criteria tables have been customized and filled in for a specific ERP acquisition case, an optional step in SHERPA methodology is to express them using a more structured notation, designed to capture the criteria in a formal way. In general, there are many reasons that support criteria formalization whenever possible, in particular:

- A detailed and formal description of the domain is obtained, which provides a comfortable and precise framework for reasoning about the ERPs involved.
- Not only the product, but also the formalization process, is interesting in itself. As usual in most contexts, during formalization many questions may arise concerning the criteria, which otherwise would remain hidden.
- From our point of view, comparison of ERPs with respect to formally expressed criteria is a step towards assuring the decisions taken during procurement. This is especially true when dealing with more than a few candidate ERPs.
- A structured and formal notation can be used as a basis for building ERP procurement toolkits.
- The existence of a widely accepted high-level language would even provide a lingua franca to which ERP vendors could adhere for elaborating uniform descriptions of their products, and it would enable ERP procurement specialists to improve their ability to search for and examine ERP solutions.

There are many existing approaches to formalization in the more general case of COTS package selection (Dong *et al.*, 1999; Guerra and Finkelstein, 1999; Maiden and Ncube, 1998). Although the actual notation used is not a fundamental point of the methodology, formalization has been carried out in SHERPA using the NoFun notation (Franch, 1998). Although originally designed for describing non-functional attributes and requirements in the component-based software development framework, NoFun has proven to be well suited to describing ERP evaluation criteria (Burgués *et al.*, 2000).

Obviously, a key point in the ERP acquisiton process is a proper evaluation of candidates with respect to the criteria considered. It seems natural for criteria evaluation to be systematized as far as possible, to avoid untrustworthy results yielding potentially erroneous ERP selection. Along these lines, ERP selection criteria could be classified into three categories with respect to their evaluation:

- **Criteria computable directly from the ERP.** Although this is the desirable case, it turns out to be the least frequent one. In addition to some simple criteria (e.g., product size, price), we can mention ERP complexity, expressed using, for instance, function points or many design measures, and also ERP quality in terms of the internal structure of the product.

- **Criteria evaluable with a systematic methodology.** In this case, a well-defined process can be defined to evaluate the criteria. As part of the process, several issues must be defined: a metric to measure the criteria; the stages during the evaluation process; and the correspondence between the results of these stages and the final score with respect to the metric. As criteria that seem to be well suited to this category, we can mention functionality criteria.

- **Subjective criteria.** In this case, the evaluation relies mainly on the skills of the ERP provider and the procurement specialists. With respect to the provider, we can mention as an example its previous experience in the customer's industry; with respect to the customer, the confidence in the provider and its product.

We believe that all criteria are important, especially functional criteria, and that their consideration must be as systematic and formal as possible, and taken on board by the company.

16.5 Experiences with SHERPA

We recall that SHERPA was first derived from a real experience of an ERP acquisition for a mid-sized company, and that so far it has been (or is being) used and improved in three additional ERP acquisition cases. Furthermore, the companies which have applied SHERPA for their ERP acquisition decisions belong to four different industries. We next explain briefly this sequence of cases (referenced with coded names) where SHERPA has been conveniently combined with other tasks and tools specific to each case:

- MAGIC is a mid-sized company producing and distributing small electrical appliances for consumers through various distribution channels within the Spanish market. This company had a very problematic legacy IS developed in-house over the past ten years, technically obsolete and very difficult to upgrade, and functionally very limited and unable to deal with Y2K and the euro. Confronted with such a software renovation decision, MAGIC decided to run a business strategy planning effort and a business process analysis prior to the software renovation. Once these two strategic tasks were done, and the company had a clearer view of its current and future interests, it decided with the help of SHERPA to adopt ERP and to acquire a specific ERP tool.

- COSMIC is a mid-sized enterprise producing and distributing cosmetic products for professional markets in Spain and Central and South America. COSMIC wanted an integrated IS to replace its extensive set of small software applications, some bought and some developed in house. Y2K and the euro were also a motivation for software renovation, rather than technological obsolescence. In this case, the IS/IT manager used SHERPA, under our supervision, to organize the ERP acquisition project. Furthermore, as part of the ERP functional evaluation task, we used UML (*Unified Modelling Language* (Erikksson and Peuker, 2000) to formally specify and represent their five most critical business processes. From such specifications, comprehensive functional checklists were produced and used to evaluate the functionality of ERP candidate products. Finally, the company selected a big ERP system, as well as an implementation consulting company.

- GRAPHIC is another mid-sized company that produces packaging materials from paper and cardboard for an extensive market of industrial European firms. In this case, the IS/IT manager used SHERPA, under our supervision, to acquire an ERP solution, which is now starting to be implemented by an already selected consulting company. The legacy IS included a large subsystem developed and controlled by a single programmer, and a couple of software packages for industry-specific purposes. Owing to temporal constraints, the ERP acquisition project did not address functional criteria evaluation with as much effort and detail as in the COSMIC case. However, in this case UML is now being used to formally represent current and expected functional needs by areas and business processes, with the purpose of serving as a rich input to the implementation task, which will address process improvement along the way.

- FERRIC is a company producing iron-based components for the automobile industry and for the automobile repair consumer market in France and Spain. FERRIC has recently decided to break its relationship with a consulting firm that was implementing one of the currently leading ERP products for them. After recognizing that its prior ERP acquisition task was overly simplistic and superficial, which in its opinion explains part of the problems with the aborted implementation, FERRIC is now using SHERPA as a guide to address another ERP acquisition project. Under our guidance, the project is being set up and managed by the IS/IT manager and the Purchase and Procurement Department.

To conclude with our most recent experiences related to ERP acquisition, let us mention that the ERP acquisition experience gained by our group through our university posts has permitted us to address an important project for auditing an ERP acquisition project developed by a big hospital in the Barcelona area under the guidance of a big consulting company.

16.6 Conclusions

Our method, named SHERPA, is specific to ERPs, not too complex, but rigorous and complete enough for its purposes. It covers the whole ERP acquisition life cycle, from the search for candidate ERPs (and even from the decision to acquire an ERP versus other alternative IS approaches) to the signing of the contract with the provider of the selected ERP. Thus, we believe that SHERPA fulfils an almost empty space in the acquisition methods area.

Obviously, SHERPA can be improved in many ways, including: support for the selection of multiple candidate providers – implementation consulting firms – for a unique ERP solution; better comparison with other methods; application to COTS selection (that is, a more generic SHERPA); support for issues related to risk management; extended Phase 0; stronger link with implementation; refined lists of criteria; and combination with other methods or tools (for conducting interviews, attending demos, IS planning, IS modelling, etc.). We believe that, as shown here, SHERPA is a well-balanced method which can be the foundation for rigorous ERP selection.

Literature

Burgués, X. Franch, X. and Pastor. J.A, (2000) 'Formalising ERP selection criteria'. *Procs. 10th International Workshop on Software Specification and Design (IWSSD)*, San Diego, California, USA.

Chaffey, D. (1999) *Groupware, Workflow and Intranets*, Digital Press, Ch. 6, 'Selecting the right software'.

Conger, S. (1994) *The New Software Engineering*, ITP, Ch. 16: 'Purchasing hardware and software'.

Dong, J. Alencar, P. and Cowan, D.D. (1999) 'A component specification template for COTS-based software development'. *Procs. 1st Workshop on Ensuring Successful COTS Development*, at 21st ICSE, 1999.

Erikksson, H.-E. and Penker, M. (2000) *Business Modelling with UML – Business Patterns at Work*, John Wiley & Sons (OMG Press), USA, 459 pp.

European Software Institute (1996) *Euromethod v1*, www.esi.es, July.

Franch, X. (1998) 'Systematic formulation of non-functional characteristics of software'. *Procs. 3rd IEEE International Conference on Requirements Engineering (ICRE)*, Colorado Springs, Colorado, USA, April, pp. 174–81.

Guerra, S. and Finkelstein, S. (1999) 'Specification of COTS-based systems'. *Procs. 1st Workshop on Ensuring Successful COTS Development*, at 21st ICSE.

Helmerich, A. (1995) *Euromethod contract management*, in P. Bernus, K. Mertins, and G. Schmidt (eds.), *Handbook on Architectures of Information Systems*, Springer.

Hlupic, V. and Mann, A.S. (1995) 'SimSelect: A System for Simulation Software Selection.' *Proc. of the 1995 Winter Simulation Conference*.

ISO/IEC 9126:1991 (1991) *Information technology – Software product evaluation – Quality characteristics and guidelines for their use*, ISO, www.iso.org, 1991. (As referenced in European Software Initiative (1996) and Mayrand and Coallier (1996).)

ISO/IEC 12207:1995 (1995) *Information technology – Software life cycle processes*, ISO, www.iso.org (As referenced in European Software Initiative (1996) and Mayrand and Coallier (1996).)

Lucks, M. and Gladwell, I. (1992) 'Automated selection of mathematical software'. *ACM Transactions on Mathematical Software*, 18, March.

Maiden, N. and Ncube, C. (1998) 'Acquiring COTS software selection requirements'. *IEEE Software*, 15, March/April.

Mayrand, J. and Coallier, F. (1996) 'System acquisition based on software product assessment.' *Proc. of ICSE-18*, IEEE.

Reimann, B.C. and Waren, A.D. (1985) 'User-oriented criteria for the selection of DSS software'. *Communications of the ACM*, 28 (2), February.

SEI (1996) *Software Acquisition Capability Madurity Model Version 1.01*, Technical Report CMU/SEI-96-TR-020, www.sei.cmu.edu, December.

Sistach, F., Pastor, J.A. and Fernández, L.F. (1999) 'Towards the methodological acquisition of ERP solutions for SMEs'. Keynote paper in *Proc. of EMRPS'99 – First Int. Workshop on Enterprise Management and Resource Planning: Methods, Tools and Architectures*, Venice, 25/27 November.

Sistach, F. and Pastor. J.A. (2000) 'Methodological acquisition of ERP solution with SHERPA'. *First World Class IT Service Management Guide 2000*, ten Hagen & Stam Publishers, The Hague, Netherlands, pp. 225–33, March.

Stefanou, J. (2000) 'The selection process of enterprise resource planning (ERP) systems'. *Procs. 2000 American Conference on Information Systems (AMCIS)*, Long Beach, California, USA, pp. 988–91, August.

Verville, J. and Halingten, A. (2000) *Acquiring Enterprise Software – Beating the Vendors at Their Own game*, Prentice-Hall PTR (Enterprise Resource Planning Series), New Jersey, USA, 282 pp.

17 Relationship management: delivering on the promise of outsourcing

John Buscher TPI Managing Partner, Europe

Summary

If you can believe the industry analysts and the level of activity in the marketplace, outsourcing is here to stay as a strategic tool that is only as effective as the operator of the tool. The process for managing an outsourcing relationship can be as complex as the transaction process itself. The implications of an outsourcing transaction last far beyond the contract signing.

Many companies today may not understand the value of and the need for solid relationship management. Good relationship management requires thought, planning, coordination and dedication of resources to be successful. Senior management cannot overlook the importance of this structure and its supporting processes. Good relationship management can be used to overcome many ills inherent in a sourcing transaction.

While this area of expertise is relatively immature, it is nonetheless important if the promise of outsourcing is to be realized. The skills required to successfully manage an outsourcing relationship, the governance roles and responsibilities, the contract management process, the need to create and maintain buy-in, dispute resolution and the need for training and retaining skilled people are areas detailed in this chapter.

17.1 Introduction

In many cases, all of the emphasis, effort and energy goes into consummating the outsourcing transaction. Often the dealmakers, from both the client and the supplier marketing teams, scatter to the four winds shortly after the deal is signed. It is the unlucky soul that has been named the client contract manager that is left to determine what was just negotiated. More times than not, this is a recipe for disaster when it comes to realizing the benefits of outsourcing. You have more than likely read about such disasters before.

Fortunately, clients today realize the importance of having a good relationship management structure in place and a sound governance model by the time the deal is struck. The question is, how does one go about building this into the process and how does one operate after the deal is done? This chapter provides insights into how to achieve a successful relationship-management structure to deliver on the promise of outsourcing, based on experience in Europe, the USA and Asia during the past twelve years. First, we will provide some context, with insights into how the outsourcing marketplace has evolved.

17.2 Changes in outsourcing

The essential difference in the third wave of outsourcing is best understood by contrasting it with the two earlier waves. The first wave of outsourcing agreements were primarily long-term, fixed-cost commodity-based, infrastructure transactions with one objective in mind, to reduce cost.

Second-wave transactions evolved slightly, in that the focus on reducing costs shifted to getting variability by converting fixed costs into variable ones and extending outsourcing's scope from not only IT infrastructure to applications maintenance and development, but also to other IT-enabled business processes. Generally, both the buyer and the supplier of services would have considered these agreements a success.

The buyers were happy because costs were lowered, controllable and variable. And, if the truth were told, in the executive suites of many of these companies, outsourcing was also seen as a means of getting rid of managing expensive, frustrating, and little-understood parts of their operation.

Suppliers were happy with these long-term arrangements because good profits were almost guaranteed by the ever-improving price–performance phenomena of newer technology.

However, where these relationships fell down was when the buyer needed the supplier to be fast, flexible and innovative in response to changing business needs and competitive pressures; the supplier frequently lacked speed, agility and creativity to meet these changing demands.

The third wave is being driven by the now pervasive and invasive impact of global competition. To survive and succeed in their markets, buyer companies must become world-class in speed, innovation, flexibility and cost. Witness the ongoing e-business transformation, for example. The same pressures felt by the buyer companies to keep up and get ahead are inevitably forced upon suppliers. Thus, from a competitive standpoint, buyers can no longer afford nor accept many of the frustrations associated with their earlier cost-centric arrangements with outsourcing suppliers.

As a consequence, third wave outsourcing arrangements will give rise to a more holistic relationship-management approach centred upon the question: How can the buyer enterprise's objectives and core competences be best optimized as a whole by structuring and managing a suite of relationships, some outsourced and some not? While these new relationships will all be low-cost, importantly, they also must be near best in class in terms of flexibility, agility, speed and innovation to compete in today's market.

Business CEOs and suppliers who exploit the third wave will do so by redesigning their organizations from the ground up. This approach embodies innovative business process re-engineering concepts and governance techniques to maximize the value of multifaceted relationships. Clearly, implementing and making these new structures work will not be easy or done overnight because of existing structures, mores and agreements. However, once in place, they can for the first time deliver the full promise of outsourcing.

Some of the many questions to be answered about the third wave and relationship management include: How is it best to design and manage these new holistic arrangements? What do these organizations look like? How are they governed? Are their special tools and management concepts to be applied? What are the evolving best practices? Who are the leading third-wave suppliers, advisers, and consultants?

17.3 Beginning the process

Like the visible tip of the iceberg, signing the outsourcing deal is but a small portion of the whole outsourcing relationship. Much has been said about the outsourcing transaction process and much has been said about the success or failure of specific outsourcing relationships. The intent of the following paragraphs is to help highlight the importance of relationship management in having a successful outsourcing relationship.

Drivers of outsourcing

We all operate in a dynamic market swept by global changes such as Web-inspired, technology-infrastructure paradigm shifts, privatization, deregulation and the globalization of industries. Countless cases of mergers and acquisitions abound as companies seek to remain strong or gain strength in an e-commerce-enabled global marketplace. Likewise, the factors driving outsourcing have evolved from a focus on solving financial problems to making IT or certain business processes contribute to the competitive success of an organization through enhanced capability or capacity, improved flexibility, increased efficiency or enhanced speed to market. Outsourcing has evolved from a survival tactic to a strategic competitive tool touted by even the most respected management consultants, including Peter Drucker. The problem with any tool is that it is only as good as the 'operator' using it.

Relationship management

'Mega' deals have abounded in the outsourcing market, from groundbreaking deals such as those at Kodak and General Dynamics to more recent transactions at AT&T, Nortel Networks, MCIWorldcom, UTC, Westpac and AstraZeneca. As deals get larger and more strategic, they attract more attention from senior management, stockholders and the media. This requires the relationships to perform at least as expected. One facet that tends to get overlooked after the deal is done is how the deal will be managed. Remember that the end game is not to complete a transaction but to deliver the results that were defined by the initial objectives for an outsourcing relationship.

How does a company considering or involved in an outsourcing transaction plan for success? One can borrow from Stephen R. Covey (author of *7 Habits of Highly Effective People*) and begin with the end in mind. In this case, it means that it is never too early in the transaction process to begin developing the governance model for managing the relationship regardless of the size or scope of the transaction, number of suppliers, or the number of people affected. One of the keys to good relationship management is to make sure that, from both the client and the supplier(s) side, the people responsible for negotiating the transaction are involved in managing it initially and for some period of time.

The governance model has to be developed and refined concurrently with the transaction process such that it is a well-defined process by the time transition begins. The governance model is the roadmap by which you manage and measure daily operations, evaluate supplier performance, and cope with change.

The tools and metrics for measuring performance have to be clear and agreed. Creating metrics for activity that cannot be measured or that is irrelevant has no value. The level of detail and the type of information reported has to be meaningful to the user. If you are reporting mainframe availability and MIPS usage to a business unit leader who wants to know why customer service complaints are increasing, you are measuring the wrong activity and that executive's needs aren't being met. Metrics and service levels have to be developed from an end user's viewpoint.

Too often the client and supplier(s) go through a long and ambitious effort to close the deal, and then they relax. The first six months of the contract, the transition, is a vital aspect of the relationship for all parties. Good communications and well-handled HR issues are critical to success. Establishing credibility with users through high-quality delivery and responsive behaviour is essential. Finalizing governance and operating procedures that are successfully implemented is paramount. The transition will set the tone for the future of the long-term relationship.

A couple of other key aspects of good relationship management are well-defined change control procedures and dispute resolution. Processes for dealing with both of these situations need to be established before the deal is signed. Given a dynamic environment with rapidly changing technology and market forces, these sound processes become very critical to the long-term success of the transaction.

Planning for success is the underlying element of good relationship management. Anticipating that some change is inevitable, one must enable the core team managing the transaction to deliver on the promises of the outsourcing relationship. The skill sets and experience required are covered in the next section.

17.4 Skills for success

Previously, points were made relating to the need to plan for relationship management early in the transaction process. The need for a successful transition and the importance of setting the tone in the first year were described earlier. Once the transaction is concluded, it is essential to have the right relationship management leadership in place. What skills do such managers need to be successful?

Know the deal

Having those that are going to manage the relationship involved in creation of the transaction is desirable so that they understand the workings of the deal, the key issues negotiated, and the commitments made by each of the parties. This may not always be possible, but should be part of the transaction process. If not involved early on, the relationship leader needs to call on the people who were involved so that the knowledge can be transferred as soon as possible.

Negotiating skills

The relationship management team must have the ability to manage necessary change throughout a long-term outsourcing relationship, including changes to the deal structure, services scope, quality and flexibility. The ability to resolve disputes is critical.

Management and leadership skills

Particularly in larger transactions where multiple relationships exist, it is necessary that the senior relationship manager have well-developed managerial and leadership skills to use in dealing with the extended relationship management team, the supplier's staff and management, and the various other internal constituencies.

Programme management skills

The ability to manage multiple, complex processes simultaneously and deal with the interrelationships is important. The ability to identify and resolve problems before the impact becomes significant is crucial to good programme management.

Technical skills

The relationship management leader does not need to know every intricate detail but does need to understand the technical architecture, technical strategy and how they relate to business needs. Understanding the technical interdependencies in an environment subject to change is an essential skill. The relationship management leadership needs to know how to measure supplier performance and interpret the results from the metrics in the contract or service level agreements.

Business acumen

The relationship management team must have a sound understanding of the business needs of the user community and the evolving nature of their needs in a global market. Understanding business issues allows the relationship managers and users to communicate and solve problems. Measuring the right activities and being able to report to users and senior management in a meaningful way is a key to success.

Communications skills

The relationship management team must be proactive in keeping the stakeholders informed and in managing expectations. They must be able to communicate effectively with suppliers to transform business needs into deliverable services. The relationship manager should be good at telling the supplier(s) what to do, not how to do it. Different audiences at different levels will need tailored messages.

Procurement skills

As needs evolve during the course of a relationship, relationship managers must be able to run an efficient, cost-effective demand management process. Additionally, should the supplier's performance fall below what was contracted, a well-defined procurement process will allow the relationship manager to source with other third parties.

With such a diverse skill set required, the challenge is developing, training and retaining key relationship managers and having a succession plan as people move on to new roles.

17.5 Roles and responsibilities of the client relationship management team

Detailed below is one model of the roles and responsibilities for a relationship management team focused on application development and management (ADM). This will provide you with a sense of the structure of the team and individual responsibilities. However, the structure will vary depending on the scope, size and complexity of any given sourcing relationship or set of relationships.

Listed below are basic descriptions of the individual positions. Detailed responsibilities for each position can be found in Appendix A on page 259.

- The **Client Contract Executive** will be thoroughly familiar with and responsible for the ongoing management of the agreement, including billing activities.
- The **Client Contract Project Office Director** has primary business operating performance responsibility for the arrangement and monitoring of all supplier deliverables and commitments.
- The **Client Project Office Transition Manager** has overall responsibility for fulfilling the client's obligations under the Client Transition Plan. The successful transition of all client personnel and subcontractors to the supplier account team will ensure that performance levels and client satisfaction are maintained.
- The financial management of the agreement is critical to ensure accuracy and auditability of all related financial transactions and that proper financial controls are in place during the term of the agreement. The **Client Project Office Business Control & Risk Manager** will proactively inspect the supplier's process and procedures to ensure compliance with the agreement and with the client's audit, security and business recovery requirements. The Client Project Office Business Control & Risk Manager will ensure that all involved parties, including the supplier and infrastructure provider, are using all of the client-reviewed and approved procedures to protect data, and adherence to audit requirements. That person will also work with the internal audit and compliance groups to review supplier adherence to these requirements. The Client Project Office Business Control & Risk Manager will be responsible for approving all contract-level performance credits and track all performance credits.
- The **ADM Coordinator** is responsible for administration of the balanced scorecard assessment to determine whether committed productivity and deliverables under the agreement are being satisfied.
- The **Client Contract Administrator** is responsible for establishing and maintaining all necessary agreement-related documentation, communication logs and reference material required by the client governance team to manage the agreement effectively.
- The **Client Portfolio Manager** is responsible for ensuring that the supplier is fulfilling all portfolio-level contractual obligations. This includes authorizing work, establishing scorecard targets, analysing scorecard results and assessing portfolio-level performance credits. The Client Portfolio Manager monitors that service levels are maintained and continually improved, and that problems with the supplier's day-to-day delivery of services are minimized.

The **Client Program Managers** and **Project Managers** perform the critical role of interface with and representation of the client business community and end users. Their duties have the option to be both tactical and strategic. The Client Program Managers will participate in the requirements phase and in portions of the business design phase of any new project. Although the Client Program Managers will continue participation for the duration of any new project, their emphasis will be on communication, setting priorities, and ensuring that business requirements are being met. Client Project Managers will be familiar with which projects are covered under the baseline portion of the agreement and which will require additional funding, as these will require different approval processes.

The **Client Architecture Planning & Strategy Team** will ensure that appropriate attention is paid to the future technological direction for the client. During the term, many technological changes may occur. This team will evaluate and ensure that the client has the appropriate mix of current, emerging and stable technologies.

High-level functional matrix for contract management processes

Now that we have described some of the key roles and responsibilities in a typical governance structure, let's examine some of the key activities and identify the responsible party. Some activities are shared and some are performed independently. Table 17.1 gives some insight into the interdependence and shared responsibilities between a client and a supplier in a sourcing arrangement.

TABLE 17.1 Interdependence and shared responsibilities in a sourcing arrangement

Contract management Major functions and activities	Client/ Governance	Supplier
1. Contract Planning and Management		
Forecast annual and quarterly financial objectives	P	P
Manage overall supplier relationship (e.g. contract, performance, audit, service level attainment) via steering committees	P	P
Execute dispute resolution process	P	P
Assess performance credits	P	
Execute service level adjustment process when required	P	H
Conduct customer satisfaction surveys		P
Analyse customer satisfaction results and develop action plans	P	P
Provide data to support monthly scorecard reporting		P
Produce quarterly scorecards	H	P
Analyse scorecard results and develop action plans as required	P	P
Review key personnel results	P	H

TABLE 17.1 contd.

Contract management Major functions and activities	Client/ Governance	Supplier
2. Metrics (Quality, Customer satisfaction, Productivity)		
Define agreed-upon operating level agreements	P	H
Define agreed-upon service levels and target commitments	P	H
Define customer satisfaction survey requirements for CIO/ITS customer survey	P	P
Define balanced scorecards at contract and portfolio levels	P	H
Provide for third-party benchmark, analyse results and determine remedies if required	P	H
3. Invoicing and pricing		
Produce monthly base charge invoice		P
Approve and pay monthly base charge invoice	P	
Produce monthly project accounting reports		P
Approve monthly project accounting reports	P	
Produce monthly additional resource charges (ARC)/ reduced resource charges (RRC) invoice if required		P
Approve monthly ARC/RRC invoice if required	P	
Review monthly in-scope expense targets	P	H
Review monthly in-scope telecom expenses	P	H
Review monthly In-scope PC maintenance expenses, i.e. maintenance, LAN/intranet connection moves, adds or changes	P	H
Provide baseline and updated pricing/unit rates for full-time person ARC/RRC charges		P

H = Help; P = Perform

17.6 Creating buy-in

One key to success in a long-term outsourcing relationship is getting the various business units' buy-in. The relationship management team cannot solely be focused on managing the supplier. They must continue to interact with the business units and achieve consensus on meeting business unit needs. Like many other aspects of good relationship management, creating buy-in starts as you begin to plan the sourcing transaction. Initially, it is important to make sure that outsourcing goals and objectives are aligned with the business unit needs. It is of no benefit to have an outsourcing goal of reducing costs by 10–15% if you are not meeting business unit needs for flexibility and speed to market. Alignment of goals is a critical factor in the success of the long-term outsourcing relationship.

How do you achieve goal alignment? During the transaction creation development process it is important to have one or more representatives from the sourcing project team liaise with the business units and the executive steering committee for any outsourcing project. The project team must seek out the business units and understand their goals and objectives prior to finalizing the contract. They need to discuss how IT or the relevant business process being considered for outsourcing can enable or help achieve the goals of the business units. The business unit representative(s) on the steering committee must continually provide input on business unit needs relative to what is valuable to them.

Another element of achieving buy-in is to communicate openly, honestly and often. Keep the business unit leaders informed about what is happening and why. Spend the time to give formal updates at key milestones. This will keep the business units informed and provide them with another means of feedback. This way you avoid rumours and relying on others to communicate accurately messages or interpret feedback.

When a sourcing transaction is finalized, get the business units involved in the transition process so that they understand the changes that are going to take place, get to know the supplier(s) and have a vested interest in the process. The objective is to get the business units to feel that this transaction is something you are doing with them, not to them. You have to be able to constantly answer the question 'What does this mean to me?' from the business unit's perspective.

The successful conclusion of a transition is not always a sign that the business units have completely bought in and can be ignored until they complain. Business unit representatives need the ability to fine-tune supplier requirements and actively participate in holding the supplier accountable for contract deliverables and any resulting dispute resolution. Again, there is a strong need to communicate in order to keep the business units informed and provide mechanisms for feedback. Participation in monthly performance reviews, quarterly planning sessions and problem resolution task groups are all valuable.

Continuous business unit buy-in is critical to achieving the success and productivity objectives in any sourcing relationship.

17.7 Managing change

The one constant in the world of outsourcing is change. Issues such as globalization, the increasing pace of change in technology, e-commerce, and mergers and acquisitions drive change. It is naive to think that a 5–10-year deal will end in the same form as it began. So the question in an outsourcing relationship is, are you prepared to cope with the inevitable given that unforeseen changes will occur?

There are many consulting firms ready to advise you on change management processes. While this advice is useful and helpful, its application may be limited by the contract. The point is to include terms and conditions to deal with incremental or wholesale change in the sourcing agreement and incorporate those processes in the governance structure. Without these basic elements in place, no amount of change management advice will make you successful.

Any outsourcing agreement has to be constructed with a degree of flexibility and scalability. Outsourcing agreements must also include provisions for handling increased and reduced demand to the resource volume baselines through additional resource charge and reduced resource credit pricing mechanisms. Wholesale changes can be accommodated through the contract 'Change Control Procedure'. Additional terms and conditions to deal with change are the rights to use third parties, significant event clauses or contract termination for convenience. Any outsourcing relationship must have a reasonable exit strategy.

Having the right to use third parties allows the client to source in-scope work (with limitations) due to poor performance or out-of-scope work based on requirements for best-in-class service. This right is an incentive for the current supplier(s) to continue to perform in order to retain the current in-scope business as well as competitively bid for additional out-of-scope business. A 'significant events' provision in the contract will ease the deletion or addition of a specific service need due to a change in ownership, acquisition or divestiture. Termination for convenience, normally for a fee, allows the client to end the relationship with the supplier(s) for any reason. Termination fees should be non-punitive. The supplier should expect to be made whole on any unrecovered investment costs. Additionally, one should not be overly concerned about the contract term length if one can easily exit the contract with little cost.

Implementing the right governance team and processes is the other key aspect to being prepared for change. The governance team and to some extent the supplier(s) need to be involved in business planning so that change can be planned for in an orderly fashion rather than as a reflex response. Processes must be clearly defined and structures in place in the governance organization to identify and address change needs. An investment must be made in building and maintaining good relationships with the supplier(s). The supplier needs to have a vested interest in helping you address change either through involvement in building solutions to change related issues or through the opportunity to acquire additional or replacement work as a result of change. Consideration should be given to processes and capabilities to provide redundancy during a change transition so that business disruptions do not occur or project delivery dates are not missed.

Addressing change should be a routine part of managing a sourcing relationship, not an extraordinary event handled on an ad hoc basis in a crisis mode. A well-structured agreement and governance team can make handling change a routine part of business.

17.8 Resolving conflicts or disputes

Just as change is inevitable, so too are disputes and conflicts. The key to successful dispute resolution is what mechanisms and processes are put in place to recognize issues and to resolve them amicably.

A critical mistake some relationship managers make is that they file the contract away in a bottom desk drawer, never to be seen again. Without the contract, how can you make the supplier perform? On the other hand, you should not use the contract to bludgeon the supplier into submission. After all, an outsourcing relationship is made up of two or more parties striving for mutual gain. If one party dominates, the other will want out as sure as there are death and taxes.

If the proper governance model is in place, the right metrics are in place and the communication channels are open and functional, issues should be resolved before they become disputes that are escalated to the steering committee. Reporting should be done daily, monthly, quarterly and annually as appropriate in a proactive presentation that reviews performance relative to service levels, which includes suggested solutions to issues. More formal reporting often negates the need for difficult conversations. Both the supplier and the client have to devote adequate, properly skilled resources to manage the outsourcing relationship in order for this process to work effectively for both sides.

Even if the most effective governance model and metrics are put in place to model the contract, disputes will still arise and may fester without the people involved in the day-to-day operations on both sides knowing how to communicate and resolve issues. Additional training or reading may be appropriate in these instances. Books such as *Getting to Yes* and *Difficult Conversations* can be helpful. Trained professionals skilled in dispute resolution, like Doug Stone and Sheila Heen from Triad Consulting, can assist you in learning how to resolve disputes in an amicable way versus a win–lose approach based on who is the toughest negotiator.

Your contract should also provide some tools such as charge-backs to suppliers for missed performance levels, short paying of invoices to influence resolution of disputed items and earn-back credits for suppliers that resolve problems or improve performance. The process for escalation and dispute resolution should be clearly defined in the contract. A process to settle disagreements once the two parties reach a point where they cannot agree needs to be in place. This may be through litigation, rights to cancel the contract or taking away portions of the business, arbitration or mediation. The governance structure should support the resolution of issues.

In the final analysis, if the objectives are clear, there is a meeting of minds on expectations after the contract is signed and there is constant and clear communication, many disputes should be avoided. However, you cannot negate the need for a well-defined and expeditious dispute resolution process that is focused on keeping the relationship beneficial for all parties. In the end, either everybody wins or everybody takes his or her marbles and goes home.

17.9 Keeping outsourcing on track

Developing the relationship management function is a process many organizations are struggling with today. Previously, the roles, responsibilities, skills and qualifications of relationship managers have been described. As a quick review, the following skills are needed: communication, leadership, negotiation, procurement, programme management and technology. In addition, relationship managers must know the deal and have the necessary business acumen to understand user needs in the context of the user's business.

How do members of the transaction management team get the skills they need? Some can be obtained through training courses or certification programmes, such as project management or negotiation. Some skills are acquired through education or experience, such as procurement, technology or communication skills. However, the options for a comprehensive training ground are precious few at the moment.

How many outsourcing relationships have failed or achieved significantly less than projected due to a lack of sound relationship management? Some organizations such as DuPont have sought to build capabilities and processes internally. Others have chosen to acquire the necessary skills by hiring experienced people. No consistent pattern has emerged as to the best approach. Each organization, by necessity, is forced to invent its own approach.

Various organizations, academics and consultants have emerged in the outsourcing space with offerings to help address these needs. These offerings seem to be an evolving set that have not reached a steady state, become comprehensive and integrated in nature, or achieved critical mass. Until the market matures, each organization may be left to its own devices to provide the training/career development based on whom they know or what they discover in the marketplace.

Retention of the relationship management team is the parallel key issue in the sourcing industry today. Few organizations have developed career paths for people in relationship management roles. There seems to be a great deal of recognition for the leaders that close the deals but precious little recognition for those that manage the deals to realize the objectives. Often the reaction from management to relationship management needs is 'Why do you need those people and that budget? I thought we outsourced that.' Unfortunately, the recognition all too often comes at a significant price after some disaster has occurred once the relationship is some way down the track.

It would seem that the first step toward high retention is to get management to recognize the value of relationship management. After all, the relationship management leaders are responsible for the value their organization receives for millions to hundreds of millions to billions of dollars of expenditure. The next step would be for HR to develop job descriptions, provide certification and career paths that are not terminal and reflect the high level of diverse skills necessary to be successful as a relationship manager. Another important aspect is to make sure that the relationship managers are recognized for their contribution and the skills and experience they must possess to be effective in their roles. The more junior people that were involved in creating the relationship need to have the incentive to stay around to learn how to manage the deal and move up within the relationship management hierarchy or into other roles within a relationship management function. Organizations also have to remember that experienced relationship managers are a relatively scarce resource and subject to enticements from external organizations as well.

17.10 Summary

Outsourcing is here to stay if you can believe the industry analysts and the level of activity in the marketplace. How outsourcing is used as a strategic tool will continue to evolve. The process for managing an outsourcing relationship can be as complex as the transaction process itself. The implications of an outsourcing transaction last far beyond the contract signing. It takes many elements to produce an outsourcing relationship that can deliver on its promises. However, it could be argued that the most crucial element is the relationship management structure. While good relationship management on its own cannot guarantee success, its absence can guarantee disaster.

Good relationship management requires thought, planning, coordination and dedication of resources to be successful. Management cannot overlook the importance of this structure and its supporting processes. Good relationship management can be used to fix many ills inherent in a sourcing transaction.

While this area of expertise is relatively immature, it is nonetheless important if the promise of outsourcing is to be realized. The information in the preceding pages provided assistance in helping you understand many of the issues and how to address them. Now you may feel you know what you did not know and can intelligently tackle the issues or seek out the proper assistance to help you be successful.

Appendix A

Roles and responsibilities

This appendix contains detailed information on the various responsibilities for specific roles within the relationship-management governance structure for a specific ADM example.

The primary responsibilities of the **Client Contract Executive** are to:

- monitor supplier compliance with obligations of the agreement;
- manage the overall relationship with the supplier;
- staff and provide leadership to the Client Contract Project Office leadership team;
- work with the Supplier Contract Executive and the Client CIO Leadership team to ensure that the goals and objectives of the arrangement are met.

The primary responsibilities of the **Client Contract Project Office Director** are to:

- monitor supplier compliance with obligations of the agreement;
- monitor supplier contract-level deliverable commitments;
- track fulfilment of supplier deliverables;
- ensure auditability of supplier processes;
- manage benchmarking activities;
- staff and provide leadership to the project office team.

The **Client Project Office Transition's** primary responsibilities are to:

- approve the transition plan;
- manage the client's obligations under the transition plan.

The **Client Project Office Business Control & Risk Manager** for the client governance team performs all IT-related financial and audit related activities, including:

- establish and manage the overall budget in connection with the agreement;
- monitor that savings objectives for the agreement are being met;
- review financial analysis for all supplier-sponsored initiatives to ensure financial viability;
- manage and track all monthly charges to ensure accuracy of supplier charges, client retained costs and pass-through expenses;
- ensure that anticipated and agreed-upon supplier financial responsibilities are not converted to client retained or pass-through expenses;
- investigate variances in forecast expenses or usage;
- establish and maintain the client charge-back process and systems;
- reconcile projected resource baseline with actual utilization;
- monitor compliance with all client standards and procedures for client business policies and government and statutory regulations;
- define corrective action for all violations of client policies, including security breaches;
- review development of contract-level project risk mitigation plans;

- approve and track contract-level performance credits;
- facilitate and coordinate with client audit and compliance groups to review supplier processes and procedures;
- validate all fees.

The primary responsibilities of the **ADM Coordinator** are to:

- maintain application portfolio inventory and application demographics database;
- assist the client programme managers in monitoring the productivity of the project staff;
- audit the supplier's productivity and quality attainment;
- maintain and evaluate the balanced scorecards;
- monitor enhancements and changes to application portfolios;
- implement and manage the results of the Client CIO Customer Satisfaction Survey for the arrangement;
- provide project management support for contract-level initiatives as required.

The **Client Contract Administrator's** primary responsibilities are:

- coordinate all negotiation meetings regarding the agreement;
- develop and maintain a project plan, if applicable, for contractually required audits, reviews, etc.;
- track all software licence agreements;
- provide advice and counsel to the client team regarding contract terms and conditions.

The primary responsibilities of the **Client Portfolio Manager** are to:

- approve all service level agreement changes and shepherd through the change management process;
- reconcile projected resource baseline with actual utilization;
- establish and track supplier performance;
- authorize all work, including maintenance, on-demand and development projects;
- review and monitor supplier problem-management process and escalation procedures and adherence thereto;
- as operational problems occur, review supplier recovery and permanent fix plans and approve, as appropriate;
- approve and track portfolio-level performance against service levels and performance credits and report to Client Project Office Business Control & Risk Manager;
- monitor supplier adherence to disaster recovery procedures.

Client Programme Managers/Project Managers are responsible for all areas of the client's business unit relationship management, including:

- manage programme cost, schedule, quality;
- perform primary business partner interface;
- coordinate IS services, projects and plans among client business units;
- understand the client business unit market strategy and proactively identify and confirm business requirements in connection therewith;
- assist the client business unit in the development of the financial analysis for all proposed projects;
- take forward all new project proposals through the approval process;
- monitor that the end user is involved in the delivery of new projects as required and that delivered projects meet customer requirements;
- monitor project status;
- participate in user acceptance testing and user training;
- participate in post-implementation reviews and project evaluations;
- maintain master project plan to monitor all active projects;
- review and approve all IS project plans and identify weak project plan points and potential points of failure;
- assess project risk in conjunction with client business units;
- assist in the development of risk mitigation plans for projects;
- communicate the status of all projects to the appropriate programme managers, client business unit and client corporate management;
- conduct checkpoints and evaluate critical-path variances to ensure that projects remain on target and within cost and scope commitments;
- track and ensure resolution of project issues;
- authorize project-related change requests;
- maintain and coordinate consolidated project plans for key projects;
- participate in application design reviews, and in the development of major supplier deliverables such as business process prototypes, workflow diagrams and process models;
- develop and maintain the IS project management methodologies for the client;
- monitor productivity in each phase of project.

The ***Client Architecture Planning & Strategy Team*** is responsible for the following:

- establish and update IT strategic architecture;
- keep abreast of emerging technologies;
- monitor IT industry technology trends as they apply to client business;
- define requirements for approved end-user technologies;
- facilitate technology reviews with technology review board;
- develop and maintain the client's information technology strategy;

- work with the supplier to develop information technology plan;
- communicate technology direction and strategy to client business units;
- review transition plans for introduction of all new technologies;
- control and update foundation architecture.

Literature

Fisher, R., Ury, W., and Patton, B. (eds), (1991), *Getting to Yes*, Second edition, ISBN 0140157352, Penguin USA.

Stone, D., Patton, B., Heen, S., and Fisher, R., (2000), *Difficult Conversions*, ISBN 014028852X, Penguin USA.

Chinese walls in IT outsourcing

Roger Leenders Ordina Sociale Zekerheid
Johan Duim Atos Origin
Albert van Houwelingen independent consultant
Mario Paalvast Diod Advies
Gregg Shaffer Concert

Summary

IT outsourcing is not a universally acceptable concept. This chapter presents the results of an investigation into the obstacles that were encountered by a major global corporation in the wake of an international IT outsourcing decision. The text stresses the importance of deeply rooted cultural configurations, in this case the Chinese family business culture. In addition, the authors describe the market perspective and show the high impact of cultural aspects on an unsuccessful attempt to penetrate the Taiwanese IT outsourcing market.

18.1 Introduction

It is almost common knowledge within the global business community that business practices differ from country to country and culture to culture. This is even more so where IT outsourcing is involved. Outsourcing seems to be sensitive in almost all cultures. Trust is an essential prerequisite for two parties who enter into a multi-year contract including transfer of staff and equipment.

The authors had the opportunity to study closely the viability of IT outsourcing in a Chinese business setting.[1] Their findings indicate that the business issue they had set out to study was to a fairly high degree related to cultural aspects that normally are not brought to mind when contemplating nuts-and-bolts IT business agreements.

The authors feel that the strategic insights gained could be valuable for the international IT Service Management community and present their findings in this chapter, hoping that the readers of this Guide may benefit from the results of their research project.

18.2 Research description

The sponsor firm, a global player in the IT Services market, presented to us the case of its subsidiary in Taiwan, with a local presence over the last ten years. This subsidiary had started business in Taiwan in the wake of a single major account for which our sponsor firm provided worldwide IT services. In Taiwan, an IT outsourcing contract with this global client accounted for a major part of the business. The intriguing question brought to us by the global management of the sponsor firm touched on the apparent inability of the Taiwanese subsidiary to expand its business to other clients during the ten-year period of its presence in the local market.

This situation was aggravated by the announcement of the major customer that they would concentrate their IT services in a regional data centre outside Taiwan, thereby substantially weakening the business case of the Taiwanese subsidiary.

This development took place against the backdrop of an economic forecast of 12% annual compounded growth for the period 1999–2002 (Baty et al., 1999).

Our sponsor, the Executive Vice President for the responsible business unit, summed up the problem as follows: *'Considering our presence in Taiwan for the last ten years, what is causing the fact that we have not been able to expand our outsourcing business?'*

After accepting the assignment, we started an extensive literature search, focused on getting to understand 'how to do business in Asia in general and in Taiwan'. Based on this desktop research, an initial approach was phrased and refined into a conceptual model of our subject within the Taiwanese environment. Based on these preconceived notions, we formulated four hypotheses and outlined the required research tool: a questionnaire that would enable us to test the hypotheses. During our two trips to Taiwan, essential information was gathered by means of a series of 24 interviews with stakeholders (the management of the Taiwanese subsidiary, customers, competitors, prospects, government officials, academia). After sorting out the extensive material and testing it against the four hypotheses, we formulated our conclusions, which were subsequently presented to the management of our sponsor and its Taiwanese subsidiary.

Basically, the explanation for the stated problem should be found in either the characteristics of the local market (market perspective) or in the local performance of our sponsor firm (organizational perspective). Our approach therefore revolved around two questions:

- Is there an IT outsourcing market in Taiwan (market perspective)?
- Does our sponsor firm respond to the Taiwanese market in an appropriate way (organizational perspective)?

As the insights of our research concern proprietary information belonging to our sponsor firm which is not transmittable to other firms, we will not disclose any details about the findings concerning the second question nor about our advice. The scope of this chapter will therefore be restricted to the market perspective.

Most authorities on Asian business topics suggest that a good understanding of Asian business life cannot be developed without addressing the cultural dimension. The impact of the value system around trust, face and relationships is widely described. Do these values affect the willingness to outsource in a positive or negative way? Can we expect a strong governmental involvement with the economy? What impact does this have on the specific public policy regarding outsourcing of governmental IT facilities?

A second factor to be considered is the relative strength of economic incentives in the market to outsource IT activities. Is the situation in Taiwan, from an economic perspective, comparable to western Europe and the USA?

Prior to the authors' field work they had developed the following preconceived notion: '*There is no real market for IT outsourcing; however, from a business management perspective, the Taiwanese subsidiary is doing its utmost.*'

To test their research questions, four hypotheses were formulated:

1. The Taiwanese business culture is not conducive to the IT outsourcing market.
2. There are no incentives for Taiwanese companies to outsource their IT infrastructure.
3. The business plan of the subsidiary firm reflects the exigencies of the Taiwanese IT outsourcing market.
4. The marketing mix of the subsidiary firm is an appropriate reaction to the local IT outsourcing market.

In this chapter, only the first and second hypotheses will be addressed as these embody the market perspective, as opposed to the organizational perspective (hypotheses 3 and 4) which falls outside the scope of this chapter. In the next section, the authors will present the findings and their implications for IT outsourcing projects in a Chinese business setting.

18.3 Taiwanese business culture

The globalization of the business community in the 1970s and 1980s has led to growing interest in the differences between business partners from different cultural backgrounds. Among the best-known writers in this field are Geert Hofstede and Fons Trompenaars (see Hampden-Turner and Trompenaars, 1997; Hofstede, 1991; Trompenaars, 1993). Though these studies are insightful and relevant for every student of cultural variability, the authors felt the need to dig further: the preparatory research had led to the hypothesis that the Taiwanese business culture would not be a fertile substrate for IT outsourcing. They were in need of instruments to properly delineate the hypothesis and to test it.

Desk search

It is in this respect that the work of Richard Whitley proved of high value and relevance. His comparative study on East Asian business systems (Whitley, 1992) enabled the authors to clarify the distinctive characteristics of the Chinese family business system, especially its Taiwanese form. Through Whitley's work, the authors' hypothesis could be corroborated. The description of the Chinese family business system and its historical roots in the following paragraphs is based on Whitley (1992).

Economic exchanges take place in an environment that is shaped by many societal institutions, not all of which are necessarily rooted exclusively in economic relations. Institutions as diverse as political control structures and inheritance rules have an influence that extends in many guises throughout the economic realm and boast an impressive longevity. The integration of strong institutional environments encourages the alignment of economic practices to societal structures.

Describing important characteristics of Chinese family businesses as they matured long before industrialization and were altered by the recent industrialization phase of Taiwan, the authors feel able to point out important cultural drivers and barriers to IT outsourcing in Taiwan, the topic of this study.

Whitley categorizes the business system's characteristics in three major areas:

- ***the nature of the firm:*** what sorts of economic activities are integrated and for what competitive goal?
- ***inter-firm connections:*** how is competition and cooperation between firms organized?
- ***coordination of activities:*** what kind of authority hierarchy do we see in the firm?

Pulling together his combined observations on these dimensions, Whitley arrives at a series of configurations of hierarchy–market relations with high distinctive power among the diverse East Asian business systems.

Several characteristics of the Chinese family business configuration are illustrated in Table 18.1.

TABLE 18.1 Main characteristics of the hierarchy–market configuration of Chinese family businesses.

Economic actors	
Owner control	High
Homogeneity of expertise and similarity of activities	High in firms, medium in families
Risk sharing through mutual dependence	Low outside personal commitments
Market organization	
Degree of particularism and long-term commitment between firms	Low except for family-like partnerships
Reliance on personal networks	High
Employment and personnel practices	
Employer commitment to, and dependence on, core employees	Limited
Institutionalization of procedures	Low
Authority and control systems	
Importance of personal authority and control in hierarchy	High
Delegation to middle management	Low
Managerial role	Patriarchal

Based on Whitley (1992), p. 80, Table 3.5.

Many of the differences between East Asian business systems are interconnected, strengthening Whitley's view that only certain configurations of hierarchy–market relations are effective within a particular institutional environment. The strong emphasis – in the case of Chinese family businesses – on personal ownership and control leads to centralized decision making, but risks are managed by limiting commitments to core workers and by the limited level of capital investment. Flexibility is the key concern and so firms are highly specialized, with families sometimes diversifying through personal alliances to seize new opportunities and limit dependence on particular industries. Authority relations are highly personal; formal control systems and procedures are unimportant. Networks of personal connections between individual owners are crucial for survival and reinforce the tendency to centralize key decision making. Limited trust and family priorities restrict critical management roles to family members, or to those with comparable personal ties of loyalty and commitment.

The Chinese family business configuration is closely linked to particular features of the societies in which they developed, in our case the characteristics of pre-industrial China, which have had significant influences on the pattern of industrialization and which continue to affect the institutional environment of firms and economic activities. The present Taiwanese business culture is heavily influenced by historical processes that reach back far into the dynastic history of Taiwan and mainland China.

Historical roots

China was dominated by an imperial dynasty with absolute power that formed the centre of a bureaucratic web. The ownership of large landed estates – in other societies the power base of the landed gentry – was inextricably connected to central state offices which could be bestowed on the members of the hierarchy and rescinded by the whims of the emperor and his entourage. The dependence on central state offices for status and wealth limited the development of rival hierarchies and focused the energy of elite strata within Chinese society on the central bureaucracy.

As a result, the relations between Chinese peasantry and the political elite were affected: Chinese villages were less integrated into a hierarchy of authority and loyalty than elsewhere in South East Asia as the mandarins were dependent on the central state and were often replaced. After the fifteenth century, relations between the political elite and commoners were more commercial and impersonal than e.g. in Japan.

The lack of toleration of local power bases was mirrored in the adverse attitude of the mandarin elite against local concentration of wealth. Through the strict control on markets and towns the accumulation of private wealth was blocked as effectively as the emergence of rival political power. Already during the Han dynasty any large-scale private property could without much ado be subjected to state confiscation.

Commitment of subordinates to collective authority was therefore restricted to the minimum rather than being intense and overriding. This negatively affected the capacity of Chinese society to institutionalize collective commitment to larger units of social organization (beyond village level).

In stark contrast to the Japanese village, with its strong cohesion and relative political autonomy, the Chinese village was much less cohesive and more subject to exactions of landowners and officials.

The overwhelming importance of family ownership and control, the low level of trust of state officials and the lack of a settled system of authority relations with integrated loyalties and commitments: all of these aspects of Chinese societal institutions formed a heritage that had important consequences for the way industrialization took place in Taiwan and thereby determined the kind of business system that came into existence afterwards.

The Japanese colonization of Taiwan from 1895 to 1945 developed both the physical and social infrastructure of Taiwanese society. The development of technical and managerial skills among the indigenous population was limited. However, the infrastructure and factories built by the Japanese were dispersed throughout Taiwan.

In 1949 the Kuomintang (KMT) government came to power. An important event in the postwar history of Taiwan formed the land reforms between 1949 and 1953. After these reforms had taken effect, the small landowning family became the dominant force in rural Taiwan. Concomitant with the land reforms was the growing state control over the peasantry. Through this domination, agricultural surplus was siphoned off towards the fledgling manufacturing (export) industry. In other areas too, the KMT government acted as a centralized political executive, dominating both the bureaucracy and the legislature. In spite of its domination, the regime managed to co-opt native Taiwanese elite groups to a much higher extent than e.g. in Korea, achieving a stability that has been further enhanced by the high rates of economic growth since 1950.

Ever since, the KMT government has promoted economic development to justify its role in Taiwan when the original justification (regaining control over mainland China) receded ever more into the distance. The KMT rule in Taiwan led the highly autonomous and centralized political executive to pursue economic development tools through a decentralized private sector guided by a powerful economic bureaucracy.

We arrived at the hypothesis that the Taiwanese subsidiary should encounter severe difficulties in selling the concept of IT outsourcing to the Taiwanese market because of the existing Taiwanese business system, which we consider to be rather hostile to the concept of IT outsourcing.

Field work

During visits to Taiwan this hypothesis was verified through 24 interviews with managers of the Taiwanese subsidiary, customers, competitors, government officials and academic experts. Many of the observations could be linked to business culture traits that are a direct or indirect result of historical developments as described in the preceding paragraphs.

Comparing the exigencies of IT outsourcing agreements with the output of the interviews, three areas were discerned where the institutional setting and the requirements of an IT outsourcing market do not fit:

- firm size;
- control structure within the firm;
- government role.

Each of these will now be discussed.

Firm size

The Taiwanese market consists of firms that predominantly do not belong to the IT outsourcing target group.

Generally speaking, IT outsourcing agreements presuppose the existence of an IT function of sufficient size to make outsourcing worthwhile. In Taiwan, however, the distribution of firm sizes is heavily skewed in favour of small and very small firms, often not counting more than several employees. This category of firm comprises more than 80% of the 1 million Taiwanese enterprises.

We have seen, in the section on the Chinese family business culture, that this small firm size is tied to the powerful drive of the typical Chinese entrepreneur to keep everything in the firm under control. This drive entails a prudent stance towards external financing, a reluctance to trust non-family salaried managers and a less than enthusiastic attitude towards risk taking: risks are managed by limiting commitments to core workers and by a limited level of capital investment. Flexibility is the key concern and so firms are highly specialized.

Owing to the special circumstances under which the Taiwanese manufacturing industry came into existence, only a few capital-intensive, large enterprises came into existence, most of these government-owned.

Though this highly adaptive network of small firms has proven to be a successful economic configuration in Taiwan and far beyond, the simple fact of the Taiwanese firm size distribution precludes the development of a large-scale IT outsourcing market.

Authority and control structure

The small size of most Taiwanese firms is coupled with strong family control and large-scale reliance on subcontracting networks. Decision making rests with the family, more specifically with the *pater familias*. Decision authority is seldom given to associates outside the own kinship group. Professional managers outside the owning family are not supposed to take on an entrepreneurial role.

This concentration of power within a small group of trusted kinsmen results in a high degree of specialization in the firm's activities. Family businesses take advantage of investment opportunities preferably by spawning off a new firm and entrusting it to a trusted partner within the family or kinship group. When this is not feasible, alliances are formed that take the form of partnerships with common goals and relying on trusted investment partners. These partnerships are, however, not centrally controlled like the Korean *chaebol* and don't play a dominant role in the Taiwanese economy.

The typical pattern of business development evolves around cost cutting and expansion into neighbouring areas to increase resources. The focus lies on short pay-back periods, intense focus on cost-effectiveness and price/cost competition. Furthermore, there is a reluctance to share control or responsibility.

A mutual trust relationship, however, is the essence of any IT outsourcing agreement. Jae-Nam Lee and Young-Gul Kim demonstrate the importance of partnership quality in their study of 36 Korean organizations that had outsourced their IT functions to external service providers (Lee and Kim, 1999). Though there are marked differences between the business cultures of Korea and Taiwan, the similarity of authority hierarchical mechanisms in both societies is in Whitley's view (Whitley, 1992) sufficient to warrant adoption of the results of this study for the Taiwanese situation.

Lee and Kim (1999) establish partnership quality as a key predictor of outsourcing success. Partnership quality was found to be positively influenced by factors such as participation, communication, information sharing and top management support; it is negatively affected by age of relationship and mutual dependency.

From what was said earlier in this subsection, the authors conclude that the circumstances under which IT outsourcing may be successful do not match the institutionalized inclinations of the typical Taiwanese manager.

Government role

Though one might concede that the many small Taiwanese firms are not likely candidates for outsourcing agreements, there are of course large-scale, capital-intensive firms in Taiwan. Many of these firms are government-owned.

Here again we enter an area where institutionalized historical processes shape the role of economic actors. The role of the Taiwanese government is not clear: though it has declared itself a proponent of IT outsourcing, counterforces seem to be prevailing and we doubt wether the government sector (including most banks, airlines and telecom firms) will open up to the IT outsourcing concept. When the Taiwanese government prepared its first outsourcing project (the 'Science Park' project), the first draft of the contract was worked out in such detail that lawyers worked on it for five months. The authors consider this evidence for the uncomfortable feelings generated by the concept of IT outsourcing.

After the KMT take-over of Taiwan in 1949, the gulf between government and commerce became manifest here also: mainlanders occupied the bureaucracy and military apparatus that were effectively blocked to native Taiwanese, who then adopted business careers. When reunification as the power source for the KMT faded away, the Taiwanese government adopted a constructive attitude towards economic development, which led to the much sought-after stability that accompanied the surprising growth of wealth from the 1960s until today. As a result, the Taiwanese government we encounter today has adopted a stimulating rather than a regulating role that extends itself explicitly to the IT outsourcing field.

Since 1995 the Taiwanese government has officially propagated the IT outsourcing concept and has even adopted the role of pioneer in this field. It is definitely in a position to do so, as the government not only owns most of the banking sector (private banks have only been in existence since 1992) but also owns no fewer than 600 data centres throughout the country. Though most of the IT departments are small (fewer than 10 staff members), the total headcount amounts to 10,000 people.

The effort of the Taiwanese government to enter into outsourcing agreements has been stepped up considerably after an official visit to Australia, where one of the federal governments had successfully outsourced its IT function to another party. This visit proved to be extraordinarily influential. Henceforth the Taiwanese government firmly pursued the IT outsourcing project.

In spite of all effort, serious doubts linger as to the viability of this initiative. In talks with the government official in charge of the programme, it transpired that the project was well behind schedule. Of all the projected outsourcing deals, only one showcase project had actually been implemented. The driving motif is cost reduction: during our visit to Taiwan in the first half of 2000, newspapers announced government plans to lay off 70,000 civil servants over the next five years. The reason for the delay, according to our spokesman, is the inherently difficult question of transferring civil servants to the private sector. In regions where IT outsourcing is more accepted, this is already a difficult issue. Owing to the much wider gap between the government and the private sector in a Chinese business culture setting, a transfer of government personnel to private enterprises might be an insurmountable obstacle.

However, even though the authors got some insights in the pros and cons of government outsourcing policy, they did not feel confident to fully assess the force fields around this issue.

Conclusion

During their visits to Taiwan, the authors were able to corroborate many of the assumptions that had resulted from their preparatory research. Time and again, the interviews allowed insight into the cultural aspects we had learned from Whitley's study of East Asian business systems.

Several of these aspects were discussed in this section: the small firm size, the tight familial control structures and the as yet ambiguous effort of the government to promote IT outsourcing. These were singled out because the authors hold the opinion that each of them taken separately would be a major obstacle towards a flourishing IT outsourcing market. Though the first two aspects may be found in other parts of East Asia where the Chinese business culture is preponderant, the combination of the three and the particular circumstances under which the three obstacles are combined is a unique feature of the Taiwanese business culture.

The authors are therefore led to the conclusion that their initial hypothesis, 'The Taiwanese business culture is not conducive to the IT outsourcing market', is true.

18.4 The Taiwanese market and its actors

Though the Taiwanese business system might for historical reasons not be conducive to IT outsourcing, there still could be economic counterforces strong enough to balance the cultural disinclinations. Besides this, Taiwan is part of the modern world, producing for the global marketplace. Could we expect an influence of common Western business practice in the behaviour of Taiwanese businesses?

Guided by the economic concepts listed in Table 18.2, the authors tried to find economic and operational incentives for outsourcing in the Taiwanese Market. They see rational planning and budgeting as a prerequisite and potential driver for outsourcing. Economy of scale is a second basic element for outsourcing. From an operational point of view they conclude with a short look at IT maturity, total cost of ownership, and efficiency.

Planning and budgeting

In Western businesses, integrated planning and budgeting processes are used to keep financial and operational control of the current and future business. In Taiwan, however, planning and budgeting is more or less a directive from corporate headquarters to be 'filled in'. It is not used to forecast the future business. Let us look at a few examples in the context of the company in our study. This set of examples could be enlarged by others, gathered during the interviews with many Taiwanese businessmen working for other companies.

As described in the earlier paragraph about the approach, the authors expected a business strategy that mirrors, and reacts to, the local situation and dynamics. They also expected this strategy to be translated into a marketing strategy, and further crystallized into products, human resources, pricing and so on.

In reality they did not find anything like a complete picture. The strategic planning process shows elements of different kinds of approaches, with several blank spots and obstacles that are difficult to understand. Reasons behind these inconsistencies are not

TABLE 18.2 Main characteristics of economic several viewpoints and their implications for IT outsourcing

Characteristics	Implications of the outsourcing transaction
Anonymous selection	Selection of potential ICT suppliers is based on trust and relationships.
Asset specificity	Ownership is crucial within Taiwanese society to sustain status.
Bounded rationality	The dynamics of ICT and the duration of outsourcing contracts acknowledge the importance of relationships during the contract phase.
Competence building	One of the common reasons for a company to outsource is that ICT does not belong to their core activities.
Coordination costs	Depends on the level of trust. The lower the trust level, the higher the costs.
Dependence	Mutual dependency makes the relationship stronger.
Dynamics	The ICT environment nowadays is a very dynamic environment
Efficiency	Ownership of assets is a prerequisite to be able to leverage economy of scale principles.
Equilibrium	An outsourcing contract is too complex to establish equilibrium.
Learning	Learning is essential in building confidence in ICT relationships as well as within an ICT service provider organization as well between customer and service provider.
Mutual adaptation	Both parties will gain in fine-tuning ICT to become an integral part of the customer's business processes to achieve a win–win situation.
Networking	Owing to the interrelations in the supply chain, the networking aspect is increasing in value.
Opportunistic behaviour	An essential difference between the East and the West is the striving for win–win versus win–lose.
Perfect competition	Owing to sophisticated networks and relationships, perfect competition is hardly feasible.
Perfect information	Owing to sophisticated networks and relationships, perfect information is hardly feasible.
Social change	Changes in status, ownership, respect etc. are perceived to be more important than the social well-being of the relevant staff.
Static environment	The ICT sector is one of the most dynamic sectors.
Transaction as investment	IT outsourcing is not an investment to build a relationship: a profound relationship has to exist before IT outsourcing can take place.
Transaction relation	IT outsourcing is a strategic choice. Only a win–win relationship will sustain.
Trust	Trust is a prerequisite for any relationship and therefore any business transaction.

easy to trace. At least until the beginning of 2000, systematic strategic planning had been very limited and hardly formalized. An in-depth market analysis was lacking and a rational strategy had not been developed. Existing challenging business development ideas did not connect to earlier written plans and were not formalized, nor were these subjects for debate to change the focus from outsourcing towards these new business initiatives. This limited planning is a typical corollary of the local business culture.

In addition to the Western practice of composing a business plan to establish corporate goals for the years ahead, a marketing plan is also generated to complement the content of the business plan. The marketing plan harmonizes the business plan and is viewed as an essential ingredient in the corporation's success by providing the firm with the ability to execute its marketing initiatives. According to Philip Kotler (1999), the marketing plan is the vehicle for directing and coordinating the marketing efforts within a firm, and primarily operates at two levels:

- **strategic marketing plan:** develops the broad marketing objectives and strategy based on an analysis of the current market situation and opportunities;
- **tactical marketing plan:** outlines specific marketing tactics, including advertising, merchandising, pricing, channels service and so on.

Within the tactical marketing plan, marketing managers with a Western background typically apply a popular marketing tactic known as the four P's (product, price, place, promotion) to execute their marketing initiatives effectively. By applying the four P's mentality, marketing managers essentially exercise their marketing intelligence by carefully defining and detailing each marketing initiative.

The Taiwanese subsidiary showed a totally different picture. Most of the business ideas and the market approach were implicitly shared in the internal communication and were subject to sudden change. There was no explicit mid-term policy, translated into comprehensive plans and action. It is suggested here that the observed deviating planning process and strategy style in Taiwan has to be explained by differences between Western and Asian thinking. Many authors pay attention to the Asian mindset, e.g. Hampden-Turner and Trompenaars (1997), and give an illustrative comparison of values and management style elements (Figure 18.1). The planning behaviour observed within the Taiwanese subsidiary, the collective thinking and talking of the people about their future market, the intuitive vision of new product development, and needed relations express several elements of the Eastern value and style elements as presented in the scheme. Lack of continuity in the formal plans then all of a sudden relates to adaptability and flexibility. The differences between Western and Eastern management not only imply that we probably have to 'read' the subsidiary ideas differently, it also might have consequences for the strategies that should be applied to be successful in Taiwanese society in general.

The authors are inclined to believe that the lack of planning and budgeting leads to an IT environment that, although controlled, is not managed towards the future, which limits the awareness of the financial incentives to outsource.

FIGURE 18.1

Comparison of western and eastern values and management styles

Features	Basic values	Style	Organization	Action
Western	Individual Legal Confrontational Analytical	Rationality Structured Directive Doing	Formal Fragmented Hierarchical Competitive	Short-term Controlled Conflicting Product-focused
Eastern	Group Trust Compromise Fluid	Relationship Flexible Adaptive Understanding	Informal Generalist Integrated Cooperative	Long-term Human resource Collaborative Customer focus

Economy of scale

Economy of scale is one of the main financial incentives for IT outsourcing arrangements. The potential IT outsourcing market in Taiwan can be divided in 'government controlled' and 'the rest'.

To start with the second part, the authors' team observed that the Taiwanese business community is very fragmented: approximately 1 million small and medium-sized enterprises (SMEs) exist in Taiwan. Financial gain due to economy of scale cannot be expected within this market.

In the governmental area, large-scale data handling is more common. In 1997, the government officially presented a new approach that should 'lead the way' towards large-scale outsourcing (government brochure 'Status and Prospects of Government Computerization in R.O.C. Government' (1997)). The government started this policy several years before. As yet, the initiatives have not been succesful. After five years (a delay of three years) the first governmental pilot of approximately ten people and a value of US$500,000 has been granted. The first real major project to be issued (*Land Administration Information Management Project*), according to the official leaflet, started in 1993 (!) and was still being announced in 2000.

Operational incentives

As far as operational incentives are concerned, the authors looked into the Taiwanese IT maturity level, the concept of total cost of ownership, and efficiency. Summarizing the information from the interviews, the Taiwanese overall IT maturity should be classified at level II, according to the classification scheme in Strassman (1994) (Figure 18.2). Though this does not preclude excellent quality levels, the perception of IT is not strategically oriented. As IT outsourcing as a concept clearly belongs to the strategy level, the authors were not surprised to see that the 'value' perception of the contribution of IT outsourcing to Taiwanese firms is low. Total cost of ownership includes all organizational and technical costs necessary to execute an IT function. For example, 'desktop services' is not only the desktop and LAN but also training of staff, hidden costs for 'helping your colleague' etc. Owing to low labour costs in combination with cultural preference for status, standardization is not an important topic. Standardization, however, is the prime way to control your cost of ownership. The same argument applies to efficiency. It is easier and preferable to Taiwanese firms to hire extra staff than to initiate improvement programmes to increase the efficiency.

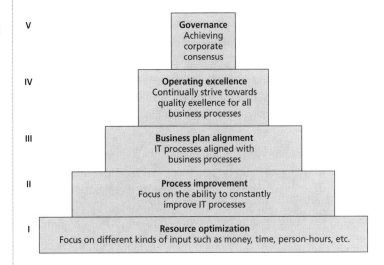

FIGURE 18.2

IT maturity model according to Strassman (1994)

Financial and operational incentives, therefore, do not have enough substance to counterbalance cultural preferences.

18.5 Conclusions

As a result of their readings and interviews with IT outsourcing subject matter experts, the authors arrive at the following conclusion and recommendations:

- Cultures have their own inertia. Business culture as a derivate thereof is a given that permeates deeper than many businesspeople foresee. General economic concepts are not as applicable as expected. The 'global village' has its distinct subcultures that are neglected only at the peril of those who attempt to do so. IT outsourcing is a 'global' concept that get its relief only in a local setting. Using IT outsourcing in Taiwan as a study object, the authors have shown that regional business configurations determine the market perspective and therewith the chances of success for the application of 'global business concepts'.

- Based upon their experiences during this investigation, the authors believe that it is absolutely essential for a global corporation to investigate and understand offshore conditions in detail, prior to launching a particular business internationally. This includes, but is not limited to, full comprehension of local business ethics, grasping the political climate, as well as testing the feasibility of a product or service.

- Furthermore, due to the vast differences between Eastern and Western business mentalities, it is essential for both local and headquarters' management to collectively determine a common ground and mutually define clear objectives and expectations.

Literature

Baty, C. *et al.* (1999) 1998. *Asia/Pacific Professional Services Trends and Vendor Market Share.* Gartner (Dataquest).

Hampden-Turner, C. and Trompenaars, F. (1997) *Mastering the Infinite Game – How East Asian Values are Transforming Business Practice.* Oxford: Capstone.

Hofstede, G. (1991) *Cultures and Organizations – Software of the Mind.* New York: McGraw-Hill.

Kotler, P. (1999) *Marketing Management.* Upper Saddle River, New Jersey: Prentice Hall.

Lee, Jae-Nam and Kim, Young-Gul (1999) 'Effect of partnership quality on IS outsourcing success: conceptual framework and empirical validation'. *Journal of Management Information Systems*, 15(4), 29–61.

Strassman, P. (1994) *The Politics of Information Management.* New Canaan: Information Economics Press.

Swierczek F. and Hirsch, G. (1994) 'Joint ventures in Asia and multicultural management'. *European Management Journal* 12(2), 197–209.

Trompenaars, F. (1993) *Riding the Waves of Culture – Understanding Cultural Diversity in Business*, Second edition, McGraw Hill.

Whitley, R. (1992) *Business Systems in East Asia.* London: Sage.

Note

1   In the first half of 2000 the authors, working for different non-related corporations in the Netherlands, formed a study team in the two-year *Executive MBA/MBI* programme of the Rotterdam School of Management (RSM). They chose 'IT outsourcing in Taiwan' as the subject of their *Executive Field Survey*. This is a major part of the programme in which students are required to apply theories and tools to an existing business problem in an international setting. This chapter is a condensed version of their report.

19 Best practice in acquisition and procurement management: the Information Services Procurement Library

John Dekker Dekker Adviesbureau (Dekker Consultants)
Lex Hendriks EXIN (Examination Institute for Information Science)

Summary

The Information Services Procurement Library (ISPL) is a 'best practice library' for the acquisition/outsourcing of ICT-related services. ISPL offers a number of books, tools and services that can assist an organization – both in the role of customer and in the role of supplier – in the acquisition and outsourcing of services and systems. ISPL is specifically oriented toward the management of such services in a variety of situations. The ISPL approach is an aid for customers and suppliers to monitor cost, risk and time schedules and to promote mutual understanding.

Experience teaches us that both customers and suppliers take significant risks in outsourcing processes. This applies not only to software development, but also to outsourcing ICT services and management. Software is often delivered too late, or at a much higher cost than anticipated. The software does not meet the (often changing) specifications, caused by developments in customer/user requirements, or by sudden leaps in technological development. The management and services do not meet the customer's expectations, or do not conform to the service level agreements that were drafted in advance (if they were drafted at all).

Research carried out in companies that have had experience of outsourcing ICT services shows that 30 to 40 percent are 'dissatisfied' to 'very dissatisfied' with the way the supplier fulfils its promises. Planning overruns have almost become usual in the delivery of information systems. For this reason, companies often employ external advisers to assist them. This does not always have the desired result. External advisers who are involved in the selection process or the information plan generally paint too rosy a picture of the added value of a company-wide integrated system.

Many services and projects fail because of insufficient risk management. The ISPL approach offers a structured contribution to risk analysis and management by providing a clear insight into the situational factors, the underlying complexity and the uncertainties that are inherent in the formulation and supply of the intended services.

19.1 The practice of procurement

CIO Insight is an American magazine on outsourcing. A recent (Spring 2001) CIO Insight survey among CIOs and senior IT strategists does more than highlight the continuing popularity of outsourcing IT applications and functions. It also points to an even more significant trend: companies are becoming increasingly comfortable with outsourcing the 'family jewels' – critical customer-facing and revenue-producing applications.

From a macro view, the study shows continued support for IT outsourcing, with 76% of respondents indicating that they had hired outside IT specialists during the past 12 months and had spent, on average, more than $1 million on outsourced IT in 2000 (see also http://www.cioinsight.com/).

Research carried out among 123 large and medium-sized companies in the UK by KPMG Management Consulting in 1999 shows that companies generally have high expectations of the 'business benefits'. For instance, 76% hope that outsourcing will allow them to concentrate more on the core business. Of the companies questioned, 67% expect flexibility in planning the workload and 65% expect a reduction in operational costs. In addition, reduction of personnel costs, improvement of customer services, company rationalization (downsizing) and reduction in management efforts are named as the main advantages expected from outsourcing. Remarkably, improving the company's competitive position does not score as high.

The research also shows that companies have high expectations of the customer–supplier relationship. Reliability (94%), a good working relationship (93%), a good level of customer service (92%), value for money (92%) and efficiency and being prepared to listen to requests (91%), in particular, scored high. Many companies hope the supplier has an understanding of the ICT requirements, is a good communicator and adviser and is able to provide an insight into the costs.

Companies are far less specific about the kind of contract they want to enter into with the supplier (unambiguous or, on the contrary, flexible) and only just over half demand that the supplier has an insight into the company's business goals.

The KPMG research shows that more than a third of companies are dissatisfied with the supplier's lack of independence and with the lack of influence over the supplier's level of service. In these companies' experience, management required more time than originally estimated to deal with supplier issues, and the supplier was not as dynamic and innovative as originally thought.

Another piece of research, by the Everest Group, shows that there are a number of recurring causes for the dissatisfaction with outsourcing processes. Outsourcing is implemented in too much of a hurry, the supplier is expected to take on an 'ineffective' or 'failing' ITC situation, 'service levels' are hardly defined because of this, the customer organization does not provide the supplier with enough information, and the result is a 'win–lose' contract between supplier and customer (or vice versa). (See also www.kpmg.co.uk)

Often, outsourcing processes appear to be prepared and implemented in a rather haphazard manner. The risks in particular (from time overruns to the failure to achieve the functional requirements or service levels) are underestimated or, even worse, not projected in time or not at all.

19.2 ISPL as 'best practice'

ISPL, the acronym for Information Services Procurement Library, is a 'best practice library' for the management of acquisition/procurements processes. ISPL was developed on the basis of experiences with acquiring and outsourcing ICT services in different countries and in companies that vary in size, in both the public and private sectors. ISPL was developed from Euromethod, a framework for the management of the technical and organizational aspects of contractual customer–supplier relationships. Experiences gained in the development of other 'best practices' for the management of ICT services were also utilized in the development of ISPL, such as ITIL for IT Service Management and PRINCE2 for project management (both methodologies were developed by the UK's OGC (formerly known as CCTA). This is why ISPL, where applicable, refers to relevant ITIL processes and ITIL guidelines.

Following ITIL and PRINCE2, the year 1998–9 saw a search for an outsourcing (procurement) management standard as a successor to Euromethod. Five European companies, EXIN (Netherlands), FAST (Germany), Ordina Institute (Netherlands), SEMA (France) and TIEKE (Finland), joined forces and, with the support of the European Commission, developed ISPL as a methodology for Procurement Management. The ISPL methodology is comparable to ITIL and PRINCE2. The basis is always the experiences of managers, advisers and experts.

In practice, such standards prove, for all parties concerned (including suppliers of IT tools and training), to be a good aid for applying 'best practice' in concrete situations. And, equally important, these methodologies are accessible to anyone; they are in the public domain and are supported by active user groups.

Acquisition management

The acquisition process is the process of acquiring a system or 'service', or any combination of both. A 'service' is every process whereby a person or a company supplies something (a service or a product) to another person or company. ISPL distinguishes two types of services, projects and ongoing services.

The aim of a project is to change a process or system within the organization. One can view this as a transition from an existing status to a more desirable situation. Examples are the design, development and installation of software, the installation of hardware and the establishment of a service desk.

'Ongoing service' refers to a longer-term service provision. Because the main issue here is maintaining an agreed level of service, this is sometimes referred to as a 'steady-state' or 'ongoing' service. Examples are hardware maintenance services, network management, service desk services, problem management and change management.

> In large companies it is still often unusual to view service provision from one department to another (the supply of a product or the support of a service) as acquisition and procurement. But in these cases too, the company benefits from the systematic application of ISPL.

> By doing so, the internal acquisition or procurement becomes much clearer and gains added value: what can or can't be done that other departments do; what planning is required for delivery; is the user organization equipped to use the products or services; is the 'truck system' approach a sensible one, or are there external parties who can do it better (quality) or faster and cheaper (quantity).
>
> Many companies do not give this issue sufficient consideration. Should we do it ourselves, or are there real external specialists who can do it better? But also vice versa: we could outsource it externally, but they don't really know anything about our 'business' so it will become a difficult process.

ISPL views ICT services in a broader context than for instance ITIL, because projects (and specifically those carried out for third parties) are included under services. Despite the differences between projects and services in the literal sense, with a view to management of the acquisition process there are many similarities.

The aim of acquisition management is to control the acquisition process. A number of stages may be distinguished in this. Depending on the purpose of the acquisition and the expectations regarding the complexity and uncertainties, an approach – the acquisition strategy – is determined. Based on this strategy, possible suppliers are approached with a request to submit proposals, from which a selection must be made. Planning and managing this tendering process is an important part of acquisition management. A subsequent stage will require preparation and planning for the delivery of the service or system. At the final implementation stage, contracts and plans must be monitored for accuracy and acquisition management is responsible for cost and risk management. Ultimately, even in the provision of so-called 'ongoing' services there comes a time when the contract needs to be terminated.

Advantages of ISPL

ISPL offers a systematic approach to the acquisition process and with it a framework to exchange and organize experiences (best practice). ISPL consists of a series of books, tools and services to assist customer and supplier organizations in managing the acquisition of services in a variety of situations. ISPL was developed for use in both the public and private sectors.

Advantages of ISPL use to customers are:

- clearer formulation of requirements;
- improvement of risk management;
- support in selecting the appropriate acquisition approach for a specific problem situation;
- a better understanding of the supplier's proposals;
- simplified evaluation of the supplier's proposals;

- simplified management of ambitions;
- improved cost management information;
- avoidance of a 'lock-in' to a specific supplier or method;
- improved decision-making process with regard to products;
- easier system acceptance through a better definition of requirements and planning;
- improved contract management.

Advantages of ISPL use to suppliers are:

- a better understanding of customer requirements;
- a clearer insight into the customer's service or system;
- improved risk management with regard to a service;
- determination of the most suitable approach for the supply of a service;
- improved ability to get clear support from the customer regarding the important design decisions of the service;
- simplified system acceptance through a better definition of requirements and planning;
- improved cost management information;
- improved contract management;
- simplified management of ambitions.

As mentioned above, these advantages apply not only where 'external' suppliers are concerned but also with regard to 'internal' customer–supplier relations.

ISPL users

Target groups that will benefit from ISPL use are, among others, procurement managers, acquisition managers, programme managers, contract managers, facilities managers, service level managers and project managers in the field of ICT. To get maximum benefits from ISPL, it should ideally be used by both the customer and the supplier. But even if used only by one party, there is a benefit in terms of improved planning and project management.

ICT has become an integrated and accepted part of today's society and is used in a large number of fields. Many organizations now rely heavily on ICT to support their aims and business needs. For many organizations, survival without ICT is no longer possible. Business managers in customer organizations must be aware of their needs and requirements and must be able to be confident that these requirements are specified and complied with by the supplier organization, independent of the question of whether these services are procured internally or externally. For this reason, service acquisition and delivery have almost become a profession in their own right.

A 1998 study by the Getronics Group into outsourcing of various types of ICT services gives an indication of the growth that may be expected in outsourcing of ICT services. Table 19.1 shows the percentage of outsourcing against total ICT service provision in 1998 and the expected figures for 2003.

TABLE 19.1
The expected growth of outsourcing in ICT services

	1998 (%)	2003 (%)
Data centre	20	45
Network services	15	45
Application maintenance	20	50
New applications development	35	60
Distributed services	25	55
IT planning	15	30
IT management	<5	10

These figures underline the necessity of learning from past experiences of acquisition and outsourcing of ICT services through the use of a systematic approach. For a growing number of companies whose core business is not ICT, bringing in specialist suppliers becomes a matter of survival in order to keep up with the rapid developments in technology and to maintain levels of service provision in this area.

The role played by I(C)T in an organization has changed from the technical translation of information requirements to day-to-day business support. This demands a more professional management-oriented structure and specific expertise. Because many traditional IT departments, especially, struggle with this transition, the question arises almost automatically of whether the organization would not be better off if (part of) the IT service provision were outsourced.

19.3 Systems and services acquisition

Acquisition and delivery of services generally use the following steps:

- defining the acquisition target;
- development of a delivery strategy;
- contracting parts of the acquisition target;
- integration of the parts into the overall service or the overall system and into the business processes of the organization making the acquisition.

In doing this, relations between customer and supplier, in particular, demand professional management. Every service organization will, in practice, be both customer and supplier. Any type of customer–supplier relationship demands its own form of management. The core is determined in the contract: a binding agreement between both parties for the provision of the service. But, in addition, a number of informal aspects play a role in the management of customer–supplier relationships.

Acquisition of services differs from the acquisition of systems or products in a number of aspects. Generally speaking, products can be specified to a high level of detail – for instance, a Pentium IV PC 1.3 GHz with a 100 GB hard disk, etc. For services, a lower level of detailing is common – for instance in terms of methods (an AS/440 expert for six months), tasks (a service desk with well-defined procedures), results (a system according to specified requirements) or goals (the realization of a specific service level). If the services that have to be acquired (internally or externally) have been formulated in terms of results and goals, more responsibility is generally placed with the supplier. In such situations the customer–supplier relationship evolves into a solid partnership, in which the primary concern for the customer is the fact that the supplied results can be checked.

The financial aspects of the contract generally depend on the differences in acquisition of services and systems. The financial and legal aspects usually form the core of the contract. The technical specification of the service or the system is normally incorporated into the technical supplement. To produce a good technical supplement, professional management of the customer– supplier relationship is necessary, in which the requirements are clear, expectations and risks are managed, customer and supplier understand each other, and ambitions and costs are controlled.

Managing expectations and mutual understanding

Effective acquisition of a service or system requires concise descriptions of the desired end result (final state) and the current situation (initial state); both customer and supplier must be clear on this.

Communications between customer and supplier are complicated if they use differing terminology that is interpreted differently by each, caused partly by the existence of a large variety of methods and approaches, each with its own concepts and notions. For instance, different suppliers may offer a customer the following products: preliminary study, opportunity study, feasibility study, functional planning, or requirement analysis. Are all these concepts equal? Do the products satisfy the same requirements and goals? How can customers assess quotes if they are based on the terminology of a specific method? How can customers be certain that the problem is sufficiently understood by the suppliers and that enough consideration is given to this in the planning and cost estimates of the project?

The successful introduction of modern services and systems requires the involvement of a number of people in different roles, with different responsibilities, experiences and backgrounds. It is essential that effective communications exist, in order to create mutual understanding.

One of the main sources of frustration in the customer–supplier relationship is underestimating costs. Costs for the acquisition of a service or system often end up higher because during the delivery process ambitions increase, often unconsciously. Controlling these ambitions requires careful management of the decisions regarding the implementation or the formulation of the service, the construction and the installation of the system. The decision-making process must be meticulously planned and implemented and must involve both customer and supplier.

Risk management

Risk management is one of the most important elements in the ISPL approach.

The simplest and most common form of risk management is: there is a goal, there is a plan for getting there and we'll deal with the rest as we go along. If things end up a little different, if they don't quite go according to plan, we'll decide what to do at that time.

In an acquisition process this strategy is rather risky, to put it mildly. After all, apart from a goal and a plan there are contracts with other parties that strongly restrict the freedom to make decisions 'along the way'. It is therefore essential to weigh up the risks in advance and to consider measures that may need to be taken. The importance of risk management within the acquisition process explains to some extent why this subject has been dealt with in a larger and more concrete context in ISPL than in ITIL and PRINCE2. The ISPL approach to risk management can also be applied outside the acquisition process, for instance in service management or project management, and has, in practice, proven to be a good supplement to ITIL and PRINCE2. In ISPL, formulating a risk management strategy is the key to the formulation of an acquisition strategy.

In acquiring a service or system, we automatically work from the assumption that it must serve the interests of the organization, that costs must stay within certain limits and that the service or system will be accepted by the users. But what if this is not the case? Or if delays occur in the delivery or if the quality of the product supplied does not meet expectations? Unfortunately, we know the answers to these questions from experience.

Risks associated with acquisition can have a direct negative impact on the business itself. Some examples are:

- demotivation in staff providing the service;
- increased service costs;
- unclear requirements;
- non-specific interfaces with other services or systems.

Let's turn the case around and force ourselves to consider which factors will help or hinder a successful implementation. This poses the question of how large we feel the chance is that something may go wrong and what the consequences will be. Let's assume that the probability of something going wrong or the consequences are so large that we have to think of measures to take. This means we can formulate a good plan for the acquisition and delivery of the service (the delivery plan) or the system by making a sensible selection of such measures.

Very simplified, this is the core of the ISPL approach.

19.4 The basic ISPL concepts

The following ISPL basic concepts can assist in understanding the basic philosophy behind contractual relations between customer and supplier:

- **Contract diversity** ISPL provides assistance in choosing the most suitable contract type and provides assistance in the acquisition planning phase in which the services and projects to be acquired are determined.

- **Situation-specific planning** Planning the implementation of a service is situation-specific. Every situation is assessed with the aid of a list of situational factors. The complexity and uncertainty are determined. Risks are identified and their probability and impact are determined.

ISPL provides assistance in defining actions to avoid or reduce critical risks and in formulating a delivery plan that is tailored to the situation in question.

- **Emphasis on decision points** The delivery plan in the technical supplement to a contract stresses decision points. Decision points consist of contractual interactions between customer and supplier whereby the customer, probably together with the supplier, makes decisions regarding the service provided. The production of piles of unnecessary paperwork is avoided because every product is linked to a decision point. The products must support the decisions that have to be taken. This approach improves the effectiveness of the production process.

Emphasis on products With regard to the implementation of projects, ISPL emphasizes the products rather than the processes that lead to those products. It describes what needs to be produced. It does not, as such, prescribe how the realization of the products must take place. ISPL does, however, certainly with regard to delivery of services, describe how the customer and supplier organization can manage the processes in order to achieve the agreed result.

19.5 The acquisition process

The customer's first activity in the acquisition process is the acquisition initiation. This involves defining the acquisition target based on the company's requirements, producing the specification for the desired services and systems, formulating the acquisition strategy and planning the acquisition based on an analysis of the situation and the acquisition target.

ISPL provides guidelines for this activity and specifically for the formulation of the acquisition strategy.

Examples of questions for which support is provided are:

- Should the acquisition take place in one or more contracts (procurements)?
- Should we use external suppliers?
- Which type of tendering should we use (open, limited, 'negotiated')?
- Do we need to start a multi-phase tendering process?
- Which contractual elements must be kept flexible in order to enable amendments or refinements (and what are the limits of this flexibility)?
- Should we buy or develop products?
- Which type of service arrangement should be used?

> Experience with a number of projects that utilized ISPL has shown that the acquisition target and the requirements are often described on a very general level. If different people (often from different departments) sit around a table to articulate, each in their own words, what the actual target of the acquisition is, very differing descriptions and demands are the result.
>
> Internal traditions within companies, competition between departments and people, wanting to protect one's own IT department, and users' scepticism each lead to a range of different expectations, acquisition targets, specifications, requirements, etc.
>
> It is essential that all these issues are expressly determined at the start of the acquisition process and that agreement is reached between departments, between people, but also between customer and supplier.

Answering the above and similar questions results in an acquisition plan, which is then the basis for guiding each of the procurement processes. Each procurement process is related to one contract.

For each contract the procurement process is a sequence of three processes: tendering, monitoring of the contract and finalizing the contract (Figure 19.1).

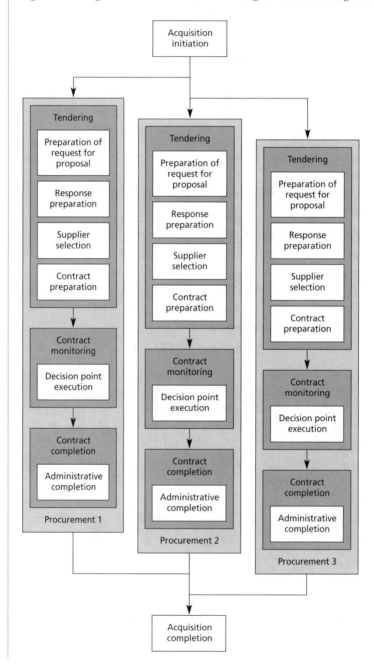

FIGURE 19.1

Acquisition processes and procurement processes

The aim of the tendering process is to select a supplier (external or internal) and to formulate a proposal for delivery of the service, and to agree a contract with the chosen supplier which outlines the products and/or services to be supplied as well as the responsibilities of each party.

During the tendering process, procurement requirements can evolve (ISPL gives this specific consideration). The tendering process consists of four activities (see Figure 19.2). The sum total of these activities results in the production of documents that are exchanged as part of the customer–supplier relationship. ISPL provides guidelines for each of these activities.

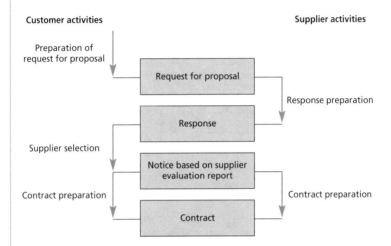

FIGURE 19.2

Activities and exchange of products within a tendering process

> ISPL recognizes a basic concept of differentiating between the service domain and the target domain. Simply put, the service domain is the organization or the part of the organization (when it concerns an internal acquisition) that will produce and supply the product or service (the supplier); the target domain is the organization or the part of the organization that will be using the service (the customer).
>
> Experience shows us that this is not the way some companies look at it. Conscious, content-related consideration of roles, responsibilities and activities are often not very far advanced. Various planning and legal agreements, however, often are in existence. Many a company has learned a lesson with this in the past.
>
> From the vague distinction between which are the supplier's and which are the customer's tasks and responsibilities, misunderstandings often result where the customer thinks the supplier will take care of it; the customer feels that it is really part of the acquisition target for the supplier to take care of it.

From the contract point of view the tendering process ends at the moment the contract is signed, and this is the start of 'contract monitoring'.

In the transition from tendering to the monitoring process, the customer's responsibility changes from managing the process to monitoring the process that is now being managed/carried out by the supplier. Within the contract monitoring process, the delivery plan is instrumental in product validation and the execution of decision points (see Figure 19.3). This process is divided into a series of decisions regarding, for instance, the system that is to be changed, the project being executed or, for instance, the service level that is to be realized.

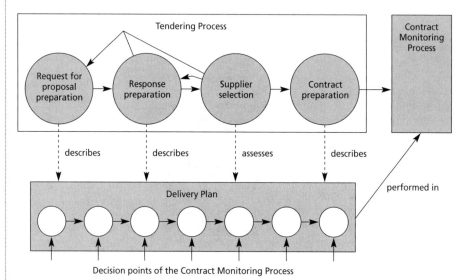

FIGURE 19.3

The tendering process with the delivery plan as an important result

19.6 The delivery plan

Within ISPL, the delivery plan is the most important management instrument in the acquisition process. The delivery plan defines the delivery process in terms of formal interactions between customer and supplier. It is important in this context to recognize the difference between the delivery process within ISPL and the delivery processes within ITIL. An ICT organization forms part of a chain in which, on the one side, ICT services are being supplied to customers and, on the other, services and products are being bought from suppliers. The IT Service Management delivery processes as described in ITIL focus on ICT service provision to customers and have the specific aim of achieving agreements and of creating planned conditions to conform to those agreements. Within an organization this is commonly referred to with a term like Service Management and Planning. The term 'Service Delivery', however, refers to the actual provision of ICT services. The latter matches ISPL terminology, where the delivery process is aimed at the supply of services (which of course can also include projects). In most organizations, the delivery process described in ISPL will therefore be considered part of service procurement. Which does not mean, of course, that the required ISPL 'best practice' may not come in very handy when a company manages service delivery. The formulation of a delivery plan is a good example of this.

A delivery plan describes the service and formulates a planning schedule of what has to be supplied. In the case of an ongoing service it describes the agreed service levels (SLAs). In the case of a project it describes the starting situation (initial state) and end situation (final state). In both cases the delivery is planned in terms of strategy, decision points and products.

The delivery plan contains the situation analysis and the strategy as well as the decision structure (including the decision points and the product description). The level of detailing in the delivery plan will increase from the formulation of the acquisition strategy, via the invitation to tender and the tender response through to the contract being awarded.

Service control

The delivery plan is the cornerstone for managing the delivery of the service and the standard for assessing the extent to which the contract with the supplier is being adhered to (contract monitoring). Such a plan is not just a requirement for 'ongoing' services. In practice, misconceptions about agreements often occur at the time of software delivery and acceptance, because a delivery plan has barely been agreed with the supplier. What exactly should have been delivered, who takes the decisions regarding acceptance and what needs to be done if a delivery is not accepted has not been documented previously.

Within ISPL, the delivery plan is based around decision points, milestones in the service delivery process where the customer, possibly in conjunction with the supplier, makes a decision relating to the service. A decision point is characterized by the decisions that must be made, the roles involved in these decisions, the transactions that take place and the products that are being exchanged. These products form the basis for decision making. ISPL provides the methodology for distinguishing decision points, products, etc. A methodology such as PRINCE2 provides the instruments to achieve product-based planning. In this regard these methods are complementary.

For every decision point the responsibilities of each party must be clearly defined. For the supplier this generally means an involvement in the decision-making process. Both the customer and the supplier must determine who takes part in the decision-making process.

> It can be useful to apply the PRINCE2 concept of the Project Board to this situation. In ISPL terms this would be the Service Board. PRINCE2 describes three roles for the Project Board: the Executive for the Business, the Senior User and the Senior Supplier.

The sequence of the decision points for a specific service depends on the service delivery strategy selected. In the case of projects, ISPL proposes decision point patterns for different strategy options. These patterns can serve as an example and can be used again when a delivery plan for a specific project needs to be formulated. The ISPL plug-ins offer specific guidelines for decision point sequences in the respective domains.

The aim of the service delivery is, of course, that products are exchanged between the supplier and the customer.

Agreements must be made about the delivery of these products. Not just about what and when, but also about the way the customer will accept the products. Therefore, for every delivery there is a series of decisions: about proposals, plans and acceptance. These form an equal number of decision points in the delivery process.

In the case of an ongoing service, management of the service provision based on the delivery plan (in which the service level agreement with the supplier is included) is a task for the service control team. Within an organization, the Service Control Team can be a part of Service Management and Planning. The Service Control Team will also have to maintain and adjust the Delivery Plan in conjunction with the supplier if Service Levels have to be adjusted in order to continue to respond to the demands of the customer of the ICT organization.

> Within ISPL there is mention only of structuring the client's organization for the purpose of monitoring the delivery process. The Service Control Team notion within ITIL (which, within ITIL, is directed mainly internally) can be applied successfully within ISPL, including as an external instrument. The chairman of the Service Control Team could act in the Senior User role in the Project Board or Service Board.

19.7 Service planning

The effectiveness of the acquisition process can be improved by 'tailoring' the process to a specific situation. An acquisition process that is designed to suit a specific situation maximizes the chances of successfully realizing a service level or system change, with minimization of risks and costs. Situational factors are those characteristics of a particular situation that cause these risks. These factors are used to determine the most suitable risk management strategy. The four activities that must be carried out in order to produce a service delivery plan are: situation analysis and assessment, risk analysis, formulation of the service delivery strategy and decision point planning.

Situation analysis and assessment

ISPL offers a set of situational factors that relate to the complexity and uncertainty of the service to be provided and the service organization providing it (the service domain) and a set of situational factors that relate to the complexity and uncertainty of the organization to which the service is to be provided (the target domain). The value of each situational factor can, generally speaking, be high, medium or low. This then results in a high, medium or low complexity or uncertainty. Table 19.2 is an extract of such a table of situational factors. Once the values of the situational factors have been determined, special consideration must be given to the factors that contribute to either the overall complexity or the overall uncertainty of the service.

> Experience teaches us that, in the case of larger procurements, it is advisable to assess not only the main situational factor categories, but to also take a look at individual sub-factors (outlined in the short description). Some situational factors have a large number of sub-factors. In such cases an overall assessment will not provide the correct input for the risk analysis.

TABLE 19.2 An example of a situational factor table

Service domain	Uncertainty factor	Short description	Certain	Moderate	Uncertain
Process	Adequacy of schedules	A measure of how tight the schedules are, due to bad estimates or urgency of the project.	–	Normal	Tight
	Adequacy of budget	A measure of how tight the budget is, due to bad estimates or constraints.	–	Normal	Tight
	Adequacy of service processes	A measure of the adequacy of the processes, approaches, strategies, culture, maturity of the service organization for the attainment of the goal of the service.	High	Normal	Low
	Formality of customer–supplier process	Compliance of the customer–supplier process to defined rules and procedures.	High	Medium	Low
	Specificity/ Novelty of service	A measure of the innovative value or the specificity of the service with respect to the state-of-the-art.	Low	Medium	High
	Dependency on other services	Dependency on ongoing services or projects that interface to the service.	None	Low	High
Information	Formality of service information	Formality of service information is its conformity to rules and structure.	High	Medium	Low
Actors	Attitude of service actors	The attitude of the service actors regarding the service. Sub-factors: perception of need, commitment and involvement.	Pos.	Medium	Neg.
	Ability of service actors	Skills, experience, knowledge and capacity of the service actors.	High	Medium	Low
	Dependency on subcontractors/ suppliers	The dependency on other parties than the customer and the main supplier. These other parties may provide products or services to the service.	None	Low	High
Technology	Novelty of service technology	A measure of how innovative with respect to the state-of-the-art are the methods, tools (including computerized tools) and techniques used by the service actors for the execution of the service.	Low	Medium	High
	Availability of appropriate service technology	A measure of the availability of the methods, tools (including computerised tools) and techniques needed by the service actors for the execution of the service. Sub-factors: delivery, support and accessibility.	High	Medium	Low

> From the start of the acquisition process up to and including the formulation of the request for proposal, the situation analysis limits itself specifically to the target domain – the organization that will be using the products or services. At this stage there is an abstract service domain, but not yet a concrete partner who will execute the project. For instance, the ability of service actors may not yet be assessable. A number of situational factors can, at that stage, not yet be assessed. However, some thought can be given to the demands that may be made on the service organization by the target domain; for instance:
>
> - software must be developed on existing platforms and within the boundaries of the current infrastructure;
> - the developers must be specialists in database technology XX.

Risk analysis

The values given to each of the situational factors are used to identify possible risks. Table 19.3 gives an example of the guidelines that ISPL provides for this. Each situational factor provides a number of risks. The probability and impact of each possible risk are determined. This way, risks that are critical to the service delivery are identified.

Formulation of the service delivery strategy

In formulating the service delivery strategy, it is customary to review a number of strategy options. The formulation of a suitable service delivery strategy involves three activities:

- defining actions to reduce the risks, to change individual uncertainty factors and to manage the complexity;
- selecting suitable strategy options for the service monitoring (or service management);
- selecting suitable strategy options for the service execution.

The strategy offered for the service monitoring (or service management) of an ongoing, steady-state service consists of 'execution control', 'quality control' and 'configuration control'. The customer and supplier must come to an agreement about the formalization and frequency of the monitoring and customer responsibilities for each of these management areas.

The column numbers in Table 19.3 indicate the situational factors as follows:

1. adequacy of schedules is tight;
2. adequacy of budget is tight;
3. adequacy of service processes is low;
4. formality of customer–supplier process is low;
5. specificity/novelty of service is high;

19 ■ Best practice in acquisition and procurement management

TABLE 19.3 Example of the guidelines with regard to risks associated with service domain uncertainty

Situational factors	1	2	3	4	5	6	7	8	9	10	11	12
Risks												
Unclear service/systems requirements				X	X	X						
Unstable service/systems requirements				X	X	X						
Uncertain interfaces					X	X						
Shortfalls in subcontracted tasks	X	X								X		
Loss of control of service	X		X	X	X	X	X	X	X	X	X	X
Delays in the deliveries	X	X	X	X	X	X		X	X	X	X	X
Poor quality of deliverables	X	X	X	X	X	X	X	X	X	X	X	X
Increased costs of the service	X	X	X	X	X	X		X	X	X	X	
Demotivation of service actors	X	X	X	X	X	X		X	X	X	X	X
Poor quality of service/system	X	X	X	X	X	X		X	X	X	X	X
Delay in system delivery	X	X	X	X	X	X		X	X	X	X	X
Service/system not accepted by actors				X		X		X				business
Unpredictable costs for the business						X						

6 dependency on other services is high;

7 formality of service information is low;

8 attitude of service actors is negative;

9 ability of service actors is low;

10 dependency on subcontractors is high;

11 novelty of service technology is high;

12 availability of appropriate service technology is low.

In the case of a project, ISPL offers eight relevant strategy options for service execution. Service execution with regard to a project is a combination of:

- description approach;
- construction approach;
- installation approach.

The description approach defines and describes the method of analysing and formulating the system, the construction approach defines and describes how the system must be constructed and tested, and the installation approach defines and describes the process of making the system operational. Figure 19.4 gives a simplified example of guidelines for the installation approach.

FIGURE 19.4

Guidelines for the selection of an installation approach

> **Which is the best installation approach to choose?**
> The standard selection for the installation approach is the 'one-shot approach'. With the 'one-shot approach', project management is simpler and the general risks of loss of control over the service domain are reduced.
> An 'incremental' or 'evolutionary' approach must be selected depending on certain situational factors.
> An 'incremental' approach is best selected in case of the following situational factors:
> - the overall complexity is high;
> - the timing schedule is tight.
>
> An 'evolutionary' approach is best selected in case of the following situational factors:
> - the overall uncertainty is high;
> - the timing schedule is tight.

Planning and monitoring of the decision points

The sequence and content of the decision points must be a reflection of the service delivery strategy. ISPL provides guidelines for the most suitable decision point sequence. ISPL also provides guidelines for the description of the deliverables that must be exchanged at the decision points.

Contract termination

After a period of time the provision of the service will finish. In planning the service, it must be taken into account that a number of activities will still need to be executed. These could include finalizing licences, removing software and data from systems, but also archiving of information and informing buyers. In addition to a possible completion of financial matters with the supplier, in this phase an evaluation of the procurement or the overall acquisition must also be planned. Specifically by means of learning points from earlier acquisitions will an organization be better able to systematically link the ISPL approach (consider the formulation of situational factors, possible risks and possible consequences) to the demands of their own organization. The guidelines in PRINCE2 on 'closing a project' give a number of more detailed procedures than are contained in ISPL.

19.8 Support in the Essentials books

The core of the ISPL approach can be found in the Essentials books, the basis of the Information Services Procurement Library. These books describe the acquisition process, the specification of the products to be supplied (deliverables) and the management of risks and the formulation of the delivery plan. Finally, there is a dictionary in which all ISPL key concepts may be found.

In the description of the **acquisition process**, consideration is given to, among other things, the way in which a consistent list of requirements can be formulated. How to achieve more clarity regarding the target of the acquisition and the content of the service is also discussed. It is of course also discussed how the acquisition strategy may be defined and how the acquisition organization may be established. Next, consideration is given to approaching suppliers with regard to requesting proposals and to the issue of how a supplier can formulate a competitive proposal on the basis of the requirements in the request for proposal. A number of options are described for the selection of the most cost-effective proposal that matches the requirements and available budget. And, finally, the technical and business aspects of the procurement contract are discussed.

In the book dealing with **specification of deliverables**, the content of a request for proposal, the response, the supplier evaluation report and the final contract are described. Based on the description of the delivery plan, drafting a proposal for a decision point and a 'decision point report' is dealt with. In addition, the service plan and the service report are described.

As mentioned earlier, **risk management and delivery planning** are important cornerstones in the ISPL approach. The Essentials book dealing with this subject outlines how projects and 'ongoing' services may be described and how situations may be assessed on the basis of aspects such as processes, information, actors and technology. Based on this assessment, risks may be identified and their probability and impact may be determined. There is a description of how this preliminary work may be used to formulate a strategy and plan decision points.

19.9 Recommendations regarding ISPL use

ISPL is a very detailed methodology for the systematic execution of an acquisition process. It is useful and necessary to have 'mastered' the methodology in order to apply it in the right manner. ISPL is not only applicable for 'large, complex' projects (say in excess of €500,000) but also for smaller projects, provided that the methodology is used in a sensible manner. In smaller projects many of the steps may be dealt with more quickly, although they can't be left out altogether. The running time of an ISPL process will not be vastly different from a 'normal' outsourcing process. The amount of information required, however, probably will be different.

ISPL provides a framework for the acquisition process. If an organization is used to defining requirements in a different manner, this is not necessarily incompatible with ISPL. It could be complementary. In coming years, procurement will play an ever-increasing role for companies, as specific specialist expertise may no longer be available in-house. A number of organizations have now experienced the ISPL approach to various kinds of information services. Experiences have generally been positive and the methods have proven to be practicable. Experience teaches us, however, that the method must not be underestimated. While the organisation has not trained its own specialists in this area, it is advisable to involve external advisers who can provide necessary knowledge and experience.

Procurement and acquisition management are on the cutting edge of line and project organization. And in many cases it also has to deal with the IT management organization. Procurement management often starts out as a project that ends up within the line organization. It is therefore necessary for the line organization to consider the place where the project is to be allocated (among other options, via the Delivery Plan and the Service Control Team).

Even this concise description of the ISPL approach shows where the main differences are compared with the 'traditional' approach mentioned earlier:

- The acquisition target is analysed and refined right at the start. Service domain, target domain, costs and benefits, as well as the parties involved and their interests, are inventoried.
- The risks are determined prior to planning. Based on this analysis, the acquisition approach is determined and the main decision points are established.

Other advantages of the ISPL approach are:

- focus on the products to be supplied, deliverables and the support in the description thereof;
- support via tools;
- the ISPL approach invites structured consultation between all parties involved. The discussion of the relevant situational factors, the risks attached and the measures to be taken lends itself well to the organization of workshops.

19.10 Information regarding ISPL

For further information regarding ISPL please contact::

- the authors of this chapter: dekkerjo@wxs.nl and lex.hendriks@exin.nl
- the ISPL user group: ispl@itsmf.nl
- EXIN: www.exin.nl

Literature

The Information Service Procurement Library (published by ten Hagen & Stam, The Hague):

– *Introduction to ISPL*

– *Managing Acquisition Processes*

– *Specifying Deliverables*

– *Managing Risks and Planning Deliveries*

– *Dictionary*

– *ISPL in the European Public Sector: guidelines*

– *ISPL for Web Engineering*

– *ISPL for Large Scale migrations*

– *ISPL for IT Service Management*

Further literature:

Dekker, John and Hendriks, Lex (1999) 'ISPL: de Information Services Procurement Library', in *IT Beheer Jaarboek* (*IT Management Yearbook*) 1999, ten Hagen & Stam.

Dekker, John and Hendriks, Lex (2000) 'Succesvol uitbesteden vereist gedetailleerde risicoanalyse' (*Successful outsourcing requires detailed risk analysis*), in *Automatiseringsgids* (*Automation Guide*), 4 Feb.

Review of part 2

In **Methodological ERP acquisition: the SHERPA experience**, Pastor, Franch and Sistach extensively describe the SHERPA procurement method, which is specific to ERP. The different phases (and the stages within a phase) of the procurement process, including all types of criteria, are elaborated. The method is primarily focused on implementation aspects of ERP applications but also covers management aspects of ERP.

An important fact is that SHERPA is not just a theoretical model but has already been used successfully in four different industry ERP procurement cases. That makes a difference to the practical applicability of this method.

Despite the fact that SHERPA is positioned as a typical ERP procurement method, it could – in our opinion – also be used to acquire other business applications, owing to its generic structure. SHERPA is in fact a light-version procurement method of great value to medium-sized enterprises. A potential addition to SHERPA would be the inclusion of the decision part in Phase 0, to become an integral part of SHERPA.

In **Relationship management: delivering on the promise of outsourcing**, Buscher focused on the client side of the outsourcing contract and looked into the organizational implications of an outsourcing deal. The competences needed on the client side are various and of a high level in order to be able to control the ICT service provider. Establishing a well-balanced service level agreement is not enough to ensure an uncomplicated service delivery from an ICT service provider. Buscher makes a good point in proclaiming that client and provider must stay in touch on all issues concerning and relating to the service delivery. So, an important element in the success of outsourcing, as seen by Buscher, is relationship management. Other recent developments in Service Level Management, such as the Kwintes project (see Chapter 32), acknowledge this pronouncement. The static piece of paper called the SLA is of course an important element, but people and processes such as Relationship Management are needed to make it really work.

The conclusions of Leenders *et al.* in **Chinese walls in IT outsourcing** didn't come as a complete surprise. In business fields other than IT outsourcing there were earlier documented observations that culture is an important factor in the success of a business concept. In the literature on the subject of ICT outsourcing, there is also a strong indication that culture is a important factor in the success of outsouring (Beulen *et al.*, 1994).

De Looff (1997), in his book on an outsourcing decision model, observes that situational factors have a great impact on ICT outsourcing. Culture could be recognized as one of those situational factors.

The other chapters in this part differ in one very important aspect from the chapter under discussion: they all reflect the situation in the Western cultures, which slightly differ from each other, whereas this research looked into the effect of a Western outsourcing concept in an Eastern business culture.

The one important question still remains: is the realization of an outsourcing concept a mission impossible in Asia for culture reasons?

ISPL, as described in **Best practice in acquisition and procurement management** by Dekker and Hendriks, can be regarded as the successor of the former Euromethod. Euromethod was a procurement management method, developed by five organizations from five different countries and with the support of the European Commission.

One of the strong points of the ISPL approach is the Risk Management method. This Risk Management method can be seen as a self-contained method, which could be used apart from ISPL in other applications, e.g. project management or service management. An important instrument in the ISPL Risk Management method is the use of situational factors to assess the elements of risk in terms of complexity and uncertainty associated with client and provider organizations. The use of countermeasures forms part of the risk method.

Although both ISPL and ITIL are products of the OCG (CCTA), ISPL is a much more coherent library than ITIL, probably due to the fact that ISPL was written in one effort, and ITIL grew into the final book-set in more than ten years.

Literature

Beulen, E. *et al.* (1994) *Outsourcing van IT-dienstverlening: een make or buy beslissing.* Kluwer Bedrijfswetenschappen (in Dutch).

De Looff, L.A. (1997) *Information Systems Outsourcing Decision Making: a Managerial Approach.* Idea Group Publishing. Series in Information Technology Management.

part 3

Metrics

Introduction to the theme

An IT service provider must be able to state clearly and objectively the quality of the services it offers and provides. But metrics (quality attributes which have been rendered measurable) are required to enable the quality of the IT services to be measured. Quality improvement programmes also require that the outcomes of stages can be recorded in quantified terms. Metrics can then be used to determine whether particular quality levels are being achieved, thus feeding the dialogue between customer and provider.

Standards

All standards in the field of IT Service Management are of the de facto standard type. Industry standards are still missing or just emerging, and *de jure* standards are only at the natal stage of development, or limited to a small geographical region. However, there are several attempts going on to grow from de facto into industry and *de jure* standards.

Whatever evolution the standards and the likely accompanying certification will show, it is clear that they will be built on the principles of metrics. Therefore it is clear that we should investigate what kind of metrics we know, and how we can use them, before we can step up the road towards certification.

Certification

Based upon such measurements, it is possible to award a certificate for that result. In certification, a distinction can generally be made between individual-oriented and organization-oriented certification. Certification is a method which can contribute to standardization, but it always indicates a stable situation:

- **Individual-oriented**: the job must be generally recognized and acknowledged. The professional group must be homogenous and measurable.
- **Organization-oriented**: there must be a stable picture of what the organization is, its goals, performance patterns etc.

There is no point in certification if a stable situation of this kind has not been achieved. After all, in that case the value of the certificate will not be recognized; it is not founded on the recognition of a goal to be pursued. The field of IT Service Management is not characterized by such a stable situation at present, certainly not worldwide. But certification does occur wherever a reasonable degree of stability has been achieved within cultures or geographic areas.

Worldwide certification is a big thing. It can actually be said that in many parts of the world there is absolutely no refresher training, in-service training or retraining which is not tied into a certification system organized in a national context, or in some cases on an even broader basis. In Australia, considerable attention is generally paid to the effect of certificates on career prospects and job mobility. The certificates found in the management field there, apart from technical and product-related certificates, are mainly certificates intended for front-office staff. Most systems in Asia are comparable, and university accreditation is also being demanded increasingly for advanced courses. There, too, people want to know what kind of paper/certificate they will get for their training efforts. Looking next to the United States, the striking feature there is the huge variety of individual-linked certificates in the management world. Again, many of the certificates are technically oriented or product-oriented, but there are also plenty of task-oriented management certificates. Such certificates are often aimed at staff in the front office of the IT organization – help-desk staff and support staff. The certificates are often issued by large associations or company groupings.

In Europe, a huge growth in the area of individual-oriented certificates in the ITIL environment is evident, and the associated training courses and exams are also being offered from Europe to other parts of the world at an increasing pace.

Content

This part contains five chapters, which describe several ways of measuring management parameters in an IT Service Management environment.

Enforcing performance guarantees based on performance service levels
André Scholz and Klaus Turowski

GQM applied in IT Service Management
Wouter de Jong

Service level measurement: Checkpoint 2000
Mike Tsykin

How to improve the quality of your support centre by certification
Eppo Luppes, Bill Sheehan and Jackie Kuflik

A standard for IT Service Management
Jenny Dugmore

A review of part 3 follows these five chapters.

part 3: Metrics

Reading instructions

The chapters in this part can be read independently of each other. There is no specific relationship between the chapters, except for their common focus on processes. The first three chapters go into specific aspects of IT Service Management. The last two concentrate on issues of standardization.

Introduction to the chapters

In **Enforcing performance guarantees based on performance service levels**, André Scholz and Klaus Turowski analyse the way that service level agreements (SLAs) can be created and apply this analysis to the handling of performance metrics for an ERP system.

In **GQM applied in IT Service Management**, Wouter de Jong describes a top-down quality improvement method that is not exclusive to IT. The Goals/Questions/Metrics model (GQM) is widely used in measurement programmes. It is one of the best-known methods of translating improvement goals into the metrics that need to be gathered, by means of a series of questions that need to be answered to reach the goals, which in turn lead to the metrics needed to answer the questions. De Jong applied this method in an IT Service Management context.

In **Service level measurement: checkpoint 2000**, Myke Tsykin emphasizes that an IT service should in fact be managed and measured at the level of the end user. Recent developments in tooling for such an end-to-end domain are making considerable progress. However, user acceptance and practical applications are still lagging behind.

In **How to improve the quality of your support centre by certification**, Eppo Luppes, Bill Sheehan and Jackie Kuflik present one of the latest initiatives to develop a worldwide standard for certification in the front-office environment. HDI's Certified Support Centre Certification Programme was designed to improve the effectiveness of the support services industry by providing a reference model for the support centre.

Another initiative, of the British Standards Institute, delivered a true standard for the UK. In **A Standard for IT Service Management**, Jenny Dugmore explains the background, the specifications and the relative position of the British Standard 15000. The standard is compatible with ITIL and could very well be the staircase to an international standard for IT Service Management.

20 Enforcing performance guarantees based on performance service levels

André Scholz University of Magdeburg, Institute of Business and Technical Information Systems, Germany

Klaus Turowski University of the Federal Armed Forces Munich, Chair of Business Information Systems, Germany

Summary

Thanks to increased use and purchase of IT services, service level agreements (SLAs) become a major part of most IT concepts and roadmaps. This contribution introduces basic concepts of SLAs. It shows how to derive service levels from specific system requirements. In addition, it describes creation of an SLA using an example of the important service factor performance, which is too often neglected within IT environments. All explanations are based on an SLA project of a major German outsourcer.

20.1 Introduction

Some big vendors offering large, standardized, off-the-shelf application systems, e.g., SAP R/3 or Oracle Applications, dominate markets for business applications encompassing software for production planning or order management. Despite all the advantages of selling and buying these large integrated application systems, there is one major shortcoming: mostly, only large enterprises can afford to buy, install, customize, and maintain these systems. Furthermore, markets for these large packaged application systems are almost saturated, as more and more large enterprises have satisfied their demand. On the other hand, there are lots of small and medium-sized enterprises (SMEs), which demand very specialized application systems together with a broad coverage of common business functionality, as the core of the related business tasks stay the same, independent of a company's size. However, most SMEs cannot afford to purchase or even maintain these large packaged application systems. This leads to two important problems: SMEs' demand for business application systems cannot be satisfied, and vendors of large, standardized, off-the-shelf application systems lose an important market.

Outsourcing and related concepts such as application hosting, application service providing, or business application services offer solutions to these problems by trying to reduce IT service costs for the customer. An IT service provider is in a position to establish several customer relations at different levels of service quality. Service levels can be introduced to distinguish between different IT service qualities, e.g., different response-time characteristics of an information system. A set of IT services together with respective service levels leads to a *service level agreement (SLA)*, which allows customers to customize an outsourcer's offer according to their demand. Despite this straightforward approach, there are still some problems to solve before an outsourcer can launch its first offer. This contribution addresses these steps and explains the derivation of service levels for a SAP R/3 solution using the example of the service factor performance. Our explanations are based on an SLA project of a major German R/3 outsourcer.

20.2 Importance of the performance service factor

Performance characteristics of information systems are critical service factors.

Performance can be defined as the capability of a system to process a given number of tasks in a determined time interval.

Many developing projects as well as productive systems fail because of insufficient performance characteristics. Often, performance was not treated as an elementary quality and service factor within the customer–provider relationship and in software development. The main focus was put on functional specification. But if we focus on semi-critical and critical systems with regard to performance, e.g. call centre solutions or (Web-based) sales applications, this factor is as important as pure functional descriptions. Many projects have had to learn this the hard way.

The projected development costs for the luggage processing system at Denver airport were exceeded by US$2 million because of insufficient performance characteristics (Glass, 1998). At the beginning of the project, the system was designed for one terminal only. But within the engineering process the system's responsibilities were enlarged. The system had to process all luggage transactions of all the terminals at the airport, but performance aspects were not considered. Because of the not unexpected flood of data, the opening of the airport was delayed by 16 months.

A study of AT&T analysed hundreds of in-house projects with regard to possible problems within development and maintenance, which lead to massive problems or failure of the projects (Avritzer and Weyuker, 1998). The results underline the underestimated importance of this factor and show that performance is still a critical factor within the development and maintenance phase of the software life cycle. That's why we explain the determination and proving of service levels at using the example of performance.

Performance can be determined and analysed subjectively and objectively. Subjective analysis describes a performance analysis from the system user's point of view. It describes qualitatively how a certain performance characteristic is perceived. Because of individual expectations and stress limits, these results are related to an individual person (Ghanbari *et al.*, 1997, p. 3). In order to evaluate subjective performance reasonably, results have to be aggregated to clusters. Clusters can be formed by aggregating evaluated application functions or user queries, or according to which workplaces initiated requests, or on which dates requests occurred.

In contrast, objective performance analysis is based on using approved measurement methods and tools. Database management systems usually offer options for objective performance analysis, such as auditing, tracing, or the logging of system characteristics in dynamic performance tables in the data dictionary. Furthermore, a series of tools for objective performance analysis is available.

Functions with objectively inadequate performance characteristics primarily have to be adjusted (see Table 20.1). Functions with subjectively adequate performance characteristics but objectively inadequate performance characteristics have to be modified since they can hinder other functions in execution. An extensive data run for a report, for example, can considerably hinder execution of other functions if many users access the same resources in parallel. However, the report itself can be subjectively uncritical.

TABLE 20.1
Subjective and objective performance analysis

		Subjective performance	
		Adequate	Inadequate
Objective Performance	Adequate	No need for adjustments	Unrealistic expectations
	Inadequate	Need for adjustments	

Functions which are subjectively inadequate but objectively adequate are problematic from the system management's point of view. This reflects unrealistic user expectations. In these cases, users have to be influenced in such a way that they accept weaker performance, at least temporarily.

20.3 Service level agreement concept

The following sections describe briefly how SLAs are structured and how service prices can be determined.

The service level agreement

Companies are faced with the fact that they have to design the cost structure of their IT services more transparently. Furthermore, they have to compare their own cost rates with the market average (Inmon et al., 1999, p. 302). Small and mid-sized companies have to outsource IT services, e.g. the development and maintenance of an application system, the preparation and the processing of mass e-mails, or a periodic data backup, to external service providers (Loh and Venkatraman, 1992, p. 7; Lacity and Hirschheim, 1993, p. 5). A written list of a specific set of IT services is collected in an IT service catalogue.

Performance service levels allow a detailed specification of performance requirements. A sufficient specification of performance requirements is the basis for a comprehensive performance analysis of an information system. Performance characteristics can be quantified by performance metrics. A performance service level contains a set of lower bounds of quantified performance metrics (Scholz and Turowski, 2000, p. 252). The more performance metrics are used, the better the performance requirements are represented.

Performance service levels are fixed in a service level agreement. An SLA describes an agreement between an IT service provider and a customer about performance and corresponding service costs. It specifies the performance characteristics and other software quality factors in addition to functional requirements. The agreement is ratified as a compromise between representatives of the customer, management, user, and developer. It is important to find a compromise solution since the performance requirements of customers often do not correspond to the performance expectations of users.

Internal and external SLAs can be distinguished (Pantry and Griffiths, 1997, p. 11). Internal SLAs are not based on a legal declaration, but the IT department has to offer the IT services at negotiated performance levels. External SLAs are a contractual framework between several companies.

Process model

The structured development of an SLA requires a process model, which is described in the following.

Services and performance service levels

The customer determines all services, e.g. the operation of an information system, in the first phase of the process (see Figure 20.1). Services are functionally specified. In addition to the functional description, each service has to be concretized with time and spatial characteristics. The complete description of all services is collected in a service catalogue.

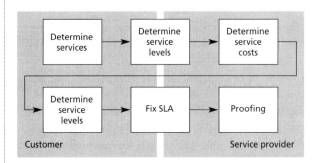

FIGURE 20.1

Process model for the development of an SLA

The service catalogue is handed over to the service provider in the second phase. The service provider determines performance service levels for each service in consultation with the customer. Performance characteristics can be specified with the help of performance metrics.

Performance metrics are specific product metrics, which can be determined on different system layers and from different perspectives. There are a lot of classification schemes of performance metrics, e.g.:

- **Perspective**: Metrics can be determined from different perspectives, e.g. from the perspective of the service provider, which can lead to metrics such as mean server utilization. Beyond that, they can be determined e.g. from the perspective of the user, which can lead to metrics such as mean response time.

- **Granularity**: Metrics can be oriented on different system granularities. Thus, they can focus on single system components, e.g. a CPU, which can lead to metrics such as CPU processing time. On the other hand they can focus on a whole system environment, which can lead to metrics such as system response time.

- **Classical subdivisions**: Performance metrics can be defined by their classical subdivisions, distinguishing three metric subgroups: throughput, utilization and time consumption. Thus, metrics also can be determined with regard to throughput, e.g. a transaction rate metric, to utilization, e.g. a CPU utilization metric, and to time consumption, e.g. a response-time metric.

- **Internal/external performance**: Another differentiation only distinguishes between internal and external performance. External performance means the time consumption of a user process, including all necessary basis system processes. On the other hand, internal performance focuses on single IT services such as a database service, but is less important; e.g. when considering integrated information systems, processes of database-based information systems induce a lot of basis processes with a versatile use of resources. Thus, in this case the informative value of internal performance metrics is low. For that reason, internal performance metrics don't play a major role within the performance specification of an SLA.

A couple of service levels due to different operation states can be defined. Therefore, an instance of every performance metric has to be assigned to every service level. Thus, different performance characteristics are defined in different service levels. Furthermore, a scale needs to be assigned to each defined performance metric. Four kinds of scales, which are based on each other, can be distinguished:

- **Nominal scale**: There is a simple value assignment of symbols or numbers, which act as a descriptor. Different values don't have a different symbol. Values cannot be ordered or added. Only an equalization check is possible.

- **Ordinal scale**: There is an operational defined criterion in a rank order. The transitivity postulate is fulfilled. Thus, the scale is in the position to define a rank order over values, and comparison operators can be used.

- **Interval scale**: Equal large distances on the scale indicate equal large differences with regard to the specific performance characteristic. Addition and subtraction operations are defined.

- **Ratio scale**: There is an absolute or empirical neutral point. All mathematical operations can be applied.

For wise application within an SLA, at least an interval scale is necessary. In the case of a sales report, three performance service levels are defined, which are specified by two performance metrics (see Table 20.2). The performance metric 'mean response time' characterizes an online access on the sales report. The performance metric 'page throughput' characterizes the paper output rate of the sales report.

TABLE 20.2 Performance service levels

IT Service: Sales Report		
Performance service levels	**Performance metrics**	
	x: Mean response time (online) in seconds	y: Page throughput in pages per minute
1	$x < 1$	$8 < y$
2	$1 \leq x < 3$	$5 < y \leq 8$
3	$3 \leq x < 9$	$1 < y \leq 5$

Performance metrics put the resource requirements of respective programme segments in relation to a planned hardware system. Since the hardware configuration of the productive system is not determined at the beginning of software development, the metrics refer to a hardware reference system. The reference system corresponds to a relative performance degree of 100%. As soon as the hardware configuration can be determined in more detail, the degree of performance is adapted to the new reference system. A tuple (performance value, relative performance degree) identifies specified performance data.

Service costs

In the next phase, a cost rate is assigned to each performance service level. In general, three techniques for determination of service costs can be distinguished.

On the one hand, actual costs of hardware, software, personnel, and so on are used in calculation models to determine service costs. Determination is simple, but the results are not transparent and do not allow market comparisons.

On the other hand, cost rates of services can be used, containing actual and future costs on the basis of ratios and estimable developments to determine service costs, because of fast development and resulting cost changes in the IT department. Costs have to be determined on the basis of a customer's requirements of the IT system. With knowledge of these costs, a customer can receive a price offer that corresponds to his or her specific requirements. In addition, this cost structure allows the customer to find out in future which services can be provided at which cost.

Further on, the target-costing concept can be applied. With the help of this concept an attempt is made to reach a fixed price for a specific service. Thus, companies can do market research to determine the prices that customers are willing to pay for a service. Resulting cost structures determine the scope of services.

The customer decides, in a further step, in favour of one or several service levels (see Table 20.3). Besides the individual requirements and budget, the decision depends on performance service levels and their costs. If several service levels are

TABLE 20.3 Example of performance service level cost rates

IT Service: Sales Report	
Performance service levels	Price in € /month
1	620
2	410
3	180

linked together, the costs of an IT service are computed by a mixed calculation. Let, for example, 5% of all service uses belong to service level 1, 15% of all service uses to service level 2 and 80% of all service uses to service level 3; total costs are computed as a sum of the weighted service-level partial costs:

Total costs = (0.05 * 620) + (0.15 * 410) + (0.8 * 180) = €236.50 per month

Fixing an SLA

An SLA needs to be fixed in a written contract. The contract consists of an extensive service specification and further significant sections. In practice, an SLA should encompass the following sections:

- **Preamble**: The preamble describes the contracting parties, general objectives of the SLA, and a mediator, who is responsible for interpretation and further modifications of the agreement. Furthermore, it states services that are not part of the agreement, but which might be expected to be part of it, to avoid later conflicts.

- **Scope and framework**: In this section, the scope of the agreement is described, e.g. involved departments, users, hardware, operating systems, and applications. Furthermore, the duty of the customer to cooperate is stated, e.g. to provide network interfaces, special types of terminals, or necessary qualification of the users.

- **Service descriptions**: The service description enumerates the services that have to be provided as well as the respective performance service levels reflecting the customer's demand. The services themselves are defined in detail in the service catalogue. For that reason, the respective version of the service catalogue becomes (implicitly) part of the SLA.

- **Reporting**: Reporting is necessary to prove that a certain service level has been met. For that reason, the SLA partners have to agree upon accuracy, measuring intervals, measuring tools, measuring methods and recording methods for each service.

- **Data security**: In this section, the provider guarantees adherence to laws, rules and guidelines concerning data security. Furthermore, physical access control and the use of security software, e.g. against viruses, are regulated.

- **Prices**: Here, prices for each tuple (Service, Service Level) that has been defined in the service description section are determined.

- **Contractual period**: This section determines the period of time for which the SLA is valid. Usually an SLA is negotiated on a one- to three-year basis. After that, most conditions will be renegotiated.

- **Termination clause**: This section regulates the contract termination modalities. Each party is in a position to abandon the contract in specific cases.

- **Contract penalty**: If a service provider fails to provide a negotiated level of service, he or she has to pay a contract penalty. In this section, all possible cases that could result from a violation of performance service levels should be considered. It should serve as an incentive for the provider to secure a proper delivery of services, but not as a means for the customer to reduce costs subsequently.

- **Organizational settlements**: This section determines the organizational structuring of the SLA. Official reporting and communication channels are determined. In addition, contact persons for certain problem areas are agreed upon.

Similar findings are reported in the literature as well, e.g. Pantry and Griffiths (1997), pp. 30–45. As an extension, the SLA should be split into a static and a dynamic part to simplify its evolution over time. The static part contains preamble, scope and framework, reporting, data security, contractual period, termination clause, contract penalty, and organizational settlements. The dynamic part includes service descrip-

20 ■ Enforcing performance guarantees based on performance service levels

tion and prices, which can be adapted to changed requirements and environments. Each SLA is individual to a considerable degree. That's why there is no standard form for an SLA. Each section needs to be negotiated individually and precisely.

20.4 Proof of service levels

After fixing the SLA, the meeting of service levels during operation has to be proved. A service level is called 'proved' if the outcome of the corresponding metric lies within the bounds given by the service level's definition.

The proof of a service level is mandatory for customers since this is their only way to assure quality. Besides quality assurance, monitoring and proving, service levels offer an important way for providers to improve profitability. Take e.g. a service whose response time is constantly on a better service level than agreed. In this case, it might be possible to run it on a server with weaker performance, which in turn is less expensive, and, further, to preserve more expensive resources for SLAs with higher requirements and maybe a better return on investment (ROI).

In the following, we describe how the distribution of transaction response times in a SAP R/3 environment can be monitored and proved (see Figure 20.2). First, raw (measurement) data is needed. A monitoring program that is part of SAP R/3 provides this

FIGURE 20.2

Proof of response-time characteristics

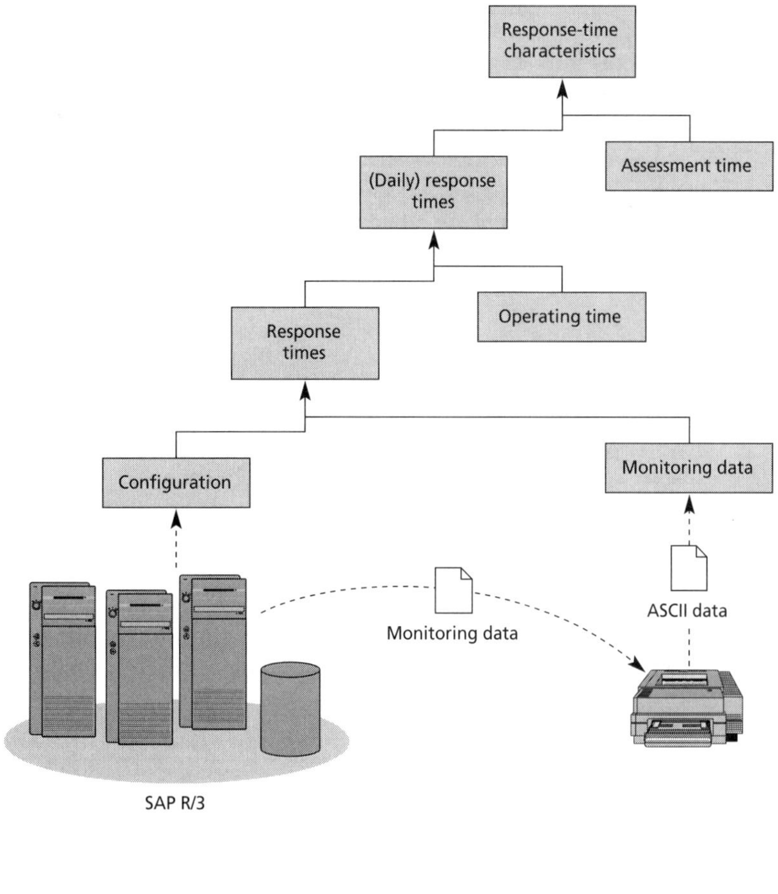

information. The monitor within SAP R/3 reports, for each dialog process and for each application server, the starting time, working time, kind of transaction, and user. However, this information may not be accessed from outside R/3, but it is accessible by a program written in ABAP/4. For that reason, an ABAP/4 program is used to store the monitoring data in an ASCII file. With this, the information can be processed by information systems outside SAP R/3. In the next step, raw monitoring data is filtered by eliminating times caused by system transactions or by the monitoring process itself.

By combining data concerning the hardware configuration with filtered monitoring data, response times are obtained which relate to specific application servers. If a working day is taken as a whole, it has to be broken into time intervals that are feasible for dialog processing (operating time), and those that are not feasible for dialog processing. After filtering data concerning the non-operating time, daily response times are calculated. Finally, together with the agreed assessment time (e.g. a month or ten days), the distribution of response times is calculated (response-time characteristic).

20.5 Conclusions and outlook

SLAs are a powerful concept for ensuring the service quality of purchased or in-house IT services. Service levels can be determined at defined prices. Metrics are in a position to quantify service levels. The determination of metrics has to be analysed very carefully, because it has to be ensured that all metrics can be measured and proved while providing the service. That's why early integration of all SLA partners within the project is important.

Performance is a critical service factor of a software system. A service provider has to ensure a defined level of performance. Therefore, it is wise to pay attention to performance not only during the operation of a system while providing a service but also during the development or purchase of a software system itself. If a service provider intends to purchase software, benchmarking results should be analysed and compared with the own-system environment. Results should come from third-party consultants or independent benchmarking organizations, because most software providers use idealized cases for their benchmarks.

If a service provider intends to develop software, performance-oriented system development techniques should be used. An efficient technique is 'performance engineering'. It considers performance as a design objective throughout the whole software system development process. Performance objectives and analyses of the respective design structures are continuously compared. In the early stages, response-time metrics can be quantified using estimation formulas, analytical models, simulation models, and prototypes. Deviations lead to an immediate change in the software design. Thus, performance engineering is able to guarantee an adequate response-time characteristic of the productive system. Performance engineering of software systems needs an approach converting the whole software development process. For this purpose, practical models of integration are already available (Rautenstrauch and Scholz, 1999).

Literature

Avritzer, A. and Weyuker, E. (1998) 'Investigating metrics for architectural assessment'. *IEEE Fifth International Symposium on Software Metrics*, IEEE: Bethesda.

Ghanbari, M., Hughes, C.J., Sinclair, M.C. and Eade, J.P. (1997) *Principles of Performance Engineering for Telecommunication and Information Systems*. Inspec/IEE: London.

Glass, R. (1998) *Software Runaways – Lessons Learned from Massive Software Project Failures*. Prentice Hall: Upper Saddle River, NJ.

Inmon, W., Rudin, K., Buss, C. and Sousa, R. (1999) *Data Warehouse Performance*. John Wiley & Sons: New York.

Lacity, M. and Hirschheim, R. (1993) *Information Systems Outsourcing. Myths, Metaphors and Realities*. John Wiley & Sons: Chichester.

Loh, L. and Venkatraman, N. (1992) 'Determinants of information technology: outsourcing. A cross-sectional analysis'. *Journal of Management Information Systems*, 9(1), 7–24.

Pantry, S. and Griffiths, P. (1997) *The Complete Guide to Preparing and Implementing Service Level Agreements*. The Library Association: London.

Rautenstrauch, C. and Scholz, A. (1999) 'Vom Performance Tuning zum Software Performance Engineering am Beispiel datenbankbasierter Anwendungssysteme: Reduktion des performancebedingten Entwicklungsrisikos'. *Informatik Spektrum*, 22(4), 261–75.

Scholz, A. and Turowski, K. (2000) 'Service level agreements of performance requirements'. In J. Bon (eds), *World Class IT Service Management Guide*. Ten Hagen & stam: Amsterdam, pp. 249–56.

21 GQM applied in IT Service Management

Wouter de Jong Department of Information Systems and Software Engineering, Delft University of Technology, the Netherlands

Summary

Business depends more and more on IT and therefore requires adequate services at low cost. Many IT service organizations struggle with the questions: are we doing the right things, and are we doing them in a cost-effective way? In other words, they have doubts about the effectiveness and the efficiency of their IT services.

For effectiveness, it is important that the right tasks are executed in the right sequence to realize the agreed IT services. For efficiency, it is important that the right tasks are scheduled to the right people in order to avoid queues and people wasting time. For a guarantee that these requirements will be met in the future it is important to use a well-proven methodology to achieve the abovementioned goals. A well-proven methodology that suits these purposes is the Goals/Questions/Metrics (GQM) methodology.

In this chapter we present the results of a research project in which GQM is used. We found that the answers to seven questions are necessary and sufficient to achieve several different goals concerning evaluation of the effectiveness and efficiency of the tasks in IT service processes in a uniform way. We evaluated three cases, each with a different goal.

21.1 Introduction

The integration of ERP applications, e-commerce and telecoms in the primary business processes makes the business depend more and more on the proper functioning of the IT infrastructure. This requires that a reliable IT infrastructure has to be guaranteed at a reasonable cost and that IT service management has to get a closer relationship with the management of the primary business processes. This means a requirement for 'better services at lower costs'. In other words, the effectiveness and the efficiency of the IT service organization must be guaranteed at high standards.

Effectiveness can be increased by a proper sequencing of the tasks in a process flow to make sure that this sequence ends in the realization of the desired IT service. For an evaluation of this aspect (the process-oriented approach) all the defined tasks need to have a well-defined input and output object to ensure the link to other tasks (see Figure 21.1).

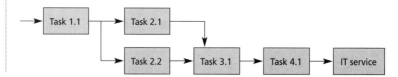

FIGURE 21.1

The sequencing of tasks

Efficiency can be increased by a proper scheduling of the tasks into an organizational unit and the determination of priorities to avoid both queues and a waste of time. Figure 21.2 shows the allocation of several tasks to an organizational unit with limited resources, sometimes even limited to one employee, which means that if one of the tasks is active, the other tasks have to wait.

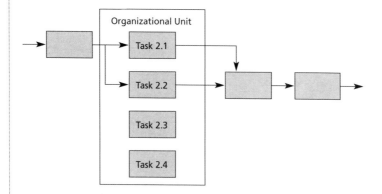

FIGURE 21.2
The scheduling of tasks

For an evaluation of this scheduling aspect, it is necessary to be able to define a finite duration and an execution trigger for every task in order to be able to optimize this scheduling. The time element, the non-linearities in the queues and the unpredictable firing rules sometimes even make it necessary to apply a simulation approach to this evaluation.

21.2 Modelling the process flow

IT managers often consider a transition from a task-oriented approach to a process-oriented approach in order to improve the effectiveness and/or efficiency of the IT service organization. For this transition it is necessary to model the process flow and to determine all the activities that have to take place within the processes. This investigation can be initiated for a number of reasons, e.g.:

- the design of the required process diagrams to verify that the IT service requirements are really met;
- the prediction of the performance of the processes by means of simulation;
- the desire to calculate the number of employees, in FTEs (Full Time Equivalents), that are needed to realize the IT services;
- the cost calculation per service product;
- the optimal scheduling of personnel.

This means that there can be many different reasons for the modelling activities, so it is obvious that other details have to be taken into consideration. In all cases, however, the tasks have to be linked to processes and scheduled to employees.

The modelling process starts with an investigation of all the departments or organizational units that participate in the processes we have to model. The activities necessary for the realization of the IT service processes are usually organized and managed in a number of organizational units or departments with specialized knowledge and/or skills. The traditional task-oriented structure of such line organizations is described by Looijen (1998) and depicted in Figure 21.3.

Today, many IT service organizations have adopted a process-oriented approach, as described in the IT Infrastructure Library (ITIL) (CCTA, 1989). To ensure that the IT services are realized in an effective and efficient way, the process management has to follow the process flow from the start to the resulting IT services; see Figure 21.4.

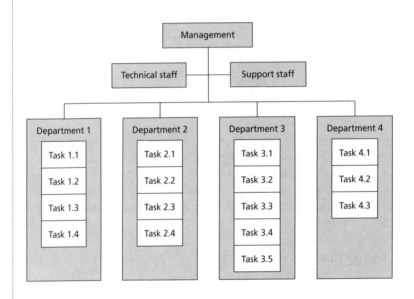

FIGURE 21.3

Traditional structure of an organization

FIGURE 21.4

The process flow in the line organization

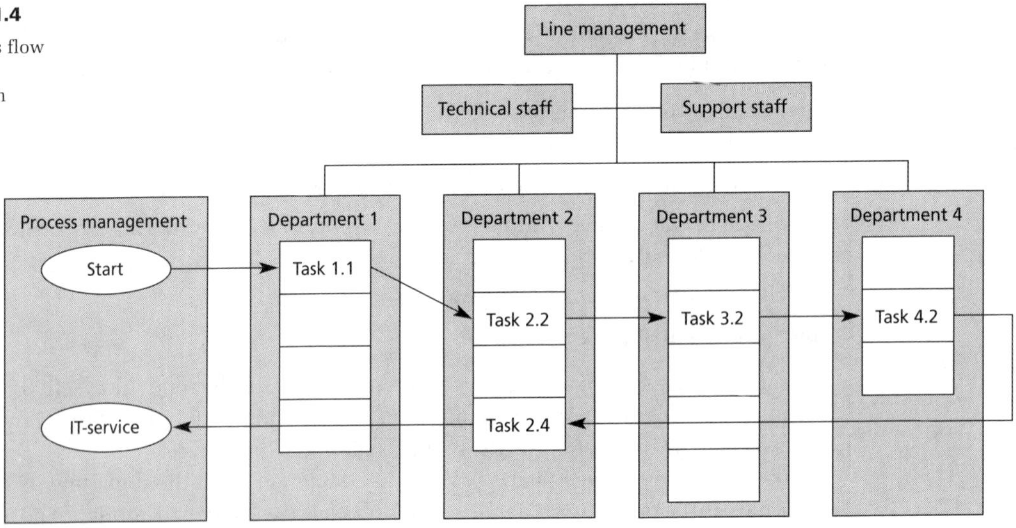

IT service processes often require many different knowledge skills, so in many cases the process managers cover more than one department. Their interest concerns only the tasks participating in their processes, which sometimes results in conflicts of interest between the line and process management. This becomes even more serious if more than one process manager has a claim on the same human resources.

21.3 Simulation of the processes

Simulation of the processes is performed using a dynamic modelling approach such as that of de Vreede (1995), in which the tasks are allocated to the executing actors. The allocation of the tasks to actors or eventually to workgroups with several equally skilled actors is necessary because the time dependency has to be made explicit: after all, people can do a lot of things, but not at the same time! The building of an allocation model starts with the drawing of a diagram where all the tasks performed for a specific process are placed in a sequence and are allocated to the actors in the organizational units.

A simple example is given in Figure 21.5. The example describes a simplified Help Desk process: The dashed line represents the flow of first-line incidents where the incident can be solved by the Help Desk (actor 1) with the help of the operator (actor 4). The continuous line represents the flow of second-line incidents, where the assistance of the incident controller (actor 2) and the support of the software and hardware maintenance departments (actors 3 and 5) are necessary. The lines represent the flow of objects, such as incident calls, problem reports, and new software or hardware solutions. As can be seen in Figure 21.5, most actors have to carry out more than one task and for this reason it is necessary to ensure that the workload for every actor (or workplace) is well balanced.

In this example, it is clear that the tasks form a central role in modelling the process flow: horizontally, they are the minor building blocks in the sequence of the process flow; vertically, they are the minor building blocks in the task allocation to actors.

In the next step the dynamic data of the process has to be collected concerning the frequencies of the incoming objects (incident reports in this example) and the processing time of each task execution. In most cases this data will depend on the type of the incoming object.

If the diagram and the dynamic data are available, it is quite simple to make a running simulation model with one of the modern simulation tools.

21.4 Goals/Questions/Metrics

To find out which information we have to collect about the activities in the processes to model and how these activities can be placed in sequence to contribute to the desired IT services, we used the Goals/Questions/Metrics (GQM) approach, which is briefly described in this paragraph. The GQM method was originally developed by V. Basili and D. Weiss, and expanded with many other concepts by D. Rombach. GQM is a result of many years of practical experience and academic research. A detailed and practical description can be found on the Internet (http://is.twi.tudelft.nl/gqm), along with all the literature references.

FIGURE 21.5

Example of a task–actor diagram

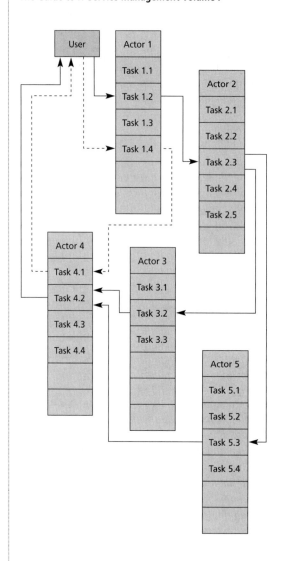

In the Goals/Questions/Metrics approach, first the goals of the research are defined, then the questions that have to be answered are derived and finally the metrics (the relations between the data) are specified. The measurement of the specified data, which form the results of the inquiries, is set up to answer the questions so that the goals can be reached. (See Figure 21.6.)

This is a very simplified description of the method, but we can see that the questions form a central part in this approach; they largely depend upon the research goals and form the basis of the realized metrics.

For the research, a number of possible goals were specified, which were based on the different reasons for the research. In this chapter we will elaborate three of them as an example:

FIGURE 21.6

The Goals/Questions/Metrics approach

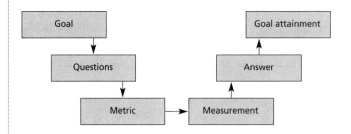

- **Goal 1** the creation of process diagrams in order to show how the IT management tasks contribute in a consecutive way to the resulting IT services;
- **Goal 2** the prediction of the dynamic performance of the IT service processes by means of simulation;
- **Goal 3** the calculation of the number of FTEs that are needed to realize the services.

21.5 Seven Questions Matrix

In the research, we found that we needed an answer to seven questions, to be able to achieve all of the abovementioned goals: four questions to determine the process structure (for the evaluation of effectiveness) and three questions concerning the dynamic data (for the evaluation of efficiency):

Questions for the process structure:

- Which *tasks* have to be performed?
- Which *input* object is required?
- What is the *output*?
- What is the *destination* of the output?

Questions concerning the dynamic data:

- What *triggers* the task?
- What is the *frequency* of task execution?
- What is the *duration* of the task?

In the questionnaire we positioned the questions concerning the dynamic aspects in the middle of the sequence of questions because this data concerns the internal processing of the task between input and output and this is a more logical sequence in the interviews. (See Figure 21.7)

FIGURE 21.7

The seven elements of the Seven Questions Matrix

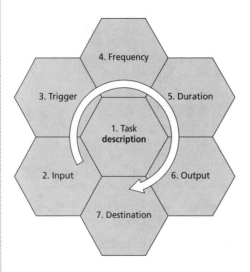

Summarized, it shows that for the realization of all the defined sub-goals we could ask the employees in the processes concerned to answer the following seven questions:

1. What do you have to do?   → task description
2. What do you require to do it?   → input
3. What makes you do it?   → trigger
4. How often is it done?   → frequency
5. How long does it take?   → duration
6. What is the result?   → output
7. Where does the result end up.   → destination

If we have to draw process diagrams, it is only necessary to gather the descriptions of all the tasks that are fulfilled, the sequence of these tasks (input/output relation) and the objects that follow the arrows in the diagram (questions 1, 2, 6 and 7). To make a working simulation model, the data about time elements also have to be added (questions 3, 4 and 5). These consist of events that trigger task execution, their frequency and the duration of every task. For the calculation of the number of FTEs, only the frequency and duration of every task are necessary.

These subsets are depicted in Table 21.1.

TABLE 21.1

Relation of goals and questions

Questions	Description	Input	Trigger	Frequency	Duration	Output	Destination
Goals							
Process diagrams	x	x				x	x
Simulation	x	x	x	x	x	x	x
FTE calculation	x			x	x		

The questions must give us detailed information about the following subjects:

1. *Task description*: an activity to bring an object (or a person) into a specific status. A task description should consist of a verb (to describe the activity) and a noun (the description of the object to be processed). From the task description it must be clear which status the object should reach after processing; i.e. it should be clear when the 'job is done' (the task is finished).

2. *Input object*: the object that is being processed – that is, transformed into another status or into another object or even more than one object. Such objects can be, for example, hardware or software components, but also documents such as functional specifications, test procedures or management reports.

3. *Trigger*: triggers decide when a specific task will be carried out; there can be a diversity of trigger types:
   - Clock triggers: for example, every Friday at 15.00 a backup is made.
   - Events: for example, an incident registration starts as soon as a customer calls in.
   - Schedules: for example, roll-out is planned for Sunday 24 March between 01.00 and 06.00.
   - Deadlines: for example, the tested module should be delivered before 18 June.

4. *Frequency*: the number of task executions per time interval; for example: twice a week, once in a lifetime, or about 24 times a day.

5. *Duration*: the amount of time the execution of the task requires, from start to finish. Often this duration depends on the type of object to be processed; if these relationships are known, the durations should be specified in a duration table. Sometimes the execution of the task can be interrupted and resumed later, depending on the priority.

6. *Output object*: the output object should be defined for further use in another task within the process or it should be an element of the resulting services of the entire process. It is very important to define an output for the task, because the realization of this object or the reached status of the object indicates that the 'job is done', and at this time the measurement of the duration will stop.

7. *Destination*: the destination of every output should be defined. This destination can be either a colleague who is using the object for further processing, or the customer, who needs the final result of the IT service organization to do other work in the primary business processes. It can be either a product (an information system consisting of hardware, software and/or datasets) or a service (aspect) such as support to use the information systems or a document that proves compliance with the agreed service levels (management reports). Even an invoice for payment can be considered output. If no destination can be defined, the result of the task cannot be processed further and the processing of the task should be questioned.

21.6 Work in practice

Depending on the goals of the specific research, we used the questionnaire in three cases. Although it is not always necessary to answer all seven questions, it is advisable to ask for the complete set in order to avoid vague task descriptions such as 'maintaining availability' (no start and stop) and 'attending a meeting' (no defined output). In the cases, we had the following goals:

- **Goal 1** Drawing a process diagram to verify the effectiveness of a process;
- **Goal 2** Running a simulation model to verify the dynamic characteristics;
- **Goal 3** Defining the required number of employees by FTE calculations.

Goal 1. The process diagram

The first goal consisted of drawing a process diagram to verify the effectiveness of the Change Management process of a Dutch IT organization. The sequencing of the tasks had to make sure that the agreed IT services were realized. For this reason, all the tasks in the process were placed in sequence in a process diagram to show the process flow from the request for change to the final realization of the changes in the IT infrastructure.

It showed that a complete process diagram concerning the realization of a service request could be drawn with the answers to the four mentioned questions (see Figure 21.8). In this diagram not all the arrows are drawn, as it would make the picture rather confusing. The input/output relations were explicitly defined in a separate table.

For this goal, only the input and output of the tasks and the destination of the output is required; the dynamic data concerning trigger, frequency and duration are not necessary yet. They become important for the next goal.

Goal 2. The performance simulation

For the second goal (verifying the dynamic performance of the process), the dynamic values about trigger, frequency and duration had to be collected as well. With this data the questions about the maximum number of changes to be processed in a specific time interval and the mean time of a change realization could be answered. The simulation model is based on the same case as the process diagram of goal 1. Running the simulator gave a good evaluation of the utilization of the human resources, the mean time for the realization of changes and the number of objects in the queues (see Figure 21.9).

It showed that a complete set of answers to the seven questions was necessary and sufficient to build a working simulation model which showed the dynamic performance of the process. Seven answers for every identified task were sufficient, without further additional questioning of the personnel involved.

During the building of the simulation model we found that in the process model some links were not specified correctly. In a simulation model this omission is automatically detected because of a deadlock in the simulator.

Goal 3. The FTE calculation

The third goal in this evaluation consisted of the calculation of the required number of staff (technical and support personnel) to realize the IT services. For this reason, only the data about the frequency and duration of the identified tasks is necessary. These values are listed in the first two columns in the spreadsheet (Figure 21.10).

The tasks are now grouped into two types: processing tasks and facilitating tasks. The processing tasks have a direct contribution to the services delivered: direct user support and IT service processes. The facilitating tasks have no direct relation to the final result, but they make the processing tasks possible. Examples of these tasks are 'handling e-mail' and 'time registration'. In the spreadsheet these tasks are summarized separately and the total number of hours per week is subtracted from the total work hours per week to find the number available for the FTE calculation.

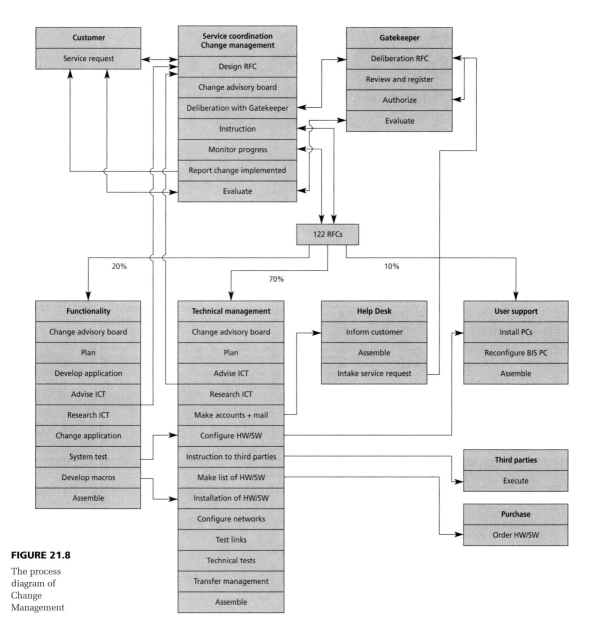

FIGURE 21.8

The process diagram of Change Management

FIGURE 21.9

Simulation model of the Change Management process

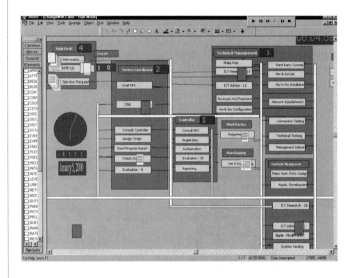

In the example, the first series of tasks, numbered 1 to 41, consisted of processing tasks. They could be allocated to the identified user support and IT service processes. The facilitating tasks were summarized separately to 12.8 hours per week (hpw). This means that of the original 36 hours only 23.2 hpw are available as a basis for the FTE calculation of the processes. These FTE numbers are then separately summarized per process; see the six columns in the marked block in the spreadsheet in Figure 21.10.

FIGURE 21.10

The spreadsheet with the FTE calculations

	Processing tasks					Supp	SLM	Av	CfM	Inc	ChM	Sec
1	Prepare and modify documentation	0.5	240	2.00	ChM	0.09					0.09	
2	Create reports	1	120	2.00	SLM	0.09		0.09				
3	Install new equipment	1	240	4.00	ChM	0.17					0.17	
4	Replace hardware component	2	60	2.00	ChM	0.09					0.09	
5	Create service-overview	1	120	2.00	SLM	0.09		0.09				
6	Restore data	2	60	2.00	Av	0.09			0.09			
7	Create new account	22	15	5.50	ChM	0.24					0.24	
8	Change account	34	10	5.67	Chm	0.24					0.24	
9	Check database back-ups	5	30	2.50	Av	0.11			0.11			
10	Distribute IP adresses	0.5	120	1.00	ChM	0.04					0.04	
11	Check logfiles	2	60	2.00	Sec	15.00	2	2.00	1.00	1.00	4.00	3.00	2.00
32	Fill in logbook	5	15	1.25	SLM	0.05		0.05				
33	Periodic preparation of data extraction	1	120	2.00	Supp	0.09	0.09					
34	Support user	20	15	5.00	Supp	0.22	0.22					
35	Registration incident call	32	10	5.33	Inc	0.23				0.23		
36	Check configuration	1	240	4.00	Cfm	0.17			0.17			
37	Modify CMDB	12	30	6.00	Cfm	0.26			0.26			
38	Solve problem	10	30	5.00	Inc	0.22				0.22		
39	Check entry authorization	5	10	0.83	Sec	0.04						0.04
40	Export data from database	1	60	1.00	ChM	0.04					0.04	
41	Measurement for availability	1	120	2.00	Av	0.09						
		total number of FTEs				17.63		2.3	2.23	1.19	1.43	4.45	3.91	2.04
	Facilitating tasks	freq./w	min.									
42	Process e-mail	5	60	5								
43	Register timetables	1	45	0.75								
44	Travelling Zoetermeer – Driebergen	1	120	2								
45	ICT mgmt meeting	0.5	30	0.25								
46	Reading professional magazines	1	60	1								
47	Training	0.1	480	0.8								
48	Reading manuals	3	60	3								
				12.8		1 week:	avail. 36 hr-		12.8	23.2			

It shows that, with a limited number of questions, an overview can be made of the costs per service process. This overview is depicted in Figure 21.11.

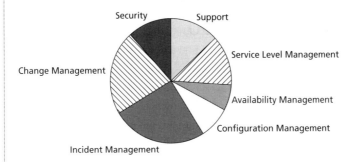

FIGURE 21.11
Graphical representation of the costs per IT service process

21.7 Conclusions

Although it was not easy to identify all the tasks in a complete and uniform way, and we found out that not all the mentioned tasks could be positioned within the processes, it proved to be very useful to determine the characteristics of the processes in a standardized way by applying GQM as a method. It showed that there were a lot of remaining tasks, but all the remaining tasks could be classified as a set of facilitating task types and they were reduced from the available number of hours per week. In this way a clear evaluation could be made of the contribution of the IT service personnel to the specified IT service processes.

In the first case we modelled the process flow and could show that the requirements concerning the desired IT services were really met. The second case made the performance indicators of the process visible in relation to the process parameters. The third case gave us an indication of the necessary number of employees for the realization of the IT services. The most important result of the research was the increasing awareness of the personnel involved of the benefits of a process-oriented approach. We didn't give them the exact answers, but we helped them to ask the right questions.

Literature

Looijen, M. (1998) *Information Systems, Management, Control and Maintenance*, Deventer, Holland: Kluwer Bedrijfsinformatie.

CCTA (1989) *IT Infrastructure Library*, Central Computer and Telecommunications Agency [new OGC], UK.

de Vreede, G.J. (1995) *Facilitating Organizational Change*, Doctoral dissertation, Delft University of Technology, ISBN 90-5638-006-0, Delft.

22 Service level measurement: checkpoint 2000

Mike Tsykin Fujitsu Australia Limited

Summary

Direct measurement of service levels (as represented by end-to-end response time) is now relatively common, thanks to the new generation of measurement tools. However, commercial acceptance of it is not meeting the expectations of tool developers. This chapter analyses the situation and makes a hopeful prediction for the future.

22.1 Introduction

Measurement of service levels and particularly end-to-end response time (ETE RT) is one of the most necessary facilities for capacity management practitioners. The subject is much debated, but practical approaches and tools for open systems were lacking for a long time. Over the past two to three years, quite a few ETE RT measurement tools have appeared on the market. However, user acceptance and practical applications are still lagging behind.

The objectives of this chapter are:

- to review the history of measurement of ETE RT;
- to review and classify the available tools;
- to discuss possible new metrics;
- to discuss the reasons for the relatively slow acceptance of ETE RT measurement tools and the remedial measures.

22.2 Historical perspective

Measuring computer service has been achieved in many different ways over the past 40 or more years. Initially, with single-tasking batch systems, the measure of service was simple – how long it took to execute a particular program. This metric naturally progressed to the concept of throughput – how many programs or jobs could be executed in a given amount of time. With this progression, and the birth of performance tuning, came the idea of measuring the performance or efficiency of various critical parts of the system such as the CPU, input/output devices, and memory usage. Over a period, these performance/efficiency metrics came to be regarded as indicators of how well a system was doing its job, and operating systems were instrumented as a matter of course to provide various metrics, ranging from simple measurements to the results of complex analyses.

22 Service level measurement: checkpoint 2000

As operating systems improved, and multi-tasking and online systems became the norm, these system metrics became the common indicators of how well the system was servicing the organization. They were there, and it was easier to use what was available than to make alterations to applications to record service-level information directly.

Slowly, however, as users became more computer-literate and organizations began to exercise tighter control on data processing budgets, more sophisticated ways of determining service levels were demanded. Suppliers of database software, network and terminal controller equipment, began to 'instrument' their products to provide better measures of how well their particular product was operating. Users demanded that IS departments provide guaranteed service to the organizations concomitant with their spending on equipment and software. And so Service Level Management was born, and evolved. Towards the end of the so-called 'mainframe era', it even became possible to measure ETE RT directly, using the (then) latest terminal multi-controllers. Thus, measurement of transaction-based ETE RT became possible.

In mainframes, a transaction is assumed to be a single protocol block (the SDLC protocol is the dominant one in such an environment) or a message as seen by a transaction monitor (e.g. CICS). Either one of these closely relates to a meaningful user interaction; therefore the approach worked. Attempts to combine such transactions into more meaningful units (Natural Business Units or NBUs) started, but the environment changed radically. Open systems arrived in force.

The roots of these are in scientific and personal computing. This means that various derivations of the TTY (teletype) protocol became dominant. As opposed to SDLC, this is a byte-mode protocol. Therefore, the correlation between user action and protocol block disappeared. Furthermore, complex transaction monitors went out of fashion. The result of this on the measurement of ETE RT was devastating – it simply became too hard.

However, the need remained. Indeed, it even increased due to the advent of outsourcing (both external and internal). In addition, end-user computing was evolving, with its emphasis on service. And so, development continued.

The first tools started appearing on the market in 1997–8. The number of available tools increased rapidly, but acceptance remained cautious. This is still the case, although the recent focus on Internet Quality of Service (QoS) may change the trend in the future.

22.3 ETE RT – approaches to measurement and tools

Concepts

It is useful to define ETE RT formally. In the words of Maccabee (1996), ETE RT is: 'The time between the start of a users' request (indicated by depressing of a key or a button) and the time when the user can use the data supplied in response to the request'. As such, it adequately describes the level of interaction between a user and a computer system that he or she uses. Traditionally, the concept is applied to a single interaction between a user and a system – that is, a transaction. It is assumed that a transaction is a self-contained unit; therefore ETE RT thus derived represents a service level.

For the purposes of this chapter, let's accept this concept of a transaction with one qualification: a transaction may or may not be directly measurable. If it is not, but a measurement is still required, there is no option but to emulate or simulate it.

ETE RT may be broken into discrete components. The most common breakdown is into client, network and server components. This may become complicated if a network of servers is involved in servicing one transaction (multi-tier client–server implementations). Further, depending upon a protocol, each of these components may be further broken down. Therefore, there are several ways in which transaction-based ETE RT may be measured. McBride (1995) proposed one such. Snell (1997) identified three types of ETE RT measurement tools. In 1998, Tsykin and Langshaw expanded and modified Snell's classification. At the same time, independently, Scott and Conway published a similar one.

This chapter modifies and expands the Tsykin/Langshaw classification to reflect the current developments. It is presented below.

There are four approaches to measurement of transaction-based ETE RT:

- 'benchmarking' and emulation;
- application instrumentation;
- 'wire sniffing';
- client instrumentation.

Let us look at each one separately.

Approaches to measurement

Benchmarking and emulation

- *Description*
  - Benchmarking. This approach involves three essential steps:
    1. Intercept user transaction (for instance, access to a Web page) and modify as required. Alternatively, an artificial transaction may be scripted.
    2. Reissue this transaction(s) using 'robots' from one or more locations. Robots would measure ETE RT and its components.
    3. Collate and analyse results.
  - Emulation. This is a variation of benchmarking, except that 'packets' of data (e.g. issued by the *ping* command) are used instead of intercepted or scripted transactions.

- *Advantages*
  - These approaches are intuitive, conceptually simple and acceptable to most people.
  - They are 'active', in that they work regardless of whether there are actual users on a system being measured. Therefore, they are suitable (and widely used) for the measurement of availability, either throughout a period or at a certain time (e.g. before the start of a morning shift).

- They support quite a sophisticated approach to troubleshooting, including identification of problem segments via triangulation.
- They are available as either services or products.

Disadvantages
- They are 'intrusive'. This means that they impose explicit additional load on the system. The extra load need not be large, but the situation may not be philosophically acceptable to many managers.

Penetration

Lately, these have emerged as the dominant form of ETE RT measurement. Emulation is, understandably, the preferred approach in a scientific community. Benchmarking is the mainstay of the Web QoS measurement.

Products (in alphabetical order)
- @watch (Quicksand Development)
- AlertSite (AlertSite)
- EnView (Amdahl)
- Envive (Envive Corporation)
- Keynote (Keynote)
- Netcool (Micromuse)
- NetScore (Anakara)
- PingER (SLAC)
- Proctor (Dirig Software)
- Quotient (Fujitsu)
- Tivoli (IBM)
- Trinity (InfoVista)

Application instrumentation

Description

In this case, transaction points are inserted into user applications, which are then monitored. The most widely known version is ARM (toolkit available), but other versions exist also, particularly in the Web area.

Advantages

This is the most suitable approach for application tuning. It enables tracing of the application (depending upon positioning of transaction points within code).

Disadvantages
- It requires changes to source code of applications, and therefore commitment by suppliers and customers (customized applications).
- Rollout implications impede acceptance by users.

- Commercial benefits to suppliers are (at best) unclear, which impedes development.

Penetration

At present, a minimal number of applications are instrumented. This is not expected to change rapidly.

Products (in alphabetical order)
- BEST1 (BMC)
- Info Vista (Info Vista)
- MeasureWare / PerfView (HP)
- Patrol (BMC)
- S3 (Nextpoint Networks)
- TME10 suite (IBM/Tivoli)

'Wire sniffing'

Description

This approach involves interception of network traffic, analysis of the packets and attribution of those to certain transactions. The rest is conventional analysis. Two possibilities exist for traffic interception:
- 'Raw' network traffic is monitored, decoded and analysed.
- Communications traffic on a server or a client is used. This approach, strictly speaking, should be categorized as an 'instrumented client' (see below). However, it is included here due to the obvious similarities with the other 'wire sniffer' approach.

Advantages

This is a technically clever approach, which provides a comprehensive analysis of network performance and some idea of application response time.

Disadvantages
- A hardware-based probe (either dedicated or a board in 'promiscuous' mode) or instrumentation of the operating system is required. In this case, either a 'shim' or LSP (layered service provider) may be used.
- Architecture is limited in not supporting data on server performance activity.
- Results are particularly dependent upon placement of the probes within the network.

Penetration

Small as yet.

Products (in alphabetical order)
- Chariot (Ganymede)
- EcoScope (Compuware)
- Hypertrack Performance Monitor (Trio Systems)

- NetScout Application Flow Management (NetScout)
- SLM (Fujitsu)
- Sniffer (Network Associates)
- TNG Response Manager (CA)
- various LAN monitors, et cetera
- VitalSuite (Lucent)

Client instrumentation

● *Description*

This approach involves interception, decoding and analysis of operating system events on a client workstation. Given the penetration and messaging architecture, the logical choice of a client platform is Windows. However, the approach is as useful for other 'intelligent' (instrumentable) clients. Of particular interest are Web-based applications.

● *Advantages*

- An architecturally advanced approach, because it allows tracing of all users of operating system services, be they applications or systems products.
- It does not require special hardware, nor instrumentation of applications.
- Within the framework of this approach, ETE RT is easily available as one of the monitored metrics.
- The most flexible approach of all.
- Particularly suitable for product development and debugging.

● *Disadvantages*

- Requires instrumentation of operating systems.
- Presents logistical problems in multi-platform, multi-OS environment.
- Presents problems with measurement of Web activity, due to the coding of popular browsers (neither Internet Explorer nor Navigator uses Windows events much). To overcome that, a combination of 'wire sniffing' and instrumented client has proved useful.

● *Penetration*

Small, but growing.

● *Products (in alphabetical order)*

- ARO (CA)
- OpenView (HP)
- ETEWatch (Candle)
- FSE (Concord)
- SLM (Fujitsu)
- SmartWatch (Landmark)
- Tivoli (IBM)

Summary

All the four approaches described above are now in use. The first one – benchmarking – is the most popular at this stage. This is likely to continue. The second (instrumented applications) and the third (wire sniffing) became 'niche offerings' and are likely to remain that way. The fourth (instrumented client) enjoyed the initial burst of popularity and then faltered somewhat owing to the technical limitations. These are being overcome and the popularity should return in the future.

22.4 Direct measurement of service levels

Objectives

The objective of Service Level Management (SLM) is to manage the service provided to users. Therefore, the first and necessary step is to measure such service.

As McBride (1995) points out in relation to SLM: 'What cannot be measured cannot be managed.' However, he then proceeds to discount client-based measurement in favour of application-based measurement, and suggests that ARM (instrumented applications) should be used for measurement. The author disagrees. It stands to reason that measurement of levels of service should be done from the user's perspective – that is, on a user's workstation and for the user's units of work (such as a business transaction, NBUs or equivalent).

Naturally, it is desirable to trace a transaction across the network, as it 'skips' from server to server. From the point of view of *measurement* of service levels, though, it is not, strictly speaking, mandatory. It is mandatory, however, to:

- measure and understand the user's activity at his or her workstation;
- do so soon – the need will not wait;
- do so for a representative part of a user population, if not for all of it – that will make the measurement meaningful;
- do so relatively cheaply – otherwise, it will not be of practical use.

These are the objectives of direct measurement of service levels regarding ETE RT.

Concepts

As said above, the most popular metric for service levels is response time. But is this a real measure of service or just another indicator? With complex, client–server environments and multi-tasking GUI workstations, such wait times are simply indicators of service levels, and may not be very good ones at that. That is not to say that response time is useless – rather that it must be considered in the context of many other factors. Further, the ETE RT metric alone does not support the proper understanding of service levels necessary for Service Level Management. To put it another way:

- increasingly complex environments mean increasingly complex ways of measuring service;
- analysing the service provided by computer systems which are heavily integrated into an organization's operations requires more understanding of the organization's operations and user workload profiles.

The way in which a service is provided to an organization by that organization's computer infrastructure is a very complex issue, relating not only to items such as response time, but to how users utilize the infrastructure. This chapter does not aim to canvass these matters in a way that they deserve to be addressed. The reader is referred to other chapters in this publication for proper treatment. However, two relevant matters will be briefly dealt with here:

- metrics that may be used in the measurement of service levels;
- the current level of acceptance of Service Level Measurement by the market.

Metrics

Metrics are best grouped by their intended usage. In the case of Service Level Measurement, there are two main applications:

- monitoring and reporting;
- troubleshooting.

These will be dealt with separately.

Monitoring and reporting

Thus far, two metrics have proved the most popular ones in measurement of service levels: ETE RT and availability. These are looked at below.

- ETE RT – traditional end-to-end response-time measure defined above. It may be successfully measured by the benchmarking, instrumented applications or instrumented clients methods.
- Availability – the critical metric, defined as time during which an application is available to be used. Therefore, only active methods (i.e. benchmarking) may be used to measure it. Other methods are passive, that is, they rely on actual user activity. This means that if there is no activity – there is no measurement.

Troubleshooting

In troubleshooting, composite metrics are not sufficient. In order to be able to find a problem, one must know the details of ETE RT. It was mentioned earlier that ETE RT might be split into one or more (depending upon the level of client–server nesting) groups of three functional components:

- server part;
- network part;
- client part.

Server and network parts were explored in detail previously and are well enough understood. However, a client component presents challenges. These stem from the fact that it too is a complex, powerful, multi-tasking platform. Therefore, for troubleshooting purposes, we must be able to measure the interrelations between applications on a client platform. Some metrics suitable for this purpose are listed below:

- ***Application Busy-Switch Time (ABST).*** The time period between an application becoming busy and the user switching away from it. This metric describes a 'level of patience' by a user. Consistently low ABST (say, 1–2 seconds) may indicate that a user expects a delay and does not wish to wait.
- ***Application Cycle Time (ACT).*** The time period between successive switches of focus to an application. Low ACT would indicate a consistently and frequently (but not continuously) used application.
- ***Inter-Application Time (IAT).*** The time period from when focus switches away from a specific application until that application receives focus again.
- ***Application Active Time (AAT).*** The time period from when an application receives focus until focus is switched away from that application. (Note: IAT + AAT = ACT)
- ***Consecutive Wait Count (CWC).*** A count of the number of times the wait cursor was active when focus switched from an application, and still active the next time focus switched to the application.
- ***Application Switch Table (AST).*** A table with applications as row and column headings containing counts of the number of times focus switched from one application (row) to another application (column). It is useful in identifying user work profiles. An example is presented in Table 22.1.

Focus switched from application A to application B 23 times. Focus switched from application B to application A 9 times.

TABLE 22.1 Example of an application switch table

	Application A	Application B
Application A	x	23
Application B	9	x

Several refinements are possible based on the AST. For instance, as well as switch count, the AAT of the application which is losing focus could be calculated – i.e. the AAT specifically for situations where this switch occurs. Similarly, the AAT of the application being switched to could be calculated. The AST could also contain a count of the number of times the wait cursor was active in the application being switched from/to when the switch occurred.

The author believes that only the instrumented client approach is suitable for this task. Please refer to Tsykin and Langshaw (1995) for more details.

Market acceptance

As mentioned above, Service Level Measurement for open systems has been around since the late 1990s. However, market acceptance remains disappointingly slow – in fact, so much so that one of the pioneers of the instrumented client approach (Landmark Systems) withdrew from this market segment in November 2000. An analysis of this slowness of acceptance is presented below.

22 Service level measurement: checkpoint 2000

Service Level Möbius Strip

It is interesting to compare the situation to the Möbius Strip – an endless loop discovered by August-Ferdinand Möbius during the nineteenth century. A sort of 'Service Level Möbius Strip' is presented in Figure 22.1.

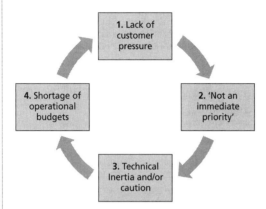

FIGURE 22.1
Service Level Möbius Strip

Brief explanations for the points in the boxes are presented below.

1 *Lack of customer pressure.* In the author's experience, suppliers are not yet under pressure to adopt the directly measurable metrics (such as ETE RT) as part of SLAs. The reason is that customers are not yet comfortable with the concept and therefore are unsure of the implications of SLAs constructed in those terms on *them*.

2 *'Not an immediate priority'.* To misquote an Australian saying: 'When you are up to your eyeballs in crocodiles, it's hard to be interested in weather.' That is, let's worry first about *meeting* the Service Level Agreement, and then we can decide how to monitor it. This makes sense, because the majority of SLAs *still* do not include ETE RT requirements. Availability is usually included, but it is either:

 - defined as application uptime (application is running), which does not necessarily mean that it is available, or
 - calculated from Help Desk records (if there are no complaints, the application is assumed to be available).

3 *Technical inertia and/or caution.* Large networks grow ever more complex. Frequently, this means that different organizations (departments, in the case of systems managed in-house) are involved with the management of networks, servers and clients – all contributing to the final ETE RT. Naturally, suppliers are reluctant to accept non-performance penalties (normally stipulated by SLAs) for problems associated with other suppliers.

4 *Shortage of operational budgets.* Industry is competitive; to get a deal one has to quote the lowest price. SLA monitoring is not *really* a priority for anyone. So, once the competitive bidding starts, this is the first area to be hit. Therefore, once the contract is awarded, perpetual SLA measurement and reporting problems are inevitable.

The way out

The situation will remain as it is – until customer demand for ETE RT measurement emerges. It is happening already, albeit slowly. It is hoped that chapters such as this will help to speed it up by demystifying this essential area.

Some hopeful signs are emerging already. Web Quality of Service (QoS) measurement is sometimes credited with 'saving the Web' in 2000. This claim appears to be somewhat excessive – the Web, being a sociological as well as technical phenomenon, was never in danger of disappearing – but it is true that the focus on user experience is important. ETE RT requirements are starting to find their way into service level agreements. Just recently, a well-known corporation tied a bid/no-bid decision in a major outsourcing tender to the availability of Web-based ETE RT measurement. More to come soon….

22.5 Conclusion

This chapter reviewed the history of the development of, and existing approaches to, measurement of service levels, as well as the tools available as at the year 2000. Objectives and the concepts of direct measurement of service levels, appropriate metrics and market penetration were also looked at. It is hoped that this will be of use to readers.

22.6 Disclaimer

All brand names are Registered Trademarks and Requested Trademarks of their respective owners.

Literature

Literature on the subject is voluminous. The author of this chapter cites a very limited selection and asks authors whose contributions were inadvertently omitted to accept his sincere apologies.

Maccabee, M. (1996) 'Client/server end-to-end response time: real life experience'. *Proc. CMG96.*

McBride, D. (1995) 'Toward successful deployment of IT service management in the distributed enterprise'. *Proc. CMG95.*

Scott, D. and Conway, B. (1998) *Tools for Measuring Application Availability and Performance.* Gartner Group; COM-03-8396; 28/4/98.

Snell, M. (1997) 'Tools solve mysteries of application response time'. *LAN Times*, 14 (5); http://www.wcmh.com/lantimes/97/97mar/703a034b.html

Tsykin, M. and Langshaw, C.D. (1998) 'End-to-end response time and beyond: direct measurement of service levels'. *Proc. CMG98.*

23 How to improve the quality of your support centre by certification

Eppo Luppes L-iT Counselling & Consulting, the Netherlands
Bill Sheehan Help Desk Institute Inc., USA
Jackie Kuflik Help Desk Institute, UK

Summary

The support centre is the front office of the IT organization. It has day-to-day contact with the customers of the organization and supports the delivery of IT services. Therefore, the quality of this support centre is crucial to the perception of IT quality in the eyes of the users, and thus for customer satisfaction. A smoothly operating support centre is the business card of the IT organization.

For that reason the Help Desk Institute (HDI) has developed a certificate for support centres, to facilitate the auditing of these centres against a worldwide standard.

23.1 Introduction

In past years, IT has grown to what we have now, a chaotic world with numerous different objects of management. Twenty years ago we were working on monolithic systems. User support was done by the system manager and was considered a logical extension to his or her task. This was the era of Systems Management. Life was easy!

With the introduction of the client–server concept and the personal computer more or less at the same time, complexity increased. The system manager needed to spend more and more time on supporting his or her users (Figure 23.1). Dedicated help desks were formed and special processes and procedures introduced.

Systems Management evolved into Service Management. The IT Infrastructure Library, better known as ITIL, describes the Service Management processes and procedures needed to bring structure into the dynamic world of IT.

If this trend continues, the chaos will increase and become unmanageable (Figure 23.1). The self-help within organizations will increase and many users will miss the boat.

New solutions will bring some relief, but the main objective in this fast lane is to become better than your competitor.

When Service Management evolves into Customer Relationship Management, the focus is increasingly on the customer. In our e-conomy the difference between success and failure is often only one 'click' away. The position of the support centre, the consolidated help desk, is crucial to the business's success. This means that processes and procedures in the support centre and the perception of the customer become important issues. Customer satisfaction surveys can do something, but certification of your support centre hasn't been available worldwide, until now.

FIGURE 23.1

Self-help vs. professional help

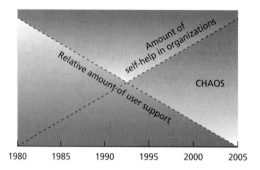

Help Desk Institute

The Help Desk Institute (HDI) is a member-centric organization, focusing on the needs of internal and external support organizations and the vendors who support them. HDI's mission is to:

- set the standards for the industry;
- establish certification and training programmes;
- provide access to industry resources;
- encourage member collaboration.

HDI's vision is to lead the customer support profession worldwide. HDI provides targeted information about the technologies, tools and trends of the help desk and customer support industry, as well as customized training and certification programmes for both the individual and site support organization. HDI also provides numerous opportunities for members to network with their peers, via participation in one of HDI's more than 50 local chapters, in its international branches or in HDI-hosted gatherings. HDI is one of the leading support services associations, with more than 25,000 members around the world.

HDI's Certified Support Centre was developed by an open industry standards committee for the support industry. In 1998, the Help Desk Institute took a leading role in forming the HDI Open Standards and Site Certification Committee. This initiative is an international effort with participants from the United States, Canada, Europe and Japan working jointly to define the criteria and methodology for support centre evaluation. The committee is dedicated to creating an industry-wide blueprint for support centres to follow. Committee members include representatives from a wide variety of leading organizations (see Table 23.1).

TABLE 23.1

Organizations who formed the standards committee

Bank of America	North Highlands
CSM Europe (UK)	Service Management International
Japan Help Desk Centre	Sprint
NCR Corporation	Sun Microsystems
Pink Elephant	Wolbersen Associates (Germany)

23.2 The Site Certification Reference Model

The Help Desk Institute's Site Certification Programme has been designed to conform to existing international quality standards, such as the European Foundation for Quality Management (EFQM), the Malcolm Baldrige National Quality Awards, and ISO9000. If you are already acquainted with any of these quality certification programmes, then the HDI Site Certification Reference Model will seem familiar (see Figure 23.2).

FIGURE 23.2

Site Certification Reference Model

The Reference Model is most closely based upon the EFQM framework, with modifications to adapt the standards to be specific to the requirements of support centre organizations. It is, in essence, a quality process model. Its structure and elements define the manner in which an ideal, high-quality support centre would function.

The purpose of the Reference Model is to provide an overall framework and context within which specific standards for certification can be defined. Composed of eight distinct elements (five 'enabling' factors and three 'performance results' areas), the model defines and focuses attention on the areas most critical to a support centre's performance and long-term success. Enabling factors are those activities or resources that allow support centre to achieve its objectives successfully. Results areas measure and assess the degree to which performance objectives are being achieved.

Each of the eight elements of the Reference Model is associated with a specific set of standards that determines a support centre's maturity within that element. The Certified Support Centre standards are analogous to ISO9000 in that they require quality processes and procedures to be defined, documented, followed and measured. But they are not prescriptive in nature. Differences in objectives and approach among organizations are acceptable, as long as the standards are met.

Familiarity with the Reference Model elements will allow an auditor to view the many individual standards in a logical relationship to one another within a comprehensive overall structure.

Model elements

Leadership

Leadership defines how managers and employees in team leadership roles define success and inspire and motivate employees. Effective leaders guide the formulation and evolution of statements of purpose, ensure that they are communicated and understood throughout the entire organization, and provide visible support and encouragement as individuals and teams seek to carry them forward. Fostering meaningful teamwork, resolving communication, resource and priority issues, and inspiring an environment of cooperation and enthusiasm are each important aspects of effective leadership.

This element addresses such fundamental issues as establishing concrete connections between service objectives of the support centre and the business objectives of the enterprise, according to support centre requirements, with reasonable priority, and fostering communication and teamwork.

Policy and strategy

The mission, vision, goals and objectives of the support functions must clearly and effectively support the business purposes of the enterprise. As with any business activity, they must contribute to the organization's ability to achieve its stated goals. Policies and strategies translate purposes and objectives into plans that can be acted upon, measured and revised as required and that achieve the desired results. Specific plans must be established to define the way in which the organizational goals will be achieved. To be useful, plans must lead to the achievement of measurable results and be coordinated with the plans of the larger enterprise.

Policy and strategy are concerned with establishing clear objectives and plans. Statements of vision and mission, the establishment of goals and objectives, and the existence of appropriate strategic and operating plans are evaluated here.

People management

The creation of an environment that motivates people to perform at their peak is crucial to the success of any support centre, and one of the most important responsibilities of support management. People must know what is expected of them. The support staff must have, and maintain, the required set of skills to respond effectively to customer requests for assistance. Meaningful performance feedback, peer and management recognition, and opportunities for technical and professional growth are proven motivators.

Job descriptions, training and development plans, periodic performance appraisals, equitable compensation, and reward and recognition programmes are the tools for developing a satisfied and motivated workforce.

Resources

The support operation must have access to the resources and tools necessary to achieve the objectives established for it. These may be infrastructure-related or support-specific. They include financial and human resources, physical facilities, communications infrastructure and processes, specialized organizational knowledge and competences, hardware/software tools, and third-party partnerships. Support technology such as incident and problem management systems, knowledge bases, remote access tools, and Automated Call Distributors (ACDs) can provide significant increases in support centre efficiency, which translates directly to cost savings, superior service, or both.

The standards related to this element assess the presence, quality and adequacy of the infrastructure within which a support centre operates.

Processes

The support function must have in place processes that allow it to be successful. These must be well defined, documented, communicated and understood. Efficient processes for call recording and tracking, triage, management escalation procedures, performance measurement, quality improvement, effective knowledge capture and distribution, information management and communication, change control, customer satisfaction and service level management, financial controls, etc. are the necessary foundation for a successfully operating support function.

The existence, documentation of and conformance to appropriate processes are a prerequisite for consistently successful performance. The standards associated with this element assess the degree to which the organization defines, documents and follows its processes.

People satisfaction

The perception and feelings of its people towards the organization will significantly influence its long-term success. The people providing support must be well motivated to perform the support function. They must understand why it is important, receive satisfaction from their work, and feel supported in and valued for their efforts. Measurement of such key factors as absenteeism and turnover, attitude and enthusiasm can reveal the extent to which the staff regard the support function positively.

Direct employee feedback, measured turnover and sick day rates are used as measures of overall employee satisfaction with the support centre operation.

Customer satisfaction

The perception of customers of the success of the support function in satisfying their needs and expectations will ultimately determine its overall success. All customers have alternatives for obtaining the support services that they perceive they require. For the support centre to earn the position of favoured provider, the organization's culture must recognize, value and support the effort to provide customers with effective and efficient support. It must be valued at a senior level and visible throughout the organization. Normally this is reflected in the existence of effective service level agreements and customer-centric performance measures. The collection and meaningful use of customer feedback, the ongoing measurement and management of satisfaction levels and the establishment of an effective collaboration between the support function and its customers will create the long-term customer loyalty that all businesses seek to earn.

Formal surveys, complaint counts and measures of customer loyalty comprise the standards associated with this element.

Performance results

The organization's measured achievements in relation to its planned performance and the results of all internal processes are the final standard by which value and success will be judged. Measurement processes must be objective, reliable and realistic. Results must be clearly communicated to the appropriate audiences. Performance objectives and results must either be achieved, or the reasons for any variance must be well understood, and appropriate actions taken to achieve the standard or revise it.

Various measures of financial and operational performance, tracked and trended, comprise the standards for this result element.

Quality model

Malcolm Baldrige and ISO9000 are general quality standards and are recognized worldwide. The Site Certification Standards Committee agreed that they wanted to pattern their standards with the worldwide ones but with a specific focus on the support centre industry service. The HDI Certification Standards were created to be complementary to these other standards and not as a replacement.

Within each standard, four categories were defined which reflected the level of maturity of the support centre. These can be viewed within the Site Certification Standards document, available for downloading at http://www.hdi-europe.com/certification/standards/standardssite.pdf.

23.3 Site Certification process

In the Site Certification process, three steps can be distinguished: Site Readiness, Site Preparation and On-Site Audit. We will discuss them separately.

Site Readiness

In Figure 23.3 the Site Readiness step is outlined. The first step an applicant takes is to understand the need and the possibilities on how to improve the quality of the support centre. The applicant browses the Web, consults HDI or a Certified Auditor, or asks for help from a third party. All activities are targeted towards better knowledge of the success rate of a Site Audit to follow.

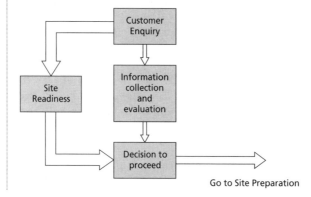

FIGURE 23.3
Site Readiness

A Support Centre Assessment, comprising a questionnaire with 190 questions in six key areas of success, can help the applicant to calculate its readiness for a Site Audit.

Site Preparation

After the Site Readiness step, the applicant has a perfect view of the good and bad in the quality of the Support Centre. The applicant can then decide to proceed. It will do so (Figure 23.4) by choosing a Certified Auditor from the list of available auditors. Usually the best basis for selecting auditors is their geographical whereabouts and language, but since all auditors have passed the same exam, have achieved the requirements and standards defined by HDI, have been trained in the same way and have regular contact, the choice of auditor should not affect the outcome of the audit. All auditors are highly skilled and experienced people who have been working in the support centre industry for a long time. They all underline the auditors' 'code of ethics', a set of guidelines which each auditor is expected to abide by.

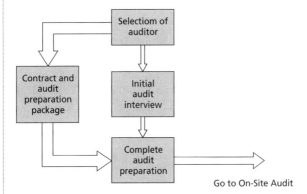

FIGURE 23.4

Site Preparation

The applicant receives a pre-audit package. This package is the preparation of the actual audit. It gives the applicant the opportunity to collect reports and 'evidence' of areas of interest that are being audited. When this site preparation is completed, the final step is to arrange the on-site audit.

On-Site Audit

The On-Site Audit (Figure 23.5) is always executed by an HDI Certified Auditor. This On-Site Audit will take some days to complete and will consist of interviews, observations and checking the available documents. The Support Centre Standards are the guiding principles for the audit.

When the On-Site Audit is completed, the certified auditor compiles the results and reports his or her conclusions. This report, including the 'evidence', will be sent to the master auditor. The master auditor oversees the performance of the certified auditor.

If the master auditor disagrees with any aspect of the outcome of an audit, or when the outcome is not well documented, both the auditor and the master auditor can decide that some issues need to be resolved by the applicant. The auditor will contact

FIGURE 23.5

On-Site Audit

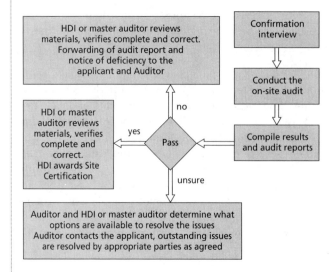

the applicant to resolve the issues and the applicant can try again to get the certificate. Where the score adheres to the criteria, an applicant will achieve certification. This will be announced to the public and the applicant.

If the score does *not* meet the criteria set for the certificate, the applicant is notified accordingly.

Importance of certification

The fact that a support centre has been granted the certificate is evidence for the organization and to the industry that this particular support centre is meeting the criteria set in the Support Centre Standards. This has a positive impact on the quality and the constant monitoring and improvement of the quality of the support centre. Certification of the support centre has many advantages:

- more exposure in the market;
- higher customer satisfaction;
- better morale with the employees of the support centre;
- more satisfied customers means more satisfied employees;
- benchmarking opportunities;
- increased competitive opportunities;
- more marketing power.

Employee certification

But, most importantly, the certification process provides the information needed to plan strategically for future success. The training and testing involved allows organizations to pinpoint accurately where they stand in terms of current best practices and recognized standards.

The people are the business, and motivated people are the key to successful business. This also applies to the support centre. Next to Site Certification, it is just as important to have the employees certified. This is the Individual Certification programme and three levels of training and certification are available:

- **Help Desk Analyst**: in today's increasing complex IT environment, it is crucial for help desk analysts to provide unsurpassed technical and customer service.
- **Help Desk Senior Analyst**: this certificate is meant for individuals with extended experience in support centres. It targets the ability to use technology and processes to optimize the performance of the support centre.
- **Help Desk Manager**: this certificate focuses on the management of support centres – the correct utilization of service level agreements, the operational management of a support team, various forms of performance measurement, people management, etc.

23.4 Future directions and conclusion

Support Centres searching for a 'best-of-breed' quality standard will be best served by adopting the objectives for both site and individual performance set by the Help Desk Institute. The HDI Best Practices Survey for 1999–2000 describes the growing demand for certification, with approximately 40% of the membership adopting the HDI Individual Certification Programme.

Without doubt, the support centre business community is a global one. As organizations and their customers demand constant support, so will the growth of the global support centre continue with either 'follow the Sun' or 24/7 operations. As the speed and quality of communication methods develop, organizations may consider the option of locating their support centres (or outsourcing) to other countries and not just other regions of their home country. Maintaining high standards for multinational support centres in an organization means relying on a certification programme that is recognized globally and has effective application in different countries, cultures and languages. These organizations can rely on the HDI standard – one that is audited by a certification body and team who understand the global picture and can apply it to the local installation.

Support centres searching the globe for the right support staff can now rely on an Individual Certification programme that transcends borders, allowing the hirer to search effectively for suitably certified professionals who can offer other skills, such as another language, without the need to compare qualifications country by country.

The Help Desk Institute is, the authors believe, the first organization to offer a global standard that aims at international recognition for service performance quality. Ongoing communication between all parties in the standards maintenance process ensures a certification that keeps current with the fastest-growing industry in the twenty-first century.

24 A standard for IT Service Management

Jenny Dugmore Service Matters, UK, Chair of British Standards Panel BDD/3

Summary

The BS15000 Specification for IT Service Management is the world's first standard for service management to be published. It is aimed at both providers of service management services and businesses that either manage their own IT requirements or outsource them.

BS15000 specifies interrelated management processes, and will form the basis of a service audit. The specification is supported by the management introduction DISC PD0005 Code of Practice for IT Service Management and PD0015 IT Service Management – Self-assessment Workbook. Used together, the set provides comprehensive best practice – what needs to be achieved and how to set about achieving it.

24.1 Introduction

Developments in information technology

Developments in information technology increasingly allow us to communicate by electronic means quickly, cheaply, and on a global basis.

A high proportion of the world's population can now receive electronic services from an ever-increasing number of organizations, both public and private sector. These services are often available 24 hours a day, throughout the year. The global scope of the internet has led to true worldwide communication, with services, news, and vast quantities of information freely available via electronic means.

Business drivers

Technology is revolutionizing the way that organizations and individuals transact business, and obtain goods and services. As a result, IT is becoming even more deeply integrated into business processes. Senior managers who understand their environment recognize that correct strategic alignment between IT and key business objectives is a critical factor to their success.

First-mover advantage

The trading world has seen a rapid escalation in the rate at which organizations attempt to move into a new market space. This is happening because commercial organizations recognize that by getting first into an identified market they can gain that all-important brand recognition. In turn, this brings the possibility of market dominance.

Many of these organizations are new start-ups, generally small and nimble. They are set up for the very purpose of gaining that first-mover advantage.

Other organizations, perhaps long established or simply unable to move fast enough to be first in a new market, still need to enter and grow their share of new markets, often in the face of intense competition. At the very least, established organizations need to hold onto their share of longer-established markets.

Organizations targeted at new markets are generally strongly reliant on the effective application of new technology or technology used in new ways. In reality, few organizations can even retain their existing place in the market without effective use of technology. Where an organization operates in a multinational or global market, the situation is often even more extreme.

The role of information systems and IT services

In the fight for market share, information systems and IT services play an essential part in an organization's ability to deliver. The quality of service may even determine whether they survive. For an organization, its competitive edge may be dependent on the quality of the 'humdrum' service it delivers day by day.

It must be concluded that reaping the benefits of developments in IT and associated infrastructure is not merely a matter of delivering services electronically; the customers must actually use them and be happy to do so. Customers will be lost if the service they receive is seen as unreliable or unsuitable for their needs.

It is also increasingly accepted that winning new customers is far more expensive than retaining existing customers. A customer who is unhappy also cascades a negative view far more widely than a happy customer. This damages the supplier's ability to win new customers because of damage to the brand and image.

The pressures on businesses and the resulting pressure on IT suppliers are illustrated in Figure 24.1.

FIGURE 24.1

Business pressures

The scope of service management

Operational service and IT Service Management processes are ceasing to be the poor relation of the industry and are coming into their own as central to an organization's business success.

Public sector services

Widely accessible electronic service delivery is also an increasingly important means of improving public sector services. This is also usually linked to an expectation that there will be an increase in public sector value for money.

Some public services are effectively a monopoly, because the customer has no option but to use them. Nevertheless, 'customer retention' under these circumstances provides no grounds for complacency.

Providing poor services carries the hidden cost of badly damaged credibility for the public service. There is also the more tangible cost of inflated overheads from the need to respond to and handle the complaints that under these circumstances are made by large numbers of customers. Rework and recurring problems both add to the cost of a service.

It is also largely pointless to invest in services that fail to meet public expectations because, for example, they are unreliable, unresponsive, or unavailable for use when needed. The investment will be wasted and there will be a barrier built up against any new attempts to introduce technology-based services.

Only by adopting a planned and methodical approach to service management can a significant contribution be made to satisfying public expectations on the quality of electronic service delivery.

Credibility of IT services

Increasing pressure to provide a high quality of service, usually at a reduced price, is something faced by most of the IT service industry. This adds pressure to an industry where a proportion of services already have low credibility with the customers, for historic reasons.

A single failure in a service will be remembered long after a series of successes has faded from memory. Judgements can become increasingly emotive and subjective.

Many organizations face a vicious cycle of demands that make it harder to deliver and therefore result in lower customer satisfaction. This often leads to cuts in the available funds, in turn making the situation more difficult to deal with. A typical cycle of demands and resulting problems is illustrated in Figure 24.2.

FIGURE 24.2

The vicious cycle

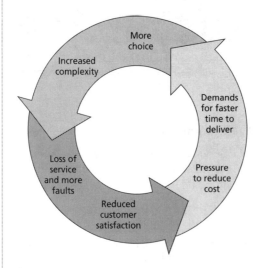

Independent and objective judgements

The lack of independent public standards for service management has left service providers under additional pressure. Historically it has not been easy, and in some cases it has not actually been possible, to prove that a service is compliant with industry best practices.

In addition, many people in this situation have not even been able to assess the effectiveness of the service they deliver. Instead, they may have to use informed guesswork or a proprietary method to decide whether or not they are approaching service management in the best way. It has not been easy for a judgement to be made about why a service may be deficient, and how that deficiency can be corrected.

In the context of BS15000, 'IT Service Management' comprises a set of interrelated management processes. Taken together, and if the quality criteria are met, they are intended to ensure that the customer is satisfied (and therefore retained), regardless of whether the customer is an organization, an employee, or a member of the public using a public service.

Effective implementation of service management processes should also lead to a service that, while not necessarily cheap, is cost-effective and within the agreed budget for the service.

24.2 What is service management?

There are a variety of processes within the commonly accepted understanding of service management.

There are also many organizational forms across which the service management processes may be split. To complicate matters, many organizations name and rename the key processes and functions within service management according to the current dictates of organizational form, which may also change frequently.

Historic precedents commonly influence names. The selection of names also needs to recognize the connotation of certain terms to a specific organization.

The scope of the document set described here covers the main service management processes, which are considered to be:

- service design and management processes;
- relationship processes;
- resolution processes;
- control processes;
- release processes.

Each core process is the composite of sub-processes, as shown in the diagram in Figure 24.3.

In addition to the core processes listed above, it covers component processes as described below:

- **Configuration Management and Change Management** as two separate but closely linked components are part of Control Processes. These are not only central in Figure 24.3 but are also central to the processes themselves, influencing the effectiveness of all processes.

FIGURE 24.3

Scope of service management

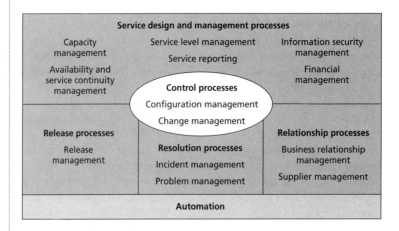

- **Information Security Management** is part of service management. However, a separate standard, BS7799, covers this subject in much more detail than the service management standard. BS15000 contains security and business continuity requirements compatible with those in BS7799.
- **Availability and Service Continuity** are covered as part of the service design and management process. This component takes into account the need to consider longer-term issues, and not just to focus on improving service levels by fixing problems faster. This also recognizes that service levels and resilience should be considered early in the development of a new service.
- **Service Level Management** is one of the key components, focused on service level agreements and fit-for-purpose services built and delivered with a clear understanding of the customer's requirements.
- **Service Reporting** is a theme that is common to most service management processes – service management is not actually possible without suitable metrics as input. In this sense it is a fundamental component of service management.
- **Capacity Management** covers all aspects of resourcing, not just bandwidth and data storage capacity.
- **Financial Management** covers the identification of and accounting for service costs, without actually being prescriptive about whether a profit or cost centre is best, or even whether costs should be recovered at all for in-house service suppliers. As a minimum, it is a process that allows a judgement to be made on whether or not the service is good value for money.
- **Business Relationship Management** covers relationships between supplier and customer. It incorporates elements of customer satisfaction management.
- **Supplier Management** is included and applies to all organizations, even those where a third party provides a small proportion of the service, or even if the supplier is also dependent on other third-party suppliers in turn.
- **Incident and Problem Management** are both included as components, in line with the industry's documented best practices. These are towards the reactive end of the proactive–reactive spectrum, unlike many other aspects of service management.

Release Management is a component that can be summarized as release, roll-out and global deployment, quickly, while also 'getting it right first time'. When release processes are effective, there is a reduction in the ensuing support costs, with service management being fundamentally proactive and not reactive.

24.3 Developing standard BS15000

Standard BS15000 did not spring out of a void. Instead, it was produced as the logical and necessary step following production of other best practice material. It also followed recognition of an industry need for such a standard, partly as the IT service industry matured.

For the British Standards Institute (BSI) the first stage was the establishment of a specialist group, in the late 1980s. This group, known as BDD/3, was asked by the BSI to work on the subject of service management.

Who is involved in the development?

The mainstay of the development work is the BBD/3 group. It is composed of experienced practitioners, from a wide range of public and private sector organizations, with a mix of backgrounds and experience.

Including the author as chair, representatives from the following organizations have been and continue to be involved:

- BSI – Sharon Sinatra
- OGC[1] – John Groom
- British Computing Society (BCS) – Shirley Lacy of Change IT
- itSMF-UK – Aidan Lawes, CEO of itSMF-UK, the British chapter of itSMF International, a user group focused on service management with equivalent chapters in many other countries
- National Audit Office (NAO) – Ian Petticrew
- Ivor Macfarlane – co-opted member from Guillemot Rock, and also author of the *BSI Workbook on IT Service Management* described below
- Ivor Evans – co-opted member from Ivory Consulting
- Lynda Cooper – co-opted member from Xansa
- Don Page – co-opted member from Marval Software
- Hilary Faul – co-opted member from BBC Technology.

Peter Lickiss, Controller of Technology, of the British Broadcasting Corporation (BBC Technology Ltd), has been the sponsor for the work of BDD/3.

There are also a large number of people and organizations involved in reviewing the draft versions. These were from the public and private sectors, from the UK and non-UK, responsible for service improvement and day-to-day delivery.

The BSI and BDD/3 are extremely grateful to these people and their organizations, although space limitations have prevented them being individually listed here.

Code of Practice for Service Management

Following an extended stage of work, BDD/3 published the first product, BSI/DISC Published Document 0005. This was the first edition of best practices for core processes in service management.

This first edition covered only the core processes in service management. It sold well, despite the limited scope, confirming that there was a real need for products of this type.

The second edition

Much encouraged, the group assessed the business need in more detail. As a result of this assessment, the group opted for fast-track production of a second edition. This second edition was produced far more quickly than the first and was published within two years, superseding the first edition. It also covered the full set of IT Service Management processes and was more detailed.

The Code of Practice was also reformatted to be a convenient A5, 'pocket size' that can be carried around and referred to by managers as and when required and as and when time permits.

An award winner

The BSI won an itSMF award for the second edition of PD0005, the management introduction to service management, in 1999.

Management introduction to the Code of Practice

The format was refocused as a management introduction to service management, complementing other best practice material. It also built on a newly agreed relationship with organizations, in addition to the BSI, who are responsible for best-practice material.

Each process and constituent is described in a standard format, covering business benefits, key features and, inevitably, potential problems. The latter is included to help understanding of where existing service management has failed, or the risks if service management is to be implemented for the first time.

Topics included also cover the role of automation in service management, issues on service management, service improvement and the implementation of service management.

Finally, a glossary of terms is included, 'for the avoidance of doubt' in an industry that is notorious for its use of jargon. This is aligned with the glossary of terms used in the OGC's ITIL[2] books, under an agreement between the BSI and OGC dating back to 1995.

As the development of a glossary had been a fraught and unproductive stage for BDD/3, this agreement was particularly welcome.

The Code of Practice is consistent with the OGC's ITIL publications which further explain the recognized methodology of service management.

Target audience

Who does the BSI recommend should read this Code of Practice? The following list represents the bulk of the target audience:

- newly appointed managers;
- anyone faced with introducing a new service or with supplier management of an existing service;
- managers who need to make or adapt to major changes;
- anyone faced with improving a service, ranging from one aspect of the service through to the whole of a service delivery organization;
- frustrated customers who are unhappy with their service, but don't understand 'why it doesn't work properly'.

What are the benefits of the Code of Practice?

The Code of Practice is essential reading for anyone who wishes to gain an understanding of service management in today's challenging environment.

The Code of Practice gives an understanding of the scale of service management and the interfaces between the different processes, for both new and experienced managers.

The Code of Practice provides an understanding of the full range of processes within service management for practitioners, instead of what may have been a limited and parochial view of just their own part of it.

Having an understanding of how their part of service management fits into the whole means that practitioners are more effective and are likely to be better prepared for taking on more responsibilities. Finally, they will also gain an understanding of the best practice for their own area, what might have gone wrong in the past, and what they may need to do in the future.

Many services are composites of different elements from different suppliers. A very high proportion of services are provided commercially via a competitive process. Business-to-business relationships, commonly known as 'B2B', are an increasingly common feature of service management. A better understanding of relationship management is also a benefit from the Code of Practice – for the customer, the supplier and those responsible for supplier management.

All changes benefit from a high standard of service management as a foundation. Organizations going through major changes may be facing new services being implemented, upheaval caused by new markets, new competitors, take-overs and mergers, changes to legislation through to a natural disaster or other major disruption to normality.

Customers who are unhappy with the service, but who are unable to understand what is going wrong, benefit from knowing what is industry best practice, as a baseline for identifying their specific concerns.

In practice, the Code of Practice addresses a number of important issues which, if properly addressed, will help to promote confidence in electronic service delivery and increase customer satisfaction.

Self-assessment workbook

Following the launch of the second edition of the Code of Practice, the BSI also produced a self-assessment workbook. The workbook was produced during mid-2000 and has sold well.

The group BDD/3 was involved in reviewing the workbook, taking care to keep it aligned to the Code of Practice. It was also aligned to the BSI specification standard for IT Service Management, described below.

The new workbook is suitable for self-assessment by any organization providing service management. It provides a suitable structure for self-assessment of service management processes, and is most suitably used by someone familiar with the Code of Practice and related best-practice material.

It can be used by someone acting in the capacity of an independent auditor or by a manager who wishes to get an understanding of the quality of the service delivered, based on self-assessment.

For those organizations that believe they already comply with the best practices outlined in the Code of Practice, it provides a means of assessing whether this compliance is actual or imagined.

The workbook now sits alongside the Code of Practice as part of an service management document set. It also maintains compatibility with the UK Government's OGC's ITIL. The compatibility extends to the use of the ITIL glossary of terms for both BSI and OGC documents.

The workbook is designed so that the essential provisions of the Code of Practice for IT Service Management are distilled into a simple-to-use set of questions, with space available for answers within the workbook itself.

In summary, the workbook provides:

- a comprehensive set of questions to assess compliance with PD0005;
- a ready-made checklist of best practices, saving time and money for any organization that uses it;
- a tool in an integrated approach to best practice in service management;
- the first steps for achieving compliance with BS15000, described below.

BS15000 specification for IT Service Management

Having successfully defined best practice for service management, the BSI committee BDD/3 then moved on to develop a complementary audit specification, published in November 2000.

The group was also motivated by the view that managers and practitioners were faced with questions that they were unable to answer objectively and confidently. The questions include:

- Is your supplier providing the IT services you need?
- How do you know you are providing the services that are needed?
- How do you prove the quality of what you are doing?
- How do you avoid the recriminations that come from unmet expectations or, more simply, from poor quality services?

It was seen to be the logical next step for the group to produce something that could be used as:

- a yardstick for organizations to measure their performance against best practice;
- the basis for a certification scheme to help service management suppliers advertise their capabilities;
- a certification scheme that will help potential customers for IT services to specify their requirements;
- a statement of the minimum requirements that are felt necessary for implementing best practice service management;
- evidence of activities to enable effective, independent audit.

The specification also covers the essential underlying requirements of planning, professional competence, service quality, and auditing.

Passing an audit to this new standard proves to your customers and to your staff that you have achieved the highest level of service management.

Conversely, it can also highlight the areas of the service that are below acceptable standards and, at the same time, highlight areas for improvement. Should areas of improvement be identified by an assessment, the benefits to be gained from implementation of best practice in service management include:

- improved customer service and customer retention arising from satisfied customers;
- focused service that supports the business strategy;
- cost efficiency, for example the avoidance of overheads from handling complaints, problem prevention, and good control of the assets that are used as part of service delivery;
- reliable and consistent service quality – the 'no surprises' service.

What does BS15000 cover?

BS15000 covers the same IT Service Management processes as the Code of Practice and the workbook.

Like the other two documents in the set, it has a strong process focus. As for the Code of Practice, this approach was deliberately adopted as it represents the most effective approach to describing best practices that apply to all organizations, as processes are independent of organizational form, scale or sector.

24.4 How does BS15000 fit with other best-practice material?

Together, the three components form an integrated approach, illustrated in Figure 24.4. The diagram shows the link to ITIL and internal procedures and work instructions.

The links between the BSI document set and the OGC ITIL set was no accident. Its origins lie in an agreement involving BSI, itSMF and OGC, which set out how the BSI's Code of Practice would form a management introduction to the detailed material comprising the revised ITIL books.

The agreement was then extended to adoption of a common glossary of terms and the preservation of the link between the workbook and the specification to the ITIL document set. As a consequence of building on this agreement, a single picture of the best practice guidance can be constructed.

FIGURE 24.4

Relationship between best practice materials

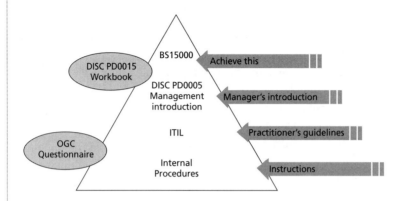

BDD/3 feels that the integration is important in demonstrating the synergy between the BSI initiatives and ITIL. In addition, it also shows how an organization needs to consider internal procedures as a part of a comprehensive and properly tailored best-practice approach.

The detail of process and procedures will vary from organization to organization, taking account of the differences of sector, geography, size, attitude etc., but they too can all fit in with the generic best practice.

24.5 Practical use of the document set

Service improvements

In practice, many of the benefits of the set of documents comes from the ability to identify areas for service improvement, to provide specifics for service improvements and as a measure for the actual benefits delivered by improvement programmes.

The best-practice material also emphasizes the need for metrics to be used as a core element of the service management, touching all areas. The metrics are also fundamental to service improvement. Unless the service levels and costs are understood, managers responsible for service improvements have to work blind, basing plans on subjective opinions and guesswork.

Reporting of metrics is not in itself adequate. All too often, although there may be a great deal of activity focused on collection and reporting of metrics, there are no actions following on from the new understanding of the strengths and weaknesses of the service. The net effect, then, is to increase the costs of service management (and of the service), with none of the gain that should come from service improvements. Producing reports without using the information can be counterproductive as the perceived value of the metrics is devalued in these conditions.

The need to close the loop in collection and use of the service management metrics is illustrated in Figure 24.5, which shows the full cycle of metrics in use – combined with customers' views. The latter may arise from customer satisfaction measurement or service reviews, discussion of service level agreements, or even the feedback from complaints and escalations.

FIGURE 24.5

Links to service improvements

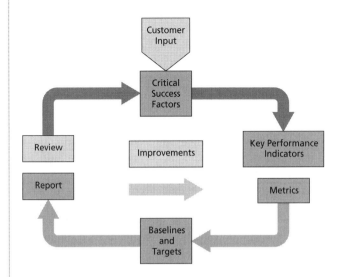

Whatever the name adopted for metrics (critical success factors, key performance indicators and the more pedestrian 'actuals'), the loop must be closed. No organization failing to do this can claim best practice and would certainly fail an audit under BS15000.

Managing service improvements

Whatever the nature of a service improvement programme, there is an almost universal cycle of 'pain before gain'.

Very few improvements can be made at no cost, or without a change to the people, processes or technology that form the service management functions.

Initial enthusiasm for plans to deliver service improvements can be hit by the amount of time the early stages take to deliver tangible benefits. At this point the negative sides of any change can loom large in the minds of those involved, enthusiasm drops and if left to spiral out of control will damage the service improvement to the point where the negative views result in it losing momentum or even being halted.

The slower build-up of benefits means that they are not seen or are delayed, as shown in Figure 24.6.

FIGURE 24.6

The pain before the gain – life cycle of a major change

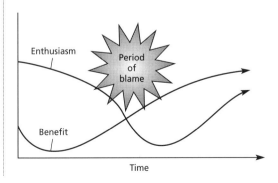

Mature service management

A sign of maturity that will be identified during an audit is the mix of reactive and proactive (preventive) activities.

A service based on processes that are dominated by reactivity is at best a starting point for service improvement – the best of best practices are much more likely to be dominated by activities that prevent problems, and don't just fix them faster and faster.

Examples of preventive activities include management of risk changes from Change Management, service reviews identifying trends very early, and a high standard of service level management that means the supplier understands the customers' needs so well that the needs can be anticipated.

A service that neglects the preventive and proactive processes is one that is unlikely to meet the requirements of best practice under BS15000.

Perhaps even more significantly, it is unlikely to meet the needs of a customer for more than a very short time – something that would be manifested as degraded customer satisfaction and increasingly serious complaints about increasing costs.

24.6 Next steps

Formal certification

BDD/3 has already started work on the next stage, including new editions, the auditor's overview and input to auditor's guidance and a certification scheme reflecting the requirements of BS15000. This is the next stage on from the assessments and audits done with the support of the self-assessment workbook.

The intention is to provide a certification scheme that gives the industry and the public at large confidence that organizations that pass the independent, external audit and gain certification under BS15000 deserve the accolade and do conform to the standard.

A new group has been spun off from BDD/3, as BRD/6. This group is the audit and certification committee. The work of BRD/6 is separate from the work of BDD/3, although links will be retained between the two. The audit and certification committee is settling scheme rules. It is covering how the auditors themselves will be tested and accredited as suitable to carry out the certification process.

The group will also produce the guidance that will be given to those auditors that are acceptable, on the audit process and how they must follow it.

What will BDD/3 be doing now?

In parallel with this activity, the committee is also updating the existing management introduction for Service Management, PD0005. It has also produced an auditor's overview, known as a Code of Practice, BS15000 Part 2. This is the companion for the auditing specification BS15000 Part 1.

- BS15000 Part 1, the specification, is being revised in line with the feedback from practical experience with the standard, some early adopters having used extensively all documents in the set.

The existing management introduction PD0005 is being revised and will be re-issued as a third edition, with changes in line with BS15000.

The committee will then be in a position to submit the standard for international status. Serious consideration is being given to this already.

Early adopters

BDD/3 has recognized the need to understand the practicalities of using BS15000 in the audit process. For example, does it set unrealistic expectations with required standards so high that no organization will ever be certified? Are the requirements sufficiently clear as to avoid the need for a large bureaucratic overhead as part of the audit? Does the document set lend itself to auditing best practices and a certification scheme?

There also needs to be a decision on whether the logical and sensible next step is to move to an international standard.

To this end, the group has encouraged 'early adopters' of the standard. Each is being helped by a member of BDD/3 to use the standard to assess not only its service management, but also the effectiveness of the standard itself.

From the managed early adopter process, the group is collating feedback that will answer some or all of the questions on the next steps. Spin-off from this is an 'Early Adopters Group', facilitated by BDD/3, where each organization involved in the early adopters scheme can exchange experience and views on the standard. As the move to an international standard is a real possibility, the early adopters include both multinationals and organizations based outside the UK.

Without the very substantial input of time and resources from organizations such as the early adopters, the experience gained from the early stages of use of BS15000 would be of much less value and the IT industry would lose valuable input to the continuing development of best practices.

We have come a long way together since the beginning of both the BSI work on service management and the OGC's work on ITIL in the late 1980s. There is, however, still much to do.

24.7 How you can get copies

A discount is available when PD0005 is purchased with PD0015 IT Service Management – Self-assessment Workbook and BS15000 Specification for IT Service Management.

Call BSI Customer Services on +44(0)20 8996 9001 for more information or to purchase the standard.

Notes

1. OGC was previously known as CCTA.
2. ITIL® is the Information Technology Infrastructure Library, covered in more detail elsewhere in this publication. ITIL is a registered trade mark of OGC – Central Computer and Telecommunications Agency.

Review of part 3

In **Enforcing performance guarantees based on performance service levels**, Scholz and Turowski use different levels of service with different prices for each level. That way, a customer can use the business process impact as a guideline to determining the required service levels. They clearly state that service agreements can only be useful if the performance can be measured adequately. They make a plea for an integrated approach: involve the exploitation departments in the development or procurement phase. Furthermore, they state that performance should be a design target within the development process. This fits very well with the experience of a lot of organizations that struggled for years with development departments that 'threw new software over the wall of Operations'. Recent developments, as are shown in e.g. the R2C model, in ISM and in ILM in part 1 (Models for managing information systems), show that organizations tend to have a type of integrated service team that will have the responsibility of managing entire life cycles. Such a structure will be able to ensure that performance metrics will be used as design targets, as Scholz and Turowski indicate.

In **GQM applied in IT Service Management**, Wouter de Jong illustrates the value of the chosen method in the fact that it helped to reduce the task management problem to a simple set of questions, making it manageable in terms of efficiency and effectivity. He encounters, however, some other problems in IT management that make it hard to interpret the results.

First, the fact that process-oriented management of an IT service organization is not a widely introduced habit, let alone a successfully implemented habit, makes it hard to isolate the effects of management from issues such as culture, (in)competence, and emotional structures in organizations. If the role of a process manager is regarded as that of a traditional project manager, as de Jong sometimes found in the organizations used in his experiment, then it is clear that the situations in the experimental environments were not typical of a modern process-oriented service organization. A well-educated process manager would probably have only the company interest in mind, and would not put team or project interest above customer values.

Another problem is that people are not standardized. You simply can't measure them and add them up by using superficial parameters. Knowledge, skills and the like can be estimated, but human interaction, soft skills and other tacit factors that can't be measured play very important roles. Therefore it is hard to reach believable results by only using hard measures and leaving out the tacit ones. A translation of measurement into FTEs (function task equivalents, i.e. persons) should make use of many other values as well.

In the seven questions, the 'skills' factor is missing. Again, this is a less mechanically measurable factor, which might explain why it is omitted from the list. On the other hand, it should be clear that 'required skills to be able to execute the task' are at least as important as the duration or the input of a task. After all, not all employees are equal, and we can train people to learn.

But all that is in fact exactly what the author tried to achieve. By facilitating the discussion to this level of detail, de Jong has shown that the GQM method offers help in reducing IT management problems to a set of simple questions that lead to measurable parameters, which in turn can provide the answers to the original questions. The experiment itself, in this case the simulation of a task model in an IT service organization, is no more than the means to illustrate this point.

Point taken.

In **Service level measurement: checkpoint 2000**, Mike Tsykin emphasizes that service should – at least – be managed at the level of the customer. After all, that's what counts for the customer: the way the IT is supporting the business. In practice, we often see very scattered patterns of management of IT: customers have several suppliers of parts of their IT's infrastructure, and they have to manage all these partial domains in such a way that the combination of the parts – at the level of the end user – gives the expected (required) result. Why not start your management paradigm at this customer level, Tsykin asks. If you organize your IT support with this end-to-end perspective, you might just end up with the support you need for your business.

This is very much in line with the Integrated Service Management (ISM) model in part 1 (Chapter 8), which describes exactly the nature of this complex, integrated IT provider environment. Tsykin takes the same approach, and zooms in to the world of tooling required to implement such end-to-end management. He focuses on end-to-end response time (ETE RT), and classifies the available tooling into four categories. The analysis provided gives insight into the kind of tools and technical approaches used.

In such an approach it is always good to consider the variability that customers display in the definition of service. For example, the definition of availability, given by Tsykin, is of a rather strict nature, often found in customer practice: if a user doesn't use the application, then availability is not measurable. An alternative way of interpreting availability is related to a different principle: if the user doesn't use the system, then the issue of availability cannot be applied: in that case the system can be down but that won't influence the availability result. Downtime, in this interpretation, starts at the moment a customer (user) finds that he or she can't use the system, and calls in an incident. Such a view should be supported by a proactive attitude towards preventing such incidents in order to have impact at the level of the customer. If this second interpretation were to be followed by Tsykin, then passive tool systems could also be applied in measuring availability. So in the end the SLA, and thus the kind of business functions supported, seems to determine whether or not such tools could be used.

The reader should not, however, forget that end-to-end response time is not the only factor that should be considered in defining required service (levels), although it is among the most important. Tsykin's analysis can help people develop their perspective on IT management, stimulating them to search for an approach that can be practised with available tools. And even if there are very few organizations that manage the provided end-to-end service at the customer's level, and even fewer that apply such management in terms of business functions (!), this is definitely an issue that will receive great attention in the near future. Organizations will need to get 'in control' of their IT environment, and maximize the contribution of IT to business. In the absence of well-structured information databases that support the selection of available tools, we will just have to work with information such as that provided by Mike Tsykin.

Regarding **How to improve the quality of your support centre by certification**, the Help Desk Institute has taken a fine initiative, getting an international group together, and having a go at developing a set of auditing guidelines for support centre organizations. As indicated in its name, the Help Desk Institute focuses on the organizational unit that we regularly recognize in terms of Help Desk, Support Desk, Service Desk, etc. This unit is usually concerned with handling user contacts.

In ITIL, until recently, there was one publication that also described the Help Desk. In this book, ITIL focused on incident management and reactive problem management. In the more recent publication on support processes, this was redesigned: the Help Desk – according to ITIL – is a typical organization unit, which deals with many IT service processes.

HDI, on the other hand, seems to see the support centre as a complete organization instead of a work unit in an IT service organization. The authors speak of freedom of choice for the customers, as if they could choose to get support from other providers. Another example: in one of the guidelines the support centre has service level agreements with its customers. In most organizations that certainly is not the case: users have only one support centre to turn to: their company's internal help desk. Since HDI associates the Support Centre Certification with the individual certificates of Help Desk Analyst, Help Desk Support Engineer and Help Desk Manager, it seems obvious that it concerns only the traditional help-desk environment.

This view is very common in traditional organizations in the USA, where the front office is crucial to the perception of the IT organization. Europe's ITILized help desks, however, are much more integrated in the IT organization, and not as 'powerful'. The *processes* in these organizations are more important than the *organizational structure*, emphasizing the cooperation between teams. That normally prevents the rather common occurrence of conflicts between the support centres and the rest of the organization (e.g. see the discussions in the HDESK-list, West Virginia's Network for Educational Telecomputing, in 2000, about miscommunication between the help desk and tier-2 and tier-3 departments), and it boosts the performance of the entire organization.

The fact that it is unclear whether the guidelines reflect the support centre or the complete support organization is somewhat of a handicap for the certificate: it makes quite a difference in the European versus the US perspective. The initiative of certification of support centres would probably be more effective if these effects would be emphasized in the audit guidelines.

Nevertheless, the guidelines seem to be a modern instrument to stimulate quality management in the help-desk environment. They should, however, grow into a set of guidelines that is more embedded in the entire IT service organization. Since HDI has a focus on the help desk, it would probably do best by working together with organizations or communities that have a wider focus, in order to develop a support centre certificate that will meet greater acceptance worldwide. It is to HDI's credit that it developed the standard as an open source set of guidelines. That way, any organization can evaluate the guidelines before applying them.

In **A standard for IT Service Management** (BS15000), the British Standards Institute follows the definitions of ITIL: as they say, BS15000 is compatible with ITIL. By associating with ITIL in that way, however, they also inherit the historical aspects of ITIL that are receiving more and more criticism. For example, the definition of Problem Management versus Incident Management has been an item that caused lots of discussion in the past decade. Modern process models give more refined definitions for the two processes than ITIL does in its latest version. BS15000 combines both Incident and Problem Management in the Resolution sector, emphasizing the reactive nature of Problem Management. And that is exactly the view that has recently been abandoned by modern modellers: if you can't decide whether a capacity problem should be taken care of in the Problem Management process or in the Capacity Management process, than your model probably needs a face-lift.

And placing Configuration Management together with Change Management as a core Control process doesn't seem to reflect the simple administrative role for Configuration Management as modern modellers apply it. And last but not least: the Operations Management process, ITIL's missing process, may well be recognized in the Automation sector of the model, but it doesn't seem to attract much attention from the BSI, let alone that it is treated as a process of the same nature as the other ITIL practices. All in all, BS15000 seems to be closely linked with ITIL, thereby connecting its fate to a library that is very successful on the one hand but is lacking a coherent structure on the other.

Nevertheless, BS15000 is likely to attract a lot of attention and it can be a big help for IT organizations that are starting to get service management under control. However, by sticking so closely to ITIL, a standard that is to be truly successful in the long term might require a redesign of the structure of the framework for the ITIL components. After all, ITIL was designed as a collection of best practices: it never claimed to be a structured method.

For interested readers: some web-based information on BS15000 has recently been made available at http://www.bs15000.org.uk/

Concluding remarks

Services are central in all the chapters in this part. Quantifying the metrics of service aspects is obviously important for the management of these services. We find some practical illustrations of this in the first three chapters. Customers are central in two of them, as is the case with several other contributions in part 7.

The last two chapters illustrate the maturity of the discipline of IT Service Management. Although they are focusing on different organization levels, they are an exponent of the demand for standardization that a growing discipline normally shows. Since there are no official (*de jure*) standards, the initiatives are spontaneous and rather 'local'. Whether they are successful will be determined by the way they reflect the opinion of the market with respect to the question of what the market finds best, and to what extent the proposed standards fit this market demand.

In the meantime, there are several alternatives that have developed in the same way: think of the Customer Operations Performance Centre's COPC2000 Standard, the TüV Service Check, Ziff-Davis' Support Center Practices (SCP) Certification Program, and Helpdesk2000's CORE2000. Which one of these will make it from an initiative to an industry standard or eventually even a formal standard is still very uncertain. But one thing is sure: the growing demand for management to get a grip on service quality will be the best breeding ground for the development of standards.

part 4

Maturity

Introduction to the theme

From the moment Richard Nolan introduced his 'staged model' for the application of IT in organizations in 1973, many people have used stepwise improvement models. These models were quickly recognized as suitable instruments for quality improvement programmes, thereby helping organizations to climb up the maturity ladder. Dozens of variations on the theme can easily be found nowadays, ranging from trades like software development, acquisition, systems engineering, software testing, website development, data warehousing and security engineering, to help desks, knowledge management, etc. Obviously the *kaizen* principle (improvement works best in smaller steps) was one that appealed to many.

After Nolan's staged model in 1973, the most appealing application of this modelling was found when the Software Engineering Institute (SEI) of Carnegie Mellon University, USA, published its Software Capability Maturity Model (SW-CMM). The CMM was copied and applied in most of the cases mentioned above, making CMM something of a standard in maturity modelling. At this moment there even is a project group working on the development of an IT Service CMM.

In Europe there is one standard for quality management, modelled by the European Foundation for Quality Management (EFQM). This model uses largely the same criteria as in the USA's Malcolm Baldridge National Quality Award. In the Netherlands a staged model was developed upon the EFQM base, and this model was applied to IT service organizations. In the contributions in this part you will find some of the results this has brought.

Content

This part contains five chapters. The first two describe maturity modelling applied to organizations, while the following three chapters describe maturity issues in specific domains. Thus we have:

The future of the IT organization
Guus Delen, Mark Griep, Daam Grund and John Roelofs

Professionalization of ICT-management organizations: a roadmap for ICT managers
Gertrud Blauwhof, Christine Praasterink, Frank van Outvorst, Leen van Stappen, Marco Postma, Ger Manders, Wim van Haaren

Improvement of the test process using TPI®
T. Koomen and M. Pol

Securing information now or never
Anton Griffioen and Jaap van der Wel

Quality of software development
Paul Hendriks

A review of part 4 follows thereafter.

Reading instructions

Applying maturity models requires that the current state of an organization can be measured. Therefore the prerequisite for maturity modelling can be found in the previous part: Metrics. You are advised to read some of the chapters in the Metrics part before reading this part.

Introduction to the chapters

In **The future of the IT organization**, Delen *et al.* show us the result of a multi-client study into the transformation of IT organizations. To distinguish the relative position of participating organizations in terms of their development, a maturity model for IT organizations was created, based on the CMM levels and using ITIL definitions.

In **Professionalization of ICT-management organizations: a roadmap for ICT managers**, Blauwhof *et al.* give us a growth path for the professionalization of an IT service organization. The authors use the EFQM quality model, together with the stepwise improvement that was added to it in the Dutch INK model. The chapter is illustrated with several practical cases.

In **Improvement of the test process using TPI®**, Koomen and Pol look at that very important stage, 'testing'. A lot of energy in the service provider organization is put into the processes concerning restoration and prevention of 'trouble'. That can be related to user faults, but mostly it concerns faults in the technical infrastructure, such as the network or the application programs. A lot of that energy (i.e. money) could have been saved if the infrastructure had been tested in such a way that these faults were detected before going live. Most organizations, however, do not have a very structured way of testing the creative process of development. Koomen and Pol describe how a well-structured test process can be used to contribute to high quality in service delivery.

In **Securing information now or never**, Griffioen and van der Wel make a stand for a structural approach to issues with respect to security of information. Activities in the management of security belong in a process that affects all layers of the organization, they say. This is in line with recent publications of e.g. ITIL. The authors illustrate their

Part 4: Maturity

approach with practical experiences, but they also add a step-by-step method to improve information security.

In **Quality of software development**, Hendriks examines a number of quality improvement methods in software development. Although software is only part of the IT infrastructure, it is an extremely important part, because it determines much of the functionality of the information system. On the other hand, the development sector is the source of many problems. For that reason, various quality improvement approaches have been developed. Hendriks presents some of the most important methods in use today.

25 The future of the IT organization

A multi-client study into the transformation of IT organizations

Guus Delen, Mark Griep, Daam Grund, and **John Roelofs**
KPMG Consulting, World Class IT

Summary

Organizations are not static. This is why regular research is conducted into their development. For instance, Nolan studied the development of information technology (IT) in relation to the computer organization (the supplier of IT) and the users' organization (the purchaser of IT). This chapter looks at the development of the IT organization from the perspective of both organization and change. We focus on the business and IT managers who want to use IT as an instrument for improvement or as a strategic weapon. We characterize the IT organization as a supplier of information technology. Within this IT organization we distinguish between primary and support processes. The degree to which these processes are structured indicates how far the IT organization has developed and its degree of maturity. To establish the degree of maturity and to position the organization in relation to similar organizations, we have developed a maturity model. This model is based on Humphrey's development phases and the primary processes that every IT organization has. The learning processes fit in with a study that was conducted among IT organizations in England; a model produced from that study is known as the Information Technology Infrastructure Library (ITIL).

25.1 Introduction

This chapter contains three sections. In the first section, we explain the World Class IT (WCIT) maturity model, which forms the theoretical basis for the analysis of the development of the IT organization. KPMG's vision of the changes in IT organization and the level of ambition within IT organizations is described in the second section, which presents answers to questions such as: What patterns are to be found in the growth of IT organizations? What relationship needs to be established with the maturity of the user's organization? Is the model useful and will it be accepted in practice? Furthermore, we want to participate in the process that leads to the summit: What are the characteristics of the IT organization which has evolved to the highest phase of maturity recognized at the present time? How much practical knowledge and experience do organizations in the Netherlands currently have about the latter phases of maturity? The third section presents a number of case studies. The case studies are all based on interviews with IT managers and reflect their impressions of the current and desired degree of maturity of Dutch IT organizations. We also discuss the change process that this growth should lead to. We are convinced that this chapter will lead to further improvement of the WCIT maturity model, because the IT organization is constantly developing, on the way to maturity.

25.2 The maturity phases of the IT organization

IT organization

In an IT organization we can distinguish the following processes:

Operations

When we talk of operations, we are mainly referring to the delivery and control of the IT products and services. Operations consists of activities such as installing infrastructure, operational planning and implementation of the information processing, processing and provision of backup and recovery, monitoring availability, performance and capacity.

Incidents and Problems

Incidents and Problems focuses on the changes to products and services. This process covers the handling of incidents and problem analysis. Incident handling encompasses the registration of faults and queries, the response to queries and the analysis and monitoring of progress. Problem analysis entails the taking of structural measures to prevent faults while striving for the greatest possible stability of products and services.

Changes and Configuration

Changes and Configuration encompasses the process of registration, assessment and handling, acceptance and installation (software distribution and hardware installation) of changes. It also covers the working methods for updating configuration items (procedures, applications and infrastructure) in a configuration administration.

Service Level

Service Level is primarily concerned with the steering of the IT organization. This is done on the basis of agreements with the customer about products and services. Service Level focuses on the quality of the products and services, under which we list the requirements and wishes of the customer. We conclude service level agreements for the products and services being supplied with respect to costs, availability, performance, capacity, calamities and security. These agreements are continuously reviewed and there is regular feedback to the customer. The standard agreements are included in a catalogue. This process also covers the gearing of IT policy to the business and information policy as well as product and account management in the longer term.

Development and Maintenance

Development and Maintenance focuses on the production and maintenance of products and services. This involves project-type activities such as IT trend watching, information analysis, design, programming/package selection, testing, acceptance and implementation.

Maturity phases

For each of the processes, we distinguish so-called maturity phases. The current phase of a process depends on the actual structure of the IT organization, with the maturity phases being classified according to maturity of the organization. We distinguish between Technology-led, Controlled, Service-oriented, Customer-driven and Business-driven. We will explain the maturity phases of the processes below. The maturity model of the IT organization (see Figure 25.1) presents the global process characteristics by phase of growth.

Technology-led

In the first phase of growth of the IT organization, the user is not a leader but a follower. The IT organization is technology-led. Having computerized information systems and keeping them available is the permanent focus of attention. The activities are ad hoc and heavily dependent on individual efforts. There are no formalized procedures, budgets and project planning. The tools available are not used uniformly. Little attention is given to problems and changes, with most attention going to resolving faults.

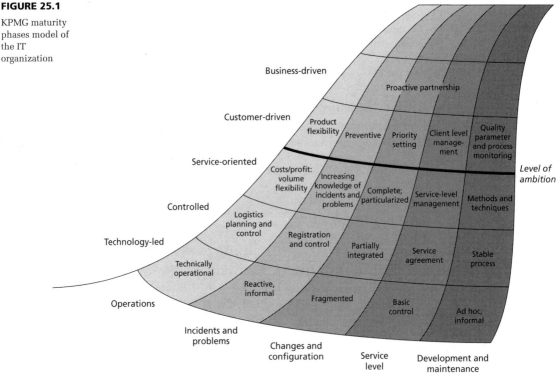

FIGURE 25.1

KPMG maturity phases model of the IT organization

Controlled

In the second phase of growth the technology is under control. The user indicates that he or she is dissatisfied. The IT organization has reasonable control of its own processes, but the processes are not targeted at the customer. A help desk, central or otherwise, handles incidents. By using service support tools for this, the organization gains an insight into the recovery, repair and response time. Risks associated with the implementation of a change are identified through the administration of configurations. With Development and Maintenance, the organization focuses on efficiency by adopting standard methods and documenting the process. Production makes almost optimal use of the tools available. The quality of the process receives more attention. The customer receives ad hoc reports in a non-standardized form.

Service-oriented

In the third maturity phase the role of the user changes. He or she states which products and services are required. The IT organization knows which products and services it can supply, which it buys in and how purchases are converted into sales. The processes are not yet really customer- driven. They are still standard services, a 'Model T Ford'. Besides incident management, problem management also receives a lot of attention. The impact of changes is studied. Development and Maintenance focuses on a short 'time to market', or control of the lead-time of the development process, the delivery of high-quality products, rapid response to new developments, and clear and open communication about products/services to be supplied with a good price/quality ratio. Production supplies high-quality services and its operations are balanced. Service level agreements for the products and services are concluded from a technical perspective (platform, applications) and the customer receives periodic reports about them.

Customer-driven

In the fourth maturity phase the user actually determines the products and services. The account manager of the IT organization concludes agreements with the customer about the costs and benefits of the product/services. The account manager must be able to translate the demands of the customer into products and services and actively respond to the customer's wishes. He or she literally seeks out the customer and provides support with the input of his or her IT expertise. For Incidents and Problems, (local) customer contact points are set up close to the customer's operational processes. The customer receives timely information about the status and progress of changes, as well as the priority setting. In development and maintenance, the organization focuses on a precise 'time-to-market' or the right timing of new IT products as a competitive advantage. The IT organization, as a whole, performs at a consistent level within the terms of the agreements made.

Business-driven

In the fifth maturity phase, the customer is not only the owner of the products and services but also steers the IT organization, which (via a partnership) proactively provides added value to the customer's business process. The IT organization is able to translate developments in its discipline into opportunities for the customer and vice versa. The customer organization will start to incorporate IT know-how as an important competence. The IT organization is more likely to be run by IT-oriented business managers. The IT organization is, itself, optimally structured and innovates continuously by systematically evaluating the processes, doing so by building up experience figures and benchmarking itself against other organizations. The IT organization will also split into a customer-driven part and an IT development and a control part. Developments in the discipline are closely followed. Openness and the self-learning capacity of management and staff are highly valued. Considerable attention to management style and culture is an important feature of this phase.

KPMG's vision of the future of the IT organization

The majority of IT organizations in the study are at the end of the Controlled phase and the start of the Service-oriented phase. The level of ambition for the coming two to three years is at the intersection between Service-oriented and Customer-driven (Figure 25.2). Our observation is that customers of current IT organizations in the Netherlands already expect a Customer- or Business-driven IT organization. The level of ambition of the IT organization is, therefore, apparently too low. To bridge this gap, we will discuss in the next section how to achieve balanced growth and the features of a Customer- or Business-driven IT organization.

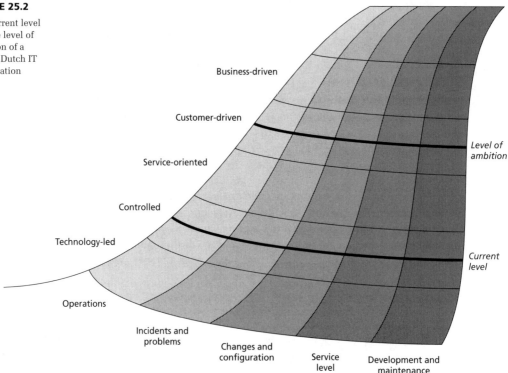

FIGURE 25.2

The current level and the level of ambition of a typical Dutch IT organization

25 ◼ The future of the IT organization

Growing in balance

To meet the expectations of the customer and withstand the competition from external service providers, all IT organizations that were involved in the study are actively changing through professionalization, by working in a process-oriented manner, through merging or selective subcontracting.

Designing and improving

Many organizations bridge the gap between the actual and desired situation with new functions such as account and product management and contractual arrangements in a service level agreement. A help desk is opened as a first sign of the new customer-driven IT organization. However, if the rest of the IT organization is not also professionalized, contacts with the customer may indeed improve but the quality of the service provision does not. Experience teaches us that unless the entire IT organization grows together, the gap between the Sales and Production functions simply widens. This does not improve the quality of the service to the customers. Therefore, organizations should not make a choice between creating a new design and improving the existing one, but have a balanced combination.

Maintaining day-to-day service

Everyone is busy with change. However, the everyday pressure, with a multitude of aspects such as new technologies, maintenance, legacy, interfacing, infrastructure etc. is so great that insufficient attention has been given to the change process and the changes required to become the ideal future IT organization. The best balance can be found by approaching it with the philosophy that you as manager are busy with changing your organization while not forgetting your day-to-day service (rather than the other way around).

Broader profile of IT management

In combination with the previous observations, it seems that when growing towards being customer-driven it is often insufficiently clear that the IT manager is also undergoing change. In the Customer-driven phase, the IT organization is really looking outward and the environment has a direct impact on the IT organization. The IT manager is more than a manager of the IT organization. He or she is an intermediary to the business. The IT manager is, together with the business managers, responsible for the balance between demand and supply of information provision. The customer makes demands on his or her qualities to make a contribution to the business, not only on the basis of his or her knowledge of IT. IT management, in this phase, does not stand for a single manager, a jack of all trades. The necessary knowledge and the skills, in particular, will have to be in balance within the IT management team.

Balance in selective outsourcing

With outsourcing it is also important to find the right balance. The organizations that took part in our study employ selective outsourcing. This involves, on the one hand, outsourcing of some parts of the service, usually based on an obligation to make a minimum effort. On the other hand, more work will have to be outsourced on the basis of hard and measurable service agreements. In the latter situation, outsourcing can only start if that part of the IT organization is properly organized.

Active input by the customer

In many IT organizations there is a lack of active involvement by the customer in the change process. Our vision is that transformation is not possible alone: they are two change paths running alongside each other. The user and the IT organization must grow together in balance. A high-quality IT organization can then only exist with a good customer base.

Relationship between tools and processes

The right balance is often missing not only in the organizational structure but also in the use of support tools. Many help-desk tools are introduced without the essential configuration database being linked to it. This makes it difficult to allocate faults and to establish the relationship with future changes and structural problems. The return on the processes can be substantially increased by using tools, that integrally support the processes. In all changes it is essential to find the right balance between the development and control of the processes, tools and the relationship with customers and suppliers. Only then can we speak of controlled growth.

Mind shift from Service-oriented to Customer- and Business-driven

In practice, there appear to be only a few IT organizations which are customer- or business-driven. An important reason is the gap between the Service-oriented and Customer-driven phases. Our experience shows that this discontinuity has a major impact. Where the first steps of growth take at least a year, the step from service to customer-driven takes far longer. Figure 25.3 shows a number of mind shifts that KPMG identified between the Service and Customer-driven phases. To take the step to a customer-driven organization it is necessary to make a break with the existing IT organization. This applies to technology, structure, employees, management and culture. The future trends, for the IT organization, are described in the following points.

Technology integrates

The customer will no longer accept that faults in the availability of services are limited by an inadequate connection in the IT infrastructure. In the Business-driven phase it even becomes so important that the infrastructure is set up as an integrated whole so that it can contribute to the added value of the business. Not only the technical integration but also the organizational integration will be tested by the customers.

Structure is transparent for the client

Visibility in the parts relevant to the client: the front office; transparency of the parts irrelevant to the client: the back office. It is important that the front office has the option to steer the back office so that agreements it makes with the customer can be met. On the other hand, the back office will have to be able to deploy flexible and efficient human

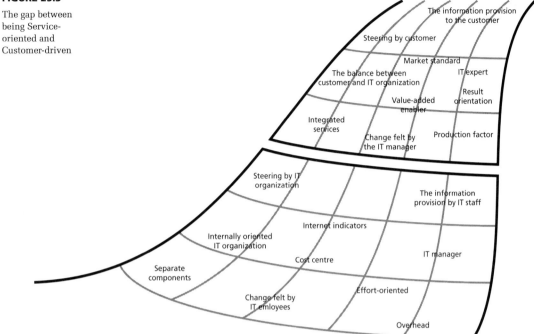

FIGURE 25.3

The gap between being Service-oriented and Customer-driven

and IT resources. For the organization of the back office, in particular, the 'make or buy' decision will also have to be continuously on the agenda of the IT management team. Furthermore, the IT organization as an integrated whole will be a part of the 'core' business change rather than a separate unit with its 'own' growth path. The IT organization enables the business to change: IT as enabler for business transformation.

Staff of IT organizations will be professional

The IT organization will characterize its employees as IT architect, IT economist, IT visionary, IT project manager, IT partner, each with a unique identity within the business management. The steering of the IT organization will also be more professional; staff will manage their own time in a network of demand and supply of areas of specialization. The entire middle management, which is now involved with accepting orders, distributing orders and setting priorities, will be kept to a minimum.

Management as a business will become management as a partner

In our view, management of IT as a partner has a great deal of significance for the skills of the IT manager. The IT manager who has climbed the ranks from programmer or operator will no longer be able to survive without the skills of the general business manager. How do I use IT to gain a competitive advantage in the market? What is the correct pace? In what way can we mobilize professionals to provide suitable IT services in response to these questions? These are questions that demand an integrated approach.

Customer-driven culture

The cultural changeover will be from Boss-driven to Customer-driven. The IT organization will have to embody a culture in which every individual manages their own work portfolio for the customer's benefit, determined by the customer. In terms of billing, this means that the customers will no longer be satisfied with covering his or her costs, but expects the IT organization to make a significant contribution to profits.

Acceleration of the mind shift

In practice, no steps are skipped. Acceleration is possible in the short term – for instance by quickly replacing the IT manager, rigorously firing unproductive staff, hiring new talent and selective outsourcing. Hired external consultants can also help with the 'push and shove'. But, ultimately, every organization must take the step itself. The step to Customer-driven does not usually fit into the existing framework, structures, standards and values.

Professionalization and standardization of the service provision

The services of the IT organization will be increasingly concrete and accessible so that the choice between insourcing and outsourcing is no longer a question of simply looking to save costs but a weapon to secure competitive edge. By professionalizing contract management in the IT organization, insourcing and outsourcing decisions can be made more quickly.

Internalized quality assurance

To respond quickly to new developments in the business means that the experts must remain with the IT organization. The learning capacity of the organization has developed in such a way that evaluation and testing of the effect of the process becomes automatic. It will become less necessary to have audits carried out by external and independent experts. The IT organization will also direct its attention outwards, to similar IT organizations, in order to increase its learning capacity.

25.4 Conclusion

The KPMG maturity phase model is more than simply a mirror. It not only gives an impression of the current situation but also indicates the direction in which the next step should be taken. The model helps to organize thoughts about the professionalization of the IT organization. The model provides answers to questions such as: How do I organize my management organization? What processes/types of tasks can I distinguish and what is their mutual relationship? In climbing to a higher phase, the soft aspects such as culture and emotion are just as important for success as the more substantive aspects. In the Customer-driven phase the customer is actively involved in the IT organization. The customer must be able to play this role. The IT organization must also be an equal partner for the customer (for instance, because problems are shared equally by the parties). In this maturity phase model we used common reference models. Besides the usual models, there are a few concrete methods available in which the method of application is described. This maturity phase model is one of

25 ■ The future of the IT organization

the supply of information provision. The model can be expanded with one for the demand for information provision. For further information, please contact KPMG, the Netherlands, Tel: +31-(0)30-6581720.

25.5 Cases

Trade organization

The objective of this organization is to sell as many products of the members (4,500) of the cooperative as possible at the lowest cost possible. In this way, the organization makes a distinction between primary and secondary systems in the application of IT. Primary systems are customized, such as logistics systems (tracking, tracing, operating carts, etc.) and a marketing system (negotiating sales). The secondary systems are preferably standard packages that are used for the purchasing and stock system (packaging material, etc.), the financial system, the personnel and organizational system and the facility management system (lease of auction space). There are 100 IT employees, 30 of whom work in the computer centre, 35 in system development, 20 in management positions (platform, databases, etc.) and 15 in the remaining positions. The IT budget for 1996 amounted to Fl14 million (€6.4 million). See Figure 25.4.

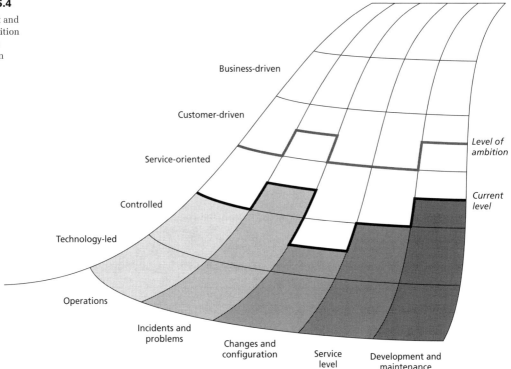

FIGURE 25.4
The current and desired position of the trade organization

The current position

Production is in the Controlled phase, where there is controlled job scheduling and more attention is given to monitoring activities. To deal with problems, this organization has a good help desk, which controls the process, answers incoming questions via the telephone and regularly carries out troubleshooting consultation. To handle changes, staff work according to a plan, an impact analysis and priority criteria. This has not yet been put into full-scale use in the organization. Service level agreements are concluded but not monitored. The service levels are also rather technical by nature, such that the client looks to further steering of the service on costs. For system development, the IT organization uses CASE tools. Projects are steered and afterwards evaluated on completion, lead-time, money and objectives. Some projects are already being carried out on a fixed-price basis. The client becomes upset about certain incidents (such as projects that run over time) and is looking at the extent to which it is possible to influence IT services. The organization needs service levels and insight into the costs. At the same time, the organization is finding it difficult to manage IT owing to a lack of professional experience. The client thinks that the IT organization should be at least service- oriented. This IT organization functions somewhat better than competing trade organizations, with whom close contact is maintained. The external service providers are used as a mirror to test 'where' the organization is.

The future

Within two to three years the organization aims for all processes to have at least reached the Customer-driven phase. On the basis of the TQM (Total Quality Management) model, they are looking at which internal business processes are controlled inadequately and how the client wishes them to be controlled. Projects will then be initiated in which the client is central. Gaining ISO certification is not the objective. Discussion is also under way with the Communications department about the image of the IT organization in the eyes of the client. The results of services and projects are discussed both internally and externally. To bring system development up to the next level of ambition, it is important to use non-IT-associated project management methods and that only jargon and methods with which the client is familiar are used. This is acquiring an increasingly important role.

Pension Fund

This pension fund is a part of a multinational. It operates as a one-stop shop with the objective of advising and informing the concern as effectively and efficiently as possible to achieve the best return on invested capital. The pension fund uses IT for its basic computer needs. No functional support is provided or decision support system supplied. For the IT management, partial use is made of contracted employees. Application development is (largely) outsourced. See Figure 25.5.

The current position

Much will change inside the IT organization in the coming year and maturity will differ greatly between applications. Nonetheless, the organization can be represented in the maturity phase model as follows. Production will be carried out with the aid of manual job scheduling. To handle problems, this organization has subcontracted the

FIGURE 25.5

The current and desired position of the Pension Fund case

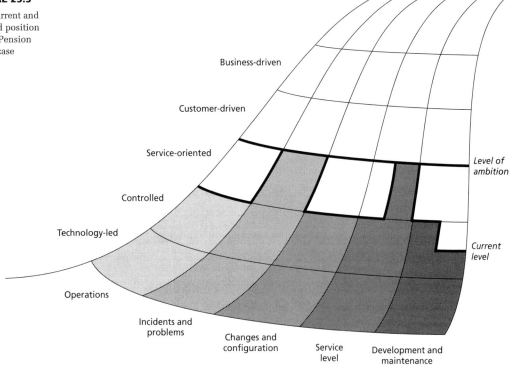

help desk to an external service provider. They will use a standard help-desk tool. To handle changes, the configuration will be set down in an organization manual. Investment decisions are made via Information Management.

Strategically and tactically these decisions will be taken by the pension fund. The operational performance will be subcontracted, whereby adaptations to software will be made on the basis of budget agreements. In the area of Service Level Management, trial service level agreements (SLAs) will be concluded with clients, although the IT organization has been entering into contracts with suppliers for some time now. Application development has been outsourced. It has proved difficult for the client to determine the desired maturity of the IT organization. The mission of the pension fund is becoming more commercial. This will have consequences for IT. The relations with both clients and suppliers are expected to become more commercial. Once the pension fund achieves the desired situation, it will become clear where the IT organization should be positioned within the model. The pension fund is positioned in the middle of the sector with respect to both the primary process and the IT process. This is thought to be the good path, but it has certainly not yet been fine-tuned.

The future

All processes should achieve the Service-oriented level. This is highly dependent on what the business demands, because this will determine where the IT organization should be positioned. The goal is for the IT organization to be Business-driven within five years. An implementation of new applications and the conversion to a new platform should act as a lever for this. Also, the introduction of a new project is intended to start the nurturing of the client, among other things, through the introduction of SLAs and quality processes.

Financial Institution I

The IT organization of this case is part of a financial institution in the banking and insurance sector which uses IT for sales, administration, investment transactions and general support. The total number of employees in the IT department is 550. See Figure 25.6.

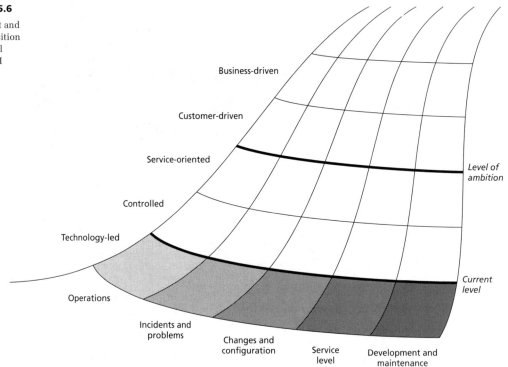

FIGURE 25.6

The current and desired position of Financial Institution I

The current position

The processes within the IT organization are all at the end of the Technology-led phase. Today's IT organization must provide its services at a reasonable price–performance ratio. This is the very least that the client now requires. This means a Service-oriented ambition. The competition, now, is generally in the Controlled phase. The organization often works with subcontractors. It wishes to spend a maximum of 10% of the IT budget on this. Here a distinction is made between niche players, such as consultants and IT employment agencies. Insight into the quality of service providers is also insufficient.

The future

The organization is striving to bring all processes to the level of Service-oriented within two to three years. According to the IT manager, one of the characteristics of this is that they should be able to operate as a profit centre. A number of measures have been taken to achieve this. The financial institution was created from a merger: the respective IT departments were recently integrated. This project is being carried out by asking a number of IT managers to break down the activities of the IT departments (product, core task to activities). This has created an entirely new organizational structure, a new function house. At a job market, all employees were informed about the new job descriptions. Interestingly, an appointment is combined with a training contract. This training contract stipulates the period in which the employee must complete the required advanced training. If they do not comply, it will affect their wages. In addition to this structural change, a start has been made, under the supervision of an external service provider, regarding the structuring of the IT processes according to ITIL. From this concept, some 30 core processes have been selected. They are now being implemented. Culture was given no explicit attention. The belief here is that culture is not created by making agreements about it, but by doing, or even not doing, certain things from which a particular business culture is born. The spotlight is not only on the organization. Standardization of the infrastructure is also an important requirement for achieving the level of ambition.

Engineering firm

The clients of this organization come from engineering firms and administrative offices. IT is used only for office computerization. This company has 20 IT employees in management positions such as the help desk. See Figure 25.7.

The current position

The IT organization is between the Technology-led and Service-oriented phases. Production uses controlled job scheduling. Monitoring is given more attention. To handle the problem process, a good service desk has been set up from which the first- and second-line incident handling is put through all processes. Structured reports are also given. Only large changes are closely controlled. The first service level agreements are being concluded. The users' organization will soon be asking for a certified IT organization. According to the clients of the IT organization, the majority of the market is in the Controlled maturity phase.

The future

The organization will meet the requirements of the user organizations and within two to three years will have achieved at least the level of being Service-oriented.

FIGURE 25.7

The current and desired position of the Engineering Firm

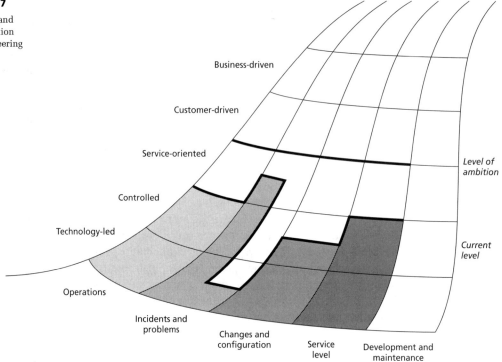

Financial Institution II

The IT organization, in this case, is a part of a financial institution in the social insurance sector. The goal of the IT organization is to supply a progressive, innovative and economically sound service to the rest of the organization. The organization controls an office computer and mainframe environment. The IT organization has a staff of 45 and the budget for 1996 exceeded Fl30 million (€13.6 million). See Figure 25.8.

The current position

The IT organization of this financial institution is defined for the processes of Production, Incident/Problem Management and Change Management. The level here varies from the Technology-led phase to Service-oriented. In the production process, there is controlled job scheduling and greater emphasis is placed on the monitoring of the production processes. To handle problems two help desks are sometimes used, but problems are solved within the department as a whole. The handling of changes is not a structural process within this organization and the first service level agreement has not yet been entered into.

The future

Within a number of years a service-oriented IT organisation should be under way.

FIGURE 25.8

The current and desired position of Financial Institution II

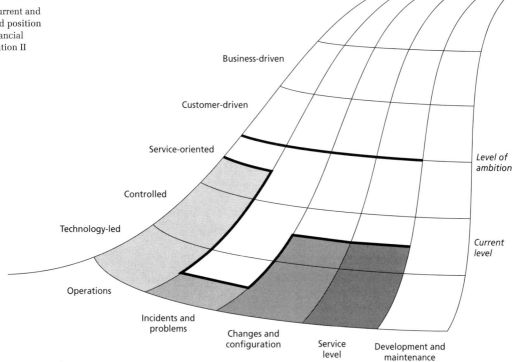

25.6 Management summary

Today's IT manager has frequently 'lost track of the IT organization'. Through professionalization, transformation, customer orientation and the use of new technologies, the IT organization has to provide ever more added value to the core business. Moreover, for many IT managers that is more than a nine-to-five job. It is, therefore, not surprising that he or she is looking for help. To provide some structure to the train of thought about the IT organization, in 1995 KPMG developed a growth model illustrating the maturity phases of every IT organization in their logical order and the relationships between the different phases. The model has proved to work excellently in practice as a mirror of the current state of affairs in the IT organization. It also provides a guide to the next step that needs to be taken, what hard and soft aspects require attention and the degree of balance needed by a manager to stimulate the development of the IT organization as far as possible. The KPMG model has been used successfully in numerous consultancy engagements with major IT organizations in the Netherlands for positioning, visioning and the formulation of a growth strategy. In 1996/97 KPMG also conducted a multi-client study of IT organizations in various departments.

Most organizations concentrate on controlling their processes, while the user organizations expect a customer or business-driven IT organization. IT managers are striving to bridge this gap in the coming few years, by focusing on new functions, balanced growth, selective outsourcing and active communication to and participation by the end user. Today's IT organizations continually improve and at the same time create new opportunities in partnership with the clients KPMG expects the IT organizations of the future to be confronted with the following trends:

- complete technical and organizational integration with business processes;
- restructuring to an IT organization with clearly distinguishable front and back offices;
- professionalization of development and implementation in the IT organization;
- the steering of the IT organization by the IT manager as a 'general' business;
- a customer-driven culture;
- acceleration of the mind shift;
- professionalization and standardization of the service provision;
- internalized quality assurance.

In short, in the coming years the IT manager will have to work more closely with the users in the business. Sometimes these users lag behind the developments in the IT field. Sometimes their ambitions are greater than the IT organization's. With the KPMG maturity model, you not only have an outstanding communication tool to successfully shape communication between users and IT organizations but also sufficient reference points for steering towards continuous professionalization of the IT organization.

Literature

Humphrey, W. (1995) *A Discipline for Software Engineering*, Addison-Wesley: Reading, MA.

Gibson, C.F., and Nolan, R.L. (1974) 'Managing the four stages of EDP', in *Harvard Business Review*, 1 January.

26 Professionalization of ICT-service management organizations: a roadmap for ICT managers

Gertrud Blauwhof, Christine Praasterink, Frank van Outvorst, Leen van Stappen, Marco Postma, Ger Manders and **Wim van Haaren**[1]
PinkRoccade

26.1 Introduction

ICT is the bearer of a new economy. The demands people make on ICT organizations are therefore heavier: 'I-conomy' depends on professional ICT management for its success.

For the professionalization of ICT organizations, a lot of use has been made of methods such as ITIL. In this chapter, we will go a step further. Because, parallel to the increasing importance of ICT, numerous ICT service management organizations have developed in recent years into organization divisions responsible for results and consisting of a few hundred staff. Process models such as ITIL are inadequate for the managers of such ICT service management organizations: they not only have to organize processes but are also involved with matters such as leadership, strategy and policy, personnel and resource management.

In order to meet the needs of these ICT managers, an integral approach to ICT management will be described in this chapter. The description is based on the INK management model (and the EFQM model on which this is based) and geared towards ICT management departments which operate as business units responsible for results, with 300 to 500 staff and providing services for internal clients.[2]

In Section 26.2, the INK model will be discussed. Section 26.3 is devoted to the growth and development phases of ICT service management organizations. In Section 26.4, we look at questions such as: How does an ICT organization reach the next level of maturity and how does the management of an ICT organization ensure that the people in the organization operate and function in an increasingly professional way? The fifth, and final, section contains tips for those who wish to work towards an excellent ICT service management organization in a structural manner.

26.2 Professionalization: a question of quality

There are numerous definitions of professionalization in use.[3] Ours is: a professional organization is an organization which is as good as its word, lives up to its customers' expectations and presents a uniform face to the outside world. Professionalization is a question of quality.

Professionalization is also increasingly becoming a matter of *continuous quality improvement*: the more the competition increases and innovation cycles become shorter, only those organizations which meet expectations and stand by agreements, time and again, will continue to play a role. The Deming circle[4] is one of the building blocks of thinking on quality and quality improvement. The four elements of the circle are: plan–do–check–act. Together, they express what is at the root of numerous quality programmes, namely the systematic planning, implementation, evaluation and, where necessary, modification of (follow-up) action so that a continuous process of improvement emerges.

INK management model

The INK management model is a management approach based on continuous quality improvement. Key themes in this management style are 'result- oriented improvement' and 'learning to excel'. In order to give some substance to these terms, nine areas of special attention are distinguished. Four of them relate to results, the remaining five to the organization. The Deming circle echoes in the model: 'good entrepreneurship', 'result-oriented improvement' and 'learning to excel' are realized by paying systematic attention to all nine areas and measuring and evaluating the results of this attention with a view to modification and continuous improvement.

The INK management model is represented in Figure 26.1. The model must be read from right to left: result-oriented improvement starts with an analysis of the results (areas 6 to 9) and then focuses on the areas in an organization via which these results can be improved (areas 1 to 5).

Result areas

The four areas of special attention on the right of Figure 26.1 relate to an organization's results and the way in which these are measured and evaluated:

[6] ***Appreciation by customers and suppliers***: this area of attention relates to how customers and suppliers evaluate the organization and its products and services.

[7] ***Appreciation by staff***: how satisfied is the organization's workforce? How high or low is absence through sickness?

[8] ***Appreciation by society***: the quality model is based on the idea that an organization continually derives people, resources and material from the world around it. The question in this area of attention is: what does the organization offer in return? How does the organization express its respect and involvement towards this environment?

[9] ***End results***: the financial and operational results form part of this area of attention. For example: to what extent has the organization managed to achieve its objectives? Has the organization lived up to the expectations of its stakeholders? Is the organization effective and efficient?

FIGURE 26.1

INK management model

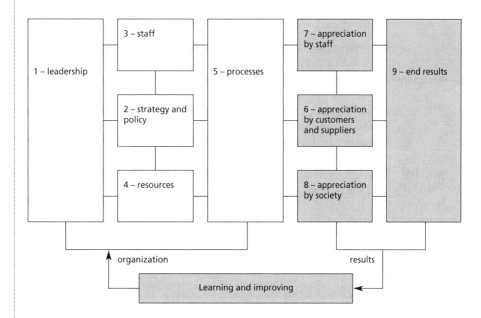

Organizational areas

The five areas of special attention on the left of the model are the 'organizational areas of attention' and enable an organization to perform:

1. **Leadership**: this relates to the attitude and conduct (the exemplary role) of all people in the organization who bear responsibility for guiding others in the organization.

2. **Strategy and policy**: this involves the question of what the organization stands for, what objectives it sets for itself and why, and how it thinks it can achieve these objectives. The way in which strategy and policy are created, communicated and implemented is also important.

3. **Staff**: this area of attention relates to realizing the potential knowledge and skills within the organization so that work can go into continuous improvement in the best possible way. This area of attention includes: the development of skills, the recognition of possibilities for improvement, the granting of power and responsibility to staff so that they are able to contribute towards continuous improvement, etc. Communication within the organization must also be considered among this area of attention.

4. **Resources**: this refers to the optimum use of resources (financial resources, materials, buildings, technology and information) without waste. Resource management also covers knowledge management.

5. **Processes**: this area of attention relates to the processes in the organization and, in particular, the way in which responsibility is taken for the establishment and continuation of an approach which results in ongoing improvement of the processes.

Control circle for continuous improvement

The relationship between the INK management model and the Deming circle is twofold and creates a control circle for continuous improvement. On the one hand, the plan–do–check–act cycle can be applied in all areas of attention. Therefore: what do we want, what concrete action is taken, how are checks made and how are evaluations made? On the other hand, the plan–do–check–act cycle links the areas of attention in the INK management model. The latter is represented in Figure 26.2: vision and mission are determined by leadership and translated into strategic policy (Plan); the implementation (Do) calls for people and resources and takes place in the block processes; control (Check) takes place via measurements in the four result areas; comparison of the results with the original objectives (Check) leads to an analysis of deviations and provides the impetus for modification, sustainable improvement and innovation.

FIGURE 26.2

Control circle for continuous improvement

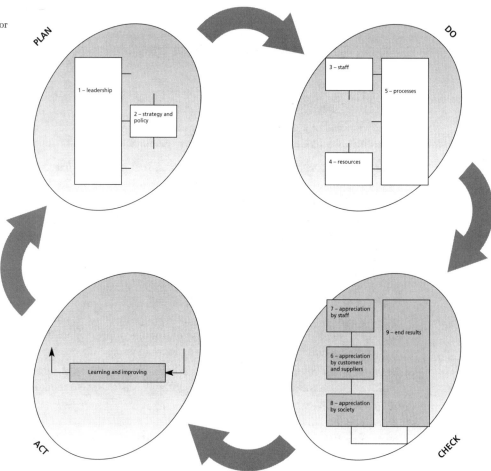

Development phases

Continuous quality improvement demands time, understanding and direction. For example: an ICT service management organization wanting to conclude service level agreements (SLAs) with its customers must have a handle on its own processes. The former assumes the latter; or, vice versa, the latter makes the former possible.

To give some direction to quality improvement, the INK model contains a guideline for organizational development. Five phases of organizational development are differentiated and every following phase contains features of the previous one. Below, we briefly explain these development or growth phases:[5]

- *Phase 1: Product- or activity-oriented* The focus is on the end product or the service. What is good goes to the customer; what is bad is binned. The question why products or services lack quality is not posed. Problems are solved reactively.

- *Phase 2: Process-oriented* Attention is paid to the primary production process and its management. Relevant questions are: How does the product or service arise? Where and why do things go wrong? and What can we do to improve this? Answers to these questions create opportunities for reactive improvement on the basis of 'measuring = knowing'.

- *Phase 3: System-oriented* The focus shifts from the primary process to the support processes, and the connection between the various processes in particular. Relevant questions are: What is the role of marketing? What is the role of finances? and How can all the sections of the total operating system contribute towards optimization of the product or the service? A system-oriented organization has been through a change in culture which is echoed in the nature of these questions; reactive improvement makes way for proactive improvement and the initiation of preventive and corrective measures on the basis of trend analyses.

- *Phase 4: Chain-oriented* The focus relates to the whole chain (i.e. the supplier, producer and customer) and the cooperation between the various parties. Keywords are: SLAs, just-in-time delivery, column-related innovation, expansion of the corrective measures from phase 3 to include customers and suppliers on the basis of win–win relationships.

- *Phase 5: Excelling and transforming* The organization is among those at the top. The process of continuous quality improvement is anchored in the culture and structure of the organization and the product or service emerges in such a way that all parties involved are satisfied. For example: wherever possible, there is 'recycling', the provisions of the Dutch Health & Safety at Work Act are applied, changes in society fuel corrective measures, etc.

Major changes are concealed behind this summary. Phases 1 and 2, for instance, are characterized by an internal orientation: all attention is focused on the primary and secondary processes in the organization respectively. Phases 4 and 5, on the other hand, are externally oriented: all attention is focused on the partners in the chain. It is evident that to realize this kind of switch in the focus and orientation of the organization, numerous changes will be necessary. This will be looked at in more detail in Section 26.4.

26.3 Development phases of the ICT organization

The INK model is a generic model for continuous quality improvement and, as such, offers little to go on when it comes to the specific questions and needs of ICT managers. We have geared the INK model to ICT organizations and, in particular, to organizations which meet the following description:

ICT departments within companies and organizations operating as business units with responsibility for results and comprising between 300 and 500 staff. The task of the ICT organization is to manage and develop products and services, and it is correspondingly organized in the form of an ICT service management division and a development division. The products of the ICT organization are: information systems (both customized and standard packages), technical management and application management. In terms of service, there is a 1:1 relationship: the ICT organization delivers services to the other departments or business units within the company.

Below, we differentiate the various development phases of the INK model into ICT organizations. We restrict ourselves here to Phases 1 to 3 inclusive – on the one hand because experience shows that the majority of ICT organizations are currently at Phase 1 or 2 and, on the other, for reasons of scale.[6]

Phase 1 – the product- or activity-oriented ICT organization

The results of a product- or activity-oriented ICT service management organization are characterized by the statement: 'It is twice as expensive, takes twice as long and produces half as much'. Many will remember the automation disasters of the 1980s and 1990s which gave rise to this statement. The causes of such failures can be found in the way in which the ICT service management organization is set up and organized. Features are: the ICT organization is run by managers who are 'the boss' of their department. Strategy and policy are mainly in the heads of the management. Quality checks are made on the end product and interim steering is hardly possible. Coordination and communication within the organization are underdeveloped and policy plans are tucked away in drawers. Staff focus on developing their speciality. Concern for personnel is in the hands of a manager; steering is on professional ability. Resources are employed to maximize the quality of the end product. Results are sometimes measured, although measurements are rarely used to improve business operations. No reports are made on the service towards customers. Insight into costs and returns exists only at a fairly high level of abstraction.

Another typical feature of a product-oriented ICT organization is the way in which products are 'tossed over the fence': in application development projects no attention is paid to (future) maintenance and management of applications and vice versa. The product quality is not guaranteed and the end result depends on the effort of individual members of staff.

Phase 2 – the process-oriented ICT organization

Prompted partly by customers who want more grip on the performance and the products of the ICT organization, attention is shifting to the primary production process. The accompanying style of management is *process-oriented*: the manager supports and encourages initiatives geared towards improving the way in which employees perform their work.[7] In process-oriented organizations, the determination of strategy and policy is also set down in a process; and managers and middle management contribute towards this, with the result that vision and operation influence each other. In comparison with Phase 1, the staff of the ICT organization experience more consistency in the method of steering. Personnel management has acquired explicit shape: recruitment and selection, uniform application of terms of employment, concern for training plans and evaluation interviews.

Resource management focuses primarily on supporting improvements in the sub-processes. Financial resources are allocated on the basis of return on investment. Often, separate staff divisions are created to get improvement processes going, under such headings as 'process support' or 'quality care'. A particularly common improvement process is ISO certification.

In a process-oriented ICT organization, criteria are applied to the changed/changing focus.[8] Information on the processes is checked and analysed by staff departments and made available to interested parties. The results of measurements lead to modification and improvement of the process. Insight into the sub-processes makes it possible to steer the organization better with the aid of criteria.

Phase 3 – the system-oriented organization

In a system-oriented ICT organization, people are aware that it is not only the primary process that influences the quality. On the contrary: all processes and their coherence are considered to determine the quality of the service. People acquire an eye for the connection between steering and support processes and the focus shifts from operational processes to tactical processes. An example of such a shift is (the arrangement of) the sub-process 'change management': change management forms part of both technical management and application management, and a prerequisite for well-functioning change management is insight into, and coordination between, the two types of management.

In a system-oriented ICT organization, strategy and policy are translated into operational plans (including budgets and performance) and communicated to all staff. In terms of management style, there is evidence of 'management by linking': the 'linker' informs the management, formulates feasible objectives, creates a well-balanced team and delegates the work. Personnel management in a system-oriented ICT service management organization is geared towards the long-term perspective of the organization (think of career development and competency management). The allocation of budgets takes place on the basis of the added value per process for the customer. Knowledge and experience are recorded systematically for the whole company and knowledge management is anchored within the organization.

In a system-oriented ICT organization, steering information must be available at all management levels. In this phase too, the criteria must be/are applied to the changed focus. On the basis of these criteria, objectives and performance can be compared. Steering takes place by interrelating the various criteria.

In Table 26.1, the above is summarized.

TABLE 26.1 Growth phases of the ICT organization

Phases	Motto	1 Leadership	2 Strategy and policy	3 Staff	4 Resources	5 Processes	6 Appreciation by customer and suppliers	7 Appreciation by staff	8 Appreciation by society	9a Financial results	9b Operational results
Phase 1 Activity-oriented	'Doing'	'The boss'	Implicit	Personnel administration / Paternalism	Cost control	'What do you mean processes?' / Ad hoc; quality and progress depend on individual effort	'Customers are a nuisance'	Specialized/substantive / 'Every man to his trade'	Socially unaware	Budgeted vs. realized	'It works – or not ...'
Phase 2 Process-oriented	'Doing things right'	'The one who thinks along'	The organization informed	Personnel management	Steering and knowledge management at process level	'Every man for himself' / Models and standards (ISO, ITIL, ASL) at operational level	'What does the customer want?'	Increasing changes / 'Don't let the lion look foolish'	Socially aware	Sub-budgets and financial returns	Reactive
Phase 3 System-oriented	'Doing the right things'	'The inspirer'	The organization involved	Human resources management	Opening up information for benefit of deployment of resources	'Cooperation' / Tactical processes (e.g. cost management, quality management)	'A satisfied customer always returns'	Added value for organization and customer	Society-oriented	Added value	Proactive

26.4 En route to an excellent ICT organization

For an ICT management department that forms part of a larger whole, it applies that: its *raison d'être* is determined by how the internal client evaluates it. Such a ICT service management organization therefore strives towards maximizing the quality for its internal clients. Or, in terms of the INK model: the realization of a system-oriented ICT organization towards all other sections of the company.

How does one realize a system-oriented ICT organization? What is needed for this? What must one do, or not do, as the case may be? In this section we briefly sketch the developments that an ICT organization experiences when evolving from Phase 1 to Phase 2 and from Phase 2 into Phase 3. By way of illustration, a couple of fragments from conversations with managers of ICT organizations are included.

Transition from Phase 1 to Phase 2

1 Leadership

To grow from Phase 1 to Phase 2, the management of a product-oriented organization must start to think in terms of processes. From 'doing' and 'ensuring that the things happen' to 'ensuring that the things happen well'.

An initial step when making such a change is not to determine the improvements oneself, as management, but to participate in improvement teams. Staff usually have lots of ideas on how the processes in the organization can be improved.

Experience shows that switching from activity-oriented thinking to process-oriented thinking takes time. Staff must, for example, learn to empathize with how others involved in the process think and not to reason primarily on the basis of their own work. It is advisable to appoint someone during improvement sessions who ensures that people think in terms of the processes.

If the processes are set down and responsibility for the process designated and allocated, it is up to the management to steer accordingly. The management must make a change: from steering only towards profit to steering on the basis of planning schedules and efficiency criteria.

> 'To realize changes, there must be clarity. Good communication is particularly important with an operation whereby one is trying to get an organization with a couple of hundred people onto the same, new wavelength. In order to achieve this, the P&O department has organized workshops for managers. In these workshops, attention is paid to what is going to change and what will be expected of the managers.
>
> What we want to achieve is that every member of staff regularly takes a critical look at how he himself functions. The middle managers create the conditions for such an attitude. They bring about the conditions under which staff work, they delegate responsibility, assess, lead, provide information etc. But they must be given the opportunity to do so. And they must be capable of doing so!

> 'During the training sessions, an inventory is made of how the organization can best support middle management in fulfilling its duties well. In addition, every participant is expected to look at his own functioning and ask himself which activities he is going to undertake and which objectives he himself sets in order to improve how he functions.'

2 Strategy and policy

The transition from Phase 1 to Phase 2 is characterized by formalization. Strategy formation is set up as a process. Questions which must be answered are: Which steps are involved in the process? Who plays which role and from which automated systems can relevant data be derived for determining the policy and strategy? Subsequently, the policy must be translated into operational plans and accompanying budgets and performance indicators and communicated to all staff.[9]

> 'For years, the strategy and the business plan were left purely to the management. Through publication in a 'staff version', the issue of a summary on the intranet and the holding of 'presentations' by the management, understanding and appreciation of the organization's course and policy have increased sharply and the distance between management and shop floor has decreased, according to the annual staff appreciation study.'

3 Staff

To realize change, it is essential to create support. Organizations which decide to change are characterized by outside pressure: dissatisfied or 'lost' customers, a concern considering outsourcing etc. This dissatisfaction in the 'outside world' is an ideal tool for creating awareness in the organization that 'things can't carry on as they are'. A customer who says what the consequences of a failing ICT service are for him or her can open people's eyes. The influx of 'new blood' and/or focused training are just as essential for bringing about change.

Activities in the context of a transformation from a product-oriented to a process-oriented ICT organization are:

- workshops in which staff and the different specialized areas which they represent meet and gain insight into each other's norms and values and in which 'walls' between departments are demolished;
- rewriting of the job profiles; it is important to treat crucial jobs as new jobs, i.e. 'remove from office' and apply for job;
- drawing up of training plans and developing courses, education and training for 'SMART' (specific, measurable, acceptable, realistic and time-bound) working;

- introducing evaluation and performance interviews;
- organizing workshops on process-oriented working, communicating and cooperating.

It is important, moreover, to pay attention to any sense of loss experienced by staff as a result of change.

> 'Personnel management needed a positive impulse. A small layer of management determined policy, so that staff were not sufficiently involved and poorly motivated. Furthermore, career policy was based too little on the potential and interests of staff. Career lines, by definition, followed the stages of programmer via technical designer and functional designer to information analyst and advisory and management functions. A long career path with inadequate opportunities for individual development. Before being able to change the career policy, we had to breathe some new life into the system of evaluation and performance interviews. Such interviews never actually took place. Now at least one performance interview a year is held. To prepare for the evaluation and performance interviews, the recording and the follow-up, checklists are made. On the one hand, as an aid. On the other, as input for training plans and career policy and to enable P&O to keep a finger on the pulse.'

4 Resources

Steering/adjusting is difficult in a product-oriented ICT organization because it is not clear where deviations in the process arise. After all, quality checks only take place in retrospect. In order to realize a process-oriented ICT organization, there must be insight into the coherence between the primary sub-processes and the impact of every process on the end result. To this end, the sub-processes must be analysed and described in handbooks. A process also needs to be put in place to ensure that these handbooks are kept up to date. By subsequently formulating standards and performance indicators, it becomes possible to make interim adjustments, to optimize the processes and monitor efficiency and effectiveness through time.[10]

> 'Signals emerged from the company that internal communication left something to be desired. A student was brought in by P&O to provide some insight into the internal communication processes. "To bring to light those places in the organization where communication does not run effectively." It was hoped that a written questionnaire held among 300 staff would help here. They were asked for their opinion on three forms of communication:
>
> *downwards communication*: the information which is received from "above", i.e. from the direct managers or higher management;

> *upwards communication*: the opportunities available to staff to express their opinion to those above;
>
> *sideways communication*: the communication with colleagues within one's own department and with staff from other departments.
>
> About 60% returned the questionnaire completed. The results were quite good, certainly considering the expected dissatisfaction. There was a reasonable degree of satisfaction regarding upwards and sideways communication. The downwards communication did badly. Staff want to be informed in good time, clearly and extensively about departmental and company matters and about other departments. Follow-up action has been discussed within the management council and with the Works Council.'

Another aspect of the transition to a process-oriented ICT organization is the setting up of a cost allocation system. This system must be based on data on and from the various sub-processes and it is therefore advisable to involve the people responsible for the process when setting up the system. The definition of a budget cycle, in which the formulating, checking and reporting are recorded, forms part of the transition. In addition, sub-budgets with financial objectives (SMART!) must be drawn up and budget holders responsible for results appointed.

5 Processes

Essential for the transition to a process-oriented ICT service management organization is a change in the way people think and work: instead of tasks, *processes* take centre stage; and, in the implementation, cooperation and 'the collective' prevail rather than 'the individual'.

The growth towards a process-oriented organization is expressed in the initiation of improvement routes and the adoption of models and standards. Two things are often considered urgent by the users/customer organization:

- the result and the time needed given system development processes, and
- dealing with technical problems.

The former can be improved by adopting a development method such as SDM or by setting CMM processes in motion.[11] The latter – the processes involving dealing with technical problems – can be improved by adopting and implementing the management model ITIL.[12]

ISO certification also plays a prominent role in this phase. In addition, tests, and the way in which these are dealt with, can serve as a means towards process improvement. By incorporating test activities into a process at an early stage, people are not confronted with mistakes at a (too) late stage.

A process-oriented organization is characterised by reactive improvement on the basis of 'measuring = knowing'. However, things do not just happen by themselves. In order to guarantee that deviations are spotted and any necessary corrective measures are taken, the

> 'Our organization strives towards avoiding mistakes. But in a situation in which risks have to be taken and in which the environment is changing rapidly, one sometimes makes mistakes. This is unavoidable to a degree. But you must not try to conceal these mistakes. On the contrary in fact: by discussing mistakes, we limit the negative consequences as much as possible and we can also learn from them and take measures to avoid them in the future.
>
> If mistakes are to be open to discussion, mutual trust is needed. In addition, everyone must realize that mistakes or deviations are not negative by definition. Sometimes you must choose between two evils and not choosing is the biggest mistake. Basically, the aim is that we learn together from them and minimize the negative consequences.'

various readings must be recorded, managed and made available to interested parties. To this end, a separate process has to be set up. In addition, work must go into developing a culture in which mistakes can be discussed and are not considered negative by definition.

6 Appreciation by customers and suppliers

The transition from an activity-oriented ICT organization to a process- oriented ICT organization is characterized by the fact that someone within the organization is made responsible for the systematic collection of information on customers and suppliers and their respective evaluation. To this end, it must first be established which target group(s) and whose opinion are relevant for improving the business operations. In addition, the management team will have to establish the (evaluation) aspects against which the ICT organization is to be measured. Subsequently, the appreciation of the target group(s) can be measured periodically and the ensuing results can be made available to the line management.

The switch to a customer-interested organization demands a change in culture. Staff in a product- or activity-oriented ICT organization often consider customers to be stupid and a nuisance, are driven by their specialization and usually strive towards 'technical elegance' rather than customer satisfaction.

> 'In the past, we used to really let fly at customers. Expressions like: "If the stupid idiot doesn't understand anything, I surely have to tell him!!" and: "He has to be told sometime that he's not always first in line!" were not uncommon.'

7 Appreciation by staff

With every transition, it is important to test staff appreciation. This applies even more in a service company and one which relies on human knowledge, like an ICT organization. Do staff experience the changes with respect to leadership, policy and strategy, personnel, resources and processes as good or useful? The answer to this question provides insight into both staff appreciation and the chance of success of the process of change: both are favourable if the chosen direction is acknowledged and considered consistent by the whole organization.

In addition to questionnaires and staff satisfaction studies, there are indirect indicators of staff appreciation. Examples are: the scale of absence due to sickness, increase and decrease in the demand for training, recruitment and selection (do staff remain proud of the organization and do they bring in new people?).

8 Appreciation by society

In order to grow from an activity-oriented to a process-oriented ICT organization it is important to determine what the company is and establish which data are relevant for the ICT organization's business operations. The perspectives and criteria which are (or can be) important in this context are represented in Table 26.2. Subsequently, the data should be measured periodically and made available to the management.

TABLE 26.2 Appreciation by society – perspectives for the ICT organization

Social	Environmental	Ethnic	Cultural
• Percentage of employees from minority groups • Time spent on voluntary work • Memberships and additional functions of the management • Educational facilities for staff and non-staff (executive level 4) • Number of places for work experience	• Number of leased cars • Number of employees who travel by public transport and/or by bicycle • Capacity ratio of the work stations • Reduction in energy consumption • Reuse of written-off computers • Burden on environment due to (number of) parked cars	• Number of complaints about discrimination • Conducting business with countries where there is evidence of violation of human rights or child labour.	• Amount spent on sponsoring sporting and/or cultural activities • Possibility for artists to exhibit their work inside the building • Amount spent on the purchase of art works

9 End results

In a process-oriented ICT organization, the financial and operational criteria are not only determined and set down but also, and primarily, analysed structurally. Which developments are taking place? Which trends are expressed in the data?

Through a focused allocation of costs and an evaluation of the results, moreover, it is increasingly easy to determine where in the organization the highest returns are being achieved.

Transition from Phase 2 to Phase 3

1 Leadership

The attitude in a process-oriented ICT organization is: 'make sure that things happen right'. In a system-oriented ICT organization, on the other hand, it is a question of 'making sure that the right things happen'. Experience shows that many ICT organizations founder on this transition. It is (too) complex and (too) threatening for many, especially in management, to see an organization as a coherent system.[13] It is therefore advisable to achieve this transition in two stages.

The first stage is (learning) to look further than one's own management or development department. Another prerequisite for evolving to Phase 3 is aligning all business units in terms of steering and assessment methods. It can help to choose a standard project method such as PRINCE2 for steering projects.

Only if there is uniformity over all the departments is the organization ready for a different management style so that, for example, management by linking[14] can be introduced. The usual organization chart is turned upside down. The staff are involved more and more in the whole decision-making process. The manager acts less like a 'leader' and more like a motivator and inspirer and clearly has an exemplary role to play here in terms of his or her behaviour.

> 'Hard work, long hours (preferably chargeable), in short: making an effort for the organization and thereby earning your salary – there's nothing wrong with that. But only making an effort is not enough. The effort must be effective, that is to say aimed at achieving a result which is measurable for the customer. Because our customers increasingly want to pay us for results rather than hours worked.
>
> Entering into an obligation to produce results has important consequences for how one works and interacts. Responsibilities are delegated more (from management, via account/engagement management to staff in the line): relations with customers and colleagues become more businesslike (expectations and preconditions must be made explicit); high demands are made on planning and checking skills (estimating well in advance, interim monitoring etc.).
>
> In my experience, it is important to prevent the transition from an "effort-obligation" to a "results-obligation" from leading to extreme individualization. Like "I'll put myself out for this but not for that". It is a question of the end result for the company, for "us". The train of thought is not "every man for himself" but "all for one and one for all".'

2 Strategy and policy

In the transition from a process-oriented to a system-oriented ICT service management organization, the process of strategy forming matures and staff become more involved and informed. An important stage is evaluation of the strategy-forming process and, where necessary, its modification on the basis of analyses of objectives, trends and periodic 'orientations'. As part of the transition, scenario planning can be introduced. By means of scenario planning, developments in the environment can be translated into strategy alternatives.

Other characteristics are that a) the vision of the ICT organization is better aligned with the requirements/wishes of the concern and b) the two visions (of the concern and ICT department) are translated into concrete, measurable objectives.

The continuous improvement of the ICT organization is also part of strategy and policy. Gradually, the results of the periodic self-evaluations using the INK management model are incorporated into the business planning cycle.[15]

> An ICT organization with approx. 250 staff wanted to make managers more aware of their role in and their contribution towards the business and the organizational development. To this end, objective interviews were introduced into the HR cycle as of 1999. Objectives are set with every manager, on the basis of three aspects:
>
> 1 Contribution towards the end results;
> 2 Contribution towards the organizational improvement;
> 3 Contribution towards the development of the staff.
>
> As this is assessed positively by both the board and the managers ('it creates a lot of clarity'), this system will also be introduced at the level of project managers.

3 Staff

A system-oriented ICT service management organization strives towards total (internal) customer orientation. To this end, attention to one's own product and process must increasingly make way for attention to the customer. Experience shows that achieving such an external orientation is a vast and time-consuming process. A seemingly simple question is, for example: how does the customer think and what does the customer want?

> 'Part of our endeavour to work in a more customer-oriented way was the project "Management of expectations". The motto of this project was: "Make your customer's expectations explicit.".
>
> Quality is determined by the customer. A customer is satisfied if the result of your work coincides with his expectations. It is therefore important to make these expectations explicit in advance and then regularly keep your finger on the pulse. Questions which can assist staff here are: Who is my customer? What must I yield in terms of time, money and quality? and When is my customer satisfied?

> It is best to start with the last one. Go to your customer and ask when he is satisfied. Let him talk, summarize, keep asking questions – until you are both satisfied about the wording of the customer expectations.
>
> Meeting the customer's expectations means that other, partly new, demands are made on staff. They must not only possess substantive knowledge but also planning, process and communicative skills. Because without a good plan you never achieve anything and without process skills and communicative skills you never find out what a customer actually wants.'

Activities which are important in the context of achieving a customer-oriented organization are:

- courses in customer-oriented working;
- training sessions on process and communicative skills;
- the organization of customer teams which transcend the disciplines of the company, with commercial people, ICT staff, project managers and staff from the support processes.

It is also important here to pay attention to any feelings of loss, to monitor the objectives (SMART!) and to safeguard the motivation of those involved – everyone is busy. Efforts which are reflected in the result act as motivators.

> 'In the project Integral Customer Contacts, it is a question of all the things which bring staff and customers into contact. Roughly speaking, two main groups can be differentiated: written and verbal contacts. This is also the subdivision used within the project. The objective of both sub-projects is to improve our customer approach.
>
> The name of the project for the activities relating to verbal communication is "Engaging". The aim is to improve how customers are received, physically or by phone. It sometimes happens that a customer is sent from pillar to post, has to wait too long, etc. The planned activities focus on communication by telephone, help-desk procedures, receiving customers and suppliers, guided tours and accessibility, and making recommendations on how we can improve verbal contact with customers.
>
> "Outgoing", the other project, focuses on written communication with customers. From letters right up to definition studies and quotes. These activities are aimed primarily at account managers, project managers, project leaders, project staff and advisers. Important decisions are often made on the basis of written communication. Think, for example, of memoranda, quotes, definition studies, etc. It is important that this is visibly improved.'

> 'Customer-oriented working means that you communicate in "customer terms" and not in "expert terms". If a customer asks whether he can make forecasts with a certain package, he is not interested in an answer involving bits and bytes, connectivity, database languages and features etc. That isn't his world! After all, you don't buy a car from someone who thinks and talks in terms of numbers of crankshaft revolutions.'

4 Resources

In the transition to a system-oriented ICT organization, non-financial steering criteria gain weight. The process managers acquire more insight into the relationship between expenditure and investment and the contribution this can make to total quality. A pre-condition for growth into a system-oriented ICT organization is the setting-up of an information system that is accessible, reliable and safe and makes information immediately available to those involved. In order to refine the information flows, the organization can make use of techniques such as the Balanced Scorecard.[16]

In addition, the budget cycle will have to be sufficiently modified in due course so that the focus of budget expenditure shifts from the maximization of financial returns to the creation of added value for the customer.

> 'The starting point of the project "Invoicing" is: our customers are dissatisfied with our invoices. They are too late, unclear, etc. Things must be improved, therefore. That is why we have chosen to introduce a new business-accounting package.
>
> Invoicing methods are largely determined by the accounting package used. The new package means a different way of invoicing. Customers can expect clearer invoices from us. The package also has consequences for our own staff, however, and the implementation was therefore preceded by an internal information campaign.'

A second pre-condition for growth towards a system-oriented organization is the setting up of knowledge management; on the one hand, to offer staff the opportunity to look beyond the boundaries of the sub-processes, on the other, to enable the organization to respond quickly and flexibly to changes in the market, and to retain knowledge.

> 'The organization of knowledge management turned out to be much more troublesome than expected because you are involved with the culture in the organization. Successful knowledge management requires people to take account of

> their colleagues. Staff must ask themselves whether others could benefit from their work or experience. But many ICT people are individualistic and, furthermore, communication in the organization must be such that they know that the other person exists and are aware of his needs.
>
> On the other hand: sometimes it is also a question of very simple things. With some departments, the staff were separated physically and, in these cases, we chose the method of taking lunch together. That works. People get to know each other, exchange experience and gradually know better where to find one another.'

5 Processes

In the course of Phase 2, many ICT organizations discover that ITIL is inadequate for covering all processes of the ICT organization. The relationships between all the different processes are made explicit and organized. The field of action application management also comes into the picture here. For the organization of application management, use can be made of ASL (Application Services Library: see elsewhere in this annual report). ITIL and ASL are interlinked and express the coherence between application management and technical management. Practice shows that, in system-oriented ICT organizations, the operational aspects of both models dominate and the said models are not yet applied across the board in phase three.

6 The result areas

In system-oriented organizations, measuring and making available data loses their noncommittal character. People formulate objectives on the basis of criteria and make managers accountable for achieving these objectives. In terms of attitude, there is evidence of a swing: managers 'long for' readings and are capable of translating results into strategy and policy formation.

In Table 26.3 the above is summarized.

26.5 'Look before you leap'

In the context of the professionalization of ICT service management organizations, four questions are important, namely: 'Why is professionalization desirable or necessary?, What are we going to do?, How are we going to do it? and What will the result be? In the introduction, reference was made to the necessity: the economic importance of ICT increases and the demands made on the ICT service management organizations become heavier accordingly. We have attempted to answer the second question – What are we going to do? – by means of particularizing the INK management model and the ensuing sketch of the development phases of ICT organizations. We also stated the intended result: an ICT organization which is universally appreciated by the other sections and departments of the organization, which radiates onto the labour market, for which staff work with dedication and pleasure, which achieves good end results and is solid in the longer term. The question remains: How are we going to do it?

TABLE 26.3 En route towards an excellent ICT organization

From Phase 1 to Phase 2	Participation and steering on efficiency criteria	Formalization	Creating support	Acquiring insight	
From Phase 2 to Phase 3	Looking further and leading less	Coordinating and making concrete	Improving customer orientation		
Phases/areas of special attention	1 Leadership	2 Strategy and policy	3 Staff	4 Resources	
From Phase 1 to Phase 2	Adopt models and standards at operational level per process	Measuring and making available data			
From Phase 2 to Phase 3	Creating (insight into) added value	Create coherence between processes	Steering on data		
Phases/areas of special attention	5 Processes	6 Appreciation by customers and suppliers	7 Appreciation by staff	8 Appreciation by society	9 End results

A question which keeps recurring in practice relates to the field of tension between 'today's troubles' and 'running the ordinary business' on the one hand, and the professionalization of a ICT service management organization and 'tomorrow's business' on the other. Experience shows that it is not a good idea to tackle all INK organizational areas at the same time. On the one hand, because this takes so much time and energy that the organization no longer gets round to its regular activities. On the other, because with such an approach there is a danger of 'little kingdoms' emerging: (ultimate responsibility for) professionalization efforts with respect to the five organizational areas incline, in due course, towards profiling and competition among one another. The consequences of this are: the process of change comes under pressure, people and resources counteract one another and the organization as a whole comes off worst.

At the same time, a certain degree of coherence is indispensable: all organizational areas of the INK model must roughly be at the same level if the organization does not want to thwart itself. The extent to which staff can show their own initiative depends, for instance, on the degree to which managers are able to relinquish the role of 'boss'. Each phase is also characterized by a specific focus and accompanying culture and, on this basis too, consistency and coherence are desirable. A cacophony of sounds, actions and good intentions has never proved effective or efficient up to now. On the grounds of the above, a project-based approach is preferable. The approach must, on the one hand, be geared towards 'horizontal' or 'integral' transformation, i.e. towards development of all organizational areas, and, on the other, be characterized by the setting of priorities (which organizational area do we tackle first?) and a sequential implementation vested in sub-projects. It is also important that responsibility for the programme of change is vested high in the organization, the coordination between the sub-projects is monitored permanently and safeguarded, and the programme is anchored in the regular cycle of business planning and control.

Experience and research in the field of change management have repeatedly shown that vision and a basis of support are among the critical success factors for organizational change and professionalization.[17] A method of change management in which both factors are safeguarded and which is also in line with the endeavour to achieve continuous quality improvement is the 'develop–design method'. There is evidence of 'designing' when (external) experts formulate new aims and a new way of working on the basis of, for example, the development phases outlined above, and then present these to the organization. Scenario planning can form part of designing. 'Designing' leads to a vision of the future and within this vision lies the power and the necessity of the procedure. 'Designing' does have its limitations, however: the method puts limits on the learning capacity of staff and, as an extension of this, the endeavour towards continuous quality improvement is not really consistent with a rapidly changing world and the accompanying need for flexibility and is at right angles to the basis of support for change needed for successful professionalization.[18] By combining 'designing' with 'developing', these limitations are negated.

With a 'development procedure', learning processes play a central role. In the context of ICT organizations in an activity- or process-oriented phase it is primarily a question of individual learning processes based on (the acquisition of) practical experience. Learning from experience or practice is viewed, in accordance with the Deming circle referred to earlier, as a cyclical process in which the 'student' goes through four phases: doing, reflecting, thinking and deciding. By doing, the student experiences something; by reflecting (feedback) on what has been done the student forms an opinion; by thinking about evaluations, expertise emerges; and on the grounds of this expertise, proposals and decisions with respect to improvement are made, the cycle is repeated and a control circle for continuous improvement arises.[19]

In a combined 'develop–design procedure', rough objectives defined earlier are fleshed out in a number of iteration exercises, together with the parties involved. By way of example: part of a vision can be to increase customer satisfaction. An initial step can consist of organizing the management processes, starting with incident management and with the aim of: a) dealing directly with 70% of all calls by phone and b) improving things with the existing staff. The help-desk team will take the lead in such a situation and determine the first step, for example registering all calls and the time taken to deal with them. The results of this registration then form the basis for the second stage and the process repeats itself until the previously defined objective has been achieved. The route of change resulting from a combination of 'design' and 'develop' is represented in Figure 26.3: as the results of a (previous) learning process determine the following cycles and stages, a non-linear process emerges within the band width of a previously defined vision.

FIGURE 26.3

Combined 'develop–design procedure'

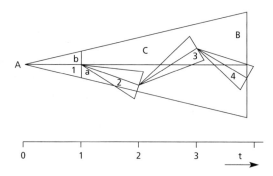

From the starting situation (A) one works step by step towards the general goal (B). Prior to every step the boundaries are set for the relevant step (design), after which these are fleshed out by the parties involved (development). After each step, the position is determined (a) and on the basis of this the boundaries for the following step (b) are defined.

In the above, the importance of support and vision for the success of processes of professionalization and change is pointed out. In the light of the question 'How can we do it?' and the 'develop–design method' described above, a number of other factors need to be added.[20] In order to professionalize a ICT service management organization, the necessity to do so must first be clear. A 'development perspective' also calls for open communication, and staff must be capable of changing or enabled to do so. The conscious organization and realization of short-term successes is also important; on the one hand, for reasons of support and motivation and, on the other, because such successes fulfil a teaching and exemplary function and can create an 'oil-stain effect'. In addition, leadership ('walk the talk') and steering on results must prevent the professionalization process from getting bogged down, and attention to consolidation and anchoring determine the degree of continued success.

> 'Why not take a critical look at your current service in the period ahead. Then we can perhaps talk about the purchase of new services.'
>
> We were receiving an increasing number of such reactions from our customers and this prompted us to initiate an about-turn. The aim was to profile ourselves on the market as a professional, commercial and service organization. That means that staff have to radiate this attitude in everything they do. In practice, this did not happen and changes therefore had to be made.
>
> In June 1993, the management launched the process of change. The organization and execution were largely in our own hands: the company director served as general project leader; six employees were responsible for the same number of sub-projects and a firm of consultants functioned as 'sparring partner'.
>
> The leitmotiv in all the projects was the 'seven-forces model', a steering model for processes of change.

> The 'seven forces' are:
> - the shock (needed for detachment and the creation of openings);
> - the spirit (the new élan);
> - the image (where are we going to?);
> - the structure (the organizational conditions under which the revamped organization can exist);
> - the success (examples which show that it really can work);
> - the balance (the new equilibrium);
> - the confirmation (the stabilization in behaviour, remuneration and information systems).
>
> As a project, the change was stopped after 18 months. Research into the culture in the organization showed that the image of staff coincided by and large with the desired culture. As a process, the change will never stop: the requirements and wishes of customers with respect to our service are changing all the time, forcing us to adopt a corresponding attitude.'

A comparison between processes of change in organizations shows that a lot of attention is paid to anchoring changes in successful projects. There are numerous examples of ICT service management organizations which have managed to achieve a certain level on a one-off basis; few have succeeded in continuing to function at the level once achieved. It is crucial in this context to make timely modifications to the different management and steering mechanisms in the ICT organization and to keep them appropriate. By way of example: if staff are judged on the basis of criteria drawn up from the perspective of a previous phase, they will not be inclined to take the step to a new phase. Modifying such criteria too late can also result in 'front runners' being punished and the process of change dying an untimely death. Attention to management mechanisms is desirable if an organization is to remain in motion and to prevent staff from falling back on old habits and cultures through either implicit or explicit steering.

The above means that expectations regarding the duration of the processes of change need not be too high. If it is to enjoy ongoing success, professionalization needs periods of stabilization and (renewed) routine formation. The picture of successful development swings: an upward trend, symbol of growth and change, is followed by a horizontal line – taking steps on the spot, which are necessary for anchoring and which form a precondition for further professionalization and growth. Paraphrasing Lynda Gratton, the keywords for successful professionalization are: meaning, soul and a human time frame.[21]

Notes

1. The authors wish to thank their colleagues Peter Aldewereld, Roel de Graaf, José Bijlstra and Hans Kateman for their support and comments.
2. The INK model was developed by the Institute for Quality in the Netherlands and is based on the EFQM model from the European Foundation for Quality Management. The INK model is described in: *Handleiding positiebepaling op basis van het INK-*

management model, 's Hertogenbosch: INK 2000; *Gids voor de toepassing van het INK-managementmodel*, 's Hertogenbosch: INK 2000. website: www.ink.nl.

3 See, for example, the magazine *Informatie*, May 1999 edition. This is devoted entirely to the theme of professionalization.
4 See, for example, T.W. Hardjono and F.W. Hes (1999) *De Nederlandse Kwaliteitsprijs en Onderscheiding*, Deventer: Kluwer.
5 The description is based on: *Gids voor de toepassing van het INK-managementmodel*, op cit.; Hardjono and Hes, op cit.
6 L. Ruijs (ed.) (2000) *De op weg naar volwassen ICT-dienstverlening. Resultaten van het Kwintes-onderzoek*, Schoonhoven: Academic Service.
7 T.J. Peters and R.H. Waterman (1982) *In Search of Excellence*, New York: Harper & Row; P. Camp and F. Erens (1994) *Meer dan 500 management stijlen*, Amsterdam.
8 See: J. Hope and R. Fraser (1997) 'Beyond Budgeting ...', *Management Accounting*, December.
9 When determining the strategy, the 'four-phase model' can serve as guideline. For how this model can be combined with the INK model, see: T.W. Hardjono (1995) *Ritmiek en organisatiedynamiek*, Deventer: Kluwer; S. ten Have (1996) *Managers moeten kiezen. Het vierfasenmodel voor organsiatieverbetering*, The Hague: Delwel Uitgeverij; M.J.M. de Vaan, C.A.G. Sneep, F.A. Drukker and S. ten Have (1998) *Strategische dialoog, Best practices in strategievorming, de onderneming aan zet*, The Hague: Delwel Uitgeverij.
10 The link between steering/controlling issues and economic information (systems) is worked out in more detail in E.G.J. Vosselman (1999) *Management accounting en controi*, Utrecht: Uitgeverij Lemma, 1999.
11 The Capability Maturity Model (CMM) was developed by the Software Engineering Institute (SEI), Carnegie Mellon University, USA. The model focuses mainly on the evaluation and improvement of system development organizations. A description can be found in *The Capability Maturity Model, Guidelines for improving the software process*, Carnegie Mellon University, 1990. Internet address: www.sei.cmu.edu.
12 The abbreviation ITIL stands for Information Technology Infrastructure Library. ITIL is a library of process definitions and best practices in the field of IT management developed in the 1980s and 1990s by the UK's Central Computer and Telecommunications Agency [now OGC]. Until recently, the series comprised ten titles: *Help Desk*, *Problem Management*, *Configuration Management*, *Change Management*, *Software Control & Delivery*, *Service Level Managament*, *Availability Management*, *Capacity Management*, *Cost Management for IT Services* and *Contingency Planning*. The first five were combined in 2000 into a publication under the title *Service Support*. The last five have been combined into a new publication in 2001, under the title *Service Delivery*. Web sites: www.ccta.gov.uk/itil, www.exin.nl.
13 Hardjono and Hes, op cit., p. 64 ff.
14 Arnold Walravens, Seminar on Team Management, Intense Course on Human Resource Management, International Executive Development Centre, Brdo, Slovenia, 11 November 1993. In: P. Camp and F. Erens (1994) *Meer dan 500 management stijlen*, Amsterdam.
15 A method for achieving this amalgamation of improvement and business planning is described in: G.H.E. Manders (1999) *Beter verbeteren met Improvaid, doelgericht en doeltreffend verbeteren van de (management)prestaties in organisaties door het integreren van het werken met het INK-model in het businessplanning & -control systeem*; PhD thesis Business Administration, Heerlen. Netherlands Open University.

16 See, for example: C.T.B. Ahaus and F.J. Diepman (eds) (2000) *Balanced Scorecard & Model Nederlandse Kwalitieit*, Deventer: Kluwer; S. ten Have, W.D. ten Have and A.P.M. Bour (1998) *Organisatiebesturing: koers uitzetten en koers houden. Balanceren met strategie en prestatieindicatoren*, The Hague: Elsevier.
17 J.P. Kotter (1995) Leading change: why transformation efforts fail, *Harvard Business Review*, March-April; J.P. Kotter (1997) *Leiderschap bij verandering*, Schoonhoven: Academic Service.
18 When choosing a strategy for organizational change, the aim of the change and the nature of the organization play an important role. For an overview of strategies for organizational change, given different objectives for the change and different types of organization, see: Berenschot/The Change Factory (1999) *Het idee verandering*, Amsterdam, Uitgeverij Nieuwezijds.
19 D.A. Kolb (2000) *Experiential learning. Experience as the source of learning and development*, Englewood Cliffs, New York: Prentice Hall. For comparable opinions, although under a different name, see: R. Espejo *et al.* (1996) *Organizational transformation and learning*, Chichester: John Wiley & Sons.
20 J.P. Kotter, op cit.
21 L. Gratton (2000) *Living Strategy. Putting people at the heart of corporate purpose*, London/New York: Financial Times/Prentice Hall.

27 Improvement of the test process using TPI®

T. Koomen IQUIP Informatica B.V., the Netherlands
M. Pol Polteq IT Services B.V., the Netherlands

Summary

Having a high-quality test process is important for service level management. This chapter presents the TPI model[1], which is based on current state-of-the-art test-process improvement practices. The model gives practical guidelines for assessing the maturity level of testing in an organization and for step-by-step improvement of the process. The purpose of such improvement could be reaching CMM[2] level 3.

The model consists of 20 key areas, each with different levels of maturity. The levels of all key areas are set out in a maturity matrix. Each level is described by several checkpoints. Improvement suggestions, which help to reach a desired level, are part of the model.

The chapter includes a general description of the application of the model, which deals with how to implement and how to consolidate the improvements.

27.1 How good is your test process?

Proper service level management in an organization is very dependent on the quality of the information systems in use. If their quality is too low, expectations of the customers are not met, leading to dissatisfied users. Also, maintaining the information system requires more resources than anticipated and means spending too much money.

It is therefore of the greatest importance for assuring the agreed service levels that the information systems are of good enough quality. This applies, of course, both to newly developed systems and to systems in maintenance. However, how do we know whether the quality is good enough? Perhaps the most important instrument to give insight into the quality of an information system is testing. If the quality turns out to be insufficient, measures can then be taken. But how good is your test process? Does it really give the required insight into the quality of the system?

These seemingly easy questions turn out to be very hard to answer in reality. Testing is often experienced as a troublesome and uncontrollable process. That testing takes too much time and costs a lot more than planned, is a frequent complaint. On top of that, it offers insufficient insight into the quality of the test process and, therefore, into the quality of the information system under test and the risks for the business process itself. But can we do something about this?

Many organizations realize that improving the test process can solve these problems. However, in practice it turns out to be hard to define what steps to take for improving and controlling the process, and in what order. A comparison can be made with improvement of the total software process, where models such as the Capability Maturity Model™ (CMM)[2] offer support.

Based on the knowledge and experiences of a large number of professional testers, the Test Process Improvement (TPI) model has been developed. The TPI model supports the improvement of test processes. The model offers insight into the 'maturity' of the test processes within an organization. Based on this understanding, the model helps to define gradual and controllable improvement steps.

27.2 Description of the model

The model is visualized as shown in Figure 27.1:

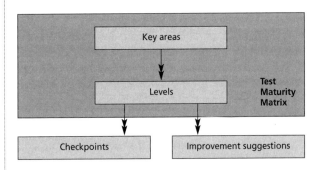

FIGURE 27.1
The Test Process Improvement (TPI) model

Key areas

In each test process, certain areas need specific attention in order to achieve a well-defined process. These **key areas** are therefore the basis for improving and structuring the test process. The TPI model has 20 key areas.

The scope of test process improvement usually comprises high-level tests such as system and acceptance tests. Most key areas are adjusted to this. However, to improve more 'mature' test processes, attention must also be given to verification activities and low-level tests such as unit and integration tests. Separate key areas are included in order to give due attention to these processes as well.

A full list of key areas is given below. An explanation is given in Table 27.1.

Test strategy	*Test automation*	*Reporting*
Life-cycle model	*Test environment*	*Defect management*
Moment of involvement	*Office environment*	*Testware management*
Estimating and planning	*Commitment and motivation*	*Test process management*
Test specification techniques	*Testing functions and training*	*Evaluation*
Static test techniques	*Scope of methodology*	*Low-level testing*
Metrics	*Communication*	

TABLE 27.1

Explanation of key areas

Key area	Description
Test strategy	The test strategy has to be focused on detecting the most important defects as early and as cheaply as possible. The test strategy defines which requirements and (quality) risks are covered by what tests. The better each test level defines its own strategy and the more the different test level strategies are adjusted to each other, the higher the quality of the overall test strategy.
Life-cycle model	Within the test process a number of phases can be defined, such as planning, preparation, specification, execution and completion. In each phase several activities are performed. For each activity the following aspects should be defined: purpose, input, process, output, dependencies, applicable techniques and tools, required facilities, documentation, etc. The importance of using a life-cycle model is an improved predictability and controllability of the test process, because the different activities can be planned and monitored in mutual cohesion.
Moment of involvement	Although the actual execution of the test normally begins after the realization of the software, the test process must and can start much earlier. An earlier involvement of testing in the system development path helps to find defects as soon and as easily as possible and perhaps even to prevent errors. A better adjustment between the different tests can be done and the time that testing is on the critical path of the project can be kept as short as possible.
Estimating and planning	Test planning and estimating indicate which activities have to be carried out when, and the necessary resources (people). Good estimating and planning are very important, because they are the basis of, for example, allocating resources for a certain time frame.
Test specification techniques	The definition of a test specification technique is a 'standardized way of deriving test cases from source information'. Applying these techniques gives insight into the quality and depth of the tests and increases the reusability of the test.
Static test techniques	Not everything can and should be tested dynamically, that is, by running programs. Inspection of products without running programs, or the evaluation of measures which must lead to a certain quality level, is called static tests. Checklists are very useful for this.
Metrics	Metrics are quantified observations of the characteristics of a product or process. For the test process, metrics of the progress of the process and the quality of the tested system are very important. They are used to control the test process, to substantiate the test advice and also to make it possible to compare systems or processes. Why has one system far fewer failures in operation than another system, or why is one test process faster and more thorough than another? Specifically for improving the test process, metrics are important by evaluating consequences of certain improvement actions, by comparing data before and after performing the action.
Test automation	Automation within the test process can take place in many ways and has in general one or more of the following aims: – fewer hours needed; – shorter lead time; – more test depth; – increased test flexibility; – more and/or faster insight into test process status; – better motivation of the testers.

TABLE 27.1
cont

Key area	Description
Test environment	The test execution takes place in a so-called test environment. This environment mainly comprises the following components: – hardware; – software; – means of communication; – facilities for building and using databases and files; – procedures. The environment should be composed and set up in such a way that by means of the test results it can be optimally determined to what extent the test object meets the requirements. The environment has a large influence on the quality, lead time and cost of the test process. Important aspects of the environment are responsibilities, management, on-time and sufficient availability, representativeness, and flexibility.
Office environment	The test staff need rooms, desks, chairs, PCs, word-processing facilities, printers, telephones, and so on. A good and timely organization of the office environment has a positive influence on the motivation of the test staff, on communication inside and outside the team, and on the efficiency of the work.
Commitment and motivation	The commitment and the motivation of the persons involved in testing are important prerequisites for a smoothly running test process. The persons involved are not only the testers, but also, for example, the project management and the line management personnel. The latter are mainly important in the sense of creating good conditions. The test process thus receives enough time, money and resources (quantitatively and qualitatively) to perform a good test, in which cooperation and good communication with the rest of the project results in a total process with optimum efficiency.
Testing functions and training	In a test process the correct composition of a test team is very important. A mix of different disciplines, functions, knowledge and skills is required. Besides specific test expertise, knowledge of the subject matter, knowledge of the organization and general IT knowledge are required. Social skills are also important. For acquiring this mix, training etc. is required.
Scope of methodology	For each test process in the organization a certain methodology or working method is used, comprising activities, procedures, regulations, techniques etc. When these methodologies are different each time or when the methodology is so generic that many parts have to be drawn up again each time, it has a negative effect on the efficiency of the test process. The aim is that the organization uses a methodology which is sufficiently generic to be applicable in every situation, but which contains enough detail so that it is not necessary to rethink the same items again each time.
Communication	In a test process, communication with the people involved must take place in several ways, within the test team as well as with parties such as the developer, the user, the customer, etc. These communication forms are important for a smoothly running test process, not only to create good conditions and to optimize the test strategy, but also to communicate about the progress and the quality.
Reporting	Testing is not so much 'defect detection' as about giving insight into the quality level of the product. Reporting should be aimed at giving well-founded advice to the customer concerning the product and even the system development process.

TABLE 27.1 cont	Key area	Description
	Defect management	Although managing defects is in fact a project matter and not specifically of the testers, the testers are mainly involved in it. Good management should be able to track the life cycle of a defect and also to support the analysis of quality trends in the detected defects. Such analysis is used, for example, to give well-founded quality advice.
	Testware management	The products of testing should be maintainable and reusable and so they must be managed. Besides the products of the testing themselves, such as test plans, specifications, databases and files, it is important that the products of previous processes such as functional design and realization are managed well, because the test process can be disrupted if the wrong program versions, etc. are delivered. If testers make demands upon version management of these products, a positive influence is exerted and the testability of the product is increased.
	Test process management	For managing each process and activity, the four steps from the Deming circle are essential: plan, do, check and act. Process management is of vital importance for the realization of an optimal test in an often turbulent test process.
	Evaluation	Evaluation means inspecting intermediate products such as the requirements and the functional design. The importance of evaluation is that the defects are found at a much earlier stage in the development process than with testing. This makes the rework costs much lower. Also, evaluation can be set up more easily because there is no need to run programs or to set up an environment etc.
	Low-level testing	The low-level tests are almost exclusively carried out by the developers. Well-known low-level tests are the unit test and the integration test. Just like evaluation, the tests find defects at an earlier stage of the system development path than the high-level tests. Low-level testing is efficient, because it requires little communication and because often the finder is both the error producer as well as the one who corrects the defect.

Levels

The way in which key areas are organized within a test process determines the 'maturity' of the process. It is obvious that not all key areas will be addressed equally thoroughly: each test process has its strengths and weaknesses.

In order to enable insight into the state of the key areas, the model supplies them with **levels** (from A to B to C). On average, there are three levels for each key area; sometimes there is a fourth.

Each higher level (C being higher than B, B being higher than A) is better than its prior level in terms of time (faster), money (cheaper) and/or quality (better). By using levels we can unambiguously assess the current situation of the test process. It also increases the ability to advise targets for stepwise improvement.

Each level consists of certain requirements for the key area. The requirements (= checkpoints) of a certain level also comprise the requirements of lower levels: a test process at level B fulfils the requirements of both levels A and B. If a test process does not satisfy the requirements for level A, it is considered to be at the lowest and, consequently, undefined level for that particular key area.

Table 27.2 describes the different levels of the key areas.

TABLE 27.2
The key areas

Levels / Key area	A	B	C	D
Test strategy	Strategy for single high-level test	Combined strategy for high-level tests	Combined strategy for high-level tests plus low-level tests or evaluation	Combined strategy for all test and evaluation levels
Life-cycle model	Planning, specification, execution	Planning, preparation, specification, execution, completion		
Moment of involvement	Completion of test basis	Start of test basis	Start of requirements definition	Project initiation
Estimating and planning	Substantiated estimating and planning	Statistically substantiated estimating and planning		
Test specification techniques	Informal techniques	Formal techniques		
Static test techniques	Inspection of test basis	Checklists		
Metrics	Project metrics (product)	Project metrics (process)	System metrics (>1 system)	Organization metrics
Test automation	Use of tools	Managed test automation	Optimal test automation	
Test environment	Managed and controlled environment	Testing in most suitable environment	Environment on call	
Office environment	Adequate and timely office environment			
Commitment and motivation	Assignment of budget and time	Testing integrated in project organization	Test-engineering	
Testing functions and training	Test manager and testers	(Formal) Methodical, technical and functional support, management	Formal internal quality assurance	
Scope of methodology	Project specific	Organization generic	Organization optimizing (R&D)	
Communication	Internal communication	Project communication (defects, change control)	Communication within the organization about the quality of the test processes	
Reporting	Defects	Progress (status of tests and products), activities (costs and time, milestones), defects with priorities	Risks and recommendations, substantiated with metrics	Recommendations have a Software Process Improvement character

TABLE 27.2

cont

Levels	A	B	C	D
Key area				
Defect management	Internal defect management	Extended defect management with flexible reporting facilities	Project defect management	
Testware management	Internal testware management	External management of test basis and test object	Reusable testware	Traceability system requirements to test cases
Test process management	Planning and execution	Planning, execution, monitoring, and adjusting	Monitoring and adjusting within organization	
Evaluation	Evaluation techniques	Evaluation strategy		
Low-level testing	Low-level test life cycle: planning, specification and execution	White-box techniques[3]	Low-level test strategy	

Checkpoints

In order to determine levels, the TPI model is supported by an objective measurement instrument. The requirements for each level are defined in the form of **checkpoints**: questions that need to be answered positively in order to classify for that level. Based on the checkpoints a test process can be assessed, and for each key area the proper level can be established. As each next level of a key area is considered an improvement, this means that the checkpoints are cumulative: in order to classify for level B the test process needs to answer positively to the checkpoints both of level B and of level A.

Test Maturity Matrix

After determining the levels for each key area, attention should be directed as to which improvement steps to take. This is because not all key areas and levels are equally important. For example, a good test strategy (level A of key area Test Strategy) is more important than a description of the test methodology used (level A of key area Scope of Methodology). In addition to these priorities there are dependencies between the levels of different key areas. Before statistics can be gathered for defects found (level A of key area Metrics), the test process has to classify for level B of key area Defect Management. Such dependencies can be found between many levels and key areas.

Therefore, all levels and key areas are related to each other in a **Test Maturity Matrix** (Table 27.3). This has been done as a good way to express the internal priorities and dependencies between levels and key areas. The vertical axis of the matrix indicates key areas, the horizontal axis shows scales of maturity. In the matrix each

TABLE 27.3

Test Maturity Matrix

Scale / Key area	0	1	2	3	4	5	6	7	8	9	10	11	12	13
Test strategy		A					B				C		D	
Life-cycle model		A			B									
Moment of involvement			A				B				C		D	
Estimating and planning				A							B			
Test specification techniques		A		B										
Static test techniques					A		B							
Metrics					A				B			C		D
Test automation				A					B		C			
Test environment				A					B					C
Office environment				A										
Commitment and motivation		A				B						C		
Testing functions and training				A			B			C				
Scope of methodology					A						B			C
Communication			A		B							C		
Reporting		A		B		C						D		
Defect management		A			B		C							
Testware management			A		B					C				D
Test process management		A	B									C		
Evaluation							A			B				
Low-level testing					A		B		C					

level is related to a certain scale of test maturity, covering a range of 13 values. The open cells between different levels have no meaning in themselves, but indicate that achieving a higher maturity for a key area is related to the maturity of other key areas. There is no gradation between levels: as long as a test process is not entirely classified at level B, it remains at level A.

The main purpose of the matrix is to show the strong and weak sides of the current test process and to support prioritizing actions for improvement. A filled-in matrix offers all participants a clear view of the current situation of the test process. Furthermore, the matrix helps in defining and selecting proposals for improvement.

The matrix works from left to right, so low mature key areas are improved first. As a consequence of the dependencies between levels and key areas, practice has taught us that real 'outlyers' (i.e. key areas with high scales of maturity, whereas surrounding key areas have medium or low scales) give little return on investment. For example, what is the use of a very advanced defect administration, if it is not used for analysis and reporting? Without violating the model, deviation is permitted, but sound reasons should exist for it.

In the example shown in Table 27.4, the test process does not classify for the lowest level of the key area test strategy (level < A), the organization is working to conform to a life-cycle model (level A) and the testers are involved at the moment when the specifications are completed (level A).

TABLE 27.4 Example Test Maturity Matrix

Scale / Key area	0	1	2	3	4	5	6	7	8	9	10	11	12	13
Test strategy		A					B				C		D	
Life-cycle model		A			B									
Moment of involvement			A				B				C		D	
etc.														

Based on this instance of the matrix, improvements can be discussed. In this example, a choice is made for a combined test strategy for high-level tests (=> level B) and for a full life-cycle model (=> level B). Earlier involvement is at this moment not considered to be of relevance. The required situation is represented in Table 27.5.

TABLE 27.5 The required situation

Scale / Key area	0	1	2	3	4	5	6	7	8	9	10	11	12	13
Test strategy		A					B				C		D	
Life-cycle model		A			B									
Moment of involvement			A				B				C		D	
etc.														

Improvement suggestions

Improvement actions can be defined in terms of desired higher levels. In reaching a higher level, the checkpoints render much assistance. Beside these, the model has other means of support for test process improvement: the **improvement suggestions**, which are different kinds of hints and ideas that help to achieve a certain level of test maturity. Unlike the use of checkpoints, the use of improvement suggestions is not obligatory. Each level is supplied with several improvement suggestions.

27.3 Application of the TPI model

The process of test improvement is similar to any other improvement process. Figure 27.2 shows the various activities of an improvement process. These activities are discussed below, with special attention for the places where the TPI model can be used.

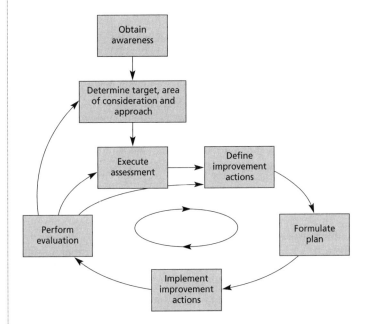

FIGURE 27.2

An improvement process

Obtain awareness

The first activity of a test improvement process is to create awareness for the necessity to improve the process. Generally speaking, a number of problems concerning testing is the reason for improving the test process. There is a need to solve these problems and an improvement of the test process is regarded as the solution. This awareness also implies that the parties mutually agree on the outlines and give their commitment to the change process. Commitment should not only be acquired at the beginning of the change process but be retained throughout the project. This requires a continuous effort.

Determine target, area of consideration, and approach

We determine what the improvement targets are and what the area of consideration is. Should testing be faster, cheaper or better? Which test processes are subjects for improvement, how much time is available for the improvement and how much effort is it allowed to cost?

Execute assessment

In the assessment activity, an evaluation is given of the current situation. The use of the TPI model is an important part of the assessment, because it offers a frame of reference to list the strong and weak points of the test process. Based on interviews and documentation, the levels per key area of the TPI model are examined by using checkpoints, and it is determined which checkpoints were met and which were not met (or only partially). The Test Maturity Matrix is used here to give the complete status overview of the test process. This will show the strengths and weaknesses of the test process in the form of levels assigned to key areas and their relative position in the matrix.

Define improvement actions

The improvement actions are determined based on the improvement targets and the result of the assessment. These actions are determined in such a way that gradual and step-by-step improvement is possible.

The TPI model helps to set up these improvement actions. The levels of the key areas and the Test Maturity Matrix give several possibilities to define gradual improvement steps. Depending on the targets, the scope, the available time and the assessment results, it can be decided to carry out improvements for one or more key areas. For each selected key area it can be decided to go to the next level or, in special cases, to an even higher level. Besides this, the TPI model offers a large number of improvement suggestions which help to achieve higher levels.

Formulate plan

A detailed plan is drawn up to implement (a part of) the short-term improvement actions. In this plan the aims are recorded and it is indicated which improvements have to be implemented at what time to realize these aims. The plan deals with activities concerning the content of the test process improvement as well as general activities needed to steer the change process in the right direction.

Implement improvement actions

The plan is executed. Because during this activity the consequences of the change process have the largest impact, much attention should be given to communication. Opposition, which no doubt is present, must be brought to the surface and discussed openly.

It is necessary to measure to what extent actions have been executed and have been successful. A means for this is the so-called 'self assessment', in which the TPI model is applied in order to quickly determine the progress. Here, the persons involved inspect their own test processes using the TPI model.

Another vital part of this phase is consolidation. The implemented improvement actions should not have a once-only character.

Perform evaluation

To what extent did the implemented actions yield the intended result? In this phase the aim is to see to what extent the actions were implemented successfully as well as to evaluate to what extent the initial targets were met. A decision about the continuation of the change process is made based on these observations.

27.4 Conclusions and remarks

To achieve satisfactory service levels in an organization, it is essential to have sufficient quality of the information systems in use. Good testing gives insight into the (possible lack of) quality of the systems, allowing corrective measures to be taken. But if the testing process is not good enough, it will need to be improved. The TPI model can help with this.

The TPI model is an objective means to gain quick insight into the current situation of the test process. The model greatly offers help for improvement in the form of key areas, levels and improvement suggestions. It supports the definition of small and controlled improvement steps, based on priorities.

The reader might get the impression that use of the TPI model automatically leads to good analysis of the current and required situation. This is not true. The model should be seen as a tool for structuring the improvement of the test process and as a very good means of communication. Apart from the tool, improvement of test processes demands a high degree of knowledge and expertise of people involved, at least in the areas of testing, organization and change management.

Literature

Koomen, T. and Pol, M. (1999) *Test Process Improvement, a practical step-by-step guide to structured testing*, Addison-Wesley, ISBN 0 201 59624 5.

At www.iquip.nl/tpi several TPI products can be viewed and downloaded. Also, questions can be asked and remarks made.

Notes

1. TPI is a trademark or registered trademark of IQUIP Informatica BV, the Netherlands
2. CMM is a trademark of Carnegie Mellon University, Pittsburg, USA
3. Traditionally, there are two main approaches to testing software: "black-box" (or functional) testing, and "white-box" (or structural) testing. White-box testing strategies include designing tests such that every source line of code is executed at least once, or requiring every function to be individually tested.

28 Securing information now or never

Anton Griffioen and Jaap van der Wel

Summary

E-commerce is now prevalent through the Internet. In several respects the importance of information supply is increasing. Securing information is gaining in importance. Also, legislation and rules are imposing increasingly higher demands. In the meantime, companies and government are constantly confronted with incidents concerning information security. The awareness that information security goes far beyond a proper password is getting across to management. But how to deal with it?

If your organization clears up the mess when any incident relating to information security occurs, punishes the culprits, honours the heroes and then proceeds to business as usual, you will have a problem. This cannot continue for ever, especially not nowadays when your organization will be accessed electronically from all sides. The introduction and improvement of information security require structural measurements involving all layers of the organization. It is a process in which three questions are at the centre: where is your organization at this moment, what is the ultimate goal and what is the shortest way to get there? In order to answer these questions this chapter describes a step-by-step method to improve the security of information. The method is based on the learning processes of those concerned with the improvement of information security. The authors draw on experiences they had at the Netherlands Ministry of Housing, Regional development and Environment, among others.

28.1 No recipe

Unfortunately, a simple recipe for securing information does not exist. In the Netherlands, decisions are made after consultation of all participants and central directives are seldom given. The learning process described in this chapter is based on this principle of consultation. Measures to improve information security are taken when people feel that the organization needs improvement. In this way a learning process is created in which the ideal situation is reached step by step, in a natural and effective manner. The result is information security through knowledge and responsibility instead of information security through obligation. The latter is expensive, as this method very often has to be controlled. Each organization has its own culture; its own primary processes and its own management. Moreover, there exist big differences in the extent to which information security has been implemented within organizations. One characteristic all organizations have in common is that improving security is a process of change. Based on our practical experience, we developed a method by which the beginning and the end of the process may be determined as well as the strategy of change to achieve the ultimate goal. This chapter offers an initial impetus for

> **Reliable information supply of strategic importance**
>
> Reliability as a property of an information system is a collective term for availability, exclusiveness and integrity. Reliability should be adequate for the demands imposed by management. A hitch in a logistics system has direct consequences for management based on minimum stock and short delivery times. In the view of a client, reliability is connected to confidence. In 1999, Microsoft informed Hotmail subscribers about a series of successful attempts at hacking and the counteractions undertaken. By such behaviour, confidence was maintained. For organizations in which information supply has a major role, reliability is part of the company strategy, because a failing information supply is translated into a reduced perspective. The share price of a US Internet auction dropped when the information supply sometimes broke down.

this method in the form of step-by-step security improvement. The method is based on the learning processes experienced by those concerned while improving information security and maintaining that level once achieved.

28.2 Who achieves information security?

In the simplest organization of information security, staff are confronted with problems while executing the job and they are forced to solve them. Not until accidents occur does the management recognize that the executors cannot fix the job on their own and, increasingly, organization levels and specialists get involved (see Figure 28.1). Thus:

- **General and technical services management.** Among them are the computer centre, the software development and operational organization, the domestic services, the financial function, etc. This group is responsible for the execution of a relatively important part of the security measurements.
- **Line management.** This level of management determines the desired level of security for the own (part of the) production process and takes care for the execution of the needed measurements.
- **Overall management.** The overall management determines the desired reliability as part of company strategy, establishes priorities and allocates tasks and budgets.
- **Security management.** This coordinates and monitors the security activities. It collects knowledge and experience on information security, by which the approach to security becomes more effective. This function can be located in several parts of the organization, but also in a special function such as an IT-security officer.

All those concerned ought to have the right attitude towards, and experience in the field of, information security. Initially, each person demarcates his or her own tasks. Between the tasks there are duplicates and gaps. The achievement of the appropriate set of combined actions will take years. The behaviour of the actors differs in each phase of the step-by-step method.

FIGURE 28.1

Persons concerned and their roles in achieving information security

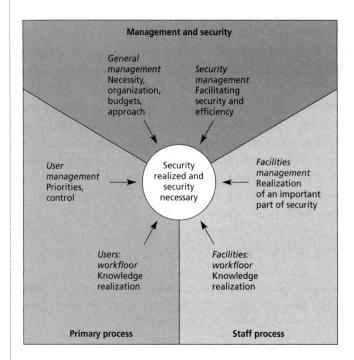

An example: investigation of security by listening to the workers

In a organization consisting of two thousand people, mainly highly skilled professionals with highly sensitive data, the management wanted to improve information security. They were obliged to do this by a ruling of the government containing a lot of details on how to deal with sensitive data. Within this organization, people doubted the effects of implementing the details of the ruling: the result would be a lot of paperwork with uncertain security effects. Especially in an organization like this, a greater effect is possible by using the knowledge and experience of the workers themselves. The details of the government ruling were used as a checklist and source of inspiration.

The result was a systematic overview of the actual way of working with security. The workers had a number of additional and reasonable wishes that were never implemented by the management because they did not understand the necessity. The main function of the investigation was to restore cooperation between workers and management on security issues.

28.3 The step-by-step method

The step-by-step method (see Figure 28.2) describes the introduction of information security. The method recognizes five phases, each of them having particular characteristics:

- *Phase 1: Ad-hoc information security*, in which an organization solves problems and continues with business as usual.
- *Phase 2: Spearhead information security*, in which an organization prevents major problems by supplying security to the most vulnerable parts.
- *Phase 3: Department-based management*, by which an organization analyses the total company situation and introduces security for all departments with similar procedures as in the previous phase. Each department will deal with a systematic approach to security for the first time. Because they lack the necessary experience, a tailor-made approach will usually arise from the existing security of the previous phase.
- *Phase 4: Strategically managed security*, by which an organization puts an effective security architecture together based on a strategic vision. A typical difference from the previous phase is the extended use of classification standards and standard packages instead of tailor-made security on the user level.
- *Phase 5: Proactive security*, in which security is one of the design aspects of new organizations, information supply and ICT architecture. Instead of the catching-up of the previous phases, security is organized systematically for the entire life cycle.

During the walkthrough of the phases, an organization proceeds from approaching information security in a non-organized way (phase 1) to increasing information security (phases 2 and 3) until costs hamper the developments. Consequently, rationalizing

FIGURE 28.2 Step-by-step method for the introduction of information security

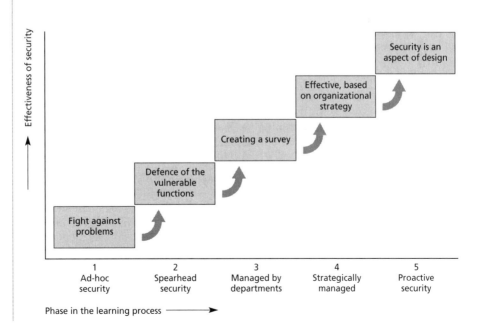

> ## A sixth phase: security within a chain of organizations
>
> Specialization and outsourcing make organizations more and more dependent on third parties. More and more information processes within organizations (within government and the business sector as well) are only part of a chain of processes. An example is communication between an organization and its customers using the Internet. Organizations pay a lot of money to maintain their firewall. At the same time, many service providers accept that hackers try, for example, to crack passwords with automated procedures that operate day and night, forcing organizations to shut off services not only for the hackers but also for some of their clients. For a safer Internet the perfect firewall is insufficient; providers have to undertake more activities to deny services to hackers.
>
> Society has to learn how to use the Internet in a safe way, which will become necessary when more and more processes are sustained by the Internet. More and more existing processes will diminish, leaving us at the mercy of the stability of the Internet which today is dictated by irresponsible nerds, sometimes 15 years old, who try the most sophisticated attack programs written by experienced maniacs. Society will have to learn how to make the Internet safe. The first step could be that big organizations with a lot at stake will press service providers to pay more attention to hackers.

the approach will further the efficiency and effectiveness of the security by the efforts of specialists, the development of standards and so on for existing systems (phase 4). In phase 5 this approach is extended to the entire life cycle of the organization and the supply of information by making security an integral part of the development. In that case the costs of information security can no longer be distinguished from the costs of realization. Figure 28.3 shows the outlined development in a qualitative manner. This graph should be put in perspective, because the effort needed in order to step to the next phase depends on the organization.

An organization with a high degree of standardization of ICT and management will proceed quicker to phase 4 than an organization in which standardization has not yet been shaped.

28.4 Characteristics of each phase

Table 28.1 characterizes each phase by the activities carried out by the relevant members of the organization. For each phase these are the following.

Phase 1: Ad-hoc information security

No priority is established for information security. Mending the damage, punishing the culprits and rewarding the heroes is the treatment in the case of incidents and

FIGURE 28.3

Effectiveness and costs: the increasing efficiency of security efforts

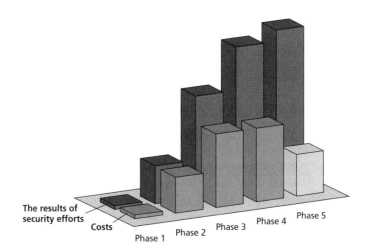

disasters. The presence of heroes, who helped out after big accidents in the past, ensures information security. Nevertheless, in parts of the organization which depend heavily on information supply, the need for a structured approach is felt in order to prevent recurrence. This provokes transition to the next phase.

Phase 2: Spearhead information security

In this phase, information security is an important issue for the most vulnerable departments and processes. Examples are protection of the financial process with a separation of functions, protection of computer centres by secured buildings, and so on. The protection of company networks by firewalls against the hackers and crackers of the internet is an issue belonging to this phase. The line management concerned have recognized the importance of information security and require a management budget for better security.

This phase is characterized by formalizing financial procedures and the introduction of ITIL procedures (or similar) within the computer centre and between the computer center and user departments.

In this phase, information security is part of the know-how of the department concerned and aims for that reason to use the techniques of that department, whether they are financial or technical. Risk reduction, from the perspective of the departments concerned, is of primary importance (a defensive approach to information security). Knowledge of information security is spread over the supporting functions and is specialized. In the personnel department you will often meet a person with knowledge of privacy legislation, in the computer centre someone with knowledge of computer centre procedures, and so on. The fragmentation of this knowledge of information security over departments may well lead to gaps in knowledge.

Through the effort of the line manager concerned or as a result of external factors (reports of the auditors, demands of clients, privacy legislation) the management will recognize the existence of risks within the organization. The need for overall understanding and overall security is growing at management level.

TABLE 28.1
Characteristics per phase

	1 Ad hoc	2 Standard department	3 Managers by managed	4 Strategically security	5 Proactive security
General Management	.....	Pays attention to security	Responsibilities, budgets for security become dear	Security is part of the organizational strategy	Security is part of organizational strategy
Security Management	.....	.....	The measures of the standard security level are described	A classification system is available	Development of new systems uses the classification system
Facilities Management	.....	Organization and procedures for maintenance and improvement	Organization and procedures for maintenance and improvement	The measures of the extra security levels are described	The measures of the extra security levels are described
User Management	.....	.....	A survey of processes, systems and their security needs is available	The choice of the appropriated security standards is based on needs and available budgets	The choice of the appropriated security standards is based on needs and available budgets
Users: workfloor	Performs security tasks based on a feeling for doing the right thing	Performs security tasks based on a feeling for doing the right thing	Performs described security measures	Performs described security measures	Performs described security measures
Facilities: workfloor	Performs security tasks based on feeling for doing the right thing	Performs described security measures	Performs described security measures	Performs described security measures	Performs described security measures

Phase 3: Department-based security

In this phase, security will be rolled out throughout the entire organization. For feasibility reasons, existing structures and procedures are adapted. This phase is characterized by the professionalism of security procedures within user departments. This approach demands the commitment of the management, because it involves a big change in working methods. Attention shifts from techniques to the company's aims for information security, which should establish the priorities for the security level. By not having standards, it is still quite difficult to withdraw exaggerated security or to remedy unacceptable risks. So servers that are too strongly secured remain in place, with high operational costs, and risks that are too big are accepted with the argument: 'We have been doing this for a long time and nothing has happened so far.'

Sometimes the wheel is invented at several places at the same time. This is the case when line departments develop security procedures meant for the staff systems (finance and personnel) they use in their departments. The inefficiency shows the necessity for specialized information security, which looks after every aspect of management and regulations. The field of knowledge of information security officers starts to shift compared with the previous phase, because the wishes of users should be translated into measures in or around information supply. Information security increasingly becomes a field of knowledge in which security levels and measures should be derived from company needs (a strategic approach to information security).

For organizations in which departments (business units) have a very high degree of autonomy, this may be the final step. The high costs of security often bring an awareness of the need for an efficient operation.

Phase 4: Strategically managed information security

In this phase, attention to the efficiency of information security increases. Common cost-cutting standards will be developed and applied by information security officers, who will arrive in the previous phase. In the meantime, tasks and responsibilities are laid down in other parts of the organization for efficiency reasons.

So packages of comprehensive measures for information supply, housing etc. arise for the several classes of security demands distinguished within the organization. By doing so, *make or buy* decisions may be required for parts of information security, such as introducing and maintaining firewall software and monitoring the operational firewall. The survey of security measures in the entire organization, which arose in the previous phase, is helpful, because *best practices* can be derived. By adding a price to the packages, a base occurs for new procedures where users may 'buy' the desired level of security and accept the obligation to introduce the concomitant security procedures.

For organizations with a usual dependency on ICT, this may be the last step toward information security. Organizations that stand out by achieving strategic advantages from ICT should look to the future. Therefore phase 5 exists.

Phase 5: Proactive information security

In this last phase, information security is more than an addition to existing information supply: it becomes a development criterion. Information security is included in the set-up of a company-wide ICT strategy. In this phase an organization follows trends in information security and anticipates risks. Each strategy is checked for potential security risks.

With standards and standardized measures, originating in the previous phase, information security is integrally involved in renewal projects. The budget explicitly dedicated to information security is relatively small and mainly destined for the maintenance of tools and trend research.

28.5 What is the ideal phase?

A direct positive relation between information security and the importance of information supply exists (see Figure 28.4). At one extreme, information supply is of hardly any importance and security may be reduced to ad-hoc measures. At the other extreme (information supply takes a strategic position), an integral approach to design and security offers efficient and effective possibilities for existing security problems.

In Figure 28.4 a straight line represents the optimum information security of an organization as a function of the importance of information supply. This graph is a tool in analysing the conjunction of the existing security to the needs of information security, as can be derived from the importance of the information supply. This straight line, which represents the optimum, separates the areas of too little information security and of too much information security.

FIGURE 28.4
The use of the step-by-step model in policy making

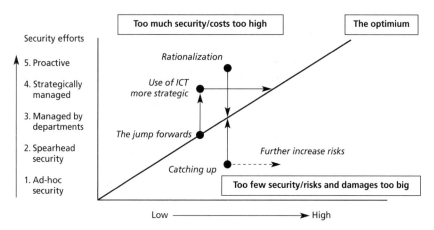

28.6 The use of the step-by-step method

A process of improving information security will probably be most successful if efforts concentrate on those areas in which the highest output is to be expected. These areas can be found by answering the next three questions:

1. **Where we are at this moment?** With help of the foregoing the information security available and what is needed in the organization will be checked. The method is used here as reference for a check on the present situation.

2. **What shall we aim at, regarding the importance of information supply?** The importance of information supply may be derived from the risks of the present situation or from the company-wide ICT policy. The method is used as reference for the conceptualization of the future information security.

3 ***What is the most effective strategy of change in order to reach the final step?*** The existing and desired situation determines the approach needed to achieve the change. In practice, three main directions may be distinguished (see Figure 28.4). Each demands an entirely different motivation by the management in order to persuade the organization to undertake the desired change processes:

- ***Catching up,*** to redress shortcomings in information security. In this type of case, the organization has usually encountered enormous problems. These problems deliver good motivation for the change process. In exceptional cases, employees deny or trivialize that things went wrong. In such a case an additional awakening programme will be needed.

- ***Rationalization,*** in which exaggerated information security is simplified. This occurs, for instance, in organizations that have recently started a network and have handled security as indicated on a network control course without taking special situations into account. The technicians concerned are usually the biggest opponents of rationalization, because a change easily gives the feeling that mistakes have been made in the past. A change path is more likely to be accepted when the path starts with the recognition that the implementation of exaggerated security was a necessary learning process.

- ***A jump forwards,*** in which the dependency of primary processes increases – as, for example, when e-commerce is introduced. A re-gauge of information security is then an essential precondition. To the organization, the jump forwards may seem to be overdone, especially if there are few problems with the present security. The essential motivation will be evoked by allowing those concerned insight into the risks of a failing information supply in the new situation. Pointing to new threads and imposing much higher demands on the back office may do the trick.

28.7 Conclusion

Improving information security is a complicated process. Of course, the reality is always more complicated than described in the method, which should be applied with due caution and know-how. The method is an initial impetus for a process-like approach and will have to be field-tested much more intensively than it has been so far. The authors welcome suggestions and other ideas.

Acknowledgements

The authors thank J. Corman, B. Kwak, W.S. Velt and W. de Vries for their inspiring contribution.

This article has been published in Dutch in *Informatiebeveiliging Praktijkjournaal*, nr. 3/2000 and in *IT Beheer Praktijkjournaal*, nr. 4/2000.

Literature

Anton Griffioen and Willem Velt in Jaap van der Wel (2000) 'Implementatie VIR bij het Ministerie van VROM' (in Dutch), *Informatiebeveiliging Praktijkjournaal* nr. 1, p. 19.

29 Quality of software development

On the road to total quality of information technology?

Dr Paul Hendriks Senior Consultant at M&I/Partners, Amersfoort, the Netherlands

Summary

It is a generally accepted fact that the primary processes of most companies depend on information technology. Often, software is an essential part of the products and services that companies provide to the market. Therefore, software has become a core competence factor for an increasing number of companies. When speaking of total quality management, the care of information technology in organizational processes and in products will have to play an important part. Information technology is, of course, more than just development of software products; it also has to deal with the exploitation and management thereof. Moreover, software development is only a small part of the costs of information technology. Despite this, software development is the source of many problems and therefore it is one of the critical elements in the area of quality management. This chapter examines quality improvement in software development. It provides an overview of the most important methods in this area. Some of the questions raised are: What is to be expected of these methods? and Where can more information be found?

29.1 Goal of quality improvement

The prime question in quality improvement of software development is: Why should an organization work on quality improvement? Why should money be invested in it? What are the benefits of quality improvement? What business goals can be achieved with quality improvement of software development? Although a growing amount of data and number of case studies have become available in the literature that describe the advantages obtained and the returns on investment that can be achieved, it is not at all straightforward to translate such results to specific circumstances. Can those results be ascribed to the improvement process alone? What activities have contributed to the results? Those questions are difficult to answer. The general tendency, however, is clear. It shows that quality improvement helps forecast the quality of products to be delivered and enables software-developing organizations to be able to deliver their products within the estimated time and budget constraints. The aim of quality improvement (Figure 29.1) is to continuously improve the quality of software development in a stepwise manner. One wants to learn from positive as well as negative lessons in the past. Improvement actions will induce changes that have to be

FIGURE 29.1

Goal of quality improvement

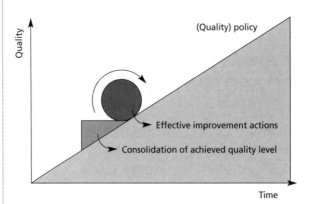

consolidated in the organization, all of these activities having the business goals of the organization in mind. The business goals have to be the leading principle that guides the implementation of improvements. In practice, these business goals are not at all clear, which creates one of the major risks for a successful improvement project. The methods described for quality improvement are the means. They have to be adapted to the specific business goals and the culture of the software-developing organization.

29.2 Different lines of approach

Methods for quality improvement of software development can be classified along different lines according to their approach. In practice as well as in research, much effort is dedicated to improving the quality of the software development process (SPI = Software Process Improvement). The starting point in this approach is that an improved software development process automatically leads to better software products that can be delivered within estimated time and budget constraints. Apart from process improvement, there is more emphasis, currently, on other P-aspects: product, people, and performance (measurement) of software-developing organizations. How to specify and validate the quality of software products? ISO9126 gives handles to focus on product quality. Increased attention is given to the people aspect of software engineering. Individual software engineers or teams of engineers are central to such approaches, not the total software-developing organization and its processes 'Performance', finally, entails improvement methods that focus on measuring. GQM (Goal/Question/Metric) is the most prominent in this area. In this chapter, the most relevant methods regarding these P-aspects will be explained.

29.3 Process

ISO standards

The oldest and most well-known standard for consolidation and certification of processes in an organization comprises the ISO9000 standard. In 2000, a new version ISO9001:2000 ('Quality Management systems') was published that supersedes –

amongst others – the 1994 versions of ISO9001 ('Quality systems – Model for quality assurance in design, development, production, installation and servicing') and ISO9002 ('Quality systems – Model for quality assurance in production, installation and servicing'). This standard is generally applicable and not specifically dedicated to software-developing organizations.

ISO delivers guidelines for application of its standards in specific fields. For software engineering, ISO9000-3 ('Guidelines for the application of ISO 9001 to the development, supply and maintenance of software') is such a guideline. Information on ISO9000 and ISO's standardization activities can be obtained from ISO (International Organization for Standardization) using its website: www.iso.ch. It is also possible to order standards directly from its site.

CMM

The most well-known method for assessment of the software development process is the Capability Maturity Model (CMM) (or more precisely the SW-CMM; the CMM for software) (Paulk *et al.*, 1993). The Software Engineering Institute (SEI) developed the model. Each software-developing organization can be characterized by one of the five maturity levels of the model (Figure 29.2). It also provides information about those processes, which have to be addressed to attain a higher level of maturity. Watts S. Humphrey (1990) describes CMM. The model originated from research into the way in which (successful) software-developing organizations organize their processes in practice. A description of the model and publications regarding its philosophy and practical use can be found at the website of the SEI: www.sei.cmu.edu/cmm.

At the lowest maturity level, an organization is in the 'initial' phase. It develops software, but development is done in an ad-hoc manner where a different approach is used for different software products. In many cases, budget and time estimates are not met if those estimations are present at all. The quality of the delivered product is unpredictable as it is based on the individual effort, knowledge and experience of local heroes. In such a situation, one has to introduce basic management activities to lift the organization to the second level of CMM: 'Repeatable'. More uniformity is brought into the software development process such that the organization is capable

FIGURE 29.2

Maturity levels in CMM

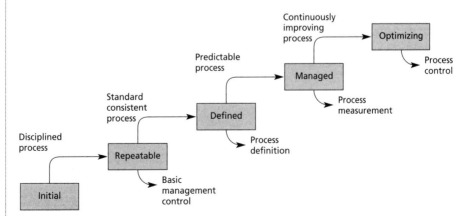

of producing similar products in a similar way with similar levels of quality. Quality assurance and configuration management are crucial facets in the transition from level 1 to level 2. An organization grows to the third level ('Defined') if it is capable of describing its software development process and manages to use the standardized software process. As the organisation comes to grips with the main parts of its development process, it can control them. However, in order to achieve the 'Managed' level of CMM, one has to quantify data regarding the software development process. That data should be analysed and used in establishing estimates in plans and changes whenever needed. At the highest level ('Optimizing'), a software-developing organization is capable of flexibly changing its development process based on the characteristics of the software product to be developed. The organization is at the stage of knowing how to handle changes.

CMM is primarily known for its five capability levels and its use in assessing organizations. The goal of such an assessment is to determine whether the software development processes are adequate enough to achieve the business goals of the organization regarding software and software development. From an assessment, an improvement plan is formulated, which describes the measures required to achieve improvements. Each level of CMM, apart from the first one, contains so-called KPAs (Key Process Areas). These are areas in which the CMM advises an organization to improve in order to grow to a higher level of maturity. Each KPA has one or more goals that describe what has to be achieved. Furthermore, the activities that help implement and institutionalize those goals are given. As such, CMM provides a practical framework that shows an organization how to improve its software development process.

An interesting new development in this context is the CMMI (Capability Maturity Model Integration) (see: www.sei.cmu.edu/cmmi). This is the effort of the Software Engineering Institute to create a framework of integrated maturity models. This framework is presented in two different ways: in the staged representation all process areas are grouped into maturity levels, as we know them from the 'normal' CMM for software. In order to successfully attain a maturity level, an organization has to satisfy the goals for all processes that are on that level. In the continuous presentation, capability levels are defined for the process area, meaning that an organization may possibly be on different levels for each different process area. This approach is more in line with SPICE and ISO15504 (see later).

Bootstrap

Bootstrap (Kuvaja *et al.*, 1993, 1994) is also a method for assessment and improvement of the software development process. It was developed in an ESPRIT project sponsored by the European Commission from 1990 to 1993. The aim of that project was to develop a useful method for software quality improvement for the European market, based on existing material such as CMM, ISO9000–3, and ESA (European Space Agency) standards. In contrast to CMM, Bootstrap is not freely available. The Bootstrap Institute operates the method (see: www.bootstrap-institute.com). One of the major differences between CMM and Bootstrap is the emphasis that Bootstrap places on the strength and weakness profile of an organization in contrast to the maturity levels of CMM. A software-developing organization does not need to master all processes to achieve a higher level. All processes are analysed to see whether the organization implements them adequately. Apart from the primary development processes such as requirements analysis, design, implementation and testing, Bootstrap also investigates supporting processes. Examples of these are project management, quality management, configuration management and, in particular, the generic management practices such as the relationship with customers and users, human resource management and process improvement. Assessments using Bootstrap have been conducted in many European countries and abroad. The data of those assessments are gathered anonymously by the Bootstrap Institute into a database for analyses. The large amount of data allows for comparing analyses and benchmarking. A specific organization can be compared to the general 'state-of-affairs' in its market.

SPICE

ISO15504 / SPICE

In 1998/1999, ISO published the nine documents that make up ISO15504. These technical reports deal with software process assessment. They are the tangible result of SPICE (Software Process Improvement and Capability dEtermination). This project was initiated in 1993 following a study by ISO, which established the need for a standard for the assessment of software development organizations. Under SPICE, lessons from existing assessment methods (including CMM, Bootstrap and Trillium) are used – particularly the practical experience gained with these methods. SPICE focuses on the software development process as a basis for improving that process (process improvement) and with a view to determining and improving the quality of the supplier in the software producer/software consumer relationship (capability determination). A large number of organizations, in over 20 countries worldwide, contributed to the development of SPICE by producing materials or by testing them in practice. Through the use of the Internet and regular meetings, it was possible for some nine documents to be delivered in 1997, within a relatively short space of time (in ISO terms). The SPICE consortium continues to work on the development of these documents, particularly on the basis of the experience gained during the third phase of the trials. The activities are being coordinated for Europe by the European Software Institute (ESI) in Bilbao (see: www.esi.es/Projects/SPICE.html). Information about SPICE is also available on the official SPICE website: www.sqi.gu.edu.au/spice or the website of SUGaR – the SPICE User Group: wwwsel.iit.nrc.ca/spice. ISO15504 consists of the following nine documents (Figure 29.3):

1. ***Concepts and introductory guide***: This provides an overview of the concepts and ideas that are fundamental to SPICE. An overview of the documents delivered by SPICE and how they interrelate is also provided.

2. ***A reference model for processes and process capability***: This describes a two-dimensional reference model, which can be used to write up the result of an assessment. The reference model comprises a group of processes and a framework for evaluating the maturity of the processes.

3. ***Performing an assessment***: This describes the requirements which an assessment needs to satisfy in order for the results to be replicable, reliable and consistent.

FIGURE 29.3

The SPICE product set

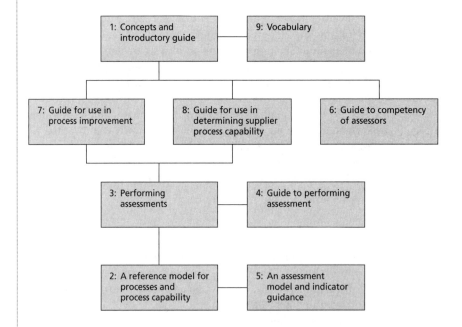

- **Guide to performing assessments**: This gives guidelines for performing assessments, interpreting the requirements, which assessments need to be satisfied (see previous document) according to the differing circumstances for assessments.
- **An assessment model and indicator guidance**: This describes an example of how an assessment is performed, based on and compatible with the reference model of document 2.
- **Guide to competency of assessors**: This comprises a description of the knowledge, skills, training and experience that an assessor must have in order to be able to perform assessments competently.
- **Guide for use in process improvement**: This sets out the manner in which assessments can be used in the software quality-improvement process. It indicates what steps may be distinguished in such a process and how they may be implemented in practice.
- **Guide for use in determining supplier process capability**: This shows how the result of an assessment may be used to demonstrate the capacities of the software developer in the software developer/customer relationship.
- **Vocabulary**: This comprises definitions of the terms used.

EFQM

The EFQM (European Foundation for Quality Management; see www.efqm.org) developed a model for evaluating the overall quality of an organization. The model is a general one, not specifically designed for software development organizations. The primary objective of the model is to support organizations in carrying out self-assessment. A Dutch variant of this model is the INK Management model (NKM) which is promoted by the Dutch Quality Institute (Instituut Nederlandse Kwaliteit, website: www.ink.nl). The nine different key areas addressed by the NKM are shown in Figure 29.4. In the methods dealt with above, the emphasis is on the management of processes, although in some cases peripheral areas (particularly resource management) are also included. NKM is markedly broader in scope. On the other hand, NKM is more a descriptive model, which provides a firm basis for assessment but is less helpful on the matter of how a particular quality level (e.g. the next one) can be achieved.

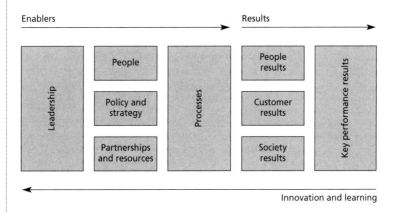

FIGURE 29.4 Areas of consideration of EFQM

29.4 Product

ISO9126

When the term 'quality' is used in relation to a software product, the speaker is often alluding to the functionality offered and the absence of defects after the product has been released. Often, however, these are not the characteristics that determine the quality of the software as far as users are concerned. They may, for example, be interested in the product's user-friendliness, availability and/or its performance over time. Attention to these quality characteristics is, therefore, essential in any communication between users and developers of software products. An essential precondition for this is that both parties know what is meant by such characteristics. A framework of terms is, therefore, required for the specification and validation of the quality characteristics for software products. The current ISO9126 ('Quality characteristics and guidelines for their use') provides definitions of quality characteristics (ISO/IEC, 2000). This standard defines six characteristics and the appendix to the standard defines a number of sub-characteristics for each characteristic. ISO is currently working on new versions of this standard. SERC,

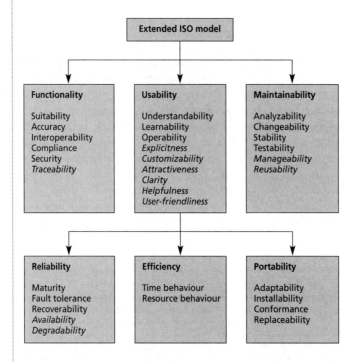

FIGURE 29.5

Quality characteristics of software products

in collaboration with a number of other parties, carried out two projects as part of the QUINT ('Quality in Information Technology') programme with a view to producing a framework of terms for the quality of software products. The results of these two projects are described in van Zeist *et al.* (1996). QUINT led to the quality model, described in ISO9126, being extended. QUINT added a further eleven characteristics which have, in practice, proven to be useful additions. Figure 29.5 provides an overview of the hierarchy of quality characteristics (characteristics added by QUINT are shown in italics). Apart from expanding the model by the addition of a number of characteristics, indicators, measuring scales and measurements, instructions have also been introduced. Practice has shown these to be the aids that enable software characteristics to be specified and validated. An indicator is a measurable property of a software product, which provides an indication of the degree to which a given characteristic has been achieved. Mean Time Between Failures, for example, is an indication of the availability of the product. For each of the indicators the measuring scale, which can be used to measure it, is given, as are the instructions for measuring each indicator. The book (van Zeist *et al.*, 1996) also details practical experiences of using the quality model.

ITIL

The quality of a product is determined not only by the product itself but also by the services supplied with the product. It is in this regard that mention should be made of ITIL – the IT Infrastructure Library. This consists of a collection of handbooks dealing with the practice of IT Service Management. Information about ITIL may be obtained from the official ITIL website: www.itil.co.uk.

29.5 People

People-CMM

In addition to the CMM, SEI – the Software Engineering Institute (see: www.sei.cmu.edu) has also developed People-CMM (also known as P-CMM; see: www.sei.cmu.edu/cmm-p). This is a framework that is comparable with CMM, the aim of which is to develop and manage the knowledge, experience and motivation of employees in the organization. Just as in CMM, the maturity of the organization with regard to human resource management is charted and improvement priorities are indicated.

PSP

In addition to activities designed to improve the software development process and the software product, increasing consideration has been given to improving the capacities of individual software developers. PSP – Personal Software Process – in particular focuses on this. PSP was also developed by the father of CMM, Watts Humphrey, who described it in 1995 (see also: www.sei.cmu.edu/tsp/psp.html). The purpose of PSP is to make individual software developers aware of their own software development process, in order to improve the quality of that process, its predictability and the quality of the result. Developers are taught to analyse and measure their work and to set themselves personal targets for improvement. PSP is introduced on the basis of a training course, which offers the opportunity to learn and apply PSP.

TSP

In 1999, Watts Humphrey *et al.* published a book in which they describe TSP – Team Software Process (see also: www.sei.cmu.edu/tsp). This is the third (intermediate) level (after CMM for the entire software development organization and PSP for the individual software engineer) at which the processes are mapped and improved. It is claimed that these three methods combined can reinforce each other. It will be interesting to see if practical experience provides evidence for the claim.

29.6 Performance

GQM

Metrics also need to be used in order to gain insight into the software development process ('to measure is to know') and to help direct the process on the basis of the measurements made. One of the most common errors made in introducing metrics programmes within software development organizations is that a wide range of data are collected without knowing how the results of measurements are to be put to use. The result is that the measurement results are not actually used and the measurement programme fails. The GQM – Goal Question Metric – paradigm of Basili *et al.* 1994; (a detailed description can also be found at: www.gqm.nl) tackles this problem by using a structured approach to the introduction of a metrics programme. First the objectives are set for the software development process and the products which will result from it. These objectives are refined in a number of questions, which are then detailed in a metric that is intended to provide answers to the questions posed. GQM distinguishes six steps in the process of introducing a metrics programme itself. The first step is to analyse the existing situation. This serves as a basis for the following step, when the objectives are identified and described. These are then set out in a GQM plan with questions and metrics. In the fourth step, the final plan for carrying out the measurements is drawn up, which also defines the environment in which the measurements will be collected and analysed. In the fifth step the plan is actually implemented and the measurement data are collected, validated and analysed. That information is then used to establish an improvement programme.

Productivity

An increasing number of commercial tools are appearing on the market, which can be used to determine the productivity of a software development organization. Various data are collected on software development projects: the effort required, running time, the size of the product developed (in terms of lines of code or function points), the quality of the product (in terms of the number of faults discovered during development and/or after delivery) and a number of characteristics of the project (e.g. the development environment and the knowledge and experience of the development team). Some of these tools contain an extensive database with data on actual projects. By adding data from one's own organization and by the use of statistical analysis, it is possible to compare the organization's productivity with the data in the database. Using statistical analysis, it is possible to make better estimates when scheduling projects. Some tools allow a comparison to be made between the actual status of a project in progress with the project schedule. The tool can then show whether the project is still on schedule, running a little late, or whether drastic measures need to be taken if the project is still to produce results within an acceptable time span. Examples of such tools, in random order, are: Estimate by SPC – Software Productivity Centre (see: www.spc.ca), KnowledgePLAN from SPR – Software Productivity Research (see: www.spr.com) and SLIM from QSM – Quantitative Software Management (see: www.qsm.com).

29.7 Finally

This overview of methods for quality improvement of software development already shows that the topic is in the spotlight. It is not only research and theoretical work, but it is rooted in the daily practice and problems of software development. None of the described methods is a silver bullet that solves all your problems but they can guide you to further improvement. An increasing number of software-developing organizations are aware that they not only have to invest in the technical infrastructure, but also and even more in the organizational infrastructure and its improvement. The number of companies that actually use one or more of the described methods is growing. If you do not use them, your competitors will!

Acknowledgements

This contribution is partially funded by the European Commission under ESSI-project 27700 ESPINODENL and the Dutch Ministry of Economic Affairs. The goal of ESPINODENL is to facilitate knowledge and experience exchange regarding 'Software Best Practice' in the Netherlands and the Dutch-speaking part of Belgium.

The main part of this chapter was written while the author was employed as project manager by the Software Engineering Research Centre (SERC), the Netherlands.

 ## Literature

Basili, V.R., Caldiera, G. and Rombach, H.D. (1994) *The Goal–Question–Metric Approach*, Institute for Advanced Computer Studies, Department of Computer Science, University of Maryland.

Humphrey, W.S. (1990) *Managing the Software Process*, SEI Series in Software Engineering, Addison Wesley Publishing Company, ISBN 0-201-18095-2, August.

Humphrey, W.S. (1995) *A Discipline for Software Engineering*, SEI Series in Software Engineering, Addison-Wesley Publishing Company, ISBN 0-201-54610-8.

Humphrey, W.S., Lovelace, M. and Hoppes, R. (1999) *Introduction to the Team Software Process*, SEI Series in Software Engineering, Addison-Wesley Publishing Company, ISBN 0-201-47719-X, August.

ISO/IEC (2000) Quality characteristics and guidelines for their use, ISO9126.

Kuvaja P. *et. al.* (1993) 'BOOTSTRAP: Europe's assessment method', *IEEE Software*, 10(3), 93–95.

Kuvaja P., Similä, J., Krzanik, L., Bicego, A., Saukkonen, S. and Koch G. (1994) *Software Process Assessment & Improvement – The BOOTSTRAP Approach*, Blackwell, ISBN 0631 19663-3.

Paulk, M.C., Curtis, B., Chrissis, M. and Weber, C.V. (1993) *Capability Maturity Model for Software, Version 1.1*, technical report, CMU/SEI-93-TR-24, Software Engineering Institute – SEI, Pennsylvania, USA, February 1993.

van Solingen, R. and Berghout, E. (1999) *The Goal/Question/Metric Method; A Practical Guide for Quality Improvement of Software Development*, McGraw-Hill, ISBN 007-709553-7, March.

van Zeist, B., Hendriks, P., Paulussen, R. and Trienekens, J. (1996) *Kwaliteit van softwareprodukten; praktijkervaringen met een kwaliteitsmodel*, Kluwer Bedrijfswetenschappen, Deventer, ISBN 90-267-2430-6, May, in Dutch.

Review of part 4

More and more often, today's IT manager is 'off the track of the IT organization'. Increasingly, the IT department has to add value to the organization's core business through professionalization, transformation, customer orientation and the deployment of new technologies. And that is more than a full day's work for many an IT manager. So it is not surprising that he or she looks for help. In 1995, KPMG developed a growth model which shows the development phases of an IT organization, places them in logical order and describes the relationships between the various phases. Delen *et al.* describe this in their chapter, **The future of the IT organization**. The model, the World Class IT Maturity Model for IT organizations, uses both ITIL definitions for arranging activities in processes and also a maturity level such as is used for instance in the Capability Maturity Model and Nolan's staged model. It is typically a management tool for improving the quality of service.

An interesting remark made by the authors is their perception of the gap between service-oriented and customer-driven processes, respectively stages 3 and 4 in their model. They conclude that the steps below the service-oriented level will each take no more than a year on average, but the step towards a customer-driven organization will cost far more time. The change that is necessary for this step requires a more fundamental change in the organization. This observation of the authors is supported by several contributions in this Guide, e.g. in terms of the cultural aspects that are dealt with in parts 6 and 7.

The model presented by Delen *et al.* is illustrated with some cases that show how the model helps in practical analysis. Although the structured presentation of the model doesn't really require such illustrations – it is clear in itself – this makes the model even more understandable.

In **Professionalization of ICT-management organizations: a roadmap for ICT managers**, Blauwhof *et al.* have considered the subject of developing the 'excellent IT organization'. In this case ITIL is replaced by new, extended reference models with a far wider scope. They used the Dutch INK model (Dutch Quality Institute, a government institute) as a base. The INK model is based on the EFQM model but adds a maturity philosophy to it. It distinguishes three simple phases: doing/doing things right/doing the right things. This maturity approach is again a stepwise approach to quality improvement, this time based upon two dimensions:

- Deming's PDCA cycle is used in the INK model: by applying the Deming cycle in an iterative way a certain maturity level of organizational development can be achieved.

- In the staged growth model of INK, the next stage is not reached by trying to get there in one big step: it takes several smaller steps to grow into the next higher level.

Blauwhof *et al.* adopted this technique for IT service organizations and translated it excellently, adding many practical cases as illustrations. In this way they determined adequate requirements for IT organizations to step up the maturity ladder, creating a roadmap for organizational improvement.

This roadmap isn't completely finished, however, since the specifications for transition to stages 4 and 5 are still missing. On the other hand, this does not matter too much: how many IT service organizations are even at level 3 today? The authors still have plenty of time to finish their work.

In **Improvement of the test process using TPI®**, Koomen and Pol emphasize the need for a well-structured test process, to be able to achieve high quality in service delivery. They do so by offering a test process that fits modern perceptions of process management, very compatible with ITIL structures. In fact, the test process can be regarded as part of the Change Management process domain, according to ITIL definitions. Although the authors have been writing about their approach for several years now, their perception of the test process aligns with the latest developments in service level management: they state the necessity of a very early involvement of the test process in the creation of new (versions of) infrastructure, comparable to the involvement of Operations in the early stages of development. This is an exponent of the proactive nature of the test process.

Another aspect of the latest views on process management is the commitment and motivation of people involved. The authors have emphasized the crucial role of continuous commitment and motivation for some years now. Thus they show that they have a very good appreciation of the human factor, now being recognized as the major component in tackling company security issues. As in security, the test process is highly dependent on the behaviour of people. A reasonably high quality of products can be achieved simply by discipline of the people involved.

The well-structured TPI model uses components that are well known and widely accepted in other fields, such as the Deming cycle and the CMM model for quality improvement, self-assessment support, best practice evaluations, and *kaizen* step-by-step improvement, making it a valuable contribution to all involved in providing high-quality service in IT. Testing clearly is a profession.

In **Securing information now or never**, Griffioen and van der Wel state that there is no simple recipe for dealing with information security issues. An analytical approach tends to help in such cases, and so the authors start decomposing the problem. They start by investigating the roles in the organization and their respective tasks in information security. From that moment on, the focus is on the organization. The step-by-step method of improvement that they present is defined in terms of management and organization, and typically describes the learning curve that an organization will go through when tackling the information security responsibility. Thus the path is made very practical.

Griffioen and van der Wel make room for ITIL in their approach, illustrating the level for the introduction of ITIL procedures (or similar, as they say). A focus on costs comes in at a higher level as well: first the security activities should be under control, then you can start managing their cost. At the highest level, security issues are integrated in the complete end-to-end chain of activities. This is similar to other aspects of management where the operations interest is embedded in the organization: in the development phase many operations demands should be taken into account, making the result of the chain manageable, not least in terms of cost (compare Koomen and Pol regarding testing issues). This approach is also reflected in several of the frameworks in part 1 – e.g. in R2C, which was the base for ASL.

The authors state that there is an optimum level of control for an organization, depending on its dependency on information supply. In this way, the cost of getting in control can be limited to that of the optimum level. Awareness is the keyword throughout this approach. Information security management cannot be achieved through sophisticated technology alone; it is – and it remains – human work.

Within the total spectrum of information technology management, the development of software occupies only part of the spectrum. Nevertheless, software development has attracted most of the attention in the field of information management for decades now. On the other hand, software development is one of the greatest risk factors because huge quantities of money are still disappearing into software development projects which do not provide the required quality within the planned time specification. Quality management of software development poses the question of how the quality of the software process and the software product can be improved. In **Quality of software development**, Paul Hendriks outlines the most important developments in the field of the software developer. The results are based on the development achieved in this field in recent decades. Elements from that world, such as the staged maturity model of CMM, have gained influence in other parts of the IT field in the meantime, as is illustrated in the introduction to this part. In the most recent developments, the field has linked up again with current general quality systems such as the model of the European Foundation for Quality Management (EFQM). None of the methods presented by Hendriks is a silver bullet, but in many cases the methods can provide assistance in efforts to obtain quality improvement. Although Hendriks illustrates that there are several widespread improvement programmes available in software development, the sector doesn't seem to adapt them intensively. Perhaps that is due to the fact that software houses have gained their money easily for decades now, and profits will come in even without a strong drive for quality improvement. For the operations environment this attitude is not applicable: they have a direct relation to the performance of the information-supporting mechanisms and they simply *have* to be successful. For that reason, it seems logical that improvement of IT service quality is initiated from the operations sector and not from the software sector.

Concluding remarks

Stepwise improvement has generally been accepted as the best, controlled method of organization change management. In IT it all goes back to Nolan's staged model of 1973. Although his ideas have been worked out similarly in various cases, it has led to different models.

Some of the models use four stages, as Nolan did the first time: Initiation/Contagion/Control/Integration. Others use five stages, e.g. Delen *et al.*: Technology-led/Controlled/Service-oriented/Customer-driven/Business-driven. Or Griffioen and Van der Wel: Ad-hoc/Spearhead/Managed by departments/Strategically managed/Proactively managed. And also the much applied CMM: Initial/Repeatable/Defined/Managed/Optimized.

Some use even six or more stages, e.g. SPICE: Not performed/Performed informally/Planned and tracked/Well defined/Quantitatively controlled/ Continuously improving. In Part 1 we find another six-stage model associated with IPW: the IPW Stadia Model, which also added a level 0 for initial stages: Not performed/Not defined/Monitored/Controlled/Proactive/Improving.

Whatever the number of stages, all models use a comparable growth model, from 'not performed' up to 'completely in control and continuously improving'.

This search for improvement mechanisms is a sign of a maturing market. By figuring out how to improve your organization, the discipline itself is no longer an issue, and that's what has been gained in the past decade.

part 5

Processes

Introduction to the theme

Processes are very popular nowadays in the world of IT Service Management. Many process models in the IT Service Management field have seen the light since the day that Hammer and Champy (1993) introduced Business Process Re-engineering (BPRE) into the world of management professionals. Their approach was one of a very drastic and almost revolutionary change in management style: processes should be revised radically to make them customer focused; empowerment of the caseworkers is essential; and IT support becomes a crucial factor.

We all know what has become of BPRE. It must have been disappointing for Hammer and Champy to see that most of the BPRE projects were unsuccessful. The BPRE movement experienced a quick death.

On the other hand, the focus on business processes and customers has – from that moment – never disappeared from the minds of managers. Processes and customer focus are very much alive in various management models. If we look at the very well-known IT Infrastructure Library (ITIL) best practices (see the chapter on ITIL in part 1 of this book), we see these elements clearly present in its structure. The structure of ITIL contains a number of best practices which are formulated as processes. Service Level Management, Incident Management and Release Management are examples.

In this part, a series of chapters is presented which have subjects very closely related to processes, in the sense of detailing or criticizing known processes and presenting quite new ones.

Content

This part contains five chapters, which elaborate on a wide range of Service Management processes.

Service Level Management
Rocky Kostick, Justin Williams and Matt Arnold

An integrated environment for managing software maintenance projects
Francisco Ruiz, Mario Piattini and Macario Polo

Kwintes project: results of a multidisciplinary research project in the field of IT Service Management
L. J. Ruijs

Integrated life-cycle management: optimizing ICT service through the central positioning of ICT objects
Wim van den Boomgaard and Ton Pijpers

Hunting the Mammoth
Jan F. Bouman and Michel van Dijk

A review of part 5 follows thereafter.

Reading instructions

Two of the five chapters presented in this part, i.e. **Kwintes** and **Service Level Management**, have the same subject process: Service Level Management. Both chapters take quite an innovative holistic look at Service Level Management. The other three chapters can be read independently of each other.

Introduction to the chapters

In **Service Level Management,** Kostick *et al.* plead for a holistic approach to Service Level Management. In this case, that means the inclusion of the organization domains People, Processes and Technology. This put them very much in line with many other approaches to service management. Another good example of the holistic approach is the quality model of the European Foundation for Quality Management (EFQM). In these approaches there is an emphasis on organization domains such as Processes, Human Resource Management and Asset Management, but also on Policy and Strategy, and Leadership. In their holistic approach, Kostick *et al.* describe three important organization areas, which deserve the attention of an IT organization.

In **An integrated environment for managing software maintenance projects**, Ruiz *et al.* analyse the work that builds up to some 60% of the professional time spent by software developers: software maintenance. This is an important sector that has been ignored for many years: for decades all the attention in the field of software development was reserved for software *development* methods. It is only in the past few years that attention has shifted to maintenance. This trend is comparable to the fast-growing attention the field of service management is getting in the world of IT. It is a typical aspect of the fact that people have always been eager to develop new techniques and methods, and were not interested in the presumed 'dull' environment of maintenance and exploitation. Nowadays IT specialists seem to find more and more satisfaction in the reward that can be found by emphasizing the service nature of IT, with customer satisfaction as the ultimate goal. In this chapter the MANTIS Big-E Environment is presented, an integrated framework of conceptual, methodological and software tools that supports the Software Maintenance process.

In **Kwintes project**, Ruijs – on behalf of the multidisciplinary project team – presents the results of a research project on the application of the well-known Capability

Maturity Model in the field of IT Service Management. The four phases of the service management lemniscate, as developed in the earlier project 'Concrete Kit', were further developed and adapted to make it possible to measure performance. Based on this result and on the application of the growth models already mentioned, an IT Service Capability Maturity Model was formulated. This model has one goal: to support improvement programmes in IT service organizations.

Another interesting management topic is control of the life cycle of information systems. This is a typical strategic process, in which important decisions are made on development, exploitation and phasing-out of information systems. In **Integrated life-cycle management**, van den Boomgaard *et al.* describe a Service Management reference framework for the management of ICT objects, as developed for the computer centre of the Dutch national Treasury Department.

In **Hunting the mammoth**, Bouman and van Dijk make some criticism where the ITIL book on Cost Management is concerned. Their thesis: 'Cost management without an analysis of the added value is like Russian roulette' is the basis of the chapter. Because every IT manager knows it is a pretty tough exercise to quantify added value, the authors have developed the so-called 'survival web' to measure added value. This methodology is explained in the chapter by means of two cases.

Literature

Hammer, M. and Champy, J. (1993) *Reengineering the Corporations: A Manifesto for Business Revolution*, Harper Business, New York.

30 Service Level Management

Rocky Kostick, Justin Williams and **Matt Arnold**
Synet Service Corporation

Summary

In summary, successful Service Level Management (SLM) requires a holistic, business-driven approach that integrates enterprise-wide process, technology and organization. These enterprise SLM processes need to be enabled, not driven, by technology. Successful SLM also requires knowledge of what elements need to be measured, how to collect and measure them and how to report their performance in a meaningful and manageable fashion.

Focus on getting the right metric for the management task at hand. This implies that the task is understood and the desired solution has been well defined. Ignore the urge to create a solution and then look for a problem to solve with it by collecting every piece of data, all the time, with the thought that someday it may be needed.

SLM also requires the IT department to be aware of how they impact the business as a whole. In other words, how they contribute to, or detract from, the business's productivity, quality, customer service or cost. IT needs to enable the business to be successful.

The bottom line is this: SLM is about more than reactionary management and producing compliance reports. It is the translation of business strategies and requirements into technology service delivery and infrastructure information. It is IT's responsibility to deliver meaningful information that the business user wants and needs, when they need it – and SLM ensures that both IT and the business units understand and agree upon what that meaningful information is.

30.1 Introduction

One of the struggles facing IT organizations and the businesses they serve is the lack of effective Service Level Management (SLM). Many IT organizations are still reacting to business needs rather than proactively delivering the services required to support and enable business strategies. Although many people believe that SLM is important, few organizations are realizing success with their SLM implementations.

By understanding the power and scope of SLM, you can build an effective strategy that allows IT operations to provide the business units what they need – real-time information that is both meaningful and manageable and available when it's needed. SLM must be driven by business need, or business impact. As more and more companies are developing e-commerce and e-business strategies, SLM is becoming mission-critical in implementing these strategies. As these new e-commerce strategies are changing the face of business, they are also changing the face of IT. The line between business and IT is becoming blurred – it is no longer easy to determine where business ends and IT begins.

Given this new era of e-business and IT's changing role in the organization, it is important to keep in mind the mutually important and valuable outcomes of effective SLM as it relates to the business. Those outcomes are increased productivity and quality, improved customer service and reduced costs.

Background

SLM is a very trendy and timely topic among business and IT professionals. However, SLM goes beyond the development of service level agreements (SLAs) and management compliance reports. Typically related to the effective deployment and management of mission-critical applications, SLM is a strategy intended to provide (and, in many cases, guarantee) levels of service from IT to business users who rely on IT applications to support their mission within the enterprise.

SLM has been used in the IT industry in one form or another for many years, usually by organizations that have realized the necessity for a balanced, service-delivery approach within IT. Service Level Management is based upon the philosophy of defining, achieving and maintaining required levels of IT service to the business user within the enterprise. Unfortunately, few IT organizations have adopted Service Level Management as a key strategy toward meeting their stated objectives within the larger enterprise. Even more unfortunate is the fact that on the path toward adoption of the distributed computing model, many organizations have left behind the orientation toward service while they struggle to gain control over new and somewhat immature technologies.

Like any set of key management processes, successful SLM requires a commitment at the highest levels of management within IT organizations. Although the rigour of adopting and implementing new management practices may seem less than appealing at this juncture in technology evolution, it appears that the alternatives may be even less appealing to those who are charged with delivering IT services to their respective companies. Failure to implement SLM or similar practices is just delaying the inevitable – and it will only get harder as the pace of technological evolution continues to accelerate.

Point of view

Our point of view is that it is imperative that organizations take a holistic, business-focused approach to SLM. In turn, this approach will yield:

- greater return on the technology investment;
- greater success in meeting the business user's expectations of technology;
- an IT organization with greater awareness of technology's impact on the business and IT's ability to impact productivity, quality, customer service and cost.

This chapter discusses, at a high level, our point of view regarding SLM as it impacts large, data-intensive organizations, by looking at the following topics:

- what SLM is;
- why use SLM;
- how to approach SLM;
- the common pitfalls regarding SLM.

30.2 Service Level Management is …

Before an organization can implement SLM, it needs to know what SLM is. We define Service Level Management as the holistic, business-focused management of converging IT and business unit perspectives. SLM ensures that business initiatives are enabled by the effective implementation of technology and that the information necessary to make business decisions is produced and presented in real time.

Fundamentally, the result of SLM is effectively using the data and information produced via the business units and IT processes to enable the organization to make informed, intelligent business decisions. In today's e-business environment, to be successful and stay competitive business units and IT must work in harmony to be nimble, efficient and effective.

SLM needs to be holistic and business-focused

The bottom line is that IT should have a holistic, business-focused attitude to the management of service levels. We believe that three critical results should be expected from effective SLM:

- **A higher return on investment in IT expenditures** By using the needs of the IT customer (in today's environment, this can be an internal or external customer) to specify the capabilities and behaviour of the IT infrastructure, costs and business benefits are understood early in the cycle. Excess capacities can be avoided, and proper ongoing management activities are understood, and can be planned for and staffed appropriately.

  The case for higher returns becomes clear when the IT infrastructure is managed throughout the life cycle of applications (design, building and ongoing management). Instead of reacting to problems, the organization, as a whole, can be more proactive by planning for resource needs from the design and build stages through to ongoing management of delivery and service levels.

- **Greater success through proper expectation setting** By working with the business user during requirements definition and planning activities, user needs become known and understood. In this way, IT analysts can help the business understand whether their expectations can be met within the fiscal constraints of the organization. Because the business unit's input was considered from the beginning, they are now 'part of the solution', rather than 'part of the problem'.

  When functionality and usability demands are combined with performance requirements, business and IT are more closely aligned on the expectations of a particular application. It is important to look beyond functionality and usability. If the performance requirements are not met, cost and inefficiency are built into the process rather than removed. By using rational design and measurement requirements that are designed, built and managed by business and IT, expectations are set and there will be fewer IT-related failures.

- **Business impact** The IT organization of any business is there to enable the bottom line of that particular business to grow. IT and the business units must work together to understand and positively promote the outcomes of productivity, quality, customer satisfaction and cost. These outcomes can appear to be mutually exclusive; however, if the benefits of each outcome are maximized then the benefits of the whole will be increased. For example, you can build an IT infrastructure that can handle more Web-based transactions faster (productivity), with greater accuracy (quality) and security than your competition. While this type of infrastructure is highly desirable, the cost can be significant. It is important to realize the synergies and trade-offs among productivity, quality, customer satisfaction and cost by working with the business units to understand their impact on the business.

SLM can be seen as having a cause-and-effect impact on the IT infrastructure. In other words, SLM becomes harder to do as the infrastructure grows in complexity, and IT infrastructure seems to become more unwieldy if there is ineffective Service Level Management. However, as companies get their arms around SLM, the ability to manage the infrastructure increases.

As technology becomes more complex and more distributed, there are more break-points and more things that need to be planned for from both a business and IT perspective. While the business should not be burdened with reasons why distributed systems are more difficult to manage, the needs of the business will have to be translated into measurable and manageable actions across the IT organization.

30.3 Service Level Management should be used to...

SLM should be used to ensure that technology is enabling the organization to deliver more value as a whole. By moving beyond a collection of service level agreements and truly delivering SLM, organizations can align the business units and IT to support the goals of the organization.

SLM goes beyond service level agreements (SLAs). However, many organizations consider SLM and SLA to be synonymous. SLAs are documents and reports prepared explicitly to define various service levels that IT is expected to deliver. Usually, SLAs are produced (per business unit, per application, per region, etc.) in an ad hoc manner that lacks harmony and consistency across the organization. Additionally, SLAs are used more to defend a particular part of the IT organization rather than align business and IT. SLAs need to be unified and comprehensive, as well as driven by business need. Business does not want or need a myriad of SLAs across the various units of IT. Business needs a few comprehensive SLAs that define the deliverables of the IT organization in terms meaningful to the business.

Through effective SLM, expectations are set from both cost and performance perspectives by having IT and the business units work together. Through the cooperative managing of expectations, there are fewer failures due to missed expectations and confusion over semantics.

30.4 Service Level Management approach

Our philosophy is to take a holistic approach to SLM by addressing the organization, process and technology components of IT operations and the business units (Figure 30.1).

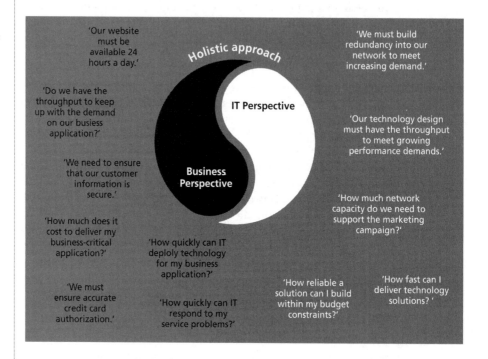

FIGURE 30.1
Illustration of the balance in perspectives that needs to be part of a holistic approach to SLM

Process

SLM requires integrated enterprise-wide processes that cut across all parts of the IT organization (as demonstrated in Figure 30.2).

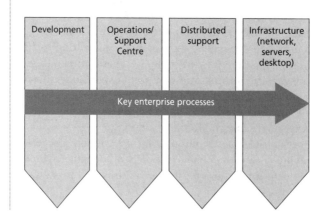

FIGURE 30.2
Some of the typical silos in an IT organization. The arrow represents the key processes that need to cut across the IT organization

30 ■ Service Level Management

To reduce the impact of the silo IT structure, key processes (such as Problem Management, Change Management, and Asset Management – see Figure 30.2) must be viewed end-to-end across the entire IT organization.

Some of the key processes include:

- **Problem Management** The discipline of taking actions to identify, record, diagnose and correct problems as they are brought to the attention of IT support personnel through either events or calls.
- **Change Management** The discipline of managing enhancements to the technology infrastructure. The goal is to meet user requirements while ensuring that change does not adversely impact the performance of the entire environment.
- **Asset Management** The function that tracks the inventory of IT components from a physical and financial perspective. This includes managing the asset through the entire life cycle, leasing, maintenance contracts and cost allocation.
- **Request Management/Customer Fulfilment** Initiates, processes and approves user requests for the acquisition, modification, transfer or disposal of hardware and software products.

These key processes are a component of the infrastructure necessary to support and enable the business needs. While the business units are not concerned with the details of problem, change or asset management, those processes need to be designed to support business requirements, both internal and external. The key processes can be viewed as a closed-loop system. For example, poor asset management will translate into poor change management. Poor change management will put a great burden on the problem management ability of the organization. On the other hand, when the key processes, or management disciplines, are being managed well, other disciplines can run more effectively. When an organization is doing a solid job of managing IT assets, change management should improve (can the enterprise successfully upgrade to NT or do those desktops in business area X need more RAM to support the NT upgrade?). When these things are known and managed, problem management can become more stable, more predictable and more effective.

While it may seem obvious, there are many examples of poorly managed IT processes that do not support the business objectives. A real-life example can be seen in the C/Net (2/5/99) story about a major online brokerage. Users of this online brokerage were barred from trading and viewing their accounts for half an hour. That problem was due to technical problems that had plagued the site for three days in a row. The outage was an aftershock from software changes that went awry. The business impact of this was tremendous – not only from immediate, real revenue loss but also from branding and image management issues that followed. This online brokerage lost customers because they could not use the technology or receive timely technical support. The poor change management translated into a support strain – unpredicted spikes in e-mails and calls to the help desk. Owing to the strain on the support environment (call and problem management), the company planned thereafter to add another 200 people to its customer service staff.

When key IT processes are designed from a broad, high-level perspective that supports the business, the people involved can understand their roles and objectives relative to supporting the goals of the organization. Cost efficiency and productivity gains can also be realized when key IT processes are managed effectively.

Organization

Most IT organizations are constructed and managed in a silo or stovepipe arrangement, as depicted in Figure 30.2, with poor cooperation among the silos. The stovepipes continue to multiply as IT moves further and further from the centralized 'glasshouse' model and becomes more decentralized through a distributed client–server environment. E-commerce business strategies and related support technology (more applications, more servers, Internet connections) increase the number of break-points in today's business environment. When it comes to dealing with the problems of technology, these break-points result in finger pointing and scapegoating within IT, failures and angry customers.

A critical success factor for SLM is executive ownership and sponsorship at the highest level of the organization. This ownership helps ensure the critical SLM activities are conducted at a level that is high enough to transcend many of the silos within an organization.

Along with the structure of departments within IT organizations, roles, responsibilities and objectives must be defined for the people working within the organization. Clearly defined roles regarding corporate strategy and business needs help make sure that IT is truly supporting and enabling the business. Some of the critical roles include executive sponsors, process owners and relationship managers. The executive sponsor(s) will ensure that various organizational barriers are removed from the SLM process.

Technology

As with all enterprise systems management disciplines, there are no 'silver bullets' when it comes to technology. The technology does not manage itself, at least not yet. With SLM, it will still be some time before companies see 'balanced' SLM from the tool perspective. META Group analyst John Warne (Director) does not expect a balanced SLM tool for a few years.

Currently, most tools, or point solutions, focus on the monitoring of particular elements. As these tools develop, the real value will be in the integration of various systems management tools and in the ability to perform effective event correlation. The performance of systems management tools is also critical. It is important that systems management applications do not consume excessive processing resources, thereby degrading response times and adding inefficiency. Additionally, the tool needs to help with reporting – one of the keys to proper SLM is doing the right reports. There is no need to report just for the sake of more data.

When working with the available technology, make sure that the SLM tool integrates with your systems management service-desk solutions, because SLM does not exist in a vacuum. It is also critical to develop business-driven service levels that are grounded in the IT organization's ability to measure those levels.

Service level objectives

Business needs drive the infrastructure. This is evident in the use of, and need for, service level objectives (SLOs). Service level objectives are a critical component in SLM. Basically, service level objectives are the interpretation of business needs into tangible, measurable IT services and objectives. Service level objectives are the by-product of the SLA process and are wholly owned by IT. These are the objectives that are defined by IT based on the service level agreements that have been negotiated with the business units. The business units do not need to know all the details or how it works – it just needs to work. Service level objectives help align IT to support those business initiatives and meet the SLA that has been defined by IT and the business units. These services and objectives must be managed during the design, build and manage phases of various IT initiatives.

Once the service level objectives have been determined for IT, they need to be further translated into coordinated action items and responsibilities for various parts of the IT organization (see Figure 30.3). The translation of business needs into service level objectives drives specific tangible, measurable services and objectives for IT operations, such as service delivery, systems management and reporting on various data elements. The source of the data needs to be determined, the applicable data needs to be collected and information needs to be derived to ensure that appropriate IT decisions, both strategic and tactical, can be made.

Operating level agreements

SLM requires translation of business needs into SLAs. SLAs require translation into service level objectives. SLOs require the establishment and management of operating level agreements (OLAs). OLAs are similar to SLAs, but they are established through IT

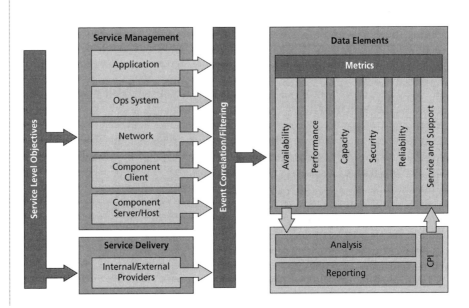

FIGURE 30.3
Illustration of the translation of service level objectives into coordinated tasks for various parts of operations (Systems Management, Service Delivery) by internal and external providers. The events then must be correlated, filtered and measured appropriately. The metrics and reports are then analysed to deliver continuous process improvement (CPI).

with both internal and external service providers. The OLAs help establish the expectations and parameters necessary to support SLAs. For example, if a fix for part of your infrastructure requires an external vendor (i.e. satellite, T1, etc.) who has contracted for three-hour resolution, IT must develop a service level agreement with that time frame built in. How much time will it take to develop a complete solution after the external provider has finished its task? These time frames and interdependencies need to be considered before the SLA can be developed and managed. For the objectives to be met, a solution involving all aspects of the infrastructure needs to be defined in order for the terms of the SLA to be met. See Figure 30.4.

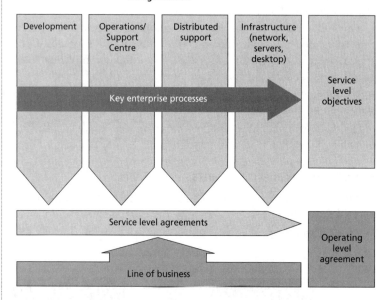

FIGURE 30.4
Illustration representing consistent, unified SLAs developed by both IT and the business units. The SLAs are then translated into objectives that IT needs to meet. Finally, operating level agreements must be made by both internal and external vendors to make sure that SLAs are met.

30.5 Common pitfalls of Service Level Management implementations

There are a few common SLM implementation pitfalls that can be easily avoided when one knows what to look for. The most common pitfalls fall into three categories:

How the organization treats SLM When organizations treat SLM as only another SLA exercise, another tool purchase, or just another way to measure the technology environment, they will most likely fail to realize the benefits that SLM has to offer. Obviously SLM goes beyond SLAs; it is more than measuring the technology environment. A tool alone cannot perform SLM. It takes a holistic approach that encompasses people, process and technology.

- ***Lack of a common vision for SLM*** Organizations typically lack a common vision, key enterprise processes viewed end-to-end and agreed-upon baseline metrics for SLAs, SLOs and OLAs. Additionally, many organizations do not have executive sponsorship and process owners necessary to ensure that SLM will be successful.
- ***Lack of business focus*** Closely related to lack of common vision, many IT departments are not in sync with the business direction of the overall organization. Clear understanding of business objectives and IT deliverables, through SLM, helps promote a healthy and profitable balance of the outcomes of productivity, quality, customer satisfaction (both internal and external) and cost. It is worth restating that when business objectives are understood up front and IT's ability to deliver to those objectives are understood, expectations can be properly managed throughout the process.

31 An integrated environment for managing software maintenance projects[1]

Francisco Ruiz, Mario Piattini and **Macario Polo**
University of Castilla, La Mancha, Spain

Summary

The objective of software engineering environments (SEEs) is to allow the integrated and automatic management of data and activities of a specific software process (ISO/IEC, 2000). In this chapter we present MANTIS, an extended environment whose aim is to help to improve the management of all the aspects that intervene in real-world software maintenance projects. MANTIS extends and broadens the concepts of SEE and methodology. MANTIS is a set of conceptual, methodological and software tools integrated in a coherent framework. These tools support the manual and automated realization of the activities that form the Software Maintenance Process (SMP).

31.1 Introduction

Traditionally, the software engineering community (scientists and professionals) have considered the maintenance process to be less important than the development process. This has been due to a number of different factors: technological, social, psychological etc. In recent years, however, everything that occurs once a software product has been delivered to users and clients has been receiving much more attention owing to the significant economic importance that it has in the information technology industry. The recent cases of the year 2000 effect and euro adaptation are proof of this.

Very recently, Rajlich and Bennet (2000) have made a new proposal of a software life cycle oriented towards increasing the importance of software maintenance (SM). These authors consider that, from a business point of view, a software product passes through the following five distinct stages:

1. *Initial development*: engineers build the first functioning version of the software product to satisfy initial requirements.
2. *Evolution*: engineers extend the capabilities of the software product to meet user needs. Iterative changes, modifications and deletions to functionality occur.
3. *Servicing (saturation)*: engineers make minor defect repairs and simple functional changes. During this stage, changes are both difficult and expensive because an appropriate architecture and a skilled work team are lacking.

4 *Phaseout (decline)*: the company decides not to undertake any more servicing, seeking to generate revenue, or other benefits, from the unchanged software product for as long as possible.

5 *Closedown*: the company shuts down the product and directs users to a replacement product, if one exists.

Several characteristics change substantially from one stage to another, including staff expertise, software architecture, software decay (the positive feedback, the loss of team expertise and the loss of architectural coherence) and economic benefits. From the point of view of the SMP, another important difference between one stage and another is the different frequency with which each type of maintenance is carried out. *Corrective* maintenance (correcting errors) is more usual in the servicing stage while *perfective* maintenance (making changes to functionality) is more frequent in the evolution stage. The other two types of maintenance (ISO/IEC, 1998), namely *adaptive* (changing the environment) and *preventive* (making changes to improve the quality properties and to avoid future problems), are usually considerably less frequent.

While the initial development stage is well documented using numerous well-known methods, techniques and tools, the other four stages (which correspond to SM) have been studied and analysed to a lesser degree. Moreover, unfortunately, the methodologies for the development process have difficulties of adaptation to the SMP because both processes have different characteristics (Ruiz *et al.*, 2000) and, therefore, the activities and tasks included may also be different and have a different instant or importance (Figure 31.1). Consequently, it is not unusual for the software industry to demand methodologies for controlling and managing this long and difficult stage, especially if we take into account the large number of legacy systems still being maintained (Briand *et al.*, 1998).

For these reasons, specific methodologies taking SMP into account are needed in order to achieve effective management of SM projects (Basili *et al.*, 1998). One of the first is MANTEMA (Polo *et al.*, 2000, 1999).

However, having said that, companies undertaking SM projects need a lot more than just a specific methodology. For software development projects, Cockburn (2000) included the following elements as minimum requirements: people, roles, skills, team, tools, techniques, processes, activities, milestones, work products, standards, quality measures and team values. With the same objective, and integrating these aspects and others in a more general framework, the MANTIS Big-E Environment

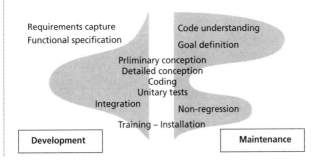

FIGURE 31.1

Development vs. Maintenance: differences

aims to define and construct an integrated environment for the management of SM projects. By using the nomenclature 'Big-E Environment' our intention is to emphasize the idea that MANTIS is broader than the concepts of:

- *methodology* in its usual sense, that is to say, a series of related methods and techniques.
- *software engineering environment* (SEE), that is to say, a collection of software tools used to support software engineering activities (ISO/IEC, 2000).

We believe that the principal advantage of MANTIS is that it integrates practically all the aspects that must be taken into account for directing, controlling and managing SM projects into one conceptual framework. This advantage is built upon the following features:

- a conceptual architecture that facilitates working with the significant complexity inherent in the management of SM projects;
- the integration of methods and techniques that have been specially developed for SMP (such as the MANTEMA technology) or adapted from the development process;
- the integration of horizontal and vertical tools by means of orientation to processes, based on the proposal *Process Sensitive Software Engineering Environment* (PSEE) and the use of standards for storage and interchange of data and metadata; and
- a process metamodel based on the international standards of ISO (ISO/IEC, AGS).

31.2 Generic characteristics of MANTIS

The MANTIS Big-E Environment for the integrated management of SM projects aims to integrate the following aspects, among others (see Figure 31.2):

- People with certain skills carry out certain roles in the project, working together in different teams (groups of people).
- These people use methodologies to construct products that conform to certain standards (norms) and satisfy quality measurements (criteria). The processes must also satisfy quality criteria.
- The methodologies require certain skills and tools. The tools facilitate conforming with the standards.
- The teams participate in activities (included in methodologies) that belong to processes encompassed by the project. Each activity undertaken helps to reach a milestone which indicates the progress of the project.

In each software maintenance project, the aspects included in the MANTIS Big-E Environment are considered from two different but complementary points of view (Derniame *et al.*, 1999):

- a real-world SMP that includes all the real activities needed to carry out the maintenance project; and
- an SMP metamodel, which is a representation of the real-world activities for guiding, enforcing or automating parts of that SMP.

FIGURE 31.2

Aspects considered in SM projects.

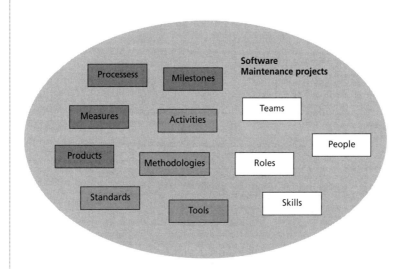

In order to achieve these objectives, the following general requirements have been defined in MANTIS:

- **Tool-oriented:** the services of MANTIS are supplied through software tools according to the philosophy of the integrated SEE. The integrated use of all these possible tools is advantageous as it increases productivity, reduces the possibility of errors and facilitates management, supervision and control. Although various proposals with these objectives in mind have been made (PCTE, ECMA/NIST, STARS etc.)[2] and their generic contributions and architectural models can be applied to the SMP, none of them takes into account the special characteristics of software maintenance.

- **Process-driven:** assuring consistency with the processes and activities described in the standards ISO12207, referring to the software life-cycle processes (ISO/IEC, 1995), and ISO14764, referring to the SMP (ISO/IEC, 1998). The orientation to processes is a very important vehicle for integration (Randall and Ett, 1995). In MANTIS, two types of integration can be dealt with simultaneously: that of the processes of the organization with the Big-E Environment and that of the tools and artefacts with the processes. This orientation is known as the Process Sensitive Software Engineering Environment (PSEE).

- **Role-based:** the organizational metamodel is based on the concept of role, also used in the MANTEMA methodology. Three roles (maintainer, customer and user) and several sub-roles have been designed.

- **Scalable:** the possibility of adaptation to the necessities of small, medium and big organizations. The tailoring process of ISO12207 is used for this.

- Selection of a **specific methodology** for the SMP, in this case MANTEMA (Polo *et al.*, 2000).

- **Support of the technical work** (more precisely the SMP) and the organizational and **management** activities (management processes). We consider that, like a manufacturing project, an SM project really consists of two types of processes: the SMP, and the management processes that provide the resources needed by the SMP and control it.

Use of the technology based on the XML standard (W3C, 2000) and *XML Metadata Interchange* (XMI) (OMG, 1999) for the data and metadata **repository**.

In Figure 31.3 we can see a summary of all the components that currently make up the MANTIS Big-E Environment. The principal components are described in the following sections, highlighting the most original aspects and those of most interest to organizations that must undertake SM projects.

FIGURE 31.3

Components of MANTIS Big-E Environment

CONCEPTUAL TOOLS
Conceptual architecture: based on MOF standard
Life-cycle processes of software: ISOs 12207 + 14764
Metamodel of SMP: Kitchenham *et al.* ontology
Process enactment metamodel: based on workflow
Measure metamodel: based on the IESE proposal

METHODOLOGICAL TOOLS
Methodologies: MANTEMA
Measures: specific suite of metrics for SMP
Interfaces with organizational processes: – Improvement based on the Niessink proposal – Project Management: based on the PMI proposal
Interfaces with support processes: – Audit – Quality Assurance – configuration Management

TECHNICAL (SOFTWARE) TOOLS
Horizontal Tool: MANTIS integrated tool
Vertical tools: MANTOOL, MANTICA, ...
Repository: based on XMI standard

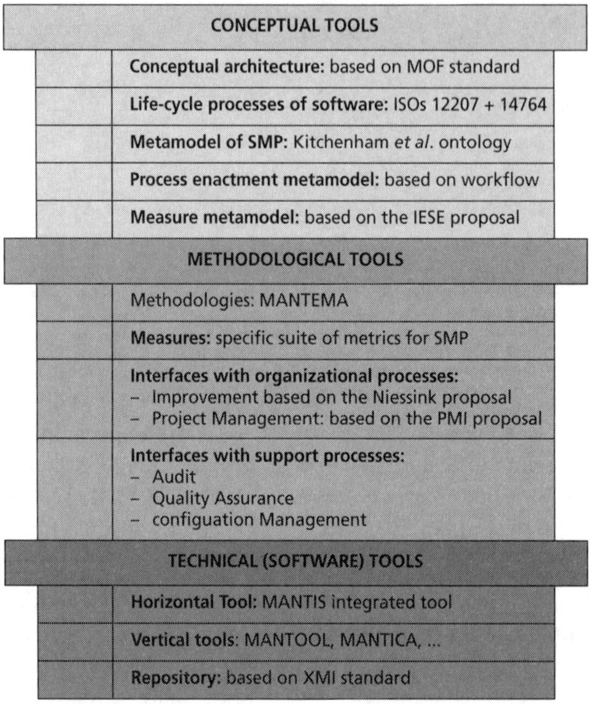

31.3 Conceptual architecture

An important principle of modern software engineering is the separation of a system into encapsulated layers which can mostly be specified, designed and constructed independently. Following this philosophy, in MANTIS four conceptual levels have been defined that are based on the MOF (Meta-Object Facility) standard for object-oriented modelling proposed by the Object Management Group (OMG, 2000). In Table 31.1 we can see these four levels of the MOF architecture and its adaptation to MANTIS.

Run-time instances of real-world and specific SM projects are found in level M0. The data handled at this level are instances of the concepts defined at the higher-level M1. The specific model used at level M1 is based on the MANTEMA methodology and a group of techniques adapted to the special characteristics of maintenance: effort estimation, risk estimation, process auditing (Ruiz *et al.*, 2000), etc. Level M2 corresponds

TABLE 31.1

Conceptual levels in MANTIS and MOF

Level	MOF	MANTIS	Example
M3	MOF model (Meta-metamodel)	MOF model	MOF class
M2	Metamodel	SMP metamodel	Activity
M1	Model	MANTEMA and other techniques (SMP concrete model)	Modification Request Study Activity
M0	Data	Instances of SMP (real-world concrete SM projects)	Modification request study no. 36 of the PATON project

to the SMP meta-model,[3] which we will discuss in the following section. In the upper conceptual level of MANTIS, M3, the SMP metamodel is represented in a MOF model. A MOF model is composed basically of two types of objects: MOF class and MOF association. Consequently, all the concepts represented in level M2 are now considered instances of MOF class or MOF association. For example, *Activity*, *Actor* and *Artefact* are instances of MOF class; and '*Activity uses Resource*' and '*Artefact is input of Activity*' are instances of MOF association.

As the level rises, we must work with increasingly abstract concepts. Between the concepts of one level and those immediately above it there are correspondences of the '*is-instance-of*' type. For example, the object '*modification request study no. 36 of the PATON project*' of level M0 is a run-time instance of the object '*Modification Request Study*' of level M1. In turn, the latter is an instance of the object '*Activity*' of level M2 and '*Activity*' is an instance of the MOF-class generic object.

By using standards for metamodelling (MOF) and for metadata interchange (XMI), we can achieve as flexible as possible an environment for defining and sharing models and metamodels. The inclusion of level M3 enables us to work with different versions of SMP metamodel, which is a requirement in order to be able to manage the process improvement.

31.4 Process metamodel

In MANTIS we propose the use of the MANTEMA methodology as a specific model (level M1) for the SMP, but organizations can use any other methodology or collection of techniques. The SMP metamodel of level M2, however, is generic and as a result must be appropriate for any situation or organization. Aiming at this generality, and also at standardization, in MANTIS, the SMP metamodel has been defined using the following basic contributions:

1. the software life-cycle processes model proposed by the standards ISO12207 and ISO14764;
2. the informal ontology proposed by Kitchenham *et al.* (1999);
3. the Workflow Reference Model of the Workflow Management Coalition (WfMC,1995); and
4. an adaptation of the IESE proposal for modelling of the measure sub-process (Becker-Kornstaedt and Webby, 1999).

ISO12207

In MANTIS, the ISO12207 standard is used to characterize the processes that can exist during the life cycle of a software product, what these processes are like and how they are related to each other. The MANTEMA methodology also uses this option because, as Pigoski (1996) says, 'ISO 12207 will drive the world software trade and will impact on maintenance'. For obvious reasons, of the five primary processes described in ISO (acquisition, supply, development, operation and maintenance), MANTIS only focuses on SMP. Nevertheless, among the methodological tools, interfaces with some of the eight supporting processes and the four organizational processes defined in ISO12207 are included. These interfaces will be discussed later. As well as the processes previously mentioned, ISO12207 includes the tailoring process which is used to carry out basic adaptations of this norm for a specific project and consequently helps to satisfy MANTIS's scalability requirement.

Ontology of SMP

The informal ontology proposed by Kitchenham *et al.* (1999) is used in MANTIS as a fundamental base for the SMP metamodel of level M2. This proposal is structured as several partial sub-ontologies referring to the maintained product, the maintenance activities, the maintenance procedure, the maintenance organization processes, and peopleware. In the MOF-based conceptual architecture used in MANTIS, each of these ontologies is a partial metamodel of level M2 which operates like a MOF package (similar to UML packages) in level M3.

In brief, each of these partial metamodels represents the following aspects of SM:

- *product* metamodel: how the software product is maintained and how it evolves with time;
- *activities* metamodel: how to organize activities for maintaining software and what kinds of activities they may be;
- *procedure* metamodel: how the methods, techniques and tools (either specific or shared with the development process) can be applied to the activities and how the resources are used in order to carry out these activities;
- *organization processes* metamodel: how the support and organizational processes (of ISO12207) are related to the SMP activities, how the maintainer[4] is organized, and what its contractual obligations are.
- *peopleware* metamodel: what skills and roles are necessary in order to carry out the activities, what the responsibilities of each one are and how the organizations that intervene in the process (maintainer, customer and user) relate to each other.

Figure 31.4 shows a summarized integrated view of these five partial meta-models (in UML diagram-class format). It is worth emphasizing that these metamodels take into account the fact that one of the major differences between development and SM is that development is requirement-driven and maintenance is event-driven; that is to say, the inputs that initiate a maintenance activity are unscheduled (random) events. In the MANTEMA methodology these events usually occur when the maintainer team receives

31 ■ An integrated environment for managing software maintenance projects

a problem report (PR) or a modification request (MR) which triggers the execution of the 'Study of the PR/MR' activity followed by other activities depending on the maintenance type that has to be carried out (Polo et al., 2000).

FIGURE 31.4

Integrated view of partial SMP metamodels

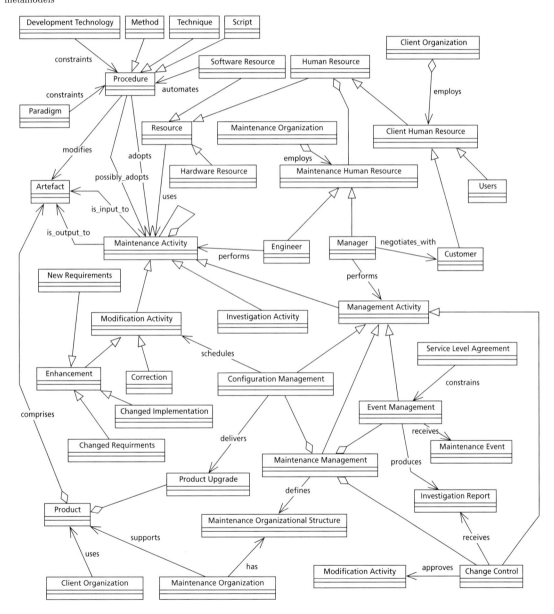

Process enactment

The usefulness of workflow management systems (WfMS) in the automation of business processes has been clearly demonstrated and, given that SMP can be considered as part of a wider business process, it is reasonable to consider that workflow technology will be able to contribute a broader perspective to SMP (which we could call Process Technology) in line with the objectives of the MANTIS Big-E Environment. Moreover, in MANTIS we try to take advantage of the similarity that exists between the software process and workflow technology: in both cases we refer to activities that make up the process, to artefacts used, modified or produced by these activities (products, documents or data), to people who participate in carrying out a certain role, to tools used (for example, software applications), to aspects of collaboration in work groups, etc. For these reasons, in level M2 of MANTIS, aspects of the *Workflow Reference Model* of the Workflow Management Coalition (WfMC, 1995) and aspects of other proposals of workflow metamodels have been included.

For the WfMC, a workflow is the automation of a business process in whole or in part, that is to say, its representation in a format that can be understood by computers. In the use of WFMS there are two clearly differentiated phases:

1. *design-time phase:* referring to the workflow conceptual modelling;
2. *run-time phase:* referring to workflow enactment.

In MANTIS, ideas from both phases are used. The central part of the SMP metamodel that represents the existing activities and their performers (Figure 31.3) must be extended in order to show in more detail how it can be broken down into simpler activities, their relationships and control flow and the possibility of automatic execution. The resulting *Process Enactment metamodel* represents the following main characteristics:

- Each *Maintenance Activity* (that is to say, its specification) and the node that represents it in the associated workflow (*MA Node*) is differentiated.

- The possibility of automated enactment activities is contemplated, for which two specializations are created, called *Manual MA Node* and *Automated MA Node*.

- Each activity can be assigned to several different roles. Each role can be carried out by several actors. The new class *Role* makes these associations possible.

- In order to represent the activities hierarchy – that is to say, to demonstrate that an activity can be composed of other activities, and these activities, in turn, of others etc. – we use a recursive representation. The class *Maintenance Activity* is specialized in two new classes: *Primitive MA* for the atomic classes that do not include other simpler activities and *Nested MA* for the classes with a complex structure, meaning those with an associated workflow including other simpler activities. Moreover, the recursion allows the use of the class *Nested MA* to represent the full specification of an SMP using the MANTIS tools (in a similar way to a WfMS).

- Lastly, it is necessary to use a workflow model to represent the internal structure of the nested activities. MANTIS uses the representation proposed by Sadiq and Orlowska (1999). The classes *Node*, *Control Flow*, *Condition*, *Or-split*, *Or-join* and *MA Node* are used for this.

31 ■ An integrated environment for managing software maintenance projects

In order to include the aspects related to the run-time phase – that is to say, information for support, administration and control of the process enactment – the following must be taken into account:

- The horizontal tool of the MANTIS Big-E Environment plays a similar role to a WfMS:
  - it allows the definition of the SMP metamodels, and
  - it allows the creation of SMP run-time instances (*SMP Instance* class).
- Each SMP run-time instance is made up of run-time activity instances which generate work items. A work item is the smallest unit of a job which is undertaken and which is controlled, managed and assigned to an actor to carry it out.

Figure 31.5 shows the resulting Process Enactment metamodel. The elements related to the run-time phase are situated on the right.

FIGURE 31.5

Process Enactment metamodel

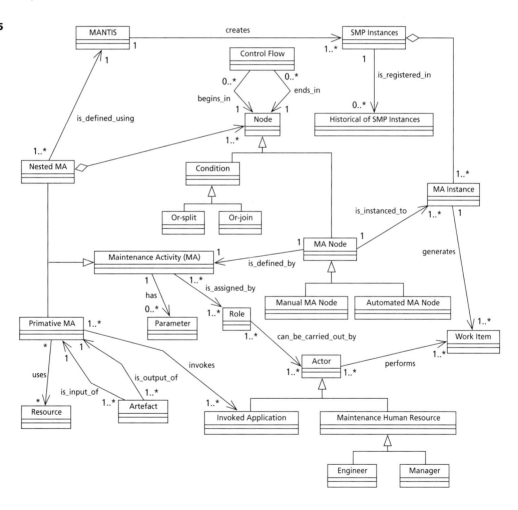

Measure metamodel

In order to manage and control any project, it is essential to measure the product that is being produced or maintained and how the project is being executed. Both aspects are fundamental for the Quality Assurance and Improvement processes. In order to do this, the *Measure* metamodel of MANTIS includes the concepts of measure, metrics, value and attribute associated with the activities, artefacts and resources, bearing in mind that the measurements can refer to both product and process aspects. In MANTIS the following aspects are taken into consideration:

- The activities, artefacts, resources and actors are appraisable elements. In order to be able to measure process enactment, the run-time instances of SMP activities, and the work items are also appraisable elements.
- An appraisable element has attributes that are susceptible to measurement – for example, the duration of an activity or the length of a code module (artefact).
- Each attribute has a specific attribute type, with the possibility that subtypes may exist. For example, the 'duration of an activity' is a subtype of 'quantity of time'.
- A metric is a formula for measuring certain types of attributes. A measure is an association between a specific attribute and a metric. Its principal property is the value obtained.

31.5 MANTIS Big-E Environment tools

One of the fundamental requirements of MANTIS is its orientation to tools. As we have already seen, due to the incorporation of workflow technology, the SMP metamodel allows the possibility of automated activities. Moreover, in order to make the integrated use of all the software tools possible, the MANTIS Big-E Environment is based on the principles known as 'Process Sensitive Software Engineering Environment' (Derniame *et al.*, 1999). A PSEE is controlled by a process engine, whose goal is to control the information flow among the performers according to the process metamodel. The process metamodel is stored in a repository, together with the product definition and process enactment information. The PSEE also has the ability to share data and metadata with the rest of the world by import/export services that use a suitable communication format.

In MANTIS there are two types of software tools:

- ***A 'horizontal tool',*** named MANTIS-Tool, whose objective is to automate the global management of SM projects in a similar way to a PSEE. However, MANTIS-Tool does not try to develop a process engine software tool, similar to those already on the market, as this task can be carried out much better by tools especially designed for this purpose. In MANTIS we propose the use of a commercial WfMS for this.
- ***Several 'vertical' tools,*** each of which is used to automate one of the types of activity included in the previously mentioned SMP metamodel.

The objective of MANTIS-Tool is to aid the global management of SM projects. In order to do this, it is important that it represents all the aspects discussed in the introduction (hence the importance of the SMP metamodel) and that it is able to communicate with other tools – either external ones (WfMS, CASE etc.) or vertical tools specific for SM. The component MANTIS-Metamod is responsible for the first: it allows the definition and editing of models and metamodels of software processes and run-time instances of specific real-world projects; that is to say, it makes it possible to work with the four previously mentioned conceptual levels.

An SM project typically generates many different forms of data. The following common data types are a non-exhaustive list:

- *product data:* source code, version and configuration management data, documentation, executables, test suites, testing results, etc;
- *process data:* explicit definition of a SMP metamodel, process enactment state information, data for process analysis and evolution, history data, project management data, etc;
- *organizational data:* ownership information for project components, roles and responsibilities, work teams information, resource management data, etc.

MANTIS-Repository must efficiently handle the storage and retrieval of all this data and metadata. In order to guarantee maximum flexibility and interchangeability with other tools and environments, this repository uses the format *XML-based Metadata Interchange* (XMI) proposed by OMG (1999). In Figure 31.6 we can see a summarized scheme of the MANTIS-Repository.

MANTOOL is a tool for managing modification-request events according to the MANTEMA methodology. The tool allows the tracking of a portfolio of maintenance projects. Each project receives a number of modification requests, which are categorized into one

FIGURE 31.6

MANTIS-Tool repository

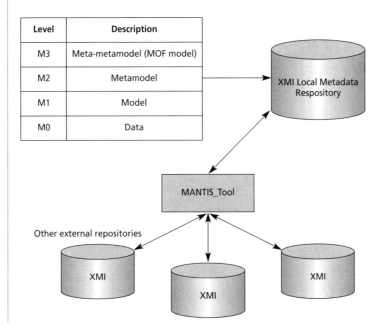

of the five types of maintenance defined in MANTEMA (Polo *et al.*, 2000). Modification requests are tracked using a screen which depends on its maintenance type (i.e. different tasks, different input and output products, people in charge, etc.). Figure 31.7 shows the screen to track modification requests of the 'urgent-corrective' maintenance type. This one consists of the five tasks which appear in the graph. There is a window area to collect the data of each task, and an additional window area to be filled in with the general information of the modification request. All these data are saved in the XMI-based repository in order to extract different types of predefined reports.

The work in some of MANTOOL's tasks can be facilitated with some 'vertical' components, such as the 'measurers'. Measurers collect source code metrics from different programming languages. Initially, only Visual Basic and COBOL programs could be measured. However, we observed that, except for a few metrics (specifically designed for the COBOL language), most of them are usable in all programming languages (lines of code or cyclomatic complexity), and some depend on the programming paradigm (i.e. number of classes, weighted methods per class, response for a class, etc.). For this reason, we have developed a set of independent tools for collecting metrics from any object-oriented programming language: the basis is to translate the source code to another format, which must not depend on syntactic details. The selected format is an abstract syntax tree written in XML which is processed using the Document Object Model (DOM) API. A first tool, which depends on the programming language (but of very easy implementation using a grammar generator, such as YACC), translates the source code to a file in XML format. Later, this file is processed with the object-

FIGURE 31.7

Tracking modification requests with MANTOOL

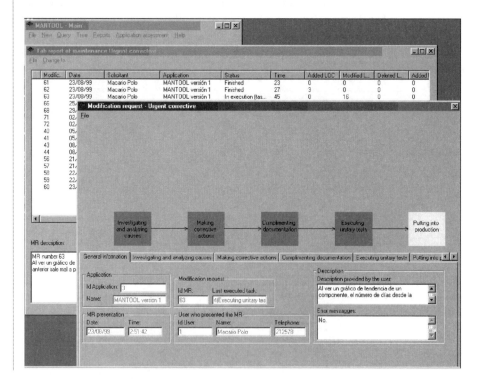

oriented measurer. At present, we have translators for C++ and Java. The standard format of the XML trees allows us to do other types of processing maintaining the language independence, such as code restructuring, clone detection, generation of test cases, etc.

Of course, all of these tools are a fundamental component of the MANTIS Big-E Environment, since they help both managers and programmers to keep the processes under control.

31.6 Other support and organizational processes

Of the eight supporting processes and four organizational processes defined in the ISO12207 standard, the MANTIS Big-E Environment pays special attention to the following: *Audit*, *Quality Assurance*, *Configuration Management*, *Improvement*, and *Project Management*. MANTIS does not attempt to deal with specific 'internal' aspects of these processes, but rather with the way in which their use can be integrated in the management of SM projects.

To this end, different interfaces between the aforementioned processes and the SMP have been defined and various specific techniques and vertical tools have been created. There now follows a brief (for space reasons) presentation of these interfaces.

Audit

In spite of the importance that the SMP has for the correct functioning of the information systems of a company, the most recent bibliographical sources devoted to the audit of information systems have paid very little attention to the audit of SMP (Ruiz et al., 2000). For this reason, MANTIS incorporates an interface with the audit process that is based on a specific adaptation to SMP of the COBIT methodology. COBIT (*Control Objectives for Information and Related Technology*) is the principal proposal recognized worldwide for dealing with Information Systems Audit. It has been performed by the ISACF (Information Systems Audit and Control Foundation) (ISACF, 1998). As a result, in MANTIS, in order to carry out an audit of the SMP, one high-level control objective and fourteen detailed control objectives have been defined, as shown in Table 31.2.

Determining the degree of satisfaction of these control objectives in a specific project allows us to respond to a fundamental question. Is the SMP being managed efficiently and correctly?

Configuration Management

At the beginning of the Maintenance process, all the software elements that are to be under Configuration Management (CM) must be identified. Policies about how to maintain the updated CM database must be also established. Later, the interfaces established with the CM process must be executed when software products undergo modification. In this context, software products are programs, full databases, tables, associated documentation, etc.

The inclusion of the CM process is determined at the M2 level of the MANTIS conceptual architecture, whereas the Concrete process to be used belongs to the M1 level.

TABLE 31.2

Control objectives for the SM audit

	High-level control objective
AI06	*Manage the software maintenance process*: the business activities are performed without accidental interruptions and the software of existing information systems is adapted to the new necessities
	Detailed control objectives
1	*Changes in the operating environment*: an organized procedure exists in order to carry out the migration of a software product from an old operating environment to a new one.
2	*Software retirement*: the methodologies of software development and maintenance include a formal procedure for the retirement of a software product when it has concluded its useful life cycle.
3	*Maintenance types*: the software maintenance types are categorized, and the activities and tasks to perform for each type have been planned.
4	*Maintenance agreement*: the relationships between maintainer and client, and the obligations of each one, are established in a maintenance agreement or contract.
5	*Improvement of process quality*: the methodology used for the SM includes techniques that increase the maintainability (ease of maintenance).
6	*Planning of maintenance*: A maintenance plan exists. It includes the scope of the maintenance, who will perform it, an estimate of the costs, and an analysis of the necessary resources.
7	*Procedures for modification requests* (MRs): procedures exist to begin, to receive and to register MRs.
8	*Managing and monitoring the changes*: the maintainer has established an organizational interface between the maintenance and the configuration management process, so that the second can give support to the first.
9	*Analysis and assessment of the MRs*: the MRs are categorized and prioritized, and there are well-structured mechanisms to evaluate their impact, cost and criticality.
10	*Verification of the problems*: the maintainer replicates or verifies that the problem, which is the source of the MR, does really exist.
11	*Record of the MRs*: the maintainer documents and records the MRs, with the analyses, assessments and verifications performed.
12	*Approval*: depending on the maintenance type of an MR, there are formal procedures that detail the approval that the maintainer should obtain, before and after implementing the modification.
13	*Modification implementation*: to implement the modifications, the maintainer uses the same methodology previously established for the software development process, but adapted to the maintenance process.
14	*Update the documentation*: the documentation (technical reports, manuals, etc.) affected by an MR is updated after finishing the modification.

When the SM process is being executed, the updating or querying of the CM database is an instance at the M0 level.

Improvement

Most improvement models are designed for the development process, and few proposals are provided for SM. One of these is the IT Services CMM described in Niessink and van Vliet (1999). This model is built on the basis that maintenance cannot be managed in the same way as development, since its nature (event-driven, for example) means that it must be treated as a service between two organizations. These authors have proposed a complete model to evaluate the maturity of maintenance organizations from a service perspective, including some questionnaires (and guidelines for their interpretation) to facilitate the analysis. The authors describe several experiences which show the validity of the model. We have used these questionnaires experimentally to evaluate the maturity of several information system departments in different Spanish public entities. These organizations have developed and maintained their own software using a stable environment for years, typically from the same maker (IBM, Computer Associates etc.). According to our experience, in these examples of the SM process (the same organization produces, maintains and uses the software), questionnaires and guidelines must be adapted to this situation.

Therefore, the original version of the IT Services CMM model can be used as the M1 instance of the Improvement process when there are two different organizations, but we must use a revised version when there is only one.

Project Management

The method for controlling the execution of a project in MANTIS is based on the proposal of the Project Management Institute (PMI) (2000). Its *Guide to the Project Management Body of Knowledge* is used to define all the sub-processes that can arise when managing SM projects (the project management model corresponding to level M1 of the MANTIS conceptual architecture). For example, the sub-process Risk Management (comprising the activities Risk Identification, Risk Quantification, Risk Response Development and Risk Response Control) uses a collection of risk factors obtained from the 14 aforementioned control objectives.

Literature

Basili, V., Briand, L., Condon, S., Kim, Y., Melo, W. and Valett, J.D. (1998) 'Understanding and Predicting the Process Software Maintenance Releases'. *Proceedings of the International Conference on Software Engineering*. IEEE.

Becker-Kornstaedt, U. and Webby, R. (1999) *A Comprehensive Schema Integrating Software Process Modeling and Software Measurement*. Fraunhofer IESE – Report   No 047.99, August. In http://www.iese.fhg.de/Publications/Iese_reports/.

Briand, L., Kim, Y., Melo, W., Seaman, C. and Basili, R. (1998) 'Q-MOPP: Qualitative evaluation of maintenance organizations, processes and products'. *Journal of Software Maintenance*, 10, 249–78.

Cockburn, A. (2000) 'Selecting a project's methodology'. *IEEE Software*, July/August, 64–71.

Derniame, J-C., Kaba, B.A. and Wastell, D. (eds) (1999) *Software Process: Principles, Methodology and Technology*. LNCS 1500, Springer-Verlag.

ECMA/NIST (1993) *Reference Model for Frameworks of Software Engineering Environments*, 3rd edn. TR-55, June. In http://www.ecma.ch.

ISACF (1998), *CobiT: Governance, Control and Audit for Information and Related Technology*, 2nd edn. Information Systems Audit and Control Foundation, USA.

ISO/IEC (1995) 12207: *Information Technology – Software Life Cycle Processes*.

ISO/IEC (1998) FDIS 14764: *Software Engineering – Software Maintenance* (draft), December.

ISO/IEC (2000) JTC1/SC7/WG4 15940 working draft 5: *Information Technology – Software Engineering Environment Services*, June.

Kitchenham, B.A., Travassos, G.H., Mayrhauser, A. von, Niessink, F., Schneidewind, N.F., Singer, J., Takada, S., Vehvilainen, R. and Yang, H. (1999) 'Towards an ontology of software maintenance'. *Journal of Software Maintenance: Research and Practice*, 11, 365–89.

Long, F. and Morris, E. (1993) *An Overview of PCTE: A Basis for a Portable Common Tool Environment*. Technical Report CMU/SEI-93-TR-1. In http://www.sei.cmu.edu/publications/documents/93.reports/93.tr.001.html.

Niessink, F. and van Vliet, H. (1999) 'Towards Mature IT Services', *Software Process – Improvement and Practice*, 4(2), 55–71.

OMG (1999) *XML Metadata Interchange (XMI)*, v. 1.1, October. In http://www.omg.org.

OMG (2000) *Meta Object Facility (MOF) Specification*, v. 1.3 RTF, March. In http://www.omg.org.

Pigoski, T.M. (1996) *Practical Software Maintenance. Best Practices for Managing your Investment*. John Wiley & Sons, USA.

Polo, M., Piattini, M. and Ruiz, F. (2000) 'Managing the software maintenance process'. In J. van Bon (ed.), *World Class IT Service Management Guide 2000*. Netherlands: Ten Hagen & Stam Publishers, pp. 213–23.

Polo, M., Piattini, M., Ruiz, F. and Calero, C. (1999) 'MANTEMA: A complete rigorous methodology for supporting maintenance based on the ISO/IEC 12207 Standard'. *Third Euromicro Conference on Software Maintenance and Reengineering (CSMR'99)*. Amsterdam (Netherlands): IEEE Computer Society Press, pp. 178–81.

Project Management Institute (2000) *A Guide to the Project Management Body of Knowledge 2000 edition*, USA: PMI Communications.

Rajlich, V.T. and Bennett, K.H. (2000) 'A staged model for the software life cycle'. *IEEE Computer*, July, 66–71.

Randall, R. and Ett, W. (1995) 'Using process to integrate software engineering environments'. *Proceedings of the Software Technology Conference*, USA: Salt Lake City. In http://www.asset.com/stars/loral/pubs/stc95/psee95/psee.htm.

Ruiz, F., Piattini, M., Polo, M. and Calero, C. (2000) 'Audit of software maintenance'. In *Auditing Information Systems*, USA: Idea Group Publishing, pp. 67–108.

Sadiq, W and Orlowska, M.E. (1999) 'On capturing process requirements of workflow based business information systems'. *Third International Conference on Business Information Systems*, Poznan, Poland, pp. 195–209.

US Air Force (1996) *Software Engineering Environment Integration Process. Summary-level Definition.* Informal TR STARS-PV03-A032/001/00, 1996. In http://www.asset.com/stars/darpa/Papers/ProcessDDPapers.html.

W3C (2000) *Extensible Markup Language (XML) 1.0* (2nd edn), October. In http://www.w3.org/.

WfMC (1995) TC00-1003 1.1: Workflow Management Coalition. *The Workflow Reference Model*, Jan-1995. In http://www.aiim.org/wfmc/standards/docs.htm.

Notes

1 This work has been undertaken in collaboration with the company Atos ODS subsidized by the MANTIS and MPM projects. MANTIS has been partially supported by the European Union and CICYT-Spain (1FD97-1608TIC). MPM has been partially supported by the Science and Technology Ministry of Spain (FIT-070000-2000-307).
2 PCTE 'Portable Common Tool Environment' (Long and Morris, 1993), 'The Reference Model for Framework of SEE' (ECMA/NIST, 1993), and STARS (Software Technology for Adaptable, Reliable Systems) (US Air Force, 1996)
3 Some authors do not distinguish clearly in their nomenclature between model and metamodel but refer to both that corresponding to level M2 and that of level M1 as 'model'.
4 The organization responsible for carrying out the maintenance.

32 Kwintes project: results of a multidisciplinary research project in the field of IT Service Management

L.J. Ruijs Cap Gemini Ernst & Young Information Systems Management

Summary

This chapter provides a brief summary of the key results of the Kwintes research project. The project was subsidized by the Senter agency at the Dutch Ministry of Economic Affairs and its goal was to define methods and guidelines to extend the principles of the IT Service Management concepts that were developed in a previous project, 'Concrete Kit'. Participants in the project are three universities (Technical University Delft, Technical University Eindhoven, Free University Amsterdam), Belasting Automatiserings Centrum BAC (Dutch Tax Computerization Centre), TwijnstraGudde and Cap Gemini Ernst & Young.

32.1 Kwintes as follow-up to Concrete Kit

The final results of the Concrete Kit project, which ran from 1995 to 1997, was the launching pad for the Kwintes project. The Concrete Kit project resulted in a simple route map for defining and measuring services.

One of the main tools resulting from the 'Concrete Kit project' was the IT Service Management Lemniscate (Figure 32.1).

In the Lemniscate model, IT Service Management contains a left loop, Service Level Management (SLM), and a right loop, Service Process Management (SPM). Within SLM the IT organization negotiates with its customers with regard to the services to be delivered and the conditions under which they are to be delivered (specifying and quantifying). The agreements that result from these negotiations are set down in a service level agreement. Then the IT organization organizes the delivery of services such that these agreements can be complied with (designing/organizing management processes). Within the framework of SPM, measurements and evaluations are then carried out to determine whether the agreements are actually being carried out. If it is necessary to adjust the process, the implementation processes are organized differently (monitoring/evaluating management processes). Another possibility is that the agreements are modified (monitoring/evaluating SLAs).

When applying the steps defined in the Service Management Lemniscate to real-life projects, it appeared that the steps were still not tangible enough. It also became clear that more than one effort or project was undertaken by the supplier to develop the service organization.

32 ■ Kwintes project

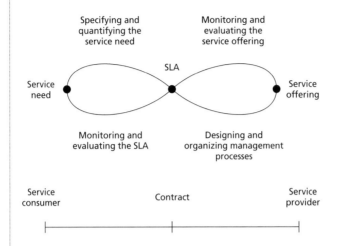

FIGURE 32.1
Service Management Lemniscate model

This resulted in the Kwintes project in 1998. Kwintes is a Dutch acronym; the English equivalent would be Quintes, derived from QUantifying INformation TEchnology Services. The research in Kwintes elaborated on the Service Management Lemniscate model of the Concrete Kit project. Again, steps were defined for the loops of the lemniscate, some additional models were introduced and, on top of all that, relationships with maturity levels were established. The entire set of models and steps resulted in a usable toolset for setting up Service Management.

32.2 The stepwise route to better service

The IT Service Management Lemniscate describes how IT needs can be used to shape service level agreements and, during the next step, the service level agreements are used to the IT service organization. In itself, this approach would appear simple to implement. Unfortunately, it was found in practice that this is not such a simple matter.

The left upper loop represents the specification of services and defining the SLA. Very often, however, from the outset enthusiastic efforts are made to close the service agreement. During a protracted and intensive process, these efforts usually lead to comprehensive SLAs which tend never to be used.

The right lower loop stands for implementation of service processes. This comprises defining the operational and service procedures, employing the human resources needed, and deploying the required infrastructure. In many cases where the SLA really is adopted as a basis for shaping the services organization, we will still find that the measuring and reporting/evaluating activities are neglected, so that the next step is negotiating the next version of the SLA.

The third movement is the right upper loop. This loop represents the efforts made to measure and monitor the services. The aim of measuring and monitoring is to check whether the level of service lives up to the SLA and, if this is not so, to correct the service level. However, situations are known where minute measurements are taken but results are only used to improve the services organization; the activities for giving feedback to the client and evaluating with the client are completely forgotten.

Finally, the fourth loop is the left lower one. This loop shows the process of feeding back the measurement results to the client and evaluating the service with the client. Here, there are also cases where evaluation meetings with the client are held scrupulously, but where the repercussions on the SLA are never discussed and changes to the SLA are omitted.

The examples above will reveal that there is generally a focus on one or two loops of the IT Service Management Lemniscate. For example, much effort is spent on writing a good SLA or compiling a good service-level report. As a result, the other activities such as measuring and evaluation receive little or no attention.

To improve attention for the entire Service Management process, an incremental approach towards implementation may be helpful. An incremental approach means that every service management step is implemented to some degree, only to go into more detail during the next round. All phases of the IT Service Management Lemniscate receive equal attention, but depth is gained by repeating the steps in a later stage.

Elaborating on this knowledge, we have identified various stages in service development by the service provider. This in itself is not a new phenomenon – in other areas this was recognized earlier. For example, the Software Engineering Institute (SEI) is an organization which strives to improve the quality of software development. To achieve this, SEI has done quite some work on developing a maturity model – the Capability Maturity Model (CMM).[1]

The CMM model for software development focuses on improving the processes of developing software. Other attempts have sought to improve other processes, but no model was available for IT operations and services.

Kwintes has taken up the challenge to develop an IT Services CMM. The aim of this model is:

- to provide guidelines for IT suppliers that help them assess whether they are sufficiently capable to deliver certain services;
- to prescribe necessary steps to be taken for the gradual improvement of service delivery in order to give IT suppliers the opportunity to evolve.

We have embraced the Software CMM framework (Figure 32.2) because it is sufficiently generic in application and is already being applied to other fields, resulting in (for instance) 'People CMM' and 'Engineering CMM'.

As we have deliberately chosen to keep to the original CMM structure, the IT Service CMM is very much the same as Software CMM. The same maturity levels of Software CMM appear in Services CMM:

- **Level 1: Initial level** The IT service process is event-driven, ad hoc, and in some cases even chaotic. Few processes are well defined, and successful results depend on individual efforts or 'heroic actions' by one or more support champions.

- **Level 2: Repeatable level** Elementary Service Management processes are in place to manage costs, progress and quality in IT service operation. The different disciplines have been organized to ensure that past achievements can be repeated for similar services or new projects.

FIGURE 32.2
The CMM framework

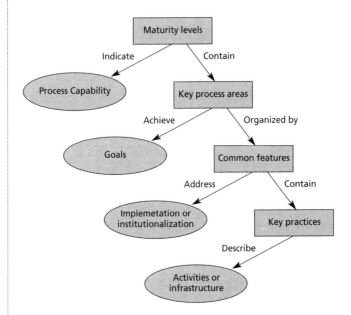

- *Level 3: Defined level* The IT service processes are documented, standardized and integrated in standard service processes. All projects use authorized, tailored versions of the organizational standard for their activities.

- *Level 4: Managed level* Accurate and detailed measurements are carried out on the quality of service. Both the service processes and the delivery processes are investigated and managed through quantified data.

- *Level 5: Optimizing level* Continual process improvements are possible as a result of quantified feedback information from processes and by the early testing of innovative ideas and technologies.

CMM describes a number of so-called key process areas for each level: process areas that have to be implemented before achieving that level. We have adopted the existing key process areas of Software CMM as much as possible (Table 32.1).

Each of the key process areas is described in terms of objectives and 'common features'. The features are divided into five groups:

1. Commitment to perform
2. Ability to perform
3. Activities performed
4. Measurement and analysis
5. Verifying implementation.

Further information on IT Service CMM is available on www.itservicecmm.org.

TABLE 32.1

Key process areas in IT Service CMM

Category	Management	Support	Delivery
5. Optimizing		● Technology change management	
	● Process change management		● Problem prevention
4. Managed	● Quantitative process management		● Service quality management
3. Defined	● Integrated service management	● Organization process focus ● Organization process defined ● Training programme	● Service delivery
2. Repeatable	● Service commitment management ● Service delivery planning ● Service tracking and overview ● Subcontract management	● Configuration management ● Event management ● Quality assurance	
1. Initial		● Ad-hoc processes	

32.3 Steps in the IT Service Management Lemniscate

Phase 1: Making agreements

The activities in the upper left loop of the IT Service Management lemniscate agreements are aimed at making service agreements that are based on the client's business situation and the IT needs to support the business processes. The agreements are prepared during negotiations between client and service provider and then recorded in service level agreements (SLAs). These SLAs form the basis for actual IT service delivery but also for the continued improvement of IT services.

In recent years, IT departments have gained a great deal of experience in defining agreements. Generally speaking, agreements about the quality of service were laid down in lists of agreements, contracts and SLAs. Nevertheless, we discovered that many agreements still fail to deliver what the client had meant in the first place. The reasons for mismatches between expected and delivered service are:

● different perceptions of the defined services between client and provider;
● focus on efforts rather than results;
● incomplete specification of IT services;
● agreements are difficult to interpret or poorly written;
● inadequate (internal) communication about the agreements;
● SLAs have 'open ends';
● no communication between development departments and operations & services.

Many IT departments focus heavily on delivering products (which product can I run to help my client?) but fail to focus on rendering services.

One of the conclusions of our research was that we should divide IT services into two – on the one hand the technical and tangible *product* and on the other the more abstract or experienced part of *services*. Of course, products are usually needed to generate service, but the two are not the same. To illustrate the difference, we have used the everyday simile of the *service kernel* and *service shell*.

Service kernel

Lying at the heart of service delivery is what we call the 'kernel'. The IT object is the kernel and therefore the basic element of the service. The kernel is usually a system or application that provides the functionality that the users need. This may be a financial system that provides invoicing and payroll administration.

The kernel or object provides a specific amount of functionality but is described in terms of a number of quality requirements: availability, capacity and performance.

Looking at the organization model of companies, we can identify more than one level of service:

- the highest level is that of the business process that fulfils the organization's tasks and that may need IT support;
- the second level is the information system that offers specific IT support to one or more business processes;
- the IT infrastructure, which is a coherent set of IT components (hardware, software and network components) that may be used by more than one IT system;
- separate IT components that support the processing, storage, distribution, inputting and exporting of data.

It is important to note here that each higher level includes its underlying levels.

Service shell

The shell surrounds the IT object and consists of a collection of environment areas – user support, changes, security and calamities. For each of these areas, arrangements have to be made. These arrangements are not directly related to the IT object (the kernel), but they are still important for the client to experience good service. For example, it is important that the supplier offers support when there are crashes or problems with the system; otherwise the users may become dissatisfied with the service.

In summary, the environment areas are the following:

- User support
- Changes
- Security
- Calamities.

The IT object (kernel) and environment areas (shell) together make up the IT services that are deployed to meet the needs of the client.

Service components and service attributes

Research has shown that there is an enormous variety of service requirements. If we hold the view of IT service as a kernel and a shell, the service requirements will relate both to the quality of the IT kernel and to the quality of the shell. Experience shows that in many cases agreements are made about the IT object, but that no or only effort-based clauses are defined for the shell.

The IT object will provide functionality that is subject to a number of quality issues. It must be available, it must be able to handle a particular number of users, commands, etc. (capacity), and it must also perform this in a particular time frame (performance).

Quality issues are also attributed to the environment areas (the shell). For instance, the functionality of user support will be defined in terms of 'the level of support' or the language in which support is offered (e.g. Dutch or English).

Other examples are the maximum number of questions that could be asked to the help desk (determines the help desk capacity), the opening hours (determines availability) and the response time of the help desk (determines performance).

When we develop this further, we can represent all issues and attributes in a table. The quality of the IT object (the kernel of the service) is described in the upper part of the table; the quality of the environment areas (the shell surrounding the service) is described in the lower part (Table 32.2).

TABLE 32.2
Issues and attributes

IT object	Functionality	Availability	Performance	Capacity
IT object				
User support				
Security				
Calamities				
Changes				

The concepts used in the table are explained as follows:

- **IT object** An IT object is an object that meets a user's information need. Depending upon usage, an IT object may be a (complete) IT system, an IT infrastructure or an IT component.
- **Functionality** The functionality is determined by the specified functions and workings of IT objects for requirements and wishes laid down explicitly and implicitly within clearly defined application situations.
- **Availability** The ability of an IT object to satisfy functions required or specified at a particular time or for a particular period.
- **Performance** The ability of an IT object to comply with the time-related aspects (processing time, response time) of the specified functionality.
- **Capacity** The ability of an IT object to provide specified functionality with a specified amount of resources.

- **User support** The extent to which support to users is delivered to ensure effective and efficient use of an IT object.
- **Security** The extent to which the authenticity, confidentiality, integrity and exclusivity of data produced by IT objects is delivered.
- **Calamities** The extent to which the continuity of the functioning and operation of IT objects is delivered in the event of downtime caused by 'abnormal circumstances'. Abnormal circumstances are natural disasters such as fire, breakdown of external communication, etc.
- **Changes** The extent to which desired or required changes within IT components are achieved.

To help service managers to specify service requirements, we have defined a number of attributes for each cell in the SLA quality table. The attributes are listed on our (Dutch language) website (www.kwintes.nl).

Developing SLAs: a structured approach

In drawing up SLAs, it is important to know all the parties involved, to select the right level of service and to make the right agreements on SLA components and attributes.

A structured approach is suggested for specifying SLAs step by step. The plan developed for this purpose breaks down into five stages:

1. **Analysis of business setting:** At this stage, the business setting in which the IT objects will be used is described.
2. **Description of IT object:** The IT object is described in terms of the functionality that it is supposed to offer and the quality issues for delivery.
3. **Importance of the IT object:** At this stage, the importance of the IT object to each user group involved is defined.
4. **Importance of the environment areas:** The importance that the client attaches to the environment areas and its quality issues is defined in more detail.
5. **Specifying and quantifying SLAs.** The agreement is written at this stage. The quality issues are specified in measurable terms, both for the IT object and for the environment areas.

Phase 2: Setting up the service

In the second loop of the Service Management lemniscate, the supplier has to implement activities and processes that will enable its organization to comply with the service level agreement. All quality issues pertaining to the IT object and the environment areas are implemented.

Much work has been done by different authors on defining consistent and usable task descriptions for the IT field. One of the pioneers in this field is Prof. Dr. Jr. M. Looijen. Readers may recall the task fields and task clusters that he defined in the early 1980s. Various groups after him have also addressed this matter. Finally, process-oriented implementation has reached full maturity only recently with the introduction of ITIL.

Despite the available research and methods, numerous problems remain unresolved when it comes to setting up a service management organization:

- Implementing a management structure can be a difficult job: should we choose task-oriented, process-oriented or hybrid?
- Procedures can be hard to implement.
- Managers are not informed about formal arrangements between other departments.
- Employees are focused on efforts rather than results.

Literature on this subject offers a variety of methods and techniques for setting up a service. Elements of the task and function-based approach as well as the process-based approach can be found in most of the publications. Practice shows, however, that many organizations are still 'failing to get there'. Why? In our view, the reason is that tasks, responsibilities and jobs are mixed up with processes and activities.

Since you cannot have one world without the other, the solution should be obvious – to combine task-oriented and process-oriented implementations in what is known as the integration model. In the integration model, operational and service tasks are defined. But despite their position in the organization, they are combined as concatenated chains into processes. In Figure 32.3, service tasks are concatenated into processes. The order of the tasks into processes may differ according to the aim of the process.

FIGURE 32.3

The integration model

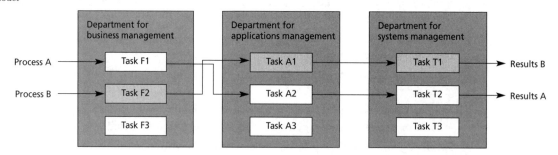

In the Kwintes project, we have made a list of the main activities that are normally performed when the support and delivery processes of ITIL are implemented. By adding the tasks to the process descriptions of ITIL, we have achieved a frame of reference that is more usable and comprehensible.

When defining service and operational tasks, we have also included tasks incurred by new technologies. One example is the task of Content Management, as used in Web-enabled environments such as the Internet, intranets and extranets.

The great benefit of introducing task descriptions is that it is now possible to establish a direct link between the SLA issues and attributes and the tasks that are needed to perform the activities that achieve the service requirements in the SLA.

The steps to implement Service Management tasks are:

1. **Selecting service processes and tasks needed to meet the SLA requirements:** This is to make sure that tasks and processes are selected to be able to fulfil the SLA quality attributes defined in the SLA.
2. **Implementing processes for service tasks:** The tasks are allocated at this stage to organizational entities. They are also placed in processes.
3. **Allocation of resources to tasks:** The tasks identified are assigned to the human resources. Various resources can be grouped together in a team, unit or department.
4. **Validation based on simulation:** A simulation of the business situation is run to show how the individual and time-related aspects perform. This simulation is used to check whether the implementation can really work for the business situation.
5. **Making task descriptions:** If the simulation model has proved that the service organization implementation is adequate, the task descriptions and procedures can be written.

Phase 3: Measuring the service level

The third loop of the Service Management lemniscate checks whether the SLA requirements are really achieved during operations. Measuring has two purposes: reporting on which service level is actually delivered and providing the supplier with management information to improve supplier processes. One benefit of measurement is the accumulation of historical data; these can be used to anticipate future SLAs.

When it comes to measuring, we have seen the following problems:

- No measurable agreements have been reached.
- There are clear agreements in place, but no measuring infrastructure.
- There is a registration system, but no internal commitment.
- Problems are resolved but not reported.
- It is difficult to establish the link between an incident and relevant service.
- Services often contain a number of different environments.
- Measuring takes time and money but generates little benefit.

Following these principles, it is possible to introduce the measuring programmes on the basis of a stage plan:

1. **Setting up a measuring programme**: The important element here is to determine what is to be measured and how. These are derived from the SLA attributes. The result of this step is a measuring protocol.
2. **Measuring**: It seems that measuring is done by making the measuring process 'transparent'. This means that the measurement must preferably be part of the regular tasks of operators. It is even better if measuring can be automated through monitoring systems.

3 ***Analysing the measuring data***: There are two types of analyses on measuring data:
- Analyses for service level reporting. For example, the number of transaction runs, available disk space on file servers, the number of questions presented to the help desk, the number of outstanding incidents and problems, etc.
- Explorative analysis. If there is a database containing measuring data, it can of course also be used to look for relationships and connections between different variables.

4 ***Feeding back measuring results***: The fourth step is to feed back the data and reports to those interested. This includes of course the client (or the client representative), but may also include the users and in-house staff. The client report is input to the evaluation of the service. Reports for own staff are designed to help in identifying improvements to the service provisioning process.

Phase 4: Evaluation of service provisioning

The final loop of the IT Service Management lemniscate is evaluation. In the previous phases, the SLA was defined, service processes were implemented and measurements done to check whether the services lived up to the SLA. The fourth loop assesses and evaluates the service with the client. This means that the service level report is discussed in a meeting between customer and supplier. If necessary, the SLA is modified as a result of this evaluation.

If all the previous loops have been organized well, evaluation is simple. However, in practice it appears that:

- too little attention is paid to evaluation of service;
- evaluation frequently leads to condemnation rather than to adjustment of the SLA.

No steps have been defined for this phase: when sufficient attention is paid to evaluation, better information, better understanding of service management and mutual trust between customer and supplier will be the reward.

For further information on the Kwintes project see the www.kwintes.org website (in Dutch).

Note

1 CMM is owned by Carnegie Mellon University, USA, and the Software Engineering Institute.

Integrated life-cycle management

Optimizing ICT service through the central positioning of ICT objects

Wim van den Boomgaard Tax and customs administration, Information and communications technology centre, the Netherlands

Ton Pijpers Atos origin Business Solutions

Summary

The method developed by the Dutch tax and customs administration, Integrated Life-cycle Management (ILM), aims at the integral control of ICT objects. The aim of ILM is to get the ICT service and ICT processes to reach a higher level and, at the same time, to improve the quality of the infrastructure. The path to integral management of ICT objects begins with an unambiguous object model and a clear management process. Together with well-defined organization tasks and roles, practical information systems and a culture atuned to integration, the basis is laid for correct, complete and current product and service portfolios. From these portfolios come the next input for the systematic implementation of platform releases and the provision of services that meet the requirements of the client. This chapter describes the ILM reference framework and its application at the tax and customs administration.

33.1 Introduction

The role of ICT service in the overall organizational policy of the Dutch tax and customs administration has become more important in the past few decades. ICT grew to become a management and improvement instrument and is an indispensable method for achieving the tax and customs administration's objectives. The ICT service function has therefore also become increasingly concerned with its contribution to achieving the objectives. The increased interweaving of information and communication technology with the organization's processes makes it necessary to raise the quality of the ICT service to a higher level. To achieve this within the Belastingdienst/Automatiseringscentrum1 (B/AC) (Tax and customs administration Computer Centre[1]), much thought is given to the rearrangement of the ICT processes and transformation to a client-oriented organization. Within B/AC, a method has been developed, Integrated Life-cycle Management, from which an important contribution is delivered and with which the gap between the sepa-

---

[1] Since the beginning of 2002, a reorganization has taken place and the computer centre is now called 'Belastingdienst/Centrum voor Informatie en communicatie technologie' (Tax and customs administration/Information and communications technology centre).

FIGURE 33.1

ICT services Tax and customs administration

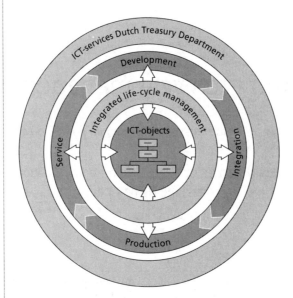

rate business processes can be bridged (Figure 33.1). ILM centralizes the objects of the ICT service and aims to manage these objects in a controlled way: better development, integration and exploitation is the result. In this chapter, attention is paid to the 'what' and 'why' of ILM, description of the reference framework, the ILM models such as the object model and the process control model, and the application of ILM within the Treasury Department. The chapter ends with a number of conclusions about the method and its application at B/AC.

33.2 ILM vision

In this section the 'what' and 'why' of ILM are examined. First, the ICT service at the tax and customs administration is analysed and then the problems that arise from that service. The following section is a description of how ILM can offer a solution.

ICT service within the tax and customs administration

New legislation and technological and social developments forced the tax and customs administration to continually renew the existing service as well as develop new products and services. These products and services are increasingly based on ICT (declaration diskettes, Digital Tax Office). The tax and customs administration Computer Centre (B/AC) supports the tax and customs administration ICT service, which optimally connects to the primary processes of the Treasury Department. The ICT services of B/AC are achieved and assisted by the following processes:

- development of the application products;
- development of the technical infrastructure;
- integration;
- production and service.

Problems

As a large ICT service supplier, B/AC has a great need for trustworthy, timely, correct and complete information and knowledge about ICT objects, not only substantive information (product information, relationships between objects, information from the market) but also administrative information (needs of the client, planning information, performance information, etc.). The then current reliability of the ICT object information and the available object knowledge was not sufficient to support the increased service demands. Specific bottlenecks experienced were:

- The information in the product and service portfolio was often incorrect, incomplete and obsolete.
- The quality of the ICT object information left much to be desired.
- There were no clear plans for the short and medium term with regard to the ICT objects, which was hindering the management cycle in terms of portfolio management and tactical planning.
- There was no uniform and centrally managed service catalogue.
- The relationships between ICT objects were insufficiently named and registered (relevant in relation to changes).
- The control of production and service was still based on the object type 'product': there was no complete understanding of the management of change: i.e. the life-cycle of services, products and the release of platforms.
- There was insufficient understanding of standardization of products and other possibilities for savings, for example with regard to the use of licences and such.
- The integration between the different links in the value chain was insufficient because, for example, during development insufficient thought was being given to quality aspects such as reparability, manageability, exploitation advantages and total cost of ownership.

This was mainly due to lack of a uniform, communicated understanding about the ICT object framework. Which objects do we deliver to the customer? What is an ICT service and what is a product? Also, it was often unclear which aspects and criteria played a role in decision making around ICT objects. Moreover, the organization was still not adequately organized with the right roles and responsibilities for product management/service management and correctly working information systems to make the much-needed object information available for the steering and execution of the separate ICT processes. An important cause of this was that the traditional, separate ICT processes, through their own dynamics and culture, were still fairly detached from each other.

Integrated Life-cycle Management

Integrated Life-cycle Management (ILM) is the method for integral control of ICT objects in such a way that product and service portfolios are available with reliable information about the ICT objects. This aims to provide the ICT processes with the correct, complete and current information to achieve an optimal service. ILM stands for:

- ***Integrated***: ILM results in uniform thinking and methodology for information about ICT objects to be commonly managed across the processes, and made widely available. ILM ensures chain integration.
- ***Life-cycle***: ILM looks at the life-cycle of the ICT objects, services, platforms and products – from the beginning until they are phased out.
- ***Management***: ILM manages on three levels. On a strategic level, the connection is found by ICT policy. ILM ensures that the focus on technology (products) moves towards services that give added value to the client. On a tactical level, the product and service portfolios (portfolio management), platform releases (release management) and service catalogues (service management) are managed. On an operational level, the life-cycle of the separate ICT objects is managed.

Added-value ILM

ILM facilitates and steers the primary ICT processes and is set up to improve the performance of these processes. Good agreements, and the sharing of information and knowledge about ICT objects (including their composition and the mutual relationships between them), ensure that the commercial, technical, organizational and financial aspects of the objects in the ICT production and service processes are completed. Moreover, ILM supports the following management processes:

- policy planning;
- portfolio management;
- release management;
- supplier management;
- performance management;
- asset management;
- cost management (incl. charging); and
- licence management.

ILM enables the management to align the ICT portfolio with the customer requirements and achieve performance improvements in the ICT service:

- Through the discontinuation of certain services and products, cost savings are possible, owing to a better insight into products with identical functionality.
- Through better tuning a more efficient process is possible, which leads to a result that better meets the needs of the client.
- Through better insight into the current portfolios and through reuse of components, a quicker time-to-market is possible.

ILM offers a unique method for optimizing ICT services, with its integral focus on the ICT objects and the ICT-facilitating processes. This object focus forms a useful extension to existing methods that are particularly process-oriented (for example, ITIL/IPW). The object focus is derived from logistic concepts, which have been used in the industry for decades with great success.

33.3 ILM reference framework

Within ILM, four sub-models have been developed. The models are designed:

- to ensure clarity and commitment for management and colleagues regarding what ILM can mean for ICT policy;
- to stimulate communication about ILM between the various parties and to adjust the various mental models with regard to this subject;
- to achieve clarity and to be able to make choices concerning the introduction of ILM;
- to provide clarity with regard to responsibilities and competences.

The ILM models relate to the following areas:

- objects;
- process control;
- information; and
- organization.

These models are now explained.

Object model

For reasons of simplicity and summary, the object model has very few levels. Within the defined levels, further levels are allowed (Figure 33.2). Within the object model the following types of objects are distinguished:

- service;
- product;
- activity;
- platform.

FIGURE 33.2
ILM Object model

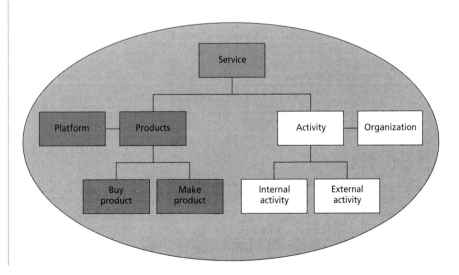

Service

On the highest level of the ICT service (seen from the client organization and its end users), we distinguish the supply of services. Services are ICT objects that contribute directly to the business processes of the client organization. Services usually have a long life-cycle and are expressed in functional terms. A service delivers a specified set of functions in a standardized form. As seen from the content point of view, services are made up of material products (hardware and software) and immaterial activities such as support by means of a help desk. Examples of services are: workstation, text processing, print service, and telephone service. The end user takes the ICT service as if it is a composite or as integrated packet services. Many of these services make use of superior platforms, with communication between application components accomplished via the underlying technical infrastructure (TIS). Each service is, in principle, a unique configuration product – that is to say, a bundling of products that are connected to a specific platform of the application (TIS architecture). In order that the packet ICT service corresponds to the agreed service level, these services and the underlying technical infrastructure must be integrally developed and managed.

Product

A product is a physical (hardware) or digital (software) object that is or can be installed on behalf of one or more services in the ICT infrastructure (e.g. Word 7.0). A product is, therefore, a building work of the ICT infrastructure and is obtained from an external supplier or from a development unit. A product (version) has a relatively short life-cycle. A product can be built up from components. Components are those parts of a product relevant for management, exploitation and logistics. This relevance needs to be analysed when new products are developed. A product can be bought or made. A purchased product is called a supplier's product or purchaser's product. A self-made product is called a 'made' product. Under this come applications and application components. A composed product is made up of purchased and/or made products. The distinction between service and product is essential. Through this distinction you disconnect the management of the ICT infrastructure from the use of ICT services by end users. This enables standardization on a product level, which leads to lower exploitation costs. The clients themselves, via the charging mechanism, can establish efficient use of the ICT services.

Service activity

A service activity is carried out on behalf of the user of a service. Examples are support via a help desk, backup of data, or the arrangement of a subscription by an Internet service provider.

Platform

A platform forms a technical slice of the ICT infrastructure and is built from TIS and application products. Within the Dutch tax and customs administration, a distinction is made between the client platform, local platform, mid-range platform and main-frame platform. A platform, particularly in a technical sense, is characterized by the hardware and system software used.

33 ■ Integrated life-cycle management

Portfolio and release

The infrastructure consists of two product portfolios: the TIS portfolio and the application portfolio. These portfolios describe the collection of products in relation to the services. In addition to the product portfolios, there is a service portfolio which describes the agreed service activities in relation to the services (Figure 33.3). Over time, platforms are released or re-released: we then talk about a platform release. Within the term of the release, the released products can be installed and managed. The same applies to the release of services to the client. A service catalogue enables the client to see which ICT services are valid and available.

FIGURE 33.3

ILM Object model's service portfolio

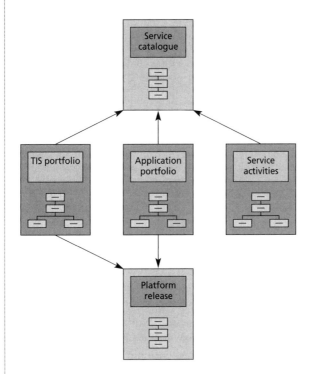

Process control model

ILM is process control. Just as a control mechanism is necessary for cash flow, there is also a mechanism to manage the 'ICT logistics', that is to say, control of the ICT objects. In Figure 33.4, the control process is shown. On an operational level, the individual objects are monitored: object management. On a tactical level, the TIS and application product portfolios are planned and controlled: portfolio management. Control of the infrastructure platforms is on the same level: release management (Figure 33.4).

ILM controls the life-cycle of the ICT objects service, product and platform release. It is about ICT business processes being able to reach the correct information about

FIGURE 33.4
ILM Object model's control process

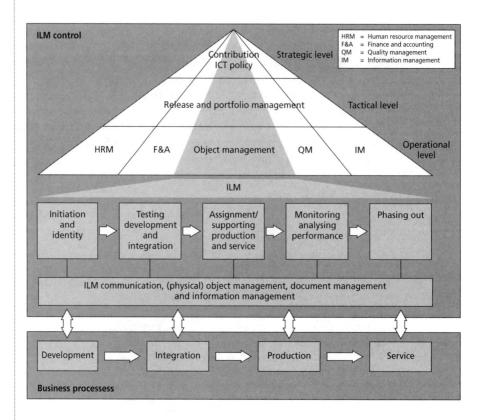

the objects at the right moment, thereby enabling the service production process to be performed as optimally as possible.

Portfolio management and release management

An improvement of the internal process performance is achieved through sorting out the product portfolios since reliable information on the application and TIS-portfolios is the primary requirement for the execution of the ICT processes. Portfolio management ensures that the development and usage of services and products is done according to plan. An improvement of the ICT service is achieved through making the service catalogue clear and reliable. On the basis of a good catalogue, communication with the client becomes clear and accountable. A revised service catalogue, with clear milestones scheduling the delivery of the ICT services, is a form of release management. Improvement of the continuity and stability of the infrastructure is achieved through platform releases. A platform release occurs through successively taking the release steps of planning, product intake, integration, testing and acceptance. The fixing of the infrastructure in time is a form of release management.

life-cycle of the service, product and platform

On an operational level, the separate ICT objects are controlled: object management of a service and product or platform. In Figure 33.5, the life-cycles of the objects are

33 ■ Integrated life-cycle management

FIGURE 33.5
ILM Object model: object life-cycles

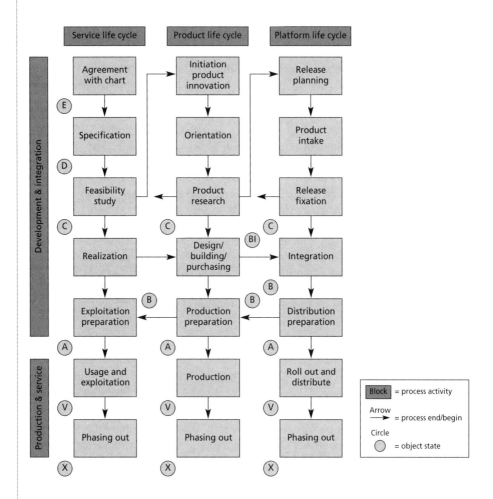

shown separately and in relation to each other. The life cycle of an object consists of a number of successive process steps. After the successful accomplishment of a process step, the object is in a certain state. This state is represented through a status. The A-status of a service, for example, shows that the service is ready for use and exploitation. To achieve A-status, the service is tested against A-status conditions. The A-status test is a part of the certification mechanism that credits the status criteria and the method of testing. The process model for the operational management of the life-cycle of the ICT service has been summarized as follows:

1 ***Initiate/identify innovation/change*** The life-cycle of a service begins with an agreement with the client. When the clients' wishes are registered and specified, the service to be developed is given E-status, and respectively D-status.

2 ***Feasibility study*** Next, a feasibility study is carried out. This study indicates whether the service can be realized and prepared for production. Sometimes, a further study regarding the possibilities of a product is necessary. Closing the feasibility study results in a sound offer. Approval of the offer means that realization and exploitation preparation can start. The service is given C-status.

3 ***Monitoring/testing realization and exploitation preparation*** Preparing for the realization and exploitation of a service is a virtual process, and a service is in essence an abstract notion. A service consists entirely of a combination of one or more products and services. Besides those from current portfolios, if necessary one can decide whether to buy or make a new product. If a product has been technically realized and functions correctly B-status is granted. Products with this status will be integrated and accepted per platform release. If the release is accepted, the products within it receive a definitive B-status. This B-status indicates that the product has been found to be technically and functionally correct and can be integrated in the technical infrastructure. If the underlying products of the service have all been tested (release-wise) and have received B-status, the service also receives B-status. This implies that the service (content-wise) is technically achieved, but is not yet ready for exploitation. Preparation for exploitation is principally concerned with the organization of production and service. The most service-oriented activities are prepared and organized on a product level. If the exploitation of the product is well prepared, A-status is granted. As soon as the service is totally prepared for exploitation and all the underlying products are prepared for production, the service receives A-status.

4 ***Supporting production and service*** Production and service are supported by ILM through the use of product information, advice, directives, performance criteria, logistical information (ordering conditions etc.) and solutions for similar problems. This is done via the certification mechanism (for instance, A-status) and the link between object type administration and object item administration.

5 ***Monitoring performance*** Obsolete services can be determined according to delivery through this process, performance information and information from the ICT market. A service can become obsolete because the functionality supplied through the service is no longer desired or an underlying product or service is technically or economically antiquated, or an underlying product or service is no longer deliverable. In these situations, V-status is granted and advice about replacement and renewal is given.

6 ***Phasing out*** An antiquated service is phased out. A phased-out service is called 'out of work'. This means that the functionality is no longer deliverable. Moreover, it must be verified with the client if the functionality remains the same, or if the service can be offered in another way (with other functionality). This version of the service then receives X-status. Any new service receives a new version description.

In addition to these six core processes of object management, there are still the supporting processes, namely the management of object information and the management of the objects themselves (for instance, original software products), which is called version management.

Information model

For each ICT business process, the information about the ICT object that can be applied in the process is enumerated (Table 33.1).

TABLE 33.1 ILM contributions to business processes

Process	Contribution from Integrated Life-cycle Management
Development and integration	ILM supplies information about performance of ICT objects in use.
	ILM supplies the service catalogue.
	ILM ensures that, when making an offer, all relevant aspects are taken into account (architecture, ICT market, management and exploitation, investment, total cost of ownership, technical and organizational feasibility etc.).
	ILM steers the life-cycle of an ICT object via the certification mechanism.
	ILM supplies information about which ICT objects are available on which platforms, and which standard application components under which conditions.
	ILM registers the result for specific ICT-object drafted architecture specifications.
	ILM registers the information about the composition of an ICT object in products.
	ILM registers product-specific issues such as platform dependence and operating systems.
	ILM gives (on behalf of impact and risk management) information about the relationships between ICT objects, that is to say: • Which ICT objects are relevant through this new object/ this change? • In which service or application is this product used?
	ILM gives information about the composition and status of the release in which an individual product is taken up.
	ILM guarantees, via version management that the right version of the software and matching documentation are always available.
Production and service	ILM gives information about which ICT objects can be ordered through individual buyers (catalogue function), while also mentioning the object characteristics, order conditions, logistical and price details.
	ILM gives information about the factual performance of an ICT object.
	ILM supports the solving of problems on a test/example level.
	ILM gives information about the level of support of the ICT object through the producer/supplier, gives an alert as to whether an ICT object is perhaps obsolete, or if there is already a successor available, and if the ICT object is already phased out.
	ILM gives information about similar related problems around an ICT object and analyses improvements/replacement possibilities.
	ILM advises about possible ad-hoc measures on continuity problems that arise or restrict on account of the ICT object concerned.
	ILM advises about the content of a change on a type (source of the change, planning, capacity, changes connected with ICT objects and existing examples of the ICT object, etc.)
	ILM gives information about which ICT objects on an item level may be ordered, purchased, delivered and used, as well as how these ICT objects are composed.
	ILM gives information about how many licences from software products are used, or that are still available.
	ILM makes important contract information available.
	ILM gives information about the active class of an ICT object
	ILM supports financial responsibility and charging.
	ILM gives information about the actual status of the ICT object, who signed this and when, if the progress is good, and if corrective conditions are necessary.

Organization model

Life-cycle management is a management function that is created to focus on specific expertise in all activities around a particular ICT object. Responsibility for the management of the life-cycle of an ICT object is, in fact, delegated to the separate life-cycle management function. The organization unit that life-cycle management fills is the 'owner' of the object and is ultimately responsible for managing all relevant aspects (planning, client demands, development, management, etc.) adequately and integrally. The 'life-cycle managers' are, in fact, the eyes and ears of the object that they manage, and they react proactively to new developments and trends. They are entrepreneurs, and direct those responsible for the development and management process. Although the 'life-cycle manager' has responsibility for good management of the ICT objects, they have no direct influence over those involved in the execution of the primary process. A life-cycle manager is, therefore, a specialist and generalist at the same time – a specialist because he or she always knows everything about the objects concerned and must be able to monitor performance, give advice and make plans; and, at the same time, a generalist because he or she need not know how all life-cycle activities are carried out, but must know which way to turn to get things achieved. A successful life-cycle manager trusts the skills and expertise of the organization in order to achieve the aims regarding the object. Life-cycle managers are, therefore, in a good position to communicate cross-functionally, to plan and to coordinate. When making decisions about individual objects, the consequences are again taken for things such as development, testing, implementation, production, use and management (Figure 33.6).

From the main ICT processes, the following roles are filled on behalf of ILM:

- *Account manager*: responsible for agreeing with the client about ICT services that are to be developed or changed; facilitated by the advice, feasibility study, establishment and acceptance of ICT services.

- *Infrastructure manager*: responsible for the release of the application and TIS products per infrastructure platform to production; ensures the integration and testing of the platform releases.

FIGURE 33.6

Organizational roles in ILM

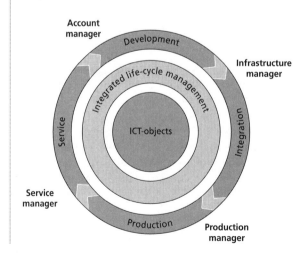

- **Product manager:** responsible for the maintenance of the application and TIS product portfolios; ensures agreements with architects, builders, suppliers, logistical managers and service managers on product research, selections and performance.
- **Service manager:** responsible for the maintenance of the ICT services; ensures agreements with the client about the actual ICT service through service level agreements (SLAs).

33.4 Implementation of ILM at the Dutch tax and customs administration

This section describes the implementation of ILM within the Dutch tax and customs administration, which, started with the introduction of a change process to put only certified products into the production environment. Further attention was given to the introduction of two information systems for the registration and management of products and services; the introduction of a life-cycle game in order to create awareness in the organization; and an ILM maturity model to gauge the ILM maturity of the organization.

Introduction of the WIPP procedure

In the past few years, the WIPP procedure (modifications of the ICT product package) has been used at the Computer Centre. The introduction of this procedure was effectively the start of ILM within B/AC. The procedure aims to put developed and modified products into production in a controlled manner. To assist this, two test offices have been set up: B-status and A-status offices. The B-status office aims to test the technical integrity of a product in the infrastructure. The A-status office aims to test the organizational manageability of a product. A product that receives A-status is an equivalent of the well-known KEMA approval stamp (Dutch industrial standard). An A-status product can be requested to be placed in the production environment without technical and organizational problems.

Introducing the SAP-COMIS and PMDB information systems

Three years ago, the ERP (Enterprise Resource Planning) system SAP was implemented within B/AC. It was deduced to register the product types in the materials-management module of SAP: SAP-COMIS (Component Management Information System). The SAP-COMIS information system formed the article base file for purchasing, stock control, ordering and asset management (Figure 33.7). In 1999 the PMDB was introduced in the organization. The product management database will play an important role in the life-cycle management of object types. The PMDB is an information system for the application and infrastructure product managers to administer the characteristics of their products. The PMDB is the central information system for the integral information collection and distribution for the ICT processes customer view, realization and implementation, production and service management. Physically this information system is (will be) coupled with the electronic distribution management system EDM, the object item service management system ITSM, the enterprise resource system SAP and the version management system.

FIGURE 33.7

SAP-COMIS framework

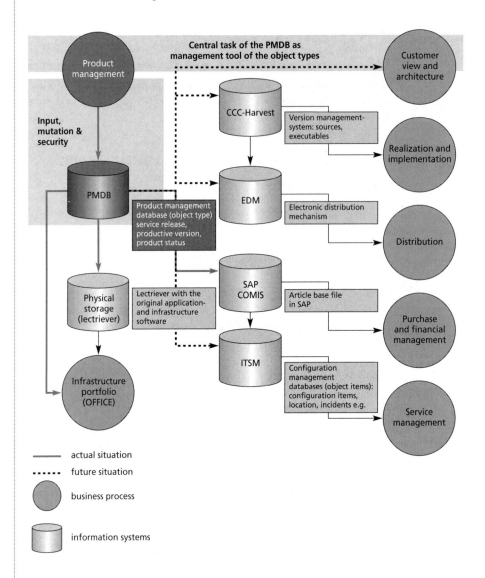

The PMDB is, basically speaking, an intelligent, electronic card-tray from which information about services, products and their underlying relationships are easy to find. To achieve this, a user-friendly user interface was developed; its functionality is shown in Figure 33.8.

Introduction of the life-cycle game

It appears that the introduction of an effective information system is not the final solution to the ILM problem. It has been ascertained that the sectors/departments usually have their own specific knowledge and view of the control of the infrastructure and related ICT services. The development and introduction of the information system does not always go according to plan. It was decided to develop a life-cycle

33 ■ Integrated life-cycle management

FIGURE 33.8
PMDB interfaces

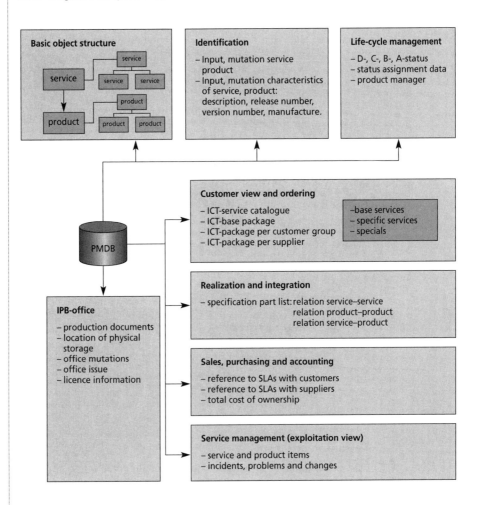

game to enable a smoother introduction of the PMDB information system. The life-cycle game is a great instrument for creating the necessary awareness for ILM in a less formal way within the organization: see Figure 33.9. The life-cycle game is a board game. Process owners go through the life-cycle of an ICT service (supply) and stop at 'bugs' in their process that concern the ILM problem. Through perpetrating the right number of interventions, team working and choosing the right strategy, the winner can receive his or her well-earned prize.

Introduction of the ILM maturity scan

By introducing the information system and playing the life-cycle game in the organization, it has been determined that not all sectors are on the same maturity level with regard to the ILM application. An ILM maturity model has been developed to measure the ILM maturity of each part of the organization. The model is based on the INK model (Institute Nederlandse Kwaliteit – The Institute of Dutch Quality). The model has five aspects that are important for the successful implementation of ILM:

FIGURE 33.9

Life-cycle game

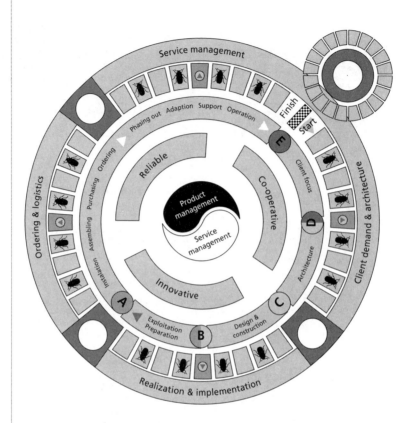

- Leadership and culture;
- Human resource management;
- Resource management;
- Process management;
- Strategy and policy.

The ILM maturity model assumes the different levels of maturity that the organization can have in the area of ILM. In total, five levels are distinguished in the model, analogous with the INK model. The maturity value is then defined acording to the level at which an organization unit scores on the five aspects of ILM (Figure 33.10). At present, the computer centre is on ILM level 2: the organization is ILM process-oriented. During the millennium transition the Year 2000 problems were solved and, while doing this, some big steps were taken in the standardization of the ICT and infrastructure. The application and technical infrastructure product portfolios were set up and the product management processes and tasks were described and carried out. At present, effort is going into describing the input and output of the product management process. There is also a need to interface the application portfolio with the technical infrastructure portfolio. And last but not least, there is a big need to couple the ICT service levels and service activities to the (technical) product portfolios.

FIGURE 33.10

The five levels of ILM

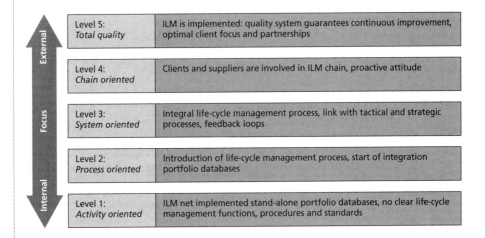

The advantage of this method is that every organization unit, in terms of the ILM maturity model, clearly controls its own current ILM situation and ILM path of growth.

Development of the Object model

In Figure 33.11 the latest version of the object model is shown. Characteristics of this model are:

- separation between service and product;
- separation between applications and technical infrastructure services;
- separation between buy and make products.

FIGURE 33.11

Current version of Object model

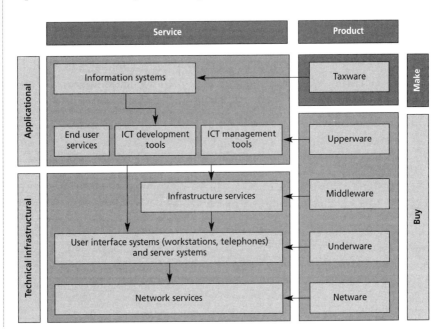

33.5 Conclusions

The reference framework contributes to life-cycle awareness, and the application has led to a number of definitive results. With regard to the ILM reference framework, the following conclusions have been made:

- ILM offers, with its integral focus on ICT objects and the resulting production process, a unique method for optimization of the ICT service process. Combined with object orientation, it forms a useful extension to existing methods that, above all, are process-oriented (i.e. ITIL, IPW). The object orientation is borrowed from logistical concepts that the industry has already successfully applied for decades.
- ILM offers four connected models with which the problem can be approached from different angles (objects, process control, organization, information) and on the basis of which ILM becomes a practical reality for an organization.
- The ILM object model makes it difficult to introduce logical structuring in the different object portfolios of an ICT service organization, which offers an overview and possibilities for standardization and, ultimately, cost saving.
- The ILM process-control model creates a bridge between development and production.

With regard to the application of ILM, the following can be concluded:
- The introduction of the certification has achieved its goal; A-status approval becomes the formal transfer from development to production.
- The article base file of the integral SAP system is constructed and becomes the basic registration to support the processes of logistics, asset management and service management.
- The product management database acts as the porch of the SAP system to manage the product portfolios, service portfolio, platform releases and service catalogue.
- ILM offers an instrument, in the form of the Maturity model, to control and guide the introduction of Integrated Life-cycle Management in an organization.

Within the ICT department of the Dutch tax and customs administration, clear paradigm shifts in the organization culture have been detected:

- from innovation to control;
- from technology to service; and
- from activity to result.

Parallel to these paradigm shifts, ILM makes a definitive contribution towards a trusted, client-oriented and professional ICT service organization.

34 Hunting the mammoth

The nonsense of cost management

Jan F. Bouman and **Michel van Dijk**
Solvision/The Art of Service

What does it cost? What is the yield? What is the added value? Relevant questions, but can you give an answer to every situation? Certainly the last one – what is the added value? – is often a problem.

What is added value? A definition:

The added value delivered by X is the consideration of the profits of X compared with the costs of X. Where profits as well as costs can be completely quantified in the same units, for example in Australian dollars, the added value is the difference between profits and costs. In other words: added value is material and immaterial yield.

34.1 Surviving

The basic understanding of profits minus costs is as old as humanity. The question is, 'have we progressed since the time when hunters and collectors wandered the prehistoric tundra? Could it be that they knew better than we do how to handle questions about costs and profits? Maybe they did a better job than we do because their society was considerably less complex. Why should one hunt if the meat and skin supplies for one's own needs are more than sufficient? Moreover, the carrots and firestone turnips acquired by bartering skins were getting on their nerves. It was time to save one's strength and avoid risks on the hunting fields because the added value was insufficient. It might be better to work on construction of a shelter because wind and rain threaten health, and thus life.

Every individual participant of the old society simply had to survive. They would reconsider ten times before economizing on activities that were of vital importance. Certainly if someone was facing starvation, he or she would dedicate additional (scarce) energy to energy-devouring activities such as hunting the mammoth. These were considerations that dealt with the added value of every effort and every expenditure of resources. Each action and each input was directly related to its contribution to the highest purpose: survival of the individual and the group (Gear and O'Neal, 1990).

34.2 Surviving in 2002

We are still surviving. It is in our genes. However, unlike the case of our prehistoric ancestors, the urge to survive has many different consequences. For the chief executive officer (CEO) it has to do with shareholders' value, and with market share, profitability and strategic policy. Managers below that level have to attain their targets, and they implement and manage company processes on a daily basis. At the operational level, people try to survive by carrying out their individual tasks, based on which they are reviewed.

Anyone at any level searches for a balance between fun, finance, future and fulfilment (see Table 34.1). This means that decisions taken, inspired by the urge to survive, will differ. In many cases these decisions are conflicting.

TABLE 34.1
4F balance

Fun	I enjoy my work.
Future	What I am doing now is relevant for my future career.
Fulfilment	My work is important. I do it for a reason.
Finance	And it pays well on top of everything else.

Source: Jan F. Bouman

If I take decisions from my own point of view about the resources of my organization, for whom or what in my organization does it have added value? This question is as much relevant to the CEO as to his or her on the colleague operational level. The view that 'added value' for people within organizations can have a completely different meaning has large consequences. Thus, the benefits of spending and costs can be reviewed in a completely different manner. How do we know that savings do not nullify the conditions for the survival of another person – or for the organization itself? And whose survival are we talking about? In other words: to whom does which added value belong and against which costs?

34.3 The nonsense of cost management

This rationale represents the core of 'the nonsense of cost management'. Often the management of an organization cuts a certain percentage of costs if business is slow. What often does not happen is the analysis of the added value of the departments, activities, resources, ideas and people concerned. One could cut something whose added value exceeds the savings and consequently cause more misery in the organization. Maybe one cuts something that is vital to survival. Cost management without analysis of the added value is like Russian roulette. Rationally it is nonsense, even dangerous.

34.4 Facilitating added value

Cost Management is not nonsense if it is an integral part of a cost/profit consideration. It must be part of the management of the life cycle of departments, activities, resources, ideas and functions. It must be possible to make a cost/profit analysis at any moment. In this way, costs can constantly be linked to added value. It is very possible that profits cannot directly be expressed in money. Immaterial profits, such as a stimulating company culture or a safe working environment, are often vital conditions for material success.

Several years ago Gartner Group expressed the development of asset management (managing company resources) in four phases (see Table 34.2). The first phase is primarily aimed at the acquisition and implementation of resources. The second phase adds administration (keeping up to date with what there is and who is using it) and management with the purpose of solving potential problems as soon as possible. In the third phase the management is performed proactively and one tries to manage the material lifetime of resources. Predictability of the 'behaviour' of resources is important at this point. Finally, in the fourth phase one manages the economical lifetime of resources with the delivered added value as the starting point.

TABLE 34.2 The four phases of Infrastructure Resource Planning

Stage	Business unit's view of IT value	TCO impact	Asset management	Operations management
1. Asset implementation	Asset implementation	Raise	Acquisition	Deployment
2. Asset utilization	Reactive efficiency	Control	Inventory	Monitoring and problem resolution
3. Asset optimization	Proactive Productivity	Lower	Technology resource management	Configuration and change management
4. Asset synchronization	Facilitation of value creation	Not applicable	Technology life-cycle	Service management management

Source: Gartner Group

The question here is: how much does the asset facilitate added value? Gartner Group calls this the development of Infrastructure Resource Planning. Today, many organizations have passed phase 2 and are trying to reach phase 3. This chapter tries to visualize phase 4 for the reader (Govekar, 1998).

34.5 Activity-based costing (ABC)

In the last few years, many large companies have been allocating costs to services and products. Before that, costs were usually linked to cost areas or departments. The idea behind this is that any company or department delivers a number of services or products to others. One wants to visualize what the cost price is so it can be controlled and, if necessary, allocated. This forms the basis for the next step in allocating costs to profits and eventually added value.

In commercial environments this has always been the case for services and products that are actually sold to customers. A company must know what the cost price is in order to determine the selling price and margin. With large and complex companies it is never easy to determine the actual cost price of an activity, service or product.

This is why disciplines such as activity-based costing (ABC) have been developed. ABC identifies the activities responsible for certain costs. Costs of activities are only allocated to products or services which are linked to that activity. If activities are 'monitored' better and more frequently, ABC will be more and more capable of seeing the mechanism that leads to certain costs. In this way, costs can be managed much better than before. For all the supporting departments, activities, resources, ideas and functions that do not have a direct relation to the end product, the situation is more complicated. For solution of the cost price problem we refer to the many publications about activity-based costing (e.g. Cooper, 1990; Perik, 2000). The World Wide Web also provides useful information.

ABC usually continues to allocate the costs to activities without analysing the profits. Referred to the above, this remains 'nonsense'. However, ABC lays down the basis for the next steps, which are that activities can be linked to services/products and consequently to profits (see Figure 34.1).

34.6 Trend

In the article 'IT cost management at the ABN AMRO Bank' the author Koen Perik describes how a large company follows the path to better financial management and control of IT costs (Perik, 2000). He indicates that having a good idea of the cost price structure of services and products is important. A move from allocating costs to cost centres (read cost areas or departments) to allocating them to service centres (services and products) is described. This trend especially applies to product- or service-related costs. Personnel-related costs remain linked to cost areas. The real link to added value is, however, one step too far. We can best illustrate the indicated trend as shown in Figure 34.1.

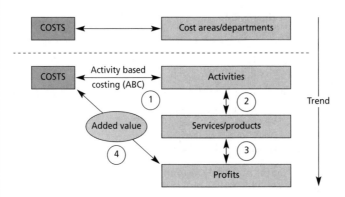

FIGURE 34.1

Cost management trend

Source: Bouman and van Dijk

In the last (lowest) step of this development, we can see that costs are linked to added value. However, this connection can only be made via the services/products. Services and products provide organizations with the right to exist by contributing to society. This means that organizations have to take the following:

1. Make a connection between costs and activities (e.g. by activity-based costing).
2. Make a connection between the activities and products/services of the organization.
3. Make a connection between products/services and the profits from them. Determine for whom these profits are relevant.
4. Determine the relation between costs and added value by determining the difference between costs and profits. The difference does not always have to be expressed in money (with immaterial profits).

These steps can be found in Figure 34.1.

34.7 Survival Web

As mentioned above, costs and profits need to be determined in order to measure added value. Added value is the material or immaterial yield (or profit) of a department, activity, project, resource, idea or function. From now on, this will be referred to as an 'object'. Figure 34.2 indicates the Survival Web. Within the Web, eight angles of incidence are projected, starting from which the added value of an object can be determined. In the example in Figure 34.2 this object can be 'Department IT Management' or 'Computer XYZ' or 'Network manager Escalon Network' (respectively department, resource or function). Before using the Survival Web a concrete object must be chosen, for which the added value must be determined.

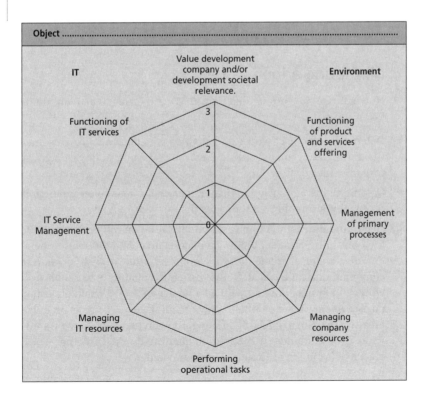

FIGURE 34.2
Survival Web

Source: Bouman and van Dijk

On the left side of the Survival Web the added value is presented from the IT perspectives, and on the right side the perspectives of the environment are handled.

IT perspectives:

- Value development company and/or development societal relevance;
- Functioning of IT services;
- IT Service Management;
- Managing IT resources;
- Performing operational tasks.

Environment perspectives:

- Value development company and/or development societal relevance;
- Functioning of product and services offering;
- Management of primary processes;
- Managing company resources;
- Performing operational tasks.

The environment is the organization or company (or division) to which IT offers its services. The same model can be applied to objects from other parts of the organization, e.g. financial policy and management, in which case the left side needs to be translated into financial angles instead of the IT angles. In the angles a certain hierarchy was added. This has to do with the fact, mentioned above, that at different levels different considerations apply to added value. Everyone has his or her own Fun, Future, Fulfilment and Finance (see Table 34.1).

34.8 Measuring added value

How can we measure added value? With the Survival Web, the following steps are taken:

1. Determine the object whose added value is to be assessed. This must be an object that fits the angles of the left side of the Web and can be a department, activity, project, resource, idea or function.
2. Determine the measuring indicators per angle. This relates to both halves of the Survival Web. Table 34.3 indicates the relevant indicators.
3. Determine the method of measurement. Different methods are available, for example Meesters and Bouman (2000). Vandecasteele *et al.* (2000) also offers starting points. For effective measurements, workshops, interviews, abstract analyses and combinations can be used. In the rest of this chapter we assume a simple interview or workshop form combined with an abstract analysis. When choosing a method of measurement, it is essential to know *what* needs to be measured. Is it necessary to measure the range of feeling of the parties involved or do we want to determine added value in an analytical way based on quantified units? In other words: subjective or objective (as much as possible) measurement.

4. Select the people involved in the measurement. It is essential that people from different levels and departments within the organization are involved. Added value can differ per person or department. Any person or department has its own needs and one person attaches more or less value to certain angles than another. Everyone has the imperative to survive. A chief information officer (CIO) will value the control of IT resources while a product manager will value the functioning of the products and services offering. That is why, for an optimal result, people from different parts in the organization need to be involved in the measurement.
5. Perform the measurement.
6. Project the measured added values into the Survival Web: add links between the projected measured values. In this way a spider's web image evolves – the *Survival Web*.

Everyone involved in the measurement will be confronted with understandings three things:

1. **Object** *What needs to be reviewed?* The object whose added value is measured.
2. **Angles** *Why does it have to be reviewed?* The angles used when determining the added value. The angles are shown in the Survival Web.
3. **Indicators** *How should it be review?* The indicators for each angle that support the bordering and reviewing from the angle (see Table 34.3: indicators per angle).

Example with information system ABC as an object. The person involved is asked: How do you review the added value of 'ABC' (=object) for the 'functioning of the IT Services' (=angle) taking the following indicators (list indicators) into account?

For reviewing the added value of an object (from a certain angle) one can use a scale of 0 to 3, where the scores mean the following:

Score 3: [object] adds large/essential contribution to [angle]

Score 2: [object] adds a clear contribution to [angle]

Score 1: [object] adds little contribution to [angle]

Score 0: [object] adds no contribution to [angle]

Each person (involved in the measurement) will apply a value for every indicator per angle. Each person will determine an average value per angle. For each angle, an average score will be determined.

Each angle has its own indicators for determining added value (Table 34.3).

34.9 Interpretation of the Survival Web

Added value can now be measured based on the added value indicators. People from different departments give a score per angle for each indicator. All information is collected and averages are determined. These results are presented through the Survival Web. Interpretation of the results can simply be determined by the percentage covered. The results of a *value scan* performed for a certain object are given in Figure 34.3. A covering percentage over 25% adds sufficient added value to decide in favour of a

TABLE 34.3 Indicators per angle

Angle	Indicator
Functioning of IT services	• Portfolio • SLA • Uptime / MTBF • Perception of customer/company • Number of resources used • Service balance: standard versus special
IT Service Management	• Quality guarantee • Policy issues (vision, goals and policy)
Managing IT resources	• Number of tools used • Quality of tools • Quick/accurate reports • Number of needed resources
Performing operational tasks	• Efficiency • Delivered quality
Managing company resources	• Acquire and implement resources • Administration and control • Proactive control • Manage economic lifetime
Management of primary processes	• Process owners • Process descriptions • Process implementation
Functioning product and services offering	• Product/service purchase • Customer content • Meet the customers' needs
Value development company and/or development societal relevance	• Market share • PR • Attraction for new employees (Investors In People)

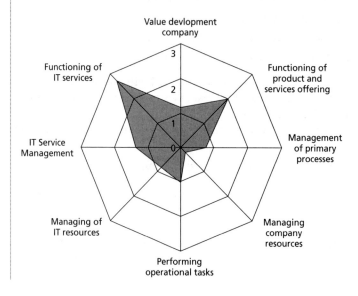

FIGURE 34.3 Survival Web example

project, an activity, a purchase of an object, continuation of an information system, etc., i.e. a decision can be made to *start* or *continue* (the object). A smaller percentage covered should lead to the conclusion not to start or continue (the object). In addition, the Survival Web provides a visual image of where the added value is experienced most or least: at strategic or operational level, within or outside IT.

34.10 Applying the Survival Web

Here are several instances of applying the Survival Web.

The new salary system NovaSal

A new salary system, called NovaSal, is implemented in a company. Therefore, a project is started to determine the added values by performing a Survival Web measurement. The goal of this measurement is to determine who acknowledges most and least added value from NovaSal. First, a specific IT angle is reviewed, combined with general angles. It seems that only those who work outside IT at the tactical and operational levels positively experience added value from NovaSal. Conclusion: because the range of IT workers (who need to implement the system) and of higher management (who decide on budgets and priorities) is the smallest, the project is at great risk (see Figure 34.4a).

If a new Survival Web measurement is performed for the same project, but from the angle of the personnel department, another image evolves. In the personnel department the need for NovaSal is seen at every level. The weakness remains the commitment of top management (see Figure 34.4b).

FIGURE 34.4

The NovaSal system

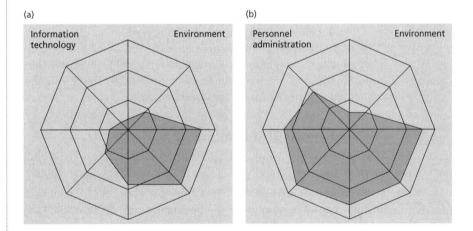

The Stock Exchange quotation

A company starts a procedure for a Stock Exchange listing. This is often a difficult procedure that can have many consequences for the culture and the organization. For each division within the company a Survival Web measurement is performed. This is important because with a Stock Exchange listing everyone has to point in the same direction. If this is not taken into account, completely different and even contradictory interests within the organization can be experienced. Figures 34.5a and 34.5b indicate the Survival Webs of respectively the IT and the Sales divisions.

FIGURE 34.5

Stock Exchange listing

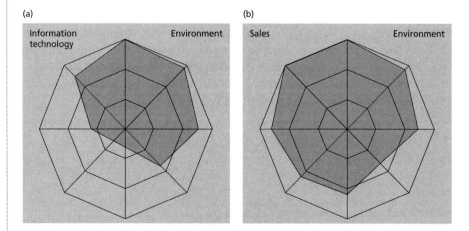

Conclusions: in both cases there is a lot of commitment at strategic level. However, on the IT side the tactical and certainly the operational levels do not appreciate the added value of a listing, possibly because people see it as a threat to their own positions. The Sales division has a different view, being conscious of the need for a listing at tactical and operational levels, probably because they expect good publicity and a positive reputation when contacting (potential) customers. In such situations one has to realize that in divisions where the change (=the object) is not experienced as an additional impetus to survive, people will resist.

In both examples the measurement is based on added values. It is essential that choices are made when measuring: do we want to measure the range of feeling of those involved, or do we want to determine (subjectively and objectively) the added values analytically based on quantified units?

34.11 Survival Web and cost savings

How can the Survival Web be used in a practical way when saving costs?

How often do we need to economize? A measure often taken in these situations is cutting resource expenditure. For example sometimes (all) contractors are removed and in some cases the employees are not spared either. These decisions are taken to get a quick financial result without thinking about the added value these resources bring to the company. Furthermore, as soon as the savings phase is over, contractors need to be hired all over again. Staff hired need to get experience to be able to rebuild the necessary knowledge that has been lost, with all the additional costs that this implies taken into account. In the end, it all turns out to be more expensive than before.

In these cases the Survival Web can offer a solution. The question 'Do all contractors have to leave?' (contractors = object) would be much too vague. For such a large group it is not possible to determine an added value for different angles. The object should be modified to 'Should we continue Project X?' (Project X = object). Scores for the different added value indicators can be provided for this direct question. Even if the outcome is that the project does not contribute sufficient added value, at least it becomes clear in which areas more added value needs to be delivered in order to continue.

34.12 Conclusions

Prehistoric hunters made the choice to hunt the mammoth by thinking in terms of added value. Because hunting was generally teamwork, one first looked at added value for the whole group and then for individual members. This was a continuing process of costs–profit analysis. The dominating motive was 'survival'.

Survival is still everyone's central motive. However, owing to the complexity of our organizations and increasing individualism, survival has mainly become a personal matter. This brings the continuity of the organization, or collective, into the discussion. Owing to the complexity, the top management, who make the most far-reaching decisions, have a limited view of the stimulators determining the survival of the company as a whole. That is why they consciously or unconsciously mainly argue from a personal survival strategy. CEO, be honest: *what are your real motives for taking important decisions about costs and expenses?*

It is vital to have a better view of the motives for survival at different levels within the organization, because it gives insight into what needs to be done to let the whole company survive. Until recently, choices were made based on the contribution of costs to cost areas or departments. In 2002 we notice a trend to cost management linked to added value. Our prehistoric ancestors had already made this link. Thus, this places question marks over the sense of cost management in its recent form. This chapter adds a path that cost management will follow: added value as yield and added value as result of the survival stimulators of all individual players.

The quantification of the added value is often a difficult business. This chapter provides practical aid in the form of the Survival Web and the eight different angles. The indicators per angle quantify the added value. The Survival Web presents the results in a simple and clear manner. Determining the added value indicators plays an important role. These indicators can differ for each organization. It quantifies the added value! Or put another way: the changes necessary to survive are quantified.

Maybe the prehistoric hunters did not do so badly. With every mammoth hunt, they thought about the added value. They had to, in order to survive. This is why mankind was able to survive and become what it is today. However, there is a reverse side of the coin. *The mammoth has become extinct.*

Acknowledgement

With thanks to Lychinta Zichem for her translation support.

Literature

Cooper, R. (1990) 'Implementing an activity-based cost system', *Journal of Cost Management,* Spring, p33–42.

Gear, M.W. and O'Neal, K. (1990) *People of the Wolf*, Tor Books; New York

Govekar, M. (1998) Gartner Group, Conference Presentation.

Hammer, M. and Champy, J. (1993) *Reengineering the Corporations : A Manifesto for Business Revolution*, Harper Business, New York.

Meesters, B. J.M.A. and Bouman, J. F. (2000) 'A service check', *World Class IT Management Guide, Edition 2000,* Ten Hagen & Stam, The Hague.

Perik, K. (2000) 'IT Cost Management bij de ABN AMRO Bank' (www.management.hbp.net), September (in Dutch).

Philips, K. and Dilton-Hill, K. (1996) 'As easy as ABC', *ABC Technologies*, 27, Winter.

Vandecasteele, J.R.M., Acda, L. Grund, D. and Burger, M. (2000) 'Visie op Performance Management in IT-organisaties', *IT Beheer Jaarboek 2000* (in Dutch), Ten Hagen & Stam, The Hague.

World Wide Web: www.bettermanagement.com/abcmauthority

Review of part 5

It is obvious that the approach of Kostick *et al.* in **Service Level Management** was not based upon ITIL. The discrepancy in terminology with the European ITIL model is striking: where ITIL speaks of Service Management, Kostick *et al.* speak of Service Level Management. The same discrepancies are found in terms such as Configuration Management and Incident Control versus Asset Management and Problem Management. In that sense, ITIL looks like a somewhat broader approach.

Kostick *et al.* make a good point when they say that management commitment, explicit process ownership, and business alignment are crucial elements in IT Service Management, where the responsibility for the IT infrastructure lies solely with the IT services provider (as in other areas: you don't tell your baker what means he or she must use to bake your bread).

Further, they name a group of activities which are not referred to as such in ITIL: Request Management. Request Management refers to the processing of user requests. This is a more general denomination of support call handling than is covered in ITIL. For example, Request Management covers production jobs such as those which occur in day-to-day operations; these are not explicitly positioned in ITIL, even though they account for a very considerable part of daily routine. In this approach, Kostick *et al.* are in line with the views on the Operations Management process which is modelled in IPW and ISM (see part 1). The vision of Kostick *et al.* is quite clearly based on practical lessons, as is ITIL, but that has resulted in a number of interesting differences, and Request Management is probably the most striking of these.

The MANTIS Big-E Environment, as described by Ruiz *et al.* in **An integrated environment for managing software maintenance projects**, is a real framework in the right sense of the word: it contains a thorough approach to what tools are needed to support a Software Maintenance process. But be careful: tools in this case must not be understood only as software tools like the ones on the IT Service Management market. Here 'tools' is meant in a broader sense: conceptual tools (the concepts used) and methodological tools (the methodologies used) are also described.

Ruiz *et al.* use several well-known concepts, among them the Workflow Reference Model of the Workflow Management Coalition, the ontology of Kitchenham *et al.* These concepts are integrated to form one process metamodel. Also, several existing methodologies (including that of the authors: MANTEMA) are incorporated in the methodological part of the framework.

In **Kwintes project**, Ruijs gives us only a basic introduction to what is realized in the Kwintes project. The Kwintes project team has made a great effort in detailing the four phases of the IT Service Management lemniscate. Very characteristic in this approach is the central position of the service level agreement (SLA). With the details of each phase, the IT organization and the client organization both have a very useful toolbox put at their disposal. Derived products such as self-assessment questionnaires are currently being developed in the follow-up project, DOCIS.

In **Integrated life-cycle management**, van den Boomgaard *et al.* distinguish themselves in their object-oriented approach to the framework. IT services are decomposed into infrastructure platforms, products and support activity patterns. Each of these objects can be decomposed to more levels, if necessary. The management of objects is the starting point for building a stable management framework that adds up to the management of services in all stages of the life cycle. The chosen decomposition method could be replaced by any other, if that were more useful for the situational characteristics of the organization applying it. The method also provides for a tool that is able to support improvement programmes for ILM. As in other service management methodologies, a growth model is described to facilitate the step-by-step implementation of ILM.

In **Hunting the mammoth**, Bouman and van Dijk compare the IT organization to a group of hunters in prehistoric times. As in the case of the hunters, it is an important issue for IT organizations to weigh the benefits and costs – in other words, to determine added value.

The authors have a point there: from the enterprise perspective, cost management alone is not enough to make the right decisions on certain measures (investments, cuts etc.) in ICT. The benefits for the enterprise as a result of the measures taken on ICT have to be quantified. The Survival Web introduced by Bouman and Van Dijk can be of great help, even when objects other than ICT are concerned. The method can support measuring the added value of decisions to the enterprise. Also, on the level of the IT organization, the method can be deployed to estimate the effect of internal measures in terms of added value. From the perspective of the whole (enterprise), the added value of a part (of the enterprise) is always important.

Looking from the other side, from the perspective of the part (i.e. the IT organization) to the whole (i.e. the enterprise), deployment of cost management is not useless. When an enterprise is planning to use a new application, which is determined using the Survival Web to be a good decision, that is a plain fact for the IT organization. Looking from the perspective of the IT organization, cost management (costing and charging for the service delivery for that application) is an effective means to achieve optimal control and efficiency in Service Management.

The tactical process of Cost Management will play an important role for IT organizations in the customer–provider relationship (charging). The analysis of the added value is important to the customer, but only the customer can make this analysis.

part 6

Organizational aspects

Introduction to the theme

In IT Service Management we introduce processes for improving the quality of the service. The introduction of processes makes sure that organizations are managed quite differently from the traditional hierarchical organizations. Processes are cross-departmental. They are focused on their output, their result, and, by running through the organization from head to tail, they are focused at the organization's output as well.

Hierarchical organizations are not capable of coping with modern, highly demanding customers, in terms of speed and flexibility. Services have to be delivered much faster, better, custom-made, etc., than ever before. Processes, implemented the right way, will contribute to this.

The implementation of processes, however, can only be achieved through an organizational change. And changes, particularly organizational changes, often cause traumas to those involved. In this case those involved not only have to cope with the organizational changes but have to improve the quality of service at the same time.

The delivery of service is a process between the provider and the customer of the service. The customer experiences the quality of service through the interaction he or she has with the supplier. The perception the customer has in the pre-delivery phase is matched with the actual service delivered. Therefore this moment of service delivery is often called the 'moment of truth'.

In the IT consumer product market a lot of standardization has been established, especially regarding the end product (e.g. PCs, network equipment). This standardization has led to a high level of process control in the products market. In the services market, however, each and every so-called moment of truth is unique. The quest for process control in IT service management has led to procedures and working instructions, best practices and process definitions, each contributing to the level of standardization in service management. Formal standards haven't been determined, however, and it will take some time before we reach that. Services will have to be measured first or, rather, they will have to be made measurable. And although the best practices of ITIL help in this respect, it is obvious from the conclusions in part 1 that more is needed.

In the meantime, all services will be unique in their own way, leaving the quality of service highly dependent on the professionalism of the individual that is supporting this service.

At the same time, the labour market is so tight that it is very hard to get all the (right) people you need. And even if you can find them, it is a continuous challenge to retain them. People have to be motivated and they have to have opportunities for personal development. And all of this has to be accomplished in compliance with the organizational goals. So, on the one hand you have the embedding of processes aiming at service quality improvement and on the other you have the human aspects that have to contribute to the continuity of this quality, along with the need to retain these people in your organization. These challenges and the way in which organizations have taken them up will be described in this part.

Content

This part consists of five chapters describing practical approaches to the organizational aspects of IT Service Management:

Embedding and managing IT processes in an organization
Richard van Bavel and Jeroen Bronkhorst

Patching the blind spot in implementation of IT process models
Peter A.J. Bootsma and Jan van Bon

Competence management
Renée Kamphuis

Knowledge management and the IT Service Management organization
A.P. Kuiper, P.M. Los and J. Sietsma

Organizational improvement and culture ... growth deserves space!
Jolanda Meijers and Hans van Herwaarden

A review of part 6 follows thereafter.

Reading instructions

IT service delivery is organized into processes more and more often. This is achieved through an organizational change. The first two chapters describe several options for such organizational change.

Whatever approach is taken, the employees will have to carry the consequences. Within the process environment the employees have to develop themselves not just for their own benefit but also for the benefit of the organization. Important keywords of this decade are: competences and knowledge. The third and fourth chapter in this part deal with these matters.

Apart from the proper organization of service delivery, the culture of the organization must be one that stimulates the development of its employees within both the individual and the organizational goals. The fifth chapter provides a vision of how the culture of an organization can be used to gain maximum benefit from it in the service delivery stage.

part 6: Organizational aspects

Introduction to the chapters

In **Embedding and managing IT processes in an organization**, van Bavel and Bronkhorst conclude that organizations often try to implement processes into an organizational structure that is not sufficiently clear in itself. As a consequence, conflicts concerning the control of the human resources may arise. The authors compare traditional hierarchical structures to the matrix organization, in the case of implementing IT service management processes. As an alternative, they show us the network organization. For these three organizational structures the authors provide practical guidelines for implementing IT Service Management processes.

Either way, if you want to change the way an organization behaves, it will affect the people working in it. And because organizational changes are tough and sometimes hard to overcome, you'd better do it right the first time. In **Patching the blind spot in implementation of IT process models**, Bootsma and Van Bon combine insights gathered from the area of Quality Management and IT Service Management. This combination results in an approach that can lead to an effective embedding of processes in an organization. Bootsma has done a thorough investigation on quality management in complex organizations. This has led him to develop a method for setting up self-directed teams, the so-called Recursive Process Management (RPM). In this chapter this method is theoretically combined with the ideas of Integrated Service Management (ISM, see part 1). In doing so, the authors make an attempt to bridge the gap between IT Service Management and Process Management.

In **Competence management**, Kamphuis describes the bottom-up approach used by KPN Datacenter to implement Competence Management. This approach focuses first on the task-bound competences for employees. These task areas are defined in such a way that they will contribute to the organizational goals. This approach yielded results within a fairly short time and appears not to be too difficult to implement. Kamphuis sees Competence Management as a means to make maximum use of the talents of employees in the organization. In doing so, the management style must invite and encourage employees to explore the scope of their talents within the organization as fully as possible. Competence Management is seen as a facilitator for People Management, a process that appears to be difficult to implement.

In **Knowledge management and the IT Service Management organization**, Kuiper, Los and Sietsma describe Knowledge Management as the process that manages the intellectual capital. Intellectual capital is, according to the authors, the means for business improvement. Knowledge is regarded as making decisions based on information, and information is regarded as data within a certain context. The authors define knowledge management as the management of the knowledge life cycle, on a strategic, tactical and operational level.

In **Organizational improvement and culture ... growth deserves space!**, Meijers and van Herwaarden give their vision on the culture of organizations. According to the authors, an organization can respond to opportunities in the environment more quickly by giving their employees as much freedom as possible. The coordination of activities must then be managed by their organizational culture. The shared values of the employees are especially important in this coordination. They argue that the lasting success of an organization depends on the speed with which it can react to the environment. Because organizations respond much more slowly than individuals to changes, the authors argue that organizations must use this speed of response by freeing the employees as much as possible.

35 Embedding and managing IT processes in an organization

Richard van Bavel and **Jeroen Bronkhorst**
Hewlett Packard, Amstelveen, the Netherlands

Summary

Output levels and the degree of customer friendliness are becoming increasingly important indicators for the quality of an IT organization. To improve these, result-oriented (ITIL) processes are being introduced into many IT organizations that (can) embrace several organizational units and that are controlled by the process owners. When doing this, it is important to embed the IT processes soundly in the (desired) organizational structure and ensure that they are adequately controlled. In practice, neither of these two things is always done properly. For this reason, this chapter presents a number of tips (best practices) that can be applied to different organizational structures.

35.1 Introduction

Many IT organizations have always had a hierarchical set-up and structure. Such a structure is characterized by organizational units managed by one or more (layers of) managers,[1] where the managers have (delegated) responsibility to implement a particular task area of the IT work field. Traditional task areas include operation and maintenance, system development, and consultancy. In order to achieve the agreed results, the manager controls the content (who does what and how?) as well as the facilities (what is needed where?).

The hierarchical organizational structure has advantages and disadvantages. One advantage is that both the customers/users and the IT employees have a single contact person who tells them what is allowed and what must be done and who provides them with the necessary resources. Another advantage is that escalation levels are (intuitively) clear (first the manager, then the manager's manager, etc., etc.).

One disadvantage is that, when providing services to a customer/user of the IT organization, IT employees from several organizational units are involved, and they may be managed differently by their respective managers. This can lead to long delays, frustration and dissatisfied customers/users. Another consequence of this is that it is difficult to measure/control the quality of these services, because there is often no consolidated information about the organizational units as a whole (nor is there anybody responsible for it).

Now that output and the degree of customer friendliness are becoming increasingly important indicators for the quality of an IT organization, result-oriented (ITIL) processes are being introduced into many IT organizations. These processes (can) embrace several organizational units and are managed by process owners. In practice, however, this type of management has been found somewhat disappointing. Process owners do indeed bear the responsibility for the processes, but they often have insufficient power to actually manage and control them. And the people who have the power either do not understand the process enough to make the right decisions, or they are driven by different interests. This chapter provides, therefore, a number of tips (best practices) on embedding IT processes[2] in the (desired) organizational structure and on the appropriate management tasks.

Scope

This chapter does not deal exhaustively with the specific execution of IT processes. However, it does discuss the management of IT processes and management from the line. The fundamental principle is that the organization has already chosen to work or start working with IT processes. More information about IT processes is available in Drake (2000).

The structure of this chapter

In order to describe the organizational embedding of IT processes, this chapter first presents an overview of different organizational structures, the characteristics of (the management of) IT processes and the way IT processes can be projected onto the various organizational structures. It then goes on to discuss management of the IT processes in greater detail from the perspectives of an IT manager, a process owner and an IT employee. It also describes the overlaps between line management and process management, subdivided into management effects, escalations and measurement values. The chapter concludes with best practices that can be applied when introducing process management.

35.2 Components of an IT organization

When setting up and managing an IT organization, many organizations look for a balance between three areas: clustering people (organizational structure), clustering activities aimed at an organization's output (IT processes), and automated support. The following is an overview of a number of different organizational structures, the characteristics of IT processes and a number of best practices regarding the way these two components can be projected alongside each other.

Organizational structures

The activity of 'Organizing' can be seen as the functional relationships between available people, resources and their activities in order to achieve particular objectives. Simply put, an *organization* consists of all of the working relationships that people consciously enter into with each other to achieve their shared objectives. Forming an organization is what makes it possible to achieve objectives that could not otherwise be achieved.

35 ■ Embedding and managing IT processes in an organization

It is a fact that tasks are distributed as soon as a company has so many tasks to execute that a single person can no longer execute them. Tasks are classified into functions for employees, and a grouping of functions results in a department or unit, the basic element of an organization. The division of labour breaks up the cohesion of the whole; after all, every department now has its own tasks and objectives. As a consequence, there is a need for coordination – not only within the department but also between the departments – in order to realize the business objectives in due course.

Division of labour can be organized in a horizontal or a vertical direction. In a horizontal direction, this is expressed organizationally by departments based on *similarity*. Departments are classified according to their function (similar knowledge or activities), product and service, market (target group) or geo-graphy. Classification according to products and services (=result orientation) in combination with market and geography (=customer orientation) is used a lot nowadays, as it caters for both the interests of the customer and the contribution required for the business process.

The division of labour in a vertical direction is expressed by clustering based on *equality*. Here, there is almost always a division between management and execution. The consequence is a hierarchy, which has the following important forms of expression: the line and staff organization and the project/matrix organization. And because management is an important part of this chapter, we will examine these hierarchical forms more closely.

Line and staff organization

The line organization is characterized by a clear, pyramid-shaped structure (see Figure 35.1a), in which management is performed from above to below. Every employee has a single superior, who allocates his or her tasks and to whom he or she is accountable. Disputes between employees are often settled at the level of the first joint manager (who can impose his or her will on both parties). Advantages of the line organization include the unity of leadership and the clear communication structure, while the disadvantage is mainly the overburdening of managers with decision making, long communication channels (loss of time and information), and often their insufficient knowledge of the material needed to make the right decisions.

The line organization can be expanded by introducing assisting staff who provide the managers with support on expertise and tasks. Management itself does not change – after all, the formal authority to make decisions is and remains in the line. The staff merely advise the line managers on the subject matter. The disadvantage of this structure is the subsequent erosion of the managerial function, the (lack of) authority of staff, costs, and the possible duplication of tasks.

Project/matrix organization

A matrix organization is characterized by its matrix structure (see Figure 35.1b). Management in such a structure is performed from different dimensions (both vertically and horizontally). Employees have functional managers (for example, project managers, product managers or process owners) and line managers to whom they are accountable (no unity of leadership). For each employee it should be recorded which

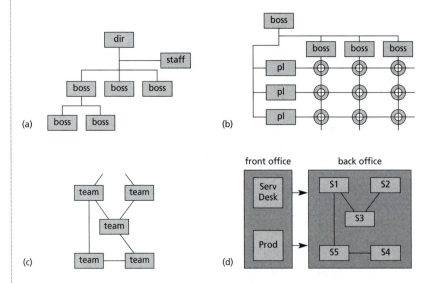

FIGURE 35.1

Organizational structures: (a) line (and staff) organization; (b) project matrix organization; (c) network organization; (d) front and back office

manager is entitled to which portion of the work capacity and which manager has which responsibilities and authority to assess and evaluate employees, as well as who will perform the evaluations. The advantages of this structure are mainly its flexibility and capacity to adapt quickly to new needs, while the disadvantages are the large overheads and the area of tension linked to the relative power among the (project) managers. If there is no relative power among the managers, the matrix degenerates into a line structure.

The project organization is a temporary variant of a 'normal' matrix organization. After all, a project organization only exists while a project is being executed, and it is disbanded afterwards.

In addition to the hierarchy, the degree to which tasks, authority and responsibilities are allocated lower or higher in the organizational structure indicates how *centralized* or *decentralized* the organization actually is. One organizational design rule is that the lower they can be located in the organization the more effectively it can function (no unnecessary communication, more control, etc.).

Network organization/hyperarchy

In addition to the forms mentioned above, the current trend of the 'hyper-archy' or network organization (see Figure 35.1c) is also worth mentioning. Whereas the line organization and matrix organization have a bilateral or trilateral relationship based on the relative power, in the hyperarchy every component can have a relationship with another component. Every component in such an organization has grown to become a specialist on specific components or services of the shared end product. In an IT organization, for example, one component can be specialized in a SAP application, another in network infrastructure, a third in server components. Various services are provided to customers both individually and collectively. The distinguishing feature of such components is their high degree of autonomy. The traditional (steep) hierarchical structures have been made 'flatter' in an attempt to increase the organization's effectiveness.

The following forms are possible:

1. network between different organizations;
2. network between business units within organizations;
3. network between (self-managing) teams in (business units of) organizations.

In the first two forms, a division of labour is again possible (the possibility of a hierarchy); in a self-managing team, all members of the team manage and make decisions on the basis of equality. However, self-managing teams must remain limited in size; after all, if they become too large a division of labour will be necessary, which will again give rise to a hierarchy. A division into new teams can prevent the formation of such a hierarchy, but if many teams are formed, the complexity among the teams and therefore the need for coordination also increases (organizational paradox). With a hyperarchy, the relationship between the components is of crucial importance, and mutual agreements should therefore be made (for example, using underpinning contracts or Operational Level Agreements). These agreements can guarantee the total chain of the provision of services.

The network structure, given its recursive nature (from team to separate organization) and the demarcation of supplied products and services for each component, easily lends itself to the creation of strategic partnerships and the insourcing and outsourcing of services. This added value is particularly important in the current Internet e-conomy.

Combinations of the forms above are also possible (see Figure 35.1d). For example, the IT organization can be arranged into product (service teams) and target group segments (front and back office), and can be (partially) structured as a network organization.

The abovementioned forms provide all kinds of opportunities for effective organizational designs. Is it possible, then, to create a generic organizational design for an IT organization? Unfortunately not, because an IT organization is not a static entity, and it can change in the course of time as a consequence of many different circumstances. For example, changes in the culture and the market can lead to expansion, cutbacks, or the redistribution of organizational components (such as 'tilting' or 'flattening'). An organization can also change from one structure to another and later revert to its original form. Therefore, no 'ideal' structure can be indicated; all of the forms mentioned are possible in practice and each has its advantages and disadvantages. The actual structuring of an IT organization is and will always be a question of customization.

Processes

To set up an effective organization, you mainly have to examine the processes within the organization. The products and services of organizations are, after all, the result of processes (executed by people or machines). The following is a short explanation of these processes.

General definitions

A process is a cohesive series of activities carried out to achieve a predefined objective (van Bon, 2000). A process description records what is being done, which input is required for that purpose and which output will be generated. One other factor that characterizes a process is that it is measured to determine the degree to which it satisfies the agreed standards. In addition, the process is evaluated periodically and, where necessary, optimized for effectiveness (aimed at the customer) and efficiency (aimed at the organization itself). Here, the objective is to achieve the agreed result as effectively as possible, in terms of both quality and quantity.

In order to keep track of the whole process, processes are managed by process owners who are responsible for the structure, continuance, operation and output of those processes. This means, for example, that the process owner must ensure that the process has been defined adequately, that the work has been distributed and completed effectively and efficiently in accordance with the process documentation, and that the output of the process satisfies the agreed requirements and wishes.

In order to distribute the work within a process, the process activities are clustered into process roles. Here, it is usual to indicate which knowledge, skills and behaviour are required to perform the process roles. A process role is not necessarily the same as a function. This subject is described in more detail below when dealing with processes in an organization.

The activities within a process can be divided into two categories: execution and management. The first category includes the activities that are characteristic for (execution of) the process. These activities are described specifically for IT management in the IT Infrastructure Library (ITIL), based on the 'best practices' of the UK government. One example is the set of activities for handling a (threatened) disruption in Incident Management. Given the scope of this chapter, it is not possible to discuss this category in any detail here.

The second category includes the activities for managing the process. These management activities consist of measuring and evaluating the process (for example, on the basis of reports) and adjusting it where necessary (see Figure 35.2). This might include both the long-term addition of new process components and/or the adaptation of existing process components, as well as short-term measures to stimulate progress. The management activities are executed by the process owner or by a delegate. In this way, for example, daily progress can also be monitored within Incident Management by an employee fulfilling the role of progress controller, or (part of) daily management can be delegated to a process manager. For effective management, however, the managers should have sufficient power in the organization.

In many organizations, IT processes support the primary business processes. With the upsurge of the Internet, IT processes can now be the same as the primary processes of an organization – for example, shops and banks that only operate on the Internet.

In more traditional organizations, IT processes are the same as the primary processes *of the IT organization*, which are supported by processes such as financial management, quality management, purchasing, internal communication, external communication (marketing), personnel management, security and resource management (facility affairs). One thing that characterizes these support processes is that they are applied more broadly in an organization, and separate organizational units have been created to manage them (for example, Personnel Affairs, Purchasing, Financial Affairs, etc.). These support processes are performed by the line manager, and this creates the peripheral conditions that enable the IT processes to function adequately.

FIGURE 35.2

Execution and management activities within a process

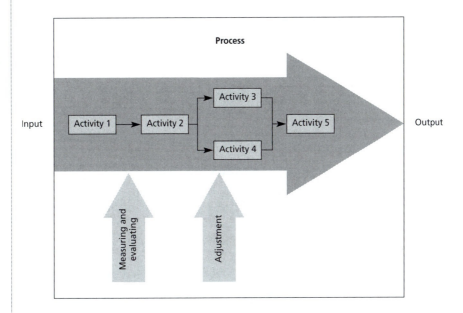

Embedding IT processes in the organization

When projecting the IT processes onto an IT organizational structure, the defined IT processes are incorporated into one or more (new) organizational units. These IT processes can, however, cover several departments (see Figure 35.3). This means that, when embedding the IT processes, the organization may be confronted with the *current* organizational structure. This structure should be tested to ensure that the processes can flow properly, and any necessary organizational adjustments that become evident from this test must be implemented. For an optimal flow of processes, the structure must be organized, as it were, around the processes.

The following options are possible when projecting the IT processes onto an IT organizational structure:

1. The existing organizational structure is retained as much as possible.
2. There is a transition from one organizational structure to another organizational structure.
3. Different organizational structures are combined with each other.

Maintaining the organizational structure

If a line structure is retained when IT processes are being introduced – by appointing an organizational unit *for each process* – the negative characteristics of this organizational structure will be retained (see the Introduction to this chapter), whereas the aim of introducing IT processes is in fact to achieve the opposite. In this organizational structure, it is possible for the role of the process owner to be projected onto a line manager. The advantage of this is that the process owner gains more power with this position, which can promote better management.

FIGURE 35.3

Process flow through an organization

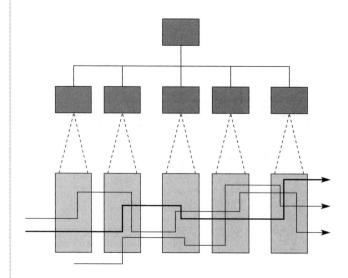

If the matrix organizational structure is retained, the management principle remains the same. After all, the organization has already experienced management from several perspectives. One dimension can possibly be added. In a matrix organization that focuses on products and geography, for example, the dimension of a management process is introduced. An expansion like this adds to the level of complexity, so the desirability of this must be carefully considered.

Projection onto an existing network organizational structure can create teams in which the same processes are executed. To prevent a situation in which every team is reinventing the wheel, it is advisable in such cases to agree which team will be responsible for the process guidelines. In most cases, therefore, this team will usually include the process owner. Another way to project IT processes onto a network organizational structure is to allocate every process, including the process owner, to a separate process team. However, the coordination required to achieve the shared result can be hindered by too many teams.

Transition to another organizational structure

When an organization switches to another organizational structure, there is always a (total) change in the relative power, and this demands a high level of adaptability from the organization. An improved process flow can justify this change, but you must be careful not to assume that the new organizational structure will automatically produce an improved process flow. Remember that processes are, in principle, independent of any organizational structure.

Switching between the different specified structures is possible provided, for example, that the necessary knowledge, skills and (power) culture are available to effectively manage a new organizational structure.

Combining organizational structures

As indicated above, there is no 'optimal' structure, and every organizational structure has its advantages and disadvantages. With this in mind, an organization can also opt for a combination of organizational structures with the aim of merging the best qualities of the various forms. Another reason for combining different organizational structures is to examine whether another organizational structure would be more suitable than the current one and in this way slowly switch to the new one. The disadvantage of combining the forms is that it increases the complexity, with all the consequences that this entails.

One very frequent combination is that of a line organizational form with a network organizational structure. This might involve a team with a line organizational form inside it, or a hierarchy in teams, or a hierarchical top layer that manages the teams.

Projecting process roles onto positions and persons

What does the projection of IT processes onto an IT organization mean for the IT employee? Within the IT processes, the process roles must be linked to IT employees with certain (new) jobs. Here, a position may consist of one or more process roles (see Figure 35.4). Depending on the policy and function range of an IT organization, process roles can be projected onto positions statically or dynamically. If the range of positions is arranged statically, there will be a fixed projection between employees, jobs and process roles that can only be adapted by a formal organizational change. In an IT organization with a dynamic range of positions, career levels are permanently linked to people who can fulfil one or more process roles at different times whenever the need arises.

FIGURE 35.4

Process roles, positions and persons

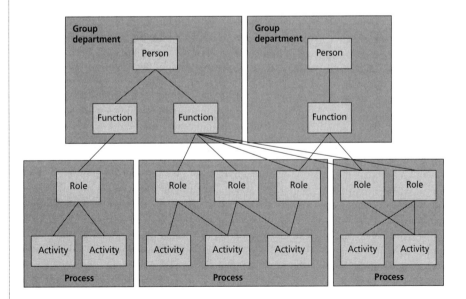

To summarize, it can be concluded that there are very many possible ways of projecting IT processes onto an IT organization. You are therefore advised to make clear choices about the organizational structure, to communicate it to the organization and to evaluate it periodically on the basis of the insights gained.

35.3 Process management and line management

Process owners, line manager(s) and IT employees should have their places assigned within the chosen organizational structure(s). This gives rise to an area of tension because of the different management influences that the process owner and IT manager exercise both on each other and on the IT employee. Because process management and line management have a major influence on the success or failure of working with IT processes, this subject is discussed in depth below, and it is assumed that the roles or functions have not been allocated to the same person[3] (see Figure 35.5).

FIGURE 35.5
Relationship between the process owner, line manager and IT employee

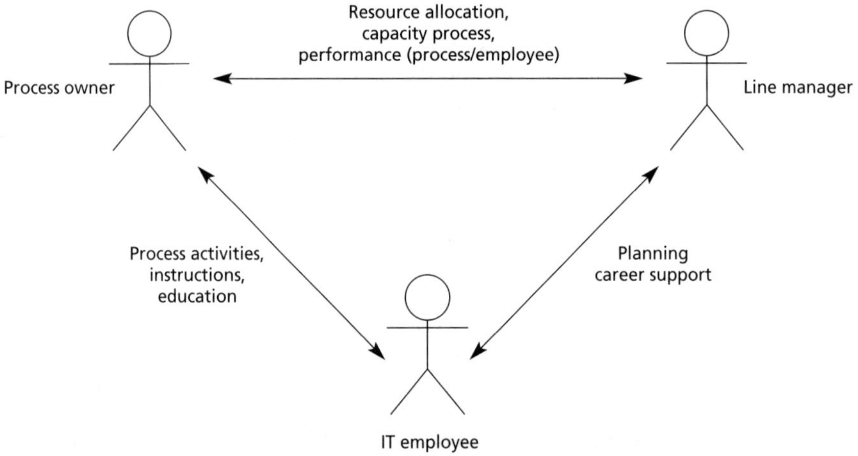

Process management

For the effective management of a process, a process owner should at least have sufficient power, insight and coordination capacities. Process owners can acquire power through their position in the organization (for example, if they hold a senior management position), through their expertise, through their relationships/contacts or through their own budget. They can acquire insight through reading the right reports and monitoring the process. One example of a coordination mechanism involves standardization of the process.

In practice, the process owner defines a process and creates a capacity estimate of the amount of work needed to get the process to run properly (effectiveness). The process owner has no resources (IT employees) of his or her own and must obtain them from the line managers. The process owner does have a budget, however, and will submit a request to the line manager for resources. When given permission to deploy an IT employee, that employee must be trained to perform the process tasks for the process. In addition, agreements must be made about to whom the IT employee in the process is accountable when executing the various tasks. The process owner gains an insight into the way the process works by reading reports about (substeps of) the process and by monitoring the process. On the basis of process indicators and current findings, the process owner can facilitate the IT employee or, following a process analysis, can decide to adjust or optimize the process.

A line manager who does not play a (controlling) process role cannot manage any employees with process roles in his or her department in the actual process area. In such a case, the line manager will function as a resource manager, and in that function will therefore try to deploy his or her employees as efficiently as possible for the various processes in the organization (efficiency). The line manager receives a request for resources from various process owners and can grant these applications. When the line manager submits an application, the function of dividing the tasks (and the managerial authority) is allocated to roles in the process for an agreed time. Within that time, the IT employee receives work from the process (role players in the process, information systems). The line manager can, however, adjust the allocation of IT employees to IT processes as long as the agreed resources are still supplied. To compensate for deployment of the employees, the line manager receives an agreed fee from the process owner.

The process role of IT employees determines which tasks, responsibilities and authority they have and to whom they are accountable. Becoming involved in the process automatically means that the employees will familiarize themselves with the work of the process and will try to complete the work properly (duty to take initiatives). They must also report to the appropriate responsible person(s) when the objective is achieved either late or early (duty to report). Therefore, an incident specialist must solve any disruptions and inform the incident progress controller on time if the recovery time for a disruption is longer than agreed. If required, the incident progress controller can initiate alternatives or escalate the incident (duty to ask for assistance by calling in the supplier, etc.).

Line management

The process owner provides information that the line manager can use for the line activities. On the basis of the expected capacity information and role descriptions, the line manager can plan his or her resources, organize future additions and train the IT employees. The process owner also provides information about the performance of the department/individual in the process. This information can be used to develop optimization and evaluation activities on an organizational level.

Every IT employee formally comes under the supervision of a line manager and can be managed as usual by this manager for the rest of the (unclaimed process) time. During the agreed time, the line manager does not have to execute any operational tasks (division of labour) for the IT employee, and this allows the line manager more time for management tasks, such as maintaining relationships/contacts, specifying objectives, financial monitoring and making the requisite resources available. The line manager remains responsible for the development, performance and evaluation of the IT employee.

Outside the process activities, the IT employee can perform normal 'line activities'. One point of focus involves drawing up a training/career plan together with the line manager. In order to implement this plan, the IT employee should have the time to receive feedback from his or her line manager (evaluation, adjustment).

Overlaps between line and process management

Apart from the differences between process and line management, both can use the same coordination and effect mechanisms. The management principles also overlap in certain areas.

Coordination of tasks

When distributing tasks, cohesion between the activities should be coordinated. To do this, the line managers and process owners can use the following mechanisms:

- *Adjustment by mutual consent* – the work is coordinated through informal communication. One employee says how it should be done and checks the other employee and vice versa. This mechanism mainly works well in smaller organizations.
- *Direct supervision* – an employee is made responsible for the work of others, issues instructions and monitors the work; the manager is responsible for the work of his or her employees and makes adjustments where necessary.
- *Standardization* – by standardizing skills, work processes and output, the result, behaviour, knowledge and know-how to be expected in particular situations can be recorded. This point is mainly focused upon in the Service Management field (ITIL).

The larger (more complex) an organization becomes, the more the coordination mechanism of mutual adjustment will switch to direct supervision and then to standardization.

Management effects

Every manager who wants to achieve particular objectives must be able to get subordinates to do exactly what needs to be done (or prevent them from doing something else). Here, the following can be used:

- *Reward (positive sanction).* Rewards can be both financial (salary, etc.) and non-financial (compliments, career prospects).
- *Punishment (negative sanction).* Punishment might include a fine, less pleasant work and fewer career opportunities.

His or her responsibility for, and authority over, the IT employee means that it is mainly the line manager who can use the above methods. The process owner can also have some bearing on reward and punishment, but he or she can use it less directly to exert influence on a role player in the process. Therefore, the process owner will have to ensure that the process is controlled properly through the correct allocation of tasks, responsibilities and authority. If this is not the case, the process owner can reallocate tasks or exert influence on employees with process roles through and with the cooperation of the line manager.

The line manager and process owner must have regular contact with each other and should work together rather than treat each other as rivals.

Escalations

In every organization, situations may occur that require extra attention. These events, called escalations, can be caused by such things as the stagnation of particular activities in the process. Such events can have very undesirable consequences for the business, and the persons responsible therefore need to take appropriate measures. Escalations can be classified into horizontal (competence) and vertical (authority) escalations.

If there are escalations, the basic principle is that the people responsible for results (process owners) will take measures supported by a line manager. Ensuring that escalations are solved as much as possible within the process also implicitly tests whether the process is working properly. However, it is important to notify the line manager on time in order to avoid (serious) negative consequences.

If an IT employee has insufficient knowledge (know-how) about how to perform a particular task properly within a process, that employee should report this to the line manager. The line manager is responsible for allocating employees to the process and monitoring the IT employee's development. To solve a problem, for example, the line manager can get other employees to help the IT employee or train the IT employee to do the task properly. If the IT employee has been assigned work for a particular level and it turns out that another level is required to complete the work, the IT employee reports this within the process to the person responsible, who can in turn approach other employees in the process who do have the right level (that is, first line, second line, etc.).

If an IT employee does not complete the tasks within the specified time, and authority is required to obtain (extra) people and resources, the employee should contact the responsible person in the process (process owner or delegate). If resources are not available, the process owner must contact the line manager. The line manager can examine whether employees can be switched around so that the tasks can still be executed properly.

If it turns out that the process owner's estimate of resources was inaccurate, the line manager must talk to the process owner about this. The process owner should then apply to the line manager for more resources.

Measurement values (insight)

Formalization and standardization of the process and the allocation of process roles in the organizational structure enable the organization to measure[4] the way in which departments contribute to processes and thereby determine the value in the operating result. This makes it possible to provide departments (and functions) with customer-oriented, process-driven performance indicators that can be measured after (or during) the process.

During an evaluation, the measured values are compared with specified standards or expectations. Corrective actions can be taken when discrepancies are detected. The IT employee is evaluated by the line manager and works in a particular process for most of the working day. The values therefore partially come from the process and partially from the line. It is vitally important that measurement criteria from these two environments are not contradictory. The line manager and process owner should therefore harmonize the desired performance indicators.

35.4 The introduction of process management

Introducing process management into an IT organization is part of the procedure of introducing complete IT processes. In order to implement this change, it is a good idea to opt for a project-oriented approach for the first six to eight months of a procedure. The basic principle here is that the project organization should try to create an adequate basis (with the emphasis on effectiveness), and this basis must be built upon by the IT organization *itself* after the project (with the emphasis on efficiency). A project-oriented approach is also characterized by a clearly defined assignment definition that must be executed within the agreed starting and completion dates under the supervision of a project manager.

In such a project, you are advised to follow a step-by-step approach that includes at least the following four steps:

- preparation;
- design;
- build and test;
- support in production.

In many cases, it is a good idea to add a fifth step: after-care. During these steps, the desired process management will be defined and assimilated into the organizational structure.

Preparation

The main *preparation* activity is to compile and work out a project plan. During this phase, the provisional roles of process owners should be defined for subsequent steps in the project. As a result of the *design* step, definitive role descriptions for process owners will be compiled, and these will be formally allocated to people during the *build and test* step.

The roles of the process owners in the project will preferably be defined by people who, based on the current situation, will also fulfil those roles in the future. In addition, it is a good idea to release the project employees as much as possible from operational duties in order to guarantee the progress of the project. If necessary, these process owners (and other project employees, where relevant) must be trained for the project during this step. This could involve various ITIL training courses (Control IT game, ITIL Foundation, ITIL Practitioner, etc.) but also, for example, team-building sessions within the project.

Besides the process owners, the relevant IT managers must also be appointed to the project organization, and they must reserve time for this – on the one hand to define the organizational consequences of introducing IT processes, and on the other hand to create the peripheral conditions that will allow the project to function adequately.

One requisite component of the project plan is to define a detailed communication plan in order to create a basis for the organizational change. This plan must indicate which project information will be released when, how and to whom. This might include the process owners introducing themselves during the initial presentation and monthly information sessions, the fortnightly publication of process information (for example, the project plan) by process owners on a project website specially created for this purpose, or a weekly meeting to be held by both the process owners and IT managers involved.

Design

The main activities in this step are the definition of IT processes on paper, the (changing) IT organizational structure and the selection of support tools. In this, the process owners play a crucial role in the project with regard to the IT process activities, cohesion between the IT processes and the support processes, the process report, process roles and functional requirements for support tools.

Here, the IT managers provide information on the possible changing nature and scope of the work in their organizational units, the desired management reports, as well as the way the process roles are projected onto functions in the IT organization. To illustrate this, one or two process-owner roles can be projected onto a (new) function. Furthermore, independent external experts with no historical and/or political agenda can be used frequently in this step.

During this step, there must be regular harmonization with departments (groups) outside the project, so that the surroundings are also prepared for (and, where relevant, can contribute to) the impending changes.

Build and test

During this step, all of the preparations required to execute the IT processes are taken. The process owners focus on installing and configuring support tools, training IT employees for their (new) process roles and functionally testing the IT processes without affecting actual operations. Depending on the basic level agreed in the project plan, the procedures and work instructions for the IT processes are worked out in detail during this step.

Based on capacity estimates made by the process owners, the IT managers define a capacity planning schedule. This involves activities such as drawing up a formal placement plan, harmonization with the works council, selecting and – where relevant – testing/training people, and informing the organization about who has been appointed. If required, the IT manager can decide at this stage to allocate process owner roles to other persons, where they must take into account that these people may have to be retrained or instructed accordingly.

This step is concluded with a formal transfer document with which the IT organization indicates that the project has sufficient basis to continue and is ready to put the IT processes into production. In addition, this document can function as a transfer document between 'old' and 'new' process owners. It is advisable to inform all the people involved, through different channels, about this milestone and its consequences.

Support in production

The main activity in this step involves the operational execution of the IT processes within the IT organization in accordance with the agreements incorporated into the process documentation. The process owners are now also formally responsible for the operation of the IT processes and for reporting to the IT managers, and they receive extra support from the project organization. Here, any misunderstandings or bottlenecks that arise are immediately tackled and, where necessary, adjusted in the process documentation.

During this step, the IT managers must ensure that the peripheral conditions have been defined so that the IT processes can function adequately. This could include extra training for the IT employees, holding job appraisal meetings and monitoring capacity planning.

As a result of this step, one or more monthly reports are created in addition to a final evaluation with which the project can be formally concluded. The final evaluation report assesses the structure, continuance and operation of the IT processes and it also provides an overview of activities that must still be carried out by the process owners and IT managers.

After-care

The main activity in this step is to supervise and coach the individual process owners and (groups of) IT employees. Here, the positive and less positive aspects linked to the daily execution and management of the IT processes are discussed on a regular basis with the IT employees, process owners and IT managers, and the necessary corrective measures are taken (for example, drawing up individual training plans, adapting process documentation or fine-tuning support tools).

35.5 Conclusion

This chapter shows that there are many opportunities for embedding and managing IT processes in an IT organization. It is important to make clear choices with regard to the organizational structure, the division of tasks between the management functions and the selection of people to perform these functions. When introducing process management, it is crucial to (continuously) communicate with everybody concerned on the points mentioned above, that both process owners and IT managers are personally supervised, and that the structure, continuance and operation of the IT organization are evaluated periodically.

Literature

van Bon, J. (2000) *IT Management Yearbook 2000*, fourth edition, first printing, ISBN 90-440-0007-1

Drake, J. (2000) *The HP IT Service Management Reference Model White Paper*, version 2.0, Hewlett Packard Consulting

ITSMF (1999) *IT Service Management, an introduction*, April, ISBN 90-804928-1-7

Jagers, H.P.M. and Jansen, W. (1991), *The Designs of Effective Organizations*, ISBN 90 207 2092 9

Keuning, D. (2000), *Organising and Managing*, ISBN 90 11 0745 2

Mintzberg, H. (1979), *The Structuring of Organizations*, ISBN 0138552703

NIG (1993) *Tasks and Functions in Managerial Computer Science*, ISBN 90 267 1837 3

Notes

1 The names 'manager', 'IT manager' and 'line manager' are replaceable in this chapter.
2 IT processes can be divided, for example, into IT management, development and policy processes.
3 In practice, the line manager can indeed perform a coordinating process role.
4 An adage: 'If a process isn't measured, it isn't managed.'

36 Patching the blind spot in implementation of IT process models

Peter A.J. Bootsma Quality Research
Jan van Bon Bureau Hoving en Van Bon, the Netherlands

Summary

Scalable process models can be difficult to implement. Many currently popular IT Service Management concepts specify which processes are needed for good service management. These concepts may range from limited checklists for process structures to comprehensive total management concepts. Examples are HP's IT Service Management Reference Model, IBM's IT Process Model and several models recently published for the IT Service Management community, such as R2C, IPW, IIM, SIMA and ISM (*IT Service Management Yearbook*, 1999). A useful characteristic of these IT Service Management concepts is scalability. Scalable process models are designed for organizations ranging from very small to very large. For instance: in the IPW model an IT service provider is expected to explicitly organize incident management and problem management, no matter how many or how few people are involved. From the process point of view, scalability is a natural characteristic. It is much like a recipe: no matter how much beer you brew, the recipe and brewing conditions remain the same. When it comes to *implementation*, however, the number of people involved and services delivered becomes important. It will determine how detailed procedures are written, how many layers of management are needed, how formal or informal communications will be, to what extent standardization is required, etc. In addition to this, at implementation time other management areas and aspects get involved, such as planning and control, HR management, communication and the company culture. Here too, size makes a difference: large organizations behave differently from smaller ones. Also, the project-wise implementation of a process model can be very different between large and small organizations. Scalable process models, therefore, cannot be installed 'off the shelf'.

Scalability makes for applicability but, when it comes to implementation, leaves many 'how-to' questions unanswered. For instance: how to choose between multifunctional process teams and functional departments? This chapter discusses an implementation strategy that reduces the gap between model and practice while remaining generic. This is achieved through joint application of a process model specific to IT Service Management (Integrated Service Management or ISM) and a generic model for self-directed work teams (Recursive Process Management or RPM). Both models are explained briefly, followed by a stepwise account of implementation issues.

36.1 An implementation framework

What kind of models do we need in order to design, set up or improve an organization? In other words, how do scalable process models fit into a larger framework? This section is our method to get the big picture:

1. To start with, organizations often have some frame of reference that helps them in designing their structure. This may include written or unwritten visions, philosophies, values, missions, strategies, etc. It provides a general direction for many decisions to be made when implementing a process model. We like to visualize this category of an implementation framework as an umbrella, covering all other categories.

2. We may further discern between synthesis and analysis. In many organizations, structures are chosen and evaluated and processes are designed and audited, plans are made and progress is reported. Switching between building up and measuring results is a natural way of developing or adjusting organizations in changing environments. The activities of synthesizing or analysing, though, are quite different. Synthesis often is a creative process with unpredictable outcome, while analysis can be a routine job with (preferably) replicable outcomes. This also influences the concepts, models and tools used for synthesis and analysis. Typical tools for analysis include requirements and criteria: questions that can be answered with 'yes', 'no' or 'to some degree'. It is the type of question found in EFQM self-assessment guides, ISO9000 standards and IT models such as COBIT, CMM, SPICE, etc. Tools and models for synthesis more often prescribe structures or flows of events, or describe methods to arrive there. The process models we started with mostly fit into this synthesis category.

3. We split up the synthesis category into 'blueprints' and 'building blocks'. Blueprints include scalable process models and templates for hierarchical structures. They usually picture the organization as a whole and have limited detail. Building blocks, on the other hand, are models for the cells, molecules and atoms of an organization, the smallest groups of individuals that are managed explicitly, for instance the 'department' or the 'project team'.

The resulting framework may be depicted as in Figure 36.1.

FIGURE 36.1

Implementation framework

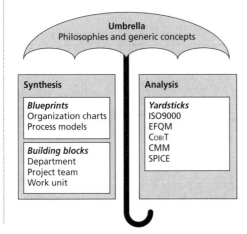

36.2 The blind spot

The building blocks category seems to be the blind spot in this framework. This category usually gets the least attention, especially the 'department' and the 'project team', which are accepted as facts of life. Everybody knows a department often carries out routine tasks, has a hierarchical leader, a plan, a budget and an undefined life span. Similarly, it is common knowledge that a project team usually has a limited life span, a time-phased plan, milestones, a budget, matrix-type relations to the rest of the organization and a non-hierarchical leader. Both departments and project teams can be stacked recursively into hierarchies, which makes them universal building blocks. For a long while, these two were all you needed to put an organization together. On the other hand, building blocks is where the action is. In order to explain this, Figure 36.2 provides a (simplified) historical overview:

- The department is probably the oldest 'cell' in organizations, with a 'genetic code' dating back to prehistoric times. It was very useful in the industrial revolution when untrained labour and routine jobs were the standard. Complexity was limited and cross-departmental issues could often be managed along hierarchical lines.

- The middle of the previous century saw the rise of project management as a new discipline. This may be seen as a reaction to growing complexity in general: larger projects, shorter lead times, increased quality requirements. To manage this, specialists needed to cooperate directly, without hierarchical bypasses. Departments and project teams complemented one another well: one covered routine tasks, the other unique assignments.

- At the beginning of this century, complexity has increased further. Organizations need to address more issues, have to do it faster and have to involve more people in decision making. Direct cooperation is no longer the domain of specialists in project teams, but now also reaches routine jobs. This has contributed to the development of a new building block, suited for routine tasks and horizontal cooperation across functional borders. It exists in many forms: process teams, autonomous task groups, mini companies, etc. The new building block is commonly referred to as 'self-directed work teams' or SDWTs. SDWTs not only enable process-oriented work, they also add to a stimulating working environment. Decision lines are shorter, which enables

FIGURE 36.2
Development of new building blocks

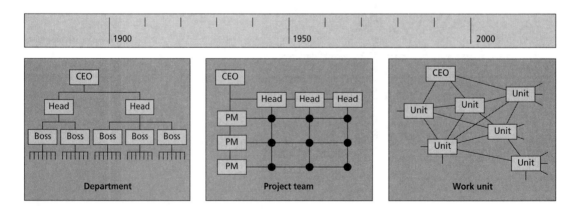

informal problem solving (a major motivator). SDWTs are also positively related to business responsibility and personal development.

When SDWTs and departments serve the same purpose (routine jobs) and SDWTs are better adapted to current complex business environments, then why not convert all departments to SDWTs? A major roadblock is that many SDWT concepts are, by design, incompatible with traditional management concepts based on hierarchy and control. Implementing such concepts often requires a major mind shift from management and employees. Many organizations would rather stick to familiar structures or restrict themselves to 'tilting' their hierarchy in the direction of their processes. Process models cannot flourish in these circumstances; they just add complexity to an environment that already has enough. The following sections show a way to make some progress in this situation:

- Section 36.3 about Integrated Service Management (ISM) goes into the complexity of the IT service environment. An adapted scalable process model is presented, suitable for use as a reference model in conjunction with an SDWT concept.
- Section 36.4 about Recursive Process Management (RPM) takes a critical look at SDWT concepts. An alternative is presented ('work unit') designed for better interfacing with hierarchical structures.
- Section 36.5 about implementation shows how the two concepts match in a redesign of an IT service organization.

36.3 Integrated Service Management (ISM)

Background

In the early 1990s, the datacenter of a large IT telecom company's organization developed and implemented IPW (for a description, see Chapter 7 in this volume), a model of a process-oriented IT services organization. Since then, a lot of experience on the subject of process-oriented organizations has been gathered, but the IPW model, originally based upon ITIL (CCTA's IT Infrastructure Library), was only slightly adapted to developments. A fundamental update never took place. Yet, in the same period a growing number of constraints revealed themselves. Therefore, the organization started looking for a new reference model that could contribute to the diminishing of these constraints. During this search, in 1999, the model ISM (Integrated Service Management) was developed and targeted at updating the traditional, operations-concentrated process implementation (IPW) and redesigning it with the strategic and tactical processes that were not yet sufficiently involved. ISM was developed in a highly structured step-by-step approach:

1. Establish the constraints.
2. Determine demands.
3. Develop premises and paradigms.
4. Develop the reference model (Figure 36.3).
5. Publish and present the model.
6. Check and apply the model in different (internal and external) environments.
7. Ongoing development.

Steps 6 and 7 are executed simultaneously.

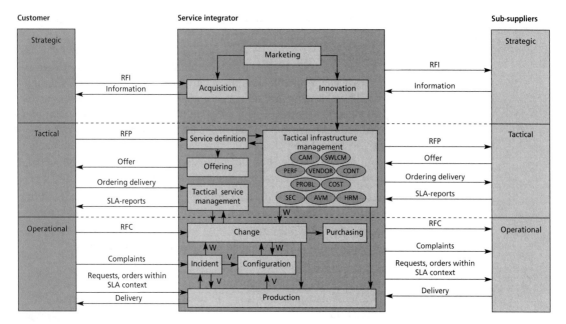

FIGURE 36.3

ISM model overview

Constraints

Seven years after the deployment of IPW, the lack of development of this method had led to several constraints. The organization was not ready for the fact that almost all services had an integrated nature: the role of service integrator had not been developed explicitly. The focus was still very much on the operational processes; the tactical and strategic processes lacked management attention; many responsibilities were not covered by the model. The product of the organization was still very much infrastructure-focused instead of service-focused. The general acceptance of process-orientation had faded away: hierarchical and project responsibilities were still valued more than process responsibilities. The new reference model should be able to cope with at least the demands to be:

- acceptable and simple;
- recognizable and applicable;
- maintainable;
- process-focused, service-focused and customer-focused;
- deductible and reproducible;
- manageable of complex and integrated services.

Paradigms

The premises are described in paradigms that will be used as building blocks for the model. The following paradigms are developed:

- **Delivery paradigm** – describing the relation between customer and supplier.
- **Infrastructure paradigm** – describing the elements used to produce the service.

- **Organization paradigm** – describing the relation between Organization, Processes and Means.
- **Management paradigm** – describing the relation between Strategic, Tactical and Operational levels.
- **Integration paradigm** – describing the integration of sub-services into one delivery.

Each paradigm creates specific values to which the model should comply.

Publication and presentation

The ISM model was published in *The IT Service Management Yearbook 1999* (in Dutch, van Bon, 1999), in this Guide (in English, Chapter 8) and it was presented at a National Dutch congress 'The World of IT Service Management', February 1999.

Checking and applying the model in different (internal and external) environments

Since 1999 the model has been presented to various parties. In the meantime the model is already being used as a reference model by several organizations. Some of them are using the model to improve their organization, some of them use it to design new functionality for support tools. In addition, the model is used for training purposes (Service Management Awareness).

Ongoing development

The experience during 2001 made it clear that ISM is well applicable for many purposes in service organizations but can still be improved in some areas. The Strategic processes, in particular, should be better adapted to company vision and mission. At the tactical level, the Tactical Infrastructure Management processes should be worked out in greater detail. These adjustments from empirical use were made in 2000.

36.4 Recursive Process Management (RPM)

Introduction

RPM (Recursive Process Management) is an integrated management concept for self-directed work teams. It outlines a 'micro management system' for 'work units', with a special focus on efficiency and transparency. RPM was conceived in 1992 as the primary product of Quality Research and has been subject to ongoing development ever since. Applications have been undertaken mostly in the Netherlands in public and commercial organizations, including IT service management. To introduce this concept, the following paragraphs discuss two of the main ingredients of RPM:

- the structure model of RPM, designed to link SDWTs to classical hierarchy;
- the dialogue model of RPM, designed for management control in learning organizations.

RPM can be implemented independently, but this section focuses on joint implementation with ISM.

FIGURE 36.4

A work unit in its hierarchical context

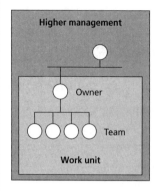

TABLE 36.1

Main characteristics of a 'work unit'

A work unit manages and operates a specific process, a sub-process or a combination of process tasks. Processes are preferably segmented in such a way that all work units deliver distinct products. Sometimes this implies multi-disciplinary teams (for instance, to improve customer orientation); at other times it has advantages in bringing together specialists in work units (for instance, to benefit from scale factors).
A work unit performs repeating tasks (production and/or coordination) for an undefined period of time (in practice, as long as the process exists). This implies demands on quality assurance and continuous improvement. It also means that a work unit is not a project team.
A work unit maintains network relations with higher management, other work units and possibly external stakeholders. Work units are also concerned with the interests of their own members. In practice, work units operate in a tension field of interests, which requires competence in relationship management.
A work unit is controlled by higher management in a participative style. This requires continuous dialogue in which top management is asking questions rather than giving orders.
One of the team members is the team leader. This implies coordination tasks and a role as spokesperson. A team leader is responsible for good communication, but not for results (see 'owner', next). Team leadership can be fixed or rotational.
The highest manager in the work unit is the owner. The owner reports to the person who initiated the work unit (mostly higher management). The owner is responsible for work unit results and work unit competence immediately after he/she is appointed. The owner, therefore, needs to be a competent person and needs a hierarchical position towards the team.
The team can be self-managed. The owner remains responsible for results, but delegates in that case specific management tasks to the team leader. Contrary to outcome responsibility, self-management is not standard; the self-management level and the development pace may vary (the implementation paragraph has a model for this).
Development towards self-management has consequences for the team size. Effective and efficient meetings must be possible, as much as members being able to recognize their contribution. Small teams (typically 5 to 10) often work best.
A specific situation occurs when a team is cross-departmental. However, the same definition applies. All involved managers participate in the work unit and the manager where all reporting lines join (however high that may be) is by definition a member and owner of the work unit. It is good practice, however, that the owner delegates all daily management tasks (who, what and how matters) to the other managers in the work unit. What remains for the owner is to inspire the work unit and the occasional arbitration, often only for a few hours per year. Work units may, therefore, be cross-departmental but may also coincide with departments, which makes the concept backwards compatible (Bootsma, 1995).

Structuring organizations

The RPM structure model is designed to *detach* the network of teams in an organization from the relatively static formal hierarchical structure. This creates more options to model the people network after the process network. To enable management control, teams are linked to managers as described below. The building block provided by the RPM structure model is the 'work unit': a team of workers complemented with managers who are directly involved and selected specialist staff (Figure 36.4). Basically, a work unit is a team with a 'shell' around it. The team inside the unit shares characteristics with self-directed work teams, process teams, and socio-technological concepts like autonomous task groups. The addition of managers and staff serves to achieve a self-reliant and outcome-responsible building block, effective from the day it is installed. Table 36.1 lists the main characteristics.

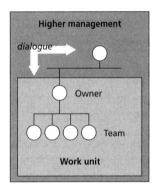

FIGURE 36.5
Dialogue between work unit and hierarchical context

Managing results and quality

Managing a network of work units asks for an adequate dialogue between top management and work unit owners (Figure 36.5). This dialogue covers various issues: process design, policy, results, quality assurance, improvement actions, personnel, labour conditions, safety, environment, etc. When top management and unit owners stay tuned to each other, there is a double bonus: work units are better informed and can make better decisions, while top managers get to trust the management skills of units and can delegate accordingly.

The practical approach

How to achieve an effective, and not least, efficient dialogue? The approach taken in RPM is to gather generic questions that can be asked of all work unit owners, for instance: 'What were the disappointing trends last quarter?', 'What causes are known?', 'What measures are taken?'. This has led to a current list of approximately 60 generic questions, designed to:

- save work and time on both sides;
- help develop a common language;

- improve understanding between work units;
- enable faster setting-up of new work units;
- enable more effective and efficient auditing.

Introducing a dialogue model with 60 questions, all at once, may not be welcomed with enthusiasm. The alternative is to start with a minor selection and to grow stepwise to a professional dialogue. The benefits are:

- further reduced initial workload and reduced resistance against change;
- more opportunities to evolve the method, develop routines and get used to increased transparency.

An example is included in the paragraph about implementation. An additional learning effect is built in by dividing difficult questions into easier ones. For instance, the list does not contain a question like: 'What are the work unit's long-term objectives?'. Instead, five questions are asked in a specific order:

1. Who are the work unit's primary stakeholders?
2. What are their main interests?
3. Given these interests, what success factors should the work unit focus on?
4. What indicators measure trends in these success factors?
5. What long-term target levels are negotiated for each indicator?

In answering these questions, the tension field around a work unit may sooner be perceived as a challenge to communication skills rather than as dilemma, bureaucracy or inertia. It may also help people to diverge from narrow perspectives like 'technical perfection' or 'minimum costs' to a balanced set of objectives that is easier to communicate to all stakeholders. Finally, it prevents the selection of indicators based exclusively on availability of measurements (such as the average time before someone picks up the phone). The list of questions is generic in the sense that it can be used in all work units ranging from technical units, support units to management teams and staff units. However, prior to implementation, the list needs to be customized to the language and culture of an organization. To achieve the intended learning effect, all questions and answers need to be published within the organization – for instance through an organization manual, bulletin boards or an intranet website (RPM includes various templates). This will increase the transparency and will create conditions for transfer of skills. Transparency, on the other hand, can also be a threat. It therefore needs to be introduced with care and requires, at least, some good examples from the top managers.

Summary

RPM work units are teams of workers completed with managers who are directly involved and selected specialist staff. Work units are self-reliant 'shops' that collectively run the network of processes of an organization, based on continuous dialogue with top management, short internal decision lines and customized self-management. Work units, in this sense, are a modern alternative to departments, suited for complex organizations with highly intertwined processes, high demands on quality and a high speed of change.

36.5 Implementation

In this paragraph, the joint application of ISM and RPM is described as a stepwise project approach. The content is drawn mostly from implementation into an IT service department consisting of approximately 70 people, the ISA department of the Philips DAP division, located in Drachten, the Netherlands. We will discuss the issues that are specific to the combination of a blueprint and a building block. The following, therefore, is a collection of annotations rather than a generic implementation guide.

Phase 1: Focus

Setting objectives

As with any organizational change project, motivating people to participate is one of the primary issues for the implementation team. A useful starting point can be to conduct intake interviews. These interviews can serve to build closer relations between the implementation team and the organization, to gather material for pilot projects and to get an overall sense of the workplace atmosphere. To mobilize people, the objectives of the intended change need a connection with real issues or problems. A sense of priority (or even urgency) may be created by asking customers for their opinions. Similarly, an employee satisfaction survey or a hidden rules survey (Scott Morgan, 1994) may uncover roadblocks. Another useful approach involves making cognitive maps that reflect the shared ideas of the management team (Eden and Ackermann, 1998). A well-formulated paragraph about the objectives is in itself a powerful change tool, worth spending a few hours on. To start with, the objective paragraph should include a line of motivation straight from the concern strategy to the intended change. If it is not relevant to the business, why bother? The other crucial line of motivation is the working environment. Somehow, the intended change should contribute to more challenging, varying or otherwise rewarding jobs, or the initiative will lack support from its primary target group. An example:

The increasing speed of change, the increasing intertwining of processes and the increasing demands on quality have been main factors in establishing this change project. They have led us to the conclusion that central control, as a management concept, has reached its limits in our organization. Adding more people to headquarters would make things worse rather than better. The only option is to reinforce decentralized decision making. At the same time this is a fortunate option for all people working here. It means that more of us will be involved in management matters and that decisions regarding daily work will be made closer to where the action is. It is also good news for young people with newly attained college degrees, starting a professional career. It means their future working environment here will be better suited for the skills and expectations of their generation.

The next thing anyone expects from a well-written objective is direction. This is about the first opportunity to get a bit more specific on the type of change that is ahead. It may ask for some explanation, for instance:

The change project sets out not just to create a new organizational chart but to create a new type of building block for organization charts: the work unit. A work unit will contain a team of workers, one or more managers and specialist staff, to form a competent group of people. This group will be focused on a specific product, able to carry outcome responsibility from day one with the perspective of developing their own degree of self management.

The remainder of the objective paragraph can gather all kinds of criteria that are important to special interest groups. An important group is middle management, where people are quite often reluctant to step into self-management initiatives. A final reminder: objectives need to be 'SMART': Specific, Measurable, Attainable, Relevant and Time-bound (or, if you wish, 'Ambitious' and 'Realistic').

Choosing and customizing tools

Language is a key to change. When a vision is formulated in appealing and unambiguous words, people will sooner be able to exchange positive views about it during their coffee and lunch breaks. Especially when fundamental changes are at stake, as with the introduction of work units, it is well worth the effort to write a glossary, a FAQ or another brief reference document. This should include a definition of 'work unit' or whatever synonym will be used. During this phase, a practical approach would be to introduce a concept text in the management team and work towards a consensus statement. Another focus point in this phase is the dialogue between management and work units. First, the basic idea of a dialogue, based on fixed questions and internal publication of answers, needs to be agreed upon. In a following step, composing a prototype question list may help building consensus and identifying issues. The result may look like Table 36.2. This example has very few questions to enable a quick start for all work unit owners. During the next phases of the project, the list may develop into, for instance, a 'compact', a 'standard' and an 'advanced' edition, to match process maturity objectives for various work units. Inspiration for questions may well be drawn from process maturity models like CMM or quality assurance standards such as ISO9000. Work unit maturity is independent from team autonomy. For instance: a well-performing and competent work unit may have a team focusing on routine tasks and, consequently, an active owner. At the same time, another well-performing work unit may have an autonomous team, saving the owner a lot of work. Team autonomy, therefore, is a dimension in itself. To avoid pushing teams into more or less autonomy than adequate, it may be useful to distinguish levels of autonomy. Each team then has its own autonomy target level and due date, independent from the work unit or process maturity level. Switching between autonomy levels is equal to shifting management tasks between owner and team leader. Table 36.3 contains the five-level model used in the RPM concept. A critical part of every management system is its representation in a model. This model may take the form of a policy note, an organization manual, an intranet website, or any description of how the organization is managed. The model, however, is not the system itself. Management systems are in the first place agreements and interactions between working people, not paper or digital descriptions of this. Nevertheless, prints and screens are invaluable in explaining the design of the management system to employees and auditors. Especially during fundamental changes in the management system, the visible description of the new system needs to be available early to serve as a prototyping and learning tool. Installing it later and using it only to consolidate stabilized practices leaves a valuable integration opportunity unused. An

TABLE 36.2

Exmple of a question list

Theme	Questions
Identity Reason for existence, who are members, who is owner, where they are located, etc.	1. What products/services does the work unit deliver? (possibly related to reference processes) 2. Who are the team members making these products/services? 3. Who is owner of this work unit? 4. How often does the owner discuss short-term progress with higher management? 5. How often does the owner discuss short-term progress with the team or the team leader? 6. How often are team meetings conducted?
Managing results Stakeholder interests. Short-and long-term objectives, measuring, making adjustments	7. Who are the work unit's primary stakeholders? 8. What are their main interests? 9. Given these interests, what success factors should the work unit focus on? 10. What indicators measure trends in these success factors? 11. To what extent are current results satisfactory? 12. What improvement actions are planned or being executed?
Managing quality What can go wrong, how to assure quality, where to describe it	13. What are the major work steps (process description, flow chart, etc.)?

intranet has a major advantage over paper manuals as it has the potential to provide all work units with a real-time publishing tool. Phase 1 is a good moment to install such a system (see the example in Figure 36.6), so it is ready for use in phase 2.

TABLE 36.3

The RPM five level role model

Level		Characteristics
5.	Entrepreneur	The teams develop their product and do internal marketing
4.	Organize	The teams propose modifications in process design and team memberships
3.	Control	The teams plan, do, check and act (PDCA cycle)
2.	Teamwork	The teams have a group assignment and meet regularly to deploy work and solve problems
1.	Professional	The teams provide quality products, but members receive individual assignments

Phase 2: Structure

The second phase is about 'doing the right things', as a prelude to the third phase which moves on to 'doing things right'. To start with, a structure of work units needs to be established. This may involve the following steps.

- Make an inventory of all current activities in all current working groups. When a management system or quality assurance system exists, this should be relatively easy. The inventory should include all control and support functions, such as human resources management, planning and control, facilities management and quality assurance.

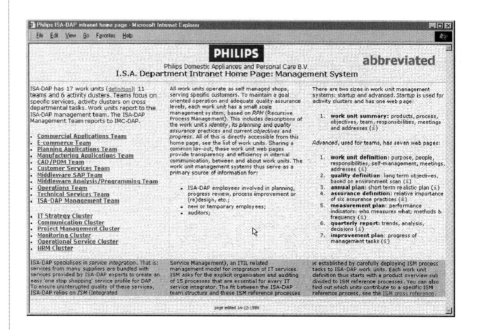

FIGURE 36.6

Intranet management site

- Cross-check with the ISM process model to find white spots: activities prescribed by the model that are not carried out in the current organization.
- Decide to adapt the current structure or redesign it. Skip the next step when adapting the current structure.
- Work top down from the ISM process model to compose a network of teams. This may be a complex puzzle, requiring several iterations and many decisions on team size, specialization or multifunctional teams, process interfaces, etc. Note that the resulting structure is a list of teams, not a hierarchy of managers. The next step is to design a flat and simple hierarchy. The art is to follow the team network as closely as possible and to ensure that most teams report to just one manager. A close fit between hierarchy and the team network, however, is a 'want', not a 'need'.
- Reallocate activities to teams, including the missing ones as found in the cross-check.
- Identify ISM processes that involve more than one member of the top management team. Form process coordination teams including one member from the top management team and all team leaders involved. In large organizations, coordination can have multiple layers.
- Transform all teams (operation, support, staff and coordination) to work units by adding managers according to reporting lines and by adding specialist staff as required. Pick team leaders or, if appropriate, let teams choose themselves.
- Check the results by answering identity questions from the dialogue model for each work unit.
- Check again with all involved managers and employees.

- Decide upon starting dates and publish the new structure through the organization manual, bulletin board or intranet.

The structure phase may, therefore, have various outcomes: for instance, a tilted organization or a functional organization with additional process co-ordination. Basically, the organization now has two structures: a dynamic work unit structure, closely following changes in the network of processes, and a static hierarchy following the work unit structure on a distance. The advantage is that changes in processes (installing or terminating processes, changing interfaces, size, workflow, etc.) require fewer changes in the hierarchical structure of the organization; the consequences are for work units only (for instance, the team changes from departmental to cross-departmental). A separate thread in phase 2 is redesigning all control, development and support functions to cater for a new audience: work units. This requires a collective effort from all staff people and support people who will be asked to deliver services to work units rather than to departments. This involves more than renaming, since work units are in many aspects different from departments. The result may include a new or adapted training programme, changes in the reward and recognition programme, adaptations in the planning and control cycle, a new audit plan, new signposts and phonebooks, etc. The amount of work in this part of the project can be significant but usually requires little outside help. Start with top staff people and agree on objectives, methods and planning first.

Phase 3: Managing results and quality

Phase three is about achieving results and quality with the newly formed work units or 'doing things right'. This needs to start with setting two types of objectives for each work unit: output and competence. To some extent, these are independent. An incompetent work unit may get good results (probably not for long) and a competent work unit may fail to do so (*force majeure* or bad luck). In both cases, having both output and competence objectives is an advantage: it may help in detecting risks or it may prevent frustrating competent people with unnecessary interventions. Thus:

- Setting competence objectives requires insight into current competence in management of processes. To measure this, the current process management practices should be compared to a standard. In our case this involves a 'process management maturity scan' in which work units are investigated along the lines of the ISM reference processes.

- Setting output objectives is much more integrated in the (adapted) management control cycle. Triggered by this cycle, management will be frequently asking work units to publish reports, plans and other documents or intranet pages.

In this phase, a limited number of questions are used to create focus on essentials and to get going with obvious improvement opportunities. Acceptance and motivation are more important at this stage than correctness or completeness. Changes should be recognizable for work unit members and customers. The ambition is moderate and the dialogue is more qualitative than quantitative. It needs to be made very clear who are expected to take action in the dialogue. The person asking questions is the same that initiated the work unit, often higher management. Answers are provided by the work unit owner. Delegation from the owner to the team is not relevant yet; the owner needs to feel at home with the dialogue first. Also, it needs to be clear that answering questions is not an audit or one-time exercise, but a recurring event in a management control cycle. The effort in writing answers can in this stage be kept to a minimum, for instance by agreeing on the amount of text. A format or work sheet is hardly necessary, but can easily be made. A template may be needed when answers are published through the intranet. When the first answers to the selected questions are gathered, it may appear that the questions have been interpreted differently or that writing styles are different. This is a good moment to discuss definitions, amount of text, keywords or full sentences, etc. There is no need to get this all on paper. A collection of good examples may do as well and may even have a better learning effect. Another aspect here is unwritten rules about transparency, such as 'hiding facts leads to mistrust', 'showing bad results yourself is better than letting others discover them'. Such rules exist everywhere (Scott Morgan, 1994) and can work for or against the organization. Setting examples is a way to influence them, for instance by openly discussing how learning from mistakes contributes to better results. During this phase, it may be useful to have coaches, facilitators or (internal) consultants available to help work unit owners and teams to get started. Another option is to offer training modules. The implementation may further include a stimulation programme for 'quick hits' or ideas. Depending on the size of the organization, a communication plan may be useful too, to ensure two-way communication between top management and the organization during the implementation.

Phase 4: Evaluate

Management systems, like the one implemented, have their own mechanism for evaluating: the management control cycle and the auditing function. Both ensure a steady stream of evaluation about both output and competence to top management. The evaluation of the implementation project, therefore, does not include output measurement or an audit, but merely checks if these functions are in place in the management system and perform as they should.

36.6 Conclusions

Implementing IT service management process models can be tricky since scalable models cannot predict organizational structures in detail. This chapter argues that there is a blind spot in the building blocks that organizations are composed from: 'departments', 'project teams' and similar. The 'department', in particular, is less adapted for current complex business environments. Newer building blocks are being developed, such as 'self-directed work teams', but these are often not compatible with the hierarchical structures. An effort has been made to close the gap between model and practice. From one side of the gap, an IT Service Management process model was used: Integrated Service Management (ISM). ISM was not used as a blueprint for the organizational structure, but as a checklist and as a model for assigning process coordination tasks in a management team. From the other side of the gap, a model for self-directed work teams was used: Recursive Process Management (RPM). RPM has been designed to connect self-directed work teams to normal hierarchical structures and to enable immediate results as well as a customized learning curve towards self-management. The combination of ISM and RPM has turned out to provide a sound implementation framework. It has made it much easier to develop flexible organizational structures and creates conditions to unify the often disjunctive functions of control and quality assurance. It has also helped to speed up the initial phases of projects and has contributed to consensus and ownership.

Literature

van Bon, J. (ed.) (1999) *IT Beheer Jaarboek* (IT Service Management Yearbook), Ten Hagen & Stam.

Bootsma, P.A.J. (1995) 'Backward Compatible Management Systems', congress paper, 39th EOQ Annual Conference.

Eden, C. and Ackermann, F. (1998) *Making Strategy*, Sage.

Katzenbach, J.R and Smith, D.K. (1993) *The Wisdom of Teams*, HarperBusiness.

Rummler, G.A. and Brache, A.P. (1990) *Improving Performance*, Jossey Bass.

Scott Morgan, P. (1994) *The Unwritten Rules of the Game*, McGraw-Hill.

Stacey, R. (1982), *Managing Chaos*, Kogan Page.

ISM home page: http://www.bhvb.nl

RPM home page: http://www.qualityresearch.nl/rpm.en.html

Papers about RPM: http://www.icce.rug.nl/qr/index/103/en.html

RPM Server demo: http://www.qualityresearch.nl/rpm-server.en.html

37 Competence management

Renée Kamphuis KPN, the Netherlands

Summary

Recently, there has been an upsurge of interest in competencies and competence management. There are also enormous differences in the way the concept 'competence' is defined and in the uses to which competencies and competence management are put. Roughly speaking, we can distinguish between two approaches: 'top-down' and 'bottom-up'. The top-down approach focuses primarily on the formulation of a mission and a strategy, then goes on to define the key qualities necessary for establishing them. Competencies can then be further differentiated and ultimately, via a number of intermediary steps, assigned to employees. The bottom-up approach first focuses on the competencies individual employees need to perform well within a defined job area. This approach naturally assumes that job areas have been selected which will ultimately contribute towards achieving the corporate mission and strategy. This chapter describes the latter approach, which is currently being implemented in the central IT organization of KPN Telecom. For this purpose, the Institute of Applied Business Research at KPN Research has come up with a set of competencies. We certainly do not intend to claim that this is the only approach. It is, however, an approach that will yield results within a reasonably short period of time and which has taken shape quite easily, even within a large organization such as KPN Telecom.

37.1 Why competence management?

In a conversation with Warren Bennis (1992), Jack Welch (Chairman of General Electric since 1981 and regarded by many as the charismatic leader of the 1990s) named the following as the three criteria with which the continued success of an enterprise can be measured:

- satisfied customers;
- satisfied employees;
- cash flow.

Creating an atmosphere of *employee satisfaction* has been increasingly recognized as a crucial success factor. This is feasible, if only for the fact that satisfied, motivated employees perform better, in the quantitative and, in particular, in the qualitative sense. Obviously this is not only true in regard to knowledge-based organizations, but its relevance there goes without saying. With respect to IT in particular, the pressure on the labour market is currently so great that maintaining employee satisfaction is an absolute necessity for retaining employees. As a rule, IT organizations are 'professional organizations', which employ many, predominantly technical professionals. According to Mattieu Weggeman (1992), it is the job of the professional to 'utilize brainpower, expertise, craftsmanship, experience and troubleshooting ability in pursuit of an organization's goals, while monitoring the efficiency of the contribution made'. It is clear that in order to achieve optimal results, the management style in this type of organization must dovetail with the situation described above. Managerial staff in professional organizations should, therefore, focus on two areas: the formulation and communication of a vision upon which company strategy and aims are subsequently based and the development of the talents and qualities of professionals, as individuals and in a team context. Good people management has become an increasingly crucial success factor. At the same time, good people management with effective coaching has proved difficult to implement and is often underestimated or given short shrift. Competence management, as described in this chapter, can be used to support people management. Depending on choices made with regard to its form and content, competence management offers a common language and a set of definitions that apply to a person's performance, specifically with respect to attitude and behaviour. It is precisely in this area that coaching can be highly effective. Yet these very aspects are often neglected during performance appraisals, primarily because of the absence of this set of definitions or because managers do not feel authorized to address particular aspects of attitude and behaviour. Obviously the introduction of competence management is no panacea. In addition, it is likely to be ineffective or counterproductive if it is implemented on its own. However, in those instances where a company realizes the importance of a conscientious management style involving coaching and is prepared to invest in it (particularly in terms of time and attention), this approach can provide a powerful driving force.

37.2 Competence management: the theory

To gain insight into the individual achievements and potential of employees, we use two terms: performance and competencies (Figure 37.1).

FIGURE 37.1

From competencies to performance

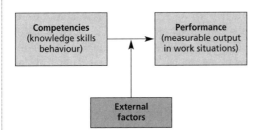

By performance *we mean the measurable output that a person produces in his/her work situation. In other words, performance is an indicator of what a person has actually accomplished.*

By competencies *we mean the combination of knowledge, skills and behaviour in an individual. Competencies are, therefore, an indicator of what a person is potentially capable of achieving.*

Source: KPN Research, Institute of Applied Business Research

Competencies are necessary for good performance but, naturally, provide no guarantee. When performance dips below par, this is often because one or more essential competencies are either absent or present to an insufficient degree. Poor performance can also be a result of external factors (work processes, manager, etc.). Although significant, these factors will not be discussed here. It is important that competencies be described in terms of *perceptible behaviour.* They should be defined in a way that is unambiguous and recognizable and based upon this description it must be possible to determine whether and to what degree a person possesses competencies. The Institute of Applied Business Research has compiled a list of 33 competencies that are used at KPN. Each one is clearly defined and described in three or five proficiency levels which, in terms of definitive behaviour, indicate exactly what is expected for a particular competence at a particular level. The definition used at KPN for 'competence' is as follows:

A competence is a set of behavioural capacities that, as a rule, enables its possessor to react effectively in a given situation.

Source: KPN Research, Institute of Applied Business Research

Examples of competencies are:
Leadership: An employee must be capable of eliciting the support, assent and/or action of others in order to attain set goals and/or pursue a certain approach. Service-mindedness: *An employee must be able to view matters from the customer's perspective and strive to accommodate customer's wishes and solve problems.*

Source: KPN Research, Institute of Applied Business Research

In addition to a set of competencies and a method for producing competence profiles, resources and methodologies are available for developing instruments that measure specific achievements and competencies. These include self-management instruments (such as questionnaires for self-diagnosis), instruments for measuring performance (such as assessment forms to be filled in by the manager, customer or others who come in contact with an employee), assessment and development centres, etc. Completing questionnaires yields scores such as the ones in Figure 37.2 (which in this case applies to Applications Management). The diagram provides insight into strengths and weaknesses and can be used to increase awareness of them. It can also give direction to coaching, further development and training. Self-diagnosis is just one possible use. But results are even more interesting when both an employee and his or her manager complete a questionnaire, preferably with the input of co-workers and customers who are in direct contact with the employee; we refer to the latter scenario as a '360° assessment'.

The analysis of *discrepancies in the scores* can be a source of much valuable information for employees. By using the completed diagram as input in the dialogue between manager/coach and employee, attention is focused on the most essential competencies.

FIGURE 37.2

Score diagram for project management

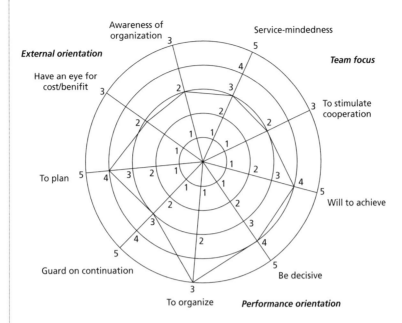

Certain elements of an individual's personality are more or less fixed (Figure 37.3). A person is 'inherently' introverted or extroverted and little can be done to change this. In cases where certain personal characteristics are essential for performing certain duties, such factors must be given sufficient consideration at an early stage, such as when applicants are first being screened. The set of behavioural competencies compiled by KPN naturally includes competencies that are capable to a greater or lesser degree of being developed. It is this area in particular that the manager/coach should focus on. Know-how is essential for good job performance. Still, this area should not receive too much attention from people management. After all, lack of know-how is usually fairly easy to determine and remedy (in many cases through training). Acquiring the appropriate experience is just a matter of time. The primary role of a people manager is to help employees determine a suitable career path, which will introduce the desired experience at the appropriate moment. Naturally, the right know-how and a good command of methods and techniques are essential for performing a job properly. However, knowledge is a threshold commodity: one's immediate contacts (principals, clients) automatically assume that this knowledge is perfectly intact. In other words, you never win points for possessing the requisite knowledge, but you lose points for not possessing it. When an individual is perceived as excelling in a particular job area, this can very frequently be attributed to behavioural aspects. Coaching of employees, then, is most effective when geared to those competencies perceived as indispensable for the job. The essence of competence management is putting employees' talents to optimal use. Competence management can be applied in various ways. On the one hand it strives to 'put the right person in the right job'. On the other hand, through sound guidance and coaching, it encourages employees to develop to their fullest extent. The first point (the

FIGURE 37.3

Approach to people management

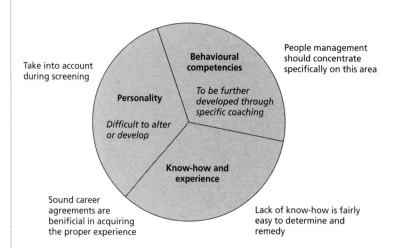

right person in the right job) can be achieved by assessing a person's potential. Employees receive scores for each of the 33 competencies based on an estimate. The scores are then compared to the competence profiles in each job area. The results indicate where someone's talents lie. Although this process is rather formally described here, by no means does a formal potential assessment always take place in practice; it often remains on an implicit level. The key truth, however, stands: sound career development requires sound insight into a person's competencies. So it follows that the competencies most essential to the job area must be developed as fully as possible. 'On-the-job' coaching is the preferred method because it allows direct feedback on behaviour. In practice, this has proved very effective, provided that feedback is given clearly and in a positive manner. 'Learning warehouses' can be developed for each competence to provide extra support. Depending on the competence, this could involve specially designed training, but didactic support of a quite different variety may also be brought into play: supervision by a mentor, an internship, reading particular books, viewing and discussing videotapes, professional assessments. Part of the training will be generic in character and part will be tailored to the job area. Developing competencies to the full could take several years. This is one reason why a common set of definitions is of such great importance. Working under a new manager should not significantly influence an employee's development. The selection and steady pursuit of a particular direction provides stability and considerably improves the chances of success.

37.3 Competence profiles for job areas

For implementation within its IT organization, KPN Telecom decided not to develop a competence profile for each job, but instead to seek broader job areas to which a particular competence profile could be applied. Such job areas (also called 'job families') include a number of positions, generally ascending in scale. For all positions within a job area, the result areas are roughly the same – although they do increase in complexity as the scale ascends. The competence profile corresponding to a job area also remains more or less the same as the scale increases. In other words, in all instances the same set of competencies is used. For each competence in the profile, the required level increases in difficulty. This approach to formulating a job family is a natural way of indicating a possible career. Since employees potentially possess the requisite qualities, they can concentrate on furthering their skills. Of course this will not be their only possible career path; depending on the competencies they possess, they can move to other job areas. Before such a move, a potential assessment is carried out, based on competencies.

A 'traditional' career path in systems development always meant starting out as a programmer, moving on to become a technical designer, then a functional designer. Finally, there was an opportunity to become a project or line manager. If we look at the underlying competence profiles for these duties, this is not such an obvious pattern of advancement after all. Here again, the primary objective is to get the right people into the right jobs (i.e. the duties to which their competencies are best suited), then encourage them to develop their knowledge and the essential competencies for that job area.

Following is a general description of the method used for defining a competence profile ('profiling') for a particular job area. Employees who are active in a job area (and are regarded by management and colleagues as the best in that area) collaborate with several managers in determining which 8 to 10 competencies from the set of 33 are the most important for excelling at that job. These competencies form the essence of the position. Creating a profile generally takes several sessions, during which participants use a structured multi-step approach to arrive at a profile and corresponding behavioural descriptions. The process is also clearly part of the result. Using a structured method to underscore the essential elements of each job area and to describe excellent behaviour is frequently experienced by participants (employees and managers alike) as highly elucidating. A final step consists of determining the level at which the various competencies must be possessed for each scale in the family of jobs (Figure 37.4). This method of describing a family of competencies is stable in that it can withstand changes in the organization. In traditional descriptions of jobs, a good deal of attention has always been assigned to place within the organization, aims of that part of the organization, and so forth. The emphasis in the new method is on the description of general result areas and linking them with the requisite know-how and competencies. Experience has shown that this method of description provides a sufficiently solid base for assessing job levels. Competence profiles must also undergo periodic revalidation. This might be necessary due to changes in the demands or circumstances of a particular job. These days, for instance, a standard requirement of IT specialists is that they be capable of making a significant contribution in multi-disciplinary teams. Just a few years ago, this was hardly the case at all: the most important criterion at the time was for an employee to be well versed (in the technical sense) in his or her field. Communicative skills and the ability to work in teams are growing in importance, also for technical specialists, and this is reflected in the competence profiles.

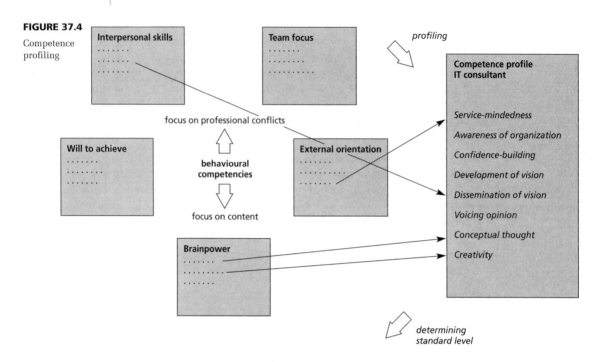

FIGURE 37.4 Competence profiling

37.4 Incorporation of competence management

Competence management might appear to be something of a new approach, but of course it does not operate independently of the existing HR policy. Competence management can, therefore, be incorporated into the organization by integrating it in performance appraisals. Directing attention to the most essential competencies for a particular position has a positive influence on the effectiveness of performance appraisals. In effect, competence management offers ready links to all aspects of human resource management. Based on competence profiles, supplementary selection criteria can be formulated when recruiting for specific job areas; and planning that applies to training and careers can be carried out in part based upon potential assessments and matching the profiles demanded by the various job areas. In many companies, job performance has always played an important role in performance appraisals. In this sense, competence management is nothing new; we've been doing it all along, only more implicitly much of the time. What competence management has to offer is mainly an explicit, common language and an unambiguous set of definitions. This increases the chance that the essential aspects of attitude and behaviour are actually named and discussed during the formulation of job requirements, performance appraisals and the assessment of potential. Herein lie the benefits of competence management. As mentioned earlier, competence management is certainly no panacea and successful implementation depends to a large degree upon whether the move towards 'management with a coaching duty' takes shape. Should this fail, employees may regard competence management as nothing more than 'just another assessment instrument' for management. True competence management requires a management style that invites and encourages employees to develop and explore the scope of their talents within the organization (and in accordance with its strategy) as fully as possible. The other side of the coin is self-management for employees, who are responsible for shaping their own jobs and careers. They must have the will and motivation for further develop-ment and self-actualization.

37.5 Future

In the future, the success of an organization will depend increasingly on the degree to which it is capable of reacting flexibly and effectively to the world around it. Flexibility is of key importance. A growing number of duties will be carried out in multidisciplinary and probably self-piloting teams that form and then dissolve, depending on the current requirements. The role of management and employees is also undergoing major changes. Far more important than an employee's position in the hierarchy is his or her contribution and added value in teams. It is these things that distinguish each employee and determine how they are assessed (as an individual, as a team, and as an organization). For management, this means a steadily diminishing emphasis on directing and controlling and a steadily increasing emphasis on facilities on the one hand and coaching and motivating on the other. Part and parcel of this situation are a 'levelling out' of the organization and jobs whose content is broader and less clearly defined, which calls for another method of describing job content than the current static one. The new descriptions will be oriented specifically towards the competencies considered important within the organization or within a particular job area and less towards the specific activities or position in the hierarchy. Competence management offers a framework for supporting these developments, defined in terms of perceptible behaviour. What do you see when a person exhibits a particular competence at a particular level? Or, what does outstanding performance look like in this job area? The behaviour an individual exhibits is determined by many related factors: personality characteristics, values and norms, motivation, knowledge, skills, and so forth. The greater the congruence between these factors, the greater the chance of the desired behaviour being authentic and, therefore, consistent – a situation that benefits company and employee alike.

Competence management will gain even more in potency when an organization specifies the desired pattern of values and norms, culture etc. in addition to its vision of excellent behaviour. After all, the more explicit this is made, the more likely individual employees will be able to assess the degree to which this pattern of values coincides with their own beliefs. This will broaden the content of the 360° assessment to include questions regarding the degree to which a person endorses and embodies the values and norms of the organization, which makes the culture of the organization an even more tangible topic of discussion.

Literature

Prahalad, C.K. and Hamel, G. (1998) *De strijd om de toekomst* Schiedam Scriptum Management.

Video 'Speed, Simplicity and Self-Confidence': a conversation between Jack Welch and Warren Bennis on the management style at General Electric (1992).

Weggeman, M. (1992) *Leidinggeven aan professionals*, Kluwer Bedrijfswetenschappen.

Knowledge management and the IT Service Management organization

A.P. Kuiper
P.M. Los RI
J. Sietsma CMC

38.1 Introduction

The appearance of a new society

The new society will be characterized by knowledge as the key factor (besides labour and capital) for production. New technologies (such as virtual images, intelligent systems etc.) will be in use in that society.

The changes generate the need for a new organizational paradigm. Since World War II, services have been the most important part of economic activities. The appearance of knowledge management has facilitated that transition from industry towards the services industry. Knowledge management manages intellectual capital. Intellectual capital is the means for business improvement.

Improvement of the services business initiates changes to the services industry, but also to industrial businesses: the structure of the economy, the structure of developments in national and regional context – they all change (Quinn, 1992.)
The 21st century will demonstrate that there is a new society with regard to:

- changed values;
- changed relationships between countries;
- changed appreciation of the arts;
- changed behaviour of companies, etc.

The beginning of this century is the beginning of a transition phase towards a knowledge society. Know-how, know-why and know-where are essential issues. Organizations increasingly become knowledge institutions, where management of available knowledge is the most critical task of management.

For these organizations, it is not enough that there is somebody who learns for the company – someone at the top who invents, rethinks, and gives commandments. That is not the way it will work in the future. Organizational structure and ways of governance and management will change. The key factor will be personal professionalism.

Guidance comes from high-level professionals with personality: they create a permanent context of visibility of their ideas that gives guidance, a sort of governance. These professionals are obliged to develop their ideas and themselves, lifelong.

In this chapter we present some down-to-earth guidance in the area of knowledge management and answer questions such as:

- What is knowledge?
- What is knowledge management?
- How can knowledge management be adapted to an IT Service Management context?
- How can knowledge management be implemented pragmatically (KIM2)?

38.2 Definitions

Many definitions around the knowledge management issue are incomplete, sometimes conflicting.

We all know the definition of data (which is considered to be normal facts), *information*, which is more than data (the specific context is meaningful), *knowledge*, which is more than information (knowledge uses information to make a decision), and *wisdom* (the ultimate stage of knowledge).

Figure 38.1 demonstrates how the value of intellectual capital improves as we move from data, via information and knowledge, to wisdom.

FIGURE 38.1

Knowledge vs. intellectual capital and value

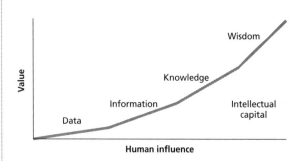

Besides the differences between data, information, knowledge and wisdom, it is necessary to look to knowledge on two levels if one wants to manage it:

- knowledge of individuals or individual intellectual capital;
- knowledge of groups of individuals or organizational intellectual capital.

Individual intellectual capital

Individual intellectual capital has much value – often more than we realize ourselves. Despite this, there are many organizations that manage individual capital very badly.

One of the reasons is that the average manager does not see the difference between the costs and the value of investments in people. It is important to recognize the differences between several kinds of individual intellectual capital, because some kinds generate revenue and some don't. Figure 38.2 helps to explain this, its four elements being described next.

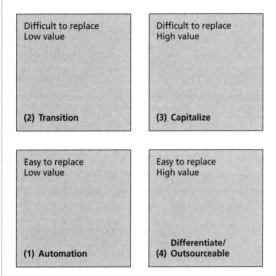

FIGURE 38.2 The value of individual intellectual capital

Easy to replace with low value (Figure 38.2 (1))

For IT Service Management organizations, the following activities belong to this category:

- backup and restore activities;
- management of repeating incidents;
- monitoring of relatively simple operational processes;
- media conversion activities (from hard copy to electronic media);
- tape handling.

Difficult to replace with low value (Figure 38.2 (2))

If this is work that uses people (and their knowledge) who are low-skilled and follow a routine, it is possible to choose a transition strategy to part 1 of the figure: computerize the work.

Difficult to replace, with high value (Figure 38.2 (3))

Activities of this kind in IT Service Management organizations are, amongst others:

- problem/change specialists $2^{nd}/3^{rd}$ line UNIX, NT, MVS etc;
- problem/change specialists $2^{nd}/3^{rd}$ line CICS, Tuxedo, Encina etc;

- problem/change specialists $2^{nd}/3^{rd}$ line DB2, Sybase, Oracle, Informix etc;
- contingency specialism;
- capacity/availability specialism.

Easy to replace, with high value (Figure 38.2 (4))

In IT Service Management organizations, examples of these activities are:

- pickup/delivery of PCs;
- implementation work regarding commodities (printers, scanners etc.);
- WAN IT Service Management;
- LAN IT Service Management.

Organizational intellectual capital

Organisational intellectual capital is different from individual intellectual capital. Individual intellectual capital is the source of innovation: from innovation by brainstorming in a laboratory to innovation arising from remarks in a sales rep's small black pocketbook. But smart people don't necessarily make a smart organization.

Imagine: one day a visitor asks the president of Amsterdam University where the quantity of concentrated knowledge in this university comes from. The answer: 'That's quite simple. Every year we accept the most brilliant people. If they leave the university four years later, with their certificate, they leave us completely innocent and completely undeveloped. They will have left their knowledge here.'

This story illustrates what organizational intellectual capital is.

Knowledge management

If you look at the development of information systems, we see the following steps:

- design the demands of the client or technological developments;
- develop by acquiring the infrastructure or information systems;
- certification of the information systems or infrastructure;
- information system management (functional and technical), including implementation;
- deletion of the information system or infrastructure.

These steps are performed on three levels:

- strategic level (based on a five-year plan, client demands and technology push come together);
- tactical level (based on a three-year plan, client demands and technology push come together);
- operational level (based on a one-year plan, client demands and technology push come together).

38 Knowledge management and the IT Service Management organization

In this way we come to a definition of knowledge management:
Management on the strategic, tactical and operational levels of the life cycle of knowledge.

This life cycle of knowledge consists of the following steps (Figure 38.3):

- identification of knowledge needed;
- acquisition (develop or buy, usage) of existing knowledge;
- certification of knowledge;
- management and exploitation of knowledge;
- deletion of knowledge.

FIGURE 38.3
The life cycle of knowledge

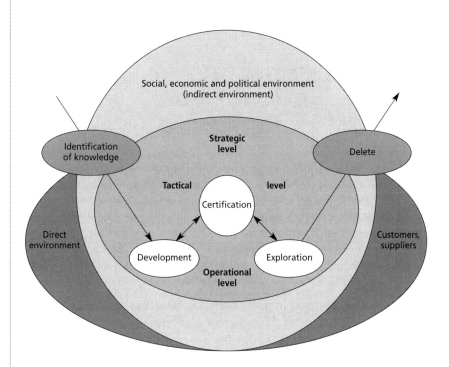

38.3 The knowledge cycle in IT Service Management organizations
General

Similar to the situation with definitions of knowledge and knowledge management, there are many views on the life cycle of knowledge. We describe one model.

Single-loop and double-loop learning

For further understanding of knowledge and knowledge management and the use of both in organizations, it is of interest to understand the difference between single-loop

FIGURE 38.4

Single- and double-loop learning

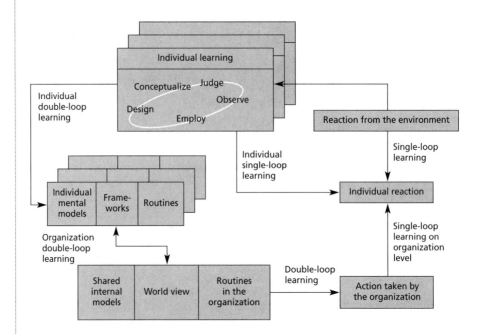

learning and double-loop learning (Argyris, 1990). Single-loop learning solves eventual existing problems. It does not solve the essential problem, that is, the source or the cause of problems we want to solve. So the system (organization) is not structurally improved after having solved problems. Figure 38.4 makes that clear.

We can see that individual single-loop learning helps to solve a problem, but does not lead to structural improvement. Not until the individual mental model has been improved can one see the improvements as structural improvement (individual double-loop learning). The same applies to generic (shared) mental models for an organization.

There is a way to move towards double-loop learning:

- Make employees aware of single-loop learning.
- (Re-)educate and train the employees in the direction of double-loop learning.
- Empower the organization.
- Repeat the steps whenever a new problem appears.

Single-loop and double-loop learning in IT Service Management organizations

The single- and the double-loop learning models are applicable in the area of IT Service Management. It is often in use (but implicitly). If we compare this model with the IPW model for IT Service Management, we see a similar learning curve especially in the cycle of incident, problem and change management (Figure 38.5).

The treatment of an incident is essentially similar to single-loop learning. Problem management is looking for patterns and structures in the different problems, and can be compared with the double-loop learning cycle.

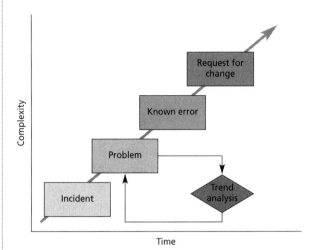

FIGURE 38.5
Problem management and double-loop learning

Looking at an IT Service Management organization from the perspective that has been offered in this chapter so far, we learn that we have hardly started adapting it in practice. Much knowledge is 'possessed' by individual specialists and the configuration management of knowledge (know-how, know-where and know-why) has not been organized. As IT Service Management is the biggest part of the complete IT life cycle of an information system, this must change.

Knowledge management from birth to death

We defined knowledge management as the management (on a strategic, tactical and operational level) of the life cycle of knowledge. This life cycle of knowledge consists of the following five steps:

1. identification of the necessary knowledge for the organization (design);
2. development (acquisition) of (eventual existing) knowledge;
3. authorization and certification of knowledge;
4. management and exploration of knowledge;
5. deletion of knowledge.

1. Identification of the necessary knowledge for the organization (design)

A vision or direction is the starting point of everything. This primary obligation of top management results in a basis for lower management to define the strategies and policies for their part of the company. That basis consists of basic rules and guidelines for allocation of resources and solving tactical problems.

A vision makes some things clear:

- What is the status that we want to realize?
- What do we think about the future?

- What will technology mean for us?
- What are the developments (social, society, political etc.) that are meaningful for us and what do they mean?

The next step is to derive a mission. That more or less gives a model of an end-state (temporary) in relation to the vision.

Finally, a strategy will be formulated, which makes clear the chosen route to achieve the objectives.

This process of defining a vision, mission and strategy is very important. It thus becomes clear what resources (knowledge is one of the resource categories) will be needed to offer products and services to the marketplace.

The knowledge resource is clustered into key knowledge clusters, which are the models of the knowledge that is needed for the organization.

It is important to understand that the vision, mission and strategy must be known and shared by all the people in an organization in a way that fits their responsibilities. So it is not exclusively paperwork, but also functions as a mind model. A mind model inspires, and helps to make decisions in different situations and conditions based on the same starting points. So vision, mission and strategy represent a shared ambition.

A shared ambition is not an idea, it is a commitment, as it is like a force that people feel, smell and taste. That makes it a strength in managing many people to pull together in the same direction.

Such a shared vision represents (partly) the thoughts and beliefs of every individual involved. It motivates, stimulates and energizes people. It is not their company, but our company!

This can be compared with the effect of a hologram (Senge, 1990). A hologram can represent a picture in three dimensions through this cooperation of several sources of light. If a photograph is cut into two parts, each half represents part of the original picture. If a hologram is divided into parts, one can see the whole original picture in any part. If the pieces of the hologram are combined, the picture does not change essentially, because the whole picture was represented in each part. The difference is that the picture becomes more and more realistic.

Possible knowledge clusters could be:

- client;
- mid-range facilities;
- high-end servers;
- local area networks;
- wide area networks;
- telematics;
- service management infrastructure;
- security management infrastructure;
- system development infrastructure;
- integration/broker infrastructure;
- middleware infrastructure.

2. Development (acquisition) of (eventual existing) knowledge

The basis for acquiring or developing knowledge is the key knowledge clusters that have been defined. These clusters represent the actual situation in the organization by function in the organization.

Ways of acquiring knowledge are:

- buying knowledge (licences, manuals);
- research programme initiatives, together with the study programmes of schools, universities, or institutes;
- recruitment;
- benchmarking and competitor analysis;
- use of scientific sources;
- visits to suppliers;
- training, conferences, seminars;
- external databases, networks;
- literature studies;
- client contacts (client surveys);
- inventory of available knowledge, etc.

3. Authorization and certification of knowledge

After making an inventory of newly created knowledge and experiences and actually creating new knowledge, we have to certify this knowledge. Successes and failures are reported and analysed to generate 'lessons learned' that can be used by the organization. They certify the different kinds of knowledge, resulting in a status:

- new area of knowledge;
- under development;
- in test phase;
- authorized;
- under Service Management;
- deleted.

4. Management and exploitation of knowledge

It is useful to look at the management and exploitation of knowledge. In fact, that means looking at the knowledge flow in an organization.

This knowledge flow can be analysed from three perspectives:

1. diffusion (distribution) of knowledge;
2. generation of knowledge;
3. exploitation of knowledge.

Diffusion
Diffusion is the spreading of knowledge all over (a part of) an organization. The most important channels are:

- communication between employees (horizontal and vertical);
- communication between departments;
- information systems;
- mass communication.

It is very important that employees in an organization are aware of the possession of (new) knowledge and that they are able and willing to share it and spread it out over the organization. There are several means of diffusion:

- manuals, rules, process descriptions, procedures;
- horizontal communication in competence groups;
- communication of functional groups;
- vertical communication;
- information bulletins;
- knowledge information systems (intranet, Internet, groupware, data warehousing, etc.);
- job-rotation;
- mentor systems;
- informal networks;
- social events or meetings;
- second opinion of colleagues;
- information sharing regarding best practices, etc.

Generation
Generation is key for the innovative competencies of an organization. Generation happens on several levels:

- the lowest level of knowledge generation is solving standard problems by existing routines;
- the second level is the development of solutions for problems by existing work procedures;
- the highest level is the development of new work procedures for problems or challenges that have not been met earlier by the organization.

Means that are often in use for knowledge generation in IT Service Management organizations are:

- multi-disciplinary teams – they provide creative tension between group members with new knowledge as a result;
- programme and/or project management that hands (new) knowledge over to line management;

- evaluation of closed activities (on concrete and meta levels);
- monthly, quarterly and yearly reports;
- simulations and what-if analyses;
- quality reviews, Fagin inspections and internal control programmes;
- horizontal, vertical and diagonal feedback;
- end-user satisfaction measurement;
- simulations (games) based upon best and worst practices;
- self-assessments; etc.

Exploitation
Exploitation of knowledge is the means of measuring the success of knowledge development. If the knowledge flow does not perform well in all its aspects, the organization will not perform well. An organization that does not exploit crucial knowledge in the way that it produces or delivers products or services is missing a trick. It is important to pay attention to the blockages that are part of mental models, for they are roadblocks against improving or renewing learning.

> A young man had a car accident and was taken to the operating theatre of a hospital. His father died as a result of the accident. The surgeon enters and says: 'Oh no, I cannot operate on him, he is my son.' How is that possible?
>
> Many people will not be able to give the answer. It is quite easy to answer: the surgeon is a woman. She was the young man's mother. Our mental model ensures that – in many cases – we expect the surgeon to be a man. That makes answering difficult.

The following means are available for the exploitation of knowledge:

- selling of knowledge;
- stimulation of the use of evaluation reports via monthly, quarterly and yearly analysis;
- organizing the know-how, know-why and know-where via knowledge systems;
- making knowledge available by competency profiles;
- promotion of the use of manuals, between peers, meetings (horizontal, vertical and/or diagonal);
- implementation (in the hierarchy) of the results of benchmarks, competitive analysis;
- implementation of human-resource management of adequate quality, etc.

5. Deletion of knowledge

As stated before: everything starts with vision. And: everything ends with vision. Vision makes it clear that specific key knowledge clusters are no longer needed in the organization. This means that management has to decide to delete these knowledge clusters; that is something that is not done in many organizations.

38.4 Implementation models

In this section we briefly introduce two models:
- the KIM2 model;
- the KIM2 model for knowledge security.

They have been developed in the context of developing an approach to the introduction of knowledge management for IT Service Management organizations.

The KIM2 model

The KIM2 model is used for preparing a knowledge management implementation and managing it. It is a concrete operationalization of some theory in this chapter. The preparation of the implementation in three stages is important:

1. Identify the triggers for implementation of knowledge management.
2. Identify and define the key knowledge clusters.
3. Define objectives for the implementation of knowledge management.

1. Identify the triggers for implementation of knowledge management

1. *Organizations have to react in a much faster way to the changing environment in order to get the perfect fit/match. Demands to be flexible are getting stronger and stronger.*
Customers want to have the product/service much faster than before. This means that organizations have minimum time to react to the demands of the customer. In order to do this, the organization has to have knowledge of all its products and services at any time and in any place.

2. *Organizations have to be empathically involved with their customers.*
Customers want to have the feeling that the organizations know them and that they have a mutual feeling about what really drives them forward.

3. *Add value.*
In IT Service Management we are seeing a much higher standard in doing business with the customer. This quality standard means that you are acting in a meaningful way and that you are making a contribution to the growth of your customer.

4. *Make knowledge accessible and transferable.*
The move by organizations to outsourcing because of focusing on their core business is getting more normal. Outsourcing makes it necessary that knowledge is transferable and accessible. In short, changing the way we organize means that people have to interact in exchanging knowledge.

2. Identify and define key knowledge clusters

It is very important for an organization to identify the clusters of knowledge being used in the organization. The clusters of knowledge could be infrastructure, customer groups on personnel groups. In any event, you don't want to maintain knowledge of clusters which are not relevant to your core business.

3. Define objectives for the implementation of knowledge management

1 *Which knowledge cluster do you focus on?*
An IT service management organization will have to write down its goals, which stipulate the need for implementation of knowledge management. Knowledge management as a primary, core goal will never lead to success. It is always derived from the goals of the business, for which knowledge management processes are necessary. But not all knowledge is important, so you will have make a selection from the total knowledge.

2 *Which knowledge management processes are necessary?*
An implicit part of the goal is to state which knowledge management processes you are going to implement in your organization. In some organizations the development of knowledge management is very important and in others the deployment or maintenance of knowledge is much more important. It depends on which type of organization you have.

In any event, in every organization you will see all the knowledge management processes we have described.

3 *Which social infrastructure is necessary?*
If we look at technology or at knowledge management processes, we state very clearly that both are very necessary for the implementation of a knowledge management model. Nevertheless, the social infrastructure is the most important thing you have to address. And in implementing and solving your knowledge problem, you not only look at technology and processes but you also specifically look at methods and techniques, which can be used to transfer techniques between the mental models of personnel. The transferring of mental models between personnel or groups of people will finally lead to greater success for your organization.

4 *How are you going to implement this?*
After having completed these three phases (Figure 38.6), implementation can start.

This structure and the sequence of phases are important. If organizations implement knowledge management without a well-defined context of triggers and key knowledge clusters, it is not possible to define objectives for knowledge management precisely enough.

Nothing is simpler than implementation of knowledge management in a broad sense. Attempts to create value by knowledge management will fail if you try to cover everything.

Only when you start implementing knowledge management on a basis of well-known needs can you avoid the pitfall of making some tacit knowledge explicit, only to find that no one wants it. Another pitfall is making a good start but finding that after a couple of months no one is using your well-defined knowledge exchange system. Using KIM2 ensures a proven method of defining the most successful areas.

FIGURE 38.6

The KIM2 model

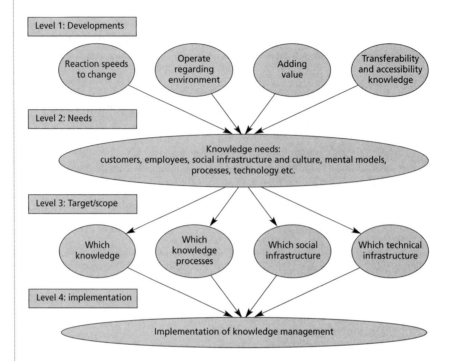

The implementation strategy itself (phase 4) depends on the number of people involved, the organizational culture, the assets to be achieved, and of course the outcome of the previous phases.

A model for security of knowledge

We have chosen this description ('security of knowledge') as knowledge management is sometimes treated as hype. We feel that without good preparation and a modest level of ambition, attempts to implement knowledge management will fail.

FIGURE 38.7

The KIM2 model for knowledge security

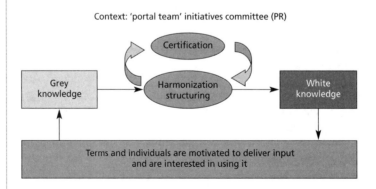

Four processes must be in place for active knowledge management (Figure 38.7):

1. Gather (and stimulate the gathering of) grey knowledge (that is, information that has not been reviewed, harmonized or structured).
2. Harmonize information and structure it (dictionary).
3. Give information a status by certification.
4. Make knowledge available for use and stimulate the use of it.

Those included are:

- Knowledge management team
  - responsible for gathering and harmonization
- Certification board (with decision power and authority)
  - for definition of status
- Portal committee
  - for creating a structure, a context for storing knowledge that is retrievable
- Initiatives committee
  - stimulates the offering of grey data or information and use of knowledge.

The advantage of handling grey knowledge in this way is that everybody can see how reliable the knowledge is. You can choose to give access to grey knowledge, but people will use it 'at their own risk', while white knowledge is certified and everybody can trust its content. In large companies you often see a formal certification process, while in smaller companies people judge reliability according to the source of knowledge and the overhead involved informal certification isn't worth it.

In any event you have to take precautions to ensure that the certification board does not create too much of a time difference between the offering and presenting of new knowledge. It is fatal if that process takes too long: people will stop offering new knowledge and find their own ways of distribution, or they will keep that new knowledge to themselves.

38.5 Conclusion

Knowledge management is important. Some people will think it is just hype. But, owing to changing economics – global marketing (which implies global competition), dynamic markets (with dynamic competitors), new developments coming along faster than ever (which implies a shorter product life cycle and hence a shorter time to invest in the learning phase and a shorter time to recover your investments) and the rise of virtual communities – networking and worker mobility organizations must use an effective knowledge management system to survive. In this new service- and knowledge-based era it is the key factor that determines the success of an organization.

However, the implementation of knowledge management is not easy. Trying to get a brain dump from all your employees or colleagues is useless (and impossible). You must determine which knowledge is worth the trouble of making accessible to others, and define a strategy for the way you handle your organizational knowledge.

The life cycle of knowledge means that you have to find out which knowledge is necessary for your organization (based on the company policy), and act accordingly.

The best way to make use of your learning power is to introduce double-loop learning, not only for your individual employees but also for the organization itself. In that way, you can reach your desired service level as soon as possible, and make your knowledge profitable.

Implementing knowledge management in your organization is no sinecure, but it is well worth the effort. But don't rush. Use a thorough implementation method such as KIM2. There are too many failures, and you should learn from the pitfalls that have befallen others. You only have one chance to implement knowledge management in the right way from the start. KIM2 is a structured way of defining your needs and goals.

Implementing knowledge management in organizations can be successful. It has already been proven.

Literature

Argyris, C. (1990) *Overcoming Organizational Defenses, Facilitating Organizational Learning*, Allyn & Bacon.

Bohn, R.E. (1994) 'Measuring and managing technological knowledge,' *Sloan Management Review*, Fall.

Choo, C.W. (1995) 'Information Management for the intelligent organization, the art of scanning the environment', ASIS Monograph Series.

Collins, J.C. and Porras, J.I. (1996) *Build to Last, Successful habits of visonary companies*, Century Business.

Drucker, P.F. (1993) *The Post-Capitalist Society*, New York: Truman Talley Books/Dutton.

Edwards, M.R. and Ewen, A.J. (1994) *360°feedback, The powerful new model for employee assessment and performance improvement*, American Management Association.

Garratt, B. (1994) *The Learning Organisation and the Need for Directors who Think*, HarperCollins Publishers.

Kuiper, A.P. and Klunder, J.H. (1997) *Kennismanagement in organisaties*, Computable.

Kuiper, A.P. and Klunder, J.H. (1998) 'Methoden en technieken bij kennismanagement', *Management Informatie*.

Kuiper, A.P. and Klunder, J.H. (1999) 'Kennismanagement in de publieke sector, hoofdstuk 8 : Methoden en technieken voor het toepassen van kennismanagement bij het Automatiseringscentrum van de Belastingdienst', Elsevier.

Kuiper, A.P. and Sietsma, J.S. (2000) *Kennismanagement in de context van IT-beheer*, Beheerreeks IT, ten Hagen Stam.

Quinn, J.B. (1992) *Intelligent Enterprise*, The Free Press.

Rogers, E. (1999) *Diffusions of Innovations*, fourth edition, The Free Press.

Senge, P.M. (1990) *The Fifth Discipline, The art and practice of the learning organization*, Doubleday.

Sprenger, C.C. (1995) *Vier competenties van de lerende organisatie*, Delwel.

Stewart, T.A. (1997) *Intellectual Capital, the new wealth of organizations*, Currency Doubleday.

Tapscott, D. (1995) *The Digital Economy*, McGraw-Hill.

39 Organizational improvement and culture . . . growth deserves space!

Jolanda Meijers and **Hans van Herwaarden**
Quint Wellington Redwood, the Netherlands

John was raised in an area with many forests. Swaying trees and rustling leaves were the wind for him. Imagine his surprise that day on the beach when he felt the wind, but could not see it. He was astonished. He had always thought that the wind was part of the trees. Wind turned out to be untouchable, invisible, but could clearly be felt. He was intrigued.

39.1 Interest in organizational culture

Culture is experiencing a great deal of interest within organizations. That is not at all surprising. Culture is playing an ever-increasing role in organizations, in both a positive and negative way. The difference between surviving and not surviving in an environment that is rapidly changing appears to depend heavily on aspects that may be characterized as cultural. In their much-discussed book *In Search of Excellence*, Peters and Waterman (1988) researched a number of 'excellent' enterprises. Five years after the book was published, a significant number of the enterprises described by the authors as 'excellent' found themselves in serious trouble. Further research showed that the enterprises concerned were capable of excellent performance with only a very specific configuration. They had adapted themselves optimally to specific market conditions, labour market relationships, production processes or the technology at their disposal. For lasting success the measure and, especially, the speed with which organizations are able to reconfigure themselves in response to altered market conditions appear to be of increased decisive importance. If possible, this is even truer for ICT organizations. For the improvement of ICT organizations, a number of interconnected aspects are important (Figure 39.1). Improvement is a dire necessity for many ICT organisations. By improvement, we mean taking the capability of an organization to remain successful and, thus, to survive at a higher level. For a more detailed explanation, we refer you to the description of the IPW Stadia Model in Chapter 7 of this book and in the *IT Beheer Jaarboek 1998*. Traditionally, a lot of attention has been given to means within an ICT organization. From the very start, the 'tools of work' have been focused on the available technology. Since the early 1990s, processes have received more attention.

Driven by concepts such as process-based working methods, ICT process re-engineering and work-flow management, function-based and hierarchical organizations have been transformed into process-based organizations that are far more focused on the client and service delivery. Up to this point, there has been little attention paid to the human being. Still, the human factor often appears to play a crucial role in the

FIGURE 39.1

The interconnected aspects of ICT organizational improvement

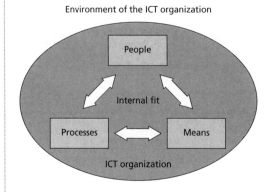

FIGURE 39.2

The human factor on three levels

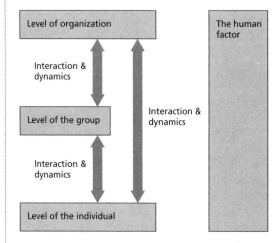

success or failure of ICT organizational improvement. We encounter the human factor again at various levels in the organization (Figure 39.2). The first level is that of the individual. On this level, we are concerned with the ICT professional him/herself. The second level focuses on the level of the group. Teams of ICT professionals work together to reach the goals set for them, in part driven by developments in the area of empowerment, 'levelling' of organizations and process-based work practices. The third level is the level of the organization. This is also the most complex level, as its scope extends to the entire group of ICT professionals in the organization. These levels interact with each other, but also with other factors. In the ideal situation, the human factor needs to be attuned to the other factors (means and processes), while the whole needs to be attuned to the environment (clients and suppliers). In general, the means factor should be attuned to the 'state' of technology, the process factor to the 'state' of the profession (best practices) and the human factor to the 'state' of society. These are, respectively, the 'technological fit', the 'process fit' and the 'cultural fit' (Figure 39.3). By 'state' we mean that which is generally in use or possible and which, therefore, serves as the reference point for the activities of an ICT organization. The

39 ■ Organizational improvement and culture ... growth deserves space!

FIGURE 39.3
Internal and external adjustment: 'organizational fit'

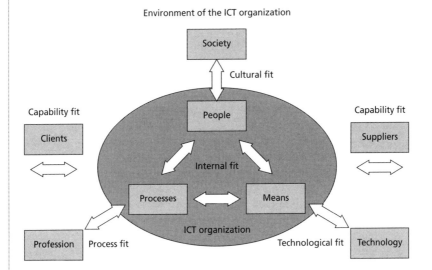

adjustment to all relevant aspects (the internal and external 'fit') is the so-called 'organizational fit'. As an organization reaches a higher level of maturity, the 'organizational fit' becomes better. If an organization is unable to attune itself to one or more of the aspects cited, problems will result in the short or longer term. In this chapter, we will concentrate on the human factor.

39.2 Developments in society

Throughout recent decades, societal developments have followed each other with ever-increasing speed. Internationalization, individualization, the 24-hour economy, hyper-competition, constant change, virtual business, e-commerce, significantly shorter product and service life cycles and networked organizations are only a few of the developments of the past five years. Developments that have been going on longer and are of a more general nature include, for example, individualization, secularization, retreating government and emancipation. Here, technology often plays the role of 'enabler'. In our contribution, we are particularly interested in consequences for the individual and, by extension, in consequences for the organization and for organizational improvement. The abovementioned developments offer opportunities as well as threats to the individual. Not only the home and work environments, but the whole world has become one's living environment. As a result of the much greater availability of information (e.g. the Internet), situations can be judged in a much wider context and everyone can make their own choices. Sprenger indicates in his 1998 book The Choice is Yours! that people are increasingly responsible and capable of choosing their own path. Don Tapscott, in his 1995 book Digital Economy, points out that place and time play an increasingly smaller role for the 'Net Generation'. The concept of 'networked intelligence' has appeared. This means that an individual can have almost the same information at his or her disposal as an organization can. However, people generally change at a slower pace than their environment does. They choose those things from new developments that fit most closely with their own ideas. For some, everything happens much too quickly. Information stress, or information overload, has become a well-known concept. These people look for a new point of stability, or they quit. They drop out or put their faith in 'Celestine prophecies'. The rise of the New Age movement is closely related to that.

39.3 Significance for the organization

Organizations also react to their environments. The pace at which organizations can adapt to new opportunities is generally much slower than that of the individual, because each organization is nothing more nor less than a collection of individuals. Wherever people congregate, agreement must be mutually reached and approved. This takes more time than an individual requires to decide whether – and if so, how – new opportunities will be used. The lasting success and, therefore, the survival of an organization depends on the speed with which it can react to the developments in the environment. The faster it can adapt, the more effective it will be. Large, well-known organizations such as IBM and Xerox almost succumbed to not being able to adapt fast enough to changed circumstances. IBM was confronted with the rise of small computers and Xerox experienced sudden competition from, for example, Hewlett-Packard because the traditional line of demarcation between copying and printing had faded. If we can accept, as stated, that an individual adapts to changed circumstances more quickly than an organization, an interesting perspective results. An organization that offers the individual the maximum amount of space will most likely remain permanently more effective, because it can adapt more quickly. In that case, cultural aspects ensure cohesion within the organization. The dominant presence of so-called 'shared values' provides direction to activities (gives meaning) and implicitly ensures coordination. In the book *Managing by Values*, Ken Blanchard and Michael O'Connor (1997) describe the enormous power of values and norms as a cohesive, inspiring and energizing factor for an enterprise, but also how the lack of them will lead to decline. The values and norms form the core of culture on all levels (individual, group and organization). In this context, Maurits Bruel and Clemens Colsen (1998) speak of the organization as a 'factory for happiness'; they see captivating people and gaining their loyalty as critical factors for success in the organization of the future. They make the proposition that ever-increasing numbers of people do not want more, but better! If that is true, ethics, identity, norms and values, authenticity and meaning are then most important, as opposed to structures, systems and monetary considerations.

39.4 Self-organizing growth and the IPW Stadia Model

Our opinion, based on the above, is that there is also a connection between the amount of freedom given to the individual in an ICT organization (the right culture) and the extent to which the ICT organization is thereby able to grow to a higher level of maturity within the IPW Stadia Model. This can also have a desirable side-effect, in that the organization may be able to attract people who identify with a higher level of professionalism, which in turn has a desirable effect on organizational improvement. In this way, an ever-stronger force for improvement is created. The reverse is just as much the case. In time, an organization that offers its people little space loses those that are most important for its success. In practice, it appears to be difficult for many ICT organizations to get out of this downward spiral once it has been entered. Often, ICT organizations cite the quality of their personnel as a problem. We suspect, however, that many of these organizations get the personnel they deserve because they give their members too little space and so encourage counterproductive behaviour patterns; they attract people who have internalized these behaviour patterns. An ascending spiral is also difficult to escape from. Some organizations and their professionals have become so addicted to improvement that they want nothing else. 'To stop improving is to stop living' has become their motto.

39.5 The role of structure

The organizational structure of effective organizations is one that gives direction but does not constrict. Network organizations and organizations that work with process-based methods appear to be able to adjust better and faster to changes than companies set up according to traditional functional hierarchical lines. An increasing number of ICT organizations are changing to process-based working methods (partially due to the above). Matrix organizations that, subsequently, need to be 'tilted' are often a consequence. In the 1980s, Galbraith stated that reducing the amount of information that needs to be processed is one possibility for the solution to the problem of having to deal with an ever more complex organizational environment. A possibility given by him is the creation of autonomic units. As a result, in the 1980s so-called 'business unit' structures were introduced on a large scale. Small units can react more quickly to changing situations and specific goals because of their size. Developing this idea further, the best structure appears to be 'as little structure as possible'. Such a structure is now often called an 'open structure'. However, an open structure can only be effective with the proper strong culture, which will serve to ensure the necessary cohesion and coordination.

39.6 The role of culture

Many scientists have described the concept of organizational culture (e.g. Hofstede, 1984; Schein, 1992). All of the definitions have a common theory that the current norms and values in the organization form the core of organizational culture. They determine the behaviour of the co-workers. Members of an organization where 'creativity and flexibility' form the core values, as in a media production company, will behave differently from members of an organization that has 'reliability and continuity' as the highest (non-verbalized) value, such as a utility company. Culture is a reliable reference point for the individual and determines how people in an organization deal with each other and their environment. In this context, Hofstede speaks of 'collective programming', Schein speaks of 'the correct way to think, perceive and feel'. Additionally, according to the latest insights, culture determines the effectiveness of an organization in large measure. Peter Senge, in his book *The Fifth Discipline*, proposes that the learning potential of an organization is the critical success factor for survival. These so-called 'learning organizations' consist of a collection of individuals exhibiting a certain behaviour that allows the organization to constantly improve itself and adapt to the environment. Cooke and Lafferty have done exhaustive research into behaviour. On the basis of their research, they differentiate between constructive and defensive behaviour patterns. In addition, Cooke and Lafferty (1987) have shown a connection between the behaviour patterns they identified and the effectiveness of individuals, groups and organizations, showing that constructive behaviour patterns have a positive effect on effectiveness and defensive behaviour patterns can impair, or even nullify, this effect. The behaviour patterns classified are further divided into patterns that affect the quality of the solutions and patterns that affect the quality of acceptance. The results gained can be seen as the product of these two factors ($R = K \times A$). Based on this research, Human Synergistics has developed an analysis instrument with which to map behaviour (Figure 39.4). The instrument has proven very useful in practice for making culture measurable on all levels (individual, group and organization).

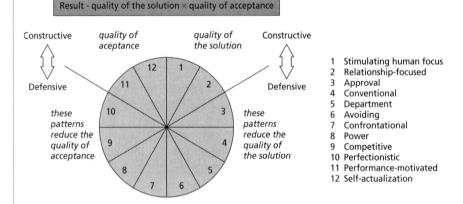

FIGURE 39.4

The Human Synergistics 'rose'

39.7 Influencing culture

Organizational culture seems an intangible phenomenon. 'Norms and values' have been internalized. Yet, organizational culture can still certainly be influenced. There are various opinions regarding the way in which culture can be influenced. Roughly speaking, there are two main streams of thought. The first assumes that culture can be viewed as a separate object and thus can be seen as capable of improvement separate from the organization. Many organizations have carried out large-scale improvement programmes on the basis of these ideas. The second stream of thought assumes that culture forms an indivisible whole with the other characteristics of an organization (structure, strategy, systems etc.) and therefore must be improved in combination with these other characteristics. An interesting view in this context is the one that states that culture must really be seen as a resultant of all the other characteristics, and thus is always a derivative. In our eyes, cultural improvement cannot be a goal in itself in any way. Therefore, it may not surprise you that we believe cultural change should be an integral part of organizational change. Mastenbroek (1997) talks about 'result-driven improvement'. In his book, *Change Management*, he states his preference for improving cultural and communications aspects from the bottom up, which should lead to the proper balance between being directed and self-direction. The central thesis of his discourse is that there is a direct connection between performance improvement and culture improvement. In our view, culture improvement is also an integral part of the entire course of organizational improvement, in all its phases. The AURRA model (Figure 39.5) is the model of preference for phasing (see also *IT-Management Yearbook 1997* and *1998*). We will discuss the attention that must be paid to culture (human beings) during the various phases of an organizational improvement project structured according to AURRA. We do not, consciously, treat the aspects of means and processes, although the cultural factor cannot be looked at as separate from these aspects.

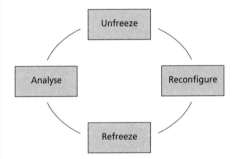

FIGURE 39.5 The AURRA model

Analyse and unfreeze

In order to be able to improve the culture of an organization, it must first be made explicit. CultureQuest is an analysis instrument, specifically meant for ICT organizations, that maps the current and also the desired culture with the use of the Human Synergistics materials cited above. As already stated, this can be done on the individual, group and organizational level. The results of a culture measurement can subsequently be used as an 'unfreezing agent'. A culture measurement describes behaviour thoroughly and opens it for discussion. Making the current culture and the gap between the current and the desired culture explicit ensures that the current culture is no longer self-evident. The results of the culture measurement serve as food for thought and give direction to possible intervention strategies.

Reconfigure and refreeze

The next step is the determination of the way in which to move from the 'current' to the 'desired'. A range of possibilities is available for improvement of the culture. With this, it is crucial that the change is structured according to the principles of the desired culture. To ensure their credibility, the 'change leaders' need to lead by example. Scott Morgan indicates (1994) that the 'unwritten rules of the game' within organizations are often more important than the 'written rules'.

The integrity of management (the extent to which the 'unwritten rules' correspond with the 'written rules') is, in our opinion, essential for a successful change process. The management influences culture in important ways, after all. At the core of a programme of culture change are often the so-called HRM instruments. Examples are, among others, the stimulation of (cross-functional) teamwork, job enrichment, coaching, redesign of reward and punishment mechanisms, redesign of decision-making processes, recalibration of inflow, throughput and outflow policies and competence management. This HRM programme can be accompanied by activities in the area of 'symbols' and 'rituals'. The change must be tangible for everyone involved. An example of changing a ritual concerns the New Year speech in an organization. Consciously having someone other than the managing director deliver this speech may be a measure that enforces the HRM measures. An example of changing a symbol is consciously changing the entrance of a building from an enclosed, glassed-in counter to an open space with a centrally placed reception desk. Selection of the proper HRM instruments is also dependent on the stage of the ICT organization's maturity, as indicated on the IPW Stadia Model ladder. After all, often more than one AURRA cycle must be completed before the desired level is reached. In this context, a relationship can also be established between the IPW Stadia Model and the People Capability Maturity Model (P-CMM), which recognizes a number of levels of maturity in the way in which HRM is implemented in an organization.

Analysis

Preferably, a change programme is closed with a new measurement, so that it may be determined whether the desired results in terms of culture improvement have been reached.

Connection

The mutual connections between the cultural components discussed (the human factor) are illustrated again in Figure 39.6. These interconnections form the basis for every intervention strategy and every AURRA cycle. External and internal dynamics lead to a particular self-reinforcing culture unless intervention takes place. The culture that originates in such a way will subsequently determine behaviour on the individual, group and organizational level. This behaviour is decisive for the performance and the capability of the organization and its members who subsequently can influence internal and external dynamics.

39.8 In closing

Starting cultural improvement requires courage on the part of an organization and the individuals who are a part of it. The organization and its members will be confronted with their own behaviour. A culture intervention demands subsequent behavioural change. That, in turn, demands courage and exertion on all levels. It is a complicated process in every organization, but even more so in an ICT organization, if possible. ICT organizations, for a large part, still consist of technically trained professionals, for whom cultural and behavioural aspects often belong to the so-called 'soft' sector.

FIGURE 39.6

Connections between driving forces

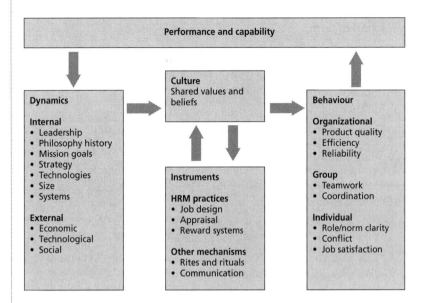

Nevertheless, ICT organizations that have the courage to make it into an integral component of their organizational improvement programme will be rewarded with permanently greater effectiveness and more success for the individuals, groups and organizations involved.

39.9 Closing thoughts

Over the course of his career, John has developed a sixth sense for 'how the wind blows' in an organization. He now works with a club where 'the wind blows' from the right direction. Although you cannot see it anywhere, you can feel it all the better for that. People stimulate and inspire each other. They are genuinely interested in each other. When the organization faces a large challenge, immediately there is an atmosphere of 'let's get it done'. Working overtime is never a problem. Decision making is primarily a collective responsibility and brought as close as possible to the 'real work'. Making mistakes is permitted; you don't immediately 'get a blast', as long as something can be learned from it. 'Celebrate failure' is a slogan you often hear. There are always many initiatives and, in one way or another, the right decisions are almost always made. Everyone has a feeling for 'the wind direction' that is difficult to describe, because everyone agrees on the direction the organization should go. Every individual gets enough space to contribute in the best way. People get a lot of freedom, but will still always act in the interest of the goals of the enterprise. Most of the time they are able to realize their personal goals at the same time. Professionalism is important to everyone. Together they try to take the enterprise a step forward each time, starting with themselves. Improvement is a core value for the entire club. John is enjoying himself very much. At birthday parties, John talks about his organization with great enthusiasm and tries to convince good friends to come and work there as well. A fresh and warm 'wind' blows; it feels marvellous. John lives on the beach now.

Literature

Blanchard, K. and O'Connor, (1997) *Managing by Values*, Berret-Koehler.

Bruel, M. and Colsen, C. (1998) *De geluksfabriek* (Factory for Happiness), Scriptum.

Cooke, R.A. and Lafferty, J.C. (1987) *Level V: Organizational Culture Inventory*, Plymouth. MI: Human Synergistics.

Curtis, B., Hefley E., and Miller A., (1995) *People Capability Maturity Model*, Version 1.0, SEI.

Galbraith, J.R. (1995) *Designing Organizations*, San Francisco: Jossey-Bass.

Gompers, R. (1998) *Organisatieculturen in veranderende organisaties*, Faculteit der politieke en sociaal-culturele wetenschappen, vakgroep sociologie. (Organizational cultures in changing organizations, Faculty of political and social- cultural sciences, Sociology Department).

Grift, F.U. and De Vreeze, M. (1998) *ABC tot IPW* (ABC to IPW), Ten Hagen Stam.

Herwaarden, C.J. van (1998) Het IPW Stadia Model: IPWSM (The IPW Stadia Model: IPWSM), *IT Beheer Jaarboek*.

Hofstede, G. (1984) *Culture's Consequences*, Sage publications.

Lafferty, J.C. (1989) *Life Styles Inventory*, Plymouth, MI: Human Synergistics.

Mastenbroek, W. (1997) *Verandermanagement* (Change Management), Holland Business Publications.

Peters, T. and Waterman, (1988) *In Search of Excellence*, Warner Books.

Schein, A.H. (1992) *Organizational Culture and Leadership*, 2nd edition, Jossey Bass.

Scott Morgan, P. (1994) *The Unwritten Rules of the Game*, McGraw-Hill.

Senge, P.M. (1994) *The Fifth Discipline*, Doubleday.

Sprenger, R.K. (1998) *The Choice is Yours!*, Longman.

Tapscott, D. (1995) *Digital Economy*, McGraw-Hill.

de Wit, T. (1997) 'Invoering van een procesgerichte werkwijze' (Implementation of a Process orientedWorkflow), *IT Beheer Jaarboek* (IT ManagementYearbook).

Review of part 6

In **Embedding and managing IT processes in an organization**, van Bavel and Bronkhorst state that a clear organizational structure is a prerequisite for implementing IT Service Management processes. The introduction of processes should not be used as a means to solve organizational problems. Process orientation is not a means of circumventing an organizational flaw.

When processes are implemented, the individual employee will receive instructions from two angles. First, there is the resource manager: the traditional hierarchical manager; and second, there will be the process manager, who is responsible for the outcome of the process. Van Bavel and Bronkhorst provide us with insights on how the processes can be implemented without creating an unclear control situation for the individual employee. This is not the first time that this situation has arisen: projects have been the cause of many problems on the employee level since the beginning of IT: whom to follow, the project manager or the hierarchichal manager?

But what about the managers? Van Bavel and Bronkhorst describe a project-oriented approach for implementing processes. They realize that the managers will have some difficulties in maintaining their role. In fact, that seems to be one of the major pitfalls in the introduction of processes: if the new responsibilities for process managers are not embedded well in the new organization, e.g. by leaving the 'old' responsibilities to the hierarchical managers, then a conflict between two management sources will be inevitable.

All in all, the authors provide some very practical guidelines on how to implement processes into an organization. Their argument that the human factors on both the workfloor level and the managerial level are crucial to the success of the effort is very important.

In **Patching the blind spot in implementation of IT process models**, Bootsma and Van Bon present a vision of a subject which has so far remained very much in the background. Many of the subjects presented have been restricted to organizations' process infrastructure and performance. The way in which the organization in question has been designed to achieve its performance has only been touched on in passing. Perhaps this is because most IT people have a technological background.

While recognition of the importance of other dimensions is growing – as the chapter on culture makes very clear – the structure of the organization continues to be an underexposed area. In an orientation study on attainments in sectors other than IT, aimed at employing the learning effects from these sectors for the benefit of the field of IT Service Management, the editor of this Guide came across a number of interesting developments in the field of quality management. Peter Bootsma incorporated many of the insights achieved in that field into a practical method for introducing quality management into complex organizations. Next, there was a joint effort to investigate to what extent the concepts were applicable in an IT environment. In this study, a method for setting up self-directed working teams, Recursive Process Management (RPM), was combined with a blueprint for a process infrastructure in a modern IT services organization, Integrated Service Management (ISM, see part 1). This exercise produced an interpretation of how the gap between theoretical model and practical working organization can be closed: patching the blind spot in the implementation of IT process models.

In the chapter, both reference frameworks that were used are explained. The illustration of the case, combining both frameworks in one company environment, offers guidance on the question of how organizational aspects could be tackled simply in a project implementing a process-oriented workflow. For ISM, other frameworks could be applied as well. Various possibilities are described in part 1. RPM, on the other hand, offers a unique addition to the toolbox for IT service organization improvement.

In Service Management practice we find a lot of organizations that are implementing processes. This organizational change is putting a strain on all those involved. Organizations must make sure that this strain is not causing good people to leave the organization. This has led to the rise of two relatively new management areas: Competence Management and Knowledge Management. Competence management is applied to make sure that the right people are put on the right job and to provide those individuals with clear career options. Knowledge management is applied to manage the knowledge in the company, by making sure the right knowledge is available to all who need it, and by making sure that the available knowledge is secured in the organization.

In **Competence management**, Kamphuis describes the efforts that her company, a company with large datacentres, software houses and end-user support organizations in the telecommunications market, has put into the area of Competence Management. This company achieved an employee turnover of only 6% in a time period in which 15% wasn't unusual for IT companies. Probably this 6% can't be all related to competence management, but the distinction is clear. Of course, the idea of putting the right people on a job isn't a new idea. The difference lies more in the improved ability to measure the competences and the definition of competence for specific tasks.

Kamphuis states that employee satisfaction is increasingly recognized as a crucial factor. Most people are striving for a organizational career. By providing them with information about their own competences and information about job profiles, employees know which competences they have to develop for their next career step. It is very important that these competence profiles are not used in reviews of the employee's performance. Employees should be able to use their own competence profiles as openly as possible, or the method will not work.

Kamphuis didn't create an extremely specific set of competences or too narrow job tasks. This would have created a very unclear picture of the necessary competences, and the competences one currently has. Defining those competences too narrowly would have ended up in the approach Taylor took when he tried to systematically analyse behaviour at work. His model was the machine, therefore his ideas are often characterized as the machine model of organizations. Each task was broken down to its smallest units to identify the best way to do each job. Then the supervisor would teach the worker and make sure the worker performed only those actions essential to the task. Taylor's method is referred to as Scientific Management, as Taylor attempted to make a science for each element of work and restrict alternatives to remove human variability or error. Scientific Management has been much criticized because it was very unpleasant for the employees.

With the history of Scientific Management in mind, we can conclude that Kamphuis has taken the right approach with her description of competence management. She presents a clear analysis of competence and competence management, without claiming that her approach is the only correct one. Just as in the relatively new field of IT Service Management, it is also true of Competence Management that there are still plenty of interpretations of the content and definitions of this subject to be found. This factor is currently getting attention in the EFQM model as one of the nine result areas for an organization, so there is wide recognition of the factor's importance. In her contribution, Kamphuis illustrates the potential importance of Competence Management for the achievement of a flexible organizational form in which management and employees contribute in the most efficient way to the organization's success.

In **Knowledge management and the IT Service Management organization**, Kuiper, Los and Sietsma describe the other upcoming management area: Knowledge Management. For the authors, there is a direct relationship between knowledge and innovation, because knowledge management manages the intellectual capital, which is the source for innovation. In knowledge management, however, it is important to realize that a significant part is determined by tacit factors. This goes for innovation too: innovation is often a matter of a radical mind shift, which leads to new ideas. There is a lot of spontaneity involved. Apart from the collection of knowledge in a system, there must also be something like the creation of an environment in which creativity can flourish to produce innovations. It is important to manage knowledge flows into, through and from the organization. Kuiper *et al.* focus on the knowledge flows through the organization.

The authors present a project approach for implementing knowledge management. Although the phases may seem very straightforward, most organizations will have trouble implementing Knowledge Management. Just the bare question of what knowledge is can make this very difficult. The authors' definition of knowledge – the ability to make decisions based on information – makes it clear that it is all about the decision rules that employees apply in their job. But these are most difficult to gather, because not all decisions are made on a rational base. If this is done successfully, the organization has gained a very valuable knowledge base from which innovations can indeed be achieved due to the combining of decision rules which otherwise would never be combined.

Competence Management is about acquiring the right competences for a certain job and Knowledge Management is about getting access to the right knowledge one needs for the job. It is all about the development of the individual employee: acquiring the right competences and collecting the appropriate knowledge. But how must this be achieved? The important question is: will Competence Management and Knowledge Management help you to retain the important people or at least the important knowledge in the organization? This is something that must be proven in practice. Competence Management has appeared to be valuable in Kamphuis' organization, as we saw in her chapter. Knowledge Management is seen as harder to implement. Where to start and what to do seem to be the important questions. But the question of whether or not Competence Management and Knowledge Management will help retain the important people has not been answered yet.

In **Organizational improvement and culture ... growth deserves space!**, Meijers and van Herwaarden come up with a visionary chapter on how this may be accomplished. They argue that the individual employee must be given as much freedom as possible in the organization. The shared values in the organization must become the controlling instrument to keep the employees on track to achieve corporate goals. Their argument is fairly simple. Individuals can respond much more quickly than organizations. If the organization wants to respond faster, it must become more like an individual. This means freeing the employee, but also creating a stimulating culture in which the employees have the same shared values.

The ideas of Meijers and van Herwaarden will seem very far-fetched for most people. But are they? The controlling mechanism is based upon relationships and sharing the same values. This fits the ideas of van Bavel and Bronkhorst on network organizations. Everything depends on the ability to perform certain tasks (competence) and to use the available information (knowledge), which contributes to the professionalism of the employees. The role of culture, as is illustrated in this last chapter, will attract more and more attention in time, since in the end it all comes down to people's work.

Concluding remarks

In this part we have seen some very interesting contributions regarding the organizational aspects of IT Service Management. Key in IT Service Management is the human factor, as is described in all these chapters, although all have a different focus. In the triad People/Process/Products this refers to the factor People, which obviously is different from the factor Process (as is illustrated in part 1).

The chapters are all related to each other, and in combination lead to a set of conclusions.

First, there are the control issues while implementing Process Management. The employee will have to work in a different manner, with different goals and within different constellations of people. Three chapters handle the control issue. One is using management theory as a point of view, the second is aimed at the level of teams and the third is about implicit process control. Can these three be used together? Yes, they can, and the combination will probably guarantee you the best results.

Second, there is a lot to say about working in teams: we can see that employees will have to work in several teams with several people in several processes. This is very important when competences are defined. But what about knowledge management? If we look at several teams/processes/people we can see that this must be a valuable issue in terms of knowledge management. Employees who are sharing ideas, thoughts, opinions, etc. will contribute to knowledge at the individual level.

The last, obvious point is that the traditional hierarchical management style is becoming a strain on successful IT Service Management. Management is more and more concerned with the question of how people can be stimulated to work together

Review of part 6

and to provide the best possible service. Effective IT Service Management may lead to less controlled teams, which can operate more freely but with clearly defined goals and sharing the same values. The keyword in this teamwork will be cooperation, working together by sharing ideas and working methods. Let's watch the gurus on modern team management theories, and see what they come up with.

Sources

http://www.onepine.demon.co.uk/ptaylor.htm

part 7

Practical guidance

Introduction to the theme

From the previous chapters it has become clear that IT Service Management and Process Management are two interconnected aspects of modern business. Services have to be delivered to the customer and this obviously should be organized in processes; traditional hierarchical organization structures are no longer fit to deliver the required service levels. This is not new; we can see it happening in many areas.

More and more organizations fall back on frameworks such as ITIL. CCTA (now OGC) has provided us with a set of books, describing best practices, which can be used for organizing service processes, although they are not prescriptive. But these books are indeed *best practices*, they are not specifically written for any one organization, or better: for your organization. In order to gain some practical support while implementing your Service Management processes you can also make use of consultants, experienced in practical implementations. This chapter will provide a third type of reference: the interesting insights that come from the practice of other organizations that have managed to implement (aspects of) IT Service Management.

Dutch Railways (NS) has been a troubled organization since the government decided that it should become a private organization. Nowadays trains have too many delays, they are too old, the employees are very dissatisfied … and the customers are very unhappy. Former CEO of NS, Leo Ploeger, gave the following comment on the developments within his former organization:

It is all about process control. You can come up with anything in the area of organizations. I have seen a lot of management gurus come by, who all had different messages. But the crux, the keyword it all comes down to, is process control: making sure that trains are running according to their schedule, that the trains have been cleaned and that they are available, that maintenance is done in time, and that new material is ordered in time.

(L. Ploeger, 2001)

Of course, this is about railways and not about IT Service Management, but that is the only difference. Both in IT and in public transport, services are delivered to customers. The clear message of Ploeger is that process control is very important. But there are other interesting aspects in this citation. First, there is the huge number of management gurus. Even in IT Service Management there are a lot of them and they all have different stories. Management gurus can be taken on board your project, but they should be used as resources, and never as a reason for jumping onto the next bandwagon.

The second interesting aspect is that customers have certain expectations regarding the service that is delivered by NS. If you look at your ticket, it doesn't say anything about how clean or how new the train should be. But the ticket does give a guarantee about the destination and the quality of your seat. And the ticket indicates how much you have to pay for this. Thirdly, NS publishes a time schedule with specific times of departure and arrival. All other aspects of the service are not specified, leaving plenty of room for the customers to create their own expectations.

In IT Service Management we regularly encounter penalty clauses in the SLA. Recently, that has also been the case in the 'NS transportation contract', the train ticket. In the Netherlands you can claim a refund when your train is more than half an hour late (and similar refunds apply in the UK). Ploeger comments:

Getting your money back when you have a serious delay! Count your blessings! What nonsense. Is that something our customers are waiting for? The customers just want their trains to run on schedule and pay a reasonable price for it.

(L. Ploeger, 2001)

This is a clear message, again. Focus your organization on the service that is delivered. And delivering services is focusing on your customers. Part of the service levels that go with delivering services can be formalized in an agreement, but there is also a part where customer expectations come into play. These expectations are the most difficult to manage, because they can differ from time to time and from customer to customer.

Content

This part contains nine contributions. They will describe practical guidelines in the area of delivering services through process management, supporting products, the formalizing of this service delivery in SLAs, and the management of expectations in this arena.

The process approach: managing chaos?
Frank van Elsdingen and Bram de Landtsheer

IT Service Management: The IT management ERP solution
Michael D. Loo

End-to-end Service Level Management
J. den Boer, P.R. Leeuwenburgh, J.J Vilé and A.C. Otterman

IT Service Management: a pragmatic direction
John Gilbey

Beauty is in the eye of the beholder
Barry J.M.A. Meesters and Jan F. Bouman

Service Level Management
Peter Sullivan

part 7 ■ Practical guidance

The management of IT service expectations
Rhion Jones and Mike Fox

Is there life after ITIL?
Lisette Favier

Russian roulette
Dick Costeris

A review of part 7 follows thereafter.

Reading instructions

This part starts with a chapter about the implementation of IT Service Management processes as an answer to the ever-increasing demands of the user population. The second chapter shows how a framework and supporting tools will help in the practice of implementing complex information systems. The third addresses the notion of service being embedded throughout these Service Management processes and shows how the alignment of these Service Management processes with the business can be established. After that, the next three chapters go into details of managing customer expectations. The notion is that Service Management is much more than formulating a Service Level Agreement. Managing customer expectations seems to be the keyword. This part ends with two critical chapters about the possibilities of using ITIL as a framework for the Service Management processes.

Introduction to the chapters

In **The process approach: managing chaos?** van Elsdingen and de Landtsheer provide a critical analysis on organizing work into processes. This process focus is applied as an answer to the increasing complexity of technology, and the increasing demand for quality and service from the user population. They start with a description of several cases in which organizations tried to improve their Service Management processes, and they show us the pitfalls they came across in doing so. They continue with the first step in the actual improvement of the management of information provision. They extend the process organization by adding a service element to it, leading to a results- oriented approach. This step in the change process is explored in detail by the authors. Finally, they describe the actual process in which the change is implemented. They go into details of the human dynamics of the change and provide practical advice regarding this change process.

In the next contribution, **IT Service Management: The IT management ERP solution**, Loo describes the practical application of a different blueprint (ITIL and HP's IT Service Management reference model) and IT Service Management products based on it in an ERP implementation at Union Carbide in the USA.

In **End-to-end Service Level Management**, den Boer *et al.* describe the end-to-end service management they implemented at ABN AMRO Bank. This end-to-end service management is aimed at connecting the various links in the service delivery chain and the streamlining of communication structures and information flows. The end-to-end service management is based on three principles:

1. one-stop-shop principle for the customer;
2. single point of service delivery to the customer;
3. alignment of all parties involved in the delivery of service.

Den Boer *et al.* wander off the traditional ITIL track regarding the role of the Service Level Manager. In ITIL this is seen as one role, but with **ABN AMRO** the role is split up. One of the roles is more concerned with the role of account manager, which is externally oriented, and the other role is more internally oriented.

In **IT Service Management: a pragmatic direction**, Gilbey provides some practical steps that must be built into the support processes in order to avoid service providers getting isolated from their user populations. Gilbey argues that the centralization of support, together with more formal defined services and Service Level Agreements, can give the user the impression that the IT service organization in getting more isolated from them. From this chapter we can pick up various means of improving communication between the end-user and the IT service organization in the light of the perceived isolation from the IT service organization.

In **Beauty is in the eye of the beholder**, Meesters and Bouman combine the rather traditional (European), mechanistic ITIL perception and the more emotion-driven perception of service management by Parasuraman, Zeithaml and Berry to achieve a customer-oriented analysis of service quality. This quality of service is much more than delivering a certain outcome. It has a whole lot to do with managing the expectations of the customers.

In **Service Level Management**, Sullivan indicates that the wider the gap between the expected and the actual service, the greater the risk of disappointment. Sullivan gives very clear pointers in the context of service delivery. This goes beyond making an agreement in a Service Level Agreement, because it is also about the management of expectations regarding the service delivery.

In **The management of IT service expectations**, Jones and Fox provide a survey of the management of expectations in an area in which large-scale IT departments support substantial groups of users. These expectations are based on an interplay between three factors:

1. management interface with the users;
2. publication of documents and formal communication of information;
3. collection of personal and reported experiences of individuals.

The authors argue that service delivery is still, for the larger part, a technologi-cal exercise. There is little experience in matching the service delivery to the expectations of the customers of the service.

In **Is there life after ITIL?**, Favier evaluates the enormous amount of attention ITIL is now attracting worldwide. She describes a number of trends in the field of IT management and investigates the way in which ITIL fits these trends. This approach goes well with the lesson we hear more and more often: ITIL alone doesn't do the trick. The question then is: to what purpose can you make use of ITIL, now and in the future, and which additional frameworks do you need alongside ITIL?

part 7 ■ Practical guidance

In **Russian roulette**, Costeris has chosen a title that suggests a dark ending to this part. This is far from true. Based on his experience, he describes the first two steps of ITIL implementation, i.e. the feasibility study and the awareness campaign. The author is clear: ITIL is a means and should therefore not be a goal in itself. Costeris' conclusion is that implementation projects are too often focused on the technical tricks.

Costeris describes how the feasibility study should be carried out and which four pitfalls can be encountered in doing so. He also describes the manner in which an awareness campaign should be handled. Owing to the fact that in ITIL implementations it is very important to generate a critical mass in order to make a change, this chapter can be valuable for those readers who are planning an implementation or who are planning an evaluation of an implementation.

40 The process approach: managing chaos?

Frank van Elsdingen and **Bram de Landtsheer** Mpire

Summary

A lot of popular models (ITIL, CMM, 6-Sigma) are available to support the process approach. However, there are quite a few issues you should consider in order to benefit fully from this 'instant remedy'. You probably want improvement because the efficiency and effectiveness of your software maintenance processes are insufficient. However, buying a pair of expensive running shoes alone will not turn you into a marathon winner, and neither will a good model by itself solve all your problems. First, you need to investigate the cause of the problem. For example, your employees lack the right attitude, or your management makes inconsistent decisions every other minute, or (internal) customers do not know what is reasonable to demand and expect from your department. Once you have analysed the problem properly, the introduction of the process approach can lead to better results. But first a lot of things have to be changed before you can achieve this goal. The process approach requires an entire business-process redesign. Boundaries between departments have to disappear. People have to be convinced that another way of working together is needed to support the 'rules' of the new process. This applies not only to the explicit rules, but also and especially to the implicit rules – in other words, behaviour. Moreover, everybody has to be convinced of the advantages for himself: 'What's in it for me?'.

In this chapter we will present the following subjects in order to find the right method of process improvement:

1. sub-optimal improvement: the so-called pragmatic improvement of processes results quite often in sub-optimization;

2. the road to improvement: a road that needs more time, but will lead to genuine improvement;

3. the road of change – the real change: adapting to ever-changing demands.

Many organizations look upon the process approach (as opposed to a hierarchical organization) as a suitable opportunity for improving the management of information systems. This approach offers a solution for the growing complexity of technical advancement and the growing demand for quality and service of the omnipotent user organization. However, is the process approach the miracle solution?

40.1 Sub-optimal improvement

Without oversight there is no insight.

It has always been very hard to find adequate resources for structural improvement activities in an ongoing business. The well-known saying, 'during sales the remodelling will continue', is certainly applicable here. The day-to-day operational activities consume, as a rule, all resources. Feasible improvements are only minor changes, the introduction of an insignificant tool or unimportant procedure. Attempts to realize a major, integral improvement are bound to fail. The net result is sub-optimization.

Examples of improvement attempts

Several approaches exist in organizations trying to improve their software processes. The selected approach depends strongly upon the prevailing hierarchy, culture and the state of the processes present. The approaches may differ, but basically they amount to one of the following cases.

'Working apart together'

Employees from to various departments are brought together to manage one or more applications. It is expected that this mixture of employees will lead to a kind of integration. Supposedly, the software management process will benefit from this higher level of integration: the people involved will meet on a regular basis and will discuss appropriate action.

The disadvantages
The workload of the departments involved determines the capacity of the employees. So, as a rule, there is too little time left for structural improvements. Departmental management is too busy keeping track of its own personnel. This prevents the joint group from establishing a new process. Cross-border meetings are time-consuming and the resulting proposals often point in different directions. Every department acts according to its own standards, which hinders working together efficiently.

'Working together together'

Assuming that employees within the same department work together more easily, several departments are combined into one. Because of the clear hierarchy, the process is managed according to a consistent approach and procedures. It is even possible to streamline the process. Forming teams dedicated to one application usually results in the best people for the most important application.

The disadvantages
The choice of teams per application points at an approach which is not result-driven. Capability and capacity are attached to the product and not to the process. Again the workload and the 'old' management prevail. The teams compete: who has the better approach? It appears to be very difficult to give priority to the other applications lacking a dedicated team. It is hard to find adequate personnel for the needs of these applications. Hardly ever do all departments take part in this internal merger (e.g. network management and operations). The over-the-fence effect remains.

In both examples this so-called pragmatic approach results in a marginally different structure of the same process. A genuine process approach is non-existent.

The process approach

In trying to work according to the process approach, management appoints process managers, aiming at a better control of the process and the products. The process managers manage the processes and the people who work in them. This means that regular management has to let go of these controlling tasks. However, quite often we see that regular management is not exempted from the matching responsibility. If process management is not tuned into regular management, you create utter chaos (Figure 40.1).

Obviously, the solution must be found in another kind of management. The structure of the organization is not decisive, but the processes and the matching procedures are. Applying the right model seems a guarantee for success. A lot has been improved since the introduction of diverse management models. However, their successes resulted in some kind of overkill. Improving every management process separately (CM, ChM, PM, SC&D etc.) usually results in sub-optimization. There is a superabundance of process identification, and every time the newly identified process seems to have a major impact on the management as a whole. In an attempt to gain control of the complexity of the management processes, automated tools are introduced. These tools need quite some management themselves. It appears that processes are very much interdependent. In no time, the software management organization is very busy servicing itself instead of the customer.

At the organization level, the awareness of the need for major changes has grown tremendously. Almost everybody is convinced that the process approach is successful only if the organization is turned through 90° (Figure 40.1). Like a spreading fire, organ-

FIGURE 40.1

Hierarchy vs. process management

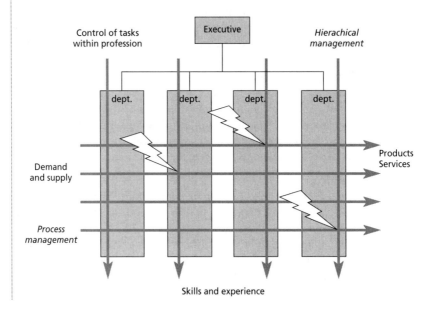

izations are tumbling over everywhere. Perhaps the seduction is that great because processes always point horizontally in a vertical organization diagram. So the organization has to be turned over in order to work according the process approach. However, a question arises: are the processes now positioned vertically, or are the departments positioned horizontally?! Whatever the case may be, one thing is clear. At the end of every process there is a customer waiting. Some people have found that the customer is also present at the beginning of the process. Only a few are aware of the fact that the customer should be involved in the process continuously.

Assuming we serve the customer from demand to supply, we identify every activity in between as a process. Every demand must be fulfilled in its own way. However, for reasons of efficiency we try to follow standards as much as possible. Recently, we learned that using standards results in higher quality. Hopefully, we have also found that blindly following standards does not result necessarily in better service. The answer to this is: keep to your procedures, but be creative when needed. This possibility will occur, as soon as we are able to call on various colleagues who can contribute to the solution using their specific expertise. The awareness is growing that service is an essential part of maintenance if we really want to satisfy the customer.

40.2 The road to improvement

Every journey begins with the first step.

The goal is clear: improvement of the information services. Only the road needs to be determined, in order to prevent us taking our first steps in the wrong direction. The first step is to move from the process-driven to the result-driven way of working. The relation is demonstrated in this very simplified formula:

Result driven = Process driven + Service

An organization has to go through two essential phases before the ultimate goal is reached. And even then there is no guarantee that there is nothing left to improve. Moreover, the necessity and the desire to grow will increase even further. Then the optimizing organization is a fact. The two phases are:

- ***Phase I: preparation.*** Careful preparation and planning are essential in order to be able to make the transition to a result-driven way of working in a later stage.
- ***Phase II: transition.*** Transition during which no organization can afford to stop and deal with everyday business.

Preparation

First something has to happen before something really happens (then at least something happens).

Without people feeling the need that something must happen, it will be virtually impossible to establish a successful transition. Management and employees alike should be aware of this fact. Changes include organizational consequences and will result in discomfort. Starting the change on the wrong foot will provoke resistance.

Loosen up management

Many managers grew up in a hierarchical organization. They are terrified of the idea of delegating part of their responsibilities. Delegation is strongly associated with a loss of power and respect. In those companies where the organization *model* is no longer strictly hierarchical, the organization *culture* often still is.

Many managers devote their time to operational tasks, because they are not able to, and dare not, delegate them. In spite of their good intentions, they only create dependent employees and thus maintain the undesired situation. The change the manager has to go through, as well as his employees, is one of uncertainty and searching for new content. The 'old' kind of management provides safety and security. Delegation of power meddles with this. Giving up security in search of a new way of dealing with management tasks is even more terrifying. A manager delegating more to his employees saves time for tactical and strategic tasks. From special literature and the massive number of seminars we visit, we know that nowadays the 'coaching manager' is hot. The goal of a coach is enabling his team to fulfil their tasks optimally, to facilitate. If he does the right things, he will receive ample respect. The manager has to move from (apparent) 'power' to 'value' and from 'awe' to 'respect'.

Besides uncertainty, managers also fear loss of respect by their colleagues: however good you are at your business, in the transition phase the rebuilding will be noticeable. In their new role, responsible employees will support and criticize their manager. This will be noted by fellow managers, especially if they are stuck in the old way of thinking. This shows that the entire management team, including the board of directors, must be committed to the change. All members of the organization have to make room for change.

Inform the employees

The employees have to be informed about the result-driven way of working as soon as possible. It is of the outmost importance that communication has already started before ideas about solutions are formed. Spread the message and stress that you are talking about immature ideas. The proof of the profitable effects of the change still has to be found. Employees play an important role in providing this proof. Avoid sentences like 'the management has decided that…'. Announce that the possibilities are to be explored together with the employees. Every initiative in the organization is welcome.

Exploration

Reasons
We have to change; there is nothing new about that. Fortunately, people in general are apt to change. They just do not want to be changed. Employees themselves have to feel that something should happen. If they are aware of the necessity for change, the change has 70% succeeded. The rest is relatively simple. That is why we first look for reasons to improve. Reasons from the point of view of the customer, of the supplier, with the aid of the ever-present 'complainer', in the company goals, in the enormous amount of good ideas at the back of the drawer, from the point of view of the competitor, because of the competitor, in seminars, workshops and training courses, during

meetings, in a chat over a drink with a colleague, and so on. Any source of inspiration for reasons of change is welcome. Collecting these reasons should not be conducted by the management or in some sort of project. Stimulate your employees to search for the reasons themselves within the framework of renewal and improvement. At that very moment they may conclude that maybe the time is ripe to act.

Possibilities for improvement
There are enough reasons for change to be found in the organization. There are also many ideas about possibilities for improvement. Most employees have ideas about how to improve their own activities. And certainly 90% of the people know for sure how others should improve their activities (the human condition!). Quite often these ideas get lost in the struggle of everyday business. People get tired of change, because they think they are being fobbed off with promises. 'Hey, that's a good idea. Put it on paper and we talk it over some time soon.' And then there is no time to work it out. This is not very motivating, but very often applied! Now is the time for a breakthrough. Moreover, a breakthrough is needed to increase the willingness to change. But be aware of the risk of too many wishes and too many expectations. However, it is amazing to see a group of people reacting so well to the newly bestowed real responsibilities. They know how to deal with major and minor issues if they get clear goals. Other opportunities for improvement are to be found in research, study of literature, courses, games etc. The use of a third party for advice is of course also a possibility. However, third parties should never take the lead in the improvement process. Even worse, they should not force the organization to follow ready-made models, procedures or packages. The consultant should always be subordinate to the integral plan for change. The consultant serves only as a 'mirror' and a 'catalyst'.

Set of requirements
A new kind of management needs a set of requirements. This set is first and foremost based on the wishes of the (internal) customer. Secondly, the wishes of suppliers and employees are taken into account. The way to do this is by making a list of contacts with customers and suppliers. Using this information, the account managers of the ICT organization evaluate the requirements with their counterparts in the customer and supplier organizations. This inventory is closely related to both the previous paragraphs about reasons and improvement proposals. And of course the activities are linked together.

Here are a few points for attention:

- Our contacts need the ability to interview their opponent in such a way that the right criteria emerge readily.
- Stating clear, unambiguous and useful criteria is an art in itself.
- Beside explicit requirements, implicit requirements should be discovered also; the latter are the key to what people experience as 'service'.
- Contacting customers and suppliers should also lead to a better understanding; customer and supplier should know, learn and appreciate that we will continue according to the new approach.
- Do not forget to manage the expectations of all parties involved.
- The company goals also entail useful requirements.

Transition

Success is not under your bottom, but under your feet.

At this point the reasoning suggests two methods of controlling: the standards of performance for the internal organization and the service level agreements (SLAs). The organization has to get accustomed to these controls simultaneously. A good change plan will be the basis for the first tangible improvements.

Standards of performance and SLAs

SLAs with clear-cut agreements are needed for communication and for servicing the customer or reviewing the supplier. The process teams are reviewed on the basis of performance indicators and corrective action is taken when needed. All requirements and standards are deduced from the list as described above, and supplemented with pragmatic knowledge and experience. Also, the company goals should be reflected in the performance indicators. If somehow they cannot be translated recognizably, this indicates that a strategic session about mission statements and vision is advisable. The experience of software maintenance people will facilitate the development of service levels. The reason is that a number of technical issues are important, but we cannot expect users to recognize and express them. In that case the maintenance expert translates the functional demands of the user into technical requirements and standards.

Use performance indicators which are, on the one hand, deduced from strat-egic goals and, on the other, beneficial for customers, suppliers and your employees. Methods like the Business Balance Scorecard are very useful provided they are used in a practical way and not as a goal in themselves. For instance, the EFQM management model (European Foundation for Quality Management) shows how performance indicators can be used in the fields of customers, suppliers and employees. Moreover, this model shows how to measure the performance of the process instead of the performance of the employee. Team-independent issues should not be forgotten – for example, aspects which are hardly measurable, such as cooperation, employee satisfaction, career opportunities. These are all issues which at first sight have nothing to do with the quality of the process, product or service. However, they play a major role in motivating the employees involved.

Getting used to operating parallel controls

Management, employees, customers and suppliers will need time to get used to performance indicators and SLAs. No doubt fine-tuning will be necessary in several places. Some criteria will appear unclear, unmeasurable and even unfeasible. It has yet to be proven that the new kind of control does work. In principle, the management of a process is more closely connected to the business. Thus this kind of management is better linked to the strategic goals. However, it also means that the individual aspects of the work are rather obscured. Previously, a unit of work (e.g. the number of concluded problems) was used as a point of control. Now, one has to trust service aspects such as the time taken to solve incidents or the mean time between failures of a system. The result-driven way of working means result-driven measurement and control. The most important criteria are at the beginning and the end of the process: from user demand to user satisfaction. Just as we have to manage the expectations of the users, we also have to manage the expectations of the ICT management.

After a period of adjustment – count on a year minimum – when the new controls appear to be working well, the previous (hierarchical) kind of management can be given up. To be clear: we are just discussing the method of performance management and the possibilities of correcting the entire process. Additional action can be taken by the personnel department concerning the need for other ways of assessing the employees.

Change plans

Change plan can be made while we are getting used to the new situation. A change plan entails process architecture, structure, control, scheduling and communication. Owing to the special nature of every individual organization, it is not very useful to present this plan here in its full entirety. However, several aspects will be dealt with in depth.

The first changes

In the meantime, the management has started the new way of managing. The next step is the transition from hierarchical management to process management. The regular managers receive another role, because sustaining the vertical hierarchy is deadly for the result-driven approach. The first possibility: they act like a kind of human resource manager. They support the same group of employees in their careers, functioning, knowledge, training etc. Beside career plans and assessment, attention has to be devoted to the professional knowledge of the employees. One way of doing this is to establish special interest groups. In these groups, experience is exchanged, guest speakers are invited and innovation training is presented.

The second possibility: the hierarchical managers themselves manage the processes. However, this means re-education in the way of learning how employees of other departments work and examining how various disciplines can be integrated into a process team. Thus the managers have to have much more knowledge of the content of work. Moreover, part of their power will disappear, because they are called upon as a manager rather than as a leader. For instance, as a team manager they participate in the *change advisory board*, or they are responsible for drafting and concluding the SLAs.

When new process managers are appointed, pay attention to the phenomenon of the best worker becoming a foreman. This person accepts the job because he likes getting a promotion. However, he is not able to manage since that is a different profession. He misses the direct contact with his mates and longs for dirty hands rather than reports and meetings. The company loses its best professional and in return gets a weak manager. Quite often this results in discontented employees. In other words, be careful in appointing the best software maintenance man as process manager or team leader. It definitely requires other qualities. Besides managing employees, it is also desirable that the process manager knows how to communicate with customers. Among other things, this job is about concluding SLAs, responding to complaints and reviewing deliverables. The perspective is outward bound rather than inward bound.

Continuity in change

The route described so far is gradual. On the road it is tempting to make turns and explore by-roads (i.e. new trends). This means a change of course. There is nothing wrong with that, but it has to be a conscious choice, for changes take time. This time should be spent; otherwise we might lose track. It is like stopping the circle of Deming (Plan, Do, Check, Act) halfway: starting new projects without checking we are achieving anything.

40.3 The road of change

The way is the goal.

Changing is a special skill. Concentrating on structure, means and techniques alone hardly allows for change. If the change has been started on the wrong foot, the organization will be rewarded with resistance. If changing is too easygoing or commitment is lacking at the top, the organization will not change at all. However, there are ample opportunities to achieve successful change. This will certainly be true, when a clear vision of the ultimate goal is supported by the entire organization, top-down and bottom-up (Figure 40.2).

Awareness

Breaking patterns: 'Everything is going well', 'Why change?', 'It's not my responsibility'. Not paying attention to this means that establishing a result-driven team leads to absolutely nothing. People appear to act in the new way, but in reality they work in

FIGURE 40.2

Model for change

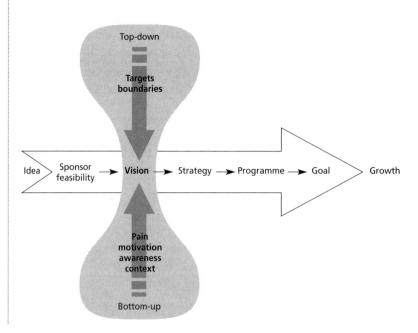

40 ■ The process approach: managing chaos?

the old way. Moreover, competition between team members will grow, because they are closer together. Who will be justified in 'his best way of working'? Who can put on the most pressure? Collaboration with new colleagues remains difficult. The team building will be very slow. In general, the untrained onlooker will not notice this, because the employees settle remarkably easily into the new structure. However, the resistance is covertly very much present.

Settling into the new situation is understandable, since people still think or even believe very much in structures (hierarchies). Since they are not free or even stimulated to leave the normal routes, nothing will change easily.

It's all about open doors, but nobody walks through them.

How can you abandon those rusty patterns? Trust your employees. You do not expect your child to ride a bicycle perfectly during the first lesson. Falling down and getting up again is all part of the learning process. And how does the caring parent react when the child has fallen? Encouraging, complimenting and showing trust in a better next time. Do you see this image in changing organizations? Everything has to go well, preferably in one go. People who make mistakes try to blame somebody else, hoping to avoid others looking down on them: our culture is one of avoiding mistakes. But is it possible ever to learn something in that situation?!

The executive (manager or project leader) will have to break the patterns himself in order to be able to break down the patterns in the organization. He or she will have to play the part of the caring parent, supporting the team in the learning phase that will be coming up. Management and change agents show in their changed attitude that this time they really want to change. The employees have already known for a long time that management is to blame. So surprise everybody, including yourself, with a different attitude:

- Let your employees feel they get more space; stimulate them in exploring.
- Set very clear limits; show them their responsibilities and powers.
- Encourage them in taking risks, in spite of going over the limit once in a while.
- Help them when they tend to lose track, instead of reprimanding them.
- Do not be discontent over failure; it is the best opportunity for learning.
- Share the experience of success and of failure with colleagues.
- Suppress the attitude of being in charge.
- Help people who ask for leadership; hardly anybody has the capabilities to be responsible from the start.
- Be aware that character is as important as skills; people whom you least suspect may come out stronger, and vice versa.

At first sight this may look soft and gentle. Most ICT workers do not like this at all. For those who are of the same opinion, consider, just for once, that the end justifies the means.

Resistance

A once-famous professor said:
'The majority knows nothing. Nothing at all!

One person always knows more than a crowd.'

And his student replied:
'Are you sure?

Once, I was of the same opinion, but the majority disagreed.'

If you think 'this will never work, it is senseless', then you are completely right. Stop now, do not even start. Your attempt is bound to fail. However, if you still have a tiny bit of confidence, go for it, all the way: there are very few other opportunities open. It is decisive that the person having ideas of change is totally devoted to them.
Vision is determined by the direction you look in.

It takes a tremendous amount of energy to remove resistance once it exists, if it is removable at all. Better pay extra attention to the way the change will start.

Stimulating

How do you get people to build a ship? Not by giving them the blueprints, but by giving them the desire to sail the seas.

Improvements are not possible without the energy of employees, without understanding or desire. You will only succeed by stimulating people, by encouraging them and by creating opportunities. Give room for practising, making mistakes and learning. And above all: continue to stimulate, show confidence and be a good example. In the new organization this is growing to be a joint responsibility. Be careful that every member of the organization (including management) does not fall back into old habits:

- not being responsible, but waiting for others to do something;
- being too much of a leader (guiding is fine);
- not comparing performance to norms on a regular basis;
- looking at norms and procedures as if they constitute the law;
- feeding back evaluations to products and processes for further improvement.

Responsibility and power

Responsibility is something many people have to get used to slowly. Some can work with it right away, others are rather afraid to go for it. Given the right amount of responsibility, people grows into it. Without any doubt, the entire process benefits considerably when responsibility is taken at the lowest level possible. While the quality of the products and the service will increase, the amount of control and adjustment 'at the top' will decrease. Thus the process will be more efficient and the response to the changing environment will be quicker.

We work in interdisciplinary teams with the right amount of responsibility and power. Those teams do not need to be self-governing, although this kind of team works quite well. But watch out. Self-governing teams only work well under good guidance. This seems contradictory. But like everywhere else, without the right guidelines and appropriate limits everything ends up in chaos.

The team is responsible for the result. Appoint a team leader who knows how to translate the guidelines into operational goals. He is able to communicate with customers, suppliers and higher management more and more. His attention to the operational process decreases continuously. Delegating power results in responsible employees. This pays off, especially when it is accompanied by the right amount of trust.

No management at all?

Of course, this kind of process cannot be created without any kind of framework or leadership. It is not desirable for people to think that all the ideas of 2700 employees can be deployed in one go. Leadership shows itself in communication. A change project will concentrate entirely on communication and not on content: communication with every employee involved. In the case of improvement of software management processes, the message will have to reach all ICT personnel. All ICT personnel, because one way or another every ICT person is involved in software management. For instance, the message is that we want improvement, but first we want to know what is going on in the organization before the route is outlined. On top of that, it is made clear that employees are invited to contribute to the solution.

Besides stimulating self-exploration, several possibilities are communicated which enable employees to organize their own initiatives. By proposing certain themes, slight guidance is imposed in a certain direction. During regular meetings, employees are even more stimulated to contribute to these sessions. It is important that managers stimulate employees, but they should not take the lead themselves. Change agents look at the developments from a relative distance. They support organizing the sessions. By the way, directors and managers are employees themselves and they are part of the change too. Here we have the right opportunity for the contributions of management. It is very important that managers cooperate in this phase, not by managing things but by doing things.

Growth

People who know their position in the operation know on whom they depend. They also know who depends on them and what the risks will be if they do not do their job properly. They know the added value of their part in the entire process. This kind of knowledge is essential for a successful result-driven approach. If they are also able to create their own situation (within certain limits), they will adapt continuously to the circumstances (Figure 40.3). The special thing about people in general is that they like to work pleasantly. This means they do not struggle on when things do not work out nicely. In a team this effect will be even stronger, because they communicate and demand responsibility. Finally, a kind of organic organization arises: continuously able to adapt to demand and supply, and aware of responsibility and the need for quality.

40.4 Controlling chaos

Improving software management processes needs more than having the organization follow the process approach. The ultimate goal is to improve the service to the customer. If everybody knows that, it is possible to work in a really result-driven way. The management should be aware that for a certain time two kinds of management, hierarchical and process management, are mixed. Probably, there is even a third kind, for the change will start as a project: project management. During this period one has to let go of the usual powers.

The employees should be aware that the organization will demand a great deal of their responsibility. The knife cuts both ways: the potentials already present will bloom fully now. No frustration, but motivation. The real improvement is the growth on the inside.

It is not possible to create freedom without creating chaos.

Restructuring a modern software management organization is a genuine change indeed, and management of change cannot be omitted.

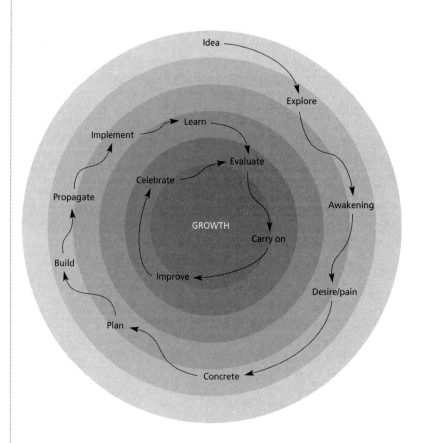

FIGURE 40.3
Circle of growth

41 IT Service Management: the IT management ERP solution

Michael D. Loo Union Carbide, USA

Summary

A manufacturing business entity, such as the Union Carbide Corporation, has numerous opportunities for improvement with the implementation of an ERP solution. From a business perspective the concept of enterprise resource planning (ERP) is well understood, both for its value as well as its shortcomings. The change impact on the business resulting from the implementation of 'world class' processes is well understood and the value equation is easily identified. One of the many processes, often overlooked from an initial strategic view, is the implementation of a comparable IT Service Management solution to complement the chosen ERP solution. If the ERP solution is SAP or BAAN or Oracle, etc., there must be a comparable solution to provide the internal manufacturing arm (information technology) with the necessary tools to implement and manage the business solution. Just like the ERP solution is for the business, the IT System Management tools and techniques and processes are the bread and butter of the IT group. An approach, similar in concept and scope, should be undertaken to implement these solutions at the same time an ERP solution is implemented in support of the core business. The same change impact that is experienced by the business should also be experienced by the IT group. This chapter deals with the implementation of a world-class IT Service Management capability in conjunction with a world-class ERP solution, SAP. It will identify the trials and tribulations and what has worked and what is hoped to work soon. It is based upon an actual implementation of IT Service Management using prescribed ITIL processes and world-class tools from several providers.

41.1 Your company has decided to implement ERP

If your company is like many large organizations, enterprise resource planning (ERP) is a fact of life and a tough one at that. There is no getting around the fact that business process re-engineering almost always means systems re-engineering as well. But it is possible to have a smooth, successful implementation if you understand the systems management infrastructure that must be in place before going live with an ERP system. There are a lot of unknowns and, in fact, 'you won't know what you don't know' when you get started. But what you should know is that systems re-engineering is part of the ERP implementation process and you should follow the business team's processes. Both you and they need to complete a discovery process to determine what parts of the company and the infrastructure will change and what will remain the same. You will need to do gap analysis to decide what parts are missing and how you will fill them. You will need to determine best practices for implementation and maintenance. Furthermore, you will have to communicate all this information to anyone who will be affected by an ERP/systems implementation – meaning everyone. The reality is that making this kind of change is difficult and a sweeping, corporate-wide change is one of the most challenging things you may ever do in your professional career. But it may also be the most rewarding. You will be part of a change that, if done correctly, can propel your business and its employees forward into a future of success. In addition, you get to do it while working with great new technology, systems and software, all the while getting paid to learn. You have to be flexible because you will not be able to see everything at once. However, good planning balanced with a willingness to roll out ERP and its related systems in an iterative process will make for a successful, manageable solution. Throughout the rest of this chapter, we will take a brief look at what business process re-engineering is and how IT management plays an important role. Then we will go step by step through the process of implementing the necessary systems management solutions, in this case HP OpenView ITSM, to create a successful ERP implementation and, for this discussion, also take a look at SAP.

41.2 A bit about ERP and re-engineering

SAP is a holistic, closed-loop system that provides the most current, close-to-real-time information encompassing operational data, analytical intelligence and contextual knowledge. Using these tools, decision makers can make informed business decisions, drive the decisions to operational systems and monitor the results. With this complete picture, managers and executives in departments throughout the company can apply the wealth of business intelligence required, when and where it is needed, to address business challenges. Many companies turn to SAP because they have lived in a legacy world, where organizations, business units and departments are distributed across the country and the globe, and each organization handles its own IT according to its own needs. This model provided lots of local control at the expense of a global view of the company. Executives and managers had little opportunity to manage the business, because they did not have access to information in the distributed units. Without a holistic view of the business, managers could not make informed decisions and, with the pace of change increasing, so that businesses needed to react upon the Internet era, the distributed model of IT had become a hindrance. Businesses looked to consolidation. They required a single solution so they could take advantage of their size for shipping and fulfilment, purchasing, and most importantly, information sharing. For example, if marketing knew what problems shipping was facing, if various areas of the supply chain knew how much was required for just-in-time delivery, and if human resources could track employee absences more accurately, the business would run more efficiently and profitably. SAP provides solutions that solve these problems; however, companies that implement SAP are often looking at major reorganization within their people, processes, and technology. Changing all three at once requires a tremendous amount of planning and coordination and IT is the backbone to make it work successfully.

41.3 Service Management (ITSM)

Service management is an IT management strategy that focuses on business needs, internal customers and the continual improvement of service quality and cost-effectiveness. The ultimate goal is an optimal balance between the costs and benefits of quality IT services through the use of service level agreements. In a SAP implementation, you might be concerned with providing the highest quality of customer services through the implementation of HP OpenView ITSM. The proactive change-management process is directed toward implementing changes in the IT environment with minimal risk to the delivered business services. But how does one define success? From an IT perspective it means that systems are available to the clients and users whenever they need them. Users do not care if you have the most sophisticated backup and recovery systems available. They just want to be able to do their jobs. So as you approach your systems planning, keep this question foremost in mind because the answer will help guide your planning: Will the users be able to access their systems and will the systems management solution I put in place allow them to continue with their work?

41.4 Getting started

Once your company has decided to consolidate information and systems, you need to ensure you have upper management buy-in and approval. Chances are good that upper management will have a direct hand in the planning and implementation of SAP, but will have less day-to-day say in what IT is doing to support the implementation. Since IT has less visibility to upper management, it is doubly important that you know you have their support, that you report to them often and that they know of any problems you are experiencing that will affect the implementation time-line (Table 41.1). As you begin your ITSM planning, remember that infrastructure requirements are part of the ERP solution, not an add-on or an afterthought. Your approach must be consistent with the SAP implementation. Naturally, many of the requirements for both SAP and ITSM are traditional and expected: high availability, continuous uptime and rapid response times. For example, if the SAP solution calls for new hardware and technology, your ITSM solution must accommodate these new boxes and networks as well as encompass compatible management capabilities. As the SAP team enters a design approach to identify processes that need to be changed, you should do the same. You need to look at your existing systems-management processes and identify which ones need to be changed and which do not. Then you should proceed to document all of them, so you have a baseline picture of your starting point. Identify the major problems first and work on them – think of it as the 80–20 rule. You will be able to go live with about 80 per cent of the implementation and the other 20 per cent will be those problems that you cannot see until users start working with the new software. You will need to design flexibly, so you can implement any changes quickly, whether they are to fix problems or simply to upgrade software.

TABLE 41.1
ITSM implementation time-line

Action	Months until go live
Strategy development	15
ERP/systems management package selection	13
Project definition	12
'As is' analysis	11
Business alignment	9
Configuration	6–9
Pilot	3–6
Go live	0

41.5 Use ITIL for best practices

As you begin the IT Service Management (ITSM) implementation, remember than you do not need to reinvent the wheel. The IT Infrastructure Library (ITIL) has been developed in collaboration with subject experts, practitioners, consultants and trainers to help organizations improve the way they use IT, and it is linked to a user group: the IT Service Management Forum. ITIL consists of several modules, each of which looks at how to provide a particular IT service. The modules can be implemented consecutively, to build IT services step by step; or simultaneously, to introduce several services at once. Each module is project-oriented, covering five stages:

- *Role definition*
  - Defining the mission statement for IT service.
  - Setting aims and objectives.

- *Raising awareness*
  - Communicating the benefits of IT service.
  - Providing general information.
  - Circulating information through seminars, meetings, brochures or newsletters.

- *Planning*
  - Producing a statement of requirements.
  - Defining detailed requirements.
  - Quantifying the workload of the new service.
  - Producing guidelines about how the service will work: its structure and relationship to the organizational structure.
  - Specifying target performance measurements.
  - Designing the process, including support for the process.
  - Producing an implementation plan.
  - Defining training requirements.
  - Describing benefits, costs and possible problems.

Implementation
- Developing and validating the process.
- Installing software and equipment.
- Customizing packaged computer tools.
- Testing the process.
- Creating inventories for software and equipment.
- Writing support documents.
- Training staff.
- Carrying out acceptance testing.
- Going live.

Post-implementation review and audit
- Reconciling requirements with reality: checking that services are providing what users want.
- Comparing actual activity levels with forecasts.
- Assessing how staff members feel about the service.
- Reviewing effectiveness and efficiency.
- Identifying benefits.
- Reviewing management of the project.
- Preparing review reports.
- Carrying out regular audits.
- Monitoring, reviewing and fine-tuning the effectiveness of the service.

By using ITIL best practices, reorganization has a basis in information and research that people can understand. ITIL also demands that each stage of the implementation undergo heavy scrutiny and stringent approvals before moving forward to ensure that all needs of all users and management are being met.

41.6 Incorporate people from everywhere

Since installation of SAP and ITSM means huge changes for all employees, it is very important that you involve as many people as you can in the planning process. Do not be afraid to include representatives from hardware, software, management, business, asset management, help desk and any third parties who will be affected, such as contractors who manage specific segments of your environment (NT, help desk, and so on). You should also include a cross-section of all users: even the administrative assistant at the front desk has valuable information that you will require in order to implement changes successfully.

41.7 Get outside help

Having outside help from your ITSM provider is invaluable. While most companies are experienced in their own businesses, the availability of experts in IT Service Management is essential to making your implementation run smoothly. Consultants can help analyse your environment and suggest solutions. They can help with detailed designs, logical and physical designs, environmental issues (heating, air conditioning, water protection, and so on) and network issues. They offer overall strategy advice and the tools to implement the processes – in this case, ITSM. Union Carbide picked HP OpenView ITSM for service management, because it is based on ITIL principles and best practices. With those assurances of standards and consistency, you can focus on the particulars of your organization.

41.8 Do systems planning

As part of the consolidation into SAP, you will need to spend time determining which applications users have been using, which ones will become part of the corporate standard and which ones will need to be replaced. There is a lot of legwork associated with this process, but it is necessary so that systems management will have a consistent view of the systems in the environment. For example, a large organization with a mainframe, dumb terminals and a mix of PCs will require standardization on a type of PC and a set of software in order to create a common client/server infrastructure. For instance, this can entail replacing thousands of desktop computers and multiple e-mail systems. At the same time you are evaluating the PC environment, you need to be working closely with the SAP team to ensure that all the IT systems changes you are implementing are consistent with the requirements for SAP. Interoperability issues are important to address all the way through and you need to ensure you have IT linkages to all the SAP functions, including finance, purchasing, cost accounting, manufacturing, and so on. For example, a company may have a help desk but no way of tracking calls or managing incidents. There would be no way to report on SAP calls to determine whether certain segments were down or not working properly. By using ITIL processes, you can:

- improve service to your users;
- provide a central record of incident statistics;
- reveal what technology and processes IT people are actually using;
- reduce user inquiries over time;
- provide a cost-effective means of customer contact;
- provide statistics to justify upgrades or improvements;
- speed up problem solving;
- catch problems early;
- prevent problems now rather than fix them later.

In another instance, an IT organization may have made changes to the infrastructure without any particular procedure in place. With an entire organization going to SAP, it is critical that the changes are made within the context of SAP and within ITIL best practices. Changes are a natural part of any developing business system. Change management ensures that they are properly evaluated and controlled. Good change management benefits both IT and the SAP implementation by:

- reducing quality problems caused by changes;
- providing a better understanding of how much changes will cost;
- reducing the number of changes that have to be backed-out;
- improving the ability to back out more easily when necessary;
- providing better management information about changes;
- improving user productivity because IT services are less disrupted by changes;
- increasing IT staff productivity;
- increasing the amount of change an organization can effectively manage.

41.9 Create a pilot

The most successful SAP/ITSM implementations are those in which ITSM was tested in a limited SAP environment for at least six months before going live. Choose a small group of people who are interested in helping to debug the system, who want to learn more about the system and who want to test it to see if it works as advertised. A pilot will provide a 'real world' setting for the verification of work processes, organization alignment, script accuracy, configuration and performance. You can make adjustments while checking that you have not strayed from ITIL best practices. Keep in mind, however, that while running a pilot can help work out many of the details, there are some problems that will not come to light until you go live at full scale.

41.10 Communicate change

When you start to implement IT Service Management, you may think that you are only installing software. But in all reality you are changing the way people have worked in your company, maybe for a very long time. In addition, the type of changes you and your SAP colleagues are talking about will not only affect a few people but may create radical changes to many existing processes, putting people into jobs they never dreamed possible. They may not like it. In fact, you might meet a lot of resistance. So it is important that you meet with your teams and with senior management and do it regularly. You will need to continually discuss the effects of each stage of the plan on the organization, what strategic approaches you will take, what kind of training is required and for whom, what your communication plan is, and how you will handle resistance to the changes. Through this process, you should check your plan and your actions with ITIL best practices to determine whether you are on track. You may find that you can skip a step and move a little faster. There are many capabilities provided with the ITSM tool that you might want to save for a later implementation. Remember you will be changing the roles of many people. Many of these people will be affected by the implementation of multiple changes. Perhaps you should save some of the lower-impact change for another implementation. You may also find that some areas need additional steps above and beyond ITIL. An example of where a specific step might need additional work is in the training area. You can never over-train but you can provide the wrong training at the wrong time. It is very important that training be provided on an 'as required' basis and that the training is specific to your implementation, not generic to the ITIL process. Most importantly, you need to communicate this information to all employees. The majority of your communication during the project will be focused on the IT management structure and the management of those individuals involved in the project. As the pilot and subsequent implementation get closer, you will need to provide detailed training for each IT associate. You may want to consider other forms of communication such as posters, T-shirts, e-mail and so on, to let everyone know what is happening.

41.11 Sometimes the best change is no change

In implementing a large-scale ERP/ITSM change, there are some things you should not change, ever.

1. Do not under any circumstances modify the source code of your third-party software. You may need to change configurations to make the software work in your environment, but you should never crack open the code. There are several reasons for this. If you start tweaking the code, you no longer have an outsourced product, and you have placed the burden of maintenance on yourself and your team. If you make code changes and things do not work, HP OpenView cannot help you fix your problems. In addition, by doing all the code maintenance yourself, you have defeated the purpose of outsourcing software installations in the first place. By outsourcing all the support of ITSM to HP OpenView, you can focus on issues specific to your company. Last but not least, if you change the code, you will have to change it again when HP OpenView issues upgrades, which will cost you more time and trouble than the tweaking is worth.

2. Do not 'reinvent the wheel' when it comes to processes. Countless companies have had successful SAP/ITSM implementations and have already developed best practices themselves using ITIL. Use their experience and advice to avoid obstacles that they have already overcome.

41.12 Going live – what to expect

As you go live with your SAP/ITSM implementation, you need to be aware of the following things:

- The users will go through a change curve. You need to manage how steep the change curve is for employees. The severity of the curve depends upon the amount and quality of the training you provide. You should consider offering coaches, rewarding excellence, and above all communicating constantly on how effective the implementation is.

- Make the change an event. Do not understate the significance of the implementation. Make it a big event. You will be changing the way a large number of people perform their jobs. Make it significant and ensure that they understand that you understand.
- Problems will arise. No matter the degree of testing or piloting, you will experience problems. Remember 'you won't know what you don't know'. Make sure that you have established a support organization that is flexible enough to respond quickly to the required changes and enhancements.

41.13 Pitfalls to avoid

There are several fairly obvious pitfalls to avoid, but in the heat of trying to get systems working, they often get left out. Thus:

- Do not go live with anything until it has been thoroughly tested. No matter how badly someone wants something to go live, doing so with untested software and hardware is asking for disaster. Always conduct pilots and always debug.
- Do not exclude anyone from the implementation process. You need everyone's input to make this work, from all levels of the company – executives down to the front-desk clerk. Everyone is an equal in adding input to the requirements and usability of the system and each one has a unique perspective on how installation of SAP/ITSM will affect his or her job. This team approach has the added benefit of bringing together people who normally do not work together, and can serve as a team-building exercise.
- Do not assume people are doing this for their health. While a project this large can be exciting, it can also be exhausting. Be sure to set goals and reward people for meeting those goals with extra pay, time off, and catered lunches and dinners. Let people know the extra work they are putting in is appreciated in a big way.
- Do not assume that all users have been adequately trained. No matter how much training you have provided, there will always be those users that either did not pay attention or who have forgotten what they learned. Be prepared to provide one-on-one coaching by placing knowledgeable users (members of the pilot group) in strategic locations. These 'super-users' should be the first-line support for answering questions and helping solve problems. This first line of defence is critical to the success of the implementation. However, if your super-users cannot provide assistance then the issue should be raised with the support team.

41.14 Now you are finished – or are you?

Once you go live with your SAP/ITSM implementation, you begin to find out 'what you didn't know'. Furthermore, if you have planned properly, you have contingencies for an iterative process – that is, you have allowed room to make mistakes and correct them. You may find that your company requires add-ons to SAP to handle special elements of your company's business, such as tax capabilities or lab sample analysis. You may require additional fall-over systems to handle outages. You might require additional ITIL processes to handle help-desk backup, so that you have a secondary system if you need to take the help desk down for upgrades. These requirements may not show up until you go live. ITSM also gives you the ability to deal with inevitable problems such as software glitches and downed printers. You will be able to gather systems information, prioritize it, collate it, and disseminate it. ITSM allows you to get a holistic view of your systems. For instance, a printer goes down and the help desk receives 50 calls about it, but the calls are received by 15 different people. Each person thinks the problem is not too bad because each person has received only three or four calls. But with ITSM, you can see that you have a problem printer. You will get a lot of pressure to have everything right on the first day, but it is simply not possible. If you waited for the perfect solution, you would still be waiting. Instead, you need to build in methods and processes for continual improvement.

41.15 Accept change, accept change, accept change

Finally, to make an SAP/ITSM implementation successful, you must embrace change. In fact, you must be a 'change junkie'. Business today, and especially technology, is changing at rates that were unimaginable even 10 years ago and to keep up you must be willing to continually explore new ideas and implement them. Remember that the impact of the implementation is as significant to the IT organization as the implementation of an ERP solution is for the business – even more so when the concurrent introduction of change to IT is coincidental to the implementation of an ERP solution for the business. This amount of change is difficult for any organization but necessary for success.

42 End-to-end Service Level Management

Design and practice at ABN AMRO Bank NV

J. den Boer and P.R. Leeuwenburgh ABN AMRO Bank NV
J.J. Vilé and A.C. Otterman Ultracomp BV

42.1 Introduction

ABN AMRO Bank NV (ABN AMRO) is a global organization. The operation and management of the ICT infrastructure is concentrated mainly at data centres in the Netherlands and is the responsibility of ABN AMRO ICT Services. ICT Services is the largest ICT service provider in the Netherlands. Why has ICT Services opted for End-to-end Service Level Management as a competitive edge in the provision of ICT Services?

Mission

The mission of ICT Services is formulated as follows:

ICT Services facilitates continual availability with adequate security of automated data processing. ICT Services performs its services at commercial rates. Maximum customer satisfaction and a contribution to the success of the bank as a whole play a key role in this.

Service Level Management (SLM) is directly associated with the preparation and contracting of service level agreements (SLAs) and is not an unfamiliar phenomenon within the ICT world. ABN AMRO already has years of experience in this field. On the basis of the mission, the implementation of End-to-end Service Level Management is regarded as a competitive edge.

What to expect?

End-to-end Service Level Management represents a new view of the SLM process, as described within ITIL. Why was the choice of End-to-end Service Level Management made? How does this concept relate to the ITIL methods? How has ICT Services addressed this issue, in view of the size and complexity of the organization? What experience has ABN AMRO gained and what has the Bank learned? This chapter makes the answers to these questions clear.

42.2 History

The need for End-to-end Service Level Management arose from the organization's enormous growth and the desire to integrate the business requirements and ICT management. Through both organic growth and growth in the diversity of the systems to be managed, the organization was divided into different (sub-)units. As a result, ABN AMRO ICT Services became a non-transparent consulting partner for the business and suffered from its growing pains. Historically, the development department was the main consulting partner for the business in order to realize its needs and requirements. As a result, management issues became obscure for the business, which consequently was unaware of the impact of its (changing) needs and requirements on the ICT management organization. ABN AMRO ICT Services had already been working with an SLM process for some years, but the process was unable to provide answers to the problems defined. It was obvious that the traditional SLM process needed improvement, but which improvements were needed in response to the situation that had arisen?

Organizational growth

Through globalization and expansion of ABN AMRO's market, ICT Services underwent strong organic growth. As a consequence, the organization was further divided into (sub-)units in order to retain the span of control.

ABN AMRO Bank has traditionally been mainframe-oriented. Through years of know-how and experience, ICT Services was able to realize a stable mainframe environment. After the mainframe era, the ICT organization faced the need to manage new technologies. This confrontation was fed by:

- changing functional requirements of the business, which led to growing use of client–server applications;

- increased attention to time-to-market, in order to retain a competitive edge. As a result of this changing market situation, the need for new functionality was met through the introduction of off-the-shelf packages. These packages, in turn, introduced specific platforms that had to be managed.

This created a complex infrastructure, in which different platforms were used for the provision of a single service to the business. These developments faced the ICT organization with the task of managing many different platforms effectively. On the one hand, expectations were high, as the business was used to the good performance levels realized with the stable mainframe environment. At the same time, the new technologies called for the development of expertise in the various platforms. In order to deploy and retain the required expertise as effectively as possible, specific management departments were set up for each platform.

Both the organic growth and the many separate 'knowledge centres' led to an increase in the number of lines of communication between the business and ICT Services. In the eyes of the business, this increase in contacts created a non-transparent ICT organization. As a result, ICT Services was not seen as a homogeneous consulting partner. Furthermore, a mismatch developed in the perceptions of the business and ICT Services. The introduction of new technologies led to changes in the ICT management organization. As a result, the ICT management organization focused more on controlling the (new) technologies and less on a good service provision for the business. In itself, this is a natural development for which there were good reasons from the point of view of ICT Services, but this was nevertheless undesirable in the eyes of the business.

Living apart together

As in almost every ICT organization, the development department is seen as the consulting partner for the business for its changing needs and requirements. In this way, information systems were developed to support the business processes of the business arm.

But because the ICT management organization was not closely involved in the dialogue between development and the business, management issues relating to the continuation of the provision of ICT Services were not taken into account in the development of information systems.

For ABN AMRO this meant:

- no insight into the impact of changing business needs and requirements on the ICT management organization;
- an exponential increase in operating and management costs through uncontrolled growth of platforms and many corrective measures after the event, in order nevertheless to manage the systems adequately;
- limited standardization of operating systems;
- increased time-to-market, because ICT management aspects were not known at an early stage and led to time-consuming extra discussions afterwards;
- limited guarantees for the provision of services, because management aspects were barely considered.

How to bridge the gap?

In an era of growing technological developments and an increasing focus on e-business and time-to-market, integrated management and development is essential. This means that SLM must focus on connecting the various links in the service chain and streamlining communications structures and information flows. The traditional SLM process must be adapted accordingly, so that contracting of 'new-style' SLAs leads to:

- guaranteed service levels, reinforced by service reports;
- a switch from individual links to a service delivery chain, or clear agreements on end-to-end service provision;
- a single contact point at the tactical and operational levels;
- full and effective responses to changing needs and requirements throughout the service chain;
- agreements based on result commitments rather than effort commitments.

Together with its customers, the ICT organization must realize guaranteed and measurable provision of services via a sound and conscious approach on this new course. This must form the basis for a clear and healthy dialogue with the business.

42.3 The challenge: design an SLM-model for 35,000 employees

The ICT Services department of ABN AMRO was originally mainframe-oriented. The SLAs and guaranteed service levels were based on substantial experience with mainframe environments. The introduction of new technologies such as client servers and the Internet placed SLM in an entirely new perspective. The challenge to design the End-to-end Service Level Management model was based on:

- eight ICT departments with separate responsibilities and customer contacts;
- approximately 4,500 ICT employees;
- 30 business areas;
- more than 100 operational information systems;
- more than 20 different platforms;
- growth towards a round-the-clock service organization;
- new business with added value and high priority (e.g. e-banking).

These facts indicate a large and complex organization with a considerable need for coordination and cooperation. Can the End-to-end model provide for this need, or is that a 'mission impossible'?

The model

SLM is the process that matches supply and demand for ICT services. This makes it the process focusing on the customers' needs and requirements. The ICT organization also saw the customer focus and the need to serve each customer as effectively as possible as a key opportunity for the development of the SLM structure. For these reasons, ABN AMRO based the design of the new SLM structure on the following principles:

- the introduction of the one-stop-shopping principle for customers;
- the provision of a single point of service delivery to customers;
- the alignment of all parties concerned, throughout the delivery chain. Concrete, clear and measurable agreements are the keys to good customer service for the various management departments.

On the basis of these principles, the following structure was chosen:

The structure chosen makes a clear and transparent distinction between a limited number of links that each participate and hold (partial) responsibility for the process (Figure 42.1). The distinction of a Front Office and Back Office within the ICT organization is a typical feature. The Front Office consists of the parties that maintain direct contacts with the customer in service provision. The distinction between a service broker organization and a service support organization in the Front Office clearly reflects the 'one-stop-shopping' and 'single point of contact' principles. The Back Office is the link in the ICT organization that secures the service(s): in fact, it is the organization's 'production plant'. Each of the service providers in the Back Office makes a contribution focusing specifically on their own area of the service delivery

FIGURE 42.1

The Service Level Management structure

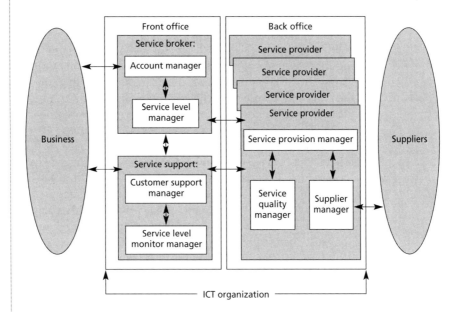

chain. Good internal agreements with the individual service providers and central monitoring and coordination of these agreements by the Service Level Manager develop the service delivery chain and make it more manageable.

Differences from ITIL Service Level Management

The Service Level Manager is the most important link within ITIL to the SLM process. The main difference between the End-to-end Service Level Management model and ITIL is the further subdivision of this role, in which the following main differences can be distinguished:

- reconciliation of the conflict of interest within the SLM role as defined within ITIL;
- explicit inclusion of the ITIL Support processes within the SLM structure;
- recognition of SLM roles within the service provider.

Conflicts of interest

In the ITIL method, the Service Level Manager is responsible for both account management with the business (external orientation) and for internal coordination, assurance and monitoring of service provision (internal orientation). The two disciplines serve different interests: on the one hand that of building up good relationships with the business and meeting its needs and requirements as far as possible, and, on the other, of ensuring the best possible service provision in the internal organization. These interests may be contrary, and combining them in a single role can lead to a conflict of interest. Where different interests can be identified, different roles must also be distinguished.

Account management with the business is a different field from coordination and management of service provision within the ICT organization. The external aspects of the Service Level Manager's position can be compared with Sales and/or Account Management. The internal aspects of this role bear more similarities to the Purchasing field. These are different disciplines, requiring different qualities of the Service Level Manager, and cannot automatically be combined.

For this reason, in contrast to ITIL, the End-to-end Service Level Management structure focuses increased attention on an effective interrelationship between the external and internal aspects of the SLM role. On the basis of this idea, the 'Service Broker' is included as a party in the process. Overall, this party can be compared with the process role of the Service Level Manager and the related tasks and powers described within ITIL. However, Account Management and Service Level Management are explicitly defined as roles within this party, with the Account Manager responsible for account management and the Service Level Manager acting as the 'buyer' of part-services provided by the different service providers. This creates a 'healthy' area of tension between the Account Manager and the Service Level Manager, while both must work together closely. The Account Manager and the Service Level Manager in fact stand 'back to back', so that each has a different field of vision but they can hear each other clearly.

Service Support processes

Ensuring the continuity of operational service provision is an important issue within SLM. In ITIL, the Service Support processes provide this continuity. In the SLM process as described in ITIL, this direct relationship is not defined clearly enough, and is dismissed as the responsibility of the individual ITIL Service Support processes. The importance of good communication at the operational level and the continuity of service provision are aspects of SLM that should not be underestimated. Good service provision depends heavily on effective interactions between the different Service Support processes.

In order to emphasize this, the Service Support organization is included in the End-to-end Service Level Management structure. This is the party that acts as an intermediary between the business and the service provider(s) at the operational level, and is responsible for day-to-day service provision (Customer Service Manager) and reporting of the performance of the services delivered (Service Level Monitor Manager).

SLM roles of the service provider

ITIL shows that Operational Level Agreements (or Service Provision Agreements) can be made with internal parties, but it says nothing about who is responsible for which tasks in this respect. In the End-to-end Service Level Management structure, these responsibilities are developed by defining the various roles. Distinctions are made here between the roles that:

- serve as single point of contact within the service provider and hold responsibility for the provider's service provision (the Service Provision Manager);
- hold responsibility for internal assurances for the service provider's service provision (the Service Quality Manager);

hold responsibility for contract management relating to agreements (so-called underpinning contracts) with external suppliers (the Service Supplier Manager).

The model explained in more detail

In a simplified form, the structure can be presented as shown in Figure 42.2.

One feature of the structure chosen is that it distinguishes a limited number of parties. Each of these parties has different relationships with the others. The following relationships are distinguished:

Service Planning *At the tactical level, the organization of the services is coordinated and planned by the business and the Service Broker. Process control and process activities of the tactical ITIL Service Management processes (similar to ITIL Service Delivery) are covered.*

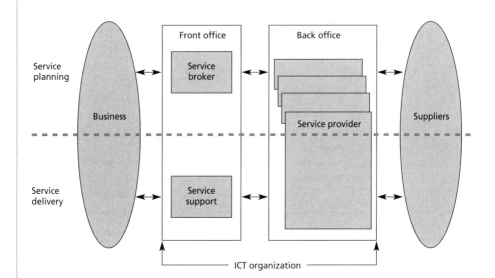

FIGURE 42.2
End-to-End Service Level Management Structure

Service Delivery *Contacts with the business concerning day-to-day operations take place through or under the supervision of Service Support. Process control and process activities of the operational ITIL Service Management processes (similar to ITIL Service Support) are covered.*

The structure forms the basis for the entire SLM process applied within ABN AMRO. On the basis of this structure:

- The document structure is described for the definition of services (Catalogues), agreements on service provision (Agreements) and quality assurance for the services to be provided (Quality Plans).
- The reports to be drawn up in order to make the service provision clear to the various parties are determined.

- The consultative structure for the various parties is shown. This involves meetings to review the performance provided in the preceding period, and to look ahead to the coming period in terms of possible improvements to the services provided.
- The roles needed for the performance of the SLM process are determined. The tasks, responsibilities and powers for each role are described.

42.4 Implementation of the SLM process for ABN AMRO ICT Services

The implementation of SLM focused on three areas:

- development of the End-to-end Service Level Management architecture;
- try-out of the architecture (pilots);
- implementation of the End-to-end Service Level Management process throughout the organization.

How did ABN AMRO manage to fuse these different areas to embed the SLM process in the ICT organisation?

SLM architecture

The project began with the development of the End-to-end Service Level Management structure that provided the most practical benefits for ABN AMRO. The SLM architecture consists of the structure and roles, the process and the model documents (e.g. for an SLA). A number of organizational units were already working with SLAs during this period and were familiar with the traditional SLM process. In order to retain and develop this know-how, the project focused on supporting these initiatives and promoting their interrelationships with the other links in the service delivery chain.

Trying out the architecture

During the development process, the architecture was coordinated with other parties concerned in the organization on several occasions. The discussions concerning this structure were confined to the conceptual level and the time eventually came to try them out in practice.

In order to try out the concepts and the models, three pilot projects were used within ABN AMRO. The choice of pilots should not be underestimated. In order to try out the entire architecture accurately, the choice of the relevant customer areas was based on the following criteria:

- The customer areas had to be willing to cooperate in such a process.
- All internal service providers, within the service delivery chain, should be involved in service provision to the customer areas.
- The customer areas should vary in terms of characteristics, so that the structure could be tried out in different practical situations.
- The customer areas should involve existing services, so that the years of know-how and experience could be used to try out the structure in practice.

On the basis of these criteria, three customer areas were chosen. Together with all service providers in the service delivery chain, workshops were arranged for these customer areas, in order to define and describe the services to be provided. A start was made on describing services for the different customer areas by drawing up a Service Catalogue for each service provider.

The service descriptions served as input for communication with the business units related to the pilot areas. These talks set the updated SLM process in motion. As a result, changes were made to the catalogues, agreements were reached with the service providers and the service provision of the entire ICT organization was described. An SLA was presented to the related business for each pilot area, based upon this process.

During this phase, the modifications needed to the architecture in order to match the practical situation of ABN AMRO as closely as possible became clear. These changes were processed into a new release of the entire architecture, which served as standard for the implementation of the process in the ABN AMRO organization.

Implementation

The implementation of the process concentrated mainly on facilitating the envisaged structure within the organization. This meant appointing and creating the SLM roles, initiating the required consultative structures, designing the reporting process and developing the process for each service provider in detail.

Certainly in a large organization such as ABN AMRO, implementing SLM is an extremely radical process. A structured and phased approach was needed. It was agreed that the implementation would take place on three tracks.

Firstly, the implementation of the process was linked to a key ICT project within the organization. This was a project for the development of the ICT organization's new services. SLM was involved in this process in order to realize secured service provision within the organization, resulting in the preparation of SLAs. In this project, the SLM process was simulated in full, by conducting a workshop with all concerned in each phase of the SLM process. The workshops kept those involved with the status and progress of the project with correct information, with advice on bottlenecks in the process, and with notification of the activities required in order to secure the required service provision within the organization.

Secondly, a track was launched to implement the (sub-)processes at all parties concerned. Within ABN AMRO, the parties themselves were made responsible for providing the required capacity, planning and progress. Through presentations and consultancy sessions, the SLM project supported each party in the implementation of the process. The consultancy was aimed primarily to co-determine the impact of the process on the internal organization. On the basis of the findings, steps were taken to transform the relevant organization into a service organization.

Finally, a match between SLM and the development path was sought. From a service point of view, the development path is nothing other than the method used to develop a new service. Through close interaction between the development path and SLM, ICT management issues were involved in the development of the service from an early stage. On the one hand, this interaction was realized by linking SLM directly to the ICT project mentioned in the first track. At the same time, it was given structural form through the direct involvement of SLM in the project started within ABN AMRO Bank to improve the development method used.

42.5 Management of change: included or excluded?

End-to-end Service Level Management requires a new way of thinking and generates changes in the working methods used to date. The process affects a large proportion of the employees in a large organization such as ABN AMRO. Implementation of such a process has a major impact and requires careful preparation. The question is how to generate a healthy breeding ground for change. Is it better to include a change process in the development and design of the SLM process, or should the change process be considered separately?

Management of change included?

ABN AMRO addressed the preparation and design of SLM on a project basis. The change process was included in the development and design of the process. The designers of the process were also those who promoted the change. In fact, it was assumed that the organization was already motivated for change.

The various managers of each department concerned were members of an SLM steering group. They were made responsible for the development and design of SLM in their own departments. This promoted awareness and involvement. It should be emphasized, however, that this does not mean that the implementation of End-to-end Service Level Management can take place at short notice. Implementation requires professional guidance over a long period.

Capacity was claimed by the project for performance of SLM roles within the various parties. The organizational units themselves were responsible for supply and allocation. The role executors were then familiarized with End-to-end Service Level Management through presentations and brainstorming sessions. Ultimately, service provision was recorded in the Provision Catalogue, through workshops for each service provider.

It was decided that the SLM structure should relate to the existing organizational structure as far as possible, to create recognition among the employees. Representatives for the various parties were brought together in workshops to discuss issues such as 'What is the relationship of my unit to the other units?', 'Which services do we actually provide?' and 'How will business contacts proceed in the future?'. This approach helps to improve acceptances and familiarization with the SLM process.

The project concentrated on assisting the role executors during the implementation process. The role executors themselves had to implement the process in their own organizational units. The implementation process was accelerated because the employees of the units performed the implementation themselves.

Exclusion of change management

Recent months have shown that a change process is not self-evident to individual employees. Many still work too much in accordance with old procedures, processes and the 'current fads and fancies'. There are always some disruptions that obstruct the structure of activities. Often, political interests in the organization also receive too little attention.

With hindsight, therefore, it can be said that including the change process proved to be less effective and efficient than expected. It is probably better to address this process as a separate, parallel track: a process aimed at creating a breeding ground for change, focusing clearly on the political, cultural and technical aspects of the organization. Such a process can be used effectively to design other process. In relation to 'value for money', we regard this as the best choice.

42.6 The experience of the first 18 months

Experience with the implementation of the SLM process is best described in terms of the various force fields that an organization encounters when a process such as SLM is introduced. How did ABN AMRO deal with these forces and how did it emerge from the struggle after its first 18 months?

SLM makes responsibilities clear, and clear responsibilities create anxiety

If responsibilities are not clear, optimal service provision is not possible. However, assigning and accepting such responsibilities creates anxiety, because they could support an accountability culture. Fears that organizational units could be called to account for their responsibilities leads to a culture of 'covering your own back' and limiting responsibilities as far as possible. This battle raged continuously within ABN AMRO during the development and implementation of the SLM process, resulting in delays in the process, or even major arguments that jeopardized commitment to SLM itself. In such situations, it is important that an independent party acts as an intermediary to remind the parties involved that the joint interests of the business prevail over the individual interests of the different parties.

SLM identifies gaps in the ICT management organization. Without a smoothly running ICT management organization, SLM has no chance of success

SLM is a process that has associations with all aspects of an ICT management organization and consequently depends heavily on the performance of that organization as a whole. SLM is a process that identifies shortcomings in an ICT management organization at an early stage and, at the same time, the process that suffers most from such shortcomings. This force field certainly played a role within the Bank. The bottlenecks in the Bank's ICT management organization meant that the process could not always be implemented in full. This led to delays in the implementation of the SLM process. In order to realize the process within the organization, management issues were identified and assigned to the parties responsible and their status and progress monitored. This did not allow any concrete service agreements to be made, but did provide for the possibility of making agreements to improve service provision. The latter has added value for the acceptance and security of the process, as the ICT organization shows that it is working to improve service provision on a structural basis.

SLM channels and reduces contacts with the customer. Customer contacts provide status and job satisfaction

The strength of SLM is the appointment of a clear contact point for the business and ICT organization for realizing service agreements. If agreements can be reached at different levels, there is no overview of the overall position regarding agreements with the business. This means that agreements may be contradictory, overlap or be incompatible. However, maintaining contacts with the business is regarded as interesting and improving status in the IT world. Within ABN AMRO, a situation had arisen in which various management departments made agreements with the business. The introduction of SLM meant that such initiatives had to be abandoned and that the points of contact for service issues were channelled. This resulted in resistance in some organizational units. During the implementation process, the ICT organization was continually made aware of the fact that simple points of contact provided added value for all parties. In order to emphasize the importance of this, the opportunity to explain the desirability of clear contact points was seized in all situations where fragmented customer contacts had given rise to problems. This awareness was reinforced by the business, which certainly appreciated the benefits of fixed contact points for ICT issues.

SLM identifies bottlenecks. Is SLM the owner of these bottlenecks?

As already mentioned, the SLM process interacts with many aspects of the ICT management organization. This often gives rise to the idea that, if management issues are raised from an SLM point of view, then SLM is also responsible for solving these issues. This argument was often used within the Bank. The trick is to ensure, using well-founded arguments, that SLM is not continually saddled with unfair tasks.

Every situation must be consciously assessed in terms of the goodwill for the implementation process that may be generated precisely by undertaking unpopular tasks. Nevertheless, the effort that goes into tasks for which the process is not responsible must be in proportion, and must certainly not be made at the expense of attention to effective implementation and operation of the process.

SLM calls for formal agreements and guarantees, which restrict freedom of action

SLM is a process that aims to realize formal agreements and issue guarantees for service provision. This gets to the root of the organization, because it provides a direct insight into the performance of the different units. While this is not a problem in itself, it does generate fears that bottlenecks in the organization will be revealed. It is often forgotten that reports are more likely to show how well an organization is performing than how bad the service provision is. However, this is another mindset that needs to change in the IT world. For this reason, measurement of service performance is often neglected, and measurement is often performed of values that in any event present the overall service provision in a good light. This made the implementation of SLM within ABN AMRO difficult. Despite years of experience with management, few parties were prepared to issue guarantees. Furthermore, many measurements and reports are produced within the Bank, but these do not focus on the service provided. As a result, service performance is not transparent and the ICT organization cannot make clear how it is performing. Appointing, delegating and providing effective advice to the role responsibility for service level reports increased attention to the measurement of, and reporting on, service provision. A start was also made on defining a basic report, which was certainly not complete but which did take the first steps towards good service level reporting. In this way, this force field was brought under control for ABN AMRO.

SLM starts with the needs and requirements of the business. SLM starts by identifying and describing the internal organization

Formally speaking, the SLM process starts with the needs and requirements of the business, but ABN AMRO opted to begin by describing the service provision of the ICT organization. In itself, this was a sound decision. It is not appropriate – certainly in the case of existing services – to conduct the negotiation with the business if the ICT organization does not know what its own services are. However, requests to describe the service provision are immediately countered with 'What does the customer want?' This is a classic 'chicken and egg' situation. The danger in this situation is that, certainly if the implementation of the process is not (yet) fully accepted, it will be used to delay the process at every opportunity. In itself, this is not an easy issue to solve. In such a situation, it is important to make a choice and to continue to announce and to justify this at all times.

Large-scale versus dosed approach to SLM implementation

SLM is a radical process for the organization. It is extremely important to transform the organization into a service organization. This will require a large-scale PR operation. For various reasons, a dosed approach was chosen within ABN AMRO, in which the process should spread like oil throughout the organisation, on the basis of proven added value. This requires a considerable effort and the art of letting loose. The effort must be made because step-by-step explanations are provided to individuals and small groups. The art of letting loose is needed because such an approach cannot control other SLM initiatives, which means that standardization is not realized. Letting go therefore also means permitting variations from the envisaged structure. The ICT organization is so large that the effort to control all variant initiatives will be at the expense of embedding the process in the organization.

42.7 Concerns and Benefits

A great deal has been achieved since implementation, but of course there is always room for improvement. Looking back over that period, one finds a fair number of points for attention, as well as successes. The design of the process also had a number of pleasant spin-offs. The flame has been lit, but how do we keep it burning? What does ABN AMRO see as the benefits and concerns?

Customer areas

The SLM process forces a clear insight into the customer areas of the ICT organization. Who can be regarded as a customer? Everyone who wants to build up a relationship with the ICT organization, everyone who wants to make agreements, everyone who pays, etc.? The ABN AMRO organization is so large and complex that first the actual customer areas of the ICT organization had to be defined. It is worth noting here that the nature of the customer must be considered carefully and decisions regarding this must be made at the right level in the organization.

Bridging function

The alignment between the business and the ICT organization has been strengthened. The structure of the process ensures the necessary bridging function between the ICT organization and the business. The business now has a single point of contact for reaching agreements on service provision at the tactical level. It also has a central access point to the ICT organization for operational issues. Nevertheless, it is important to ensure that the informal 'short lines' between the business and the Service Providers (direct contacts between the business and the Back Office) do not persist.

Expectations

What does the business actually expect of the ICT organization? Clear account management provided for improved matching and management of expectations between the business and the ICT organization. The same applies within the ICT organization. Overall, ICT service provision has been made transparent and has been recorded. Guarantees for SLAs through Service Provision Agreements has started a transition from an effort-oriented ICT organization to a result-oriented one. Clear recording and compliance with the necessary tasks and responsibilities for SLM are essential here. The danger is that business expectations should not be continually managed but that, ultimately, services should be provided in line with expectations.

Spin-offs

One welcome spin-off of the implementation of SLM within the ICT organization is the catalyzing function of the process on the optimization of the other Service Management processes. The service orientation of the ICT organization has improved in a relatively short period. These aspects are very effective in 'selling' the SLM process within the ICT organization. Care should be taken to ensure that SLM is not seen as the problem-owner and troubleshooter for all sorts of ICT management issues.

Management of change

The need for adequate management of change during the implementation has slowly become clear to every organization. Claim (and continue to claim) the necessary capacity from all parties concerned in good time. Reasons can always be found to defer the implementation for a time within the existing organization. Do not procrastinate for too long, but get started! Details will be addressed in the course of the implementation. Give the envisaged process a chance to become operational and then, after a thorough evaluation, start the discussion to realize improvements. You will not learn to walk without taking the first step!

A practical approach

The pragmatic approach of clearly linking the process architecture to be developed to the existing ICT organizational structure has had a positive effect on internal perceptions of SLM. Active involvement of the line management in the performance of roles has had a positive effect on progress. Do not allow 'current crazes' to distract you from your goals.

Cooperation

Continual monitoring and steering of cooperation between internal service providers is a vital necessity for every Service Management process, including SLM. Workshops on each SLA process, at which all parties are represented, help to achieve this. The need to identify, record and assign grey areas within total service provision cannot be emphasized enough.

Clarity and promptness

Start with the customer units that are themselves positive and motivated in order to record agreements. Then do not set the standard for the ICT organization too high. Clearly state what *can* and what *cannot* be included in a particular release of an SLA. Prompt completion of an SLM process has a positive impact on the entire process. Ensure that the points for improvement noted for an SLA are recorded and taken into account in a subsequent release. An SLA must not become a one-off success.

Measurability

'*A deal is a deal.*' As a serious consulting partner of the business, the ICT organization must be able to show how effective and efficient the provision of ICT services has been in a particular period. 'Show how well the ICT organization is performing!' It is extremely important to present the business with concrete, measurable results of the service provided. In the coming period, therefore, making service levels measurable end-to-end in such a complex ICT infrastructure is, and will remain, a key focus of attention. In such processes, it is advisable to start developing the reporting process at an early stage.

42.8 Conclusion

The End-to-end Service Level Management process has proved its added value within ABN AMRO. The development and design process has led to a highly workable and scaleable SLM standard for ABN AMRO, support for which continues to grow within the ICT organization. Now that the process has been set up, the time has come to focus on keeping it in operation. Today, SLM has become 'business as usual' at ABN AMRO…

43 | IT Service Management: a pragmatic direction

John Gilbey*

Summary

Current trends in IT service support and management – such as the development of remote help-desk services and tightly managed service level agreements – can mean that there is a risk of service providers becoming isolated from the user population they support. This chapter discusses practical steps that can be built into the management of the support operation to help avoid this outcome.

43.1 The challenge

Computing service providers in medium-sized and large organizations have a very special set of problems in the management of the interface with the customer. Many end users of the service will be highly sophisticated in their use of computers – whether self-taught or professionally trained. They are likely to have strong views on the quality and style of delivery of the computing service – views which they may not hold in respect of other business services. These views may be informed by the customers' own experience of computing as a standalone activity. The skills they have, and the benefits they can gain from them as individuals, may not scale accurately when applied to the highly integrated, networked environment that is the modern workplace. The challenge for IT service providers is to build on the aspirations and expertise of this expert population and use it as an input to the whole service development process.

As an illustration of this, I present the following example. As part of a training exercise I asked a group of IT service users, who had spent time in several parts of the computing industry, to build a list of adjectives which described a corporate computing service of which they had experience. A degree of mirth ensued while the group built their list. I then asked them to split the list into words which had positive and negative connotations. This was the result:

- **Positive:** *user-friendly, reasonably safe, learnable*
- **Negative:** *slow, unreliable, frustrating, useless, difficult, unstable, unorganized, outdated, incomprehensible, reactive, underfunded*

---

* John Gilbey is Head of Computing for a UK based life-science research organisation. He lectures in IT service delivery in the Department of Computer Science at the University of Wales, Aberystywth and is a member of the Professional Examination Board of the British Computer Society. The views expressed here do not necessarily reflect the views of these organisations.

The disparity between the two categories says much about the way the relationship between service providers and end users can fail. When challenged, the group accepted that the service they had received was probably acceptable – but their expressed perception could swamp the image of a service which is actually providing what it was contracted to deliver. The way they felt about the service they had received, and the way they expressed these views, could have a critical impact on the ability of the computing service to achieve its potential on behalf of the organization.

43.2 The objective

Computing services represent a major cost to most medium and large organizations. This cost is subject to constant scrutiny as organizations become increasingly aware of the need to demonstrate value for money and business advantage from their IT service.

Centralization of support, together with more formally defined user services and service level agreements, can give the end user the impression that they are being distanced from the IT service function. In order to avoid this, the corporate computing service can build feedback structures at all levels within the organization – to ensure the following:

- The service is meeting the actual, not the assumed, needs of the end user. Note, however, that 'needs' and 'aspirations' in this context may be two very different things. Where this creates a conflict, the reasons for it should be made clearly visible.

- The quality of the service, as seen from the desktop rather than the balance sheet, is appropriate to the business needs of the organization. There are many cases where the minimum outlay will not provide the best return on investment, so quality and metrics have an important part to play in investment appraisal.

- The user population is actively included in the discussion of service development rather than being implicitly excluded from it. The people who are the daily users of a service will have the best picture of its good and bad aspects. This is a resource to be captured and used rather than ignored or concealed.

- All the staff of the IT service group – at whatever level – are well informed about service issues and can lead informed discussions with users. This is infinitely preferable to either directing customers elsewhere for information or declaring their ignorance of the subject.

43.3 The tools

The need for good paths of communication between IT service providers and customers cannot be over-emphasized. This communication must be wholly bi-directional, driven deeply into the culture of the organization and made a visible part of the service delivery. This pathway should be the first, rather than the last, source of information and feedback for a service user.

This can be achieved by a series of interwoven mechanisms which may include some combination of the following elements:

Help desks that help

The help desk has a key role in the provision of an effective IT service, but not always for strictly technical reasons. The help desk is, in many cases, very much the public face of the IT service – and will be the element on whose performance the service as a whole is judged.

When surveyed, a group of IT help-desk users provided the following set of views – which the group sorted into the positive and negative features of generic help-desk services:

Positive	**Negative**
Helpful	*Jargon*
Knowledgeable	*Queues*
Not patronizing	*Incompetence*
Understanding	*Charging*
Not 'too busy'	*Referring calls*
Personal	*Condescending*
Targeted	*Poorly advertised*
Quick response	*Closed*
Honesty	*Inaccessible*
Reliable	*Bureaucracy*
Not too techie	*Generalist solutions*
Easy phone number	*Not returning calls*
	Voicemail/Answerphone

These comments give a very clear steer to the help desk manager, and demonstrate just how critical the balance of service must be in a technically aware environment. How the balance of costs and service delivery is arrived at in a particular organization is less clear-cut. How critical is it to the organization that customers have their problem resolved on the first call? Is it more cost-effective, in overall terms, to run a straightforward call-centre style of help desk, which refers calls on to specialists? The balance will vary in different circumstances, but having a means of gathering this type of customer feedback would be a very good way of opening the discussion.

In this case, the view was strongly biased towards 'first hit' problem resolution, with the help desk operator being able to field a wide variety of technical enquiries in a way that was supportive but didn't assume zero technical understanding. The costs associated with the provision of such a resource might be higher than for a 'call-response' type service, but there might well be a higher overall value to the organization in providing a rapid response service to key workers who would otherwise not be working productively.

The use of data mining techniques on the accumulated help-desk information set can provide important information for the IT Service Manager. By looking at trends regarding, for example, calls concerned with detailed application use, more closely targeted training plans can be developed. Similarly, frequent reports of problems with particular hardware systems can allow the troublesome or substandard kit to be identified and dealt with. This is a simple, almost user-invisible, technique which captures detailed end-user information and provides an enterprise-scale response to problems.

Regular service information

Over the years, many different techniques have been used to try to keep service information flowing out to the computer user population. How effective these techniques are in any particular case depends on a number of factors, but here are some of the most widely used.

Newsletters

Possibly the information medium with the longest pedigree, the newsletter is a staple of many IT services. They range from formal, corporate, glossy documents with four-colour printing to simple word-processed pamphlets. Their success depends on how well they fit in with the corporate ethos – in other words, whether anyone reads them. The temptation for the IT service is to include highly technical articles which are likely to be of interest only to other IT service staff. This is a temptation which should be avoided at all costs, with content being targeted on the areas which customers actually want information about.

Flyers

While newsletters may have a tendency to be buried or abandoned on arrival, flyers can be a highly effective means of getting information to users. An A4 or A5 sheet left lying on a coffee table will often be read avidly – if only because of the lack of anything more readable. Use these sheets to get across information on a single issue or some closely related points, rather than make them into 'newsletters by stealth'. Canteens, library tables, reception desks and similar drop-in points are all useful locations for this technique.

Screensaver news-tickers

Immediate service news, of the 'e-mail not available after 6pm' variety, can be handled by screensavers which scroll information. Pop-up messages are often less effective, as they tend to get concealed by other active applications. This service is also useful in another way: it provides an incentive for customers to use the standard-issue screensaver rather than one of the huge range of 'novelty' screensavers that are often in circulation.

The 'underground press'

In some organizational cultures, any document with a 'corporate' look and feel is viewed without enthusiasm. If you attempt to present service information in this environment it may be advantageous to give your publications an informal or 'underground' slant. By using authors and styles which match the culture of the customers there is a much better chance that the information will get through to where it is needed. The caveat is that you must not be seen to patronize or mislead your customers – rather, you are responding to their specific requirements.

Intranet pages

If customers are motivated enough to be actively seeking service information, then the use of the corporate intranet can be an effective means of communication. There are some important aspects of intranet provision, however, which must be recognized in this context:

- 'Under construction – come back soon' is not an acceptable part of any IT service. The chance of a user in search of service information ever returning to a page displaying this message is remote in the extreme. If the intranet is to be used as an effective service support tool, it should be populated with complete, searchable, valid data from the launch day.

- Care and maintenance of the intranet site is very important. If the customer takes the trouble to look at the pages, then the service group should ensure that the information provided is current and relevant. Too many IT service sites start in a burst of enthusiasm and then fade into irrelevance as the information ceases to be meaningful. One way around this problem is to link the job descriptions of service support staff to the maintenance of specific aspects of the intranet pages, so that the ownership of the role is never in doubt.

- Many IT support operations staff report that there are a number of core questions about the service which they spend a large proportion of their time answering. These may be of the 'How do I change my password?' or 'How do I change the font of all the headings at once?' variety. A number of organizations use FAQ (Frequently Asked Question) lists on their intranet to provide an alternative route to this information. The use of FAQs should be treated with caution as it may conceal, for example, a continuing training requirement which would have been apparent from an analysis of help desk records. Careful use of feedback frames and page tracking within the intranet pages can ensure that data are captured in usable form.

- Noticeboard functions are a simple use of the intranet that should not be overlooked. For many people, the intranet is viewed as a replacement telephone book and is their first port of call when they are trying to make contact with the IT support group. It is important, therefore, that all the contact information is kept scrupulously up to date.

Details of service development

One of the most common criticisms of IT services is that they do not pass on important information about developments in the service. Users of the service need to know about changes to the service environment, such as when the next release of desktop software will take place, how it is being tested, whether hardware or configuration changes are required and – perhaps most critically – when existing service elements are going to be withdrawn. The nightmare of a user only finding out about a service change when his or her previous working practice doesn't work cannot be allowed to happen. One aspect of service development information provision can be the publication of the active work plan for the IT service on the intranet. This could include project plans and justifications, working documents, timetables, targets and milestones. The use of open reporting enables anyone who is interested to see what is going on and, importantly, to ask the right questions if that person is unhappy with the progress of delivery.

Descriptions of services

The other thread to service information is, of course, the availability of information about the service elements themselves. Formal descriptions, as negotiated for the service level agreement, should be easily available to all service users. These descriptions should include metrics for the delivery of the service – such as how long a customer should expect to have to wait before someone responds to a help-desk service request, together with details of the escalation path the customer should use in the event of a problem. The natural extension to the service description information is a set of data which shows the performance of the service over time. Possible metrics for service performance are very varied, but might usefully include the turnover of help desk incidents, average and extremes of time to call closure, number of incidents in each predefined category of call and availability of services.

The 'local radio' model

In large organizations there is the temptation to view IT support as a single monolithic entity, and there are obvious economic benefits to be derived from running a standard service in this way. The impact on users of centralizing support for the IT operation should not be underestimated. Where customers are used to dealing with a local support group, they may feel something approaching resentment when asked to contact a call centre operation or read the standard corporate support materials to get the information or services they need. This effect can be reduced using the 'local radio' model.

In many cases, commercial local radio is provided by a large media group according to a standard formula. The playlist, format, competitions and national news gathering are determined corporately; then local presenters, news and travel information are added by the individual stations. This allows the economies of scale that stem from a national infrastructure while preserving the local front-end information valued by the audience.

The possibilities of this structure for providing IT service information are obvious, and offer the ability to provide a locally oriented service even in the largest organization. In addition to the benefits to the customer base, there is a often a greater sense of involvement for the support staff at a particular site. Staff can relate their work and contribution to the customers in a particular arena, and can tailor corporate direction to meet more precisely the local conditions.

The importance of local feedback

The involvement of local staff with the interpretation of support needs is a vital element in the correct targeting of resources. The people in the front line of support have unique information of local conditions, trends, beliefs and attitudes that can have a tremendous impact on the success of service provision. The management structure of the IT service organization needs to have mechanisms in place to enable this valuable data to be captured and used. Few things in IT service provision are more destructive than a breakdown in communication between customers, local support staff and policy makers. Take, for example, the case of a customer who wants access to a new piece of software. In the worst case, the conversation might go like this:

Customer: 'I need a copy of the new Webmeister software. Can you get me a copy?'

Local support: 'Sorry, it isn't on the supported list. You can't have it.'

Customer: 'But I need it for the new website, I can't do my job without it!'

Local support: 'Look, I can only install what is on the list – talk to management if you've got a problem with that.'

Customer: 'I'll be talking to management all right – I've never heard anything so ridiculous in my life ...'

It takes little imagination to see how this conversation could run out of control and end up as a major problem for the organization as a whole. A better outcome might be obtained this way:

Customer: 'I need a copy of the new Webmeister software. Can you get me a copy?'

Local support: 'Is that the one with the extra metadata handling? Yes, a few people have been asking about that. As there seems to be quite a bit of interest I've ordered a couple of copies for people to evaluate. Would you like to act as a tester for us? The feedback can then go to the next policy meeting and we can get the funding to make it part of the standard desktop. How does that sound?'

Customer: 'That sounds good, I'm glad you've been keeping an eye on that – I didn't know anyone else was interested.'

So instead of a customer who is about to denounce us to senior management, we have someone who is:

- impressed with our proactive service;
- going to test something out for us in the local environment;
- willing to provide structured feedback to the policy group;
- not going to go away, muttering darkly, and install it anyway without us knowing ...

Clinics

In a number of environments, the use of informal 'drop in' sessions can be rewarding. These are a useful method for capturing problems that users want to discuss in person rather than raise as a formal support request. This may be because the customer is unsure of the core problem and doesn't want to 'look stupid' to a help desk person, or it may be that the customer just wants to talk around a variety of service issues. These clinics are often best held on neutral territory, such as a seminar room or staff lounge, to which the customers have easy access. The added incentive of free coffee and doughnuts is usually enough to guarantee a good attendance, and people who come in to discuss a specific topic will often come up with a 'while I'm here ...' follow-up that they would not do through a more formal mechanism. A key aspect of clinics is that the information from customers is captured – 'help request' forms are an adequate start – and it is absolutely essential that each query is followed up, resolved and formally fed back to the enquirer.

The concept of clinics can often be successfully extended to the use of themed meetings. The meetings could run, for example, monthly with the theme of the meeting (e-mail problems, Web publishing etc.) published well in advance. These are useful as they can enable free-ranging discussion of problems, aspirations and frustrations. Both customers and service providers of all grades should be present, as this allows the discussion to be informed from all points of view – and ensures that less senior staff, who actually have to work with the system, get to present their views directly. Such meetings are hard work, as they need good preparation if they are to be successful, and might be viewed as a 'high risk' activity – but the less enthusiastic you are about hosting one, the more likely you are to need to.

Walkabouts

Some of the best user feedback comes from casual comment. Many people will pass on their feelings, opinions and ideas much more freely and naturally in a casual environment than that of, for example, a user group meeting. If support staff can have scheduled 'walkabout' time during the working week, they can act as sounding boards for user opinion.

Walkabout time can be scheduled to make this an intrinsic part of the support operation – if it isn't scheduled, there is a tendency for the time to be spent on something that is viewed as 'more important'. There will always be other jobs to do, but listening to user feedback is an important part of any successful service organization.

If walkabouts are to achieve their full potential, it is important that the IT support staff have a thorough understanding, and feeling of ownership, of the policies and practices of the service. There is little value in a dialogue which goes along these lines:

Customer: 'Why is it that I'm not allowed to have administrator access to my system?'

Local support: 'Search me. I just follow the rules – I've been told that no user gets anywhere near the administrator account and I'm not about to argue with them…'

Customer: 'Don't you people trust us? It is like living a police state!'

A better model might be:
Customer: 'Why is it that I'm not allowed to have administrator access to my system?'

Local support: 'Generally, people don't need administrator privileges – you can do most things like installing printers without them. But if there is a specialized piece of hardware you have that you need more extensive access for, we can talk about how we could best support it…'

This way, the support group finds out in detail what the customer wants to be able to do; and if the need is justified, a suitable support model can be negotiated. The user has received feedback on the real extent and intention of the policy – and hopefully doesn't go away with the impression of a huge monolithic IT service bearing down on him or her.

User representation

The common theme throughout this discussion of service provision has been the effective inclusion of end users as part of the policy loop. In a culture and a technical environment that is changing so fast, it is critically important that service providers obtain direct feedback from those who are active service users. These data need to be fed into the service development process through well-managed channels that are geared towards continuous improvement.

The capture of this information, its management and the subsequent changes to the service environment can be overseen by a group of user representatives. This group should probably be chaired by a key power user of the IT service – but in any event it must not be seen to be the property of the service provider. The role of this group is to provide a quality assurance on behalf of the user community – both in terms of the current service and the pace and direction of the IT service development. The group should have effective paths of reporting both upwards to the senior management of the organization and outwards to the whole of the IT customer base.

43.4 The outcome

With structures such as these in place, the computing service can more easily demonstrate that it is in touch with the needs of the population it supports – while ensuring that user perception is a close reflection of actual service delivery. The overall result is the provision of a better, more finely tuned, service to the organization. Central to the success of a service of this type is the quality and motivation of the staff who form the IT support service. Without their trust, understanding and active support there will always be areas of the service that do not reach their full potential. By looking after your workforce – as colleagues rather than merely as a resource – you will also be looking after the IT support needs of the organization.

44 Beauty is in the eye of the beholder

A Service Management Polder model

Barry J.M.A. Meesters and **Jan F. Bouman**
Solvision/The Art of Service

Summary

Why is Service Level Management often a very laborious process? You try to match customer expectations with the competencies of your own service organization. What is right now is wrong tomorrow. What is excellent today is nothing special next week. Despite the detailed specifications of service levels in agreements with customers, perceptions tend to shift. Parties who have service level agreements seem to have subscriptions to frustrations. What can we do to manage this problem or – better – to cope with this fact of life? This chapter presents a solution that typically matches Dutch culture of consensus in society, business and politics. It's the Service Management variant of the Dutch Polder model (Heijden, 1998). In society it proved to be a formula towards relative success and wealth for the parties involved. But, does it work for Service Management?

44.1 Introduction

A majority of ICT service providers will confirm that it is too risky to give guarantees for service that meet customer expectation 100 per cent. It simply is impossible. They say: This is Utopia. Customers should understand that there must be a balance between quality and costs. Besides, customer requirements and technology keep changing. But do providers really try? Are they really innovative when it comes to customer satisfaction?

The message of this chapter is that it is possible to give service guarantees and to approximate 100 per cent customer satisfaction. The secret is that it's not only the specification of service levels in a service level agreement (SLA) but also management of the perceptions of customer and provider. In fact, it is a 'secret' everyone knows. Why, then, don't people take the right consequences? Why isn't perception management integrated in Service Level Management?

44.2 Service level agreements

It's not new for ICT providers to try to meet expectations of customers. But, with the increasing complexity of ICT and the dependency on it, specification of service levels has acquired high priority. The level of (measurable) ICT performance is more and more decisive for the customers' business performance. Availability of an application can be of vital interest to a company. Payments for ICT services are often made dependent on measured performance of the provider. Customers generally have internal or external customers themselves, so they have to be able to cover their financial risks.

All of this stimulates concentration on service level agreements that specify detailed and quantitative service levels. These agreements include clauses that specify strict communications and escalation procedures and consequences in case of not meeting promised levels. It's a contract between two or more parties. But in many cases it also leads to lots of paper and a 'suffocating' bureaucracy.

Measurement of service levels by using so-called performance indicators is an important aspect of Service Level Management, especially when there are financial consequences to performance, e.g. throughput time of a transaction, availability of an application, average number of messages in a time-frame, CPU utilization, utilization of a telephone line or attainability of a help desk.

People are inclined to think that meeting required service levels will produce satisfied customers. Why is this so hard to achieve, despite the efforts we put into Service Level Agreements? It's because we forget to manage customers' perception: what they need, what they expect, what they feel.

44.3 Perception

In their book *Winning the Service Game*, Benjamin Schneider and David E. Bowen (1995) explain that there are ten different dimensions which determine the customers' perception of quality of service (Table 44.1).

TABLE 44.1 Ten dimensions of service quality

	Dimension	It involves
1	Reliability	Consistency of performance and dependability
2	Responsiveness	The willingness or readiness of employees to provide service
3	Competence	Possession of required skills and knowledge to provide service
4	Access	Approachability and ease of contact
5	Courtesy	Politeness, respect, consideration and friendliness of contact personnel
6	Communication	Listening to customers and keeping them informed in language they can understand
7	Credibility	Trustworthiness, believability and honesty
8	Security	Freedom of danger, risk or doubt
9	Understanding the customer	Making the effort to understand the customers' needs
10	Tangibles	Physical evidence of the service

Source: Parasuraman, Zeithaml and Berry, *Journal of Marketing*, 49 (Fall 1985)

Schneider and Bowen indicate that, to plan improvement of service, one should first assess customers' perception of the current quality (of service) they receive. Determining the customers' scores for the ten dimensions of Table 44.1 can be helpful. Then the customers should be asked to give scores on their expectations, using the same ten dimensions.

Therefore a Service Level Agreement should not only cover the rational specifications mentioned in the previous paragraph. The emotional aspects of Table 44.1 should also be addressed. A traditional service level agreement covers the tangibles and sometimes some communication, reliability, competence and access aspects. Looking at the total picture, there can still be a lot of reasons for the customer to be unhappy. On the other hand, it is possible that the provider fails to meet the measurable service levels specified in the service level agreement while the customer remains satisfied because of the responsiveness of the providers' staff.

44.4 Needs and expectations

So, beauty is in the eye of the beholder. Apart from the useful directives given by the IT Infrastructure Library (ITIL; see Section 44.16: ITIL and perception) and the service levels specified in traditional SLAs, there should be another way to meet specific customers' expectations that also respects their feelings and their 'subcutaneous' needs. Schneider and Bowen specify the difference between expectations and needs as shown in Table 44.2.

TABLE 44.2 The difference between expectations and needs

Expectations	Needs
Conscious	Unconscious
Specific	Global
Surface	Deep
Short-term	Long-term
Desired outcomes from 'service encounters' (e.g. short response time)	Desired outcomes from 'human existence' (e.g. self-esteem)
If you dissatisfy customers by not meeting their expectations, you can still recover	If you dissatisfy customers by not meeting their basic needs, you will lose them

Source: Schneider and Bowen (1995)

These needs and expectations are in fact a psychological basis of the ten dimensions of Table 44.1. It is very important to understand this whenever customer relations are involved. This brings us to the conclusion that, apart from the traditional SLA specifications, another way of determining and describing service should be introduced.

Customers don't ask to be analysed by a service provider acting as a shrink. So, detailed specification of their psychological state of mind is not desirable. Even if it were possible, it would be hard to make a formal service level agreement out of it.

This 'other way' to meet specific customers' expectations that also respects their feelings and their 'subcutaneous' needs is presented in this chapter and it is called Service Level Improvement Method (SLIM). SLIM is a variant on the service check presented by us in 'A service check', an article published by us in the 2000 edition of the *World Class IT Service Management Guide*.

44.5 ISO and quality of service

To be able to guarantee levels of quality that meet customers' expectations, one should first establish the *Quality of Service*. Generally the extent to which internal processes are organized in conformance with internal standards is considered as the measure of quality. Many companies have set up a quality system following the ISO9000 set of standards. Often, people have the illusion that acquiring the ISO certificate stands for reaching and fixing quality in the organization. An ISO certificate, however, never guarantees quality. An example is the company that produces concrete life jackets, which is able to acquire ISO certificates. An ISO certificate only proves that an organization can deliver a certain quality standard at a specific time. It doesn't prove that quality standards are really met. So, audits on internal processes don't really reveal quality.

In spite of positive expectations about the new ISO9001:2000 standards, the European standardization organization CE (Conformité Européenne) didn't really adopt the *Customer Satisfaction and Continuous Improvement* aspects. The CE footnotes referring to ISO 9001:2000 documentation say that not meeting specific requirements regarding these items doesn't have to mean that the CE standards are not met. This chapter addresses these two aspects.

The next step taken by many service providers is measurement of performance. A set of indicators is defined to get a picture of the output performance of the organization. Based on these indicators, the organization (and quality) is managed. Generally, they use financial performance indicators without involving customers. They develop their own opinions about what is important to their customers. In doing so, organizations are at risk of managing and improving the wrong aspects. Resources are allocated to projects and departments that don't really improve customer service.

Managing quality of service is more than defining and implementing processes and measuring performance. Real quality is defined by the customers' perception. Even when processes in an organization are working perfectly and the measured performance is very good, it doesn't mean that the customer is always happy, because the customer often judges quality of service based on different criteria from those made by the provider. The result can be that the perception of the customer does not match the perception of the service provider, in spite of great effort.

44.6 Quality is balance

To secure quality of service, service has three aspects that need to be balanced (Figure 44.1; Meesters and Bouman, 2000):

- *Performance*: service level agreements made have to be met. The way in which formal and non-formal agreements are met needs to be measured and reported.
- *Processes*: the way the service provider is organized. The service provider has to be organized in a manner that turns the performance (as mentioned above) into a manageable and influential activity.
- *Perception*: the performance (as mentioned above) has to be tested continuously against the expectations and needs of the receiver, without any formal agreement.

FIGURE 44.1

Quality is balance

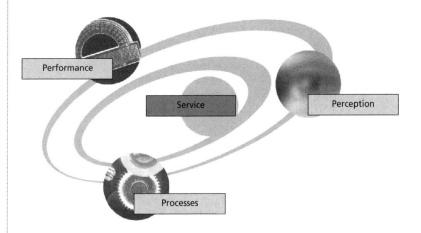

44.7 Customer: part of the organization

Many service organizations are in a stage of performing audits on processes and measuring output performance. Customers' perception is not involved because it's too difficult and often too confronting. This is an ostrich-like policy because in the end the customer always decides whether to buy or not. It's also a problem of not knowing how to handle customer satisfaction, i.e. how to measure the customer's perception and how to reach a balance between performance, processes and perception.

Involving the customer can be very confrontational. Schneider and Bowen (1995) actually say that a service provider has to make the customer part of its organization (Figure 44.2). This doesn't mean that customer and service provider have to merge. It means that the customer should be integrated into processes (how things formally work), perception (thinking and feeling) and performance (measure, ask the customer) within the service provider's organization.

As 'part' of the organization (or system), the customer can be a real threat to some established competencies. The service organization seems to be more vulnerable because the customer knows a lot. This vulnerability is a necessary stimulus to reach a higher level of quality of service (and to outrun competition).

This can work out good or bad. It's bad when the customer abuses inside knowledge and squeezes the service provider in one way or another, but a service provider shouldn't let this happen. It's good when customer involvement leads to an (almost)

FIGURE 44.2

The three-tiered view of a service organization

Source: Schneider and Bowen (1995)

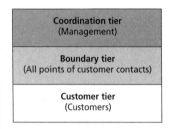

perfect match between supply and demand, to maximum trust, to a customer-for-life relationship and to survival.

Of course, there's always the choice *not* to involve the customer. The outcome will always be somewhere between the *good* and the *bad* mentioned above. If service is a unique selling point for the service provider and if it is a way to survive and to outrun competition, this can't be the right choice.

44.8 Service Level Improvement Method (SLIM)

The Service Level Improvement Method (SLIM) is a method to make the customer part of the service provider's organization.

A service level agreement often covers several years. The problem is that neither business, technology nor customer perception can be planned years ahead. Customer and provider are always changing and so are their environments. The experience of 'excellent service' will wear out fast. This means that there should be dynamic service level agreements based on (new) customer perceptions. This is what we call Service Level Improvement Agreements (SLIAs). SLIAs are products of the Service Level Improvement Method that is presented in this chapter.

The Service Level Improvement Method covers the following aspects (Figure 44.3):

- continuous improvement process;
- consensus between customer and service provider;
- concentration of the customers' perception rather than detailed specification of quality-of-service criteria;
- admission of the fact that the customers' perception of 'quality' is constantly changing (based on changes in expectations triggered by the ten dimensions of Table 44.1);
- interactive determination between customer and service provider, of quality-of-service criteria through evaluation sessions;
- dynamic Service Level Improvement Agreements (SLIAs) for periods of 6, 9 or 12 months;
- agreements, based on the perception of the customer, consisting of service criteria, scores (importance, appreciation), actions and consequences;
- a surprise element to keep the customer conscious of quality of service.

FIGURE 44.3

Service Level Improvement Method (SLIM)

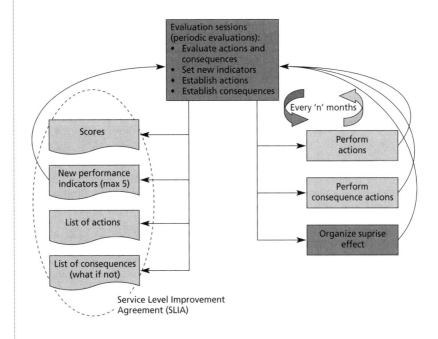

44.9 How to reach balance and to keep it

Demands, expectations and needs change all the time. Quality of service changes with it. That's why customers' service providers need a flexible and dynamic 'agreement' about service levels. This is the Service Level Improvement Agreement (SLIA) mentioned in the previous paragraph. An SLIA is a result of SLIM.

Customers prefer guarantees instead of promises. This means that, if a provider does not meet certain service levels, there should be some kind of compensation. This can be a penalty, an extra effort, a lower price or anything parties agree on. SLIM is based on constant interaction about service levels and 'what to do if not' between parties in a rather informal way and based on a balance between performance, perception and processes. Consensus: This is what the Polder model is all about. The ultimate objective is always excellent service.

44.10 The SLIM concept

SLIM aims to improve processes based on measurements of performance and perception. To get there, one customer and the service provider are brought together in evaluation sessions. Interviews and enquiries (with questionnaires) don't deliver the right effects because there's no interaction between customer and service provider. Also the (emotional) perception aspects are not 'measured' and this is very important to the perception of quality (of service). Enquiries also often contain ambiguous, unclear and incomplete questions. In an evaluation session, however, all the necessary information can be collected in half a day and parties can agree on scores, actions and consequences.

The following steps are taken during a 4-hour evaluation session:

Step 1 Determine scores

The first step is to determine scores for the quality criteria (performance indicators) agreed during the previous evaluation session. One of the advantages of SLIM is that exact definitions of the performance indicators are irrelevant. It's all about the customers' perception. Does performance meet their expectations (or needs)? No valuable time is wasted on detailed definitions that divert from the bigger picture. This is one of the essential differences from traditional Service Level Management.

The scores will be projected in a quality matrix (Figure 44.4). In this matrix, importance and valuation (appreciation) of quality criteria are related to each other. Depending on the type of criterion, branch and customer, a scale will be determined, which is important to correct processing and analysis.

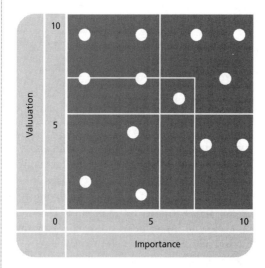

FIGURE 44.4

Quality matrix

Depending on the importance and valuation of a quality criterion, that criterion will be projected in one of the four quadrants. It is essential that quality criteria end up in the right quadrant, on the following basis:

- *Quadrant 1 (lower left):* The customer doesn't think this criterion is very important and values the performance as being low. The quality criteria in this quadrant don't deserve immediate attention to improve performance.

- *Quadrant 2 (lower right):* The customer thinks this criterion is important and values the performance as being low. Quality based on these criteria has to improve in the short term. The customer should be informed about the actions that are going to be taken to improve quality.

- *Quadrant 3: (upper left):* The customer doesn't think this criterion is very important but values the performance as being good. The quality criteria in this quadrant don't deserve immediate attention to improve performance. Investments in these criteria are not very effective for customer satisfaction because they don't think it's important.

Quadrant 4 (upper right): The customer thinks this criterion is important and values the performance as being good. The performance of criteria that are projected in this quadrant should be consolidated. Communication to customers about what is going well is important to customer satisfaction. Also, potential customers should hear it. Criteria from quadrant 2 should end up in quadrant 4 after improvements have been carried out.

Step 2 Establish action list

The projection of quality criteria in the matrix indicates fulfilment of the customers' expectations. If the service provider does not meet the expected service level, actions will be agreed in order to meet expected service levels at short notice. It is important that the customer gets the feeling that the service provider undertakes appropriate actions and commits to these actions. If, before the next evaluation, quality levels have not improved, this will become clear immediately during this next evaluation. It will almost certainly influence the customers' satisfaction. Improvement becomes a necessity!

The actions agreed during an evaluation session can be an effective instrument for the service provider to manage customer satisfaction. The customer as well as the service provider will be focused on these actions.

If the service provider does not meet expectations by failing to take the agreed actions, the agreed consequences will be taken. These consequences were agreed and described during the previous evaluation session (see Step 4. Establish list of consequences, below).

Step 3 Evaluate quality criteria

After fixing the action list, the customer determines, in consultation with the service provider, which quality criteria will be measured in the following evaluation period (generally six months) and which service levels will be used. Because of continuous change in demands, desires and expectations, this part is very important. It's the customer who indicates what criteria define the current quality of service. This interaction with customers determines the aspects of flexibility and dynamics in the Service Level Improvement Agreement (SLIA). In the next evaluation session these quality criteria will be evaluated.

A normal throughput time for an improvement cycle is six months. This is the time from one evaluation session to the next. However, customer and service provider are free to change this period. We generally recommend a six-month period in order to give the service provider reasonable time to execute improvement actions and to prove continuity of quality.

Step 4 Establish list of consequences

After defining new quality criteria and service levels, a list of consequences is established. These consequences will become 'active' if the service provider does not meet the expected (and agreed) quality level in the next improvement cycle. SLIM is based on giving guarantees. Guarantees that are not going to be fulfilled are useless. Customers are looking for service providers that will fulfil these guarantees and keep their promises. If they have good feelings about this, they want to pay for it! The list of consequences is part of the guarantee that the customers will receive. This guarantee can be financial compensation, material compensation, a free service, or anything else that suits the customer and provides the perception of a 'bleeding' service provider. With this guarantee the pressure to attain excellent performance will be higher. High quality levels will no longer be exceptions. *Quality is embedded in the organization.*

44.11 Output of evaluation session: Service Level Improvement Agreement (SLIA)

The output of the evaluation session is a Service Level Improvement Agreement. An SLIA contains detailed minutes of the evaluation session (workshop) and covers the following subjects:

- the performance indicators (agreed upon during a previous evaluation session) and the scores for these performance indicators (quality criteria matrices included);
- the new performance indicators which will be used in the following period, including the way to measure the performance;
- the list of actions which service provider and customer promise to execute, and the results they want to achieve;
- the list of consequences, which will be 'active' when the defined actions have not been executed or when the defined results have not been achieved.

The SLIA is a dynamic document, which is considered as a contract after being signed by both customer and service provider. Every period (after every evaluation session), this contract will be adapted and signed again. When this SLIA is combined with a 'classic' SLA, which contains more objective and static performance indicators, it can be an excellent framework for getting and keeping satisfied customers.

44.12 Continuation of evaluation session

In the following evaluation cycle the service provider will take care of the agreed service levels of the defined quality criteria as described in the SLIA. Continuously measuring and improving will produce the customer's expected service level. At the same time the agreed actions will be executed in order to improve the quality level of one or more quality criteria. Finally, the agreed consequences are settled in order to 'repair' customer satisfaction. However, it would not be good for customer satisfaction to be forced to use these guarantees (consequences) often. Besides, it could be a (financial) problem for the service provider. Customers demand the expected service levels and *not* compensation for not meeting expectations.

44.13 Surprise

SLIM is a method for continuously meeting the customer's expectations. However, excellent quality of service is often more than just meeting expectations. Excellence contains surprise effects (see Figure 44.3 again). A surprise cannot be defined in advance. It is a spontaneous action that sticks in the customer's memory. This action doesn't have to cost a lot of money. Timing and the impact (on the customer's emotions) are essential. Surprise effects occur when there is 'more' or 'better' than expected – when the customer's expectations are exeeded.

44.14 Conditions for evaluation sessions and the facilitator

A SLIM evaluation session should be facilitated professionally. Important aspects are:

- The facilitator should be an independent third party who manages the process of the evaluation session and who is responsible for creating conditions that stimulate results. An experienced person who has affinity with the subjects and who has sufficient authority can act as a facilitator.
- A secretary who writes down all conclusions and decisions should support the facilitator.
- Respect and equality between customer and service provider are vital. This also means that each participant should have a counterpart of the same competence level in the other party's organization.
- Understanding each other's point of view is important. There should be a positive attitude towards the other party.
- It is not a negotiation session. Great problematic differences that can dominate the discussions should be settled beforehand.
- One customer per evaluation session is best. It is important that there are only two parties, apart from the facilitator who is independent.
- Generally five service criteria are the maximum SLIM can handle. Even if it would be possible to use more criteria, it wouldn't be effective because there are always just a few aspects that really affect the customers' perception.

44.15 A case study

This case describes SLIM at Company X, an international company that develops and manufactures high-quality panelling for façade cladding and interior applications.

Company X delivers excellent service and achieves high quality levels. However, they were looking for a way to continually improve this quality in order to keep ahead of competition. They decided to practise SLIM.

The first evaluation session is always different from the others because there is no input from a previous time. Input has to be gathered from other sources. Company X performed a customer survey just a year ago. The output of this survey was used as input to the first SLIM evaluation session. There were approximately 50 service criteria gathered during the survey. After a discussion, the participants agreed that not all

50 criteria could qualify as service criteria. As stated in the previous section, five service criteria are the maximum SLIM can (and should) handle.

The evaluation session (SLIM workshop) took about 3.5 hours and had the following agenda:

1. Introduction to workshop (by Company X and facilitator)
2. Introduction to Service Level Improvement Method (by facilitator)
3. Presentation of service criteria (based on a customer survey from last year as input for this workshop)
4. Determination of the service criteria (by customer and Company X together)
5. Giving scores to importance of service criteria (by customer and Company X separately)
6. Selection of five (5) most important service criteria (by customer and Company X together)
7. Giving scores to appreciation of service criteria (by customer and Company X together)
8. Determine follow-up actions and consequences (by customer and Company X together)
9. Evaluation of the workshop (by customer and Company X together).

Company X selected criteria with importance scores as set out in Table 44.3:

TABLE 44.3 Company X importance scores

Importance of service criteria	Score
The possibility of different sizes	-> 10
Deliveries (delivery reliability)	-> 9
Specific customer demands	-> 9
Decoration switch	-> 9
Negotiation space	-> 7

After a number of discussions managed by the facilitator, appreciation (valuation) scores were determined by the customer as set out in Table 44.4. The ambition scores were determined by both customer and Company X (service provider).

TABLE 44.4 Company X appreciation scores

Appreciation of service criteria	Score	Ambition
A. The possibility of different sizes	-> 4	-> 7
B. Deliveries (delivery reliability)	-> 9	-> 9
C. Specific Customer demands	-> 5	-> 8
D. Decoration switch	-> 5	-> 7
E. Negotiation space	-> 3	-> 7

The current importance and appreciation (valuation) scores are shown in Figure 44.5. The white arrows indicate the ambitions.

The results of the evaluation session of Company X were an action list and a list of consequences for each service criterion. Below is an abbreviated example ('the possibility of different sizes') of one of those lists.

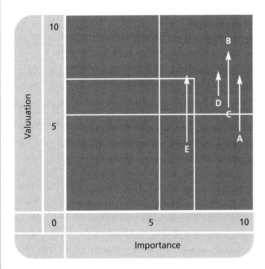

FIGURE 44.5

Quality matrix of Company X

The possibility of different sizes

- Action: *Start working group with participants from Company X and customer. Purpose is to identify the problem, to make an inventory of possible solutions, to select a future-proof solution and to solve the current problem quickly.*

- Condition: *Adjustments must be made in Company X's production process and (possibly) administrative procedures.*

- Initiative: *Company X.*

- Consequence: *Customer goes 'shopping' (to competition) or customer gets 10% discount.*

44.16 ITIL and perception

The new ITIL Service Delivery documentation about Service Level Management states that a better relationship between IT and its customers should be developed. However, the problem is that ITIL still concentrates very much on detailed specification of measurable indicators which address half or less of the ten dimensions of Table 44.1.

Monitoring of actual achievements (particularly achieving the same perception as that held by the customers) is identified by ITIL Service Delivery (2000) as one of the most difficult problems that must be addressed first as it impacts on:

- ensuring targets are achievable before committing to them;
- verifying targets prior to agreements.

ITIL addresses the 'perception problem' without really giving solutions. ITIL Service Delivery documentation apparently puts much emphasis on unequivocal definitions of terms, meanings, indicators and methods of measurement as a way to match the perceptions of customer and service provider. However, as described in the previous sections, our experience indicates that there is a danger in trying to reach perfection this way.

Firstly, both customer and service provider can develop a kind of belief that perceptions of both parties are 99.9% the same. This is never true and can lead to frustrations.

Secondly, a service agreement that covers all technical and procedural aspects addressed by ITIL still leaves some of the ten dimensions of Table 44.1 open; e.g. it is very difficult to fix or record aspects such as friendliness, freedom from doubt, respect or willingness, while they are very decisive for the customers' quality perception.

At present, many publications state that the real benefits of ITIL are very small because of the bureaucracy that is introduced into organizations. Changes breathe 'the breath of formalities and bureaucracy' as Lammers and Krewinkel (2001) say. The bureaucracy of ITIL can work against flexibility and quick time-to-market of new ideas. Especially in companies where e-business initiatives are important, slow and 'unwieldy' ICT management will be killing. Customers demand flexibility. In new ICT management, people get more freedom to act, boundaries between competencies will fade away, people and groups are innovative, knowledge will be shared and organizations will work with small, flexible units. But, most important: the customer will be leading. Professional knowledge management is vital for these developments.

The Service Level Improvement Method (SLIM) as presented in this chapter can be the new ICT Service Management's face presented to the customer. In the new ITIL documentation the term 'IT Customer Relationship Management' (ITCRM) is introduced. Service Improvement is one of the main items of ITCRM. The Service Level Improvement Method, as presented in this chapter, can be a practical guide for Customer Relationship Management, not only in ICT but also in any other area. ITIL Service Delivery documentation says that an ITCRM plan provides the following information:

- a source of reference and information;
- a way of measuring progress;
- demonstration of effectiveness;
- maintaining business continuity;
- underpinning service improvement.

The periodic Service Level Improvement Agreement (SLIA) can be the ITCRM plan as described in the ITIL documentation (2000).

44.17 Conclusions

The Service Level Improvement Method (SLIM) is a means of achieving excellent service in which customer and service provider have to cooperate closely. It is called a Service Management Polder model because of the principle of consensus. The customer has to be considered as 'part of the provider's service organization'. SLIM avoids the complicated legal constructions set out in service level agreements, covering much paper. Instead, it channels energy into active face-to-face interaction and understanding between customer and service provider.

SLIM addresses two aspects that are neglected by the European CE interpretations of the new ISO 9001:2000 standards: *Customer Satisfaction* and *Continuous Improvement*. In particular, SLIM covers the following aspects:

- continuous improvement process;
- concentration on the customers' perception rather than detailed specification of quality-of-service criteria;
- admission of the fact that the customers' perception of 'quality' is constantly changing (based on changes in expectations triggered by the ten dimensions of Table 44.1);
- interactive determination between customer and service provider of quality-of-service criteria through evaluation sessions;
- dynamic Service Level Improvement Agreements (SLIAs) for periods of 6, 9 or 12 months;
- agreements, based on the perception of the customer, consisting of service criteria, scores (importance, appreciation), actions and consequences;
- a surprise element to keep the customer conscious of quality of service.

In many cases it is more likely that excellent service will be achieved by using SLIM than by using traditional (ITIL) Service Level Management with minimum active involvement of the customer. The three most important reasons are:

- focus on the customers' perception;
- focus on continuous improvement of service;
- dynamic, ever-changing character of the agreements (SLIAs).

In some cases the best solution is the combination of traditional 'legal' service level agreements and SLIM.

SLIM can be a practical guide for IT Customer Relationship Management (ITCRM) as described in ITIL Service Delivery documentation. The periodic Service Level Improvement Agreement (SLIA) can be the ITCRM plan. However, ITIL should never be a bureaucracy that works against flexibility and quick time-to-market of new ideas.

Before using SLIM, it is important to answer the following questions:

- Is it possible to find customers who would like to cooperate?
- Can SLIM match the business culture in our company, area or society (which is a culture of consensus)?

If the answer to one of these questions is definitively NO, please don't start with SLIM. Otherwise, SLIM can be the way towards an (almost) perfect match between supply and demand, to maximum trust, to a customer-for-life relationship and to survival. In other words: a way to outrun competition for both customer and service provider.

Literature

van der Heijden, P.F. (1998) *The Flexibilization of Working Life in the Netherlands*, University of Amsterdam. Link: http://www.uva.nl/aias/publicaties/heijdenbristol.html.

ISO 9001:2000 standards, Quality management systems – Requirements (*Stage date*: 2000-12-08), International Standardisation Organisation (ISO), Geneva, Link: http://www.iso.ch/.

ITIL Service Delivery, Version 3.0, Draft for QA, November 2000, Central Computer and Telecommunications Agency (CCTA; now OCG) (UK).

Lammers, E. and Krewinkel G. (2001) 'ITIL heeft de echte problemen niet opgelost' (in Dutch, ITIL did not solve the real problems), 26 January 2001, *Automatisering Gids* (NL).

Meesters, B.J.M.A. and Bouman, J.F. (2000) in 'A service check', *World Class Guide to IT Service Management 2000*, ten Hagen & Stam Publishers (NL), ISBN 90-76383-46-4

Schneider, B. and Bowen, D. E. (1995) *Winning the Service Game*, Harvard Business School Press.

45 Service Level Management

Peter Sullivan National Data Systems

45.1 Mission

Service Level Management has at its heart a Service Level Agreement. The purpose of a Service Level Agreement is to ensure that both the service provider and the customer clearly understand what is expected of each other in the provision of the service. The wider the gap between the expectation and the actual delivery, the greater the risk of disappointment. Repeated disappointments are the harbingers of partnership failures.

In providing the following information it is intended that service providers will find themselves a step closer to establishing a practical Service Level Agreement which will assist them in avoiding some common pitfalls.

The Service Level Agreement will generally cover the manner in which the service is provided. It may stipulate measurables such as the time allowed for the service provider to respond to and clear an incident. It may also include details on escalation procedures and other areas applicable to the service delivery. The Service Level Agreement can be as simple or as elaborate as required, as long as its main purpose is fulfilled.

The smaller the 'expectation gap', the lower the risk of false expectations being generated on either side.

Adherence to the Service Level Agreement is what Service Level Management is all about.

45.2 Concern

There is an increasing prevalence of penalties for underperformance being incorporated into Service Level Agreements. This development may all too quickly lead under-resourced service providers into a financial trap, causing untold havoc for their own organization as well as creating risks for their customers. Unwary service providers may swiftly find themselves being sucked into a downward profitability spiral where once-acceptable margins begin to buckle under mounting pressure. This may eventually result in the viability of the entire support project being brought into question.

This downward spiral is accelerated by the loss of much-needed revenues which are required to resource the project. The revenue loss is directly attributable to the application of underperformance penalties. As a direct result, exposed service providers may find themselves unable to properly resource the project due to this diminished revenue stream. This in turn may force them to cut costs by reducing their project resources, which in turn may lead to further underperformance penalties being applied.

Profitability issues aside, further damage is sustained by the service providers' reputation, notwithstanding the effect that this undesirable set of circumstances has on their customer's business. This naturally leads to a rapid deterioration in the service provider/customer relationship, which further jeopardizes the prospects of service providers growing their business in the future.

45.3 Achieve clear agreement by both parties on what each party perceives the service to be

Clear communication is vital to the success of any business partnership. This is especially true in the service arena. Despite our best intentions, there is usually not enough contact maintained between the parties while everything is running smoothly.

In general, contact is limited to those situations where there is a service incident. Unfortunately, this is the worst time to discover that the customer expects one thing and the service provider delivers another. Both parties remain thoroughly entrenched in their belief that each is correct in its expectations.

It may safely be concluded that responsibility to some degree or another may be laid to rest at the door of both parties in that the Service Level Agreement was not set out in a clear enough manner to properly describe the requirements and capabilities of the parties.

For example, how is the service level measured? Is it against business hours or elapsed time? Does the measurement of an outstanding call stop at the close of the business day and resume at the start of the next business day, or does it run indefinitely until the problem is cleared?

Is the service level based on mean time to clear (MTTC) or on time to clear (TTC). MTTC is, as its name implies, based on the average of calls responded to or closed within the required time-frame. It may be further averaged out over a period of months.

For example, a Service Level Agreement requiring a 95 per cent adherence to an MTTC of 8 hours translates to the total number of hours lost in equipment downtime for that customer over a defined period, e.g. one calendar month, divided by the total number of calls in the same period; this will produce a number. When this number is expressed as a percentage it will either be greater than, equal to or less than the required 95 per cent.

$$MTTC = \frac{Total\ number\ of\ hours\ of\ downtime}{Total\ number\ of\ calls}$$

e.g. $\frac{960\ hours}{125\ calls} = 7.68\ hours\ MTTC$

The 7.68 hours MTTC would be within the required 95 per cent of 8 hours.

$$\frac{7.68\ hours}{8.00\ hours} \times 100 = 96\ per\ cent$$

45 ■ Service Level Management

A Service Level Agreement which required 95 per cent TTC is based on a per-incident measurement. This means that 95 per cent of all calls should be performed within the agreed service level requirement. For example, if the agreed TTC was 8 hours and there were 350 calls in a given month (if this was the agreed measurement period), then 333 of those calls should be cleared within the 8-hour allowance.

Additionally, it should be clearly stipulated what the measurement period is. Does the clock stop at 1700 hours or does it run, for example, on a 24-hour basis? It certainly would not be prudent of service providers to agree to be measured on downtime against a continually running measurement clock when it transpires that the customers closes its doors at 1630 hours. The service providers would therefore be severely constrained in meeting their targets.

When committing to service levels, it is important to take cognizance of distances to be travelled to site into the calculation. Any such distance allowance should take into consideration constraining factors such as speed limits and average road and traffic conditions. These distances may not necessarily be measured from each of the service provider's service points as there may not be sufficient staff at those points to provide coverage. A safer approach is to state that the distance allowance is measured from a main service point, where the likelihood of having enough staff to meet the service level, under most conditions, is high. Again, by being practical and clear in service commitment, fewer misunderstandings will be encountered.

Table 45.1 illustrates the mechanism:

TABLE 45.1 Distance allowance (example)

Distance from a designated service point	0 to 50km	50 to 100km	100km to 150 km	150km to 200km	200km to 250km	Above 250km
Standard response time allowed	2 hours	2 hours	2 hours	2 hours	2 hours	2 hours
Additional response time allowed	0 hours	1 hour	2 hours	3 hours	4 hours	Negotiable
Total response time allowed	2 hours	3 hours	4 hours	5 hours	6 hours	Negotiable

The above distances will be measured from the nearest service location of :

- Branch A;
- Branch B;
- Branch C.

45.4 Achieve clear agreement by both parties on what each party perceives the service *not* to be

It is essential that both parties understand what the Service Level Agreement specifically excludes. Agreed exclusions can be covered under time-and-materials billing, where labour, parts and travel charges are levied on a predetermined basis. In such circumstances service providers will, unless agreed otherwise with their customers, manage these calls on a 'best endeavours' basis. For example, customers may be utilizing equipment for which parts are scarce and therefore difficult to source. It would therefore be wise to exclude such equipment from the Service Level Agreement measurement. It is also important to advise customers as soon as this condition is known in order that they can take the appropriate action to offset potentially long periods of downtime.

Another example is where the customer expects the downtime clock to stop running only when the user's system has been restored to full functionality whereas the service provider understands it to be a 'hardware only' agreement.

This may mean that, in the event of hard drive failure, the service provider would have to ensure that not only was the hard drive problem repaired but also that the operating system was loaded, as well as the applications software and, where appropriate, user data.

If the service provider has committed to a very tight Service Level Agreement on the basis of hardware restoration only, this fundamental misunderstanding could seriously undermine the customer/service provider relationship as well as adding unbudgeted cost to the service for both parties.

45.5 Ensure service levels are matched to product reliability

In arriving at an acceptable service level for specific equipment, it is prudent of the service provider to ascertain carefully the anticipated or proven reliability of the equipment to be supported.

It would be imprudent to quote a high availability level for, say, a particular printer model which had a poor reputation for reliability. Such premature commitment would place the service provider at an immediate disadvantage and could readily translate into financial risk, not only from a penalty perspective but also from the cost of supporting the product. Instances of unreliable equipment appearing on the base should also be brought to the attention of customers. It may be in their interest to be able to remove such equipment from their inventory.

In any event, such equipment should be serviced on a time-and-materials basis to reduce the risk to the service provider.

One source of data on the historical performance of equipment is customers themselves. They may have access to the appropriate help-desk statistics for the previous 6 to 12-month period.

It may also prove prudent to include a caveat in the Service Level Agreement (and in the pricing terms and conditions) that service levels are based on the manufacturer's mean time between failures (MTBFs) figures. Therefore any significant variance from these figures would be treated as an exception.

45.6 Ensure Service Level Agreements cater for product complexity in terms of time to fix

Responsible service providers must be circumspect in signing off on the contents of a Service Level Agreement. They must ensure that the obligations undertaken by them are both sensible and practical.

45 ■ Service Level Management

This means that where incidents require time-consuming solutions due to the level of complexity of the systems involved, the deliverables associated with the resolution of such problems are properly qualified and 'ring-fenced'. Again it is in the interests of both customer and service provider to be aware of the realities of such situations and that they are able to share a common practical view of the potential time to implement a fix. This then affords both parties the opportunity to implement alternative strategies to optimize the potential for uptime.

No commitment on Service Level Agreement should be made by a service provider where fixes for the incident require the intervention of parties fully outside the control of the service provider, e.g. the local PTT authority.

45.7 Tailor customer service requirements to customer budget

In creating individual Service Level Agreements, it is important for the service provider to design the Service Level Agreement to match its contents with the customer's available support budget. Customers will, quite rightly, attempt to negotiate the best deal for their business. This sometimes means that they will demand 24 hours per day, 7 days per week (24×7) standby services when they can in practice only afford an 8 hours per day, 5 days per week (8×5) service.

If the service provider does not have the economies of scale in providing 24×7 services, e.g. in remote locations, or for equipment which has special support requirements, the implementation of such a service may be expensive. It is important then to be forthright in apprising the customer of the real cost of providing such a service and thus avoid the potential for widening the expectation gap.

Another pitfall to avoid is the repeated delivery of a better-than-contracted service, e.g. providing a 4-hour MTTC, when in fact the service provider is only contracted to delivering on a "Next Business Day" (NBD) service.

This at first glance may appear at odds with delivering the best service possible. However, in practice it is an unprofitable use of resources. In constantly delivering better than contracted services to a customer, the service provider is using support capacity that could be more profitably utilized in servicing new business. Furthermore, the cost of delivering such a service will not be covered by the revenues gained. If the customer pays for NBD service, then that is what should generally be delivered. If the service levels do not meet the customer's business requirements, they should be upgraded.

45.8 Ensure staffing levels and calibre match Service Level Agreement requirements

The service industry is no different from any other in that the business imperative of profitability must be satisfied to assure the ongoing viability of the organization. As time progresses, this demand grows ever more stringent and any area identified as holding the potential for cost savings is scrutinized intensely.

It is therefore an attractive proposition to skimp on the calibre of staff assigned to an account, making the cost of resources cheaper. Perhaps even more hazardous is to succumb to the temptation to understaff a project in the belief that, if difficult situations arise, these can always be managed quickly and safely.

This may be true to a certain extent; however, if the service provider's built-in safety margin is reduced too far, a vicious circle can rapidly arise if not managed correctly. As the number of uncleared calls rises due to project undermanning or too low a skill level being utilized, the help desk, through which all user calls are logged, begins to be flooded by users enquiring on the status of their previously logged and still outstanding calls.

The effectiveness of the help desk in screening calls diminishes rapidly as more time is spent in answering user queries. This then results in fewer calls being screened by the help desk and as a result more calls are issued to the service provider directly. The service provider's performance plummets as the call rate escalates. If penalties are operational, less financially able service providers may have to cut back on resources used. This then causes the call rate to skyrocket and the 'fix rate' to free-fall. More and more calls fall into penalty.

Proper resource planning and costing is essential to the correct functioning of any support project.

45.9 Ensure back-to-back agreements are in place with all contributing parties to obtain clear understanding of all requirements

Where the service provider is dependent upon a subcontractor to meet the agreed customer service levels, it is imperative that they sign off a back-to-back service agreement. This is especially true where penalties are levied on the service provider by the customer, for instances of non-conformance to the Service Level Agreement.

It should be noted that the main objective of this agreement is not to recover monies paid over to the customer where the service provider has been penalized due to the subcontractor missing a repair deadline.

The purpose of a back-to-back agreement is to ensure that subcontractors are fully aware of their business obligations and enable them to tailor their service delivery to meet the needs of the service provider. Service providers are then in turn able to meet their own obligations within the main Service Level Agreement with the customer. If, unusually, there is a requirement for the subcontractor to meet with the customer, such meetings should only be conducted in the presence of the prime contractor, i.e. the service provider. Allowing direct third-party contact with the customer may undermine the 'Single Point of Contact' call management strategy and may eventually lead to call management and escalation procedures being circumvented. Such a development is in no one's interest.

45.10 Define escalation paths and procedures and details

Even with the best will in the world, things don't always go according to plan. When disaster does strike and the service level is in danger of being breached, it is every bit as important to keep all interested parties up to date on progress and action plans as it is to work on the actual incident solution. There are few things worse in the business lives of both customer and service provider alike than being grilled by your superior on the status of a fully developed disaster in your area of responsibility and about which you know absolutely nothing.

Escalation points in any escalation system should be embedded sufficiently early on in the development path of the incident to ensure that the appropriate parties are involved in a timely manner.

Some systems employ multi-level escalation points (Table 45.2). For example, in the case of an incident with a service level of 8 hours, and where the incident has not been cleared within 3 hours of call logging, the first level of management involvement is engaged. This may apply to both service provider and customer. If a further 2 hours elapse with the incident remaining unresolved, the next level of management may be engaged. Additional levels of escalation may be invoked, depending on the importance of the call.

TABLE 45.2

Typical escalation path

Escalation level	Service provider action	Customer action
First level of escalation	Service control clerk flags to supervisor. Supervisor contacts resource assigned to incident and provides remote assistance. Supervisor advises customer help desk	Help desk advises internal first-level management
Second level of escalation	Supervisor flags to service manager. Service manager commits more capable resources. Service manager escalates within own organization and advises counterpart in customer organization of status and action plans	Customer management follow own predefined procedures which may include making alternative arrangements to lessen impact of incident on its business
Third level of escalation	Senior management now involved. Wider range of resources now engaged. Senior management now escalate to appropriate customer management, advising status and action plans	Customer management follows own predefined procedures which may include making alternative arrangements to lessen impact of incident on its business
Resolution level of escalation	Disengage resources and conduct post-mortem to lessen risk of repeat. Advise customer of outcome and any proposed changes to methodology, resources or procedures	Disengage resources and conduct post-mortem to lessen risk of repeat. Advise service provider of outcome and any proposed changes to methodology, resources or procedures

Escalation mechanisms are designed to suit the criticality of the incident. It would not be a sensible use of support resources for users to stipulate a priority-1 call for their workstation when they were just about to go on a two-week vacation with no one else scheduled to use the workstation during that period. Conversely, a call to a 'downed' network server may be rated as being extremely critical.

45.11 Ensure all Service Level Management processes are tested prior to and subsequent to live implementation

Service Level Management, by definition, attempts to ensure that the delivery of service is conducted within agreed performance criteria. When instances of nonconformance arise, these should be identified speedily and brought to quick resolution in a controlled and professional manner. This means that all applicable processes must be designed and tested prior to their use in a live environment. This ensures that their usefulness and effectiveness can be depended on once invoked. Similarly, no responsible fire department would wait until it received its first 999 call before testing its fire hoses.

45.12 Accuracy of performance measurement is paramount

There is no hard and fast rule as to whether the customer or the service provider should furnish the Management Information System (MIS) with service data for the purpose of performance measurement.

In some instances each party may bring its own data to review meetings. This arrangement, however, may simply serve to fuel the debate on the comparison of figures presented, thus preventing the proper focus being placed on actual adherence to required service performance levels.

It is therefore recommended that a single trusted source is selected by the parties and that this is used as the basis of measurement. Clearly there is no point in attempting to measure performance if the figures employed are considered suspect.

The systems, procedures and methodologies used in capturing performance data should be included in an appendix to the Service Level Agreement. This then ensures that both parties have satisfied themselves that the manner in which the data is gathered, processed and presented is in accordance with mutual requirements.

45.13 Negotiate viable penalty clauses

In choosing a service provider, it is expected that in the last stages of the selection process, the customer will extract the unique opportunities offered in a 'short-listed' situation to the fullest. It is also becoming increasingly prevalent for customers to shortlist down to a single company, subject to the selected company meeting certain conditions. These conditions are generally based on pricing, service level requirements, penalty clauses and contractual terms.

As may be appreciated, the prospect of imminent contract closure serves to exert great pressure on the over-eager or inexperienced service provider, as in the headlong rush to sign off the contract, all caution may be thrown to the wind.

It may seem therefore that the customer holds all the cards and that the would-be service provider will be ready to sign off on just about anything, including an onerous penalty clause. Both parties should, however, treat this period with great caution.

It should be stressed that the proper function of a penalty clause is not to present customers with an opportunity to subsidize their support costs by eating into the revenue earnings of the erring service provider. It is there for the specific purpose of providing an effective 'point of pain' which, when activated, will ensure that the required correctional focus is brought to bear on substandard performance.

In negotiating and accepting punitive penalties, both the service provider and customer place the sustainability of their operations at risk. A service provider who has agreed to accept large financial penalties and who lacks access to adequate financial backing will quickly lose the ability to resource the project properly. This situation may rapidly deteriorate, with the customer also eventually falling prey to this undesirable situation.

Generally speaking, all penalties should be capped and if possible should not exceed the value of the margin (profit) expected from the service. All reasonable steps should be taken to match the penalty to the actual impact caused. This means that the acceptance of consequential damages should be avoided. To accommodate the vagaries of support cycles, a reasonable period over which service performance is measured should be used, e.g. a rolling two-month period may suit some situations. The overriding criterion is that the method selected should protect the interests of customer and service provider alike.

45.14 Define what circumstances constitute a penalty action

It is important to define carefully those circumstances against which underperformance penalties are levied. Failure to meet the Service Level Agreement requirements may not necessarily constitute a penalty claim by the customer. Extenuating circumstances may have arisen which prevented the service provider from meeting its obligations.

Therefore, in order to protect both parties' interests, a list of items which comprise non-performance penalties should be drawn up and agreed. This list may include conditions such as failure to respond on time, not keeping adequate quantities of stock at the right locations, not assigning appropriately trained personnel to the project, and so on.

The following exception list is by no means exhaustive but may provide a guideline to the type of exceptions that may be included. Exceptions enable the clock to be stopped at the time that they arose and therefore prevent penalties from being levied against the service provider for circumstances outside its control.

Examples of exceptions for a hardware 'Break-Fix' contract:

- *no fault found;*
- *calls logged for types of equipment not listed in the support agreement;*
- *calls being brought about by user abuse;*
- *refused access to equipment by customer;*
- *calls being brought about due to virus infection;*
- *cancelled calls following technician dispatch;*
- *network faults (if the network is not covered by the agreement);*
- *consumable item loaded incorrectly by user e.g. user-induced paper jam on printer;*

- *the time taken to perform software reloads;*
- *PTT telephone line faults;*
- *any time-and-materials call, unless otherwise agreed;*
- *absence of electrical power, lighting etc. at site.*

45.15 Negotiate viable rewards clauses where possible

Some customers do not equate a financial benefit to their business that an improvement on the agreed service level would appear to bring. They will decide on a service level which they believe will meet their business needs. This service level would therefore be used by both parties as a yardstick with which to measure performance. Any improvements delivered on the Service Level Agreement would be viewed by the customer as merely a bonus and perhaps not worth paying the extra for in the way of rewards. The added value to the customer's operations is viewed as intangible.

Other customers, e.g. travel agencies, perceive benefit in maximizing systems availability and are able to draw a direct link to business value. Up-time can improve productivity, which in turn may lead to greater financial return. Conversely, reduced availability may lead to greater costs being incurred in recovering lost time and missed business opportunities.

Under these circumstances, such customers are willing to reward service providers for delivering results which exceed those stipulated in the Service Level Agreement. This arrangement is often to the advantage of both parties. Service providers especially benefit as they receive a monetary incentive to continuously improve their service delivery. This makes them more competitive and, at the same time, able to recover some of the associated costs in developing the service, from the bonuses received. Customers may budget for these service bonus costs in advance, as the benefit is clear to them.

45.16 Define what circumstances constitute a reward action

Where rewards for better than expected service performance have been agreed between the parties, it is important to define when these are in fact merited. It may, for example, be stated that the service provider will be entitled to a reward if the MTTC in any month is improved by a full percentage point, e.g. from 95 per cent of calls being completed within an 8-hour period to 96 per cent of calls being completed within this time-frame. If, on checking, the customer agreed that the monthly MTTC had indeed improved to the required extent, but subsequently discovered that the Repeat Call Rate had gone up by 20 per cent, it is presumed that the customer would no longer feel particularly well disposed to rewarding the service provider.

45.17 Ensure regular Service Level Agreement performance management reviews are in place

The old saying that 'communication is key' is as true today as it ever was. Regular meetings held between customer and service provider are an essential ingredient of a successful partnership. Such gatherings afford both parties the opportunity to air important issues and table new initiatives as well as greatly contribute to the establishment and development of a common dialogue.

45.18 Flexibility of ongoing service

As customers' businesses develop, so too do their service requirements. Service providers should therefore be sensitive to the constantly changing market requirements and adapt their service offerings to suit. It is important, however, to record any changes to requirements in the Service Level Agreement. This then ensures that the expectation gap is kept within manageable limits and that the associated pricing for new services or service enhancements is catered for in the main contract.

In conclusion, the creation and subsequent commitment to a sensible Service Level Agreement should be conducted in the spirit of partnership with your customer. In doing so, a document equitable to the interests and practical capabilities of both parties will be produced.

45.19 Glossary

Service Level Agreement: A document detailing the service obligations of the service provider and the customer in delivering the service. Provision is also made here to detail any customer obligations.

Back-to-back agreement Document which details the obligations of both *prime contractor* and *subcontractor*. The *subcontractor* provides *services* to the *prime contractor*. The back-to-back agreement should be structured to ensure that the subcontractor's obligations match those of the prime contractor, e.g. if the prime contractor has a mean time to respond of 1 hour for software application problems, then the subcontractor should have slightly less than this stated in the back-to-back agreement, to allow for call logging time by the prime contractor.

Prime contractor *service provider* who holds *support* contract with *customer*.

Subcontractor Company to which the *prime contractor* passes an area of support, e.g. applications software support.

Mean time between failure: The average time that a product remains operational between failures.

Next business day (NBD) service: An arrangement whereby any request for *service* received after a predetermined time will not be attended to until the following business day.

Time-and-materials service A *service* provided on a best-endeavours basis only, where labour, travel and parts are charged according to pre-agreed rates.

Repeat call: In the case of a hardware incident, a return visit to the original problem on the same device within a predefined period of time, e.g. a visit to the same problem within five days of the original service call being made.

46 The management of IT service expectations

Rhion Jones HA Ltd, UK; ITSMA, USA
Mike Fox The Transaction Monitoring Benchmarking Group, UK

Summary

The need for IT departments to improve their image and delivered customer satisfaction has been proven. Moreover, it has been firmly established that there is a wide range of people who need to be influenced and there are a variety of ways in which their expectations can be set. Formal training is just one way to encourage the use of marketing best practice, but there are signs that it could be most effective for organizations trying to establish and/or professionalize a customer liaison function.

46.1 Introduction

Both inside and outside the world of Information Technology, customer satisfaction has become a popular issue in recent years. For fast-moving consumer goods (fmcg) as for motor cars, for financial services as for retailing or entertainment, the focus has shifted slowly but steadily away from product innovation towards customer satisfaction. Not surprisingly, the weight of management attention has resulted in the adoption of widely held nostrums and a reasonably unanimous view of the dynamics of customer satisfaction. We know, for example, that satisfaction is not the same as loyalty and that a person can feel satisfied with a product yet be disloyal to the supplier and vice versa. We also know that customer satisfaction is very personal and is influenced by prejudices and predispositions of which a service or product provider is seldom aware. But most of all we have learnt that satisfaction is heavily influenced by expectations. Outside of the IT industry, huge advertising budgets and the efforts of well-staffed marketing departments have been directed at this problem. Furthermore, best practice in this area now gets close to aligning expectations to the reality of product or service delivery so that the result is a well-satisfied customer or client. Within IT departments, however, there has sadly been far less attention given to the issue of customer satisfaction. Here, in the engine-room of service delivery, there is still a technology-led culture and relative inexperience in addressing these issues. There is, indeed, a case for saying that the whole IT industry has only paid lip-service to customer satisfaction. In its race to beat the competition with the latest and fastest, IT suppliers in both hardware and software spheres have traditionally sacrificed customer satisfaction in order to achieve financial and business goals. This is the industry that for three decades had announced products when they were only half-built, launched products before they were quality-tested properly and replaced them with successor products just as they were becoming stable. Against this backdrop, it is no wonder that departments, providing a service to thousands of end users and constantly let down by vendors, developed a cynicism and an acceptance of second best when the challenge they faced required the search for consistent excellence. It is also equally no surprise to find end users and their managers often in despair at the failure to meet their IT requirements. This chapter seeks to address the issue by examining the management of expectations in the world of large-scale IT departments – supporting substantial populations of users. Section 46.2 looks at the relationship between expectations and customer satisfaction, particularly focusing on the different kinds of customer the IT department must address. Section 46.3 looks at the methods available for influencing expectations. Section 46.4 discusses the potential for training IT departments to address the issue and illustrates this potential with an example where the author developed and delivered specific courses for a UK organization that needed to improve its customer satisfaction management.

46.2 Whose expectations?

The defining characteristic of IT usage is the heterogeneity of the customer base. The immense variety of applications is, in itself, extraordinary. But there is also a range of different roles and status occupied by those who take products and services from a IT department. Everyone is, in one sense, a 'user' and many are also 'buyers'. But they all have a different expectation-set and different routes to satisfying those expectations. Figure 46.1 illustrates some of the different roles present in most large-scale IT-using organizations. Let us take some examples. Firstly, let us consider a *line-of-business director*. Such an individual might run a significant part of a major commercial business. Or he or she she might equally run an important part of a public service. What such people seek from IT is a cost-effective means of adding value to the mission of their business or activity. The return on investment (ROI) is critical. Senior budget-holders like this will often be prepared to spend more if they have confidence in the resulting business benefit. In the past, this has often been related to employee productivity. Today, imaginative use of e-commerce and other technologies opens up completely new business models. So the critical issue is *business benefit*, and the critical measure is the confidence with which they can achieve it. If we examine *departmental managers*, there is a change of emphasis. These are people who have operational responsibility for managing today's business; they may also be heavily involved in business change – as determined by the investments committed by their line-of-business director. What they require most is operational effectiveness in current systems. They are inhibited by systems inflexibility, lack of responsiveness or poor execution of change-related projects. Increasingly these are managers called upon to meet ever more demanding operational targets, yet dependent upon IT systems without being able to control them. The single most sought-after attribute is *flexibility* – in this context meaning the ability of IT to deploy its systems to meet rapidly changing requirements. Staff who make use of IT systems on a regular basis have long been called *users*, but a distinction must be drawn between them and *lead users*. All users are affected by the system interface, the quality of the functionality, and its delivery to the desktop. They are equally affected by the way the IT organization

FIGURE 46.1

Roles in IT-using organizations

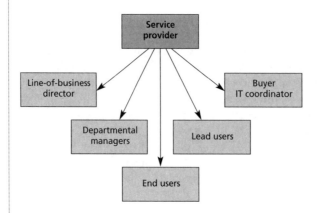

relates to its users. The nature of the help desk, the availability of assistance, and its ability to have empathy with the tasks performed by the user are all critical factors shaping expectation and satisfaction. Where lead users differ is that these are the people who often act on behalf of large numbers of users in determining when to call for assistance and what priority to give to various users. Their prime concern will be *responsiveness* and the track record of IT support in addressing the issues brought to its attention. Finally, where IT functions have adopted the purchaser–provider model, there is an increasing likelihood that user departments will have collaborated together to appoint a *buyer*; seldom, however, will the term be used. A more likely title will be IT Coordinator or Systems Manager. In essence, the role is to understand the business requirements and deal at arm's length with the IT department in order to procure the right products and services to satisfy the business needs. Budget responsibilities are usually within the departments themselves, so there is a wide variety of practices regarding financial responsibility. For these people, however, what matters is the capability of the supplier to deliver; many of them have the remit to shop around and buy from outside (or outsource) if internal resources cannot do the job. Key criteria are similar to other buying roles and include an ability to meet specification, terms and conditions, price and the quality of service. One word to capture the essence of this group's interests would be *professionalism*. Their expectations and satisfaction would be largely influenced by the supplier's standing on this factor. Almost all large-scale organizations will have the above, but in varying ratios. A major UK concern familiar to the author has about 20 line-of-business directors, about 750 departmental managers, some 25,000 users and 150 buyers. What matters is that IT departments recognize that the dynamics of expectation management and customer satisfaction work very differently for each role. To compound the problem, individuals often hold more than one role. Many managers are, of course, end users. Other managers act as buyers in the absence of dedicated resources applied to this task. The impact of this role analysis can be illustrated by looking at the different issues which matter to each role regarding two popular forms of IT service – the internal help desk and the technical support intranet (Table 46.1).

These issues are often a reflection not of the role-player's own priorities but the product of the relationship between the role and other roles. Therefore, the lead user

TABLE 46.1
Roles and their key issues

Role	Key issues re IT help desk	Key issues re technical support intranet
Line-of-business director	Reasonable cost High fix rate Good end-user satisfaction ratings	Acceptable cost Coverage % utilization Measurable cost avoidance
Departmental managers	Reliable performance Excellent escalation for priority issues	Business relevance Controllable access Deployment implications
Lead users	Excellent technical skills Reliable access Good follow-up	Effectiveness Reliability User friendliness
End users	Excellent access Empathy Ability to fix *my* problem	Ease of navigation Response time % hit rate re information required
Buyers	Service availability Clear-up rate Satisfaction ratings	Charges Frequency of updating User reactions

is interested in the overall performance of the help desk, because they have to deal with a volume of calls generated by many end users. The end users themselves have a more limited perspective and are essentially concerned with reliable access and a satisfactory answer to their *own* problems on this one occasion. Both buyers and managers are heavily influenced by the views of the staff in general. Widespread dissatisfaction by subordinate staff will inevitably affect the managers' opinions of the IT department – even if their own objectives appear to them to be satisfactorily met. Similarly, a buyer normally collects the views of key people before entering into discussions with a service provider and is most likely influenced by what he or she hears – regardless of how representative it can be. To summarize, the factors that matter vary, and role analysis is essential if IT departments are to be effective in managing customer perceptions.

46.3 Techniques for managing expectations

Expectations are shaped by the interplay of three different elements. One is the management interface to the customer base; one is the publication of documents and formal communication of information; the third is the accumulated personal and reported experience of individuals.

Management interface

Many large IT departments have now appointed customer liaison managers or account managers. They are there to represent the service provider to the customer base and their job is to manage the dialogue with the buyer as defined in Section 46.2. The advent of widespread IT outsourcing encouraged the further development of the account manager concept in IT, but its application in an internal IT department always had a different emphasis. The classic responsibility of account managers in the external world is to sell products and services. In doing so they have to get close to the client, understand the requirements and constraints and ensure that existing offers delivered sufficient satisfaction. All that the internal account manager lacked in the job specification was the responsibility to sell. But with the devolution of budgets into operating units, the liberalization of procurement rules and the growth of effective external competition, these account managers have increasingly found themselves in a selling role. If not always overtly selling, they are often defending existing business levels and seeking to prevent services being bought from another supplier. Experience shows that many appointments to these roles have been made without sufficient regard to the need for marketing skills. After all, the task of communicating with the customer base was traditionally carried out within the IT department and its formalization into a defined role was not always seen as a significant change. But the reality is that, once these roles are established and the accompanying practices of documenting requirements, holding regular service reviews and managing issues and problems take hold, they have a huge influence upon expectations. Effective customer liaison managers or account managers need three areas of expertise. Technical knowledge of the service provider's capabilities is one. Business knowledge of the operating environment and the scope for technology to contribute to success is a second. But the third is sufficient understanding of services marketing to appreciate the impact on customer expectations of the way in which this important interface is handled. The Boston-based ITSMA (Information Technology Services Marketing Association) has specialized in understanding the specific requirements of marketing IT services and has pioneered research into best practice in this fast-moving area. ITSMA defines three types of IT services:

- operational services such as installations, hardware maintenance or help-desk support;
- enhancement services such as training, network enhancements or migration to new systems;
- professional services such as IT consulting, major applications development or outsourcing.

All three of the above require different marketing strategies and a different mix of communication techniques in order to optimize the message. Few of the customer liaison staff appointed from within IT departments have the breadth of experience and knowledge to do this and are, therefore, likely to create false expectations in the customer base.

Information and publications

A second influence upon expectations is what is distributed. When asked, internal IT users and managers have often demonstrated amazing ignorance about the services which IT departments provide. Happily, this is not the situation everywhere and there is abundant evidence that communicating relevant information can succeed in moulding client perceptions. Below is a brief review of information, which can play a part in creating the right environment.

Service level agreements (SLAs)

These document the obligations of the service provider and in so far as they stipulate the detail of each service that is to be delivered, they ought to be, in principle, an important source of information about the standards to be expected. Unfortunately, they have frequently become semi-legalistic and bureaucratic. Vast numbers of unwieldy documents drafted in a defensive manner by suppliers anxious to protect themselves from liability are utterly useless as a vehicle to mould expectations. Only those in the buyer role are likely to read them and their very nature precludes an understanding of the service delivery promise. Too many suppliers believe that the existence of an SLA means that customers know what to expect. Even if customers were assumed to have access to and be able to comprehend the document, it is most unlikely that they could translate a commitment '*to escalate 90 per cent of problems unresolved at first level to second level within 24 hours*' into anything meaningful. SLAs may influence the perception of buyers but are largely irrelevant to other users and managers.

Service charters

These are marketing-style documents prepared by the supplier to convert SLAs into meaningful commitments. When properly prepared, these are a big step forward and should ideally be distributed to every end user. They serve as excellent induction-training materials for new starters and, where changes are introduced, they can provide the script for managers briefing their staff. Some have objected that the term 'charter' is misleading in suggesting a status which the document does not, in reality, have. Critics are right to point out that it has no contractual effect. But then neither does an SLA in most internal situations. Another objection is that a charter tends to focus on some promises rather than give a comprehensive picture of the supplier's obligations. But the whole point of setting expectations is to give the customer an insight into what you are proposing to do for him or her. A supermarket wanting to position itself as a value brand name will advertise competitive prices in order to lure customers into the store; it will not seek to provide them with an exhaustive price list. It knows that if it sets an expectation and then fails to fulfil it, trouble will lie ahead. Therefore, service charters, carefully designed around key promises, can be very effective.

In-house newsletters etc.

These can be remarkably useful because they can disguise the expectation management in the volume of legitimate business and human-interest stories. IT departments have a lot of news to impart but many of them do it badly. When a newsletter is used it can deflect criticism that users and managers are not being kept informed and also allow for subtle messages regarding service standards. This medium is ideal for announcing minor but important changes. A good example might be a company help desk, which expects to have more problems closing certain types of calls during the summer holiday period, because they rely on two skilled people, one of whom might be away at any one time. This is a classic expectation-management issue. In such circumstances, no one modifies an SLA. Since the volume of calls is reduced anyway, there is reason to assume that the service level will not be compromised much. However, the truth is that, when the issue does arise, the actual capability to resolve it is lower and smart companies try to influence customers' expectations accordingly. Some companies have found that it is useful to 'personalize' business messages as a means of humanizing otherwise mechanical processes. Good newsletters put IT services into a people context, with the emphasis on the individuals who deliver to members of staff. Done well, a newsletter acts to build more tolerance at the range of performance; in cases of poor performance, it can serve to dissipate anger by encouraging such reactions as *'they're only human'*.

Published performance statistics

Quality management initiatives, in recent years, have encouraged the practice of sharing operational performance data with staff and customers. Many call centres cover their walls with graphs of more colour than meaning. In terms of expectation management, this is a double-edged sword. Anyone who reads a graph that hovers consistently at or around the same level can have confidence that this is the level of service to expect. But what if this is rather higher than the contracted level of service? Does the supplier, who is successful in over-achieving, necessarily want to raise, ever upwards, the expectation for service improvements? If the key to customer satisfaction is to overachieve versus expectation, then a wise manager often dampens expectations in case of unforeseen problems. Possibly the best compromise is to report in such a way as to create most confidence in the desired service norm. Here is an example. Instead of reporting the average installation lead time variably as anything between 10 days and 20 days (leaving the customer to guess whether the supplier will be performing well or badly when his or her turn comes up), the IT department could just report the percentage of weeks when a target of 18 days was achieved. It is the same raw data, but different expectation management. There is a wide range of other information dissemination methods ranging from poster campaigns to e-mail and Web-related processes. What is needed is a mindset that recognizes that the customers' perceptions can be significantly affected by professional work in this area.

Personal experience

The third and most obvious source of expectations lies in each customer's individual experience. Traditional IT departments and the technology available to them took insufficient account of this and often created processes (e.g. batch job control) which left little scope to respond to individuals *per se*. But in a world where everyone has a PC on the desk yet works in different business environments, it is essential to recognize the differences in personal priorities and the way in which people could react differently to the identical supplier experience. Recent research in customer satisfaction and customer loyalty has highlighted the importance of each transaction. A customer might be the recipient of a service on many occasions during the course of a year. Yet it is only necessary for one experience to go badly wrong, causing the supplier's reputation to suffer in the mind of the customer. This is why leading IT organizations now perform a special kind of survey called Transaction Monitoring. This means asking the client '*how was it for you?*' after an engineer site visit or a help-desk call or after software installation. This is also why there is considerable interest now in benchmarking the results of such surveys. Since they are fairly simple questionnaires and are not as complex as corporate-wide satisfaction surveys, it is becoming possible to compare perceptions across the internal IT world. In the UK, several of the largest IT functions meet together as the *Transaction Monitoring Benchmarking Group* and are beginning to exchange data on such matters. What the data shows and what all focus groups reveal is that an identical service can yield vastly differing perceptions. This is a result of expectations, which are created in the mind of the customer and which are the result of two inputs – external and internal. The external inputs include those covered by the above-mentioned items such as publications. Internal inputs include the predisposition of the individual as well as the accumulated experience of working with or receiving the products and services of the supplier.

46.4 The potential for training IT services managers in marketing

If it is accepted that expectation management needs more attention in order for IT departments to achieve higher satisfaction ratings from their customers, then it is fair to consider what are the best methods to bring this about. IHA has worked with the ITSMA in Boston to develop courseware for IT Services Marketing. This in itself has been instructional for identifying a whole host of situations where the *IT environment makes different demands upon marketers.* The speed of technological change is such, for example, that in other industries, product development staff can go out and interview their current clients and ask them what they want to see in the next product; this does not work in IT. Few clients understand or appreciate what is just around the corner technologically. So when IBM asked its customers what they wanted in the late 1970s or early 1980s, they responded by asking for more and bigger mainframes; nobody talked about the PC. So there is now a definite body of knowledge about how to market IT (as opposed to other) services. We are also learning how to adapt these techniques to fit the internal situation. In 1999, one of the UK's leading public services invited IHA to develop a special course for its customer liaison managers. These had been appointed from a variety of backgrounds and were in daily contact with buyers, managers and users of all kinds in a very large, culturally diverse and complex organization. The course was entitled *Services Marketing for IT Departments* and was held off-site over two days. As well as using ITSMA methods, it used three role-playing and group exercises designed to give the managers greater confidence in dealing with challenging issues. The first exercise involved the preparation for a discussion with customers who needed a new application. Experience shows that many misunderstandings arise in the services required from an IT department if they do not meticulously research the customer's business requirements at the outset. This case study gives managers practice in asking the right questions. The second exercise is a Help Desk Focus Group, which is a well-proven way for managers to learn how different personal experiences can influence individual perceptions. The third exercise is a full-scale role-play to give managers experience with the dynamics of the purchaser–provider relationship. Two teams are set up. One represents the customer – a mixture of buyers and managers. The other team represents the IT function, including a customer liaison role. Both teams prepare with detailed briefs and the course moderator chairs a review meeting where the tensions of the situation are managed and lessons are learnt.

The *Help Desk Focus Group Simulation* was developed from real-life experiences and involves course participants advising management about actions required to improve user perceptions of the help desk. Course members are given eight summaries (400–500 words) of the experience and perceptions of very different users of the help-desk. These range from technical users who are critical of the skills of the help-desk staff through to managers who rely on hearsay and end users who are regular and highly satisfied users. By examining the minutiae of each one's experience, course members learn the complex correlation with customer satisfaction perceptions and are able to consider which operational improvements are likely to yield the best return in terms of customer opinion. A major conclusion of this simulation is that the user base must be segmented and services tailored to meet very different requirements wherever possible.

The result of the training course was that the participants gained more confidence in using well-proven marketing techniques in the internal IT environment and were able to make informed choices about which ones were best applicable to their own corporate culture.

47 Is there life after ITIL?

A literature study into the future of the updated IT Infrastructure Library

Lisette Favier Compaq Computer BV

Summary

When looking at the current status of IT management in organizations, one notices a marked interest in ITIL (IT Infrastructure Library). Most CIOs are aware of its existence as a result of a growing interest in IT management and increasing management costs. In the *World Class IT Service Management Guide 2000* the author reflected the content of ITIL against developments to be expected by IT organizations. Now, with ITIL being revised recently, the updated ITIL components are being held up to the light of future developments again. In other words, what is the future of updated ITIL?

47.1 Introduction

ITIL is the abbreviation for Information Technology Infrastructure Library. This library consists of books describing five principal elements of IT Service Management: Business Perspective, Managing Applications, Deliver IT Services, Support IT Services and Manage the Infrastructure. The description is derived from a collection of best management practices. The objective of ITIL is formulated as follows: 'to facilitate improvements in efficiency and effectiveness in the provision of quality IT Services and the management of the IT Infrastructure within any organization'.

In this chapter the content of ITIL is reflected upon developments with which IT organizations are expected to be confronted in the coming years. Before dealing with these developments, we will first describe the current status of ITIL. It is assumed that the reader is familiar with the basic concepts of ITIL.

This chapter does not judge the quality of ITIL or whether the interest in ITIL is justified or not. Shortcomings or limitations, other than those related to the future, are therefore not discussed.

47.2 ITIL: current state of affairs

Publications concerning ITIL do not so much deal with the content of ITIL but, rather, with its implementation in an organization. What is remarkable is that in practice the utilization of ITIL remains confined to the implementation of two of the five principal elements: Supporting IT Services and Delivering IT Services. Although this was noted by both Looijen (1998b) and Grift (1998), neither of them provides any explanation for this phenomenon, nor can an explanation for this limited implementation be found in the literature.

A possible explanation could be that ITIL has only been used in the Netherlands since the early 1990s and therefore is not yet sufficiently mature for full implementation. Another explanation could lie in the fact that most problems arise in the areas related to the two elements mentioned and that this is where the need for proven practical experience is the greatest. A third explanation for the limited implementation can be sought in the vicious circle in which ITIL finds itself: as implementation is confined to Supporting IT Services and Delivering IT Services, CIOs are not aware of the existence of the other elements. The other elements are not implemented, with the result that they remain unknown. By the way, there is a chance of this vicious circle being breached by promotion activities around the updated elements of ITIL. In addition, a library element named Planning to Implement Service Management, which is under development by CCTA (now OCG), might also broaden the utilization of the ITIL elements.

Knowledge of ITIL alone is definitely not enough to arrive at management processes that have been organized in conformity with ITIL. Grift noted a growing awareness that the implementation of ITIL is nothing more than an organization improvement process. He identifies a number of aspects that must be taken into account to arrive at a successful implementation of ITIL ('successful' being defined as achieving the desired situation). The aspects involved are the following: vision and strategy of the IT management, corporate culture, management style, quality and quantity of personnel, and costs. Looijen (1998b) places ITIL in a more scientific approach for implementation of an IT management organization. He calls this the Managerial Step-by-Step Plan.

47.3 Expected developments in IT management

A number of expected IT management developments and their possible consequences for IT (management) organizations are reviewed in this section. These developments concern 2002–2005. The review is used in the next section as the basis for forecasting the possible future of ITIL.

The selection of developments is based on the Compendium definition of IT management (van Bon, 1998): *the maintenance of a system or service, according to the agreed demands and in the specified circumstances.* In this definition he implicitly distinguishes three elements: the IT infrastructure, the information systems and the management organization. The literature on possible future developments has, therefore, been examined from these three angles.

Some of these developments described by the various authors overlap to a certain extent. These commonalities have been used to cluster the developments in IT management:

- a further shift within IT organizations: from a focus on technology to a focus on the user, his or her business and the added value of IT services;
- more outsourcing of non-strategic IT functions;

- changing composition of internal IT management organizations;
- shifting applications development away from the internal IT organization;
- increased cooperation between business management and IT management;
- implementation of e-business services.

User-business-focused management organizations

Focus on the users and their business

The shift continues from a management organization focused on technology to an organization which places the emphasis on its users and the service it provides to its users. A growing number of IT management organizations are introducing functions such as account management, product management and service management. The entire management organization will have to participate in this growth if a gap between 'sales and production' is to be avoided. After all, if the rest of the management organization is not professionalized, contact with the user may improve but not the quality of the service to that user (Bosselaers *et al.*, 1998).

In the coming years, the managers of IT management organizations will have to find a balance between sustaining current service levels and preparing future service provision (Bosselaers *et al.*, 1998). In a user-business-oriented management organization, their role will also change: managers of IT organizations will be involved in continuously changing their management organization, while the daily provision of services will have to continue (instead of the other way round).

In the coming years this shift will lead to changes in the product and service offering of IT management organizations (van der Zee, 1997). These changes will take place in the *composition* of products and services provided by IT management organizations on the one hand, and the *manner* in which they are offered on the other.

Active input by the user

The IT management organization cannot achieve the above by itself: the active input of the user is essential. Bosselaers *et al.* (1998) typify this input as follows: 'The user and the IT organization must work together in balance. A high-quality IT organization can only emerge if the user group is providing adequate input.'

Proactive management

In the future, users will expect a more proactive attitude from IT management organizations. An IT organization in which the user business is the focal point will have to demonstrate its involvement with its users. This means that it cannot afford to wait until user demands have penetrated the IT management organization, but will have to adopt an attitude that is characterized by a proactive itemization of users' latent and potential needs and requirements (van der Zee, 1997).

This again demonstrates the importance of functions such as account management, product management and service management by IT management organizations. Markus (1996) even predicts the emergence of two new functions geared exclusively to proactive user support. The first function is that of *IT use facilitator* that she defines as follows: 'Someone who works closely with people to help them learn new tools and discover new work methods'. The second new function involves proactive management at strategic level through *IT public goods facilitators* or *change agents*. These facilitators support (inter)organizational units in identifying the required IT services in the medium term.

It is expected that a proactive attitude of IT management organizations will be supported better in the coming years by the utilization of modelling and simulation technology. Stumpel *et al.* (1997) describe how simulation models can be used to plan and optimize infrastructures from a technical point of view (required bandwidth, design of client–server applications, etc.). Looijen (1998a) defines simulation as one of the phases in his Managerial Step-by-Step Plan. Simulation models can also be used to plan and optimize the *design* of management organizations. For example, the question of how many help-desk agents will be required in the case of future expansion of IT services can be answered in this way.

Selective outsourcing of IT functions

All the publications studied on the future of IT management predict an increase in selective outsourcing by IT organizations. The authors also recognize that this type of outsourcing will concern IT functions that are not directly related to the primary business processes.

Creation of partnerships

At present, selective outsourcing is usually based on a performance obligation to be met by one or more suppliers. Bosselaers predicts that, in the coming years, outsourcing based on a performance obligation will be replaced by measurable service agreements, risk-sharing arrangements and professional contract management between the supplier and the internal IT organization. In this context one no longer refers to suppliers but to IT partners, which implies a much more proactive attitude. After all, a partner is expected to contribute to ideas about current and future IT services at all levels (operational, tactical and strategic). A supplier can no longer afford to work according to the 'your wish is our command' principle as this is far too reactive.

Other reasons for outsourcing

According to Rockart *et al.* (1996) the reasons for outsourcing will also change in the years to come. At present, outsourcing is often used as a cost-saving measure and to compensate for the lack IT expertise and skills within the IT organization. In the years to come, this cost-saving motive will be replaced by using outsourcing as a weapon towards achieving a competitive edge. By entering into partnerships with external parties, the internal IT organization expects to be able to respond better to the demands made of the efficiency and flexibility of the IT infrastructure, thereby achieving and maintaining a lead on the competitors. It is expected that the second motive (supplementing IT knowledge and skills) will continue to exist.

As in the previous cluster (a shift towards user-business-focused management organizations), developments in selective outsourcing will lead to changes in the role of CIOs in IT management organizations. They will have to develop into mature partners for external parties, into well-informed buyers and into strong negotiators, and will have to gain fulfilment from 'seeing a job well done, not just from doing it' (Rockart *et al.*, 1996).

Composition and structure of IT management organizations

Some authors expect the composition of management organizations to change in the next few years. The IT organization will need a different type of employee and will also identify other functions. In addition, the organizational structure of the company itself will also change.

Characteristics of employees and functions

Two functions in support of proactive management have been described above: that of IT use facilitator and change agent. Rockart *et al.* (1996) also find that an IT management organization that focuses on the user and his or her business will no longer consist of only system professionals, but will also need business consultants. These are the people who are able to estimate the added value of IT services, who are able to talk to users about it and convert the added value into IT solutions (at both tactical and operational levels). The literature also refers to functions/roles such as IT architect, IT economist, IT visionary, IT project manager and the external role of an IT partner.

All these types of employees are personally responsible for the correct performance of their duties. Not only do they deal with the assignments they receive; they are also actively involved in finding and distributing the work to be performed. Each employee personally manages his or her work portfolio on behalf of the user (Bosselaers *et al.*, 1998). Personal skills required include customer-friendliness and commercial insight. In addition, the employees 'of the future' will be expected to be self-auditing, have a growing learning ability thanks to an outward focus and must regard the evaluation and testing of processes as a matter of course. This must be reinforced by appropriate career counselling, assessment systems and a motivating reward structure (van der Zee, 1997).

Managing such a group of professionals will make high demands on the skills of the managers at IT management organizations. A number of the required management skills have already been described (finding a balance between current and future services, dealing with external partners).

Structure of IT organizations

In the years to come, IT management organizations will continue to work with a clearly (user-)recognizable front office with a professional back office behind it (Rockart *et al.*, 1996). The front office has direct control of the back office, without being hampered by hierarchical relationships. The involvement of the back office is usually based on a make-or-buy decision.

Whether or not to centralize the IT management organization, and all possible forms between these two extremes (centralized versus localized) is a regular topic of research and one that is the subject of ever-changing insights. In the literature on the future of management organizations, only Rockart *et al.* (1996) venture to discuss this topic. They predict that in the years to come a mixed form will evolve with the following characteristics. A vision of IT services will be formed at central level, where the strategy will be determined and the primary operational tasks performed. At local level (e.g. at the business unit level), priorities are set with regard to the centrally formulated strategy. The criteria that determine the priorities are derived from the requirements generated by the primary process of a specific organization unit. In a number of years, these local parts of the IT organization will no longer have their own growth plan or annual plan, but will have become an integral part of a specific business plan.

Application development out of the internal IT organization

Although application and system development is beyond the scope of a management organization, changes in this area most certainly affect the management. Markus (1996) describes a future in which application and system development moves away from the IT organization: on the one hand towards the users and on the other hand towards external developers. This shift is caused by the need for more rapid development of applications from a competitive point of view: the time-to-market of new products and services is becoming shorter and application development must keep pace with that. Markus also predicts that more 'customer-off-the-shelves' software will appear with which users can develop their own business applications. The IT use facilitators referred to above will play an important role in supporting users of this software.

Cooperation between business management and IT management

In the years ahead, IT opportunities will be identified by CIOs as well as business managers. This will make business management and IT management jointly responsible for the balance between the demand and supply of information provision and IT services (Bosselaers *et al.*, 1998). This development will affect the CIOs of the future as well as the business managers of the future. The CIO will have to have extensive knowledge of both IT and business processes. The business manager too will have to have insight into the possibilities of IT and serve as an enabler of business processes at operational, tactical and strategic level. Probably a role can also be played in this context by the IT use facilitator and the change agent.

In this way CIOs and business managers will be able to strengthen each other for the benefit of the organization. Currently, more and more CIOs seem to become participators in the Board of Directors of companies. Bosselaers describes this development as follows: 'The IT manager who has progressed from programmer or operator will be unable to survive without the skills of the "general" business manager. How can we use IT to achieve a competitive edge in the market, at what speed and in what way can we mobilize professionals to provide suitable IT services in response to these questions. Questions that demand an integral approach.'

Implementation of e-business services

Redmond (2000) states it very straightforwardly: e-business services require e-service management. E-service management is characterized by:

- critical information systems to support the main business processes;
- high level of services (365 × 24 hours availability, performance and security);
- international distribution of customers, suppliers and employees;
- customers, suppliers and employees having high expectations.

According to Wiebolt and Wong (2000) and the abovementioned characteristics, an IT organization managing e-business services must be able to make healthy, strategic decisions, gain control of the infrastructure in an efficient and effective way, keep in close touch with customers and provide 100% reliable services. And there is one aspect on which authors about e-service management agree: swiftness in decision making and acting is absolutely key!

47.4 Discussion: ITIL and the future

In this section the developments (keep in mind that they are still predictions!) are viewed in terms of the current, updated content of ITIL. This will ultimately lead to a conclusion on the future of ITIL. Although it is stated in Section 47.2 that only two of the five principal elements were found, all elements of ITIL are taken into consideration below.

Developments within the context of ITIL

Shift to user-business-focused management organizations

The shift to user-business-oriented management organizations described above is generally strongly represented in ITIL, and particularly in the form of the ITIL processes Customer Relationship Management, Service Level Management and Service Desk. The Service Level Management process could probably be subdivided into the three following processes: Service Level Marketing, Account Management and Product/Service Management, in view of their increasing importance in the future. The persons responsible for these processes must also be in charge of offering products and services in terms that can be recognized by the users and which are tuned to the needs of the users.

However, what is lacking in ITIL is a management process at strategic level that is geared to the systematic identification of IT developments and with which the CIO can prepare himself/herself for future services while maintaining the current service level. As the principal element, Business Perspective, is still under development at the time of publication, it is not clear whether this gap will be filled by the Business Perspective element.

Although ITIL contains a number of proactive components (such as the Problem Management and Capacity Management processes), these are still too limited when seen in the light of the expectations. The deployment of the IT use facilitator and change agents could alleviate this limitation to a certain extent. Besides this, a number of processes could be expanded with simulation activities geared to the organizational structure of IT management.

The changing structure and design of internal IT management organizations

In the future, high demands will be made on employees and managers of IT management organizations: greater responsibility, self-auditing characteristics and commercial insight, to name but a few. A number of new roles and functions will also develop. Although this may not seem obvious at first glance, it could be useful to add a human resource component to ITIL that includes general and IT-specific human resource aspects. This component will support managers at all levels and may prove a useful tool for the employees themselves. In the updated version of ITIL, the importance of HR aspects has been recognized partly. The 'best practices' on Service Desk contains recommendations on soft skills, education and training, staff profiles, roles and functions. In other ITIL processes, the description is limited to roles only. In addition, interesting research has been done recently by Schreuder (2000) on ITIL impacting the quality of labour.

The localize/centralize issue is recognized by ITIL. Any organization that uses ITIL for the design of IT management will have to make a decision on this issue. It goes without saying that the considerations in favour of either can be collected per subject and entered in ITIL (as is being done and *only* being done for Service Desk so far).

Selective outsourcing of IT functions

Outsourcing is described in ITIL to a very limited extent, although publication of the Business Perspective book is expected to supply this need. Until then, supervision of the suppliers is geared solely to operational level and is reactive by nature ('Your wish is our command'). If ITIL is to have a future, it will have to be expanded to include guidelines for the management of partnerships at strategic, tactical and operational level. The Information Services Procurement Library (ISPL) that appeared in 1999 could possible play an important role in this, together with the Business Perspective book. This expansion is shown in Figure 47.1.

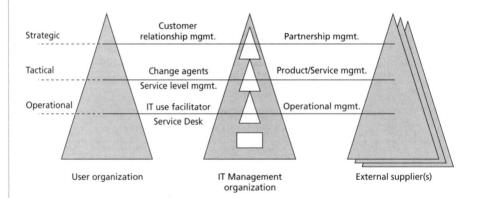

FIGURE 47.1

Management of partnerships

Shift in application development: away from the internal IT organization towards user organization or supplier

The shift of application development to the user organization or supplier will have a significant impact on Release Management and Change Management processes. In current Release Management, all activities take place in isolated environments: the development, testing, operational and archiving environments. It will become an extremely complex task to manage these when new versions of applications are developed and tested outside the IT management organization. Although the complexity of this is recognized by ITIL, it does not suggest a way to deal with management of components developed outside the IT management organization. It remains to be seen whether the Release Management function will still be able to meet its main objective in the future: to ensure that hardware and software being changed is traceable, secure and that only correct, authorized and tested versions are installed. Pressure will also increase on the performance of the Change Management and Configuration Management processes, enforcing even closer cooperation. It may be possible that technical tools will be developed to support these processes in the future.

Increased cooperation between business management and IT management
The growing cooperation between business management and IT management is already covered by ITIL, and in the same capacity as described at the beginning of this section: by direct contact between the user organization and the management organization at both tactical and strategic levels.

Implementation of e-business services
E-service management is not (yet) distinguished within ITIL as a specific area of service management, although the basic ingredients are covered by (updated) ITIL: Security Management, Capacity and Availability Management and several aspects of Continuity Management. In addition, there is some awareness in the updated library for international distribution of customers and employees of IT management departments. For instance, the possibility of having a 'virtual' Service Desk or a 'virtual' Change Advisory Board is, to some degree, discussed in the Service Support element of ITIL.

However, the most worrying part of the requirements for managing e-business services is definitely 'swiftness in decision making and acting'. Is an IT management organization, using the ITIL best practices, capable of delivering e-services in a fast and flexible way, but at the same time in a secure, reliable and cost-conscious way also? The answer to this question is not so much found in the *contents* of ITIL, but probably much more in *implementing* the ITIL 'way-of-working' in an IT management environment (which is beyond the scope of this chapter). However, it is not unlikely that within a few years these implementation experiences with e-service management will lead to new 'best practices' to be added to ITIL.

Table 47.1 reviews the results of the reflection as described above.

47.5 Conclusions

In summary, it may be concluded that the relationships maintained by user and management organizations will become a powerful tool in the future. It could well be that this strength should be reinforced by expanding the objective of ITIL: 'To facilitate improvements in efficiency and effectiveness in the provision of quality IT services and the management of the IT infrastructure within any organization, *in close cooperation with customers and IT Partners.*'

A distinct shortcoming is the current lack of the management of partnerships (probably resolved in the short term with publication of the Business Perspective book), lack of a management process for the systematic survey of IT developments and a partly lacking the human resource component. In addition, the Release Management process will come under pressure. And, finally, ITIL's capabilities of managing e-services are not clear yet: the fundamentals are present, but the actual performance depends on the implementation of the best practices.

TABLE 47.1 Future expectations and ITIL

Developments in IT management	ITIL compatible?
Shift towards user-business-focused management organizations	*OK/Partly*
• User and business key	OK
• Balance current/future service by IT management	Partly
• Changed products/services package	OK
• Active input by user	OK
• Proactive management	Partly
Selective outsourcing of IT functions	*Work in progress*
• Development of IT partnerships	Work in progress
• Other reasons for outsourcing	N.a.
Changed structure and design of IT management organizations	*Partly*
• Characteristics of employees and functions	Partly
Structure of IT organizations	*OK/partly*
• Front/back office	OK
• Centralized/localized	Partly
Shift of application development away from IT organization	Major impact on Release, Change and Configuration Management.
Increasing cooperation between business management and IT management	OK
Implementation of e-business services	Partly; basic components are present

Therefore, the conclusion is the same as before ITIL was updated: in its *current* form it will encounter difficulties in the future owing to these shortcomings. The strength of relationships between the user and the IT management organization may compensate for these defects, but probably not to a sufficiently adequate level. However, if the (IT) management of an ITIL-compatible management organization is aware of the future limitations of ITIL and implements suitable measures in time, there is no reason to throw ITIL overboard. ITIL certainly has a future as long as the conditions described above are met.

Finally, the extent to which ITIL contains *superfluous* subjects is another approach to the issue that may be interesting to include in the debate. It may even supply an answer to the question of why only two of the five elements are used in practice.

Literature

van Bon, J. (1998) Inleiding, in: *IT beheer jaarboek 1998*, Ten Hagen & Stam Uitgevers, The Hague, pp. 15–18.

van Bon, J. (1998) 'Compendium IT Beheer', in: *IT beheer jaarboek 1998*, Ten Hagen & Stam Uitgevers, The Hague, pp. 163–206.

Bosselaers, T., Griep, M., Dodok van Heel, J., Vandecasteele, J. and Weerts, R. (1998), 'De toekomst van de IT-organisatie', in: *IT beheer jaarboek 1998*, Ten Hagen & Stam Uitgevers, The Hague, pp. 61–73.

Grift, F.U. (1998), *De vergeten dimensie van ITIL*, website for Quint Wellington Redwood Nederland BV.

de Jong, W. (1998), Simulatie als tool binnen IT-beheer, in: *IT beheer jaarboek 1998*, Ten Hagen & Stam Uitgevers, The Hague, pp. 255–60.

Koops, E. and Hinfelaar, J.A.F. (1998), 'ICT-beheer: hoe minder hoe beter', *Automatisering Gids*, 42.

Looijen, M. (1998a), 'Beheer van informatiesystemen: een beheer stappenplan', in: *IT beheer jaarboek 1998*, Ten Hagen & Stam Uitgevers, pp. 27–38.

Looijen, M. (1998b), *Beheer van informatiesystemen*, Kluwer Bedrijfsinformatie BV., Deventer.

Markus, M. L. (1996), 'The Futures of IT Management', *The DATA BASE for Advances in Information Systems*, 27(4), 68–84.

Mulder, L. (1997), 'Een SWOT-analyse van ITIL', *Interprominent*.

Redmond, H. (2000), 'Een verkenning van e-service management', *IT Beheer Magazine voor IT Service en Security Management*, 4, 41–4.

Rockart, J.F., Earl, M.J. and Ross, J.W. (1996), 'Eight imperatives for the new IT organisation', *Sloan Management Review*, Fall, 43–55.

Roelands, R. (1998), 'Infrastructuur beheren is organiseren', *Computable*, 21, 47.

Schreuder, K. (2000), *Wat doet ITIL met mensen*, Paradoxale en andere gevolgen van ITIL voor de kwaliteit van de arbeid, Amsterdam.

Stumpel, E.J.H.M., Gootzen, H.G.P. and Ribbers, P.M.J (1997), 'Betere beheersing met proactief beheer', *Computable*, 33, p. 25.

Wiebolt, J. and Wong, I., (2000), 'IT Service Management en het Internet: het beheer van e-services', in: *IT beheer jaarboek 2000*, Ten Hagen & Stam Uitgevers, pp. 327–37.

Zaal, R. (1998), 'Statische modellen maken IT-beheer star', *Automatisering Gids*, 42.

van der Zee, H. (1997), 'Transformatie van de IT-organisatie', *Holland/Belgium Management Review*, 53, 63–74.

48 Russian roulette

Dick Costeris Ordina

Summary

The exciting game of Russian roulette is played with a handgun, in which one bullet is loaded at random. The participants in the game place the gun, one after another, against their heads and gently squeeze the trigger. Usually the game ends when the first participant dies. A reason for playing this game is considered 'the kick'; (not) killing yourself seems to be very exciting.

Of course, the chances of surviving the game are influenced negatively by putting more and more bullets into the gun.

The thesis of my chapter is that Service Management implementations can be compared to playing Russian roulette, and that poor preparation is equivalent to placing additional bullets in the gun.

48.1 A bizarre comparison?

Well, maybe you are right. Of course the title of a chapter always has to be a bit intriguing, but to state bluntly that a Service Management implementation might be killing for a company….

However, I hope that you will discover, while reading this chapter, that there is more to an ITIL or Service Management implementation than simply rolling out a registration tool and writing down a book full of procedure descriptions.

A few years ago I attended a discussion where one of the participants stated that he knew not one successful ITIL implementation in the Netherlands. This particular remark triggered me in doing research on this subject. It's an intriguing statement. As an external consultant and service manager, I was initially convinced that a lack of insight caused this statement (of course, my own implementation projects had run fine…) but then I started to think again. Were my own ITIL projects really successful? Did the implementations I had supervised really contribute to the company's goals? In the many discussions that followed, but also at many of the seminars I visited, time and time again the contribution of ITIL to the business processes was a hot topic. Of course I encountered difficulties myself in my own projects, and finally I realized that the majority of the problems people experience in Service Management or ITIL implementation projects had *nothing* to do with the methodology itself but *everything* with the impact of such an implementation on the organization. So that's what I focused on. A lot of the things I have seen and experienced in the past few years are included in this chapter.

Maybe you'll recognize the situations; maybe you have already instinctively or consciously avoided them. Learn from it. I wish everyone a smooth implementation.

For the sake of definitions: when I refer to an ITIL implementation, I am talking about the implementation of one of the ITIL processes, such as Change Management or Service Level Management. A Service Management implementation, however, is considered to be the implementation of a *client-focused IT-service-providing organization*, based on the ITIL processes. A Service Management implementation includes the implementation of one or more ITIL processes but is certainly not limited to that.

Generally I will be speaking of Service Management, but this chapter applies just as well to single ITIL processes. On a more detailed level you will encounter the same problems and questions as the ones I'm discussing here. Finally, when IT Service Provisioning is mentioned here, a reference is being made to the whole package of customer-focused IT services, provided by a (usually internal) IT department.

48.2 IT today

It's a fact that the role of Information and Communication Technology (ICT) has increased strongly over the past few years. Companies are becoming more and more aware that the information they use is of strategic value, even to the extent that the survival of their business depends on it. A logical result of this is that the means for transporting, storing and processing this information and the underlying data is becoming increasingly important.

Of course there are, and probably will always be, companies with a low or even non-existent need for ICT. A company producing wooden shoes just for the village where the company is located (speaking of small markets...) won't need an extensive ICT infrastructure. However, times are changing and new opportunities occur. As soon as this little company opens a virtual store on the Internet, selling its wooden shoes all over the world, the need for a reliable ICT infrastructure becomes evident.

This results in increasing demands on the ICT infrastructure of companies. Business processes will no longer settle for generic ICT support but demand tailored services, fit to their specific and changing needs.

Where dependency of the business processes on the ICT infrastructure grows, the demands on these infrastructures will grow too. The reliability, but also the changeability and scalability of both physical infrastructure and information systems and procedures (the ICT infrastructure) become more and more crucial. Looking at traditional IT departments, organized on a product basis (for instance, with a network department and a mainframe department), you will see that they have a hard time coping with these new demands and changes. Good examples of this kind of environment are Web-based organizations, who have to compete in a very dynamic market with continuously changing demands made by (in most cases) unknown customers. With traditionally organized IT departments they do not stand a chance.

But in other (non-Web) environments you can observe the same problems too. Users of the IT infrastructure are no longer just following the directions of the IT department. They understand more than ever the possibilities of IT and try to incorporate these possibilities in their own work. Their managers, responsible for business processes, do the same. They demand an optimal support for their business processes, tailored to their needs. This, however, means a conflict of interest with the IT department, managing the IT infrastructure. From their point of view, stability and standardization are primary goals.

There seems to be an obvious solution to fulfil these needs. We'll just implement Service Management, and our problems will disappear miraculously. It almost sounds like a TV commercial.

48.3 The Reality

Day-to-day business appears not to be as bright and shiny as the commercials want us to believe. The same applies to Service Management. When you start asking around to see how IT users experience support in this area, you usually don't hear success stories.

I encountered a great example during a seminar last year, where five representatives of 'the business' were sitting on a stage in front of an audience of ITIL worshippers. Sad stories all around. The business felt completely misunderstood by its own IT department. The demands were not honoured; IT staff had no grasp of the requirements made by their business processes. So they pleaded enthusiastically for the next hype: to outsource as much as possible of their IT department, arguing that doing so was the best way to get a grip on their IT services. And of course: the things that you are not good at doing yourself, you should not do at all!

The response from the audience was predictable, of course. Misunderstood? *MISUNDERSTOOD?* If there was one group that suffered from misunderstanding it was without any doubt the IT department! All the relentless efforts to keep things running and controlled weren't appreciated at all. *Their* needs weren't recognized, and now the business wanted to start outsourcing the department? This was a reverse reality.

Yes, there are companies where things do work and IT users are satisfied indeed with the IT services they are offered. This seems to be, however, a minority. Therefore, let's have a look at the reasons why the gap between 'business' and 'IT' is often so wide, and why it seems so hard to cross this gap. I will be focusing on those situations where a decision is made to implement IT services using Service Management.

48.4 A different world

Let's be realistic. Most organizations do not have ICT service provisioning as a primary production process. The goals of the organizations are usually defined in totally different areas, whether it concerns the production of paint or the running of a hospital. That IT services can be very important or even crucial is something else. IT service provisioning has a supporting role in these primary business processes. The Tree of Aims, presented in Figure 48.1, illustrates this.

In the Tree of Aims the assumption is made that organizations usually focus on quality, flexibility and control of cost, each to a certain degree. For some organizations the control of cost is paramount; others have flexibility as a central motto. There are companies, like Ericsson for example, stating that 'being first' is more important than 'being best'. However, being first can only be achieved through a large amount of flexibility. The fact that, in this case, cost control usually is not paramount speaks for itself.

FIGURE 48.1

Tree of Aims

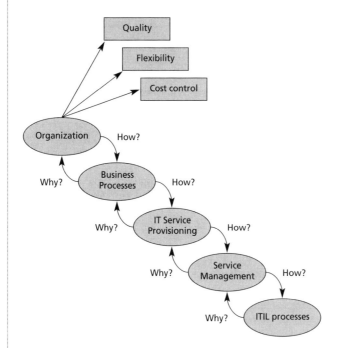

Walking top-down through the Tree of Aims, the first step is from Organization to Business Processes. The meaning of this step is that, in order to reach the organization's goals, you could decide to implement business processes that are contributing to the effectiveness and efficiency of the organization. Using business processes is a possibility, but there are other solutions. This is the meaning of the 'How?' arrow. So, you could contribute to the effectiveness and efficiency of the business processes by using IT Service Provisioning. Creating effective and efficient IT Services can be done by using Service Management (or any other of the approximately 25 methodologies available in this area today). Finally, Service Management can be filled in, you guessed it, by using ITIL processes.

I often use the Tree of Aims to explain the position of IT Service Provisioning, Service Management and ITIL in organizations. The bottom line in the argument is that underlying layers have to contribute in a positive way to the higher layers in the tree. Indirectly, ITIL and Service Management, if well implemented, contribute to the organization's goals of quality, flexibility and cost control.

Of course this thesis is the absolute favourite of the managers that are responsible for the business processes within the company. All those IT whizz-kids simply have to do their jobs in such way that they contribute positively to our effectiveness and efficiency! And to be frank: we don't care how they do it, just as long as they do it.

Here lies the gap.

Whereas the business processes are directly busy realizing their contribution to the oranization's goals, the IT service-providing departments do that in an indirect way. The fact is that they play a supporting role and will stay that way, regardless the importance of their activities for the organization.

The power of the IT departments seems to indicate otherwise, sometimes. In this situation, however, it comes down to a *mutual dependency*. The business processes cannot do without the IT services, while the latter have no right of existence without the business processes.

48.5 A solution

In accordance with the Tree of Aims, you could improve this situation by implementing Service Management. I don't say that this is the solution to all problems; it is just one of the possibilities. Choosing such an approach is thus a problem in itself. If a client asked me to implement ITIL in its organization, my counter-question immediately would be 'How did you determine to use this methodology?'. The answer to this question is the basis for accepting or refusing the assignment (in that form, that is).

We are touching the core right now of why Service Management implementations and ITIL implementations are often such harsh and worrying activities.

Why does a company decide to use Service Management for reshaping its IT Service Provisioning? Everyone starting such an implementation should ask themselves this question, because you don't know whether Service Management is the right methodology for that company, for that situation. When you accept an assignment to implement Service Management, you'll have to be convinced that Service Management is indeed a good solution for the company's problems.

48.6 Let's go for it!

Let's assume that you have the impression or – even better – the conviction that implementing Service Management might mean a positive contribution towards a high-quality IT Service Provisioning. So you decide to accept the assignment.

For the rest of this chapter I make the assumption that the person accepting the assignment is an external (Service Management) consultant. Not too many companies have the internal expertise to do Service Management implementations themselves. On the other hand, even if they are capable of doing so, it is sometimes explicitly decided to give the assignment to an external party. To what extent the involvement of the organization is required in these implementations will be shown later in this chapter. The fact is that the majority of Service Management implementation projects in the Netherlands are led or coached by external consultants.

As stated earlier in this chapter, creating an IT management environment according to Service Management principles is no easy job. Stories from the real world sometimes draw an ugly picture. For example, take the situation where a management team hands out the assignment to 'implement ITIL'. Gradually, it becomes obvious that this team is not very united in its expectations on this subject. Remarks such as 'but we already have a help desk, don't we?' or 'change management only slows down operation, so we won't implement it' indicate that a lot of work still needs to be done.

Besides this confusion, what about the kind of blunt resistance you can encounter during the implementation of Service Management? In fact, the implementation of Service Management is actually a reorganization, an organizational change due to the switch from a hierarchical structure to a process-oriented structure. There is more on this transformation later in the chapter.

I encountered a nice example of resistance during the implementation of an Incident Management process. The support engineers involved appeared very reluctant to enter into the registration tool the amount of time they spent on solving an incident. They saw it as a means of management control and an intrusion into their freedom of acting (the Big Brother syndrome). The goal of the management, however, was to use these data to determine workload in order to hire additional support engineers when the workload became too much.

All kinds of resistance can also occur within the business processes, especially if you don't take the time to take a really good look at the actual situation within these processes, the tasks they perform, and the problems they experience. I very well remember the conversation I had with a production manager who remarked irritatedly that he wasn't interested at all in that help-desk rubbish. The thing I had to take care of was that the computers, on which he was so dependent, kept on running. By the way, yesterday the system had been down for five minutes again. Did I realize what a mess that had caused? He gave me a clear message: focus on availability and stop introducing questionable remedies like help desks in all those cases when IT had failed once again.

There are strong arguments in favour of doing a Service Management implementation right the first time. What we must not forget is that we are talking about a lot of money here, not only because of hiring external expertise but also because of the claims that are made on the internal resources.

There are also less measurable aspects, such as a growing resistance to change, damage to the reputations and demotivation of the people involved, casting a shadow on future developments. Even if new implementation attempts are made, the challenges in this area will definitely be larger.

48.7 Where do things go wrong?

We have gradually become aware of the fact that the implementation of Service Management is more than inventing processes, writing books full of procedure descriptions or implementing a Service Management tool. We are dealing with a real organizational change, if not a reorganization. And even IT departments nowadays are beginning to see that, in an organizational change, all kinds of 'tricky' and complex factors play a role, such as culture, human behaviour and commitment.

What I am experiencing time and time again is that a kind of 'standard approach' seems to exist for Service Management or ITIL implementations. A management decision is followed by hiring external expertise, leading to a project to implement one or more ITIL processes. This is usually combined with the implementation of a registration tool, supporting these processes. In the optimal case, an analysis is done to determine where the organization is hurting most (for example, with one of the numerous organizational maturity scans); however, the results are in general only used to determine what the size and order of the process implementations should be.

Conclusion: the focus lies on the technical approach, and not on the 'softer' aspects such as the management of expectations, attitude, communication and so forth. Here lies a guarantee of failure.

48.8 Think first, act later

How unique is Service Management where these problems are concerned?

Looking at the way we run projects, you'll see that it is considered standard to look at the risks involved in a project before it actually starts. Such an analysis tries to describe and value all the aspects in and around the project that can influence the outcome of it. Knowing the risks, you can anticipate them.

Although I almost never see it happen in real life, this investigation of risk is also a part of Service Management implementations. In almost every serious book on ITIL or Service Management, you'll find that the introduction of a management process starts with a *feasibility study*. The objective of such a study is to determine the factors that hamper the implementation (or even block it), and the factors that have a positive influence on the project results. In fact, when conducting a feasibility study you follow the ground rules of strategy: determine where you currently are, put a mark on the map to indicate where you want to be, and plan your marching route. This last step, the determination of the way you intend to meet your objectives, should start *after* conducting a SWOT analysis. In such an analysis, originating from the world of strategy, you determine the strengths and weaknesses of the organization, and then relate these to the external opportunities and threats. These aspects influence the achievement of the goal(s) you set, sometimes in such a way that the goals become unreachable. A graphical representation of the SWOT analysis is shown in Figure 48.2.

FIGURE 48.2
SWOT analysis

48.9 The structure of a feasibility study

The structure of a feasibility study is relatively simple.

The study starts by creating an overview of the *current situation*. In what respects is IT supporting the business processes today? What parts inside or outside the organization are involved? What is the performance of the participants? Where lies the pain in the organization? Important points for attention during the determination of the current situation are the scope of the feasibility study (what is included in the study and what is not), the identification of all parties involved and the creation of measurable results. With this last remark I mean that you have to try as much as possible to create measurable values that can serve as a basis for improvement activities. Don't, for example, conclude in the feasibility study that the IT department is too slow in answering the phone when a user calls with an incident, but instead try to collect data on the amount of calls, the number of IT employees answering the phone, the average waiting time, etc. Quantification is the keyword here. I realize that this is not always an easy task. One of the most important reasons for starting a Service Management implementation is usually the demand for a greater grip on the IT service provisioning. In the current situation, therefore, these measured values are hard to determine.

After creating an insight into the current situation, we start to determine the *desired situation*. In other words: what does the organization want to achieve? Of course the management of a company does not start an implementation of Service Management just for fun, or because it is an interesting topic of discussion while playing a game of golf (I really hope I'm not wrong about this…. Well, such an attitude of course would have been noticed in the previous stage of the feasibility study, the determination of the current situation, wouldn't it?).

Explicitly stated or not, ideas exist on what people want to achieve with a Service Management implementation. Maybe in vague terms, maybe well defined, these ideas exist in the minds of those involved. In the previous stage we determined the parties involved, so now we have to interview them, in order to capture these expectations and ideas in as coherent a way as possible. It is obvious that you must avoid the pitfall here of just writing down all the criticism of things that don't run smoothly in the current situation. Being negative is easy, but what are the solutions? What needs to be done in order to improve things? When you are in the middle of this current situation it is often hard to make such leap of thought. However, the consultant guiding this process can be helpful here. Based on his or her own experience, the consultant should be able to make a reasonable projection of the consequences of the Service Management implementation in the organization. Another important aspect is that you check this newly defined desired situation with all parties concerned. Each group you identified in your determination of the current situation should be involved in the discussion of the desired situation. Take care that a coherent image is developed, supported by all parties. Here lies a direct connection with the awareness activities, which are discussed later in this chapter.

These first two stages of the investigation are relatively simple. The real challenge appears as soon as we try to determine the marching route, the road the organization has to follow to reach the desired situation. It is less hard to define where you want to go than to define how you will travel. As a good adviser, the consultant will present proposals for the approach, the order of the activities and the estimated time needed. This of course needs an intensive dialogue with the parties involved. Not only must there be a solid foundation for the desired situation, but also for the way this final goal will be reached. Elements such as the amount of change the people involved are subject to, or the contribution they are supposed to deliver, can definitely be subject of discussion.

As described earlier in this chapter, you have to make a SWOT analysis before you start planning your activities and general approach. The way you are going to do things is heavily dependent on the strengths and weaknesses of the organization, in combination with the opportunities and threats that may occur.

48.10 An example

An organization suffers from poor IT support. End users are complaining because they don't know when their problems will be solved. They make all kinds of agreements on this matter with the IT department, but these remain vague and aren't written down or confirmed. This situation highly iritates the management of the business processes, because they see loss of production without swift action from the IT department. And if an IT representative appears, it's not clear how long it will take before production is at its normal level again.

On the other hand, the IT department is extremely busy. The highly motivated employees, having a lot of fun in their work, run throughout the whole company to solve problems as quickly as possible. Wherever they think the need is highest, that's where they run to first. There is no registration of data whatsoever, there's no time for that. Customers need to be helped as quickly as possible. Recognizable, so far?

A decision is made to restructure the IT department. And, of course, Service Management will be used to do the trick. The business process management states that they want clear and unambiguous agreements on resolution times and availability. This seems to appeal to the head of the IT department, because it will save him a lot of ugly phone conversations.

The SWOT analysis shows the following. The strong points of the IT department are the motivation of the employees, the available budget and resources to make the necessary changes, and a management team that is united in its opinion that the desired situation really needs to be realized. A weak point is the fact that the head of the IT department is actually not very motivated. He wants to go along with the wishes of the management team, but sees many problems related to this approach. Besides that, the employees of the IT department are very motivated to help their customers, but on the other hand they are very attached to their freedom to solve things the way they think is best. An external threat is the possible merger with another division within the holding, with consequences for both the business processes and the IT department.

In itself this case offers quite a few angles to define some scenarios. The truth, however, is usually a lot more complex. All kinds of, sometimes hidden, agendas can be used that become somewhat clearer after a thorough investigation.

Implementing changes in an organization really is an art form in itself. Very much attention has to be paid to the 'softer' aspects of the organization.

48.11 Traps

The first pitfall lies in omitting the feasibility study. It is a fact, unfortunately, that this study is rarely conducted. Of course you can start immediately by describing the ITIL processes, bringing in a new registration tool and educating the employees, but this approach is equivalent to starting a tour around the world without consulting a map or even having the faintest idea where you are going.

The second pitfall lies in the focus on technique. It is my experience that far too much attention is paid solely to defining the operational processes, creating detailed procedure descriptions and manuals, and training the employees in order to have them understand the methodology. This is, however, only a small part of the job! Questions like 'WHY do we choose ITIL/Service Management?' and 'WHAT does this really mean for myself and the environment I am working in?' are rarely heard. The softer aspects of the implementation process, like managing expectations and the cultural influences, are strongly ignored. You may expect from an external consultant that he or she has a keen eye for (and acts upon) these aspects, and is not preaching the ITIL dogma as a mere technocrat. Be aware of the consultant that says 'This cannot be done, because ITIL says…'. Immediately accompany this person to the front door and make sure he or she never enters again!

The third pitfall lies with the management of the company – to be more specific, in their awareness of the changes at hand. The determination of the level of awareness in the several participants ought to be a part of the feasibility study. But try to imagine the following situation.

A Service Management implementation is preceded by a feasibility study. The outcome of the investigation clearly shows some severe obstacles blocking a successful implementation. So improvements are needed in the organization to create a solid foundation for the implementation of the Service Management processes. Yet, arguing from a business perspective, the management of the organization strongly urges you to start the implementation ('*because we are desperately in need of a service desk for our customers…*'). It looks like the management is strongly supporting the implementation. Alas, they do so with the wrong motivation.

This is a tricky situation, especially when you are acting in the role of the external consultant. Your customer really wants you to get busy, but on the other hand you know that the requested goals are hard or even impossible to reach. The question still remains whether you, in your role, are able to deal with the identified obstacles. An example of such an obstacle is, for instance, a strong 'island' culture (every manager has his or her own kingdom), frustrating all attempts to work in a process chain.

The fourth and final pitfall I wish to mention regarding feasibility studies is the idea that conducting a feasibility study once will do the job. You must realize that the world around you is changing constantly, not least because of the organizational changes you yourself are causing! Not only may the structure of the organization change, but the attitude of the participants in the change is subject to changes, too. Adversaries may become brothers in arms, and vice versa. Be (and remain) alert to the signals, look out for them. And keep on investigating whether the goal that was defined at the beginning of the change process is still feasible. If you are not certain, it is a wise idea to repeat the feasibility study. Monitoring and controlling remain continuous activities.

Mind you: conducting a feasibility study is no guarantee of success. The same applies to omitting the feasibility study: it isn't a guarantee of failure. Of course there are more aspects that influence the success or failure of a Service Management or ITIL implementation.

Being or becoming aware of the force field around the implementation, the individual motivation of the 'players' involved and the constant monitoring of both the positive and negative aspects you determined in the feasibility study substantially increase the chance for success.

48.12 And now for something completely different: the awareness campaign!

This has already been mentioned during discussion of the feasibility study. Something should be done about 'awareness'. Alas, there is no word as ambiguous or vague within Service Management as 'awareness'. Of course everyone agrees that 'awareness' is necessary and even important, but few are able to tell you what exactly this means. A hint is given by the name 'awareness campaign', which seems to indicate that you have to think in advance, that a certain strategy lies beneath it. Well, we'll see.

As soon as a customer decides to reorganize its IT organization by means of Service Management, the average consultant usually indicates that an awareness campaign must be started, because we seem to have learnt from the past that such an activity increases the chance of a successful implementation. End users and their management explicitly need to understand the importance of implementing all these processes, and how everyone will benefit.

Well, does it really work that way? A colleague of mine described the awareness campaign as 'running a PR circus'. This attitude bothers me a bit. It creates the impression that a forced approach to the target audience is necessary to convince them of certain ideas. That way, in my opinion, there will be far too much one-way traffic in communication. Awareness will be initiated only when people feel recognized in the things concerning them.

What does 'awareness' mean?

Awareness means 'cognizance', 'consciousness'.

Obviously the organization needs to become conscious of a few things. This is, in my opinion, something quite different from 'we need to tell the management explicitly how beautiful the world will look after implementing Service Management'. Especially in those cases where the proposal for implementing Service Management is coming from the IT department, the previous thought often rules.

Unfortunately there is often a lot of (historical) friction in the relationship between those who manage the IT infrastructure and those who use it. Both parties feel highly misunderstood.

Who (the target)

As discussed earlier in this chapter, the feasibility study is used to determine the bottlenecks that could block a successful implementation of Service Management.

These bottlenecks can appear on many levels, both in groups and in individuals. The awareness campaign is supposed to break down these bottlenecks or, at least, make them manageable. It is a fact that these bottlenecks are found as often in the IT department as in the rest of the organization.

This means that an awareness campaign cannot be limited to a specific part of the company (like, for instance, the IT department), but should extend to the whole organization, the company's management included.

What (the message)

When you are discussing the implementation of Service Management in an organization, you are discussing how to *change* the organization. Changes, by definition, create resistance. The more abrupt, unexpected, or unclear the change, the larger the instinctive resistance of the organization will be.

Looking at the organization as a whole, we see that its composition is not of a homogeneous nature. So a generic solution, resulting effectively in a positive contribution to the success of the change, is rarely found. Each separate part of the organization has its own goals: the Sales Department is primarily concerned about turnover, the Production Department is focusing on producing as effectively as possible, and so forth. The IT infrastructure provides them with means to do their job as effectively and efficiently as possible. So IT supports these business processes. From the perspective of these business processes, it is absolutely unimportant in which way they are supported, just as long as they are supported effectively. As an example of this situation, I quote the general manager of a hospital, who said: '*Our primary concern is taking care of our patients. If we fail, these patients suffer the consequences. Of course IT helps us in doing our jobs as well as possible. But I really could not care less if I have to use Windows NT or Novell, for that matter.*'

For the IT department, however, the perspective is a completely different one. A choice of either Novell or Windows NT is to them a fundamental one. Choices of the network topology, hardware and software – these are all decisions that will have an impact for many years to come. The 'horizon' that an IT department is coping with usually lies much further away than the one that the business is focusing on.

In these situations, I always use the term 'mutual dependency'. The business depends heavily on IT support. However, without the business an IT department has no right of existence. Business and IT department are mutually dependent on each other.

The goal of awareness is, in my opinion, to create a broad understanding of this dependency. IT employees have to learn why their efforts are so important to their customers, and why their customers are so important to them. When you, as an IT employee, don't understand that you cannot reboot a server in the middle of the day for minor maintenance reasons, you are not fit for the job. Business processes take priority over IT processes, because IT processes are supporting them. Constant changes in the IT infrastructure are defensible from a business point of view, although most undesirable from an IT management perspective.

On the other side, the business processes (especially their managers) should understand the dilemmas the IT department is coping with, and not easily declare them as subject to their own activities. In Service Management the customer takes a central position but is not the dominating or only factor.

As long as this understanding does not exist on both sides, there will be no awareness and the implementation of Service Management will be in severe jeopardy.

How (the medium)

The keyword seems to be 'communication'.

Sounds easy, hm? We all know that when changes in an organization fail, the 'communication' is to blame. That is, the lack of it, or the failure to do it right. However, the first rule in communication is that the responsibility for the communication lies with the sender of the message. So, if you are initiating a change, you can never blame the failure on 'the communication'; it is you that has failed.

An approach I often see being used is the missionary approach. The great news of Service Management is preached zealously by its followers, usually the external consultants. Workshops are organized, training is given just to convince the organization of the necessity to implement Service Management. That is in fact the assignment they were given by the management of that same organization.

This approach, however, has far too many characteristics of 'one-way traffic' communication, since such a missionary is rarely converted himself… With a bit of bad luck, no one in the organization will be prepared to cooperate and facilitate the changes. Not the IT department, because they feel they are being forced into a restraining jacket, and not the rest of the organization because they do not recognize their own interests in the newly proposed situation. The example of my discussion with the production manager concerning help desks versus availability, mentioned earlier in the chapter, shows this in a painfully clear way. Availability and its optimization were of major importance to him, so the IT guys should focus on that….

When (the timing)

When do you actually start the creation of awareness? Earlier in this chapter, when I described the determination of the current situation in the feasibility study, we concluded that a broad acceptance of the implementation was crucial. Apparently you have to start awareness activities at a very early stage. There is a certain dilemma involved here. You conduct a feasibility study in order to determine whether you want to start a Service Management implementation or not. But it looks as if you have to start creating the right 'environment' for this implementation while you still are not sure whether you want to implement or not! This seems to be a classic 'who was first, the chicken or the egg?' story. Yes, a minimal common foundation is necessary just to be able to determine whether or not a Service Management implementation is feasible. So, yes, as a consultant you will have to find a way to provide this, even during the feasibility study. Awareness activities are generally directed towards the key players found by the consultant in his or her investigation, but the major focus remains on the feasibility study. When the study has shown that an implementation is possible, a full-blown awareness campaign can start.

Lifespan of the campaign

How long do you have to run an awareness campaign? Well, at least until the implementation has finished. Isolated activities, performed once to get the employees involved in what's happening, won't work – certainly not in the long run. As in TV commercials, the power lies in repetition. Of course you need to bring some variation to the activities you offer. Repeating the same message over and over again without any variation will lead to symptoms of fatigue and finally to rejection. Any willingness to participate will have disappeared by then.

48 ■ Russian roulette

Do things stop when the implementation is finished? In my opinion: no. As time goes by, Service Management organizations, especially when they are under a lot of pressure, tend to grow 'softer', less effective. Emphasis easily shifts to resolving things fast instead of resolving things right. Registration of incident data, for example, becomes more and more concise, attention to the customer declines and agreements appear to be less concrete and hard than they originally seemed. When you notice this kind of behaviour, it's time to unleash the awareness campaign again.

Actually, it is better to prevent such behaviour instead of organizing a full-blown awareness campaign when things get out of hand. A continuous, subtle awareness campaign, constantly reminding the parties involved of the reasons why we are doing the things we are doing, appears to be quite effective.

Creating awareness is a *process*, with predetermined goals, followed by activities and results. Processes repeat themselves, comparing results to the original goals, and if necessary adjusting the activities within the process. There is no difference between the basics of ITIL processes and those of creating awareness. They both follow the generic scheme shown in Figure 48.3.

FIGURE 48.3

Generic process scheme

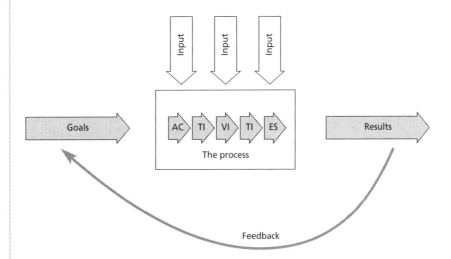

But how do you do it?

Is there some standard recipe for properly conducting an awareness campaign? Sorry, not that I know of.

As an external consultant you need, after starting such a task, to investigate thoroughly where the pain and resistance in the organization exist. After having done so, you have to investigate whether there are circumstances (opportunities or threats) that can help you or work against you in your efforts. This is done with a good feasibility study.

The results of the feasibility study offer you a possibility to focus on specific sources of resistance. Be aware of the fact that there is more in an organization than just those elements who are resisting. I mention this because I want to stress the fact that in an awareness campaign you shouldn't neglect organizational entities you classified in an earlier stage as 'no risk' or 'minimal risk'.

An awareness campaign is a snapshot, taken at a given moment. It is entirely possible that, later, some group in the organization will start to feel neglected, creating spontaneous new resistance.

Every organization is unique. There are no golden rules. This means that high demands are made on the consultant's ability to identify the problems and situations within the organization. While selecting a candidate for such a job, this property needs to be screened thoroughly.

48.13 Conclusion

Do organizations really play Russian roulette when they start a Service Management or ITIL implementation? It depends. Of course, ITIL is not the solution for all the problems in the area of IT infrastructure management. Yet I am convinced that the methodology is a good one. If properly implemented, Service Management helps you to set up clear and measurable IT services, and to break the deadlock between changing and demanding clients on one side and an IT department that is unable to cope on the other.

You are, however, playing Russian roulette when you start an implementation within an organization that is not ready for such an adventure. There is an obvious parallel with the old (maybe stale) joke of a managing director, complaining that his company is performing so poorly. The consultant advises him to start using IT, so that all his problems will be solved quickly. Indeed, they will. But not quite as the managing director expects...

You certainly are playing Russian roulette when you think that introducing a Service Management tool and a bunch of procedures equals a Service Management implementation.

Personally, I am convinced that the role of the external consultant is crucial. This expert in the area of organizational change should be able to manage both the 'soft' and 'hard' aspects of his or her assignment. But the consultant should always have the guts to refuse the assignment when he or she is convinced that the assignment is not feasible.

Comments on this chapter

I am very interested in comments on this chapter. Discussion usually broadens the perspective. So please be so kind as to share your thoughts on this matter with me. My e-mail address is Dick.Costeris@insyst.nl.

Review of part 7

In **The process approach: managing chaos?** van Elsdingen and de Landtsheer describe the result-driven approach, in which a service component is added to the process-driven approach. The process-driven approach is all about the organization of a sequence of activities to meet a specific goal. In their chapter they try to focus process-driven organizations even more on the process approach. The authors state that at the end of each and every service management process there will be a customer of that service. In doing so, they clarify that all activities within the process-driven approach must be focused on the customers of that process.

Van Elsdingen and de Landtsheer go into detail on the organizational structure when processes are implemented. It is clear that an employee cannot be managed by two captains. The authors do not state that the line management must disappear, but they do say that it must be made clear that line managers do not control the process activities. Processes are managed by their own management. The different roles of line management and process management are very interesting in respect of the management of employees. The authors do not elaborate on the way the roles of line management and process management should be organized in the organization, but it is a very interesting topic in its own right: defining a new management domain in terms of process management leaves only the employee management role (i.e. human resource management) to the original line manager. Here we find *the* most important failure factor in many process implementation projects: installing a new management paradigm and simply forgetting to remove the old one.

Van Elsdingen and de Landtsheer also discuss the effects of organizational changes on employees. They specifically focus on managing the resistance of employees to the change. Two important conclusions can be drawn from this chapter:

1. Managing processes is all about managing people.
2. Processes must be focused on improving the service to the customer.

These two conclusions lead to the understanding that employees, acting in service delivery processes, must be made aware of the customer who is at the end of the process. Because ICT supports the business processes of an organization, ICT is in the role of supplier: a customer–supplier relationship exists between ICT and the business. But in how many cases can we see this sense of a customer–supplier relationship in a service desk of an organization, and what conclusions can be drawn from this sense? Recent publications and symposia have shown us the increasing requirements regarding the social competencies of employees on service desks. Since service desk personnel appear to have the highest turnover rates and the lowest salaries, there still seems to be a long way to go.

In **IT Service Management: The IT management ERP solution**, Loo shows how the introduction of an ERP system was facilitated by using a process-based IT Service Management approach at the same time. In the case of Union Carbide, a faster and more flexible introduction of the ERP application was made possible by the parallel introduction of the IT Service Management solution. Many structural problems could be avoided by working with a fully developed Service Management framework and the associated products. Loo deals with the practical introduction of this kind of combination and indicates what you should watch out for in a similar project. As well as the frameworks from part 1, the role of culture and communication as covered in part 6 emerges as an important factor in this contribution.

In **End-to-end Service Level Management**, den Boer *et al.* cover the very interesting discussion of whether or not the activities of Service Level Management (SLM) can be handled in one role. They argue that two different roles must be created. One of these roles is responsible for the external part of SLM and the other is responsible for the internal aspects. In this analysis they come up against one of the practical shortcomings of ITIL. The single role of the ITIL Service Level Manager has a hard time bridging the gap between the ICT organization and the business. This in itself is not a new topic. In part 1, the ISM model also describes this distinction. What makes den Boer *et al.*'s chapter so interesting is that they actually implemented this in a very large service organization.

Den Boer *et al.* conclude that Service Level Management is responsible for connecting the various links in the service delivery chain and for the streamlining of communication structures and information flows. When we compare this with the chapter by van Elsdingen and de Landstheer, we can see that Service Level Management is responsible for focusing the employees on the service customers. The question is how this can be done. From the chapter it is clear that Service Level Management must gain a very good insight from the various Service Management processes. These insights must then be communicated and used for improvement. Normally this is achieved by creating reports. Because there are two roles within Service Level Management, this reporting must also be divided according to the two domains: how the customer perceives the service that is delivered and what the monitoring of the agreed service levels says about the performance of the service management processes. It is a shame that in the literature on Service Management little can be found about reporting as an instrument, or about how the required information can be generated.

Den Boer *et al.* give us some very practical guidelines on how this End-to-end Service Level Management can be implemented. They have already gained the insight that when approaching this, you are dealing with an organizational change. The authors conclude that this organizational change can't be considered too lightly, but must be managed appropriately.

The implementation of End-to-end Service Level Management has led den Boer *et al.* to provide a bridging function between the ICT organization and the business. This is a subject also described by Gilbey in **IT Service Management: a pragmatic direction**. In his chapter he provides several practical guidelines for making sure that the ICT organization doesn't get isolated from the user population they support. Gilbey takes a different perspective from den Boer *et al.*, who are only concerned with the tactical organizational level. Gilbey looks at it from the operational level, i.e. from the help-desk point of view, but also from the tactical level in which he would like to use user representatives.

Gilbey provides several guidelines. Crucial to the success of the service delivery is the quality and motivation of the IT support staff. The employee is core, and therefore the effects on the employee should be considered in the change process.

According to Gilbey, the quality of service delivery is established by the human factor. But this human factor exists on both the customer side and the supplier side. Where products are manufactured and sold to the customer, the quality of the manufacturing process is stimulated by standardizing the production process. The input, throughput and output are measured. Standardization, however, is much harder to accomplish in service delivery. One of the instruments for standardization of the service is established by formulating a Service Level Agreement between the supplier and the customer of that service. This Service Level Agreement formulates performance indicators that the service delivery must meet.

But, then again, the quality of the service is influenced by the human factor. If there is one thing that is erratic, it is the human factor. This has some consequences:

1. The service cannot be delivered in exactly the same way twice, because at the heart of the service delivery is the moment of interaction between supplier and customer.

2. Even if it were possible to deliver the service in exactly the same way, the perception of service quality would differ because the expectations of the customer would not be the same.

This leaves us with quite a challenge.

In **Beauty is in the eye of the beholder**, Meesters and Bouman combine the rather traditional (European) mechanistic ITIL perception with the more emotion-driven perception of service management put forward by Parasuraman, Zeithaml and Berry, and Schneider and Bowen. Parasuraman *et al.* received great acknowledgement for their perception of communication between customer and service provider in their famous GAP model, whereas Schneider and Bowen stand up for reasoning from the customer's point of view. Along these lines, Meesters and Bouman illustrate the latest views on IT Service Management, which have evolved over more than ten years of practical and conceptual experience with this discipline. In their model they add the factor 'perception' as a key element for improving the quality of services. They do not stand alone in this view, as is illustrated by Jones' and Fox's contribution to this part. Jones and Fox emphasize that it is of the greatest importance to concentrate on the way the customer perceives the service provided.

Meesters and Bouman concentrate not only on the internal processes of providers and their technical output, but also on the requirements, expectations and perceived quality from the customer's point of view. This is very much in line with state-of-the-art developments in the services industry. The method described by Meesters and Bouman concentrates on high-value customer groups. The authors underpin their view with a modelled approach, using some of the valuable elements of ITIL on Service Level Management – thus preserving what was good but adding what was necessary. Their approach illustrates the evolution of Service Management, but also the evolution of customers: stepping up the maturity ladder brings customers and service providers closer to each other. It's like Maslow's pyramid: you have to achieve the lower levels to be able to reach ultimate happiness.

Business–IT alignment is attracting more and more attention. Since customer and provider are learning to communicate, the customer's real demands are attracting more and more attention. As Meesters and Bouman state: 'It's all about the customer's perception.' Be nice to your customers, they say; surprise them pleasantly, once in a while. That helps to maintain the relationship. And they are right.

Their statement is one for the more mature teams of customers and service providers. In practice, both have to travel up lower rungs of the ladder in order to reach the described level of communication and cooperation. Many issues in this Guide will help these teams through those stages, and once they have climbed up, they are ready to apply the lessons of Meesters and Bouman.

In **Service Level Management**, Sullivan handles the pointers with which he believes Service Level Agreements must comply. According to Sullivan, the Service Level Agreement can be used as an instrument to manage the expectations of the customer of the service. Service Level Management is all about the adherence to the Service Level Agreement. Sullivan emphasizes that, in formulating this, it is essential that adherence is being sought between the IT organization and the business. Sullivan gives us some practical guidelines for this.

In **The management of IT service expectations**, Jones and Fox also address the issue of customer satisfaction and how this can be managed. They do not relate this to the Service Level Agreement, but adhere more to the introduction of a customer liaison function, thus following the lines of Gilbey and den Boer *et al*. This means that from three different viewpoints the necessity of a more externally focused Service Level Management function is emphasized. When implementing Service Management processes, this obviously becomes a topic that is worth investigating.

What is very interesting in the chapter by Jones and Fox is the distinction between different user types. These different types will all expect a different kind of service. It is therefore important to identify these user types and act upon that. In managing customer expectations, the understanding of these different user types is an essential part. Jones and Fox state that this requires a person that has a lot of contact with these users. The traditional Service Level Manager is not the right person for this job.

Compaq's Lisette Favier posed a relevant question when she wrote: **Is there life after ITIL?** From the history of the Dutch *Yearbook* it is obvious that you can find numerous useful additions and variations to ITIL. Combined with additions in other publications in books and magazines, you can build a library that covers a fast-growing amount of IT management ground – far more than ITIL does. This is a sign of growth in a young discipline on its way towards maturity.

In a fast-growing number of countries, ITIL is introduced as the panacea, the silver bullet for all IT management problems. Of course, no framework will ever have such a function. Frameworks are the result of contemporary thoughts about 'directions of escape'. In a fast-evolving discipline such as IT management, a framework has to evolve fast as well. Favier indicates a number of omissions in ITIL, however – among them the lack of attention to the human factor. Personal competencies, such as customer friendliness, empathy and commercial skills are emphasized elsewhere in this Guide as important factors in a Service Management strategy. This is caused to a high degree by the management concept of OCG, the owner of ITIL. The reviewing strategy of ITIL costs a lot of time and causes a lot of fuss between parties that want to be involved, and new topics are covered at a slow pace.

On the other hand, there is a good side to this strategy. Favier emphasizes the usefulness of ITIL in situations where one is aware of these shortcomings. And that, by the way, goes for all the frameworks and models presented in this Guide: their benefits vary with the circumstances in which they are applied, and no model is complete. The responsibility for a useful application of ITIL is in the hands of the user. One thing we can say is that ITIL will have a long future as long as this rule is met.

In **Russian roulette**, Costeris zooms in on the first few stages of an organizational change process. Costeris illustrates his ideas in the context of an ITIL implementation, but it applies to a wide range of frameworks. His message is relatively simple: ITIL is a means and not a goal in itself. The Feasibility Study and Awareness Campaign stages will appear under different names in different Change Management methods, but the message will remain the same. Because a lot of companies are focusing on the implementation of ITIL, the two stages are passed too fast: 'we already know what we want' seems to be the message. This is not true at all. Thinking in terms of solutions will not make the organization aware of its real problems. And building a house on a bad foundation is and will be a lost cause.

Costeris emphasizes that when the choice is made to implement ITIL, the implementation must be made in full consciousness of what is at stake. 'Making a success of your choice' must be the slogan for this. Only by consciously going through all the necessary implementation steps will the implementation of ITIL (or any other framework) seem less than Russian roulette.

Concluding remarks

According to Ploeger, transporting people by train is all about two things: process control and customer expectations. Is Service Management in IT any different? Not according to the authors in this part. We have seen chapters that go into details of process control and chapters that deal with customer expectations. But, most importantly, we have seen that process control and managing customer expectations can team up. Therefore, Service Management in public transport is very similar to Service Management in IT. This makes you wonder whether we can't learn more from other areas (other than IT). There might just be a lot to learn from, for example, process control in the petrochemical industry or the management of customer expectations in hospitals.

We'll see what the next edition of this Guide will bring us.

Literature

Ploeger, L. *Trouw*, Monday 23 July 2001, p. 9

World Class IT Service Management Guide 2000, p. 73

part

E-management

Introduction to the theme

For anyone who had missed this: we live in a New Economy. Informants state that the accompanying revolution has a similar impact as historical milestones such as the invention of the art of printing, the transition to the age of machinery, or the invention of the first aeroplane. It is particularly the ICT and Web technology that facilitates this New Economy. As usual in cases like this, the question arises: can we manage this e-volution with the traditional paradigms and instruments, or should we adjust by developing alternative mechanisms and means?

In this part of the book we find some elaborations on different aspects of this New Economy, by authors who have had a good deal of experience in both worlds. They should be able to determine the consequences in terms of e-management, e-service and e-business.

Content

This part contains three contributions. The chapters describe the effects of e-business on management structures in various cases.

Service Management and the Internet: managing e-services
Jeroen Wiebolt and Ingewang Wong

Management of a website: what's new?
C.D. Deurloo, R.J.C. Donatz, R. van der Pols and F.J. Snels

Vision in the BLUR of eManagement
Michiel Borgers and Paul van der Spek

A review of part 8 follows thereafter.

Reading instructions

The three contributions in this part can be read in an arbitrary sequence. The reader should, however, have some knowledge in terms of processes, management principles and the like, since the chapters build on a comparison of traditional versus new circumstances.

Introduction to the chapters

In **IT Service Management and the Internet: managing e-services**, Wiebolt and Wong discuss a very relevant current development. Now that IT is becoming highly integrated with the business processes in many companies owing to the rise of e-business, it has become even more important to adopt a process-oriented approach. In their analysis, Wiebolt and Wong discuss the special characteristics of e-business environments and state how the extremely high demands which are placed on such environments can be translated into demands made of the management organization.

In **Management of a website: what's new?**, Deurloo, Donatz, van der Pols and Snels discuss the differences between traditional information systems and websites and the implications these differences have on the management of a site. They test the practical applicability of one of the frameworks in part 1 (ASL/R2C) and discuss the consequences for the implementation of management and maintenance.

In **Vision in the BLUR of e-Management**, Borgers and van der Spek deal with the demands of the New Economy on service management. The eCommerce Framework that they use will show a lot of effects for companies that step into e-business. The effects on IT Service Management are analysed and compared with traditional environments.

49 Service Management and the Internet: managing e-services

Jeroen Wiebolt HPC Benelux
Ingewang Wong HPC South-East Asia

Summary

Today's IT is now at the front line of the business – in fact today's IT organization *is* the business. Moving to an Internet-based business effectively turns the IT enterprise inside out, inviting customers more or less into the heart of the IT infrastructure. The Internet-based business model, based on the concept of e-services, requires a shift in the traditional approach to IT Service Management. Although, in the past, the essence of IT Service Management already defined IT in terms of services instead of defining IT from a technology perspective, service-oriented thinking is key in order to cope with the changing business environment. This chapter will provide a set of insights into managing e-services, based on the knowledge and experience of Hewlett-Packard Consulting worldwide.

49.1 Internet today, e-services tomorrow: an introduction

The Internet today (referred to as 'Internet Chapter 1') shows an increasing number of businesses getting wired to their employees, customers and partners. Key business processes get linked to the Net and a critical mass of consumers is coming online. In a growing number of industries, e-business and e-commerce are fundamentally changing the competitive landscape. New and rapidly expanding companies are shaking up the markets and are becoming a threat to companies who still do business the traditional way. The Net has become a means for new opportunities, sharing risks and above all economic growth. In this environment, IT Service Management plays an important role, but still for most of the time it is based on 'website thinking', focused on (aspects of) IT services. What will the next Internet wave, 'Internet Chapter 2', bring us? Chapter 2 is not only about changing the way businesses behave but is also about changing business. It is the era of the digital or network economy, an economy based on a whole new, technology-oriented, business model referred to as the 'service-centric' or 'utility' model.[1] In 'Internet Chapter 2', companies package, market and deliver their strategic business processes as electronic services, to be provided through the Internet. Successful companies will figure out how to best leverage not only their core business offerings but also their proprietary processes, data, IT resources, relationships, knowledge and experience. Through the service-centric business model, IT (finally) has begun to touch every facet of business life; the concept of electronic services will make the Internet more and more an invisible piece of infrastructure. Owing to the increasing importance of the service-centric business model, IT Service Management from a strategic point of view will be a critical success factor for companies to survive the next Internet wave, not only because of its financial benefits but also in terms of increased risk and responsibility to ensure the complete transaction from the first mouse-click through to the delivery of services and goods.

49.2 What is an e-service?

An e-service for streamlining your travel, an e-service for doing your taxes, an e-service that monitors your health, e-services for enterprise resource planning, an e-service for online storage, an e-service for research. These are just a very few of the common examples of e-services.[2] In Figure 49.1, a graphical overview of the various ways that e-services can be considered is shown. Any combination of assets (i.e. proprietary service, business process, application software, IT resource, data, knowledge) that is made available via the Net to drive new revenue streams and/or create new efficiencies can be termed an e-service. In theory, any company that has these types of assets can make money in the e-services world by turning these assets into a service made available via the Internet. In reality, those companies that succeed in thoroughly defining a strategy, creatively finding (new) markets and efficiently deploying and managing these assets are the most probable to make e-services a success.

FIGURE 49.1
The anatomy of an e-service

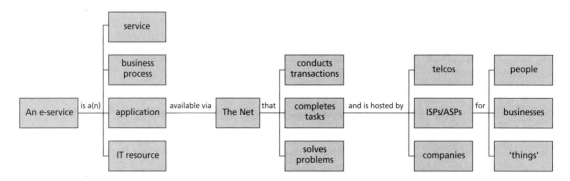

49.3 How to become part of the e-services world

The road from exploring the e-services arena, defining business visions and models towards realization of the idea into a fully operational e-services environment, is a bumpy one. To get there, organizations need to understand their e-service opportunities (What is our business potential?), their readiness (Where are we on the Internet spectrum?) and the steps to take (What requirements must we meet to get there?).[3] The present position of a company, the desired destination and the challenges along the way have to be laid down in a business model, which will address issues on how to innovate through e-services and how to plan, implement, operate and, above all, manage e-services. An important part of achieving a fully operational e-services environment consists of improving and managing the people, processes and technology in this new 'digital economy'. From this point of view, IT Service Management plays a major role in the e-services world. A model for IT Service Management is presented in Figure 49.2. Based on the HP IT Service Management reference model,[4] the most significant topics regarding the delivery of electronic services and IT Service Management will be discussed.

49.4 E-services and IT Service Management

Managing the 'Chapter 2' e-services entails a great deal more than managing the 'Internet Chapter 1' IT services. The complexity of these new e-services is way beyond what we experience today. Speaking of end-to-end service, when many elements make a service and many providers (telecom operators, ISPs/ASPs, local IT organizations, and many more) are involved in the delivery of these services, this requires significant efforts to deliver a transparent e-service to the customer. Providing an e-service is a difficult undertaking, definitely not 'business as usual'. E-services must be highly available, reliable, billable and of course manageable. A recent Gartner Group report indicated the expectations and demands of an e-customer as being 24×7 business hours, a maximum response time (stay/leave a site) of 6 seconds and an average opportunity window (time spent at a site) of no more than 12 minutes. The key to the success of e-services from a Service Management point of view will still be end-user satisfaction, but the end user now can be a (potential) customer, a business partner or a vendor and the competition will be 'just a mouse-click away'. Managing e-services will, therefore, be answering the following three strategic questions:

- Is the service there when the customer needs it?
- Does the service keep pace with the customer's demand for 'Internet time'?
- Is the service safe to use?

In the next four paragraphs, these questions will be answered using the process-clusters of the HP IT Service Management reference model (see Figure 49.2).

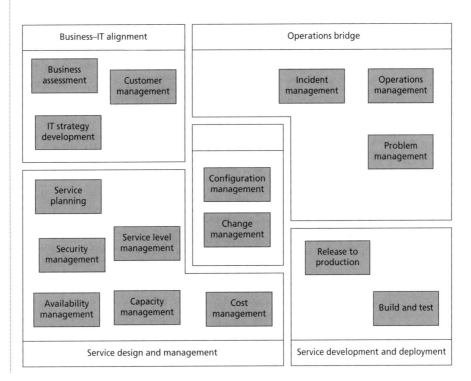

FIGURE 49.2

The HP IT Service Management reference model

49.5 Business–IT alignment

In the e-services world, business strategy and IT strategy are completely intertwined. In the Business–IT Alignment process-cluster, one of the starting points for developing or (re)defining the IT strategy consists of mapping the organization's business strategy onto today's IT business landscape. Key parameters when mapping business and IT are Chain Control and Customer Focus:

- **Chain Control** (vertical axis in Figure 49.3): the level at which a company wants to have control over the value-chain of IT components, in parallel with the supply-chain integration strategy of, for example, the automotive industry.

- **Customer Focus** (horizontal axis in Figure 49.3): the level at which a company is aiming at a position in the back-office (infrastructure-based services, for example telecom operators providing bandwidth) or front-office area (having direct customer contact).

Figure 49.3 shows a sample overview of the landscape for the industry (generic business-archetypes are used), based on the two selected parameters: chain control and customer focus. The arrows indicate in which strategic direction companies are currently moving. Although they are not positioned specifically in this diagram, the rapidly growing number of brokering companies will become more influential in e-business. When developing and implementing the Business–IT Alignment processes, filling in the four quadrants in detail can provide some new and useful insights. Typically, companies have to gain insight into the following subjects:

FIGURE 49.3

Business–IT Alignment, positioning companies by core business

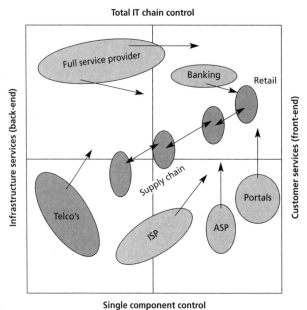

- blank spaces marking opportunities for the business and IT organization;
- companies with similar directions in other industry segments may be eligible for strategic partnerships or cooperation;
- linked companies in the chain may provide outsourcing solutions for e-services;
- other companies heading towards your company's position in the quadrant are potential competitors.

Along with traditional business assessment and strategy development methods such as SWOT, Value Chain and Maturity Analysis, the above-mentioned method provides input in defining a detailed strategy for the design and management of e-services, as offered by the IT organization.

49.6 Service design and management

In the HP IT Service Management reference model, the ITIL tactical processes are positioned in the Service Design and Management process-cluster. Although the other process groups are also important, the major pressure in the e-services arena lies on these tactical Service Design and Management processes. Since the business importance of e-services is increasing, this requires strong guarantees on the availability, capacity, contingency, security and financial aspects of a service. Figure 49.4, the main consequences of a tactical process level for an IT management organization, are shown based on both the level of chain control and the level of focus towards the customer. Decisions made on the level of chain control and positioning towards the customer have the following impacts on the aforementioned tactical processes.

FIGURE 49.4
Service design and management consequences of e-strategy

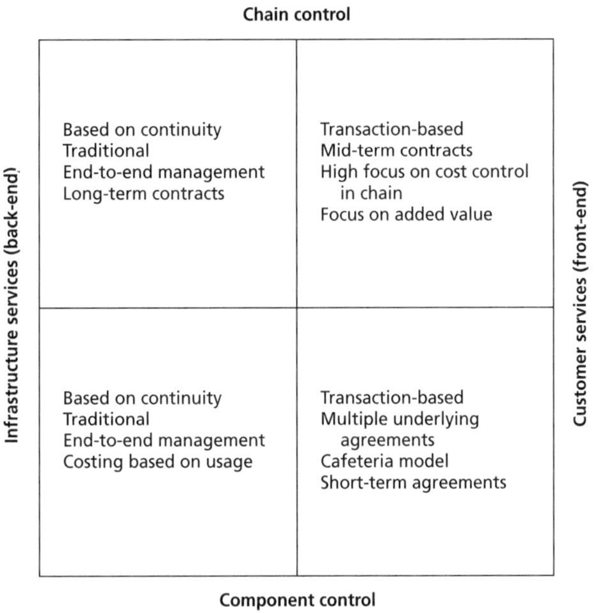

	Chain control	
Infrastructure services (back-end)	Based on continuity Traditional End-to-end management Long-term contracts	Transaction-based Mid-term contracts High focus on cost control in chain Focus on added value
	Based on continuity Traditional End-to-end management Costing based on usage	Transaction-based Multiple underlying agreements Cafeteria model Short-term agreements
	Component control	**Customer services (front-end)**

Security Management

Both businesses and customers require a level of comfort before they will do any kind of transaction over the Internet. This involves the level of integrity and availability of the needed service as well as the performance level of the service. Trust and control are the main issues here. When choosing a high level of chain control, it is easier for IT organizations to guarantee the quality of services (since they are able to fully manage the interfaces between different IT components and give directions regarding the relationship with suppliers). An even more important aspect is the higher level of security inherent in chain control. Owing to the increase in cash transactions and the exchange of personal and confidential data via the Web, Security Management must be set up in order to protect the access control and transactions made via the Web. Setting up Security Management will be accompanied by higher costs of services. In the case of a component control strategy, securing the service is slightly more difficult, since there are more components/providers in the service chain.

Capacity Management

From the e-service customer standpoint, performance can be measured and is measured in seconds. Lack of speed or unresponsiveness can be lethal for an e-service. Currently, owing to all the publicity about the new business opportunities, speed and responsiveness are translated into online, real-time, end-to-end transactions. In order to meet these high demands, Capacity Management requires very high organizational and infrastructural investments. An important role has to be played by the management of an organization in validating the real business needs and proposing (less expensive) alternatives for these investments: there are still no institutions or authorities that regulate the Internet and can provide performance guarantees about Internet connections. Through massive Internet usage and capacity limits, customers will be faced with decreasing performance, since the trend is still showing growth. Any service level agreement with response-time guarantees for Web-based transactions runs a risk. The approach should be to seek alternative and more reliable ways of making transactions, such as call-back facilities and e-mail response. The main point of the Gartner one-liner, '12 minutes and 6 mouse-clicks of attention from the average customer', is to draw the customers' attention (visibility) and to be attractive. When closing the deal, services should switch to one-to-one customer contact to establish trust. Nevertheless, dealing with e-services means a shift towards proactive management of the infrastructure and an investment in the capacity- and performance-related elements of an e-service. Based on the chain control strategy, exclusive use of IT resources will solve capacity and performance issues in a more natural way, due to the span of control. When based on the component control strategy, a service built up from a combination of several providers/companies will provide more constraints and complications for Capacity Management. Components or sub-services can now be shared by multiple companies, which will put more emphasis on Service Level Management aspects such as negotiations, terms and conditions of service, etc. Eventually financial models (in terms of pricing) could be used as regulating instruments to solve Capacity Management issues. This will occur especially when the defined services are relying heavily on performance (such as guaranteed response-times for real-time services).

Availability and Continuity Management

Availability Management is a critical process in the e-services world. Customers want and need to access an e-service 24 hours a day, 7 days a week. Any kind of downtime can be harmful to the quality of service as perceived by the customer. Mission-critical computing is vitally important; all customer relationships (image) and the company's revenues have become entirely dependent on the reliability of the complete service chain. Availability in the e-services world specifically deals with the choice between transaction-based and continuity-based services (see also Figure 49.4). In transaction-based services, response time will be the typical subject of negotiations, whereas with continuity-based services (facilitating multiple customers, for example telecom connections) availability is the major subject. Here, the link with Operations Bridge processes is very clear.

Cost and Service Level Management

Along with Availability Management, Service Level Management and Cost Management form the critical backbone of a profitable e-service. A significant example can be found in the telecom business. This is depicted in Figure 49.5. For the customer, the service is very obvious: making a phone call to a recipient. Nowadays, the build-up of this service is becoming more complex, since setting up the connection (i.e. service) consists of multiple providers, with the corresponding number of service level agreements or contracts. As a result, the billing and charging of the service provided is becoming increasingly complex as well. Very often this accumulation results in unexpectedly high bills for the

FIGURE 49.5
E-service analogy, international roaming service

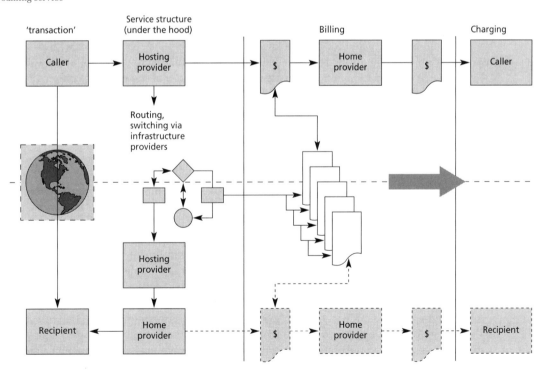

initiator/caller, but also in charges to the account of the recipient. The lessons that can be learned from traditional service providers such as telecom operators are twofold:

- Since (IT) organizations must become service-oriented firms, in the e-services era billing and charging of services become increasingly important to become profitable as a business.
- Terms and conditions for billing and charging must be clear to the customers to avoid 'jack-in-the-box' surprises. Managing the expectations of customers contributes in a positive way to customers' perception of delivered quality and the professionalism of the provider.

In addition to incorporating the above-mentioned experiences and best practices in e-services Cost Management, further knowledge can be applied in the e-services Service Level Management area. The topics mentioned in the previous paragraphs, such as security, performance, availability, reliability and costing, must be negotiated in the Service Level Management process. Even more than the cellular phone roaming example for a phone call, e-services transactions can involve money matters (Internet banking). As previously stressed, failure of service can in some ways have a dramatic impact on the revenues of an organization. Therefore, in the negotiation phase of the SLM process, it has become more important to consider the following topics:

- *legal affairs:* contract negotiations, terms and conditions, exclusions, compliance rules, content responsibility;
- *finance and administration:* contract negotiations, replicating or integrating billing systems, financial models.

Depending on the level of chain control that an IT organization has defined, policies should be formulated for service level agreements, in close cooperation with the business units of the organization, as well as other facilitating departments such as Legal, Finance and Administration. This is necessary because of the growing complexity due to the parties involved in the service chain. Since the impacts of e-services are no longer restricted to IT, it is mandatory that all organizational departments are properly aligned to provide the services in a controlled way.

49.7 Service development and deployment

In order to fully leverage the e-services world, service development and deployment require specific attention. When answering the three strategic questions mentioned above, two subjects in this field need to be addressed: first, the increasing speed of development and deployment of an e-service, and, secondly, the control of development and deployment of the service. The combination of people, processes and technology for e-services must be carefully selected and implemented; however, there will always be 'the need for speed'. Staying one step ahead of the competition by rapidly deploying new services and responding to new opportunities is essential; the time-to-market is nowdays often measured in days instead of months or years. To be able to deliver rapid control, key issues in the e-service development and deployment process cluster are, therefore, flexibility, modularity and scalability. Moreover, there is also the link back to the IT Strategy Development process where the strategic (make or buy, in-house or outsourced) decisions have to be made. In parallel with the increasing number of parties in the service chain which claim a brokering/intermediating role, there is an increase in the demand for brokering software which will provide control of these brokering activities. In the actual development of services, registration and tracking are mandatory functional requirements. Transactions must be traceable and measurable (a good example is a courier service like UPS or DHL, where customers are able to trace their parcel during the logistic process via Web interfaces), in order to provide the detailed data required for controlling the transactions. This data will become increasingly important, since in the near future transactions will be closed with minimal human interaction: WAP-based services, for example, use built-in software intelligence, but to maintain control it is necessary to log the essential information for eventual analysis. From an IT perspective, registration of this data will also serve the operational processes such as Incident and Problem Management and the tactical process of Performance Management, where from a business perspective the organization requires this information for billing and legal purposes.

49.8 Operations Bridge/Configuration and Change Management

The e-services world demands that organizations operate more like a service provider (ISP/ASP). To ensure that every person, business or device that accesses an e-service gets what they expect, operational management processes have become increasingly important. From this point of view, execution of the processes in the Operations Bridge and core stability (Configuration and Change Management) process groups have to become second nature. If an organization offers an e-service to customers and the service becomes integrated into the customer's business processes, the customer expects to receive service support all the way. Support must be given in a simple, uniform way of describing and accessing services and resources, so that they can be readily found and used. Due to the fact of IT becoming the primary business of an organization, the implementation of the Operations, Incident and Problem Management processes will be very dependent on the nature of the e-services, all focused on optimizing customer satisfaction (through, for example, 'e-service call centre' solutions and built-in business support options). The Operations Bridge processes play a major role in the customer contact area, and therefore help in evaluating and managing the customer's experience instead of just the IT experience. Even more than in the IT Services world it is essential to be proactive and to anticipate problems before they arise: 'You need to know what your customer's experience is before the *Wall Street Journal* does.' The Configuration and Change Management processes in the e-services world have to be designed to accommodate rapid innovation (time-to-market) on the one hand and the reliable implementation of changes ('a constant flow of non-disruptive changes') on the other. Since it is estimated that about 85 per cent of all incidents are as a result of unplanned and undocumented changes to an environment and since an e-business requires 100 per cent availability and reliability, it is absolutely mandatory that a Change Management process be defined, implemented and followed explicitly for the e-service environment. There is a need to manage changes for configuration items that directly affect or are affected by the e-service. In the case of flexibility and scalability, the e-services can change more quickly, having different configurations, different Service Level Agreements with different providers. Here Configuration Management needs to ensure that all hand-offs, ownership and individual procedures are adequately covered. This is because of the multitude of parties involved in a service chain that also have to link up their CMDB with each other: depending on the chosen strategy and partnership, integration or at least intensive data-sharing on the configuration items is one of the consequences of e-services on the CM process.

49.9 What's next?

In this chapter, we have tried to provide an answer to the questions of how to manage e-services from an IT Service Management point of view. The answers to these questions have to be found in making sound strategic choices, gaining rapid control of the infrastructure, ensuring an optimal encounter with customers and providing bullet-proof services. Traditional IT Service Management will not suffice when doing business in the e-services world; the new digital economy has the need for new insights. It is, therefore, imperative to enhance the current Service Management best practices in such a way that they will reflect the business processes of an e-services organization instead of the management processes in an IT services organization. The Internet in general and e-services in particular can facilitate this change by allowing us to use this technology to change the rules.

Notes

1 John D. Brennan, *Service Centric Computing: The 21st Century Model*, Andersen Consulting.
2 www.hp.com/e-services/strategy
3 John E. Mann (1999) 'E services roadmap', *The IT-Journal*, Third Quarter, Hewlett-Packard.
4 J. Drake *et al.* (1998) *The HP IT Service Management Reference Model*, Hewlett-Packard.

50 Management of a website: what's new?

C.D. Deurloo, R.J.C. Donatz, R. van der Pols and **F.J. Snels**
PinkRoccade Atribit, the Netherlands

Summary

Websites are becoming increasingly popular and important to business processes. This emphasizes the importance of maintenance and control of websites. This chapter will describe the differences between traditional information systems and websites and the implications these differences have on the management of the site. The focus is on Business Function Enabling and Application Management.

50.1 Introduction

In recent years, there has been a vast increase in the popularity of the Internet (technology) within companies. A growing number of companies have been or are developing an internet site or an intranet. Internet technology is increasingly being used as an aid and extension to existing business processes such as sales and internal communication. The impact of websites and Internet technology on the business processes of organizations is, therefore, increasing, which emphasizes the importance of maintenance and control of websites. Future maintenance and control normally receives little attention during the design phase of a website. In practice, this results in a lot of problems. Even in organizations that have set up a maintenance and control function, problems occur when a website requires changes. Most problems are caused by the fact that the Maintenance and Control function for websites requires a significantly different approach in some aspects compared with traditional information systems. In this chapter these aspects are identified and discussed using two models for maintenance and control: Application Management, an ITIL-like model for service management of applications, and Business Function Enabling, a model ensuring a consistent fit between business requirements and ICT services. It will become clear if and how these models support the required maintenance and control processes for websites. This chapter will use a couple of sample cases to show the importance of website management. The differences between traditional information systems and websites and the implications that these differences have on the management of the site will be described. The focus is on Business Function Enabling and Application Management. Since there is no essential difference between the technical management aspects of websites and those of traditional information systems, these aspects will not be covered in this chapter.

50.2 Problems encountered

The problems encountered by organizations can be placed in four categories:

- business goals;
- management;
- maintenance and control;
- technical and structural aspects.

Business goals

Business goals are often neglected when an organization is building a website. Even the goals of the site itself are often not clear. Large organizations start too hastily because they are afraid of 'missing the boat'. Having a website becomes a goal in itself. In smaller organizations, starting a website is often the 'pet project' of the IT manager or the CEO. Once it is there, management becomes enthusiastic about the potential of the site and the site tends to grow gradually. In both cases, the business goals are hardly mentioned. This implies that the goals of the website remain unknown for the organization and even its management. At the same time, substantial support is asked of the business managers and business unit managers, as they are the sources of site content. This is one of the main reasons for the business units' lack of commitment to provide proper maintenance for the website. As an example, a medium-sized Dutch company wanted to change its image. A website seemed to be the ideal way to reach this goal. Good thought was given to content, layout and presentation of the site and an external design studio built the site. However, there was no anchoring of the website within the organization. Building the site started as the CEO's 'pet project'. He thought building the site was a good idea because it could support the envisioned image change. This goal was achieved but since there were no other business objectives stated, the goal of the site remained unclear to the organization. Nevertheless, business managers were expected to contribute to the site by updating the content on a monthly basis. A few months later the CEO left the company, leaving the site without a sponsor. The website received no management attention for over a year.

Management

The introduction of a website has an impact on many parts of an organization. Several departments and areas of an organization are involved in building the site and supplying the content. This is true for Internet as well as intranet sites. Management of the site and alignment of the parties involved are essential, during development and upon completion of the site (especially because so many parties are involved). In reality, however, we see that there is often no management of the site and insufficient alignment between the parties involved. It is common practice that nobody is held formally responsible for the (content of the) website. This results in a lack of budget for building, maintaining and controlling the site. A company wanted to create its own intranet site. An investment proposal was presented to the board. This contained the initial development costs. The financial manager, who also carried ICT, was implicitly responsible for the project. The project was conducted by the IT department. This led to the situation where control was triggered from a technical point of view instead of the business. The board never realized that content and input for this site had to come from the organization and that alignment and control required a business point of view. The result was that the Web pages received little to no updates and their content did not coincide with the needs of the users; therefore utilization of the intranet did not match expectations.

Maintenance and control

As with traditional information systems, the actual use of a website starts after the site has been completed. The focus, however, is on development and completion of the site, sometimes combined with a promotional campaign to create awareness of the site's existence. The maintenance and control are in most cases hardly acknowledged or the emphasis is on technical management (keeping the website online). A website possesses a highly communicative character, which makes it crucial to keep the content up to date. The lack of awareness regarding maintenance and control, as well as insufficient funding, are the reasons that many websites are not updated regularly. There are too few changes in the content and not enough attention to Application Management (that is: management of the website structure). After the development of Internet site was completed, the organization became very enthusiastic. It wanted to have a website that followed the changes in the organization. In the meantime, the development team ceased to exist and there was only a minimal budget from which the technical maintenance could be financed. The technical manager of the site only made sporadic changes in the content of the website because it had to be done during his spare time. Soon the content of the site was no longer up to date. Little thought had been given to the management of the website's structure (Application Management), which in turn caused the breakdown of the site's initial structure and the appearance of 'broken links' on the site.

Technical and structural aspects

In many organizations, a website is regarded more as a communication tool, such as a newspaper, than as the information system that it should be. A website is rarely regarded as actually a piece of software with its own structure and restrictions. This is another reason why many sites do not receive the required professional IT support they should have. In many cases, somebody – for instance a communications manager – receives training in HTML and is made responsible for the changes in the website. In a large organization with an infrastructure of several networks and servers, the intranet site was not given the attention it required. The communications manager was made responsible for the site. Once the development of the site was complete, the technical assistance stopped. The communications manager was not capable of performing these tasks. Owing to his lack of technical knowledge, the maintenance of the website was insufficient. Subsequently, this led to a decline in use and support of the website by the organization. This went so far as to create further confusion, when eventually nobody knew which server was used as the web server. Since many problems with management of websites are caused by the differences between websites and traditional information systems, it is obvious that knowledge of the differences and their impact on maintenance and control is essential. The following section will provide fundamental insight into websites and the differences between websites and traditional information systems.

50.3 Analysis

Is there a solution to the problems encountered by many organizations? To answer this question, websites will be explored in a fundamental way.

A website as an information system

Like any other information system, a website contains hardware, network, system software and 'the application environment'. The application environment is made up of HTML (HyperText Markup Language) pages or similar types of solutions. HTML is a hybrid environment:

- It contains a variety of possibilities to add information, text, images and graphical effects and to present these in almost any style required.
- It also contains a clearly recognizable (but quite rudimentary) programming language; there are links (go to's) to other pages and other programming facilities such as applets, input commands and scripts/controls to execute processes. This defines HTML as a programming language and a website as an information system.

Therefore, this definition of a website will be used: a website is an information system based on Internet technology and comprises technological communication possibilities (networks, browsers, Web pages, applets) that make it possible to access information and data in a user-friendly way.

There is a distinction between websites and their underlying information systems

From a functional point of view, three aspects can be distinguished in a website: layout, content and data (Figure 50.1). *Layout* determines the 'look and feel' of the website and is strongly related to the overall image of the website. The effort put into this aspect has the purpose of making the site pleasant for its visitors and providing it with the image desired by the organization. All of this can be accomplished with pictures, sophisticated graphic design, moving images, logos, colours, appealing headers,

FIGURE 50.1

Functional aspects of a website

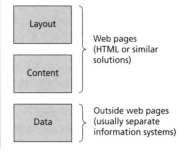

etc. The *content* is the information that is presented on the website itself. This is mostly text with some additional tables and graphics. The content contains the message the organization wants to send to the world. Furthermore, websites often offer access to external *data*. These are data accessed from underlying information systems or data-servers (Figure 50.2). These are mostly data from information systems that support business processes (e.g. order and time-sheet systems). Sometimes these systems are developed as a dedicated system for the website such as, for instance, an e-commerce system. These systems are an implicit part of the website but are developed as normal information systems with the aid of ordinary development tools like Oracle and SQL. The distinction between content and data ensures that the communicative character of the website is emphasized while the underlying systems hold their business-process character. This distinction makes allocating responsibilities and management tasks regarding the website and the information systems clearer.

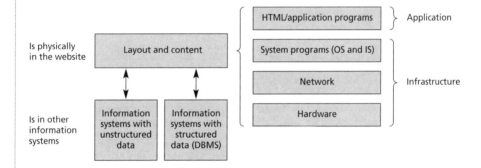

FIGURE 50.2

The structure of websites

The differences between websites and traditional information systems

A website is an information system. There are, however, some important differences from traditional systems. These are summarized in Table 50.1. Since these differences have an impact on the management of websites, the five most important differences are described more extensively below:

1. **Functional needs and technical implementation are strongly linked.** The traditional distinction between functional needs and technical implementation does not apply to a website. This is caused by the dual character of HTML implementations dealing with both content and presentation, creating an inseparable bond between business function and its representation in the application structure.

2. **Websites serve a more or less undefined purpose.** (Initial) design of a website is not directly linked to a business objective, nor is the business purpose that the website serves fully clear. Nevertheless, the website will be the organization's window on the outside (Internet) world. The design and development phases dealing with business objective and related questions require extra attention and broad, company-wide involvement.

TABLE 50.1 Differences between websites and traditional information systems

Aspect	Traditional information systems	Websites
Technical bases	Tables and programs	HTML and applets
Technology	DBMS, programming language	Web browser
Purpose	(Support of) business process: ● Register, save or mutate data ● Calculations or selection on these data	Communication or spread: ● Information ● Links to information
Users	Well-defined group of users	Undefined group; sometimes the whole world
Scope	Specific business process	Company
Developers	Designers and programmers	Graphics department (layout) IT department (site) Public relations/communications manager (content)
Base unit	Structured data	Free-format text
Layout	Finite and depending on infrastructure	Almost infinite possibilities
Structure	Depending on data, not depending on functionality	Depending on content; new page = new system
Change frequency	Data very high Programs relatively low	Content fairly high

3. ***Different types of control are required.*** Control of websites is more directed by enabling communication and less by content or message; the website controller acts more like an information agent bringing supply and demand together.
4. ***Different types of users exist.*** At least two types of users can be distinguished: the internal users responsible for the website itself and the visitors or 'surfers'. This requires a different approach to communication, the website itself being the means of communication.
5. ***Short life cycle.*** Websites are, by nature, strongly linked to the organization, its business and its presentation. Frequent changes occur, mostly causing a short life cycle (1–3 years) for the website and high costs of deprivation.

50.4 Application of models

As previously stated, websites are information systems. Does this imply that they should be managed as such? When defining the maintenance and control processes for a website, it is important to recognize the main differences with conventional information systems. What kind of impact do the aforementioned differences have on maintenance and control? Can the models used for implementing maintenance and control for traditional information systems also be applied to websites? The following

50 ■ Management of a website: what's new?

paragraph will explain how the models developed for information systems can be used for websites as long as the differences between the two kinds of systems are kept in mind and the necessary adaptations to the models are made.

By projecting the differences on the models used for maintenance and control, Business Function Enabling and Application Management (see Figure 50.3[1]), it becomes clear that most processes can be implemented in the same way as for traditional information systems. However, the characteristics of websites have an impact on other processes. These processes require a specific implementation. This section will focus on this group of processes.

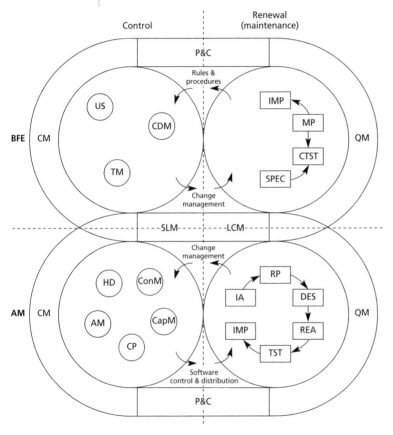

FIGURE 50.3

Models for maintenance and control

General management processes

In this chapter, we have already examined the problem caused by an organization's mismanagement of its website. Maintenance and control models for traditional information systems contain some overall processes that surround the Maintenance and Control processes. These processes are: Service Level Management, Cost Management, Quality Management, Planning & Control and Life-cycle Management. In these processes, several performance criteria such as uptime, number of interruptions, goals, costs, frequency of changes, anticipated lifetime and organizational fit are controlled and adapted. The importance of these (in the model) surrounding processes is significant for websites. Experience shows that these processes receive little attention during development, maintenance and control of websites. This causes the low manageability of websites. Life-cycle Management aims at active control over the suitability of information systems. The suitability of information systems to business processes, the potential of those systems and the continuity of the infrastructure can trigger fundamental changes. Life-cycle Management for websites is different compared with traditional information systems, which have a lifetime of more than 10 years. Websites, however, have a lifetime of no more than 2 to 3 years before they are rebuilt from scratch. Dynamics cause the rapid ageing of websites, but websites are also more related to the organization. There is often a new 'look' and organizational structure and thus a new website. Developing a new website is often a good decision because of their rather small size and low integration in the business processes. When websites become larger and more integrated in the business processes, rebuilding is no longer an option. A controlled situation will produce minimal demand. A well-planned and adequate structure of the website is important to be able to make frequent changes efficiently. It is, therefore, important to make the right choices to ensure flexibility and to monitor them during the process of renewal. As websites tend to have a short life cycle, it is questionable whether implementing Life-cycle Management extensively is a good choice. In the future, when the lifetime of websites increases, the importance of this process may also increase.

Renewal processes for Business Function Enabling and Application Management

Information systems and websites change continuously. For websites, this is even truer than for traditional information systems because information and content keep changing. There should be attention paid to the renewal processes that create these changes. These processes have a functional side (triggering the change, guiding and testing its implementation) and an application (changing software and documentation). Looking at websites, we can see two types of renewal:

- ***fundamental renewal***: a process comparable to that of traditional information systems; large parts of websites are renewed, often triggered by changes of layout, image of the site and changes in the organization;
- ***renewal of the content***: for traditional information systems this process is carried out within Business Function Enabling (Data Definition Management and Data Management). Traditional information systems do not have to be changed because

data and programs are separated. This is different for websites: HTML pages contain content and commands, so changes in the content can only take place in the pages of the site; the impact on the structure is often small, but the number of changes is very high. In the long term, the effect is significant. Since there is often a lack of knowledge to keep the website well structured, the structure of the site deteriorates.

With respect to websites, the processes Application Management and Business Function Enabling are mixed, which causes restrictions for the content manager or the structure of the site. A solution for this problem has not yet been found:

1. The functional manager (content manager) or the content owner changes the pages of a website, but becomes responsible for the technical quality of the site in the process. The pro of this solution is that changes can be made quickly and efficiently. The con is that the functional manager becomes responsible for something he or she is not trained for and for which he or she should not be responsible.

2. The functional manager changes the content him/herself with some restrictions. He or she retains the option to change pages but has some restrictions regarding the distinctive split and structure of information, and accepts layout restrictions. The functional manager becomes jointly responsible for the technical quality of the site. The advantage is that the structure of the site remains better.

3. The functional manager supplies content to the application manager who makes the actual changes. The advantage of this solution is that the technical structure of the site is preserved and an optimal layout can be established. The disadvantage is that the process becomes time-consuming and expensive.

For designing a website it is recommended to make the structure as generic as possible, which allows for changes in the content without obligatory changes in the structure of the website.

Control processes for Business Function Enabling

The goal of these processes is to keep, from the user point of view, the information system working and up to date. The clusters of processes to be acknowledged here are: User Support, Corporate Data Management and Tactical Maintenance. Each is described further below.

User Support

One of the most important processes of User Support is the help-desk process. Websites often have two types of help desk:

- the webmaster (who takes care of technical comments and sometimes questions about the content);
- contacts (often per set of pages), where information can be obtained.

The contact can be a specialist (in this case there is often more than one mentioned on the site) but sometimes there is only one entry point. It is recommended (as for traditional information systems) to keep User Support so that there is one place that monitors the performance of the site. Most organizations try to keep their help desk for traditional information systems skilled (able to help users immediately). Keeping the help desk of a website skilled is very difficult because of the scope of websites. The solution is to let the help desk help the users to find the specialist who can answer the question. To meet the demands of users regarding reaction time it is necessary to translate these demands to the second line (specialists who can answer the questions). User communication is also different for websites. Since users of traditional information systems are employees and have to be authorized as users, they are always known. This is not the case for visitors to websites. Compared with users of traditional systems, visitors to websites are complete strangers to the organization. There are ways to get information about the visitors: asking questions, counting the number of 'hits' and monitoring how long visitors stay; but this is almost entirely one-way traffic. Communication, briefing and training are hardly possible. The only adequate medium for communication with users is the website (for intranets this is somewhat different). This has to be kept in mind in the design of the site. The quality of the site strongly influences user communication. This process can be enhanced by effective monitoring and control.

Corporate Data Management

Data Definition Management and Data Management form this process. In websites there is no distinction between data management and design. This is the juncture between functional and application management described earlier. Corporate Data Management forms the process that changes the content of websites and keeps it up to date. More than one party will be involved in supplying the content. Several parts of the organization will participate in this process. There should be one party that is responsible for the content of the site. This is the webmaster who, like a newspaper's editor, has overall responsibility for the content.

Tactical Maintenance

The last processes in this cluster are the Tactical Maintenance processes. These processes take care of the long-term suitability of the systems and their demands. The emphasis is on triggering the continuous processes of Application Management. The next paragraph will look further into that topic.

Control processes for Application Management

The Application Management model comprises several processes to keep the system performing compliantly. These processes are Contingency Planning, Availability Management, Configuration Management and Capacity Management. The added value of a website is often strongly influenced by these processes. This is caused by the lack of feedback possibilities from users/visitors. If, for example, the website is malfunctioning, users/visitors will not (be able to) give feedback, which is bad for the organization's desired image. This requires specific attention, while in practice it is hardly ever done. Continuous monitoring is also desirable. The processes that take care of this are mentioned above. The process of Configuration Management aims at the management and location of the objects within a website. Compared with traditional information systems, this process is more complex and intensive because the dynamics of websites are much more complex. This is caused by many aspects: the content of the pages (the programs of a site) changes more often, web pages contain more additional objects (such as images, tables and applets), the outer world changes faster (links to other websites) and the infrastructure changes faster (new browser versions, etc.). It is important to stay attuned to the latest developments because there is strong competition: 'inviting' sites are visited sooner and more often. The possibilities to support this process are still in the early stages, but are showing great potential.

50.5 Conclusion

In this chapter, we focused on the importance of implementing the Maintenance and Control processes for websites. We have stipulated three reasons for this: a website is an information system; there is no real distinction between structure and content due to HTML technology; and, from a control point of view, websites should be separate from their underlying information systems. It is important to realize that the differences between websites and traditional information systems require a different approach when it comes to the control of these systems. The different approach is especially triggered by the communicative character, the 'first time right' concept and the short life cycle of websites. Existing methods for maintenance and control can be used as a base. Some processes must be tuned to the specific needs of websites. Due to the nature of a website, it is recommended to combine certain tasks, especially those dealing with the content and presentation of a website. Tactical Management and Lifecycle Management processes will become increasingly important when websites grow in size and are not easily replaced by new ones. General Management processes require the same attention and definition as for any other information system, although this is not always recognized for websites as it should be.

Note

1. The models are not addressed in this document; background information can be found in other articles (*IT beheer Jaarboek* 1997 and 1998) or by contacting PinkRoccade Atribit.

51 Vision in the BLUR of eManagement

eBusiness and eManagement are here, but what is new?

Michiel Borgers and **Paul van der Spek**
Cap Gemini Ernst & Young

Summary

BLUR is a vision of the new world, picturing how products and consumers are changing fundamentally, fuelled by the opportunities created by a connected society. The effect that this has on businesses also has its effects on ICT Service Management. In this chapter the changes in the world of ICT Service Management will be examined, using existing and new models. For the new challenges that arise from these changes, practical tools will be provided, which can be used by organizations to tune their ICT Service Management to match the requirements of an eBusiness.

51.1 Stronger dependencies

ICT has changed the world and will do so even more in the near future. The use of ICT in organizations is claiming an increasingly important role, making these organizations more dependent on their technologies than ever before. As organizations increasingly offer their services using ICT components, the dependency grows stronger. To help organizations get a clear view of where they stand in eBusiness developments, the eCommerce framework was developed.

eCommerce Framework

The eCommerce Framework (Table 51.1) categorizes a number of possibilities for the use of ICT within organizations. Naturally the use of a website or e-mail is there, but also processing of online client orders, knowledge distribution, integrated distribution of products and even creating new markets. These services are categorized into five aspects within an organization: marketplace, customer connections, supply chain, support/employee, and fundamentals. The first categories are focused on growth and the last on increased efficiency. The potential of ICT possibilities increases with tighter integration with business processes. This growth is classified in the framework as eInformation (low integration) to eConomy (full integration).

Using the Framework, an organization can evaluate its position and maturity in the eWorld. If an organization has just begun using ICT, most initiatives are likely to be eInformation or eCommerce initiatives. Looking at the services mentioned in the

TABLE 51.1

The eCommerce Framework

		Transformation			
		eInformation	eCommerce	eCompany	eConomy
Growth	Marketplace	• General portals	• Focused eUtilities for market commerce • Market portals	• Combine offer with business partners • Market utility • Make new markets	• Hybrid markets • Virtualized value network • Market, not brand, identity
Growth	Customer connections	• Online catalogues • Company/product information • FAQs • Electronic coupons	• Online customer orders • Online product configuration • Order settlement	• Virtual sales/distribution • Open enterprise to customers/suppliers • Flow through orders • Loyalty programmes	• Channel portfolio optimization • CRM for market • Market loyalty programme
Efficiency	Supply chain	• 'Informated' products • Research supply base • Electronic product information • 'Push/pull' supplier information	• eProcurement • Electronic distribution • Data sharing with suppliers • Online commitment	• Micro-transactions • 'Direct' fulfilment • Integrated distribution	• Market inventory • Market orders • Market distribution • Market of one
Efficiency	Support/Employee	• Online manuals • Online directories • On-line communications • Job postings	• On-line T&E • Benefits selection • Training registration • Knowledge dissemination	• Distance learning • Employee self-service, HR, travel, knowledge • Employee as customer	• Employee portals • Market administration utilities
Efficiency	Fundamentals	• Secure site • Web infrastructure • Reliable source • Log-on name	• Secure transactions • Web integration • Trusted transactions • Individual identity	• Secure company • End-to-end integration • Trusted company • Confirmed identity	• Secure market • Market integration • Trusted third party • Encrypted identity

Framework, it is obvious that an increasing number of organizations are moving towards eConomy services. Numerous companies put their job offers on the Internet and automate data exchange with suppliers. This move towards eConomy companies comes with an essential dependency on ICT for the realization of company goals.

Role in the value chain

As the eBusiness implementation within an organization grows mature, the primary function of ICT shifts from a supporting activity to an essential component in the primary chain. The dependence on ICT becomes critical to the company processes where ICT is used as an enabler (Porter, 1985). In a conventional organization, people are a critical component in the primary value chain and ICT is used to support these people. In an eBusiness, people do not perform an essential role in the primary chain; this role is taken over by ICT components. ICT is no longer just the lubricant; it has become part of the machine. Business–ICT alignment is the key in this respect. The role people take in the organization shifts from a controlling role to a correcting role. This development is illustrated in Figure 51.1.

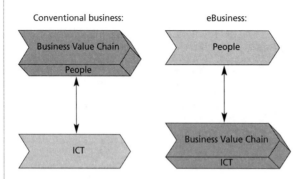

FIGURE 51.1

Role of people in the value chain

Whereas in a conventional organization the value chain depends on transporting products between different physical systems, in an eBusiness application the value chain depends solely on the transportation of information between different information systems. In fact, the primary activities and the ICT systems merge (Borgers, 1999). These shifts are related to business as well as ICT and must be jointly analysed.

BLUR: business change

The effects of doing eBusiness on existing business processes and ICT can be clarified using the BLUR model (Davis and Mayer, 1999). BLUR stands for the new world that has been shaped by the possibilities of eBusiness, now and in the future. The world is a BLUR, in which Speed, Connectivity and Intangible value are the driving forces, i.e.:

$BLUR = Speed \times Connectivity \times Intangible\ value$

The speed at which all aspects of the economy move has a major impact on businesses and consumers. Information is generated and distributed more rapidly and grows old sooner. The information is accessed by systems that are more and more connected and integrated. Bar-code scanners, PDAs, mobile phones, computers, etc. are all being connected to access information anywhere at any time. The intangible value of the new possibilities this creates is increasingly an important portion of the total business value. The elements of BLUR are discussed in more detail below.

Speed

The speed of the service provided is critical for market share. Long delivery times for products become unacceptable and data needs to be processed in real time. As an example, it is taken for granted that financial transactions are processed instantly by a bank. An unreachable or slow Internet portal will discourage consumers and affect revenue. An availability of 7×24 will prevent consumers from looking next door.

Not only is the speed of service provisioning business-critical, but the time-to-market of new products and services is equally essential. Market developments are accelerating, companies that keep up with the pace attract customers. Delivering new products and services regularly is becoming a discriminating ability for companies.

The changes in the product or service portfolio also have consequences for the organization. A new product means retraining staff, a new service may force a change in company processes. A company offering dramatically new products and services may even need to change the corporate strategy.

Connectivity

In the future everyone will be connected. For companies, connectivity means a potentially global market and an extensive choice of suppliers. Being able to reach customers as well as suppliers has always been good business practice. Optimal information exchange requires connecting with the systems of customers and suppliers. Automating the information exchange makes human checks redundant, saving time and money, while increasing quality.

An increased internal connectivity will pay back through increased efficiency and effectivity. Where Marketing has online access to sales figures, the cost of collecting the data is lower and more effective because of the ability to follow market developments closely. If procurement and production are guided by real-time sales and marketing information, this will result in smaller or no supplies. Also, the connectivity with employees can be improved. Synchronizing the business agenda with a (personal) PDA is an example.

Intangible value

The intangible value of a product or service is determined by the way it is tuned to the profile of the individual customer. The level of personalization influences the sense of value an individual experiences. For a company, therefore, it is important to know not only the market in general but also the differences between individual customers.

A carefully chosen customer profile can help deliver an optimal service. Determining the profiles needs systems with a certain level of intelligence. Since the customer profile is not static, it needs to change with the customer. The service should change accordingly.

As mentioned before, the speed of new and/or improved products or services is important to attract returning customers. Customers value low-cost added functionality for existing services. In the world of software this is common practice, issuing upgrades for the price of the added functionality. The business needs to have products or services evolving continuously.

51.2 The effects on ICT Service Management

The previous section showed that eCommerce offers many opportunities to businesses. But the penetration of ICT into the business has side effects as well. The management and exploitation of ICT have to be addressed to guarantee the continuity of the business. For that reason we'll take a quick look at the history of Service Management. The effect of eBusiness on Service Management is discussed and challenges for eManagement are identified.

From Systems Management to eManagement

Modern challenges require a flexible and business-savvy Service Management organization that has evolved from Systems Management to Service Management to eManagement. Failing to address these challenges will have an immediate impact on business results. The combination of availability, performance, flexibility and security increasingly controls business value.

The need for true integration of business and ICT is reflected in requirements for the people involved, the business processes and the way technology is used. The eManagement Evolution model (Figure 51.2) shows how these requirements have changed over the years as Service Management has needed to cater for an environment defined by mainframes, client–server systems and, eventually, an e-enabled business.

FIGURE 51.2

The eManagement Evolution model

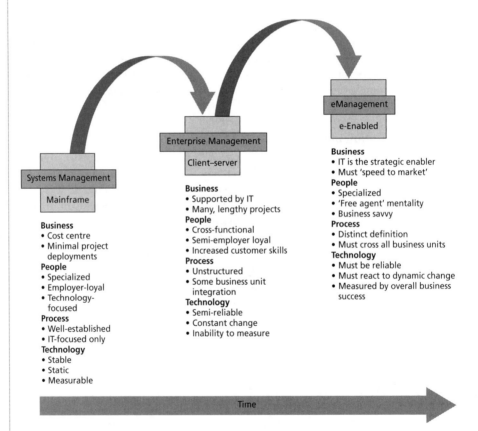

BLUR: eManagement

BLUR will affect ICT Service Management in a number of ways. The consequences can be illustrated using the effects of BLUR; Speed, Connectivity and Intangible value. The consequences for ICT Service Management are closely linked to the consequences for business.

Speed

The frequent business changes in response to the market requires an ICT Change Management process that is optimally implemented. If ICT management is unable to process changes fast enough, it could result in loss of market share for the business. However, reacting immediately to all changes that occur can also result in a grinding halt of business. It is therefore important to adjust the priority and speed of changes within ICT management to the priority and change needed from the business.

The relationship between ICT components and delivered products and services needs to be explicit. When a product or service is changed and changes must be made in certain applications, this may change the use of, or dependence on, systems. ICT staff needs to be retrained on a regular basis to keep up with the rapid introduction of new technology.

Business demands 7×24 service, which means that systems need to be available 7×24. Already many SLAs agree on continuous availability of systems but often with no guarantees or without round-the-clock support. Offering non-stop service does not only mean more human resources; it may also involve negotiations with unions, rescheduling batch jobs, planning on necessary technical capacity and replanning of maintenance windows.

The ICT organization needs to be set up to be flexible. In practice, this means that the service provisioning needs to go with the flow of a changing business demand. The ICT organization must make certain that control over the ICT infrastructure is maintained, while avoiding bureaucracy. This has consequences for the use of (ITIL) processes and procedures. Not only is retraining needed for new technology but the business knowledge also needs to be refreshed regularly. Having business-savvy ICT staff comes at a price.

Connectivity

The fact that systems of different parties interconnect has immediate consequences for ICT management. The responsibility of ICT management is spread over multiple organizations, which demands strong cross-organizational co-operation between the corresponding ICT organizations. The moment that an error occurs somewhere in the chain, all parties must know how responsibilities are divided and only a combined effort will get business back online. This kind of close cooperation needs to be part of the agreements.

Different organizational units using the connected ICT systems increases the importance for ICT management to improve its view on the use of the systems. In this way, the right people can be called if an error occurs; but it also helps in diagnosing an error. The mapping between business processes and ICT components needs to be set up and managed.

A high level of connectivity with customers and suppliers demands a multitude of communication channels. Examples are Internet, WAP, telephone, EDI, mail, etc. Not only should the channel match the local culture or even the individual, but the channels need to be perfectly synchronized. This synchronization can only be achieved if all technical and functional relationships are known.

ICT systems are modified so that consumers can use and change data on back-office systems without interacting with employees. Online banking is a popular example, having consumers enter their own financial transactions; but ordering goods through the Internet will also increase in popularity. For ICT management, these are new and often invisible users accessing the systems. ICT management must realize that these users require a different approach.

The use of new connection technology enables product innovation. The success of the mobile phone as an access device will increase as more WAP applications become available to consumers. The introduction of new technology and its potential for business should be closely monitored.

Intangible value

Increasing demands on personalization have their impact on ICT Service Management. The continuous flow of market data and personal profiles needs to be managed. All data need to be verified and personal profiles must be used well or not at all. A ninety-year-old should not receive offers for mountain bikes. Security is an issue here, not only because of privacy laws but also to avoid the theft of valuable market data. Management of market data and consumer profiles must therefore be well managed.

So, maintaining consumer profiles and delivering tailored services or products is of permanent importance for business. The intelligence required for these matches needs to be developed and asks for specifications from the business of what functionality is needed. These systems form the basis of intangible value; developing and maintaining the systems is important.

Challenges for eManagement

So BLUR has an effect on both business and ICT. In the subsection above, we discussed how the required (reliable) speed, connectivity and intangible value pose new challenges for Service Management. Looking at Table 51.2 we see a number of effects that eCommerce has on Service Management. Analysing these issues, four Service Management areas of challenge can be distinguished:

- Change Management;
- Service Level Management;
- Functional Management;
- Business–ICT Alignment.

Change Management poses a challenge within eManagement as the ICT organization has to deal with the effects of the speed of new changes required by the business and the use of new technologies. The need to know the relationship between ICT components and business processes is related to Service Level Management. Functional Management has to deal with managing new, invisible users as well as maintaining intangible value through functionality.

Issues such as continuous maintenance, End-to-end Performance Management over the Web, flexible outsourcing and rapidly changing ICT configurations are but some of the effects of doing e-business. Connectivity means dispersion of responsibilities,

TABLE 51.2 Consequences of eBusiness for business and ICT management

BLUR	Consequences for business	Consequences for ICT management
Speed	• Faster delivery of products and services • Real-time processing • 7 × 24 service provisioning • Frequent changes in product and service portfolio • Continuously changing organization	• Speed of change adjusted to the requirements of the business • 7 × 24 ICT management • Known relationship between ICT components and products and services • Up-to-date knowledge of ICT components • Flexible ICT organization
Connectivity	• Stronger connections with third parties such as consumers and suppliers • More relations with customers and suppliers • Stronger internal dependencies, e.g. between departments and employees	• Stronger cooperation with suppliers and partners • Known relationship between ICT components and business processes • Known relationship between systems • Contact with new and invisible users
Intangible value	• Availability of market and consumer knowledge • Intelligence in products and services • Product and service development (R&D)	• Data management • Use of new technologies

increased importance of functional ICT management and a complex infrastructure. Business–ICT Alignment needs to deal with the aspects of the business–ICT services such as a 7 × 24 ordering and delivery.

51.3 The eSM approach

To realize an eManagement organization that is BLUR-resistant, i.e. tackles the challenges mentioned above, a different approach is needed. The approach is similar to conventional approaches used in Service Management (SM) environments but has a very distinct focus. Perhaps that for that reason, only a lower case 'e' is used in 'eSM'.

To understand the focus of the eSM approach, we will first explain the basic principle of the conventional Service Management approach. The approach is not only process-oriented, since ICT Service Management is not based only on the implementation of ITIL processes. The conventional SM approach is based on the three pillars of People, Process and Technology.

- *People*: the People pillar is related to the organizational issues of ICT Service Management. Example subjects are organizational structure, tasks and responsibilities, education and skill levels.

- *Process*: naturally the processes are one pillar of the approach. Mostly ITIL or a model derived from ITIL is used. But other processes can be used as well, such as the TMN model, or the OSI model which is often used in the USA.

- *Technology*: the tools to support the ICT Service Management. Service Management and System Management tools are the most obvious, but also tools such as a knowledge management system or a document information system are within the scope of the third pillar.

The three pillars support the main platform, which is used to develop three methods: Diagnose, Process and Integration. The three methods have their own approach to reach a particular objective, as will be discussed below.

As mentioned before, the eSM approach is very similar to the former SM approach. Nevertheless, there are differences to handle the specific eBusiness challenges that were discussed. So all of the three methods have a special focus to the four challenge areas: *Change Management, Service Level Management, Functional Management* and *Business–ICT Alignment.* The general objectives of the three methods are described, as well as the way that the focus is adapted to suit the need to address the challenge areas.

eSM Diagnose

The eSM Diagnose is a diagnosis method to determine the extent of the effectiveness and efficiency of the ICT Service Management. With eSM Diagnose you can make a snapshot of the ICT Service Management so that improvement opportunities can be identified. The deliverables of the Diagnose study include a description of the 'as is' situation as well as an Improvement Project Calendar.

In the eBusiness environment the four challenge areas mentioned receive special attention. The speed of completing change requests is investigated and compared with business needs, and also related to the quality of the implemented changes. As for Service Level Management, the quality of the agreements with suppliers is investigated and compared with the requirements from the business. A close examination of the interaction with the unknown user shows if the interaction is taking place in the business organization. Also, the frequency of business and ICT discussions of joint concerns and opportunities is investigated, together with the effects of those meetings.

eSM Process

A special method is developed for Process Re-engineering, because in many organizations the process flow is inaccurate. Focusing on one or more Service Management processes, the objective of this method is to adapt the process flow(s) to obtain a more effective or efficient way of working. If a Diagnose has already been done, the first part of the eSM Process, the review of the current state, can be skipped.

To implement an eManagement environment that suits the business requirements, the focus of Process Re-engineering should be on one of the four challenge areas. When adapting Change Management, the focus should be on the balance between speed and quality, e.g. formalizing all steps will result in unacceptable delays where time-to-market is critical. For Service Level Management, the focus is on the relationship between the business processes and possible services that can be offered by the ICT organization, and general service levels need to be defined as opposed to detailed service levels per service. Implementing Functional Management and Business–ICT Alignment should be focused on the connection between the business processes and the ICT processes on the strategic, tactical and operational levels. Because the business processes are enabled by ICT, a mismatch between the two parties may result in immediate loss of revenue.

eSM Integration

The third method within the eSM approach is eSM Integration. This method addresses all three pillars of Service Management and the goal is to (re)define and implement a entire ICT Service Management environment. This method will be used when ineffectiveness or inefficiency of the ICT Service Management cannot be solved by redefining processes only. This method will be also be used when a major change takes place within the service offerings and/or client organization(s).

It is too complicated to explain all the Service Management issues which are related to specific areas within an eBusiness environment. For the Process pillar, a rough view was given earlier in the description of the eSM Process method. For the People pillar, one should focus on the flexibility of employees. The ICT infrastructure is in a constant state of change, so a stable ICT infrastructure is not realistic, but high risks are unacceptable. Employees must be able to adapt and judge. Training of the system managers is important because they need to deal with the latest technologies every day. For the Technology pillar, you need to be sure that system management tools can handle the newest hardware and software. Manual software installation (because the software distribution tool can't handle the software) is annoying at best.

51.4 Conclusions

Rome wasn't built in a day; evolution takes time. However, since the eBusiness world is reality today, ICT Service Management must be quick not to fall behind. ICT Service Management will have to make the transformation to eManagement to address the challenges it faces today. In this chapter, several methods and models are supplied to support eManagement development.

The eWorld is BLUR and BLUR means speed, connectivity and intangible value. For the business this means a reassessment of the business's position, as well as seeing ICT in a new perspective: as a critical enabler for doing business.

For ICT this means connecting both fast and new services. For ICT Service Management the stakes have been raised, and with them visibility. The trade-off between stability and efficiency on the one hand and flexibility on the other has never had this much effect at a corporate level.

The rise of eBusiness and so the BLUR effect provides four new challenge areas to ICT Service Management on the path to eManagement: Change Management, Service Level Management, Functional Management and Business–ICT Alignment. To cope with these challenges the eSM approach has been developed, based on the 'old' Service Management approach. Within this approach three methods are developed, all with a particular objective: eSM Diagnose, eSM Process and eSM Integration.

The four challenge areas, Change Management, Service Level Management, Functional Management and Business-ICT Alignment, have one thing in common: they shape the relationship between business and ICT. A well-organized business–ICT relationship has always been important, but now it has become essential.

Literature

Borgers, M. (1999) 'Business gericht ICT-Beheer', *Informatie*, December (in Dutch).

Davis, S. and Mayer, C. (1999) *Blur: The Speed of Change in the Connected Economy*, Addison-Wesley.

Porter, M.E. (1985) *Competitive Advantage. Creating and Sustaining Superior Performance*, The Free Press.

Tiggelaar, B. (2000) *Internet Strategie*, Addison-Wesley (in Dutch).

Review of part 8

In **Service Management and the Internet: managing e-services**, Wiebolt and Wong take one of the frameworks in part 1 (HP's IT Service Management reference model) as their base and show that the position of the end user is very central in an e-business situation. Flexible and secure environments with a high level of availability are very important for successful e-business strategies. For e-businesses, the time-to-market is so much less than for traditional businesses that this makes specific and very exacting demands on the whole design of the management organization. And because of the high integration of IT and business processes, the difference between the two areas largely disappears for the primary support processes. This makes the business focus of IT support a critical success factor for e-business. This observation will be music to the ears of those who are involved in the structuring of IT management organizations in the light of quality improvement projects. There will be an increasing need for increasingly efficient management organizations to help meet the demands of the future.

Traditional IT Service Management will not suffice when doing business in the e-services world, the authors state. They argue very well that there are new requirements in terms of extra pressure on speed, availability, flexibility and the like, but those could easily be regarded as the flexible parameters of the traditional management model. Since the authors use the same model for the analysis of e-management as for the analysis of the traditional environment, it might seem that the principle is still upright: the model works, but the e-circumstances have changed dramatically. This requires even more attention to Service Management, since more and more of the business in the New Economy is in fact made up of information technology.

In **Management of a website: what's new?**, Deurloo *et al.* opt for the user's perspective as their starting point, while Wiebolt and Wong take the demands made of the service provider as their angle of approach. This focuses the former's contribution on the functional management (Application Management) of the website as an information system.

In practice, many websites are lacking in quality. Although e-business is flying high, the implications on the organization are, for the most part, not understood. The introduction of a website has an impact on many parts of an organization. The fact is, however, that organizations tend to forget the lessons they learned in the management of traditional information systems, when they start a website. Therefore, the question in this chapter's subtitle could be answered by 'Nothing at all, so why don't you apply the management lessons you've learned?'. But again, in practice, it doesn't work that way.

For instance, the insufficient awareness of the need for maintenance and control and the insufficient funding of websites are the reasons why many websites are not updated on a regular basis. And a website that is not updated regularly is a dead website. As Wiebolt and Wong state, flexibility and time-to-market are crucial.

Furthermore, Deurloo *et al.* state that there are some important differences between websites and traditional information systems. In their analyses, they conclude that a website introduces new components in the infrastructure of an information system.

The differences between data, content and layout leads to adjustments in the management concepts. In fact, the technique that enables the high degree of flexibility that Wiebolt and Wong emphasized, causes the main difference between traditional systems and websites. Techniques based on HTML or any other Web-programming language make it possible to change the functionality and behaviour of the system in seconds.

Deurloo *et al.* analyse the implications of such characteristics upon the management organization. Two of the management domains in the Threefold model of the Delft school (see part 1) seem not to withstand the new demands: Application Management and Functional Management are merging and repositioning in the case of Website Management. Maybe this illustrates that the Threefold model is no longer an adequate paradigm, since the authors show that there are various solutions for this situation available.

All in all, their conclusion is that adjustments in the implementation of several processes are necessary, but they seem to be able to manage with 'the old paradigms'.

In **Vision in the BLUR of eManagement**, Borgers and van der Spek emphasize three characteristics of the New Economy: speed, connectivitity and intangibles, together the factor BLUR. The former three are investigated with respect to the effects of e-business. Although the authors show that there are effects on both the business and the service provider, they only illustrate this with quantitative effects like 7×24, high demands on Change Management and Configuration Management, flexible organizations, security issues, etc. The effects of e-business seem to be limited to focusing effects on matters that were already determined to be important in the traditional environment. As the authors themselves state: 'the e-Service Management approach is very similar to the former Service Management approach'. Both are dealing with the traditional triad of People, Process and Technology.

Borgers and van der Spek implicitly use a kind of maturity model in their analysis, although they do not name it as such. But with their denomination of companies in the state of eInformation, eCommerce, eCompany and eConomy, they definitely present a series of original titles for stages of integration in e-business. And although they show a high level of detail in their description of e-business effects, they too seem to get away with the old paradigms.

Concluding remarks

All authors seem to agree on one thing: e-service management looks different from traditional service management. On the other hand, none of them is able to show major differences in the structure of the management models, as is confirmed by some of the authors. Speed, flexibility, scalability, availability and the like differ a lot, but that doesn't bring about completely new paradigms. The only physical difference is the shift from the traditional tight bond between software and the functionality of the system: the introduction of HTML and its successors will require a new definition of 'software'. The 'old' paradigms, however, seem to withstand the storm of the New Economy.

Maybe that is the result of the strong focus on processes of the last decade: a process-oriented company was presumed to be very flexible and effective, and should be able to adapt quickly to changing circumstances without having to reconfigure its entire organization.

part 9

Tools and instruments

Introduction to the theme

For some reason, tools are very important in the practice of IT Service Management. Although a tool or instrument (Product) is only one of the three basic elements (the three P's: People/Processes/Products) that are needed to run an IT organization successfully, in a number of cases it appears to be the most important one. The other two P's are frequently overlooked or thought to be included in the tool.

The reason behind the importance of tooling is not clear. Maybe the explanation is that it is the only tangible element of the three P's and therefore the easiest element to implement. Others say that it can be explained by the fact that the technocratic IT organization tends to solve its organizational problems in an IT manner, i.e. with software tools. The fact is that tooling is an important issue nowadays: it's big business.

There are a lot of tools of all kinds and for many purposes. IT Service Management tools can be divided into technical tools and non-technical tools. Starting with the last category, these tools are the models, methods and frameworks to support IT Service Management. In this view the ITIL best practices could also be regarded as tools. The technical tools can be subdivided into two categories: system management tools and management tools.

System management tools are measurement/monitoring tools, e.g. for measuring and monitoring the performance of a network environment. The management tools support the management of an IT organization. Many of these have workflow capabilities and consequently they have a close relationship with the Process element of the three P's and thus with many non-technical tools, as described earlier.

Content

This part contains two contributions. The chapters describe two different tools for utilization in the IT Service Management field: an Enterprise Management tool and a Service Level Management tool. Thus:

Enterprise Management Software implementation
Niranjan Prasad, Sankaran Velunathan and Shyam Sundar V.

A business-focused Service Level Management Framework
Paul Maestranzi, Ron Aay and Richard Seery

A review of part 9 follows thereafter.

Reading instructions

The contributions deal with two different technical tools and are not interrelated. These chapters can consequently be read in any sequence.

 ## Introduction to the chapters

In **Enterprise Management Software implementation**, Prasad *et al.* deal in greater depth with the third dimension in organizations. After the detailed treatment of Processes (part 5) and People (in part 6 on organizational aspects), it is now Technology's turn. Prasad *et al.* deal with this by analysing the deployment of Enterprise Management Frameworks versus Point Solutions.

In **A business-focused Service Level Management Framework**, Maestranzi *et al.* combine the ITIL Service Level Management best practice with the SAS Rapid Warehousing Methodology to form a Service Level Management framework and toolkit.

52 Enterprise Management Software implementation

Niranjan Prasad, Sankaran Velunathan and **Shyam Sundar V**
Infosys Technologies Limited, India

Summary

Enterprise Management Software is a tool to help organizations simplify the management of their IT environment. It encompasses management of the network, databases, servers, applications, performance and more traditional issues such as backup, help desk, security and workload management. Enterprise Management Software should straddle multiple platforms, integrate functional interoperability and minimize operational and opportunity costs. It should also fulfil the business requirements of the organization – the relationship between IT functions and business processes should be clearly mapped. In this chapter, we will discuss various issues involved in design and customization of the software and the implementation in Infosys Technologies Limited (ITL).

52.1 Why Enterprise Management Systems?

Enterprise Management Software (EMS) packages and vendors have been 'all the rage' for the past few years. One reason for this recent popularity is that they promise to help meet the key challenges confronting support departments today. These challenges are:

- managing complexity;
- being cost-effective;
- ensuring quality of service;
- supporting business imperatives.

If we examine the marketing material offered by the major EMS vendors, some of the promises of EMS are:

- myriad technologies bridged;
- consistent paradigm;
- costs are checked, fewer personnel are required across various platforms;
- proactive problem solving;
- predictive and self-manageable products.

It is no wonder that senior IT managers have taken a huge interest in EMS. For if they manage to meet the challenges successfully, the stakes reached will be quite high. To appreciate the ingredients of a successful EMS implementation, let us consider the aforementioned challenges.

Complex IT environments

The scope of IT infrastructure is expanding rapidly. Technical approaches to networks, databases and applications continue to diverge. Diverse technologies are prevalent in IT today. In addition, there is a plethora of fragmented management solutions. Hence, there is a great need for integration in managing today's IT infrastructure. The control of a complex IT environment yields a lot of data. We need to look at this data in a meaningful way. We may want to segregate data by various parameters such as resources, servers or links, user/user groups, location, analyst, or by some combination of these. We may wish to automate critical operations, which is effected through triggers and alarms, event-driven actions and notifications. Finally, the dynamic IT environment implies that analysis and forecasting are vital. An EMS facilitates most of these activities.

Cost–benefit considerations

The Enterprise Management Software may not be a viable investment for everyone. Obviously, the larger the organization, the greater the economies of scale and hence the EMS investment is more likely to be cost-effective. Our analysis of the investment made at Infosys gave us some interesting insights. We also surveyed the material available from the Gartner group, IDC, Forrester and other IT consultants[1,2,3]. There are three main cost heads: the software, the hardware and the opportunity costs. The four main benefit areas are the opportunity costs of the saved downtime, the hardware and software savings, and the benefits of increased customer satisfaction. These are discussed in some detail in 'ROI considerations'. The benefit from EMS is mainly the opportunity for cost savings. This is driven by the size, growth and diversity of the IT infrastructure of the firm.

Quality of service

Today, the concept of service management through service level agreements has really caught on.[4] Two characteristics of the present-day IT support environment are:

- complex relationships between user problems, network events, changes to the IT environment, and corporate assets;
- increasing investments in IT driven by the rapidly changing, competitive and global economy.

As soon as a piece of IT infrastructure, such as a router, fails, critical business functions may begin to suffer. We have stated the importance of opportunity costs; systems failure results in lost revenue. The aim is to maintain/increase the level of service while keeping costs down. The internal help desk is expected to operate like a stand-alone business, but without the corrective forces (profit orientation and threat of losing customers) of a free market. In the absence of these forces, help desks (and, indeed, internal service departments in general) are adopting a new competitive mindset, namely Service Level Management. The internal IT department enters into an agreement with the rest of the organization to deliver a certain level of performance. This is usually in the form of service levels for various call categories. The service levels are characterized by time limits. To discourage hasty closures, a limit is usually placed on the percentage of reopened calls, or a defined level of customer satisfaction is targeted.

Service Level Management entails four key activities:

1. *Planning.* The support department and the rest of the organization determine what services will be provided, at what levels and for what ends.

2. *Delivery.* This includes Problem Management, integration with network and systems management, empowering the end user, Asset Management and Change Management. User empowerment encompasses keeping the users updated with relevant details on their requests, offering 24-hour support and supporting remote/mobile users. An integrated asset management solution automates tracking and auditing, which was a great help in meeting the Y2K challenge. Change Management technology manages the complex workflow involved by notifications and approvals, by analysing/monitoring the daily activities and by informing everyone involved in the change, namely the end users, support analysts and help desk, about progress and problems.

3. *Measurement.* It is crucial to ensure the service levels provided. Much of the measurement is built around monitoring the terms set out in service level agreements (SLAs). Help-desk solutions provide a real-time view of the SLA status of the calls, thus ensuring that service levels are continually met. Real-time metrics include the number of open calls, ageing of open calls, workload of various groups and analysts, and problems by asset or severity.

4. *Calibration.* The process of planning, delivering and measuring the delivery of customized support is a continuous process because competitive pressures, technologies, capabilities and needs change over time. Planning is the foundation of Service Level Management; calibrating the plan keeps Support responsive to the continually changing conditions throughout the organization.

The various EMS features that help enhance the quality of service in the IT infrastructure are:

- automation of critical operations;
- programmed actions for events;
- predictive capabilities that facilitate proactive measures and decrease downtime (the user can be kept updated on issues more accurately);
- Reliability of service. Help-desk software makes the service repeatable and predictable, i.e. standardized. There are a host of tools that do this; for example, one can attach a template to a certain class of requests. This template contains the workflow for that request and helps monitor the successful execution of all the stages by automatically sending notifications and reminders.

Business imperatives

EMS today facilitates some of the top business imperatives:

- *Globalization.* Most EMS has a remote control option whereby field workers and mobile users can be supported. Software can be delivered to far-off offices.

- **Customer focus.** This has been the buzzword of the past decade and indeed, customer orientation is only increasing in importance. EMS usually comprises tools to pull up customer details such as the user's contact details and computing environment, their past requests, the service level they have enjoyed, etc. The end user can be empowered by providing him or her with access to a knowledge base holding solutions for common requests.
- **Process orientation.** The concept of the process has helped increase operational efficiency. EMS allows one to monitor all the IT resources supporting a particular business process.
- **Knowledge management.** 'The difference between a company's market value and book value can be directly attributed to its intangible assets. Knowledge grows when shared and used; unused knowledge deteriorates.'[5] The day-to-day operations knowledge in an organization is usually lost when the domain expert quits. This knowledge can and should be captured. It can then be used by others to come up to speed and the availability increases the level and usage of this knowledge in the organization. EMS facilitates knowledge management by building databases of cases; for example, a particularly tough or a new problem is marked as a candidate for the knowledge base and the technician involved provides a solution. Such solutions are periodically reviewed by an expert panel and uploaded into the knowledge base.

Cost of competition

Once a technology is known to give competitive advantage to the practitioner, it soon becomes merely the cost of competition. If EMS overcomes the technical challenges and delivers on its promises, it will become the cost of competition for a) large businesses, b) high-growth businesses, and c) businesses with diverse IT environments.

52.2 Choosing the right EMS

Initial planning[6,7]

Vision and mission

The vision and mission of the support centre should be clear – the scope of the support centre and the range of services it plans to provide must be defined. Only then can one go forward making decisions regarding processes, tools and people that support high efficiency levels, knowing that such decisions support the strategic goals of the organization.

Goals

Next come the goals – they break down the vision into quantifiable levels of achievement.

Processes

Various processes should be mapped: organizations, departments, work groups, and footnotes for work-step definitions should be included. The strengths and weaknesses of current procedures should be understood. The various metrics for measuring and controlling performance should be decided upon beforehand.

ROI considerations

The return on investment (ROI) should be evaluated by considering the following cost and benefit heads. Cost heads are:

1. Software;
2. Hardware;
3. Opportunity costs:
   - initial research time and expense;
   - training costs;
   - customization and integration costs;
   - costs to expand, extend, or upgrade the tool.

The major opportunity cost savings have been studied by IDC:

- Productivity – deployment, operations and user administration;
- Availability – user productivity and prevention of lost revenue;
- Efficiency – scalability, travel savings.

Benefit heads are:

1. Software: all the management software you will not be investing in;
2. Hardware;
3. The benefits of customer satisfaction are difficult to assign a value to, but they are priceless:
   - change in customer retention;
   - gain or loss of revenue from changes in customer retention;
   - impact on customer productivity when poor services cause customers to stop calling;
   - public relations impact from customer satisfaction.
4. Opportunity costs avoided:
   (a) Productivity – deployment, operations and user administration:
     - time to log; to assign; to resolve a call;
     - time required to develop/maintain/ distribute self-help solutions to customers;
     - time required to prepare productivity, status, and root cause analysis reports;
     - time required to identify and notify key staff and customers of problem situations;
     - time required to document the problem resolution and provide feedback.
   (b) Availability – user productivity and prevention of lost revenue:
     - increase in uptime – this should be quantified in time units. The valuation of this marginal increase in available time is difficult. We suggest that only a small fraction of this be assumed as contributing directly to revenue;

- ability of customers to resolve more of their own problems;
- speed with which the customer can contact the support centre;
- speed with which the customer can get problem resolved;
- increases in customer's abilities to use tools of their job.

(c) Efficiency – scalability, travel savings:
- time savings on deployment of resources, such as servers;
- the user–analyst ratio should go up once the EMS stabilizes;
- remote management yields tangible savings in travel or outsourced support.

The project horizon should be taken as 10 years. The opportunity costs require the most number of assumptions. The positive cash flows arising from opportunity cost savings are critical in evaluating the financial viability of an EMS project. Here, the important thing to note is that the increase in available time is a marginal one and should not be blindly multiplied by productivity. Instead, a fraction of this time (we suggest 25 percent) should be valued. The positive and negative cash flows should be listed and discounted at the organization's weighted average cost of capital. Be concerned if the NPV is negative (!), or if the payback period is more than a couple of years. The problems of valuing intangibles is present throughout this ROI exercise – how does one value the opportunity costs of dissatisfied customers?

Involving users and analysts

Involve users and support analysts. Interactions with users will provide inputs to the services desired, level of self-help required, prioritization of requests, response and resolution times for the critical requests, the technologies supported, etc. Interactions with support personnel will provide inputs to the level of information required for request resolution, measures to prevent recurrence, best ways to save solutions for future reference, distribution of tasks between first- and second-level support, etc.

The framework or point solution decision

The framework is the technical concept that is supposed to deliver many of the benefits of an EMS. The first is a consistent front-end reduction in training costs and increasing ease of operation. The second is an object-oriented architecture to ensure easy scalability. One of the most attractive features of a framework is the possibility to see business views, where the IT resources related to a business function such as marketing or production can be strung together in a single view.

Typically, there are three layers in a framework architecture:

- In the lowest layer we have the agents, who reside on IT resources.
- The next layer contains information on the state of resources across the organization and the logic for responding to various scenarios. This is implemented through distributed objects.
- Finally we have a common repository for storing all the classes of resources. This layer provides integrated views of all the resources and provides a lot of management functionality.

Other common components are guaranteed messaging, a standardized common GUI and an event console and correlation engine. In addition, a framework encompasses procedures and methods inherent in specific applications, but organized by the framework. Frameworks purportedly offer benefits such as reduced maintenance through shared services, such as a single data repository; better integration between management tools; reduced training; and a single point of event correlation for the entire enterprise. It is not guaranteed that, because there is a framework, all these products will clip together into a seamless whole. Every framework is made up of bundled-together services, files, applications and protocols. Although the underlying framework services are improving, we have to deal with the details of making sure that all these pieces work in our environment. As Mary Jander's article[8] elaborates, there is a lot of disgruntlement among IS managers over the implementation hiccups and after-sales costs of EMS packages. What keeps them coming back for more is the potential of the frameworks and their powerful APIs to get a lasting grip on the control of complex networks. A point solution approach implies buying the best of breed solutions for various functions. This has the obvious advantages such as the best functionality, reports, ease of use, etc. There is a narrower scope of implementation and greater focus on the specific discipline. On the flip side, point products may or may not be integrated with different but related functions. The number of management views and overhead also increases. There is now a growing trend to use best-of-breed solutions that can filter input from the framework's databases.

Selecting the appropriate tools

Greater self-help by the end user implies lower cost of support and greater satisfaction for the technical segment of the users. Keeping in mind the interests of all segments of users, technical and non-technical, the tools that the user can use and the technology that can be delivered to the user should be considered.

Facilitation of communication to end users

Users need to be told how long a job will take, whom to contact, where to check updates on the status of their requests and any changes in the status quo. So there arises the need for publishing contact details, notifications and a forum for announcements.

Self-help

New self-help tools allow customers to directly access answers to their everyday questions, thus decreasing incoming calls to the support centre and encouraging customers to help themselves. Expert systems and knowledge bases used by the support people are now being made available to customers through Web or e-mail interfaces. Self-help tools work best for customers who do not mind working with technology, mobile workers and those who do not have access to the support centre. If self-help tools are easier to use than existing options, or if no other options exist, customers will use them.

Remote solutions

Remote control packages allow support centre agents to take control remotely of a customer's computer or conference with the end user. The host computer's screen is displayed and the agent takes control of the remote user's mouse, activating commands as needed to resolve the customer's service request. When remote technology is employed, customers view the problem being solved and often will know how to resolve it themselves if the problem recurs. Available for most operating systems, remote tools can shorten call duration and reduce call volumes by educating customers during the problem resolution process. Diagnostic tools allow support centre agents to test a remote client system, reducing repair time by providing information about the correct parts to effect repairs. Conferencing tools allow multiple people to connect to discuss an issue. Video-conferencing tools allow remote agents literally to see what is being described – particularly important when viewing hardware or the environment.

Monitoring tools

Monitors are automated tools that test for conditions that may require intervention. An example of recently developed monitoring technologies is the Desktop Monitoring Interface (DMI), a kernel of code that runs at each desktop developed by the Desktop Management Task Force (DMTF). The code alerts the support centre and/or the customer of errors or out-of-tolerance conditions. Self-diagnosing tools such as DMI can trap system interruptions, detect changes in workstation configurations and provide two-way communications to servers. These tools can also automate corrective actions, resulting in lower call volumes and shorter call duration. Monitoring tools also provide a public relations benefit because they are proactive. Customers are impressed when they hear, 'We know about the problem and are already working on it.' Even more impressive is the ability to contact a customer about a problem they did not even know was there.

Tracking and help-desk tools

A help-desk management system is the core tool of a customer support centre. A help-desk management system allows efficient management of the call resolution process by consistently logging questions and problems, establishing links between call records and the customer database and call history repository. This type of system also allows support centres to diagnose problems, identify root causes, analyse trends, and measure the performance of both the support centre and its customers. In the absence of such a tool, you would have to create performance reports manually, based on data that would be manually gathered and maintained; or you would not report performance at all. Without a help-desk management system, customer requests get lost or pushed aside, leaving support centres almost always in reactive mode. When support centres operate in reactive mode, problems are always urgent and important, staff become overworked and customers are rarely satisfied. With properly customized help-desk software, support centres are more likely to reach a proactive mode. Customer profiles and histories are maintained and call routing algorithms and escalation policies ensure high levels of service. Trends and training requirements can be identified in advance and recurring problems can actually be prevented.

Reporting

Most support reporting can be categorized as: [9]

- **quantity**: number of calls, workloads;
- **performance**: response and resolution times, percentage of calls closed within the limits prescribed in the SLA;
- **quality**: usually measured by customer surveys and can be administered through the EMS;
- **value**: the value added to the organization by the support centre – this can be approximated by an internal transfer pricing mechanism.

Apart from the abovementioned reports, the call history can be used for **root cause analysis**. Root cause analysis may identify the central problem, ways to expedite solutions and ways to distribute this solution. Reporting on the workloads can help with staffing and service level decisions. Quality reporting is an indicator of the maturity of the support organization.

Knowledge tools

There is an important distinction between information and knowledge. In many organizations there is an abundance of information in the form of notes, memos, lists, problem reports and other bits and pieces of data collected over time. Individuals in the support centre possess knowledge from assimilating the information into a form they can use to resolve problems. The most successful support centre people are those who remember who worked on a similar problem in the past or where they saw information about a particular issue. The new model for support is to systematically collect information and turn it into knowledge by organizing the data, putting it in a database in a consistent form of issue/process or symptom/solution. Knowledge tools involve two primary integrated technologies and several peripheral technologies. The most powerful knowledge tool is an expert system. Expert systems allow for storage and retrieval of knowledge in a way that helps you get the necessary information quickly and easily. An expert system allows a novice to wear the hat of an expert. By simply accessing knowledge using a decision tree structure (a series of yes or no answers), a rule-based system (using if-then paths), or a case-based system (using 'keyword' systems), first-level agents can provide answers to complex technical questions in a matter of moments. As you can imagine, this means major savings in training time and costs. However, for an expert system to be useful it has to be filled with knowledge. Knowledge consists of the actual answers to problems formatted in a manner that allows the expert system to retrieve it. An example of knowledge might that be the on/off switch for an XYZ printer is located underneath the front right corner. The knowledge is expressed in language the retrieval engine understands. Another knowledge tool is a reference library. Customers can directly access information through vendor reference manuals, CD libraries, e-mail libraries, electronic books and commercially distributed information bases. All these tools are relatively inexpensive and allow customers to avoid a call to an agent. Customers can automatically download the latest software patches, FAQs, training tutorials and vendor information, as well as post questions for feedback from peers.

Software distribution and asset management

These tools allow for the distribution and installation of software and upgrades onto remote LANs, servers and workstations without sending personnel to a specific location, thus simplifying the troubleshooting process, decreasing training costs and standardizing the desktop environment. Software management tools also will help ensure compliance with licensing agreements. A similar tool called Asset Management can maintain inventory control, costing, chargeback, and version control for hardware, software, networks and communication devices. Asset management tools help improve problem-solving capabilities by providing current configuration information about a customer's system. Asset management tools can be integrated with software management tools, call management tools and configuration polling, allowing better financial controls and reduced budgeting efforts.

Telephony tools

The two main telephony technologies are Interactive Voice Response (IVR) and Computer Telephony Integration (CTI). IVR allows users to query computer systems or route the call to the appropriate support personnel. IVR systems can serve as call routing units, they can identify customers and provide 'screen pops' of customer information and call handling scripts to support analysts. IVR can also be used to automate customer surveys. CTI uses Automatic Number Identification (ANI) codes to identify callers and provide 'screen pops' of customer information, open tickets and call handling scripts to support analysts before the analyst speaks to the customer.

A process for selecting support tools

Tools should be selected based on the vision, strategies for support and current infrastructure. They should definitely not be selected in an ad hoc manner, say because of the presence of a 'pet' feature. Tool decisions should not be fragmented ones; rather, they should keep in mind the needs of the present and the future.

Define requirements

As each environment has its own unique features, it is important to document specific requirements. This is one of the key steps in a successful EMS implementation and is discussed in some detail in 'Requirements analysis and design'.

Develop a vendor shortlist

Only a small number of vendors can be seriously evaluated. The areas identified as critical for operations are the elimination criteria. These five criteria should be further ranked and the weights considered when scoring the various products.

Formal procurement process

The best value in procurement agreements is obtained by organizations with formal procurement strategies. Request for Proposal (RFP) is a method for detailing the desired solution. An RFP also serves as a tool for formal and consistent evaluation of vendor offerings. The RFP should be part of the documentation that leads to a legal contract. All stakeholders in the support process must provide input.

Rating the tools

First, eliminate all options that do not meet criteria that are critical to your operations. Next, rate the remaining solutions on functionality. Thus, you should know how each product performs each function. The total of the scores on various functions yields total scores for the products. The final contenders should become very clear. The final decision can be taken based on detailed RFP and proof of concept demonstrations.

A long-term relationship with the vendor

EMS implementations are long-term commitments. As EMS is a total solution and is expected to deliver considerable business benefit over the long run, the vendor should be a business partner. The vendor too will be interested in a long-term relationship with repeat business in additional products or annual maintenance contracts. Nobody knows the product like the vendor does. Some ways to leverage vendor strengths are:

- having your vendor train at your site rather than sending one person to class and expecting that person to train everyone else;
- having your vendor assist on site in the initial set-up and customization;
- preparing extensive background data on your organization, your needs and your objectives before the vendor's training and support personnel arrive; and
- acting as a reference site for the vendor in order to get special attention.

52.3 Requirements analysis and design

Once the EMS has been chosen, the next step is to decide the functionality provided by the EMS. The out-of-the-box functions can be deployed immediately. It is best to hit the ground running. We begin with the following activities:

- hardware sizing;[10]
- a feasibility analysis is done to identify the risk areas,
- the system architecture is mapped, and
- these are reviewed with the vendor.

The functionality that requires customization is a much more demanding exercise.

Requirements analysis

Next, we do something very akin to requirements analysis in software development. We want to find out the requirements of the various users of the EMS.[11] Thus, we have to keep in mind the roles of the major actors – the end user, the support analyst and management. These and other support centre issues are discussed in great detail in several excellent websites, such as the ones maintained by Phil Verghis,[12] Dennis Lapcewich,[13] Noel Bruton[14] or Future Technologies.[15]

End-user requirements

The user is typically interested in self-help, a single point contact, timely feedback and ease of tracking. The typical method of collecting detailed requirements, especially end-user requirements, is by interviewing a representative sample from the interest groups and through focus group interviews. The questions usually focus on function, performance, information flow and content. The emphasis is on the 'what' rather than the 'how'. A common pitfall to guard against is that users love to talk about perceived solutions when queried about needs. These inputs are then classified into needs at several levels. These needs become the guiding principles of the subsequent customization. For an interesting discussion on needs analysis and service design in general, refer to Ramaswamy.[16] End users are primarily interested in speedy resolution of their problems. Ideally, they would like to receive no information other than the message that their problem has been solved. In a less than ideal world, though, they would like to know:

- the expected resolution time when they log a call;
- the status of their open calls;
- any development that impacts their open issues – this is usually effected through notifications;
- if the problem they are facing is a known problem and whether the solution can be easily accessed.

Support analyst requirements

The support analyst's main concerns are that the software should ease the workflow, supply relevant knowledge and keep track of work commitments through notifications and reminders. It is usually insightful to look at this from the perspective of the major processes the EMS is intended to support. Key processes for the support centre include:

- Customer trust/loyalty;
- Service management (telephone, fax, e-mail, Web, walk-in):
  - service request ownership (first, second and third level);
  - problem identification, isolation, resolution and follow-up;
  - ticket logging, dispatching, escalation and tracking;
  - service level agreement compliance.
- Software distribution;
- Asset management (desktop hardware and software);
- System administration;
- Network administration;
- Web administration;
- Analyst and end-user training;
- Knowledge management;
- Special projects.

52 ■ Enterprise Management Software implementation

These processes are further divided into sub-activities and mapped to the existing and possible functionality of the EMS. The critical work-steps are determined by estimating the financial impact on the organization – basically the opportunity cost of not getting the work done. These critical areas are automated as far as the software allows, using a mixture of triggers and alarms, event-driven actions, and notifications (pagers are used in critical situations). Most of the problems are solved at the operations level. Here, analysts should be able to:

- see the problem description, user environment and history;
- check the related resources;
- push software to (remote) users;
- troubleshoot remotely;
- look up solved cases for similar problems;
- pull up in-house or packaged knowledge bases;
- see what percentage of calls they are closing within SLA;
- check which resources are attached to the maximum number of problems.

Management requirements

Management's emphasis is on performance and trend analysis, scheduling and inputs to staffing, planning and forecasting, and reporting. Managers are interested in information that helps them achieve their goals:[17]

- ***comfort information***: a few daily figures on the state of the business in their domains of responsibility;
- ***internal operations data***: a few key figures indicating how things are going (including exceptional situations), together with progress information about planned projects and future assignments;
- ***trigger information***: warning or alerting data that suggest potential problems;
- ***problem information***: dealing with a crisis or an important project that demands daily attention until it passes;
- ***information for outside dissemination***: performance figures and reports before they are released;
- ***external intelligence***: information about the environment and reports on competition.

It is possible to create views of functionally related resources, e.g. the mail system with its mail servers, gateways, links, virus-wall and firewall. Middle management is probably most concerned with reporting, which was discussed in some detail in 'Remote solutions'. Top management would like to look at the financial performance of various projects. This phase of activities yields a requirements specification document that guides subsequent activities.

Design

In actual practice, organizations and their managers do not maximize the potential of computer-based information reporting systems. In such organizations, both top management and the Management Information Systems department must share the blame. The IT department's part in the blame stems from the misconception that management's information needs would be fulfilled by reports that are merely produced as by-products of processing the daily transactions of the enterprise. Top management's slice of the blame is carved by abrogating their management responsibilities and allowing the misconception to persist.

Critical success factors

To elicit 'real' information requirements, a technique known as the critical success factor (CSF) approach may be employed. The CSF method is not new. It is based on the concept of 'success factors' introduced by Ronald Daniel[18] in 1961. However, Dr John Rockart of MIT[19] was the first to apply the concept in the information systems arena. The methodology has been further popularized by Rockart[20, 21] and other researchers[22, 23] and is now being increasingly used by MIS departments and by consultants, as an aid to information systems planning[24]. Although critical success factors vary widely by industry and across firms, they generally originate from the same sources. The Rockart research team at MIT has identified the following as the primary sources of CSFs:

1. **industry-based factors**: CSFs determined by the characteristics of the industry itself;
2. **competitive strategy, industry position, and geographic location**: CSFs derived from whether the firm is a dominant or minor force among competitors, the niche it occupies or the basis of its competitive strategy;
3. **environmental factors**: CSFs arising from areas over which an organization has little control but which affect performance, such as energy costs, government regulations, changes in customer demands and the economic cycles;
4. **temporal factors**: CSFs springing from issues such as modernization of the physical plant, which become critical for a short period of time;
5. **managerial position**: generic CSFs associated with each functional management position;
6. **managerial world view**. CSFs rooted in the perspectives brought to their jobs by managers, especially in regard to leadership.

The use of CSFs is not an all-round remedy as, ultimately, there is no substitute for good thinking and hard work. In an interesting article, Tom Davenport makes the following four recommendations:

- Consider the key drivers of cost, revenue growth and profitability.
- Use lots of statistics, but only simple ones.
- If you cannot get the exact data you need to determine a leverage point, substituting several related (though less robust) measures that coincide is 'close enough'.
- Get out into the field and muck around.[25]

So we suggest approaching the major roles with a CSF perspective.

Workflow

When a particular request comprises several activities, some of which may be done in parallel while others are dependent on their predecessors, there arises a need for managing the workflow. Otherwise, the maximum time wastage happens in between tasks. Also, change occurs constantly within the organization. A typical example is when an employee leaves – several tasks need to be performed. Resources allotted to the employee are released; his/her various accounts are deleted, etc. Automating the notifications at the end of each work-step can facilitate these workflows. All parties concerned can view these calls right from the start and all members of this 'team' know when and why there is a hold-up. This eliminates redundant communication and ensures better coordination.

Issues

There are several types of customization that may be carried out. The front-end look and feel, or menu-driven changes from within the EMS, are the easiest to handle. Sometimes, it may be simplest to write queries on the package databases. However, when you want to add objects or modify the database tables, it is imperative to follow the procedures defined in the package. These changes may have far-reaching effects! Rigorous commenting and documentation standards should be maintained. Migration issues: do remember that just about the time you have finished your customization, another new version will be released. The customization should be capable of migrating to the latest version or there will be a huge waste of effort. If a third party is conducting the implementation, make sure than the work is well defined. It is even more important to follow documentation standards.

52.4 Implementation issues

The implementation of EMS is a major challenge as the vendor, the client and sometimes third parties are involved in complex two-way and three-way arrangements. This requires tremendous human resource management skills. The basic skeleton for task management is the project plan, which tracks various activities and sub-activities, the time and resources required for each and how delays squeeze the time and resources for the remaining activities. For successful implementation of Enterprise Management Software in any environment, the following steps are important.

Test environment

Since, in many instances, the Enterprise software is used in a mission-critical environment, it is imperative that the modules be tested before deployment. Hence, during the project implementation, it is necessary that a test environment be set up and always available. In the test environment, the following steps should be used.

Modular implementation

The Enterprise Management Software has a number of modules, which are interdependent, for providing business benefit to the organization. For example, the Help Desk and the Asset Management modules are interrelated. The Network Management and Event Management modules are interrelated. The successful implementation of these modules simultaneously is quite crucial for successful interoperability of the modules. Hence, a modular implementation of the project is essential.

Resource and configuration management

Since a number of modules are implemented in parallel, resource is a major constraint for the implementation. Configuration Management is also a critical factor as we have a number of modules being installed in various permutations across a large variety of hardware, with frequent updates and patches.

Customization

During implementation of Enterprise Management Software, customization plays a very crucial role in getting tangible benefit from the product. A product is likely to need extensive customization in many aspects for meeting the business requirements of the customer. In many instances, the actual requirement can be met only after extensive customization is carried out.

Deployment

Once the customization has been done and stability ensured in the test environment, the modules are moved to the live production environment.

Bridging the product limitations

During the implementation, there will be many instances when the product is not able to meet the requirements of the customer. Enterprise Management Software being a new and evolving field, timely technical support from the EMS vendor is vital. This requires a constant and rapid feedback channel to be available between the implementers, customers and the developers of the software. This has to be ensured for successful implementation of the project. Once this gap between the product feature and the business requirement is communicated to the developer of the product, the business benefit emanating from the product will be increased.

Training the support analysts

The usage of the product by the support analyst is very critical for success of the implementation. Hence, the necessary training must be given to the support analysts to use EMS effectively. The best method was found to be a demonstration followed by hands-on sessions.

Educate end users

Gaining acceptance of any new technology usage, particularly one that asks customers to interact directly, requires education. When considering the customer base, education is a two-phase process. The first phase involves a marketing campaign to sell customers the benefits of using the new technology. If customers do not understand and buy into the reasons for using the new technology, they will not be interested in learning how to use it. The second phase is more traditional usage training. In conjunction with the awareness or marketing campaign, you need to provide customer training. Few technology tools are intuitive to all people; therefore, you need to provide training on the tools you are asking customers to use. Training is generally more effective when provided in several short sessions rather than one long session. One method is to provide an introductory session that provides people with the basics of the product and how to get started. Then, a few weeks later, provide follow-up training on advanced features.

52.5 Infosys case study

Infosys Technologies Limited is a software services company with its headquarters in Bangalore. It has development centres located in five cities in India, as well as offices spread across several continents. It has around 4,500 desktop users and about 1,500 mobile laptop users located across all these offices. Its network spans different platforms ranging from Windows NT to different combinations of Unix, mainframe, open systems, etc. with different applications and databases running on them. The management of this complex environment necessitated the use of Enterprise Management Software. Infosys chose Computer Associates' Unicenter-TNG software. For implementing this Enterprise Management Software, the general guidelines below were followed during implementation:

- choosing the right vendor;
- requirement analysis;
- design;
- implementation;
- enhancement requests;
- documentation.

Choosing the right vendor

The different EMS products in the market were analysed for their features. A proof of concept (POC) demonstration for the different EMS was arranged at the customer site. Each product was rigorously tested in this POC and the key features promised were tested in a simulated environment. Pricing was obviously considered, though it took a back seat to functionality. Contact was established with customers of each of these products who had deployed the product in their environment. Their experience with the product when using it in their environment was taken into account before deciding upon the solution. Infosys chose CA's Unicenter-TNG over its competitors because of the better collaboration of the EMS with the Microsoft platform, the most common environment in Infosys.

Cost–benefit considerations

There is considerable ambiguity in calculating the financial impact of outages and downtimes. No one really knows how much managing complex networked environments costs. After all the years of implementing management platforms, and analysts' studies, what it really costs to get control remains a complete mystery.[26] Nevertheless, this has not deterred vendors and solution providers from advertising various ROI studies and the like. We have done a conservative estimate of expected cash flows for the implementation at Infosys Technologies Limited. A detailed list of the various cost and benefit heads are given in 'ROI considerations'. The interesting find was the breakdown of expected costs and benefits. There are three main cost heads – the software, the hardware, and the human resource and training costs. These are discussed in some detail in 'ROI considerations'. The split is approximately 75:5:20 (Figure 52.1). As expected, the software costs dominate, but the interesting thing is that human resource and training costs far outweigh the hardware costs. The breakdown of the benefits is even more interesting. The three main benefit areas are the opportunity costs saved; the hardware and software that were not purchased; and the human resources and training benefits. The split is 85:5:10 (Figure 52.2). Thus, the benefit from an EMS is mainly the opportunity cost of the saved downtime. This is driven by size, growth and the diversity of the IT infrastructure.

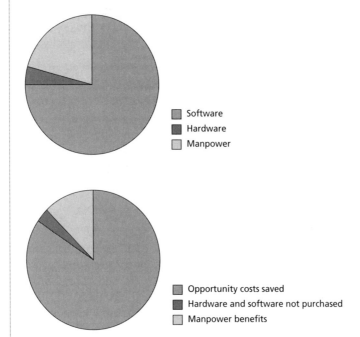

FIGURE 52.1

Analysis of EMS costs

FIGURE 52.2

Analysis of EMS benefits

Requirements analysis

At Infosys Technologies Limited, the implementation exercise started with requirements analysis. Discussions were held to identify the business requirements of Infosys from the Enterprise software. For each one of the modules to be implemented, discussions were held with the vendor so that the business requirements from the modules were clearly understood. These requirements were extensively listed before moving to the design stage of the implementation. The key requirements were:

- automating routine tasks;
- obtaining workflow for the tasks;
- multi-platform and multi-location;
- scalability;
- network and asset management;
- problem isolation for troubleshooting.

Design

Infosys has a distributed network with offices located in different parts of the world. Each location had some common as well as some unique characteristics in its network. Thus, there were some requirements unique to each location. The modules to be implemented in the various locations were selected based on the requirements of each location. The sizing of the hardware was done during this design phase of implementation. Computer Associates had tested their modules on several hardware combinations and had results and benchmarks for these. These were complemented by additional testing in our test labs. Furthermore, the future expansion of the Infosys network was also tailored into the hardware sizing of the project. The architectural design of the whole system, quite crucial for successful implementation, was completed in this phase of implementation.

Implementation

Infosys had created a test environment for the Enterprise Management Software. Initially, the capability of the product was tested in the simulated environment. The performance of the product was compared with the business requirements of Infosys. As mentioned earlier, since most of the implementation was conducted in business-critical environments, the test environment performance was closely monitored before deciding to go live with the product. In the live environment, the tested capabilities of the product were implemented and the business benefit from the product was analysed. Even after testing in the test environment, there were considerable practical problems faced in stabilizing the set-up. Hence, the live implementation was scaled up slowly. There were several iterations of movement between the live and test set-up, before successful deployment. In particular, great importance was given to event correlation activity for business benefit. The different events that were detected were classified into various levels of importance. Based on the level of importance, the alerts and event message actions were selected. The key modules implemented in Infosys were:

- the basic framework;
- network management;
- event management;
- help-desk management;
- remote management;
- anti-virus module;
- asset management.

Enhancement requests

During the implementation of the product in Infosys, there were instances where the current version of the product could not meet the requirements. Then, such issues were taken up with the developers of the product along with the implementers. Product enhancements or newer versions were obtained from the developers that could meet our requirements. This was also an important feature in the implementation of the Enterprise Management Software in Infosys.

Documentation

The documentation of the implementation procedure is a very important aspect of project management. All the steps involved in the implementation have been clearly documented to ensure the availability of the knowledge base for future use in enhancement and redeployment of the product.

52.6 Future directions

- Currently, implementation is a black hole, and controlling creeping project costs and clearly identifying goals are critical requirements. The clock is ticking and the vendors know that it is critical to overcome these difficulties. EMS vendors are focusing on this in a big way. For example, Tivoli Enterprise offers a very structured approach that documents architectural and procedural imperatives in great detail, while Hewlett-Packard uses tactical integration and the best Service Management features to offer a non-framework solution. CA has similar ongoing initiatives.
- Move to the Web – most EMS suppliers are rushing to move their solutions to the Web. This indicates a move to technologies such as Java and XML and abandonment of the problems with the SNMP and client–server model. Web technologies promote similar look and feel, facilitate better access, put lesser load on networks and have better scaling and integration features for future developments.
- Increasing emphasis on service management and support for SLAs.
- Improvements in automation of data collection and discovery as well as status and configuration management.
- Better real-time performance management aided by historical and statistical analysis. The predictive aspect of EMS needs further development. Neural network technology is the latest entrant here to provide advanced predictive capabilities.
- Advances in fault tolerance, automated response and decision support features, leading to self-healing networks.
- Increased support for Enterprise Storage Management and Storage Area Networks.

Notes and Literature

1 http://www.forrester.com/
2 gartner11.gartnerweb.com/public/static/home/home.html
3 http://www.idc.com/

4　http://www.tivoli.com/products/documents/whitepapers/ slm_wp.pdf
5　Karl E. Sveiby, in http://knowledgecreators.com/km/kes/ kes2a.htm
6　http://www.renpartners.com/file_ list_ access.html
7　http://www.networkcomputing.com/1003/1003f1.html
8　http://www.data.com/issue/990921/framework.html
9　Noel Bruton, in a discussion on the help desk mailing list. Bruton Consultancy for Help desk Best Practice; noel@bruton.win-uk.net; http://www.bruton.win-uk.net
10　Roger S. Pressman, (1992) *Software Engineering: A practitioner's Approach*, 3rd edn, McGraw-Hill, pp. 138ff.
11　Roger S. Pressman, (1992) *Software Engineering: A practitioner's Approach*, 3rd edn, McGraw-Hill, pp. 174ff.
12　http://www.philverghis.com/helpdeskfaq.html
13　http://www.ksasystems.com/prolink
14　http://www.bruton.win-uk.net/
15　http://www.ftechnologies.com/
16　Rohit Ramaswamy, (1996) *Design and Management of Service Processes*, Addison-Wesley, pp. 55ff.
17　I.F. Jackson, (1986) *Corporate Information Management*, Prentice-Hall.
18　D.R. Daniel (1961) 'Management information crisis', *Harvard Business Review*, September–October pp. 111–116.
19　J.F. Rockart (1979) 'Chief executives define their own data needs', *Harvard Business Review*, March–April pp. 81–93.
20　J.F. Rockart (1982) 'The changing role of the information systems executive: a critical success factors perspective', *Sloan Management Review*, Fall pp. 3–13.
21　J.F. Rockart (1982) 'Current uses of the critical success factors process,' *Proceedings of the Fourteenth Annual Conference of the Society for Information Management*, September pp. 17–21.
22　G.B. Davis (1979) 'Comments on the critical success factors method for obtaining management information requirements', *MIS Quarterly*, September 1979, pp. 57–58.
23　Jenster, P.V. (1986) 'Firm performance and monitoring of critical success factors in different strategic contexts', *Journal of Management Information Systems*, Winter pp. 17–33.
24　Michael E. Shank, Andrew C. Boynton and Robert W. Zmud, 'Critical Success Factor Analysis as a methodology for MIS planning', *MIS Quarterly*, 9(2), pp. 121–129.
25　http://www.cio.com/archive/060196_ dave_ content.html
26　'But how much does it cost?' http://www.networkcomputing.com/1003/1003f1side8.html

53 A business-focused Service Level Management Framework

Paul Maestranzi SAS UK
Ron Aay SAS Netherlands
Richard Seery SAS EMEA – International

Summary

With the advent of corporate globalization and e-business, increasingly IT organizations are called on to demonstrate the value they deliver to the business. This invariably has a major impact on the way in which they operate as both a supplier and customer. In the past, data centres were run as huge cost centres that at best broke even or at worst ran at a loss. There were huge operational inefficiencies and inevitably bad customer experiences. This ultimately resulted in a large number of corporations outsourcing their IT organizations to specific companies specializing in IT delivery (facilities management). This is not so different in today's marketplace, especially in the area of e-business with Internet Service Providers (ISPs), Application Service Providers (ASPs) or Management Service Providers (MSPs).

Many of today's IT organizations outsource certain activities such as storage management, desktop environments or networks. But not all corporations want to outsource; in fact, many are spinning off their IT organizations as a separate (but still wholly owned) business with their own strategies, goals, objectives, budgets, targets and management teams. In these modern IT organizations, their customers and customer services are the key to success. Not surprisingly, IT organizations are now concentrating more than ever on the quality of service and the cost of production. IT customers, on the other hand, are more concerned with the purchase costs associated with IT and also the quality of their delivered service.

The IT framework that ensures customer satisfaction is a 'Service Level Management Framework' (SLMF). This chapter highlights the major issues concerning the Service Level Management dilemma of the modern IT organization and how the SAS SLMF fits into the picture, based on our experiences at customer sites.

53.1 Introduction

In today's environment, the 'bottom-line' primary role of the IT organization is to ensure that business users can quickly and easily input and access relevant information to assist the decision-making processes. Also, in fast-moving organizations such as telecom providers, cyber centres and B2C initiatives, providing new services quicker than the competitors becomes absolutely essential. Their competitors will attempt to copy that service, but that may take up to six months, by which time it has become more difficult to gain a share of the market. IT has a crucial role in providing these services quickly and effectively.

IT organizations have to become more outward-looking; they need to understand future sales and marketing activities and business strategy to ensure they understand the needs of the business. By understanding these requirements and the value IT can contribute to the business, the internal processes of the IT organization can be aligned to the business. Even the traditional bricks and mortar organizations are moving quicker, offering new services such as Web banking, merging and partnering with others. IT organizations must streamline their processes to ensure rapid time-to-market; they can no longer afford to take years to implement business processes. IT has to move at the same speed as the business and in the same direction if it is to become a valued business partner.

To fulfil this role, it is not sufficient just to improve the IT processes and add process automation, integration and communication tools. It is also necessary that the IT organization becomes both service-oriented and customer-focused; in other words, IT must understand the business needs and actively contribute to the effectiveness and improvements in the business.

Historically, the majority of IT organizations were centred around mainframes running monolithic business applications. With the advent of distributed processing in the early 1980s, the explosion of the World Wide Web in the mid-1990s and e-based business in early 2000, the requirement to provide access to business information has resulted in a much more complex IT environment. Furthermore, the distribution of processing leads to distribution of the IT personnel and diversification of the skills required.

This distribution of the IT function and personnel means that the migration from a mainframe-centric environment to a distributed environment is not straightforward. Processes in place at the data centre – for example, for Change Management and Configuration Management – were not integrated but worked because of the proximity of the personnel and hardware. Selection of the existing systems management and process tools was most likely on a case-by-case basis with little thought about future integration. With distributed computing, the integration of existing processes becomes necessary, as well as the creation of new processes. It also becomes more challenging because we lack good process, application and user information on these platforms. A further complication arises when the environment has both mainframe(s) and distributed processing and when different applications have different processing requirements in these different environments. Briefly, the requirements we encountered in the modern IT organization are:

- Regard the consumers of IT services as customers and not users.
- Understand where the IT function adds value to the business.
- Become less introspective and more outward-looking, and business-focused.
- Focus on process as well as technology.
- Develop business-justified IT processes.
- Implement measured, accountable IT processes.
- Maintain a cost-justified balance between insourcing and outsourcing.
- Implement end-to-end processes and discard fragmented processes.
- Implement accurate service-billing mechanisms.
- Adopt a proactive organization.
- Develop service-oriented roles.

53.2 Service Level Management

Service Level Management is the process of negotiating, defining and managing the *quality* levels of IT services that are required and that are *cost* justified. The goal for Service Level Management should be clear and quantifiable. It should not be a service level report that only IT staff understand or that is not manageable anyway.

Some examples of quantified results are:

- IT services are catalogued.
- Quantifiable IT services are stated in terms that are clear to both the customer and the IT service provider (service definition, cost and quality).
- Internal and external targets are defined and agreed.
- Agreed service targets are achieved and maintained.

Figure 53.1 demonstrates the two sides of Service Delivery that have to be balanced by the IT organization in order to meet the demands of the Business.

FIGURE 53.1

Balancing the quality of service with the cost of service

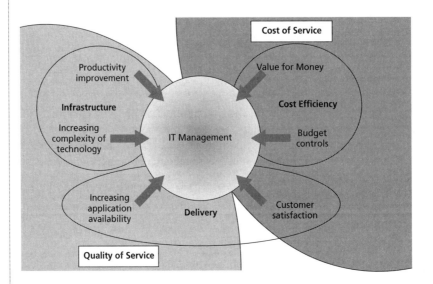

Service Level Management incorporates the management of hardware, software, people, knowledge and processes, and extends to aggregate and consolidate management information about the quality of service delivered. The principal components of Service Level Management consist of:

53 ■ A business-focused Service Level Management Framework

- the costs associated with the manufacturing and delivery of IT services;
- maintaining the quality of delivered services.

It is the challenge today of IT management to bridge the gap between the business and IT by demonstrating that they understand the needs of the business and the impact that IT has when it is unable to deliver. At the same time they have to deal with the increasing complexity of technology and applications that now span tens to thousands of servers across multiple platforms and networks, possibly even partitioned. Additionally, they have to show that they are providing value for money; it is very easy for IT infrastructures to become overloaded with technology and bypass the needs of the business.

A recent enquiry among a large number of CIOs, IT directors, service delivery managers and platform managers has yielded the following quotes:

- 'My IT organization is running at loss.'
- 'We have ineffective IT processes and procedures.'
- 'My customer base is unsatisfied and is looking elsewhere for their primary IT service provider.'
- 'I am losing customers.'
- 'Benchmarking has shown we perform less effectively and efficiently (in costs) than average.'
- 'The company wants to outsource our IT.'
- 'I have no understanding of my customers service culture'.

IT is effectively evolving into a more commercial animal. So much so, that the major issues are:

- the profitability (or loss) of services provided;
- increasing the profitability;
- more competitive and effective IT processes;
- increased customer satisfaction;
- improved customer retention;
- reduced fear of outsourcing.

IT has become process-oriented, catering for business processes. Figure 53.2 shows the relationship between these processes and the Service Level Management process. It certainly shows part of the issues in SLM.

To address the business pains that an IT organization is experiencing, a strategic solution to control and manage their business in delivering business benefits is required. This not only has internal advantages but certainly helps IT managers in discussions with the business to become a business partner. For instance, the chief financial officer (CFO) would finally understand where costs are going and the value that comes from it. The CFOs of today are not just interested in costs but need information about the intangible assets as well. They like to make decisions based on the value of a process to the business. Would this not make our lives a lot easier, compared to the stressful discussions about budgets and being too expensive?

FIGURE 53.2

Relationship between IT processes and Service Level Management

Source: *Service Level Management* by Jay Niessen and Paul Oldenburg

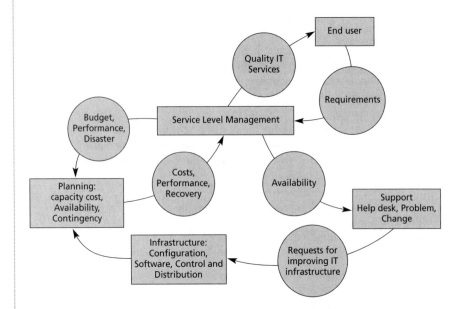

By managing the business needs and expectation, IT can improve the probability of ensuring that the quality of delivering service and the costs associated with service delivery are optimized to both IT and the customer. A very attractive commercial by-product is that the business-to-IT alignment process has begun. This process has much to do with the way in which the customer and the business measure the IT organization's performance, an accepted industry approach is to apply 'The Strategic IT Scorecard'.

Managing customer expectations can be controlled by IT in the following ways:

- service availability and delivery;
- service contingency;
- attitude to the customer;
- plans and processes;
- understanding of the business importance;
- introducing Service Level Agreements.

Service Level Management has a major role in the IT Scorecard (performance) measurements. Figure 53.3 highlights Service Level Management's role in the creation of the IT Scorecard.

The Balanced Scorecard is the brainchild of Kaplan and Norton and was first introduced in the early 1990s (latest version, 1996). The balanced scorecard looks at the business from different perspectives, usually the four shown here, but they can vary in number and name:

- To achieve our vision, how should we appear to our customers?
- To succeed financially, how should we appear to our owners?

FIGURE 53.3

The IT Scorecard

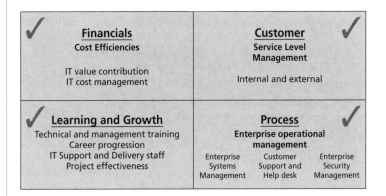

- To satisfy our customers, at what business processes must we excel?
- To achieve our vision, how will we sustain our ability to learn and improve?

The perspectives ask the question, 'What do we have to do in each in order to achieve our chosen strategy?'. There is a cause-and-effect relationship between each of the perspectives (see Figure 53.4).

FIGURE 53.4

The IT Business Perspectives Cause-and-effect relationship

This is one of the powerful features of this framework since it goes beyond output measures, like profit, and tries to identify what you need to do to get the output you want. This can get quite complex and should be unique to each organization.

The Old World idea that companies are represented by the bricks-and-mortar assets it owns has long been untrue. Companies are valued based on the market's perception of their future earning potential and this is based more on their intangible assets, such as knowledge, than on the things that can be touched.

This is not new to an IT audience who has long appreciated the value of the software developed, which has a book value of nil. But IT departments themselves have rarely tried to value this for the organization.

Putting strategy into effect is clearly a problem, and a CEO will more likely fail not because of bad decisions but because he or she is not able to mobilize the organization to execute the strategy. This is really a call for help, and since IT is so central to most organizations and IT areas are used to managing projects and delivering service levels, the IT department can play a significant role (Figure 53.5).

FIGURE 53.5

The role of IT in an organization's strategy

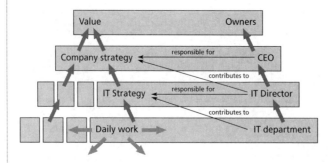

That's not to say that the IT department is the only answer, of course. Many areas of the company will contribute in their own ways. This can often make it difficult to identify IT's unique contribution. The value comes from aligning the IT activities around the corporate strategy, and reducing the number of driver activities, although most organizations find that some level of non-value-adding activity is unavoidable.

The IT department can support the corporate strategy, driving it forward and amending it. In this way, IT will be seen as a major force in implementing strategy, and this skill may be a significant percentage of the share value.

So far we have introduced a Service Level Management strategy aligned to the business, and how it can be used as part of an IT Scorecard, which demonstrates the value of the IT organization to the business. The focus of the rest of this chapter will be on the Service Level Management Framework, which provides the input to the customer perspective of the IT Scorecard.

53.3 Service Level Management Framework (SLMF)

It was clear to SAS that we could not leave the deployment of a Service Level Management framework to just tooling but also had to deliver a framework. Since SAS lacked the benefits of theorizing about it until it was 100 per cent perfect, this framework is based on best practices. SAS combined the IT Infrastructure Library (ITIL) with the SAS Rapid Warehousing Methodology and experiences from the field. SAS named this framework the 'Service Level Management Framework' (SLMF). The SLMF is used for planning, managing and executing IT Service Management. It has been developed to focus IT management strategies to receive a high return on investment through rapid results. There is a reference guide that provides an overview of the framework, plus guidelines for planning and executing IT management programmes. There is also a one-day training course presenting the theories and practices of the reference guide.

Furthermore, SAS used existing tools and expanded them to a knowledge solution for SLM, which could provide a repeatable process with rapid results and consistent message.

Overview of the SAS Rapid Warehousing Methodology

The SAS Rapid Warehousing Methodology (see Figure 53.6) outlines a plan for implementing integrated warehouse environments:

- maximizes business benefits;
- optimizes IT human and system resources;
- maintains consistent information;
- minimizes the impact of change;
- supports quality management standards.

Three principal attributes that make the SAS Rapid Warehousing Methodology successful are:

- business focus;
- detailed project definition and requirements-gathering workshops;
- use of Rapid Application Development (RAD) approaches.

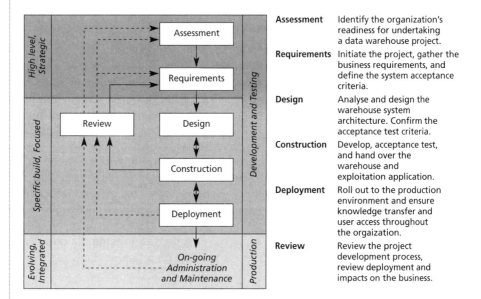

FIGURE 53.6
The SAS Rapid Warehousing Methodology

Introduction to the IT Infrastructure Library

Originally a set of about 60 books developed in the late 1980s as a set of best practices for IT developed by the CCTA (Central Communications and Telecom Agency) of the UK government, EXIN was contracted to maintain and publish the books. It is mostly used in the UK and the Netherlands, although an organization called itSMF also promotes it in the USA. The books describe best practices in a number of IT service areas, including:

- Help Desk
- Problem Management
- Change Management
- Configuration Management

- Software Control and Distribution
- Availability Management
- Contingency Management
- Capacity Management
- Cost Management
- Service Level Management.

The role of ITIL in the SLMF (Service Level Management Framework) is to:

- provide the basic foundational tools for defining service levels;
- provide a standardized terminology for the description of Service Management processes.

53.4 Defining an IT Service for the business

The goal of Service Level Management is to define a measurable service, which meets the needs of the business for both *quality* and *cost*. Monitoring compliance with this commitment requires each subcomponent of the service to be measured and combined to provide a complete picture of the quality of service and cost to the business. Also, one has to take into account the business patterns in order to plan and be ready. Thus measuring and combining is the first step; keeping a history of all this knowledge is essential for powerful and correct analysis and planning for the future. The solution therefore varies according to the type of business. For example, an investment bank may require a guarantee of trade confirmation within 30 minutes of execution, while an airline ticketing system requires near instantaneous response. Irrespective of the solution, every business has a service which is critical to its survival; therefore a Service Level Agreement process can be defined to implement an SLM-based solution.

The SLM process diagram can be used to provide the business with a pragmatic approach to implementing an SLM solution that provides rapid results aligned to the business (Figure 53.7).

53.5 Service Level Agreements

A Service Level Agreement (SLA) is an agreement between the IT service supplier and its customer(s). It is an agreement that states the level, or scope, of service that will be provided by an IT organization.

It is a tool that simply:

- clarifies expectations;
- defines the service level(s);
- provides a framework for setting goals.

On the other hand, it is NOT:

- a 'contract';
- a weapon to beat the the IT service provider;

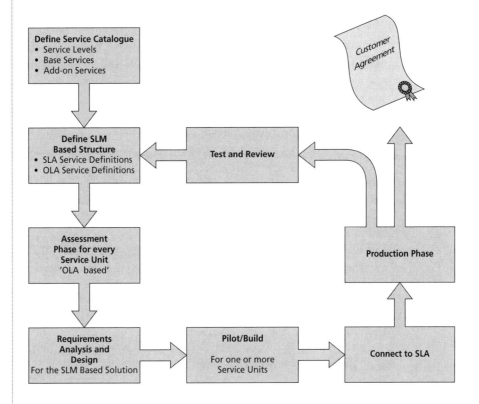

FIGURE 53.7

SLM process diagram: defining a Service Level Management-based solution

- a fence between IT and the business;
- 'static' – it is a dynamic document.

The foundations of an SLA are:

- catalogued services;
- defined services;
- measurable by IT;
- understandable by the customer.

There are a number of steps required in putting Service Level Agreements in place within the framework of Service Level Management. These steps are outlined next.

Define the business services

A 'business service' is simply an offering or application that is presented to the business, for example an airline flight booking service. These services need to be catalogued.

Define the IT services

IT service definitions must relate very closely to business service definitions. Taking the above business service example, this business service relies heavily on a number of IT services (i.e. computer terminal operation, booking database services, networking services, security services, change services, etc.). The IT service definitions that participate in this airline booking service must relate to the business service directly.

The task of compiling IT service definitions is encapsulated in the phrase 'Workload characterization'. This process helps the IT organization to evaluate the cost of manufacture and delivery of the supporting IT services to the business. In addition, the expected quality of service delivery can be assessed at this stage.

Negotiate Service Level Agreement

This phase includes the task of the IT supplier negotiating service contents and Service Level Agreements with their customer(s). By this phase, IT must be very sure of the *quality* of service and the *cost* of manufacture, production and delivery. On the other hand, the IT customer must be aware of the cost and quality of purchased services.

Set the business driver(s) into place

Once Service Level Agreements have been agreed by IT supplier and customer, they must be put into place and acted upon. This may involve a number of changes in both IT and business practices; for example, the purchase of new computer hardware, hire of new/additional IT staff, development or redevelopment of business applications, etc.

Drawing up Service Level Agreements

At this stage the SLA needs to be formalized but, remembering that the SLA is not a contract, it should rather represent:

- clarification of expectations (the level of service the customer can expect from the IT supplier and vice versa);
- defined service levels (the quality and cost of services that have been agreed and purchased);
- a goal-setting framework (performance, availability, contingency, costs, discounts, etc.).

Once these steps have been fulfilled, the purchased service will be actioned. From then on, a regular and formal review process will need to be established. This is an ongoing 'review' phase, where IT personnel review the quality of delivered services on a regular basis (this reporting interval is normally aligned with the validity of the time-scale of the SLA), and act upon the quality with contingency and financial processes. For example, if the airline booking system is not available within the agreed service period, the IT operations organization should resolve the issue within a certain period of time (as agreed in the SLA); if it cannot, financial discounts should be applied to the agreement.

These steps are presented in Figure 53.8.

53.6 Defining the SLM-based structure

This section utilizes the idea of a scenario to depict the definition of an SLM-based structure.

FIGURE 53.8

Defining the Service Level Agreement

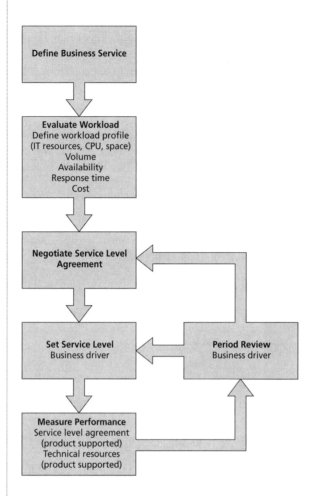

Service definition(s)

The scenario: An IT outsourcer has defined the following service types:

- problem resolution services (related to physical infrastructure, operating systems, applications and audited services, etc.);
- request services (related to installation, movement, change, restoration, procurement, etc.);
- customer services (related to security and help-desk services).

Each of these services is now broken down into smaller sub-components (Figure 53.9), which describe, more specifically, the type of delivery and for what it is required. For this scenario, we concentrate on 'Customer Services'.

Service sub-types of Customer Services are:

- security services;
- help-desk services.

FIGURE 53.9

Defining service sub-types

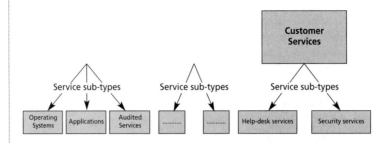

For each of the service sub-types, categories have to be defined for which metrics can be defined and measured. At this level you are able to define Operational Level Agreements (OLAs) for each of the sub-type categories. As a result, the OLAs are combined to form the SLAs required to meet the business requirements.

Service sub-type categories of 'help desk' are (Figure 53.10):

- availability;
- telephone answering;
- politeness.

FIGURE 53.10

Defining sub-type categories

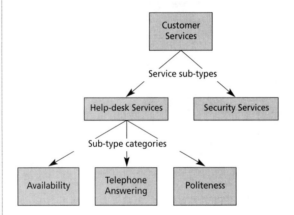

Defining the Service Level Agreement

At this point we have established a business process that has many IT processes underneath. Because of this we are ready to set the service level and thus further an SLA with the customer. Again, for the scenario the service sub-type category selected is 'telephone answering' (see Figure 53.11).

SLA foundations:

- Definition of service needs to be understandable to the customer...
  - 'Business service definitions';
- .... and measurable to the IT supplier
  - 'IT service definitions'.

FIGURE 53.11

The IT helpdesk Telephone Answering process

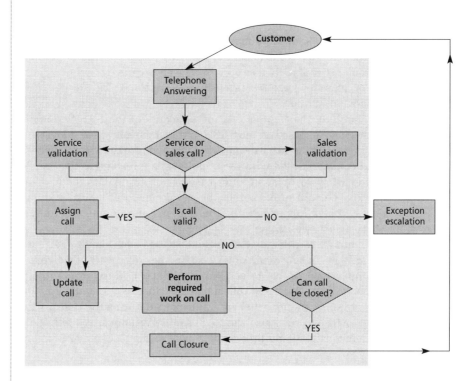

The task of compiling 'IT service definitions' is encapsulated in the phrase 'workload characterization' or 'workload evaluation'. This process enables the IT organization to evaluate the cost of the IT services that support business services. Keeping with the original scenario of customer services and specifically the 'Help desk' services sub-type and sub-type category of 'Telephone answering', the business process of IT customer services help-desk telephone answering is documented as shown in Figure 53.11.

From here, the service level quality and costs can be defined by IT, and at the same time cost-justified.

For example, customers may wish to purchase various services at 'tiered' costs based on service quality (in this case quicker and successful turnaround time of a service call to the helpdesk).

53.7 Service Level Management application

A Service Level Management application balances customer service requirements with the structure of the IT organization. By defining process parameters for each service and system process, the Service Level Management application has all the management information necessary to run a successful IT department.

When an agreement is in place for the delivery of services to the customer, internal targets are defined to deliver these agreements. This margin allows the IT personnel to use extra time for corrective actions. Every party that takes part in delivering the service agrees the internal targets.

If external suppliers are involved in the delivery of IT services, the contract with the supplier should reflect the internal target to ensure that the Service Level Agreement with the customer can be met. Contract negotiation must also involve the customer so that mutual expectation levels are not excessive.

For a Service Level Management architecture to be effective, it should be an enterprise-wide solution.

Therefore, the implementation concepts of the SAS Service Level Management Framework are based on the SAS Rapid Warehousing Methodology.

Because of the need to implement an enterprise-wide Service Level Management architecture, married with the 'top-down' approach that the SAS Rapid Warehousing Methodology adopts, an enterprise or corporate data model can be achieved very quickly. This, in turn, enables the development of logical and physical data models very quickly, thus expediting the implementation and roll-out of the Service Level Management application.

Figure 53.12 illustrates how the Service Level Management process and the SAS Rapid Warehousing Methodology can be integrated very effectively. The questionnaires and interviews of the Assessment Phase are used to develop the first concept of the corporate data model and this model is further refined during the Requirements Phase. The physical data model(s) are implemented during the Construction Phase. The continual review process of the SAS Rapid Warehousing Methodology simplifies the implementation of multiple models by ensuring that similar tasks are not repeated.

FIGURE 53.12

Using the SAS Rapid Warehousing Methodology to implement a Service Level Management application

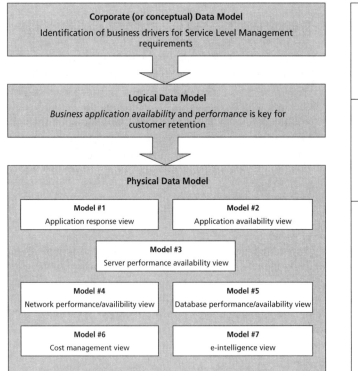
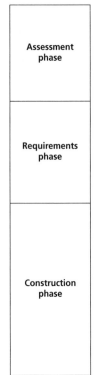

53 A business-focused Service Level Management Framework

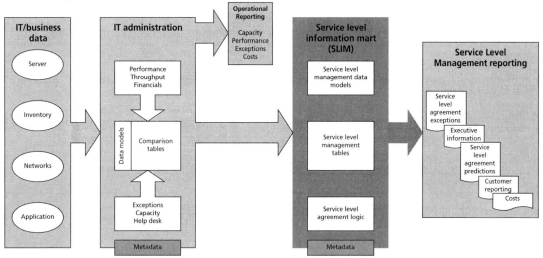

FIGURE 53.13

Service Level Information Warehouse (SLIW)

Developing the model

Figure 53.13 illustrates the basic architecture for the Service Level Management Framework architecture. The process of developing the SLMF/SLIW model includes the basic steps set out in Table 53.1.

TABLE 53.1

Developmental steps for the SLMF model

Determine IT standards	Document the IT standards, user interface standards, or IT practices that must be followed during the project.
Define the target IT architecture	Define the configuration of the operational systems that will be required to support the warehouse. This information should include documentation of the following elements about the hardware and software: • flexible reporting (to suit diverse organizational structures and procedures); • a powerful analysis platform for correlation analysis and planning based on historical behaviour and possible future scenarios; • a user interface that is suitable for different levels of user, by fulfilling their needs without any spurious information (noise); • a quick and efficient administration process; • ability to read any IT and business-related data (irrespective of the volume and the originating source); • an efficient data warehousing architecture to act as the foundational structure for retaining raw data while, at the same time, applying business views (for example, Service Level Management views) of the organization.
Create subject model	Within the concept of Service Level Management, subjects are the critical services or processes that are negotiated in the Service Level Agreements. These subjects are identified and prioritized in the Service Level Management Requirements Questionnaire.

TABLE 53.1
cont

Define source data for loading the Service Level Management warehouse	Define the repositories in which the operational data are stored and the estimated data volumes: • Repository • Platform • Volumetric.	
Define sources of data for updating the warehouse	Define the data sources that will be used to refresh and update the warehouse, the methods by which they will be updated, the frequency of the updates, and the repository platform: • Repository and platform • Frequency of update • Layout of update source.	
Determine available security features	Determine the current security features available at the operational system and data repository level.	
Identify IT personnel and resources to support the project	Identify the individuals in the customer's organization who can provide information about the IT infrastructure and who will support the project team at various points in the project.	
Identify production system, IT and operating support staff	Identify the IT and operations staff who will be required to support the warehouse operation, maintenance, and administration environment. These IT operations and support staff should be included in the warehouse construction process to facilitate easy and complete knowledge transfer.	

The following details the function of each component of this architecture.

IT and business data

This represents the raw operational data that can be:

- generated by various system, network, database, or application monitoring systems;
- database financial information.

IT administration

This is the heart of the Service Level Information Warehouse. All operational data resides within the IT administration component. There are two aspects to this component:

- installation;
- data management.

Installation

This consists of:

- declaration of the IT Service Level Information Warehouse (including all structural options);
- identification of operational data (that is, the location of incoming raw data);
- registration of the operational data in the warehouse.

Data management

This consists of:

- gathering operational data;
- storing operational data;
- summarizing operational data;
- archiving operational data.

IT administration metadata

The metadata contains the components of the data dictionary and information describing the stored data in the data warehouse. The metadata includes, but is not limited to, information about the following:

- the jobs that create and update the warehouse;
- repositories and platforms where the data resides;
- transformation rules for the data;
- views that have been created;
- business descriptions and definitions;
- other notes and comments.

Operational reporting

The supporting Service Level Management disciplines, such as Capacity Planning and Performance Management, require reporting facilities. Capacity, performance, database and network activity tables reside within the IT administration component. Therefore, standard reporting facilities support the management and monitoring of service level agreements. Such standard reports may include:

- ad hoc reporting;
- day-to-day reporting;
- tactical reporting.

Transposition

The information, gathered and summarized within the IT administration component, is input to the Service Level Information Mart (SLIM). This information represents the business application and raw IT resource activity (e.g., application response breakdown and server processor utilization).

This transposition of operational data to a Service Level Management view extracts the relevant information from the operational data and writes this information into SLIM tables.

Service Level Management administration

The Service Level Management administrator:

- defines the Service Level Management data models (gathering supporting information using the design phase tools);
- transforms the Service Level Management data models into service level subject views;
- compiles the service level subject table logic;
- transforms the logic into physical programs;
- uses the programs to populate the SLIM.

Service Level Information Mart (SLIM)

The SLIM is essentially a data warehouse containing a subset of the data collected in the IT administration component.

At this stage, all the inputs are available to populate the service level subject-related tables (that is, the raw IT and business-related data (from the IT administration component), service level agreement logic and service level subject-table definitions).

The service level logic (held in reference tables) is coupled with the service level subject tables and evaluated against the incoming IT and business data and raw IT resource activity tables.

The content of the service level subject-related tables resolves the following questions:

- *What* is the service level?
- *To whom* is the service level aligned?
- *What* IT resources make up the service?
- *When* is the service level active?
- *What* is the status of the service level?

For reporting and analysis flexibility, the service level subject tables are stored as multidimensional databases.

Service Level Information Mart metadata

Similar to the IT administration metadata, the SLIM metadata holds information describing the stored data (e.g., the time of the last data warehouse update).

Reporting

Service Level Management is an enterprise-wide discipline. This results in the fact that many people within the organization may wish to view or generate their own service level reports. Examples of the types of reports that may be required are:

- an executive overview of the IT department and how it is supporting its Service Level Agreement;
- reports for the group leaders of each (sub)group within the IT department;
- individual reports (for example, by department) per service level agreement.

These reports can be presented in a number of ways (hardcopy, e-mail, web-based, desktop).

To support the delivery of IT service to the user community, IT specialists also require reporting functionality. The requirements of this audience differ from the Service Level Management reporters as they have a more technical focus. IT specialists need to report against their particular areas of responsibility. For example, network specialists may want to measure the effectiveness of their network components.

53.8 Supporting IT functions

The principal supporting components concerning the quality of the delivered service agreed by IT and customer within the scope of the SLA lies within core IT operational functions. These functions are numerous but contain such disciplines as:

- Availability management
- Contingency management
- Inventory management
- Computer performance management
- Software control and distribution
- Security management
- Network management
- Capacity management
- Cost management
- Problem and help-desk management
- ...

Within the scope of Service Level Management, these functions should address the following example questions:

- *Capacity management*: 'Are you anticipating my future needs?'
- *Cost management*: 'What exactly am I paying for?'
- *Availability management*: 'Will I be able to get the service when I need it?'
- *Contingency management*: 'What if ... happens?'
- *Change management*: 'The network is down again... OK, what did you change?'
- *Software control and distribution*: 'How much pain are you going to put me through on the next release?'
- *Problem/Help-desk management*: 'Are you there for me?...' 'Help!...'

These operational functions are critical to the success of a Service Level Management Framework.

53.9 Conclusion

Service Level Management is traditionally a 'classic' discipline to IT. With organizational globalization and IT outsourcing become prevalent in today's business, IT is beginning to see the rich rewards of deploying a Service Level Management Framework concept. But of course this poses many challengies to IT organizations, especially with the current IT skills shortage and the complexities of IT operational infrastructures.

The prime advantages of deploying Service Level Management in the modern organization are:

- customer satisfaction;
- customer retention;
- increased competitiveness;
- increased profitability;
- happy shareholders;
- healthy organization;
- less risk to business;
- quicker time to market.

If these advantages can be realized by the IT organization, then they are organized for success.

IT must support the business goals of its organization; this can only be done using a top-down approach from the organization to ensure that any Service Level Management implementation supports the value proposition of each and every business unit. Tools such as a Strategic IT Scorecard can monitor and communicate the progress of the IT department's strategy and business value to the organization. By accomplishing this, the IT organization will understand and meet the needs and expectations of the business and deliver real value to their organization. IT is the most strategic weapon in today's organization; understanding its value and contribution to the business is paramount to its success.

Literature

Kaplan, R.S. and Norton, D.P. (1996) *The Balanced Scorecard: translating strategy into action*, Harvard Business School Press, Boston.

Acknowledgements

A publication of this type is only possible through the collaboration and experiences of many individuals. The following contributed material and/or reviewed the various drafts: Luc Mertens, SAS Belgium; Gloria Miller, SAS EMEA–International; Andy Parks, SAS America; Andreas Norens, SAS Sweden; John Wilkes, SAS UK; Christine Ritter, SAS UK.

Review of part 9

The analysis by Prasad *et al.* in **Enterprise Management Software implementation** reflects various aspects from earlier chapters: process models, strategy organization, culture, communication and all the other subjects that have been deemed important. They emphasize the huge benefits to be gained from successful EMS implementation, but they also illustrate that (as with implementation of an ERP solution) the implementation project is a complex one. For instance, Prasad *et al.* state that EMS implementation projects should have a horizon of 10 years. Nevertheless, they are convinced that a good business case for EMS can be made. Their analysis provides a very detailed manual for the whole process, from the determination of requirements through to implementation, illustrated by a case study.

In **A business-focused Service Level Management Framework**, Maestranzi *et al.* focus on one of the crucial ITIL best practices: Service Level Management. The first half of the chapter is dedicated to Service Level Management in more general terms. In this part an overview is given of the importance of SLM as a front-office process of the IT department in an enterprise. An IT (Balanced) Scorecard to measure the performance is included. Also, an SLM framework is introduced, containing a great number of well-known ITIL elements. Up to that point, nothing really new has been presented. The second half of the chapter is the innovative part: a Service Level Management software tool based on warehousing technology to give intensive support to the execution of the SLM process. The strong point of the tool is the automated performance-measurement possibilities, resulting in detailed reporting functions.

Concluding remarks

This part shows only a very limited number of the tools available to IT organizations. Especially in the more technical sense, a huge number of tools have been developed and deployed throughout the world.

In many cases, IT organizations tend to look for tools when searching for a solution to organizational problems. The previous parts, however, have shown that there are many other solutions to these problems. It is worthwhile stating that most of the problems cannot be solved by introducing another technical tool: organizations should work on their processes, and on their people and organization, and the tool should be last in the game. Nevertheless, choosing the preferred implementation order of Process → People → Products seems to be a reality only in greenfield situations. In real life, starting at the tooling end appears to be far too tempting.

part 10

Compendium for IT Service Management

54 IT management glossary

Introduction

Background

One of the most important aspects of a useful glossary is that it should be practical – it should tie in with the practices and terminology used in the real world. This glossary was written after an extensive survey of the terminology used by a wide range of companies and has been reviewed by a panel of experts and industry specialists. The terminology follows the pattern set by ITIL publications and similar works.

Procedure

A number of authoritative sources were used when compiling this glossary and a great deal of valuable support was received from the editorial board. The members of this board committed a great deal of time to selecting the most appropriate sources. We would particularly like to thank Marcel Spruit of Delft University of Technology. The members of the editorial board were: J.W. van den Brink (Pink Elephant), D. van Gelder (Cap Gemini), J.J.J.M. Heunks (Proface), W.J.J. Kuiper (Atos Origin), Professor M. Looijen (Delft University of Technology), J. Stegink MBA (Mediaan/ABS); the chairman was J. van Bon (chief editor). J.A. Dijkstra (Netherlands Standardization Institute) lent valuable support to the first edition in 1997. This wide range of board members ensured that we could benefit from a broad spectrum of experience.

Internal consistency

One of the main requirements of a glossary is that it should be internally consistent. This is ensured by the use of a number of terminology trees and by defining each term only once in the document. When used elsewhere in this glossary, defined terms are printed in italics.

Terminology trees

Various terms are defined in coherent sets, in a number of terminology trees. For example, the term 'information system' was found to be crucial (see Figure 54.1). The breakdown of this concept into its constituent parts forms an important thread throughout the document. All terms are defined at the level of the information system, unless specified otherwise. Various hierarchical structures can be applied, depending on the objective, subject, position in the service chain, and other aspects. The term 'quality' was found to be particularly difficult to analyse. The glossary uses a non-hierarchical definition (Figure 54.2). The term 'process' was divided into the operational activities, and the control activities related to the progress of the process (Figure 54.3). Furthermore, terms were always analysed in the context of Service Management domains and related business processes (Figure 54.4).

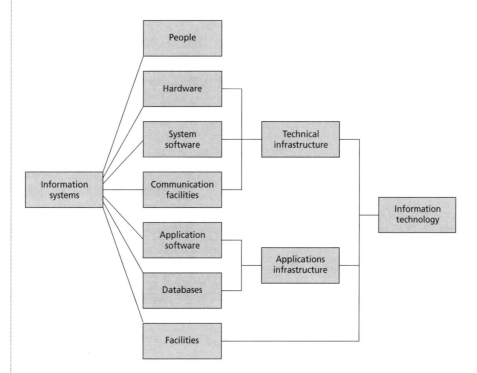

FIGURE 54.1
'Information system' terminology tree illustrating the levels of aggregation. The elements incorporated in a concept can themselves be divided into their constituent elements.

Guide to the document

Many terms in this glossary, such as 'system', are in general use, but here they are defined in the IT context. When reading the definitions it is important to remember that these should all be placed in the context of IT management. General IT terms (e.g. account manager, test, cost) have not been included as it was assumed that these are defined in other IT glossaries. However, such terms were included where they have a special meaning. Purely technical terms (e.g. LAN, incremental back-up) have not been included unless they were relevant to providing the context for other terms.

Job titles (e.g. change manager, problem manager) are included. However, functions depend on the organizational structure and therefore cannot be covered by standard definitions. In small organizations, responsibility for a number of areas may be borne by one

FIGURE 54.2

Terminology tree for 'Quality': a non-hierarchical definition

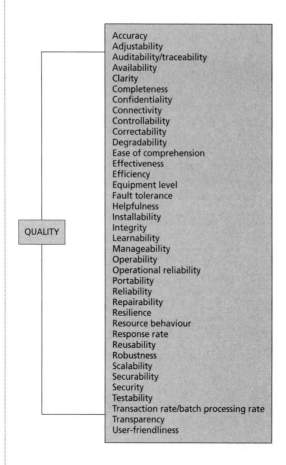

FIGURE 54.3

Terminology tree: 'Process'

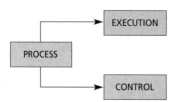

person. Similarly, in large organizations it is not always necessary to allocate areas of responsibility to the same personnel at all times. Thus, these terms refer more to roles than to specific functions. Obviously, an area of responsibility – for example, control in change management – may be addressed by a function (here: the change manager).

FIGURE 54.4
Reference framework for Service Management processes and domains

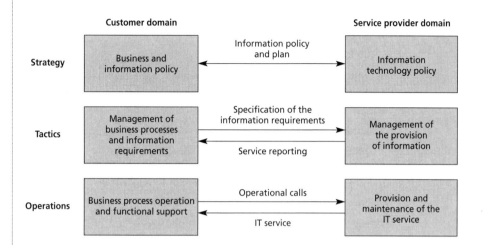

Acceptance Time when a *system* or *service* is accepted.

Acceptance environment *Environment* in which *acceptance tests* can be carried out.

Acceptance test Test to determine whether a *system* or *service* meets the specified requirements.

Access control Discipline which aims to control access to objects.

Accuracy Degree of certainty that *data* accurately reflects reality or an aspect thereof.

Adaptive maintenance Form of *maintenance* which aims to comply with changed requirements.

Additive maintenance Form of *maintenance* which aims to comply with supplementary requirements.

Adjustability Extent to which *software* settings can be made and changed.

Agreed service time Period when a *service* is available for use, according to the *Service Level Agreement*.

Alert Warning to the *users* of a *service* or *system* about a relevant *incident*.

Application Combination of *software* and *database* used to program the functionality of an *information system*.

Application maintenance *Maintenance* of one or more *applications*.

Application management Element of *management* which aims to keep one or more *applications* operational.

Application software *Software* element of an *application*.

Architecture Representation of the selected hierarchy and structure of the components of a *system*.

Asset management Process in which *infrastructure* objects are entered in the administration, but without their interrelationships.

Audit Assessment by an authorized body.

Auditability Extent to which it can be concluded which activities resulted in a particular *event*.

Authentication Verification of the identity of a person or *system*.

Authenticity Extent to which the source of a message is verifiably correct.

Authorization Granting privileges in a given situation, to a person or *system* with respect to a specified object.

Availability Extent to which a *system* or *service* is available to the intended *users* at the required times.

Availability management *Process* to make and keep *information systems* available, and the *service* provided for this purpose in accordance with specified requirements.

Back-up Secondary copy for use in the event of the loss of the primary copy.

Baseline A snapshot or a position which is recorded.

Baseline security The *security* level adopted by the *IT* organization for its own *security* and from the point of view of good 'due diligence'.

Batch processing rate Rate at which batch jobs are executed.

Benchmark Tests to compare one or more *quality* aspects with a standard or the results of the same test in a different situation.

Biometrics Discipline which studies certain unique aspects of living creatures, for *authentication* purposes.

Bug An *error* in the *software*.

Build The final stage in producing a usable *configuration*.

Building environment *Software* package used to design and produce *software* or other components.

Business request Request from the *customer environment* (business) for new or modified functionality.

Bypass See *workaround*.

CA Abbreviation of *Certification Authority*.

Call Report, question or request from the *user* of a *service* or *system*.

Call centre See *help desk*.

Capacity management *Process* to optimize the *availability* of the required resources.

Capacity planning Activities resulting in a *capacity plan*.

Category Classification of a group of items, e.g. *Configuration Items, change requests* or *problems*.

Certificate Document issued by an organization to verify that a specified standard is adhered to.

Certification Authority *Trusted Third Party* which issues and manages *certificates*.

Certify Issue a *certificate* to indicate that a specified *system*, person or organization complies with a specified standard.

Change Modification to a *system* or *service*.

Change Advisory Board (CAB) Representative group of stakeholders which assesses *change requests*.

Change control The *procedure* to ensure that all *changes* are controlled in terms of progress and *quality*.

Change management *Process* of implementing *changes*.

Change manager *Role* responsible for *change management*.

Change processing Undertaking *change management* activities.

Change request See *Request for Change*.

Charging Charging a *customer* for the costs incurred on its behalf.

CI Abbreviation of *Configuration Item*.

CI level Lowest level at which uniquely identified *configuration items* are distinguished.

Clarity Ease with which a *user* can understand the issue at stake.

Clean desk Tidy *workplace* without documents lying around.

Client See *Customer*.

CMDB Abbreviation of *Configuration Management Data Base*.

Communication facility Collection of *IT* resources used to provide communication *services*.

Compatibility Extent to which a *system* can be exchanged or combined with another *system* without special modifications.

Completeness Certainty that nothing has been omitted from or added to correct *data*.

Complexity Umbrella term for a number of aspects which make it more difficult to assess the issues at stake, i.e.: scale; heterogeneity; distribution; dynamic nature; interconnection; functionality; *management*; use.

Compromise Situation which arises when unauthorized persons obtain full or partial access to confidential *information* or if there is a *risk* of such access.

Computer Electronic *data* processing unit.

Computer center See *data centre*.

Computer platform *Computer* with the *system software* installed on it and any peripherals connected directly to it.

Computer system See *computer platform*.

Confidentiality Extent to which *data* are only accessible to a well-defined group of authorized persons.

Configuration Coherent set of *infrastructure* components.

Configuration baseline Configuration of a product or *system* established at a specific point in time, which captures both the structure and details of that product or *system*, and enables that product or system to be rebuilt at a later date.

Configuration item Component of a *configuration*.

Configuration management *Process* of identifying, recording, verifying and reporting all relevant *configuration items* as well as their status and the relationships between them (structure).

Configuration management database (CMDB) *Database* with the *information* about all relevant *configuration items* as well as their status and the relationships between them.

Configuration manager *Role* responsible for *configuration management*.

Configure Creating a *configuration* using *configuration items*.

Connectivity Extent to which *systems* can exchange *data*.

Contingency plan See *disaster recovery plan*.

Contingency planning and control See *IT Service Continuity Management*.

Continuity Extent to which a *system* or *service* is available without interruption.

Controllability Extent to which the *quality* aspects of a *system* or *service* can be controlled.

Cookie Packet of *data* sent by a website to a *user* accessing that website, and stored on the *user's* hard disk.

Correctability Extent to which an object can be repaired after the occurrence of an *error*.

Corrective controls See *corrective measures*.

Corrective maintenance Form of *maintenance* which aims to rectify non-compliance with the defined standards.

Corrective measures Measures to repair objects damaged in the course of an *incident*.

Cost management *Process* providing financial *data* to facilitate finding an optimum balance between price and *performance* throughout the business.

Costing Identification, forecasting and allocation to cost centres of costs and expenditure.

Cracker A *hacker* with malicious purposes, i.e. to steal or damage the *information* in the *system* that was hacked.

Cryptanalysis Decrypting secret *information* without the use of the relevant *keys*.

Cryptography The discipline of encoding *information*.

Customer Recipient of current or future *product(s)* or *service(s)* which are normally paid for.

Data Objectively apparent representations of *information* (knowledge) in a storage medium.

Data collection A collection of *data* with a defined structure.

Data infrastructure *Data collection* which is accessible to one or more *applications*.

Data mining Looking for previously unknown patterns or relationships in *data collections*.

Data warehouse Structured *data collection* to provide users with correct and accurate *data* when they require it.

Database Structure for a *data collection*.

Data centre Organizational unit responsible for the *operation* of the central *IT infrastructure*.

Decryption Converting an encrypted message to the original message (plain text).

Definitive Software Library (DSL) Collection of all tested and accepted *software* which is available for use.

Degradation See *degradability*.

Degradability Ease with which essential functions of the *system* or *service* can be restored after an *incident*.

Delta Release A delta, or partial, *release* is one that includes only those *CIs* within the *release* unit that have actually changed or are new since the last *full* or Delta Release.

Detection controls See *detection measures*.

Detection time Time between the occurrence of an *incident* and its detection.

Detection measures Measures to identify actual or potential *incidents*.

Development environment See *building environment*.

Digital signature Digital mark added to a message to demonstrate its *authenticity*.

Disaster *Event* which has such an adverse impact on a *service* or *system* that significant work has to be undertaken to restore the original functionality.

Disaster recovery Continuing *IT services* after a *disaster*.

Disaster recovery management See *IT Service Continuity Management*.

Disaster recovery plan Plan describing how the *IT services* will be continued with alternative resources in the event of a *disaster*.

Distributed computing Cohesive processing of *data* by a number of physically different *systems*.

Distributed system *System* whose components are spread over more than one location.

Documentation Documents on paper or other media, describing or explaining pertinent matters.

Domain Defined set of components from a larger group.

Downtime Time between occurrence of an *incident* and the time the *system* or *service* is restored, during which a *system* or *service* is unavailable.

DSL Abbreviation of *Definitive Software Library*.

EDP-audit See *audit*.

Effectiveness Extent to which the activities serve the defined objectives.

Efficiency Extent to which activities are carried out at an acceptable cost and effort.

Encipher See *encryption*.

Encryption Making *data* inaccessible using an algorithm and a *key*.

End-user See *user*.

Environment Set of objects within which an object operates.

Equipment level Extent to which the additional *user* requirements are met, as a result of which the *users* develop a positive attitude towards the *system*.

Error Activity of a person or *system* which does not correspond with the prescribed or expected mode of operation.

Error control The *management* of activities to resolve *known errors*.

Escalation Informing or engaging another party when a defined or contractually agreed situation or *event* occurs.

Escalation threshold Defined limit which when exceeded initiates *escalation*.

Escrow Delivering sources to a third party for safe keeping.

Event Situation indicated by a defined signal or *data*.

Exclusiveness See *confidentiality*.

Expert system *System* which uses artificial intelligence to obtain results.

Exploitation See *operation*.

External audit See *audit*.

Facilities (environmental) Entities constituting the basic *infrastructure* on which the *technical infrastructure* and *applications* can run (electrical power supply, cooling, etc.).

Facilities management Either used in terms of *outsourcing* or in terms of the *process* that manages the basic (environmental) *facilities*.

Failure See *incident*.

Fall back Using alternative *facilities* in case of an undesired situation.

Fault See *error*.

Fault tolerance Extent to which a *system* continues to operate when one or more parts are affected by an *incident*.

First time fix rate Commonly used *metric*, used to define *incidents* resolved at the first point of contact between a *customer* and the *service* provider, without delay or referral, generally by a front line *support* group such as a *help desk*.

Fix *Change* made to solve an observed *problem*.

Fix notes Compare *release notes*.

Flexibility See *adjustability*.

Full release All components of the *release* unit that are built, tested, distributed and implemented together.

Functional maintenance Form of *maintenance* which aims to *change* a *system* in response to changed requirements.

Functional management Aspect of *management* concerned with supporting *users* and specifying the functionality required by the *users*.

Hacker Someone who gains unauthorized access to a protected *computer system* or *network* without malicious purposes.

Hardware Set of physical electronic resources.

Help desk Central point for reporting *incidents* and requesting *user support*, normally taking care of operational *user support*.

Helpfulness Extent to which a *system* or *service* supports the *user* by giving instructions during its use.

Hoax Chain e-mail concerning a non-existent *virus*.

ICT Abbreviation of *Information and Communication Technology*.

Impact Extent to which adverse consequences, including damage, may occur during an intended or unintended *incident*.

Impact code Simple code assigned to *incidents*, *problems* and *changes*, reflecting the degree of *impact* upon the *customer's* business *processes*.

Incident Any event that is not part of the standard operation of a *service* and that causes, or may cause, an interruption to, or a reduction in, the *quality* of that *service*.

Incident call See *call*.

Incident control The *procedure* to ensure that all *incidents* are controlled in terms of progress and *quality*.

Incident management *Process* which aims to resolve *incidents*.

Incident processing Undertaking activities as part of the *incident management process*.

Information Meaning assigned to *data* on the basis of defined agreements.

Information and Communication Technology See *Information Technology*.

Information function Collection of *information systems* and their *support*, as well as the functionality they provide.

Information security plan See *security management* and *security plan*.

Information security policy See *security management* and *security policy*.

Information system Coherent *data* processing functionality for the control or *support* of one or more business *processes*.

Information Technology Set of objects which, together with the personnel, form the *information systems*.

Information Technology Infrastructure Library The UK's OGC IT Infrastructure Library – a set of guides on the *management* and provision of operational *IT services*.

Infrastructure Object or group of objects available to one or more other objects.

Install Connect a *system* or its components in an *environment*.

Installability Extent to which a *system* can be *installed* in a specified *environment*.

Integrated life-cycle management (ILM) *Management process* to optimize *ICT services* by managing the *ICT* portfolio.

Integration Combining *systems* and subsystems into a larger unit, to provide new functionality.

Integrity Extent to which *data* corresponds with the actual situation represented by that *data*.

Interactive processing rate Rate at which interactive instructions are carried out.

Interface Place where two or more *systems* meet or are connected.

Interfaceability Extent to which *systems* and subsystems can be connected to exchange *data* through the *interface*.

ISO Abbreviation of *International Organization for Standardization*.

International Organization for Standardization (ISO) Organization that issues international standards.

Interoperability Extent to which a *system* is able to cooperate with other *systems* offering the same functionality.

Inventory management See *asset management*.

ISO quality standards International standards for *quality management*, published by the *International Organization for Standardization*.

IT Abbreviation of *Information Technology*.

IT infrastructure Collection of technical components of the *information system*.

IT audit See *audit*.

IT Service Continuity Management (ITSCM) *Process* to ensure adequate technical, financial and *management* resources to provide continuity of *IT services* in the event of a *disaster*.

ITIL Abbreviation of *Information Technology Infrastructure Library*.

ITSCM Abbreviation of *IT Service Continuity Management*.

Key Bit string of a defined length used to decrypt an encrypted message.

Key Performance Indicator (KPI) The measurable quantities against which specific *performance* criteria can be set when drawing up the *SLA*.

Knowledge-based system See *expert system*.

Knowledge engineering Study of the application of artificial intelligence.

Known error *Status* assigned to a *problem* once it has been diagnosed and the potential solution has been identified.

KPI Abbreviation of *Key Performance Indicator*.

Learnability Extent to which a *user* can learn to use a *system*.

Legacy system *Application* whose technical lifespan has been exceeded, but which is still being used.

Life cycle Successive stages which a *system* goes through.

Life-cycle management *Process* consisting of subprocesses: development, introduction (commissioning), *operation* and *maintenance*.

Live environment See *production environment*.

Load See *workload*.

Logging Automatic or manual recording of *events* and circumstances associated with a *process* or *system*.

Logical control See *logical measure*.

Logical measure Measure implemented with *software*.

Maintainability Extent to which a *system* or *service* can be modified through *maintenance*.

Maintenance Making *changes* to one or more objects of an *information system*.

Maintenance window Agreed time frame in which *maintenance* can be carried out.

Manageability Extent to which a *system* or *service* can comply with the defined requirements in the given situation.

Management Maintaining a *system* or *service* in accordance with the relevant requirements and situational factors.

Mean time between failures (MTBF) Mean *uptime* between two *incidents*, or the average time during which the *system* is not affected by *incidents*.

Metric Measurable element of a *service process* or function.

Modification See *change*.

Monitoring Continuously or intermittently observing the activities of a *system* or *service*, as well as recording anything unusual.

MTBF Abbreviation of *Mean Time Between Failures*.

Network Collection of communications objects between at least two *hardware* and *software* nodes, using specified communications protocols.

Nonrepudiation Extent to which evidence can be provided so that a message cannot be denied.

OLA Abbreviation of *Operational Level Agreement*.

Open Systems Interconnection A standard description or 'reference model' for how messages should be transmitted between any two points in a telecommunication network.

Operability Extent to which a *system* is easily used by the *user*.

Operations Element of *management* concerned with keeping the *information system* operational in accordance with the agreed requirements after *acceptance*.

Operational Level Agreement (OLA) An internal agreement covering the delivery of *services* which *support* the *IT* organization in their delivery of *services*.

Operational reliability Extent to which a *system* operates without interruption or *failure*.

Organizational control See *organizational measures*.

Organizational measures Measure implemented through tasks, responsibilities and *procedures*.

OSI Abbreviation of *Open Systems Interconnection*.

Outsourcing Delegating all or part of the activities or responsibilities of an organization to an external organization.

Owner Person or body who owns something and has full authority over it.

Password Secret character string used for *authentication*.

Patch Temporary *software change* to *fix* a *problem* in the short term.

Performance Way in which a task is executed.

Performance indicator (PI) Measurable parameter quantifying a *performance*.

Performance management *Process* of measuring, continuously implementing and improving the *performance*.

Physical control See *physical measures*.

Physical measures Measures implemented through physical objects.

PI Abbreviation of *performance indicator*.

PKI Abbreviation of *Public Key Infrastructure*.

Portability Extent to which a *system* can be transferred between *environments*.

Preventive controls See *preventive measures*.

Preventive maintenance Form of *maintenance* that aims to prevent a *system* from not complying with the defined requirements.

Preventive measures Measures which aim to prevent *incidents*.

Priority Relative weight of an activity compared with other activities, determining the sequence of execution.

Private key Key for a cryptographic algorithm which is only known to those entitled to use this *key*.

Problem Condition with an unknown underlying cause that gives (may give) rise to one or more *incidents*.

Problem analysis *Process* which aims to determine *known errors* on the basis of defined *problems*.

Problem control *Procedure* to ensure that all *problems* are controlled in terms of progress and *quality*.

Problem management *Process* which aims to solve all *problems* which are encountered.

Problem manager *Role* responsible for *problem management*.

Problem processing Undertaking the *problem management* activities.

Procedure Description of a coherent set of activities, stating the parties responsible for implementing them.

Process Coherent set of activities intended to achieve a defined objective.

Process control The *procedure* to ensure that all *activities* are controlled in terms of progress and *quality*.

Processing rate See *transaction rate*.

Product Singular or composite object with a specified functionality.

Production *Process* which provides the *product* or *service*.

Production environment *Environment* in which the *production* is implemented.

Production plan Document defining all activities to be implemented for *production*.

Public key *Key* used in asymmetric cryptographic algorithms, known to all parties exchanging encrypted messages.

Public Key Infrastructure (PKI) *Infrastructure* facilitating confidential communication based on asymmetric *encryption*.

Quality Extent to which a *system* or *service* fulfils written and unwritten requirements.

Quality assurance All planned and systematic activities implemented to provide adequate confidence that the *quality* requirements will be fulfilled.

Quality control Operational techniques and activities used to meet the *quality* requirements.

Quality level Measure of the *quality*, expressed as a quantifiable parameter.

Quality management That part of the *management* function that is concerned with determining the *quality policy* and its implementation through the planning, implementation and evaluation of *quality* aspects.

Quality plan *Document* setting out the *quality assurance* activities, resources and activities.

Quality policy Overall goals of an organization with regard to *quality* and the means and resources to provide it, expressed formally in *management*-level instructions.

Quality surveillance Continual *monitoring* and verification of the *quality procedures*, methods, techniques and *processes*, and the analysis of records to ensure that specified *quality* requirements are being met.

Quality system Organizational structure of responsibilities, *procedures* and resources required to implement *quality management*.

Quality system review Formal evaluation by senior management of the *quality system* in relation to *quality policy*.

Query Formal question to extract *data* from a *data collection*.

RA Abbreviation of *Registration Authority*.

Reaction time Period between the initiating *event* and the initial reaction to it.

Recoverability Extent to which a *system* can repair itself after an *incident*.

Registration Authority (RA) Body registering *users* for a *Certification Authority*.

Release Issue of an object in accordance with the defined specifications.

Release management The *process* that ensures that the correct *versions* are available and used at the required locations.

Release notes The *documentation* supplied with a *release* to identify aspects which have been changed or deserve attention for other reasons.

Reliability Extent to which a *system* or *service* is reliable.

Repairability Extent to which a *system* can be repaired after an *incident*.

Replaceability Extent to which a *system* can be replaced without impairment of the functionality.

Repressive controls See *repressive measures*.

Repressive measures Measures which aim to limit the damage after an *incident* has occurred.

Request for Change (RfC) Formal request to implement a *change* to one or more specified *configuration items*.

Resilience Ability of a *system* to perform adequately even when one or more components malfunction.

Resolution Action that will resolve an *incident*.

Resolution time Period between the *detection* of a *incident* and its *resolution*.

Resource requirements Volume of resources needed to operate a *system* or *service* in a defined manner.

Response rate Rate at which the *system* processes transactions at a defined *load*.

Response time Period between the initiating *event* and the time at which the result is available at the specified location.

Reusability Extent to which a *system* can be used again, in full or in part, in another *system*.

Review See *audit*.

RfC Abbreviation of *Request for Change*.

Risk Likelihood that a *system* or *service* is affected by a *threat* in such a way that an *incident* and damage result.

Risk analysis Identification and assessment of the expected damage associated with defined *events*.

Risk management *Process* which aims to reduce *risks* to an acceptable level.

Robustness Extent to which a *system* resists adverse external influences, including incorrect operation (whether accidental or malicious).

Role A set of responsibilities, activities and *authorizations*.

Safety Extent to which protection is provided against undesirable and dangerous situations.

Scalability Extent to which the capacity of a *system* or *service* can be adapted to changing needs.

Secondment Use of external personnel.

Secret key See *private key*.

Securability The extent to which a *system* can be made secure against *threats*.

Security Cohesive set of activities, methods and resources intended to protect one or more objects against a reduction in the required level of *confidentiality*, *integrity* and *availability*.

Security management *Process* of managing a defined level of *security* on *information* and *services*.

Security manager *Role* responsible for *security management*.

Security plan Description of the actual or envisaged *security* measures and the organization to implement them.

Security policy Strategy with respect to *security*.

Service *System* or functionality made available for use, supported by the *IT service provider*, that fulfils one or more needs of the *customer* and that is perceived by the *customer* as a coherent whole.

Service achievement The *actual service* levels delivered by the *IT* organization to a *customer* within a defined life-span.

Service catalog See *service portfolio*.

Service desk See *help desk*.

Service Improvement Programme (SIP) A formal project undertaken within an organization to identify and introduce measurable improvements within a specified work area or work *process*.

Service level Level of *quality* of the *service* provided to the *customer*.

Service Level Agreement (SLA) Written contract between a *customer* and *service provider*, defining rights and duties with regard to agreed *service levels*.

Service Level Management *Process* of definition, negotiation and *management* of the required *service level* and costs.

Service level report Reports on actual *service levels* during a defined period, as agreed in the *Service Level Agreement*.

Service level requirements List of *service levels* required by the *customer*.

Service management See *management*.

Service opening hours See *agreed service time*.

Service point See *help desk*.

Service portfolio Detailed description of the available *services* and *service levels*.

Service provider The *role* performed by any organizational units, whether internal or external, that deliver and *support IT services* to a *customer*.

Service Quality Plan (SQP) The written plan and specification of internal targets designed to guarantee the agreed *service levels*.

Signature See *digital signature*.

SIP Abbreviation of *Service Improvement Plan*.

SLA Abbreviation of *Service Level Agreement*.

Smart disk Type of smart card used for *authentication*.

Software Programmed element of *information systems*.

Software control and distribution See *release management*.

Spamming Sending a mass of e-mails to an unsolicited recipient, or sending the same message by e-mail to large numbers of people indiscriminately.

Specsheet Detailed specification of what the *customer* wants and what consequences this has for the *service provider*, such as required resources and skills.

Spoofing Pretending to be somebody else.

SQP Abbreviation of *Service Quality Plan*.

Standard Instruction for designing, constructing, testing, operating or using.

Standardization Imposing or adopting one or more specified *standards*.

State Defined condition which a *system* is in.

Steadiness See *robustness*.

Support Set of activities carried out by a person or body to make other activities, which may be carried out by other people or bodies, more effective or efficient.

Support centre See *help desk*.

Support desk See *help desk*.

Surveyability Extent to which the *system* shows the *user* what functions it can provide.

System Object, or collection of associated objects, which together provide a specified functionality.

System opening hours See *agreed service time*.

System software *Software* specific to the *computer system* it is installed on, which makes it possible to *install applications*.

Technical management Aspect of *management* concerned with the *operation* of the *IT infrastructure* and the *maintenance* of the *technical infrastructure*.

Telematics Combination of telecommunications and *information* science.

Test environment Specific *environment* provided for an object, in which it may be tested.

Testability Extent to which it is possible to determine through tests whether a *system* meets the defined requirements.

Threat Situation which may have an adverse impact on the reliable *operation* of a *system* or *service*.

Tier-one support The *support* at the first point of *customer* contact that deals with quick responses, without dispatching the *call*.

Tier-three support The *support* that is most time-consuming, and needs maximum expertise, dealing with calls which are dispatched by *tier-two support*.

Tier-two support The *support* that deals with *calls* which are dispatched by *tier-one support*, requiring additional knowledge or power.

Timeliness Extent to which a *service* is available to its intended users at the required time.

Tool *System* to *support* an activity.

Traceability See *auditability*.

Transaction rate Rate at which a *system* processes defined transactions.

Transferability Extent to which a task or responsibility can be taken over by another person or *system*.

Transparency Extent to which a *system user* is only presented with the functions or components relevant to them.

Transportability See *portability*.

Trojan horse Harmful *software*, hidden in an ordinary program, that does its harmful work when this program is executed.

Trusted Third Party (TTP) Third party who is trusted by all relevant parties.

TTP Abbreviation of *Trusted Third Party*.

Tuning Actions carried out on a *system* to improve its effectiveness or efficiency.

Underpinning contract Contract for the supply of *products* or *services* required to fulfil agreements made in other contracts or *Service Level Agreements*.

Upgrade New *version* or *release*.

Upgrade notes Same as *release notes*.

Uptime Period during which a *system* is available, to the next scheduled or unscheduled *incident*.

Urgency Extent to which an action requires immediate attention.

User Authorized person using a *system* or *service*.

User acceptance Extent to which *users* consider that a *system* or *service* meets their needs.

User support *Support* provided to the users of a *system* or *service*.

User-friendliness Extent to which *users* find the *system* or *service* logical and pleasant to work with.

Validity Extent to which a *system* or *service* fulfils requirements imposed for a specified period.

Verifiability See *auditability*.

Version Issue of the object in accordance with defined specifications.

Version control See *Release Management*.

Version number Number identifying the *version* of the program.

Virus Harmful, self-replicating *software*, which needs a carrier.

Work instruction Description of one or more activities in a *procedure*.

Work-around Alternative solution to an *incident* which will produce an acceptable outcome for a limited period.

Workload Extent of resource use in a defined period.

Workplace Location where physical objects are present which are normally used by just one person.

Worm Harmful, self-replicating *software*, which doesn't need a carrier.

Acronyms

CA Certification Authority
CAB Change Advisory Board
CI Configuration Item
CMDB Configuration Management Data Base
DSL Definitive Software Library
ICT Information and Communication Technology
ILM Integrated Life-cycle Management
ISO International Organization for Standardization
IT Information Technology.
ITIL Information Technology Infrastructure Library
ITSCM IT Service Continuity Management
KPI Key Performance Indicator
MTBF Mean Time Between Failures

OLA Operational Level Agreement
OSI Open Systems Interconnection
PI Performance Indicator
PKI Public Key Infrastructure
RA Registration Authority
RfC Request for Change
SIP Service Improvement Plan
SLA Service Level Agreement
SQP Service Quality Plan
TTP Trusted Third Party

WE'LL TACKLE ALL YOUR ITIL CHALLENGES

interProm USA
Enterprise Service Management Excellence

Don't go for second best! Choose for the winning team that is one of the very few all-round ITIL players in the market with more than a decade of hands-on experience in:

- ITIL project management
- ITIL technical consulting
- ITIL process consulting
- ITIL assessments
- ITIL audits
- ITIL workshops
- ITIL material reselling
- ITIL certification training
- ITIL tool implementations

For more information, please visit our "ITIL-dome" at www.itilportal.com

This message is brought to you by InterProm USA Corporation, www.interpromusa.com

MARVAL®

Helping you deliver a better service

www.marval.co.uk

The Planet's ❖ No. 1 ITIL Compliant Service Management Solutions

Marval's award winning MSM Suite provides everything you need for a company wide, quality driven and structured approach to Customer Service Delivery

HEADQUARTERS

Marval Software Limited

Stone Lodge · Rothwell Grange · Rothwell Road
Kettering · Northants · NN16 8XF
Tel: +44 (0) 1536 711999 · Fax: +44 (0) 1536 712999
E-mail: info@marval.co.uk

EUROPEAN OFFICE

Marval Benelux

Reeuwijkse Poort 303 · 2811 NV · PO Box 49 2810 AA
Reeuwijk · The Netherlands
Tel: +31 (0) 182 390909 · Fax: +31 (0) 182 390900
E-mail: info@marval.nl

MAKE IT TO THE TOP

ITIL certificates: for professionals only!

IT Service Staff: Your ITIL Foundation Certificate guarantees insight into IT Service processes.

IT Service Specialist: With your Practitioner Certificate you have proven abilities in the specialized and practical aspects of one of the service processes.

IT Service Manager: The Manager's Certificate provides international credentials that you have clearly demonstrated your ability to implement and manage IT Services.

There is an ITIL-certificate for each milestone on your journey to success in IT Service Management!

EXIN, the examination institu for information science, deve international qualification standards. EXIN is well-know for its ITIL exams.

For more info, visit:
www.exin-exams.com

Telephone: ** 31 30 234 48
E-mail: info@exin.nl